Everyday
Public Speaking

Everyday Public Speaking

Mark V. Redmond
Iowa State University

Denise Vrchota
Iowa State University

Boston • New York • San Francisco
Mexico City • Montreal • Toronto • London • Madrid • Munich • Paris
Hong Kong • Singapore • Tokyo • Cape Town • Sydney

Editor in Chief: Karon Bowers
Senior Development Editor: Carol Alper
Series Editorial Assistant: Jenny Lupica
Marketing Manager: Suzan Czajkowski
Production Supervisor: Beth Houston
Editorial Production Service: NK Graphics
Composition Buyer: Linda Cox
Manufacturing Buyer: JoAnne Sweeney
Electronic Composition: NK Graphics
Interior Design: Denise Hoffman
Photo Researcher: PoYee Oster
Cover Administrator: Joel Gendron

For related titles and support materials, visit our online catalog
at www.ablongman.com.

Between the time Web site information is gathered and then published, it is not unusual for
some sites to have closed. Also, the transcription of URLs can result in typographical errors.
The publisher would appreciate notification about where these errors occur so that they may
be corrected in subsequent editions.

Library of Congress Cataloging-in-Publication Data
Redmond, Mark V., 1949–
  Everyday public speaking / Mark V. Redmond, Denise Vrchota.—1st ed.
    p. cm.
  Includes bibliographical references and index.
  ISBN 0-205-38661-X
  1. Public speaking. I. Vrchota, Denise. II. Title.
  PN4129.15.R43 2007
  808.5'1—dc22

                                                                    2006044793

Printed in the United States of America
10 9 8 7 6 5 4 3 2 1   10 09 08 07 06

Photo credits begin on page 505, which constitutes a continuation of the copyright page.

Brief Contents

Table of Contents

Chapter **3**

Speaking Ethically   58

Chapter **4**

Connecting with Your Audience: Delivering Your Message   82

Chapter **5**

Listening: Being an Effective Audience Member   114

Unit Two • Building a Presentation

Chapter

Getting to Know Your Audience   138

Chapter **7**

Researching and Outlining Skills   166

Chapter 8

Supporting Your Presentation:
Language, Reasoning, and Argument   194

Chapter   **9**

Supporting Your Presentation: Evidence, Argument, and Support Strategies   214

Chapter 10

Supporting Your Presentation: Visual Support   242

Chapter **11**

Organizing Presentations   272

Chapter 12

Managing the Organization: Introductions, Conclusions, and Transitions   306

Chapter **13**

Responding to Audiences   338

Unit Three • **Presenting to Specific Audiences**

Chapter **14**

Making Presentations to Positive Audiences: To Inspire and Inform   358

Chapter **15**

Making Presentations to Neutral Audiences: To Interest and Inform   390

Chapter **17**

Making Presentations on Special Occasions: To Recognize and Remember   458

Student Preface

*I*f you are questioning the value of taking this class because you believe that you will never give a speech in your life, you might be surprised to know that in a way we agree with you. If, in your mind, a speech is one person presenting to a large audience of hundreds or even thousands of people, we agree that such opportunities might not present themselves to you. That type of speaking situation is not what this book is about.

Think about your life. Have you given a report to a campus organization of which you are a member? Have you spoken to your religious group about an upcoming mission trip? Does your work require you to train new employees? Looking to your future, do you see yourself visiting your child's class at school to explain your job to the children? Do you see yourself making a project report to a group of managers at your office? Do you see yourself speaking out at your town council about a controversial issue that is being considered?

If you have experienced or can see yourself in any of these situations, you will be giving speeches. All of these are examples of what we refer to in this textbook as everyday presentations. We have written this textbook to prepare you for the everyday speaking events you are likely to encounter now and in the future and to enable you to present yourself and your ideas credibly, confidently, and ethically. If you do find yourself giving a speech to an audience of hundreds or thousands, the skills and theory we discuss in this text apply to that situation, too.

In addition to preparing you for everyday speaking events, there are academic, personal, and professional benefits that you will enjoy as a result of this experience. One researcher compared students who have taken a speech course to students who have not and found that taking public speaking helps you gain confidence in your speaking abilities, increases your self-esteem, and generally leads to a more positive and confident self that will extend to other areas of your life.[1]

You will also enjoy benefits in your career. A classic study of one thousand personnel directors identified oral communication, or speaking, as the skill that is most important in helping graduating college students obtain employment.[2] Presentation skills were also ranked second in importance for successful job performance. According to the results of this study, the speaking skills and experience you acquire in this class will benefit you professionally.

What can you expect to find throughout this textbook, and how will it help you to practice and enhance your everyday presentation skills?

We hope you will find the book discusses topics that are helpful to you in a way that is easily understood. We pretested this book with students in an introductory public speaking class and asked them for feedback: What did they like? What did they not like? What was helpful or not helpful to them? The resulting textbook that you are reading is the product of our toughest critics: students. We trust that the feedback they gave us has resulted in a book that is useful to you.

An integral part of this book is found on **MySpeechLab,** an online resource you can gain access to by following the instructions with the access code that you'll find packaged with this book. It contains video clips of sample speeches given by students and other speakers. Whenever you see this icon **MSL**, you will be able not only to read the examples in your text but also to view the related video clip. You'll also find the text in e-book format online, as well as various study aids, supplemental activities, and tests.

Throughout the chapters there are several boxed features designed to enhance your learning:

Act and Reflect. In these features, activities relevant to practicing the concepts and skills discussed in each chapter are followed by questions to help you assess your responses to these activities. In many chapters, these boxes are designed to help you prepare your own speeches by working through the component of the speech that is discussed in that chapter; a few include video clips. We urge you to work through the Act and Reflect boxes in each chapter.

A Question of Ethics. Effective communication requires decision making, some of which involves ethical considerations. The ethics box in each chapter contains questions that challenge you to explore your own code of ethics and apply it to related scenarios.

Everyday Examples. In each chapter we have included examples taken from newspapers, magazines, Web sites, and so on that illustrate the extent to which speaking is an everyday activity. We hope you will enjoy and learn from these.

Getting to Work. After reading a chapter, you might wonder where to begin applying the concepts and skills discussed in the chapter. At the end of each chapter the "Getting to Work" feature helps you apply the information in that chapter to your own everyday speeches.

Video Experience. Most chapters include an activity that invoves analyzing a speaking situation on video and then answering questions about it.

We hope that you find this textbook useful and when the end of the term arrives, that this is one textbook you will elect to keep for future reference as you continue to give everyday presentations throughout your life.

---

[1] Sproule, Michael. (1997). *Speechmaking: Rhetorical competence in a postmodern world* (2nd ed.). Madison, WI: Brown & Benchmark, p. 26.

[2] Curtis, D., Winsor, J., and Stephens, R. (1989). National preferences in business and communication education. Communication Education, 38, 6–14.

Instructor's Preface

Our primary goal in writing *Everyday Public Speaking* was to provide instructors with an innovative approach to public speaking that prepares students for the variety of everyday speaking situations they will experience during their lifetimes. In our experiences over the last thirty years of helping learners understand the art and science of speaking, we have concluded that traditional approaches to teaching speech are not necessarily helpful to learners, especially undergraduate students. We have also concluded that traditional approaches do not reflect the current forums in which presentations occur. In seeking an alternate approach, we have focused on understanding and adapting to specific audience types and grounded the speaking strategies in contemporary theory and research.

Our Guiding Principles

As we indicated in the preface to students, we believe that most speaking experiences occur in small environments with small audiences in attendance. The more personal nature of these everyday speaking environments intensifies the need for a speaker to consider the perspective of each individual in the audience. Although a clearly structured message continues to be a necessity, and attention to delivery is imperative, the changing relationship of speaker–message–audience requires a different approach to the teaching of speech. Our approach emphasizes that speakers understand the qualities that make up positive, neutral, and negative audiences and adapt accordingly. Your course, in concert with this text, should prepare students to develop arguments, to develop and select appropriate support material, and to choose and present visual support, as well as to organize key points and introduce and conclude presentations for these audiences. The development of presentational decision making might be more challenging to teach and to learn than a prescriptive approach; however, it prepares students for the broad range of everyday presentations that they will encounter throughout their lives.

The approach taken in this text is meant to invigorate your teaching of public speaking, providing material that reflects and builds on the realities that characterize today's audiences. In using this text, you may be challenged to adapt a slightly different pedagogy, but in so doing, you will create a foundation on which your students can develop the ability to make decisions that lead to effective everyday presentations. To help you make the transition from previous public speaking approaches, we have included a variety of aids both within this textbook and in the accompanying supplementary materials, such as the instructor's manual, and the online resource, MySpeechLab, with video features. The following principles guided the design of this text.

Focus on Everyday Presentations

As we wrote this text, we considered public speaking, in its broadest sense, to include everything from impromptu comments made in response to another person's report at a meeting to a formal address before a large forum of listeners. We use the term "everyday presentations" for two reasons: first, to help students appreciate the fact that they will encounter occasions to speak more often than they realize and, second, to avoid some of the preconceived notions students attribute to the term "public speaking." We hope students will realize making an everyday presentation is less daunting than making a *public speech*. Some students believe that they don't need public speaking skills because they will never be called upon to give a public speech. Traditional approaches confirm this view by focusing on the formalized or ceremonial event in which a speaker presents a message of major importance to a large audience. In contrast, this text prepares students to speak in a variety of situations that people face as a part of everyday life.

To help students appreciate the scope of everyday presentations, the text is filled with examples that reflect a wide variety of everyday speaking situations. Articles are included as sidebar material reflecting everyday presentations.

Focus on Audience Type

This text, drawing on Theodore Clevenger's classification of audience types, focuses on positive, neutral, and negative audiences. Rather than imposing the somewhat artificial bifurcation of speech types as informative or persuasive, this text is organized according to the audience's attitudes and interests. The goal of the speaker must be developed in concert with the audience. Each of the three audience types is further divided according to variations in their knowledge and motives. These classifications can be readily translated into meaningful classroom activities, such as students polling classmates to determine if they will be speaking to a positive, neutral, or negative audience. For example, a student speaker might decide she wants to convince students to vote in the upcoming presidential elections. However, if the students are already motivated to vote, then she is speaking to a positive audience and her presentation should focus on inspiring and confirming their attitude. If she had mistakenly regarded them as a negative audience (opposed to voting), she would have delivered an ineffective presentation trying to convince them of something they already believed.

Individual chapters are dedicated to the three types of audiences (positive, negative, and neutral); in addition, chapters on style, evidence, organization, and introductions and conclusions also acknowledge and advise regarding choices for the three audiences. Even the chapter that discusses approaches for responding to audience members' questions considers the audience type.

Once students understand that audiences are a key element in determining the nature and manner of the presentation, they are in a position to effectively adapt to a wide variety of speaking situations. Ultimately, creating speeches based on audience type results in a greater likelihood of effective and successful presentations.

Suggestions Grounded in Research and Scholarship

In writing this textbook, we discovered that public speaking as classroom content is not an area rich in research. To avoid passing on what might be tantamount to folklore, we have worked to identify research—germane, but not always within the area of rhetoric—as the foundation for suggested strategies. For example, we use research on learning, cognition, and how people process information, to establish strategies for increasing attention and retention of the content of a speech. Such grounding increases the confidence you and the students can have that the related strategies are effective.

Focus on Students Strategically Evaluating and Responding to Speaking Situations

The Chinese proverb "If you feed a man a fish, he will eat one day. If you teach a man to fish, you feed him for a lifetime" applies to the approach we advocate in this text to develop your students' "fishing" skills. Rather than teaching students to do one particular type of speech in a classroom correctly, the goal is to teach them to understand the dynamics of public speaking, the nuances of audience types, and various strategies they can use. Paramount among the needed skills is critical thinking: the ability to think critically and clearly is essential to being able to speak thoughtfully. The text includes several features designed to foster critical thought about topics and presentations, such as the *Act and Reflect* feature and *Thinking Back, Thinking Ahead*.

Focus on Engaging the Students

The material in this text is of little value if the students don't read it, don't understand it, or can't relate to it. Recognizing this, we have focused on writing in an engaging, interactive style that includes a wide breadth of examples to which students can relate. Theories and research are presented in a way intended to increase accessibility to students, thus increasing the likelihood that they will read and apply the information. The text activities encourage students to assume active or interactive roles as learners. In addition, activities to guide the students through the process of developing their own speeches should further engage them.

Text Features to Facilitate Student Learning

If you are an experienced teacher of speech, you might, understandably, be reluctant to change your approach to this course. However, the learning aids in this textbook, the teachers' manual, and other supplements are designed to ease your transition to our approach. You will find the overall organization of the text designed for both immediate and global needs of students and instructors. For example, since most instructors want students to begin speaking early in the term, we provide the fundamental information necessary for students to make their very first classroom speech in the second chapter. Feedback from several reviewers helped in determining what information instructors would like their students to learn first, so the beginning of the text includes chapters on the nature of everyday presentations, delivery, ethics, and listening.

In a similar way, we designed features to enhance student learning. As mentioned in the student preface, we used feedback from students on an earlier version of this text to help us determine which features to include. The result is a student-tested text with the following pedagogical features:

- **Act and Reflect** features, in which students examine key concepts throughout each chapter and reflect on how they apply; many of these include activities to help students work on their speeches in the classroom

- **Everyday Examples,** sidebar material with stories that appeal to students
- **A Question of Ethics,** a feature in which various ethical issues are raised for discussion and analysis
- Inclusion of examples geared to capture the interest of a varied student readership
- Numerous speech excerpts to illustrate the concepts, many available in video format on the accompanying MySpechLab online resource
- Clear objectives, marginal key terms, and highlighted key concepts and terms within the body of the text
- Clearly identified sets of guidelines and strategies to aid in the development of effective presentations
- A **Getting to Work** segment at the end of each chapter in which chapter content is made operational for the reader
- Comprehensive chapter summaries
- **Thinking Back, Thinking Ahead,** exercises at the end of each chapter that encourage review of the chapter material, focusing on how students can apply it to preparing their own presentations

The exercises provided throughout the text can be implemented in a variety of ways: as classroom activities to stimulate discussion, to supplement daily lectures; as student assignments; and as stimuli for reflections in student journals.

In similar fashion, we urge you to explore the pedagogical applications of the video speeches available through MySpeechLab. These speeches can be used as examples of various skills and concepts discussed in the textbook; they can be the focus for reflection papers for journals; and they can serve as the stimulus for class discussion. In many instances, despite the inclusion of an example or speech within a specific chapter, we encourage you to explore other ways each speech can exemplify concepts, skills, and so on.

Three additional appendixes can be found on the e-book version of *Everyday Public Speaking.*

Our Partnership with Instructors and Students

If you teach other courses in addition to public speaking, you have probably realized the special nature of a speaking class. Students engage in personal and professional development; opportunities abound to know students; long-term relationships may result. We hope we have provided you with the tools and assistance to approach your speaking class in a way that we believe will better prepare students to become effective speakers and contribute to their personal and professional development.

Instructor's Supplements

Print Resources
- **The Instructor's Manual** has been written to guide both experienced instructors and those who are new to teaching public speaking. Since the approach represented in this text is different than other texts, we, as the authors, decided to write the accompanying manual ourselves. This helps ensure continuity between the approach reflected in this

text and the suggestions provided in the manual. We hope all instructors will find the manual helpful. The manual includes debriefing questions for use with the activities throughout the chapters as well as assignments for practicing and learning the concepts in the text. Examples are given of the speaking assignments for the three audience types and suggestions for ways to launch lectures and organize your classes.

- **The Test Bank,** prepared by Morgan L. Ginther of Iowa State University, includes more than 850 test questions, including multiple choice, true/false, short answer, and in-depth essay formats.

- **A Guide for New Public Speaking Teachers: Building toward Success, third edition,** by Calvin L. Troup of Duquesne University, is designed to help new teachers teach the introductory public speaking course effectively by covering such topics as preparing for the term, planning and structuring the course, evaluating speeches, utilizing the textbook, and integrating technology into the classroom. It includes a brief guide on teaching ESL and teaching suggestions and student activities designed to accompany The Allyn & Bacon Classic and Contemporary Speeches DVD.

- **Great Ideas for Teaching Speech (GIFTS)** by Raymond Zeuschner, California Polytechnic State University, provides descriptions of and guidelines for assignments successfully used by experienced public speaking instructors in their classrooms.

Electronic Resources

- **MySpeechLab** is a state-of-the-art, interactive, and instructive online solution for introductory speech and communication courses. MySpeechLab combines multimedia, video, activities, speech preparation tools, research support, tests, and quizzes to make teaching and learning fun! Integrated video footage, indicated by this icon in the text, **MSL**, is included in MySpeechLab, available at www.myspeechlab.com.

- **The Computerized Test Bank** (composed of the same questions found in the printed Test Bank) is available through Allyn and Bacon's computerized testing system, TestGen EQ. This fully networkable test generating software is available on a multiplatform CD-ROM for Windows and Macintosh. The user-friendly interface allows you to view, edit, and add questions, transfer questions to tests, and print tests in a variety of fonts. Search and sort features allow you to locate questions quickly and to arrange them in whatever order you prefer. Available on request to adopters. Also available electronically through the Allyn & Bacon/Longman Instructor's Resource Center.

- **PowerPoint for Everyday Public Speaking,** prepared by Tiffany L. Park of Cape Fear Community College, is a text-specific package that consists of a collection of lecture outlines and graphic images keyed to every chapter of the text and is available electronically through the Allyn & Bacon/Longman Instructor's Resource Center.

- **Allyn & Bacon Classic and Contemporary Speeches DVD** presents a collection of over 120 minutes of video footage in an easy-to-use DVD format. Each speech is accompanied by a biographical and historical summary that helps students to understand the context and motivation behind each speech. Contact your Allyn & Bacon sales representative for additional details and ordering information.

- **The Allyn & Bacon Student Speeches Video Library** includes American Forensic Association videos of award-winning student speeches and videos with a range of student speeches delivered in the classroom. Contact your local Allyn & Bacon sales representative for ordering information. Some restrictions apply.

- **The Allyn & Bacon Communication Video Library** contains a collection of communication videos produced by Film for the Humanities and Sciences. Contact your local Allyn & Bacon sales representative for ordering information. Some restrictions apply.

- **The Allyn & Bacon Public Speaking Video** includes excerpts of classic and contemporary speeches as well as student speeches to illustrate the public speaking process. One speech is delivered two times by the same person under different circumstances, to illustrate the difference between effective and noneffective delivery based on appearance, nonverbal, and verbal style. Contact your local Allyn & Bacon sales representative for ordering information. Some restrictions apply.

- **The Allyn & Bacon Digital Media Archive for Communication, version 3.0**, CD-ROM contains electronic images of charts, graphs, maps, tables, and figures, along with media elements such as video, audio clips, and related Web links. These media assets are fully customizable to use with our preformatted PowerPoint outlines or to import into the instructor's own lectures (Windows and Mac). Contact your Allyn & Bacon sales representative for additional details and ordering information.

- **The Allyn & Bacon Public Speaking Transparency Package, version II** contains 100 public speaking transparencies created with images and text from our current Public Speaking texts. The transparency package is useful for providing visual support for classroom lectures and discussion on a full range of course topics. Contact your Allyn & Bacon sales representative for ordering information.

- **The Allyn & Bacon PowerPoint Presentation Package for Public Speaking,** available electronically, includes 125 slides that provide visual and instructional support for the classroom, including material on communication theory, visual aids, and tips for organizing and outlining speeches. A brief user's guide accompanies this package.

Student Supplements

The following resources are available to help students learn and study the material for the public speaking course.

Print Resources

- **Research Navigator Guide for Speech Communication,** prepared by Terrence Doyle, Northern Virginia Community College, is designed to teach students how to conduct high-quality online research and to document it properly. Pearson's new Research Navigator is the easiest way for students to start researching their speeches. Complete with extensive help on the research process and exclusive databases of credible and reliable source material, including EBSCO's ContentSelect Academic Journal Database and the *New York Times* Search by Subject Archive, Research Navigator helps students quickly and efficiently make the most of their research time. The guide is available on the Web at www.researchnavigator.com or value-packed with any of Allyn & Bacon's public speaking texts.

- **Speech Preparation Workbook,** prepared by Jennifer Dreyer and Gregory H. Patton, San Diego State University, takes students through the various stages of speech creation—from audience analysis to writing the speech—and provides supplementary assignments and tear-outs forms. Contact your Allyn & Bacon representative for ordering information. Some restrictions apply.

- **Preparing Visual Aids for Presentations, fourth edition,** prepared by Dan Cavanaugh, is a 32-page visual booklet designed to provide a host of ideas for using today's multimedia tools to improve presentations, including suggestions for planning a presentation, guidelines for designing visual aids, storyboarding, and a PowerPoint presentation walk-through. Contact your Allyn & Bacon representative for ordering information. Some restrictions apply.

- **Public Speaking in the Multicultural Environment, second edition,** prepared by Devorah A. Lieberman, Portland State University, helps students learn to analyze cultural diversity within their audiences and adapt their presentations accordingly. Contact your Allyn & Bacon representative for ordering information. Some restrictions apply.

- **Outlining Workbook**, prepared by Reeze L. Hanson and Sharon Condon, Haskell Indian Nations University, includes activities, exercises, and answers to help students develop and master the critical skill of outlining. Contact your Allyn & Bacon representative for ordering information. Some restrictions apply.

- **Study Card for Public Speaking**. Colorful, affordable, and packed with useful information, Allyn & Bacon's Study Cards make studying easier, more efficient, and more enjoyable. Course information is distilled down to the basics, helping you quickly master the fundamentals, review a subject for understanding, or prepare for an exam. Because they're laminated for durability, you can keep these Study Cards for years to come and pull them out whenever you need a quick review. Contact your local Allyn & Bacon representative for ordering information. Some restrictions apply.

- **Pathways to Careers in Communication**. The National Communication Association's booklet provides information about the discipline, its history and importance, information on career possibilities, and other available resources for investigating communication studies. Contact your Allyn & Bacon representative for ordering information. Some restrictions apply.

Electronic Resources

- **News Resources for Speech Communication with Research Navigator** is one-stop access to keep you abreast of the latest news events and for all of your research needs. Highlighted by an hourly feed of the latest news in the discipline from the *New York Times,* you will stay on the forefront of currency throughout the semester. In addition, Pearson's Research Navigator™ is the easiest way for students to start a research assignment. Complete with extensive help on the research process and four exclusive databases of credible and reliable source material including the EBSCO Academic Journal and Abstract Database, *New York Times* Search by Subject Archive, and *Financial Times* Article Archive and Company Financials, Research Navigator helps you quickly and efficiently make the most of your research time.

- **Allyn & Bacon Classic and Contemporary Speeches DVD** presents a collection of over 120 minutes of video footage in an easy-to-use DVD format. Each speech is accompanied by a biographical and historical summary that helps you to understand the context and motivation behind each speech.

- **Allyn & Bacon Public Speaking Website, second edition** prepared by Nan Peck, Northern Virginia Community College. Access this website at www.ablongman.com/pubspeak. Contains modules built with enrichment materials, web links, and interactive activities designed to enhance your understanding of key concepts. The Web site helps you build, organize, and research speeches while learning about the process of public speaking.

- **Interactive Speechwriter Software, version 1.1** (Windows), prepared by Martin R. Cox, is an interactive software package for student purchase that provides supplemental material, writing templates (for the informative, persuasive, and motivated sequence speeches, as well as for outlines), sample student speeches (text only), and more! This program enhances students' understanding of key concepts discussed in the text and is available for Windows. Contact your Allyn & Bacon representative for ordering information. Some restrictions apply.

- **Speech Writer's Workshop CD-ROM, version 2.0,** is interactive software to assist students with speech preparation and enable you to write better speeches. The software includes four separate features: (1) a speech handbook with tips for researching and preparing speeches plus information about grammar, usage, and syntax; (2) a speech workshop that guides you through the speech-writing process and includes a series of questions at each stage; (3) a topics dictionary containing hundreds of speech ideas—all divided into subcategories to help you with outlining and organization; and (4) a citation database that formats bibliographic entries in MLA and APA style. Contact your Allyn & Bacon representative for ordering information. Some restrictions apply.

- **Public Speaking Tutor Center** (access code required), at www.aw.com/tutorcenter. The Tutor Center provides students with one-on-one interactive tutoring from qualified public speaking instructors on all material in the text. The Tutor Center offers students help with understanding major communication principles as well as methods for study. In addition, you have the option of submitting self-taped speeches for review and critique by Tutor Center instructors to help prepare for and improve your speech assignments. Tutoring assistance is offered by phone, fax, Internet, and e-mail during Tutor Center hours. For more details and ordering information, contact your Allyn & Bacon sales representative.

Acknowledgments

To paraphrase a famous saying, *It takes a village to create a book*. What you hold in your hands is the product of many people's efforts. We are indebted to those who have taught us, both formally in the classroom and informally in our everyday interactions. As teachers, we are also indebted to our students, from whom we are constantly learning. As scholars, we are indebted to our colleagues, who offer advice and encouragement and challenge us to produce our best efforts. And so we give our sincere thanks to all of those who have influenced our understanding and appreciation of public speaking.

Since only our names appear on the cover, a number of other individuals need to be recognized for their contributions to development and production of this textbook. We feel fortunate to have begun our journey with Karon Bowers, who shared our vision of public speaking as everyday presentations. We greatly appreciated her initial and continued support for this project. That support was continued by Brian Wheel, who championed our text during the writing and rewriting that took place. A number of individuals provided logistical support, kept us on track, and helped in the development of various aspects of the text that we often take for granted, and many of their names appear on the copyright page.

We particularly thank Beth Houston, the production supervisor, for her behind-the-scenes work on managing the actual production of the text, including selecting photos. Deb Hanlon has coordinated the development of supplemental materials in a masterful manner. Martha Ramsey had the unenviable, but appreciated, task of copy editing our manuscript and ensuring that our commas were in the right place and, more importantly, that our writing made sense. Thanks to Tonnya Norwood, Dawn Nebelski, and Cynthia O'Dell at NK Graphics for turning our Word files into a well-formatted and well-designed textbook.

Additional thanks go to three students here at Iowa State University. Nick Redmond used his computer skills to enhance some of our initial graphics and to locate articles and videos on the Internet that are incorporated in this text. Kate Pickett began the process of securing permission to use various copyrighted materials in the text, and Jessie Stefanski helped organize those requests.

This printed edition of the text evolved by rewriting drafts reviewed by a number of instructors from across the country. Each graciously shared his or her thoughts, reactions, and suggestions, thus contributing to the final refinement of the text. We gratefully acknowledge the contributions of these reviewers as follows: Kenneth R. Baldridge, Indiana University Southeast; Samuel Todd Brand, Meridan Community College; LeAnn M. Brazeal, Kansas State University; Sue E. Brilhart, Southwest Missouri State University; L. Karen Brown, Cape Fear Community College; Joni M. Butcher, Louisiana State University; Crystal Church, Cisco Junior College; Nancy J. Eaton, Westfield State College; Debra J. Ford, the University of Kansas; Anne Goding, SUNY New Paltz; Donna Goodwin, Tulsa Community College; Lawrence A. Hosman, University of Southern Mississippi; Hillary Johnson, Marist College; David Klope, Mt. Mercy College; Linda Kurz, University of Missouri, Kansas City; Sheryl Lidzy, Murray State University; Kay McClanahan, University of North Carolina, Pembroke; Jan McKissick, Butte Community College; Shellie Michael, Volunteer State Community College; Marjorie Keeshan Nadler, Miami University of Ohio; Gloria Nicosia, Kingsborough Community College; Michael J. Pane, Gaston College; Daniel M. Paulnock, Saint Paul College; Cami Pierce, Murray State University; Darrell Pond, North Carolina State University; Jerry Thomas, Lindsey Wilson College; Esin C. Turk, Mississippi Valley State University; Melinda S. Womack, Santiago Canyon College; Archie Wortham, Palo Alto College.

Finally, we have two special acknowledgments we would like to make. The first is to a group of students in a public speaking course here at Iowa State University who participated in a trial run of this text. They were provided with a bare-bones copy of the book—no special features, no photos, no cartoons, no graphics, rough artwork, and only limited supplemental articles of interest. Despite this, they amiably took on the task of reading the text and applying the material to the development of their own presentations. Most importantly, they provided us with invaluable feedback about the overall approach as well as the content. Their contributions have resulted in a better textbook, and we wish to acknowledge them for their efforts: Jessica Culhane, Katherine Dencklau, Chelsea Desousa, Amy Diekevers, Cynthia Johnson, Laura Johnson, Ross Kelderman, Shannon Kirton, Ilana Mainaga, Crystal Nord, Ashley Osgood, Kasey Pfab, Amanda Sadowski, Collin Schmidt, Mayarih Sharif, Jonathan Sheller, Scott Sturm, Karen Tarara, and Katelyn Verhoef.

Our final acknowledgement is for someone we could easily list as our third author because of the contributions, hard work, and time she devoted to the development of this text. We cannot begin to thank her enough. To Carol Alper, Senior Development Editor at Allyn and Bacon, we offer our heartfelt appreciation for her constant dedication, commitment, and grace. Her greatest contribution was that she believed in us and in this text.

Chapter 1

The Fundamentals of Everyday Presentations

Goals

 To understand what everyday presentations are

 To appreciate how much you are and will be involved in everyday presentations

 To understand how presentations can be seen as influence, as spoken communication, and as connection

 To be able to identify and utilize four guiding principles of presentations

To understand the three audiences types: positive, neutral, and negative

Scenario 1.   George is listening to a proposal by one of his fellow managers. After the presentation, George speaks in response to the proposal, identifying three issues that he believes need to be addressed before adopting the proposal, and explains his reasoning.

Scenario 2.   Michelle is part of a project team working on the design of a new manufacturing process. Each month she meets with the executive board to give them an update on the team's progress.

Scenario 3.   Juan is an active volunteer with several youth groups in his community. He is appearing before the city council to request additional funds to help improve facilities that are used by these groups.

Scenario 4.   As part of her senior seminar in religious studies, Jasmine is expected to make an oral report on her research paper examining the early impact of Islam and Christianity on Africa.

Scenario 5.   The Minority Student Committee is requesting permission from the college to hold a diversity awareness day on campus. Jamal and other members of this committee are explaining their plan and arguing their case before a group of college administrators.

Each of these scenarios represents a form of everyday presentation. The presentations given in these scenarios vary in many ways which we will discuss in this chapter and throughout this text. Some presentations are spontaneous; others are carefully planned. Some involve providing explanations to receptive audiences, while others are requesting support from an audience that might be hesitant to provide it. This chapter is geared to creating a clearer understanding about the nature of such everyday presentations and to helping you establish a foundation for developing your presentational skills and style. ●

Definition of Everyday Presentations

The term **everyday presentations** is used in this text as an all-encompassing term that includes any presentation in which individuals intentionally and strategically deliver an oral message as part of their daily lives. Most people engage in a number of presentations almost daily, as part of their professional lives or as part of their involvement in community activities: project updates, briefings, training sessions, sales pitches, and team meetings. In most everyday presentations, the speaker plans a message and is looked upon by the audience as the primary source of information for a given period of time. Often the everyday presentation is only part of a broader communication event. For example, you might give a briefing on an issue to a group of fellow managers that then shifts into a group discussion of the issues and policies you presented. On the other hand, there are also times when you might be called on to make a more formal presentation before a large audience where interaction is restricted. The audience size is one of several dimensions on which everyday presentations vary.

While this is neither a large audience nor a formal situation, this is an everyday presentation. ●

Variations in Audience Size and Characteristics

"Public" speaking or making a presentation means you have a large audience, right? Not quite. A **presentation** involves any interaction in which two specific and exclusive roles are enacted: the role of speaker and the role of listener. This means that the minimum number of people you need as an audience is ONE. One-on-one presentations simply require one person to play the primary role of speaker and the other the role of listener or audience. For example, a salesperson meets one-on-one with a client and gives a fairly standardized, organized, well-planned message (presentation) with the intent of persuading the listener. In some ways, making a presentation to one person is simpler than making it to several people because you can adapt

everyday presentation Any presentation in which individuals intentionally and strategically deliver an oral message as part of their daily lives.

presentation Any interaction in which two specific and exclusive roles are enacted: the role of speaker and of listener.

and modify your message to match your listener. As you add more people to your audience, it becomes more challenging to deliver a message that has the same impact on all of them. Suppose you were selling life insurance. In delivering a one-on-one presentation to a forty-year-old single mother, you could discuss how the policy fits her specific needs—her age (years till retirement), occupation, and the number and age of her children (how long they will need financial protection). On the other hand, if you are delivering the presentation to twenty listeners who vary in sex, age, race, and ethnicity, you need to use a variety of appeals to be sure to meet the needs of your diverse listeners. Variations in audience characteristics affect the very nature of the presentation. A presentation to a group of middle school students on local community development issues would differ from one on the same topic to the local chamber of commerce.

Planning and Preparing

The most formal everyday presentations entail considerable planning and preparation; every word is carefully considered and perhaps even written out; for example, a presidential address or a CEO's annual report to shareholders. At other times, the presenter might develop a set of carefully planned notes from which to make extemporaneous comments. And at other times, people are called on to speak on the spur of the moment, drawing from their expertise and knowledge, when, for example, commenting on another person's proposal at a team meeting. You might not think that the impromptu comments people make in team meetings in response to a briefing are a "presentation" because the comments are spontaneous and short. However, the impact of such "impromptu" presentations can be significant. Their goals include providing additional information, counter-arguing, presenting an analysis, or expressing an evaluation. You might have to think quickly and speak effectively while challenging a colleague's proposal. The failure to present an effective "counter" presentation might result in the adoption of poor or damaging proposals. While presentations vary in the detail of preparation and planning, all speakers are guided in making presentations by their purposes or intentions.

Presentations as Communication

As you prepare to give a speech, it's easy to become so concerned about what you're going to say, how you're going to say it, and being nervous that you forget that the focus of your effort is *communication*. Everyday presentations are used as a way to connect us with other people, to communicate ideas to several people at one time, and to speak face to face with others. In this section we first discuss the general nature of communication and then cover three ways to think about the communicative nature of presentations: presentations as influence, presentations as spoken communication, and presentations as connection. All of these three approaches are important

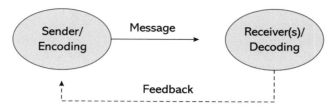

● FIGURE 1.1 Linear Model of Communication.

and are sometimes overlooked. Taking them into account as you prepare and deliver presentations will increase your overall effectiveness.

Understanding Communication

Communication in its most basic form is simply acting on information or a stimulus.[1] The "acting" part of the definition means that something happens, some change occurs. The only way for a presentation not to be communication would be if no one heard it. The act of simply getting someone's attention means you have caused that person to change—to focus on you. People don't have to agree with or be persuaded by a speaker for communication to take place; even evoking disagreement or rejection of one's claims is "action," is a "change." A presentation is a specific, narrow form of communication that is concerned with the impact of intentional and strategic messages on other people.

Components of Communication The most basic model of communication consists of the following components and concepts:

Sender: a person who is stimulated to create a message to convey an idea

Encoding: the process by which a person puts an idea into words and behaviors

Message: the product or behavior of the sender who is transmitting in an attempt to connect with a receiver

Receiver: a person who responds or is affected by a message

Decoding: the process of interpreting the meaning of what the receiver perceives

Feedback: the response a receiver displays or expresses in reaction to a message

These components create a linear model of communication that consists of a sender sending a message to a receiver, with minimal feedback from the receiver to the sender (see Figure 1.1). When you think about a speech, this model seems to fit pretty well; however, the model suggests no impact by audiences on speakers until the speakers are done sending messages. The reality is that speakers are affected by their audiences even while the speakers talk. When all the parties involved in a communication situation are affecting and being

communication Acting on information or a stimulus.

● **FIGURE 1.2** Transactional Model of Communication.

affected by one another simultaneously, this is called **transactional communication** (see Figure 1.2). While only one person might actually be "talking" at any given moment, the expressions and behaviors of those who are "listening" are affecting that speaker. As you sit in your classes taking notes, your behaviors affect your lecturers. The size of this impact varies and is probably more obvious when the audience is smaller, as in a one-on-one situation; nonetheless, there is a transactional impact. When you are in a communication situation, you are concurrently sending and receiving messages.

Communicating to Meet Needs Communication is goal driven—we have goals we're trying to accomplish. Communication occurs in order to fulfill some needs the participants have. People are motivated to communicate; they have some reason for participating—for expressing something and for listening. Effective presentations depend on having a clear understanding of your own reasons for talking and your audience's reasons for listening. Understanding your reasons for talking means you should be able to answer the question "What do I want to happen when I have completed my presentation?"

Shared Meaning Once stimulated to express something, individuals have lots of options about how to encode or assemble messages that reflect their thoughts and intentions. The words and accompanying nonverbal behaviors are based on people's experiences, and those words evoke variations in meaning for each person. The word "dog" might evoke an image of the pet poodle you had as a child but an image for another person of being attacked by a dog while jogging. People all attribute meaning to what they perceive, and the degree to which different people assign the same meaning is the **shared meaning.** One goal of effective communication is to achieve shared meaning—to elicit from your listeners the same meaning you have in your mind. Accomplishing shared meaning with a diverse audience while giving a presentation is particularly challenging. One's cultural background, race, and ethnicity impact the attribution of meaning in differing ways. The word "dog" may evoke a number of divergent images among the numerous audience members, many which you might not have even considered. As a speaker, you must develop a sensitivity to the language you use and to other people's possible interpretations. Watch the nonverbal reactions of audience members for cues to confusion or unexpected reactions (like laughter or grimaces) to terms you use. If necessary, seek clarification directly from the audience about their reaction.

transactional communication When all the parties involved in a communication situation are affected and affecting one another simultaneously.

shared meaning The degree to which different people assign the same meaning to what they perceive.

The preceding discussion might seem to suggest that giving presentations to one person at a time would be more effective than giving them to collective audiences. However, there are several inherent advantages to giving presentations to multiple-member audiences:

1. Presentations to such audiences can be an efficient means of connecting with a large number of people at one time. Making one presentation to thirty people is a lot more efficient than making thirty presentations to one person at a time.

2. Presentations to such audiences ensure that the same message is delivered to everyone. No two presentations are ever alike, and variations can mean that one audience gets one message while a second audience gets another. This is not to say that even when thirty people listen at the same time their interpretations are the same.

3. Such an audience can produce a collective response that is advantageous to the speaker. The reactions of audience members are contagious: the reactions of several people influence the reactions of any given individual. If someone has an indifferent attitude while attending a rally on some campus issue, and the audience cheers and responds enthusiastically, that person, too, might start cheering.

Presentations as Influence

Communication by its very nature is influential. **Influence** is any change that occurs in response to a stimulus. As mentioned earlier, whenever communication occurs, there is change. Inherent in your composing and sending messages to other people is the desire to have some impact on them. Sometimes that desire may be nothing more than wanting them to like you, but at other times it might be to change their behavior. Implicit in a teacher's attempt to "inform" students about a concept (like the definition of "communication") is an attempt to convince the students that it is worth listening to, worth learning, valid, and important. Do the students believe the teacher? Are they persuaded? If the students "learn" and accept the definition, then they are influenced.

In every presentation you are confronted with the question "What do I want from my audience?" The fact that you want something means that you are trying to influence your listeners. In giving a speech to your classmates, you probably just want them to like you, to validate your identity ("Tell me I'm a good speaker, aren't I?"), and not to make it worse if you make a mistake. You accomplish your goals by applying certain strategies. For the goals just listed, you might try to be humorous, tell a personal story, articulate well, avoid rambling, and practice your speech so you won't make embarrassing mistakes. Sometimes, you exert influence simply to secure the audience's interest and attention. When instructors want students to really pay attention to some information they are explaining, they often say something like "This will be on the test." That statement is an explicit attempt to influence the listeners to pay attention.

influence Any change that occurs in response to a stimulus.

By permission of Tony Cochran and Creators Syndicate, Inc.

Presentations are designed to influence behaviors, thoughts, and feelings. Just because you influence one of these three doesn't mean you have influenced the other two. For example, you might find yourself emotionally aroused by a sermon about the need to help others who are less fortunate, but after you leave your place of worship, you might make no changes in your behavior to help others. You might be convinced of which candidate would make a better president but not be motivated enough to vote on the day of the election.

The amount of resistance you encounter from any audience can be placed along a continuum, as shown in Figure 1.3. On one end are audiences who are already acting in a manner supportive of the speaker's goals and need only for the speaker to voice them; at the other end are highly resistant audiences who are actively working against the speaker's goals. The various presentations you deliver in your life will fall all along this continuum, and you will need to adapt your persuasive strategies accordingly.

● **FIGURE 1.3** Continuum of Resistance.

Minimum Resistance   Maximum Resistance

Audience is already engaged in desired behavior	Audience holds supportive views	Audience holds opposing views	Audience is currently working against you

Examples:

Speaking to a rally of volunteers working in support of a political candidate	Advocating exercise and diet changes to a new class of weight watchers	Speaking to a union group about the need for a pay freeze	Advocating gun control to the National Rifle Association

ACT&REFLECT

1.1: Listening to Written Messages

ACT • Find a complex newspaper article or text passage that you have read and understood (for real fun, use the instructions for filling out an income tax form). Read it out loud to a friend who has not read it. Ask him or her what it meant and whether he or she enjoyed it. Find another friend to read the article to himself or herself. Ask him or her what it meant and whether he or she enjoyed it.

REFLECT • What did the friend's response to hearing the material tell you about listening to messages that are meant to be read? Who understood the message better? Why?

Presentations as Spoken Communication

What would your day be like if you were not allowed to speak? While a lot of us use email and instant messaging to interact, we still depend heavily on our ability to speak out loud to other people. **Spoken communication** is that communication that occurs through the articulation of words. The meaning and impact of those words are modified by variations in tone of voice and the use of nonverbal cues such as facial expressions or gestures. For example, stories and narratives can take on an almost magical quality when spoken. The use of a spoken medium versus a written one has an impact on the type of information that can be conveyed and on one's ability to comprehend the information. One study found that listening to a presentation that was written to be presented orally produced greater comprehension than listening to a magazine article.[2] However, for both texts, reading resulted in greater acquisition of information than listening, though reading required more mental effort. It is much more challenging to convey substantial textual or visual information to someone through speech than through writing. (Imagine trying to describe a complex spreadsheet without any visual reference.) Act and Reflect 1.1 illustrates this point.

Because presentations are face to face, nonverbal cues occur that enhance the quality of and give meaning to the spoken words. **Nonverbal cues** include any behavior people exhibit other than words; this includes the voice, gestures, facial expressions, body movement, and posture. Presentations must be given face to face to utilize the full range of available nonverbal cues. There are several benefits inherent in giving presentations face to face:

spoken communication Communication that occurs through the articulation of words.

nonverbal cues Any behavior people exhibit other than through words.

1. Presentations can be used to effectively highlight information while presenting and developing key issues.
2. Speakers can immediately adapt to audience feedback (displays of confusion/boredom or questions) by providing additional explanation and examples.
3. Key information can be presented and emphasized with vocal and visual cues.
4. Nonverbal cues allow you to effectively convey sincerity as well as other emotions.

Four Guiding Principles

What do you need to know to make a good presentation? While some books provide extensive lists of do's and don'ts, our approach is to offer a set of principles for developing and making effective presentations. These principles include: understand and adapt to the audience and context; think strong to speak strong; balance style and content; speak with sincerity and thoughtfulness; and establish or maintain a positive relationship with the audience. As you read these principles, think about how they compare to your own notions about presentations.

Understand and Adapt to the Audience and Context

Whether you are speaking to one person or five hundred, creating and delivering a message that has been adapted to your listeners enhances the quality and effectiveness of your presentation. **Adaptation** involves using your understanding of the audience and the situation to select strategies tailored to the audience's needs and interests. You can use examples that are salient to the audience and that elicit and sustain their interest. There are a number of questions you can consider in analyzing your listeners. The answers you develop should be used in making decisions about your goal, the information to include or exclude, and the types of examples and evidence you will need.

- "If I were sitting in this audience, what would I want to hear?"
- "How is this audience different from me?"
- "What does *this* audience want?"
- "Why is this audience here?"
- "What do they think of me?"
- "What are their attitudes toward my topic?"
- "What do I want from this audience?"
- "Is the audience in a position to provide what I want?"

adaptation Using your understanding of the audience and the situation to select strategies tailored to the audience's needs and interests.

Bono is a successful spokesperson for his various causes partly because he is able to adapt to his audience—in his manner, his appearance, and his message. ●

You must also make an analysis of the presentational situation. For example, you should realize that a classroom filled with other students is a different context from a boardroom filled with company executives. You need a sensitivity to how situations differ and an ability to adapt your presentations accordingly.

One question (discussed in more detail in Chapter 6) that relates to analyzing the situation is "Why is my audience here?" In giving speeches to the other students in your class, the answer probably is "Because they are required to be here for the course." There is initially little motivation for the other students to obtain the information that you have to share. On the other hand, in professional settings, your audience might be there because you have information that they need in order to make vital decisions for the organization. The difference in these audiences is a factor in how much time and effort you have to devote in your speech to motivate them to listen.

For the next several weeks, your classroom will be the context for your presentations, and you should assess it accordingly. You have an opportunity to begin developing good speaking habits within the safety of a classroom. The classroom context limits the type of everyday presentation you will get to practice, and it is up to you to recognize differences and adapt what you learn in the class to other presentational contexts.

A Question of **Ethics**

Consider your responses to the following scenarios:

1. At the end of Jack's presentation, an audience member asks Jack if previous results support his proposal. Jack doesn't know the answer to the question but for two minutes speaks eloquently and with confidence in a deliberately ambiguous way; then he takes the next question. How ethical is Jack's behavior?

2. A student did not have time to adequately research statistics on the rate of crimes on campus required for a final speech. Since the student needs a C to pass the course, the student makes up some numbers that sound reasonable to the audience. How ethical is this behavior?

3. Spenser has just finished explaining his proposal for modifying employee workloads. Kaylene responds to Spenser's proposal by ridiculing him, attacking his research, and pointing out mistakes in his overheads. Has Kaylene acted unethically? Why or why not?

Think Strong to Speak Strong: Speaking Reflects Thinking

"Speech is the mirror of the mind," according to the ancient Roman philosopher Seneca, who lived from 3 B.C. to A.D. 65. These words continue to hold true today: your presentations reflect your thoughts, and that means good thinking is fundamental to good speaking. Effective speakers have the ability to think through an issue and develop supportive arguments before speaking and even as they speak. Unfortunately, we can also expose our inability to think clearly through our presentations and provide proof of the old Irish proverb "Everyone is wise until he speaks." What's your impression of the politician who gave the following response to a question about using Hawaii's health care program as a model for the nation?

> Hawaii is a unique state. It is a small state. It is a state that is by itself. It is a—it is different than the other 49 states. Well, all states are different, but it's got a particularly unique situation.[3]

So what was your impression of the speaker's thinking? The statement was made by former vice president Dan Quayle and is one of several examples he generated that often seemed to undermine his bid for credibility and support.

You might have expected that a textbook on making speeches would place the speaking and performance of the presentation at its core. However, the most critical aspect of delivering an effective presentation is the quality of thinking that accompanies the preparation of a speech. Creating an effective speech requires strong **critical thinking skills** (that is, the ability to observe, analyze, synthesize, and evaluate information), whether to improve effectiveness in making impromptu speeches or to ensure successful development of planned ones. When planning a presentation, you need to spend time just thinking about your speech: thinking about the issues, deliberating over the points to include, considering the audience and the context, identifying and clarifying your goals, and developing effective arguments, illustrations, and examples. As your thoughts crystallize, notes and outlines will aid your ability to critique, edit, and modify those thoughts.

Balance Both Style and Content: Speak with Eloquence and Sincerity

"Be sincere; be brief; be seated." —Franklin D. Roosevelt (1882–1945)

In the classical sense, "style" tended to be a term referring to the manner in which a speech should be given as prescribed by the situation. Speakers were expected to carefully select their words, employ metaphors, and attend to delivery all for the purpose of providing the most effective speech. We will use **delivery style** to refer to creating an effective and distinct manner of delivery. In general, you should be yourself; be interpersonal; relate to the audience on a personal level; share who you are; demonstrate an understanding of your audience; and develop and maintain a relationship with your listeners. Some speakers try to take on a "public speaking" personality and to use a very formalized voice. There are some situations when that style is appropriate. For the vast majority of situations, a personal, connecting style is more appropriate and effective.

Some speakers emphasize the substance or content of their presentation over their delivery style, believing that if they provide good, solid information, how it is delivered is unimportant. Sometimes this content emphasis tempts speakers into providing as much information as they can in the time allotted. However, such recitation of facts and figures fails to recognize the difference between a spoken presentation and a written document. Speeches should not be simply the reading of a written document. To maximize the potential impact of a speech, you need to take advantage of the spoken and transactional nature of presentations.

Classical rhetoricians like Cicero emphasized the use of metaphors and the inclusion of extended narratives or personal stories as ways to enhance a speaker's style. The noted political communication scholar Kathleen Hall Jamieson, in her award-winning book *Eloquence in an Electronic Age,* argues that speakers whose presentations are being delivered through the media have adapted a new form of eloquence. While Jamieson's sense of eloquence is based

critical thinking skills The ability to observe, analyze, synthesize, and evaluate information.

delivery style An effective and distinct manner of delivery.

on mediated presentations, the underlying theme applies to face-to-face contexts as well. **Eloquence** is defined as a speaking style that is personal, is conversational, does not emphasize the argument, uses storytelling and narratives, and utilizes strategic sharing of personal experiences and feelings.[4] The use of vivid imagery in presentations has been identified as an important factor in charismatic leadership. One research study found that presidents who used words that aroused a sensory experience (used imagery) in pivotal addresses were more likely to be seen as charismatic and to be rated as great presidents.[5]

A speaker with an ineffective delivery style forces the audience to work harder to listen and understand; and they will do so only if they believe the information is important to them. The speaker can interfere with the flow of information by being too quiet, going too fast, speaking with a strong accent, or injecting too many vocalized pauses or nonfluencies (like "ums" or "ahs"). A speech strong on style but with little content is effective if the audience is only interested in passing time, being entertained, or in forming an impression of the speaker. However, imagine going to a class where the instructor had great style but no content—you might have trouble with the exams.

The emotion and sincerity of this speaker impacts the audience as much as the content of his words. ●

The most effective speaking style reflects thoughtfulness and sincerity: the content should reflect consideration and deliberation of the issues, and the style should reflect honesty and openness. Your content needs to reflect clear thinking. A **sincere** person speaks honestly, openly, genuinely, without airs or pretense, and from the heart. Audiences evaluate and respond positively to a speaker's sincerity. You need to believe in what you are speaking about. If speakers don't believe in what they are saying, why should the audience? Audiences assess the degree to which presenters speak from the heart. Sincerity can even offset disorganization and poor delivery. As listeners, we are moved by personal stories, by honesty, and by speakers' commitments to what they are saying. You have probably seen news clips of people talking about personal tragedies or traumas in their lives; while they may lack polish, the sincerity with which they speak moves you. As much as you can, you should also speak with sincerity when giving presentations (Act and Reflect 1.2). Jack Canfield, who originated the *Chicken Soup for the Soul* series of popular books and is a noted motivational speaker, provided the following advice.

Tell the truth and speak from your heart. If you do that, 85 percent of what you do will come naturally. Your body will move, you'll make eye contact, you'll penetrate the audience, you'll tell jokes if you're supposed to, you'll be in-

eloquence Speaking style that is personal, conversational, does not emphasize the argument, uses storytelling and narratives, and utilizes strategic sharing of personal experiences and feelings.

sincere Speaking style in which a person speaks honestly, openly, genuinely, without airs or pretense, and from the heart.

ACT&REFLECT

1.2: Speaking with Eloquence and Sincerity

A C T • Think about an issue that is important to you. Prepare a two-minute presentation in which you talk about this issue and why it is important to you. Focus on speaking with eloquence. Include personal stories, share information about yourself, incorporate an interpersonal style, and speak sincerely. Present this in class. Listen carefully to each of your classmates' presentations.

R E F L E C T • What was your response to your classmates' presentations? How did you react to those who spoke sincerely but whose ideas were contrary to your beliefs? What were your reactions to those who seemed less sincere and less eloquent? What does this tell you about speaking eloquently?

vulnerable. People will connect with you because you are talking about your own life, your own heart, your own passion.[6]

Establish or Maintain a Positive Relationship with the Audience

One presentation goal that might not be apparent is to establish and maintain a positive relationship with the audience—to make a connection with them. Think about the strategies you use in your daily life to get people to like you—things like emphasizing commonalities, being polite and respectful, or displaying a sincere interest in the other person. The same strategies can be applied to presentations. For example, two strategies for maintaining relationships identified by interpersonal communication researchers Laura Stafford and Dan Stafford seem particularly applicable to audience relationships: positivity (being positive and cheerful) and openness.[7]

Being cheerful and showing a positive regard for a partner elicits liking;[8] in a similar vein, a speaker displaying such qualities is likely to elicit a positive response from the audience. In addition, in interpersonal relationships, displaying liking for one's partner often generates a reciprocation of that liking from the other;[9] similarly, displaying liking for your audience members increases the probability that they will like you in return. On the other hand, if you approach an audience with a lack of enthusiasm or a negative attitude, they may respond in kind.

We expect our friends to be open with us and share important information. If we find out that a friend has been holding back important information, it can damage the relationship. The same is true when giving presentations. Talking with others through presentations helps maintain positive relationships as long as the speakers are seen as being open and sharing relevant information. Discovering that the speaker was not forthcoming and withheld important information can be detrimental to the audience's trust in the speaker and the relationship.

What happens if the speaker has a negative relationship with the audience? The first thing to do is determine the reason for the negative relationship. Some possible reasons include the following:

1. The speaker is associated with something that is viewed negatively by the audience. For example, a member of the Sierra Club speaking to a meeting of the logging industry or a member of the National Rifle Association talking to an audience with family members killed by firearms probably would evoke negative reactions.

2. The audience might have a negative attitude toward the speaker because they have a negative reaction to the situation. A group of college students placed on probation for driving cars while under the influence of alcohol who have to listen to a lecture by an expert on an early Saturday morning are likely to have a negative attitude toward the speaker.

3. Regrettably, people are biased, and they hold these biases against speakers. Your race, sex, ethnicity, accent, age, body size, hairstyle, clothing style, and so on can all evoke a negative reaction from the audience.

4. Previous negative experiences with the speaker may result in a sustained negative attitude. You've probably taken classes from instructors toward whom you have developed a negative attitude during the term because of their behaviors, treatment of you, teaching style, and so on.

Strategies for diminishing these negative responses include establishing common ground and showing understanding of the audience and appreciating their perspectives. Establishing common ground, common interests, and common goals not only gains the audience's interest but also increases the audience's acceptance of the speaker. Displaying understanding, concern, empathy, and connection with the audience will make it more difficult for them to maintain a negative attitude because people don't expect those they dislike to act this way. Displays of concern and empathy might be seen as insincere and therefore manipulative, rather than compassionate.

People are more likely to trust people who are part of the groups they associate with than people who are considered the "out-group."[10] In talking to a negative audience, the more you can establish yourself as part of the audience's in-group, the more influence you are likely to have.

Sometimes the best approach is the direct approach—address the negative attitude in your presentation. This lets the audience know you understand them: you realize they have a negative attitude, and you understand why they have it. You can then present information to counter the reasons for their negative attitude. For example, in making a proposal to a church committee, a member who is viewed as obstinate and difficult to work with by other members might say:

I know many of you think I'm a bit bullheaded at times and that makes it hard to work with me, but one reason I'm that way is because I care deeply about what happens to this church and sometimes I don't realize when I should agree to a compromise. For that I apologize. I also hope you won't let your feelings toward me interfere with your support for a project that I'd like to propose that will be good for the future of this congregation.

In this example, the speaker displayed understanding of the audience's feelings, provided an explanation, made an act of contrition, and asked the audience to set aside their feelings in judging the merits of the proposal. This strategy may not get the audience to think the speaker is any less bullheaded, but hopefully they will be more tolerant and will listen objectively to the proposal.

Everyday Example

Becoming an Effective Public Speaker

Here comedian Al Franken writes about his failures at maintaining positive relationships with audiences:

Take for example the first commencement address I ever gave. It was at Hartford State Technical College, where I was a last-minute replacement for Undersecretary of the Navy Warren Untemeyer, who had been delayed by an unexpected indictment. Funny story. The message my housekeeper passed along led me to believe I was speaking at *Harvard*, not *Hartford* State Technical College. By the time it was straightened out and I had arrived in Hartford from New York, via Cambridge, I was so tired, disappointed, and frankly, angry at the graduates, that I'm afraid I allowed my feelings to color my judgment on what sort of speech to give. I took a very hard line with that year's class from HSTC.

I began with a quote from Goethe, whose most famous work, *The Sorrows of Young Werther*, deals with the depression and eventual suicide of an obsessive univer-sity student. Here then is my first, and second-least suc-cessful, commencement address:

When I was first asked to speak at Hartford State Technical College, I jumped at the opportunity. Because, you see, I thought I had been asked to speak at Harvard, which would have been quite an honor. But instead I am here with you, the nation's future air conditioner repairmen. Let's try to make the best of it.

Goethe once said, "A useless life is an early death." In Goethe's terms, most of you are already dead. Because most of you will live useless lives. You will, you will, and you will. [Here I pointed for dramatic effect at several particularly useless-looking graduates and then at a man who I later learned was Dr. Jonas Salk, discoverer of the polio vaccine, who was there to receive an honorary degree and give a serious address to contrast with my supposedly humorous one.]

If Dr. Jonas Salk were here, he would tell you the key to living a useful life like his is to expect the unexpected. [And here I proceeded to tell several anecdotes about the discovery of the polio vaccine which Dr. Salk had intended to tell himself, thus expanding the scope of the disaster.]

But back to Goethe, and please remember that I prepared this speech for Harvard students, so it will probably be way over your heads.

As the booing began, I became hostile and openly combative and concluded my address, amid a flurry of catcalls and thrown objects, by giving the graduates and their families the finger.

Let's take a look at what I did wrong. First, there was my housekeeper, who was responsible for the entire debacle. She simply had to go. Second, when challenged by an unexpected situation (speaking at Hartford rather than Harvard), I had behaved irrationally instead of trying to adapt to the new environment as Dr. Salk would have done.

But did I learn from my mistakes? Yes and no, but mainly no. A year later I was asked to speak to the graduating class of Lewis and Clark University in Portland, Oregon, where I received an honorary doctorate along with Connie Chung and Wolfgang Puck. This time my strategy was to start my speech with a bit of extremely personal information that would get the audience on my side. See if you can tell what went wrong.

Friends, family members, distinguished faculty, graduating seniors, Connie and Wolfgang. Three weeks ago I was diagnosed with pancreatic cancer. [Wolfgang's gasp could be heard over the shocked silence of the crowd.] *It is a lethal and particularly painful form of the disease. I was told I had at most six months to live. Some of you probably pity me. But don't pity me. See, I pity you. Because while I have been sentenced to death, you have received a far harsher judgment. You have been sentenced to life. Without parole. You have, and you have, and you have.* [And here I did the pointing thing.]

Aside from repeating the pointing mistake, what did I do wrong? Should I have just given up making commencement addresses? Or could I learn from my mistakes? Maury Povich, Connie's husband, took me aside and, after recommending an oncologist who had recently appeared on his program, gave me the key. "Al," Maury began, "personally I loved your speech. But I think you may have lost the crowd by being so negative. Remember, this is a big day for them. They want to be inspired and uplifted. Not criticized and harangued."

As I listened to Wolfgang explain to a delighted audience how life was like a pizza, I realized that Maury had a point.

Source: Al Franken, Ph.D. (hon.), *Oh, the Things I Know!* Copyright © 2002 by Al Franken. Dutton Publishing (pp. 6–9).

An Introduction to Positive, Neutral, and Negative Audiences

There are three types of audiences, those who want to hear you praise the things they already believe, those who don't care, and those who are hoping you fall down and break your leg on the way to the podium.

This statement describes, somewhat pessimistically, the three audience types that we will be discussing in this text—the positive, the neutral, and the negative. As you've read, the most effective speakers are those who adapt to the audience and the situation. The focus in this text will be on three dimensions that differentiate audience types: the audience's attitude toward the topic, their interest in the topic, and their knowledge of the topic. Audience attitudes can fall anywhere on a continuum from very positive to very negative. For ease of discussion, we divide that continuum into three chunks: positive audiences, neutral audiences, and negative audiences. Audiences also vary in terms of their level of interest or in commitment to an issue. Think about the issues you care about and those you don't. Do you care about local politics, student government, effective job interviewing skills, United States aid to Africa, home schooling, graduate school, automobile safety, child abuse, United States–Canada relations, quilting, or copper mining in Michigan? Besides having varying levels of interest in these topics, you also probably have varying degrees of knowledge about them. Thus, a speech to an informed, interested audience who support home-schooling should be considerably different from a speech on home-schooling to an audience who is uninformed and uninterested.

In addition to attitude, interest, and knowledge, you should be aware of the audience's attitude toward you as the speaker and to the situation itself. Sometimes you must address people with whom you have strained relationships or who have been forced to attend your presentation (for example, taking a required course). To be an effective speaker, one must adapt to all these variations in audiences.

The audience's attitude toward the topic is such a fundamental factor in making presentations that we have organized this text around it. Each of the three audience types (positive, neutral, and negative) dictates the goals you can set and the strategies you should follow, and we will discuss these in subsequent chapters. However, an audience is likely to include some listeners who are positive, some who are neutral, and some who are negative, thus constituting a mixed audience.

The Positive Audience

Most of the time people speak to **positive audiences**—audiences who are interested in what the speaker has to say, open to learning information, and often in agreement with the speaker's positions on issues. While we consider positive audiences to be those who have an interest in the speaker's presentation, a positive audience may not be informed about an issue and therefore may not have formed an attitude toward it. This means there are two types of positive audiences:

positive audience An audience that is interested in what a speaker has to say, open to learning information, and often in agreement with the speaker's own positions on issues.

supportive audience A positive audience that is interested in the topic or issue, has a positive attitude toward it, and is knowledgeable about it.

open audience A positive audience that is interested in the topic or issue, has no established attitude toward it, and has little or no knowledge about it.

Supportive audience: a positive audience that is interested in the topic or issue, has a positive attitude toward it, and is knowledgeable about it. Examples: student supporters attending one in a series of presentations on expanding campus recreational facilities; managers listening to a summary of the company accomplishments during the past year.

Open audience: a positive audience that is interested in the topic or issue, has no established attitude toward it, and has little or no knowledge about it. Examples: students attending a campus lecture on the impact of global trade on the job market; parents attending a school board presentation on a proposed new method of teaching math in the elementary schools.

One obvious difference in your approaches to speaking to these two audiences is the need to provide more fundamental information to the open audience with the intent of developing a positive attitude toward the issue. Your goal with the supportive audience might focus on inspiring, maintaining, or confirming their positive attitude, or moving them to some action.

The Neutral Audience

At times you are obligated to make presentations on topics to which audiences are indifferent—although it is almost impossible to have information about an issue and be truly neutral. Neutrality is a relative term; the lack of any intense feelings one way or another toward an issue probably leads people to see themselves as neutral. The communication scholar Theodore Clevenger used two dimensions to categorize neutral audiences: interest in the topic and knowledge of the topic.[11] These dimensions are reflected in the following three types of **neutral audiences** discussed in this text:

Apathetic audience: an audience that has a neutral attitude toward the topic or issue and has little or no interest in it but is knowledgeable about it. Examples: employees attending the mandatory semiannual training session on work safety; college students listening to a student speech on the danger of AIDS.

Detached audience: an audience that has a neutral attitude toward the topic or issue, has little or no interest in it, and has little or no knowledge about it. Examples: members of a Midwest community business association listening to a speech on efforts to save the manatee in Florida; a group of high school seniors listening to a lecture on how to plan for their retirement years.

Ambivalent audience: an audience that has a neutral attitude toward the topic or issue but that has both interest and knowledge of it. Examples: a group of voters listening to several candidates for mayor in their town; a church board listening to several proposals for renovating the church.

While all three types share a neutral attitude toward the topic, the apathetic and detached audiences both lack interest toward the issue. The difference between these two is that the apathetic are knowledgeable and the detached are not. A speaker's first goal is to increase listener's interest. Ambivalent audience members differ from both, in that they have interest and knowledge but are neither positively or negatively in-

neutral audience An audience that lacks positive or negative feelings toward an issue; the audience members consider themselves neutral.

apathetic audience A neutral audience that has a neutral attitude toward the topic or issue and has little or no interest in it but is knowledgeable about it.

detached audience A neutral audience that has a neutral attitude toward the topic or issue, has little or no interest in it, and has little or no knowledge about it.

ambivalent audience A neutral audience that has a neutral attitude toward the topic or issue but has both interest and knowledge of it.

clined. Ambivalence can be created either because (1) people have conflicting beliefs (based on what they know) or (2) people's thoughts conflict with their feelings (or vice versa).[12] There are probably lots of issues on which you have been ambivalent—unable to make a decision, despite interest and knowledge: for example, where to go to college, whom to support for a political office, or what to do after graduation.

The Negative Audience

Speaking to a **negative audience** is probably the most challenging presentation you can face. In your everyday presentations, you will face audiences whose position on an issue contradicts or opposes the one you are advocating. As a speaker, your goal becomes to change the audience's attitude—to persuade them to accept your position. In general, a negative attitude toward an issue is based on some knowledge of the issue; thus negative audiences are usually informed. However, sometimes negative audiences lose interest in the issues; in essence, they become apathetic. This results in two types of negative audiences you will face:

> **Passive negative audience:** an audience that is knowledgeable about the issue, opposes the speaker's position on the issue but has lost interest in the issue. Examples: a group of graduating college seniors listening to an administrator talk about the need to raise tuition in the future; managers who oppose the current company reorganization that has been instituted listening to plans for the final steps.

> **Active negative audience:** an audience that is knowledgeable about the issue, opposes the speaker's position on the issue, but has interest in the issue. Examples: a group of union members listening to a member of management discuss the need to cut health care benefits; members of a Young Republicans campus group hearing a speaker advocate government support of birth control and abortion.

In the case of the passive negative audience, the speaker must first arouse their listeners' interest in the issue again before attempting to change it. The level of opposition an audience holds differs and is reflected in the continuum of resistance discussed earlier. The general goal in speaking to negative audiences is to move them to some degree toward the positive side of the continuum. How far you move them depends on how strongly they oppose your position. Later in the text we will present a number of persuasive strategies you can employ to try and reduce the amount of resistance held by negative audience members.

The Mixed Audience

As part of a senior course devoted to developing professional skills, you are giving a presentation with the goal of enrolling students in the alumni association for fifty dollars. Will you be facing a positive, neutral, or negative audience? Most likely the answer is "All of the above." Some students in your audience are likely to be gung-ho supporters of your school and happy

negative audience An audience whose position on an issue contradicts or opposes the one a speaker is advocating.

passive negative audience An audience that is knowledgeable about the issue, opposes the speaker's position on it but has lost interest in it.

active negative audience An audience that is knowledgeable about the issue and opposes the speaker's position on it, but has interest in it.

to become members; other students probably have not considered the idea and are neutral; while others may be unhappy with the school or have tight budgets and thus opposed to becoming members. Most of the audiences you face will probably be more of this mixed type than uniformly one type. So what strategies should you use? Do you give three speeches in one—one for each audience type? Do you determine who the majority are and design a speech for them? The answer to these questions is "It depends." It depends primarily on your goal and the relative representation of each audience type. If your goal is to get as many students to sign up after your presentation as you can, then you would probably ignore the negative members because you are unlikely to move them to join after just one speech. The positive members need just a little more information about how to go about joining, which can be handled quickly, so your focus might be on convincing the neutral members to join.

Speaking to **mixed audiences** requires the use of a wide range of strategies— some aimed at the more neutral members and some aimed at the more negative members. In essence, you are attempting to cast a broad net that will capture the largest audience without losing your effectiveness. Applying too broad a range of strategies might mean you are ineffective with everyone. You need to strike a balance between narrowly and broadly focusing your strategies.

You might think that in mixed audiences you should always talk to the majority or perhaps just to the positive and neutral members. However, there are times when your focus might be on the minority or just the negative members. You need to iden- tify your "target" audience. For example, in making a presentation to an audience that includes managers who support your plan to acquire a new piece of equipment, your speech might be more directed to the vice president, who opposes the plan but who controls the funding.

In speaking to a mixed audience, there is the risk of losing the interest of one of the subgroups while directing comments to another, for example, repeating infor- mation already known by some of the audience members. One strategy to use in this situation is to announce that you are directing your comments to a specific portion of the audience. For example, at a commencement address the speaker might say, "Right now I want to direct my comments to the parents of those who are graduating today. You have provided . . . " This type of comment heightens the attention of part of the audience and reduces the concern of other members of the audience about how the points apply to them. However, the speaker needs to let the peripheral audience members know when the comments are being directed back toward them: "My final comments are for everyone here today."

● GETTING TO WORK

The Process of Becoming a Presenter

Interest in developing effective public speaking skills has been around for a long time. One observation about public speaking from an 1896 text, *The Modern Speaker or Complete Manual of Elocution,* still applies today:

mixed audience An audience composed of various proportions of positive, neutral, and negative audience members.

Oratory in all its refinement, belongs to no particular people, to the exclusion of others; nor is it the gift of nature alone; but, like other acquirements, it is the reward of arduous efforts, under the guidance of consummate skill. Perfection, in this art, as well as in all others, is the work of time and labor, prompted by true feeling, and guided by correct thought.[13]

This course and the experiences you have in it are only a part of the process and labor needed to develop your presentation skills. That development began before you got to this class, as you acquired your language skills, developed your personality, and engaged in various presentations associated with other classes and organizations. The process will continue long after you leave. Your development and improvement as a presenter depends on continuing the process after you finish this text.

The development of effective presentation skills involves continual self-assessment, actively seeking feedback, participating in a variety of presentational opportunities, modifying your behavior, and continuing to learn. As you read this text, you will be asked frequently to reflect on your own thoughts and behaviors. You need to become aware of your presentational strengths and weaknesses so that you can develop your most effective style. As you read about the various options and strategies, assess which ones will work for you and develop a plan for incorporating them into your presentational repertoire. You might recognize that you have a tendency to say "um" a lot, but unless you develop a strategy for reducing these vocalized pauses, little will change. Each student begins this class with varying amounts of previous presentational experience, and some students will appear to be quite polished. However difficult it is, focus on your own performance and ways to improve it. Your ability to improve from one presentation to another is more important than how well your presentations compare to those of your classmates. Use the questions in Act and Reflect 1.3 to initially assess your competence in some of the skills covered in this chapter.

Generally, the more you practice and engage in using a skill, the better at it you become. As part of the process of developing your speaking skills, you should try to engage in as many presentational experiences as you can and reflect on them carefully and critically, even after you complete this course. Along with reflecting on how you did, actively seek feedback from people you trust. Try to get a sense of how the audience responded. What features did they particularly like about your presentation? What suggestions do they have on how you could have done better? You need to be open to whatever feedback you receive, and to let your responders know that you desire honest feedback that can help you improve your presentations.

You are never too old to learn. This adage applies to presentational skills as well. Education about presentations is an ongoing, never-ending process. After you graduate, you should continue your study of presentations. Organizations often offer additional presentational training sessions for employees; take advantage of those opportunities. Scanning the Web turns up a variety of resources on making presentations, and there are a large number of popular books on the subject. In examining that information, remember that any advice that is provided is just that: advice. You need to assess what will work for you, what is your comfort level with the advice, and what fits the situation.

ACT&REFLECT

1.3: Assessing Your Basic Presentational Skills

ACT • Which of the following are your strongest skills and which are your weakest?

1. Use of logical arguments to persuade other people
2. Use of stories and emotional appeals to persuade other people
3. Adapting my message as I gain feedback from listeners
4. Use of nonverbal cues to enhance my verbal message
5. Sensitivity to the differences among people and ability to adapt to those differences
6. Thinking clearly and conveying my thoughts successfully to others
7. Deciding the best strategies to use in any speaking context
8. Talking to audiences in a conversational style
9. Talking to audiences sincerely and thoughtfully
10. Ability to be myself in front of a group of other people
11. Ability to relate to groups of people on a personal basis
12. Ability to build, sustain, and repair relationships with audiences

REFLECT • How have you come to acquire the strengths you have? In what ways will your weaknesses hamper your ability to give effective speeches? What can you do to strengthen your weak areas?

SUMMARY

Presentations encompass a wide variety of interactions that are characterized by the enactment of two roles: one who speaks and others who listen. Everyday presentations are those in which people intentionally and strategically deliver oral messages as part of their daily lives. The preparation and planning that are needed for everyday presentations also vary, as these presentations range from impromptu comments made on the spur of the moment to highly planned and structured formal speeches.

Communication is a transactional process in which all parties are simultaneously sending and receiving information. Presentations are attempts to influence others through spoken communication. Audience resistance to our attempts to influence them range from those who work in support of the speaker's issue to those who work against it. Face-to-face oral presentations allow information to be highlighted, immediate adaptation to audience feedback, and an opportunity to enhance the quality and meaning of the message through a variety of nonverbal cues.

This text is built on several guiding principles

of presentation, as follows. (1) Understanding and adapting to the audience and the situation is important for effective presentations. While many texts provide prescriptive rules, our approach is to develop your ability to make effective decisions that best suit your presentation style. (2) Your presentations should be thoughtful and deliberative. Good thinking is critical in the development of your presentation. (3) You need to balance speaking style with content in developing an eloquent presentation. Eloquent presentations involve the use of personal stories, self-disclosures, a warm tone, and sincerity. Ideally, a presentation reflects both a speaker's thoughtfulness and sincerity. (4) You should develop and maintain a positive relationship to enhance the effectiveness of your presentations. Be aware of the relationship that exists between you and your audience.

Audiences can be classified according to their attitude toward, their interest in, and their knowledge of the topic. These factors contribute to the categorization of audiences as positive, neutral, or negative. Positive audiences are interested and have a positive attitude toward the topic; they can be divided into supportive audiences, who are knowledgeable, and open audiences, who are unknowledgeable. All three types of neutral audiences have a neutral attitude; apathetic audiences are knowledgeable yet uninterested, detached audiences lack knowledge or interest, and ambivalent audiences have both knowledge and interest. Finally, both types of negative audiences have knowledge of the issue and oppose the speaker's position; the active negative audience has an interest in the issue, and the passive negative audience does not. Understanding differences among these audience types should help you become more effective and deliberative in your selection of the best strategies. These audience types provide the major structure followed in this text.

VIDEO EXPERIENCE

Check out the following video clips.

1. In the first clip, a resident of Wichita, Kansas, makes a request of the city council to promote fee waivers to public facilities and attractions for those who are pushing other people in wheelchairs. He speaks about his own positive experience visiting San Diego, which has such a policy. His sincerity makes his presentation particularly potent.

2. The second clip provides an example of speaking to a positive audience. An enthusiastic speaker addresses a positive, supportive audience who have met one morning in Batavia, Illinois, to protest changes in Social Security.

THINKING BACK, THINKING AHEAD

1. Think about the lecturer you have enjoyed the most. To what degree did the lecturer influence you? Did the lecturer probably intend these? How effective was the lecturer in fully utilizing the spoken nature of presentations? How much did you feel connected with the lecturer? What did the lecturer do to connect with you? In what ways are lectures different from the types of presentations you are likely to make? In what ways are they similar?

2. Our claim that strong thinking leads to strong speaking is easy to make but harder to accomplish. Think about some specific issue on which you are confused and uncertain. How likely is it that if you could speak effectively and coherently about this issue? What could you do to improve your thinking and therefore improve your speaking?

3. You are likely to be doing some kind of introductory speech in this class (or perhaps you already have). How would you classify the "audience" of students, in terms of being positive, neutral, or negative? Why? What might be the most important information to share in this speech, if the students are viewed as a supportive audience? As an apathetic audience?

NOTES

1. F. E. X. Dance and C. E. Larson, *Speech Communication: Concepts and Behavior* (New York: Holt, Rinehart & Winston, 1972).
2. D.L. Rubin, T. Hafer, and K. Arata, "Reading and Listening to Oral-Based versus Literate-Based Discourse," *Communication Education, 49* (2000): 121–133.
3. K. Sack, "Political Memo: Quayle's Working Hard to Give a Better Speech," *New York Times*, October 7, 1992.
4. K. Hall Jamieson, *Eloquence in an Electronic Age: The Transformation of Political Speechmaking* (New York: Oxford University Press, 1990).
5. C. G. Emrich, H. H. Brower, J. M. Feldman, and H. Garland, "Images in Words: Presidential Rhetoric, Charisma, and Greatness," *Administrative Science Quarterly, 46* (2001): 527–557.
6. Jack Canfield, interview in L. Walters, *Secrets of Superstar Speakers* (New York: McGraw Hill, 2000), 161.
7. L. Stafford and D. J. Canary, "Maintenance Strategies and Romantic Relationship Type, Gender, and Relational Characteristics," *Journal of Social and Personal Relationships, 8* (1991): 217–242.
8. D. J. Canary and L. Stafford, "Maintaining Relationships through Strategic and Routine Interaction," in *Communication and Relational Maintenance*, edited by D. Canary and L. Stafford (San Diego: Academic Press, 1993), 3–22.
9. S. Sprecher, "Insiders' Perspectives on Reasons for Attraction to Close Other," *Social Psychology Quarterly, 61* (1998): 287–300.
10. J. M. Olson and M. P. Zanna, "Attitudes and Attitude Change," *Annual Review of Psychology, 44* (1993): 117–155.
11. T. Clevenger, *Audience Analysis* (Indianapolis: Bobbs-Merrill, 1966).
12. I. Ajzen, "Nature and Operation of Attitudes," *Annual Review of Psychology, 52* (2001): 27–58.
13. H. D. Northrop, *The Modern Speaker or Complete Manual of Elocution* (Philadelphia, J. H. Moore Company), 4.

Chapter

2

Planning Your First Presentation

Your First Presentation

Identify a Topic
- Expertise
- Experience
- Commitment

Know Your Audience
- Cultural Composition
- Demographic Characteristics
- Knowledge and Interest

Formulate Your Speaking Goal

Identify Major Points

Select Support Material
- Personal Experiences
- Other Sources
- Supporting Major Points with the Brain in Mind

Organize Your Presentation
- From Most to Least Important Points
- From Least to Most Important Points
- In Chronological Order
- In Topical Order

Create an Ear-Catching Introduction
- Motivate Your Audience
- Introduce Your Topic
- Preview Your Major Points

Construct a Memorable Conclusion
- Reinforce a Point
- Establish Closure

Insert Transitions

Practice and Prepare Notes
- Achieve "Prepared Conversation" Delivery
- Prepare Helpful Notes
- Practice Your Presentation

Manage Speech Anxiety
- Be Yourself
- Breathe Smart
- Be Picky (PCCI)

Getting to Work

Summary

Goals

 To help you plan your first presentation

 To inform you of a basic procedure for planning all presentations

 To alert you to points in the planning process when you will need to make decisions

 To challenge you to reflect on your own presentation skills

To suggest ways you can channel counterproductive nervousness into productive energy

How can the instructor expect us to give a presentation next class period? Even if it is supposed to be about myself, I've never given a presentation before. Even if it only has to last three minutes, we haven't even covered the material about how to give presentations yet. I thought that's why we were in this class: to learn about presentations. I think this is too soon and it's not fair.

Perhaps you currently find yourself in the same circumstance as this frustrated student. It's the first day of class, and your instructor has assigned a three-minute presentation to be delivered to the entire class at the next meeting. You are supposed to introduce yourself to the class, but you don't really think there is anything about yourself that anyone would want to hear. You expected to give presentations at some point in the term, but this assignment is too soon. You aren't certain about what to do or where to begin. Before you get too worried, read this chapter. ●

Your First Presentation

This chapter will assist you in preparing for that first speaking assignment by guiding you through the planning process that will result in a presentation. As you plan this initial presentation, you will also become familiar with the critical points in the planning process when you will need to make decisions for any other presentation you might give in this class or in the future. In addition, because you will have read this chapter, each topic we discuss in the remainder of the text should make more sense to you because you will know how it "fits in" with the overall process of planning a presentation. Finally, although you will more than likely be a confident speaker, we conclude with suggestions that will help you channel any nervous energy you might experience into energy that will work to your advantage as a speaker.

Identify a Topic

For your first presentation, your instructor will most likely ask you to talk about a topic you are very knowledgeable about: yourself. Your assignment might require you to discuss a specific event or piece of information such as "your greatest accomplishment" or "your career choice," or you might simply be told to introduce yourself to your classroom audience in a speech that lasts for a specified period of time. If this seems like a challenge to you, you have lots of company. For many students, talking about themselves is the most difficult topic they will ever discuss. Why is this so? For some people, talking about themselves might be too close to home, making it difficult to think of anything to say; others are modest or shy, and the prospect of discussing one's self is not enjoyable; still others might think of so many things to say about themselves that it is difficult to choose. Your first challenge is to select a few qualities—no more than two or three—about yourself that will give your classroom audience a chance to get to know you. What follows will help you identify some attributes or characteristics about yourself for this assignment, as well as to start a list of possible topics for other speeches you will give in this class in the future.

When you have the choice of a topic for a presentation, the best topics for you to speak about are those topics about which you already know something. Another way to explain this is to say you should choose topics about which you have **expertise**, or about which you are currently knowledgeable; topics with which you have "hands-on" **experience**; and topics that you are committed to, or that you believe are important.

Expertise

If you had to stand up right now and speak, without preparation, about anything you chose for two or three minutes, what would you talk about? There are probably any number of things you could discuss: your major, your hobbies, your family, your opinions on subjects of importance to you. Any subject you are able to discuss

expertise Significant amount of knowledge you have of a particular subject.

experience "Hands-on" practice you have with a particular topic.

The "best" topics for a presentation are those for which we have experience, expertise, or commitment. In the photo, what topics present themselves that this volunteer might consider for her speeches? ●

for a few minutes "off the top of your head" is an area where you have at least some **expertise** and is a good possibility for your first introductory speaking assignment. When you have the option of choosing a subject for other speaking assignments this term, you should also consider topics on which you have expertise. Ilana had expertise, for example, about her native state of Hawaii. Because she lived in Hawaii, she was able to discuss her native state in a more expert manner than someone who had not lived there:

> Imagine a place where there is no daylight savings time, there is no snow, and people around you are saying "Maui no ka oe." If you can imagine a place like this, then you're imagining Maui, my birthplace. And since I lived on Maui for about thirteen years, I can pretty much say "Maui no ka oe" as well. "Maui no ka oe" means "Maui's the best," and I can pretty much vouch for that and there are five things that I would recommend tourists should do.[1]

MSL

Experience

How do you like to spend your spare time? What skills do you possess? The second criteria, **experience,** has to do with the time you spend engaged in various activities or in pursuing knowledge about various issues or topics. The experience you gain from your continued involvement also enhances your expertise. When you speak on a topic about which you have experience, you are not simply relating something you have read about or heard on television; you are discussing something about which you have hands-on experience, and the knowledge resulting from that experience adds to the mastery and credibility with which you discuss the topic as well as the way your listeners perceive you. Laura spent much of her time playing poker. The time she spent playing made her not only familiar with the rules of the game but also able to make connections to her academic work from the skills she acquired. If Laura had simply read a set of rules for playing poker, she might not have acquired the other knowledge that resulted from her experience that she imparted to her classroom audience:

MSL

> One of the most straightforward things it [poker] does is, it helps you improve your mental math skills. You have to be able to calculate probabilities on the spot to know that, well, "I need one card to complete my hand, there is only a couple of 'em out there in the deck and that doesn't leave a very good chance that you're gonna get it . . ."
> And with this knowledge of probabilities you learn to make calculated risks: weigh the pros and cons and kind of find out the relationships of the risk and the benefits.[2]

Commitment

Finally, besides expertise and experience, you should feel a sense of importance or commitment regarding the topics about which you speak. We are using the term **commitment** to mean that you believe that the topic is an important part of your life or that it represents an important viewpoint, worthy of the time and effort it takes you to create and give a speech about it, and also worthy of the time your audience devotes to listening to your speech. If you were to speak on a topic about which you felt little or no commitment, would you be able to involve your audience, let alone be involved yourself? If you aren't talking about something that is important to you, it will be difficult for your audience to find your topic important; thus your speech is not likely to be as effective as you would like, and you may not reach your speaking goal. Shannon, for example, felt very strongly that children should not compete in athletics. Her viewpoint resulted from her own experiences as a competitive gymnast when she was a child. Her strong opinion about the topic motivated the audience to consider their own opinions about competitive athletics, particularly for children:

MSL

> I feel that there are many characteristics about exercising in competitive sports that are a problem. And since I was a gymnast myself, I have personal experience in some of the negative outcomes of competitive sports and many of us seem to get caught up in the positive attributes of competing in these types of activities. I want you to also recognize there are many costs, as I see it, as well.[3]

As you prepare your first introductory speech, take the opportunity to introduce to your audience those issues about which you have expertise, experience, and commitment (see Act and Reflect 2.1). To help identify possible topics to discuss in this first speech, as well as to begin to

commitment Your belief that a topic is intellectually or emotionally important.

ACT&REFLECT

2.1: Brainstorm a List of Topics for Your First Speech

ACT • In your notebook, set up a table as shown here. Give yourself three minutes to brainstorm a list of possible topics. Remember that when you brainstorm, your goal is quantity, not quality. When the time is up, check each topic for which you have expertise; next, check each topic for which you have experience; finally, check each topic for which you have commitment. The topics with three checks are the best for you to consider for your presentations.

Topic	Expertise	Experience	Commitment
1.			
2.			
3.			
4.			
5.			

REFLECT • Using just the topics for which you were able to check that you have expertise, experience, and commitment, select two or three you would like to discuss in your first speech. Save the others for possible topics for future speeches.

build an inventory of topics for future speeches, take some time to think about yourself now: What are you already knowledgeable about? How do you spend your time? What is really important to you? Developing a list of potential topics means you'll never have to say, "There's nothing I know about that would be interesting enough for a speech."

Now that you have some ideas for good topics to discuss in your first speech and others, it is time to think about your audience.

Know Your Audience

The more a speaker knows the audience, the more the speech can focus on audience needs and concerns. For this first speech, you may not know any of your classmates; however, in the first few days of class before you give your introductory speech, if you take the time to observe your classmates, you should be able to acquire enough information about them to assist in preparing your speech (see Act and Reflect 2.2).

Cultural Composition

Considering the **cultural composition** of your audience will help you to make decisions about what is and is not familiar, what is and is not acceptable, what is and is not important to your audience. After discovering that some members of her classroom audience were opposed to policies regulating affirmative action, believing these policies promoted underqualified individuals, Maya, a Hispanic honors student, provided an example that included herself and two other classmates to refute this misconception:

> The next misconception of affirmative action is it promotes underqualified individuals. A lot of the time we might think "Oh, this person only got into this school because they were Black or they were Mexican." But this is not always the case . . . Ilana and myself and Cindy are in [she explains a campus program for minority honors students] and this is an academic scholarship only for minority students and is designed to enhance the diversity of the campus while still maintaining academic competitiveness. . . . They have stringent requirements with GPA.[4]

Demographic Characteristics

In addition to the cultural composition of the audience, speakers should consider **demographic characteristics** of audience members. Demographics are factual characteristics such as age, major, hometown, sex, and religious preference. Ross used demographics to encourage his classroom audience to begin to vote in campus elections:

> I've done research about voter turnout in various venues and I'll just go over those very quick here. The first one I'll talk about just reflects residence hall students . . . there's about half the class that does live in the residence halls. Last spring we had our election in the residence halls and there's five thousand students who live in the residence halls at that time. Of these four hundred and forty actually voted. That's about 9 percent. That's pretty low.
>
> Now for those of you who don't live in the residence halls, you would have been able to vote in the government of the student body election, which was also in the spring, that effects all students. . . . For that, oh, there were about twenty-seven thousand students who could have voted, and of that, about five thousand voted. As you can see about 18 percent voting.[5]

Knowledge and Interest

If you are able to identify some general areas in which your audience has interest and/or knowledge, you may be able to use that information to develop a speech about related areas of interest and knowledge. Scott knew his classroom audience were avid supporters of the university football and

cultural composition The cultures or ethnicity represented by members of your audience.

demographic characteristics Factual characteristics of audience members such as age, major, hometown, sex, and religious preference.

ACT & REFLECT

2.2: Describe Your Audience

ACT • Even though you have only been in this class for a brief time, what is your impression of your classroom audience? Write a description of your classmates in a few sentences.

REFLECT • What have you learned from this description that will help you develop your speech of introduction?

basketball teams. Basing his approach on the interest in those sports, Scott talked about the importance of supporting what he labeled "lesser sports":

MSL

> Most of us have all experienced "big" athletics like football and basketball. . . . But a lot of people I've noticed haven't really gone to some of the smaller athletic events that are closer to the action, so I thought I'd introduce you to that part of campus sports.[6]

At this point, you have had a chance to consider those facets about yourself about which you are expert, experienced, and or committed that could be included in your introductory speech, and you have also considered what you currently know about your classroom audience. Your next step is to formulate your speaking goal. That is, what do you want to accomplish as a result of giving your first speech and how will you accomplish it?

Formulate Your Speaking Goal

The **speaking goal** is what you want to achieve as a result of presenting your message. Although the assignment for this first speech is to introduce yourself to your classroom audience, you still need to decide how you want your classmates to view you and what you will tell them about yourself so they will view you as you want them to. Do you want your classroom audience to view you as a friendly person? If so, what details about you will create that image? Maybe you want your classroom audience to view you as an outstanding athlete. In that case, the way you introduce yourself might differ from that of the friendly person. Or perhaps it is important that your audience view you as a campus activist.

speaking goal The objective you are striving for as a result of your speech.

In that case, the information you reveal about yourself will differ from those of both the athlete and the friendly person. In your speech of introduction, you might not ever identify yourself to your audience as a "friendly person" or an "outstanding athlete" or a "campus activist," but having an image in your mind of the type of person you are that you want to present to your classroom audience will serve as the guide to the qualities about yourself you choose to discuss, the details you provide for each of those qualities, and the way you present the information. Maybe you have decided you want your audience to view you as a friendly, easygoing person. Notice that on the sample planning tree in Figure 2.1, we have entered this speaking goal under the heading "My Goal." See also Act and Reflect 2.3.

Identify Major Points

After you have formulated your speaking goal, your next step is to choose a few key pieces of information about yourself that will help you achieve your goal. These key pieces of information are called the major points of your speech, and they should not only be related to your goal but also help you support and develop your goal. If you want your audience to view you as an excellent athlete, for example, the major points of your speech should all be geared to showing your audience that you possess athletic talents. If you completed the brainstorming activity earlier in this chapter, the topics you identified as your areas of expertise, experience, and commitment will be helpful to you now.

● FIGURE 2.1 A Sample Presentation Planning Tree.

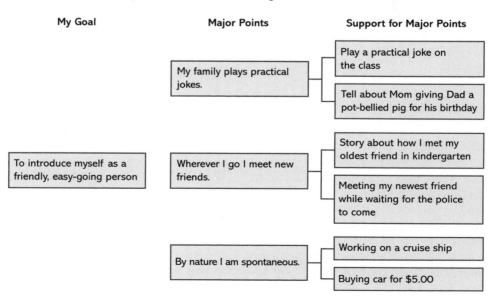

ACT&REFLECT

2.3: Draft Your Speaking Goal

ACT • You are in charge of creating the first impression of yourself to your classroom audience. What would you like that first impression to be? Complete this statement: "My speaking goal is to present myself to my classroom audience as _____. Enter this speaking goal on Figure 2.2 in the left-hand column.

REFLECT • Considering your speaking goal, what about yourself should you tell your audience that will support that goal?

● **FIGURE 2.2** My Presentation Planning Tree.

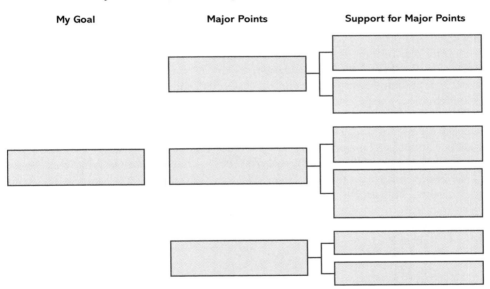

How would you support the speaking goal of introducing yourself as a friendly, easygoing person? On your checklist you might see words such as "family," "friends," "pets," "vacation," "road trip," or "picnic," along with other words that support or illustrate the image of your friendly, easygoing personality. Because this first speech is likely to be rather brief, you won't be able to talk about all of those qualities; instead, choose the two or three terms that are most important to you or that you believe will most clearly illustrate the image you wish to present to your classroom audience. If you need some help deciding on which two or three will work the best, try this:

State your speaking goal: "I am a friendly, easygoing (FEG) person."

Now imagine one of your classmates asks you: "Why do you believe you are a FEG person?"

What is the first thing that comes to your mind? "Because everyone in my family is always playing practical jokes on each other."

Your classmate asks you: "What is another reason you believe you are a FEG person?"

You reply: "Because everywhere I go, I make friends."

Your classmate asks you a third time: "Is there any other reason you believe you are a FEG person?"

You reply: "I'm very spontaneous. I've done some major things on the spur of the moment."

These two or three qualities about yourself will more than likely become the key points of your speech of introduction.

Select Support Material

Now you have a basic framework or outline for your first speech. However, you can't just stand up in front of your audience and say, "Hi, my name is Aurelia. My family is constantly playing practical jokes on each other; I make friends wherever I go; and I'm a very spontaneous person known to do all sorts of things on a moment's notice." If your audience is momentarily distracted, they might miss one of the pieces of information about you. It is also possible that some of your classmates will introduce themselves in similar ways, and your speech could blend in with the speeches of everyone else. Your next consideration is to decide what you will tell your classroom audience about your major points that will allow them to feel they not only know you but view you as an individual different from your other classmates. What you choose to say about your main points is referred to as "developing" or "supporting" your main points. This means you give additional information that supports each main point that in turn will support your speaking goal. For your speech of introduction, you have several options available to you for developing each of your main points (see Act and Reflect 2.4).

Personal Experiences

Since you are introducing yourself to your classroom audience, most of your support material is likely to be based on personal experience. Give examples: the best family practical joke ever played on you or the most unusual circumstance in which you met a friend or the most dramatic example of your spontaneity. Provide details and descriptions so your classroom audience will feel that they know the people you are discussing or that they were present at the events you are relating to them.

ACT&REFLECT

2.4: Identify Your Major Points

ACT • Working with the speaking goal you have formulated for yourself, identify all of the items on your topic matrix that you believe are related to your goal. Of these, select two or three items that you believe will best create the image of yourself that you want to achieve with your classroom audience. Enter these items in the middle column of Figure 2.2.

REFLECT • Why do these two or three qualities best present you in the way you wish to be presented? What evidence can you think of that makes these the best qualities you can discuss to introduce yourself to your classroom audience?

Other Sources

Your instructor will probably not require you to use sources other than yourself on your first speech, but don't overlook a line from a song or a poem if it is relevant to what you are saying about yourself. If you helped build the largest pizza in the world, quote the record book that acknowledges this feat. If there is a song that describes your feeling about making friends, sing a line (or at least say it). Quote what your favorite relative says about your family's practical jokes. The integration of information from other sources moves you from the role of conversationalist to the role of presenter.

Supporting Major Points with the Brain in Mind

Cognitive research, which shows that the way you present information can help your listeners understand and remember that information, provides some additional ways you can develop and support your key points and give your presentation a little more "zip." Some of the conclusions of research that will help you in constructing your first presentation are as follows.[7]

Guidelines for Supporting Major Points with the Brain in Mind

1 Incorporate **social activity** in your presentation by designing ways your audience can participate. Ask one or two members of your classmate audience to volunteer to briefly describe the best practical joke they have experienced. Or ask them to tell by a show of hands whether they would describe themselves as spontaneous. See if you can think of other ways to actively involve your audience.

social activity An opportunity you give in your presentation for your audience to participate.

2 When new knowledge is linked to something the audience is already familiar with, the new knowledge becomes easier to understand and remember. Maybe your campus newspaper has run a series of articles about the social, emotional, and physical benefits of having a large circle of friends. You could refer to that series of articles to introduce your own adventures in making friends.

3 Your audience is likely to listen to new information if **emotional appeals** are used to present it. Relate an example of your spontaneous nature that will make the audience laugh. Are there other ways you can appeal to the emotions of your audience?

4 Audiences are responsive to newness, to **novelty.** Remember that your classroom audience will hear several speeches each class period. How will yours be memorable? Play a practical joke on the audience. Introduce your speech in another language you learned from a friend. Show your spontaneous nature by bursting into song. Be sure, though, that you can tie your novel method to the point of your presentation. What are ways you can add novelty to your speech?

When you say or do something unexpected you can capture the interest of your audience and help them remember you. ●

We have advised you to identify two or three qualities about yourself that will become main points and develop your speaking goal. How many pieces of support should you be prepared to present for each of your main points? See Act and Reflect 2.5. A good rule of thumb for this speech of introduction is to have two pieces of support for each main point. You will be limited in the time you have to speak on this speech (as well as on every other speech), but if you begin with two ways of supporting each main point, you can make modifications as you continue to develop your speech.

Now you are ready to think about the order, or organization, of your main points and corresponding support material.

Organize Your Presentation

emotional appeals Issues, examples, or experiences in your presentation that will elicit an emotional response from your audience.

novelty Information, an approach, or an exercise that is unfamiliar to your audience.

You now know what you want to tell your audience about yourself. Your next decision is to identify the order in which you plan to present and discuss these major points of your presentation. Organizing major points in the body of your

ACT&REFLECT

2.5: Identify Support for Your Main Points

A C T • Make a list of personal experiences that will illustrate each of your main points. Is there information from other sources that you might be able to use? What about techniques from cognitive research? Identify two ways that you will develop each of your main points. Enter these two pieces of support in the third column of Figure 2.2 on page 37.

R E F L E C T • Do the personal examples and other support materials you have selected for each main point make sense to you as logical ways to explain your main points? If not, what changes can you make so they will appear logical?

speech works in the same way as when you are speaking in any other situation: you organize what you want to say so that your points have an **internal logic,** that is, in a way that shows their relationship to each other, so that they make sense to your listeners and so that the order emphasizes the key pieces of information you need to make your point. In the example we have been using, the first point is the practical joke tradition in your family; the next, your ability to make friends; the last, your spontaneous nature. You could arrange these three points in a number of ways, for example:

From Most to Least Important Points

First, I'd like to discuss the most important thing in my life: my family and, in particular, their ability to play practical jokes.

Next to my family, my friends are of great importance. Happily, I can make friends with just about anyone I meet.

Finally, I am a spontaneous person, and that has led me on some major adventures.

From Least to Most Important Points

Looking back on my life, I'd say I'm a pretty spontaneous person.

My spontaneous nature has helped me make many friends.

However, of greatest importance in my life is my family and their tradition of playing practical jokes.

internal logic Organization of the main points of your presentation to show how they are related to each other.

In **Chronological Order (in order of time)**

From early on in my life, I knew my family was a bunch of practical jokers.

When I was in high school, it became clear I was very good at making friends.

Recently I've realized my life has been very adventurous, and I attribute that to my ability to be spontaneous.

In **Topical Order (according to the way the points relate to each other)**

I've always been a spontaneous person, and that has led me on great adventures in my life.

Being a spontaneous person is the reason I've always been able to make friends easily and in a variety of situations.

My spontaneity has also allowed me to fit right in with my family, a group of people who are always playing practical jokes on each other.

Any of these organizational patterns for your major points would work for this speech of introduction. You might also be able to think of other arrangements for these major points. Rarely, if ever, are you going to find yourself flipping a coin to identify the proper organizational option. Your speaking goal, the knowledge you wish to present to your listeners, and the manner that will "showcase" these pieces of information in a way that will be received by your audience are the criteria you should consider in selecting the appropriate organizational pattern for your major points.

Having organized your main points, consider how you will prepare your audience by constructing an introduction that stimulates their interest and makes them want to listen to you (see Act and Reflect 2.6).

Create an Ear-Catching Introduction

The introduction of your presentation serves a number of important purposes: it motivates your audience to listen to you; it introduces your topic—in this case, yourself; and it previews your major points. The introduction is your opportunity to make a first impression on your audience and influences whether they will continue to listen to the remainder of your speech. You can see that the introduction is an important part of your presentation, and on this first speech, you will be challenged to accomplish everything the introduction must accomplish but in a very brief period of time.

chronological order Arrangement of the main points of your presentation in order of time, usually in the order in which the events described occurred.

topical order Presentation of the main points of the body in such a way that they relate to each other.

Motivate Your Audience

First, attract the attention of your audience and motivate them to listen to your speech. As soon as you begin to speak, say something about yourself that will allow you to create a

ACT&REFLECT

2.6: Organize Your Main Points

ACT • Arrange the major points of your speech in some way that you believe will make sense. Consider the ideas given here for organizing your main points or arrange them in some other way that you believe works well.

REFLECT • Will the organizational framework you have chosen allow you to attain your speaking goal, enable you to present the information you want to present to your classroom audience, and "showcase" the information so your audience will remember you? If not, is there another way you can arrange your major points so that you can discuss them more effectively?

positive first impression of yourself and make the audience want to become acquainted with you and listen to the rest of your speech. What could you say that will fill this tall order? You could always introduce yourself: "Hi, my name is Karen." You could tell what you plan to say: "Today I'm going to introduce myself to you." You could relate a personal experience that demonstrates to the audience the type of person you are: "When I was in middle school . . . " Which of these ways of introducing yourself to your classroom audience do you think would make your classmates want to learn more about you? Audiences tend to like stories, so consider relating a personal experience that will introduce you as the type of person you wanted to be identified as when you developed your speaking goal. See Act and Reflect 2.7.

Introduce Your Topic

Next, introduce your topic, in this case yourself, to your classroom audience and give a few, brief demographic characteristics about yourself. "I'm Karen. My hometown is Chicago. I came to this campus to study horticulture." As you can see, a demographic characteristic is a factual characteristic about yourself. Your hometown, your major, the number of brothers and sisters you have, whether you live on or off campus, all of these are possible demographic characteristics you could relate to your audience.

Preview Your Major Points

Finally, briefly preview the major points you will discuss in your speech to help your audience anticipate what you will say and, therefore, make it easier for them to be good listeners. "To introduce myself today, I will tell you about my family, my friends, and my spontaneous personality."

ACT&REFLECT

2.7: Creating Your Introduction

ACT • Develop a brief, personal experience that you can use to begin your introduction. Identify the details you will need for your classroom audience to understand and appreciate your experience while keeping it brief.

REFLECT • Does the experience prepare your audience to hear the remainder of your speech of introduction? Does the experience create the type of first impression of yourself that you want the audience to have? If not, what changes can you make?

A well-developed introduction is your first opportunity to influence your audience to listen to your speech. A memorable conclusion is your last.

Construct a Memorable Conclusion

Now you must create a memorable conclusion for your speech of introduction. The conclusion says "The End" in a way that is memorable to the audience and that sounds like an ending. Creating a memorable conclusion is not necessarily an easy task. Although it is a slight exaggeration, if you were to keep track of the total time that you spent preparing your presentation, that same amount of time might be sufficient to allow you to create a conclusion that would be memorable to your audience and say "The End" effectively. If you end a presentation in a weak or confusing manner, or the only reason the audience knows you are finished is that you stop talking, the power of your total presentation is diminished.

For your speech of introduction, there are two purposes to be accomplished in your conclusion: to reinforce a point you have made in your speech that you want your audience to remember and to complete your presentation with a sense of finality, or **closure.** See Act and Reflect 2.8.

Reinforce a Point

The conclusion is your last opportunity to emphasize a point that you want your audience to remember from your presentation. You might want your audience to remember your main reason for speaking (in this case it was to introduce yourself); you might want your audience to remember one or all of your major points; you could also use this opportunity to summarize your speech or to state your speaking goal.

Since this is your last opportunity to influence your audience, identify what you would like them to remember from your presentation and say it one last time. In the example we are

closure A statement in the conclusion that defines the ending of your speech.

ACT&REFLECT

2.8: Construct Your Conclusion

ACT • Review the content of your presentation. In a nutshell, what would you like your audience to remember about you? Write one or two sentences that capture this. Spend a few minutes thinking of a cordial, personal way to establish closure.

REFLECT • Does your conclusion reflect the image you would like the audience to have of you? If not, what changes could you make so your conclusion will leave the audience with the picture of you that you created through your speech?

using, the speaker describes a practical-joke-playing family, the ease of making friends, and the quality of spontaneity. If this were your speech, would you want the main thing your audience remembers to be that you have a family who like jokes? Would you prefer the audience remember you as someone who easily makes friends and is spontaneous? Select the quality or qualities you want to emphasize one last time: "So today I'd like you to remember that I am open to new experiences, and that has enabled me to make friends with ease everywhere I go."

Establish Closure

After you have restated the point or points you want your audience to remember, the last item to include in your conclusion is to say "The End." Establishing **closure** in the conclusion defines the ending of your speech, in much the same way that attracting your audience's attention in the introduction defined the beginning. For your speech of introduction, you need to establish closure briefly, cordially, and with a personal note to your audience. You might say: "In this room I see all of my newest friends. I look forward to getting to know you and to being in class with you."

Insert Transitions

The final content decision you must make is to insert transitions. The three major parts—the introduction, body, and conclusion—of your speech need to be connected, and relationships between and within these three areas need to be clarified through the use of transitions.

Transitions are words, phrases, and sentences that connect parts of your presentation while allowing you to move from one part to another. In your speech of introduction, there are several points at which you may need to insert transitions. Within the body of your presentation, you might need a sentence, or even two, to connect the major points you present: "My openness to meeting and making new friends might be related to my spon-

> **transitions** Words, phrases, and sentences that help your audience move from one part to the next.

ACT&REFLECT

2.9: Identify Your Transitions

ACT • Identify the places in your presentation where transitions are needed. What transitions will you insert at these points?

REFLECT • How do your transitions help to shape your presentation? Are the relationships of your points more clear through insertion of your transitions? If not, what other transitions could you insert instead?

taneous personality." However, if you are connecting two sentences, you could simply say "also," or "another point is . . ." or "however." A rule of thumb regarding transitions is that to connect larger parts of your speech, you need longer transitions, such as sentences; to connect smaller or shorter parts of your speech, you can use words or phrases.

Transitions deserve some thought. Although transitions should not be obvious, they are important, because they highlight what is important in your message and they help your listeners make sense of the information you include in your presentation and to understand the relationships of the points to each other (see Act and Reflect 2.9).

Although the content and organization of your speech have now been established, your next task is what actually makes your presentation a presentation: preparing your notes and practicing your message.

Practice and Prepare Notes

The content of your message is important, and the manner in which you present your message is also important. The "you" in your presentation is what is referred to as "delivery."

Achieve "Prepared Conversation" Delivery

In a presentational context, **delivery** is the means by which you create and maintain a relationship with your audience, and it is the way you give meaning to your message. Delivery pertains to everything about you that communicates your message to your audience, with the exception of the words you choose. Decisions such as where you stand as you present, the facial expressions you display that enhance your message, the people with whom you maintain eye contact are all decisions related to delivery. Everything about your delivery should focus on your audience, on building and maintaining a relationship with them, and on presenting a message that means what you intend it to mean. If you don't appear to be a credible source of your message, it is possible your audience will not attend to you or bother to listen.

delivery Everything about you, except for the words you choose, that communicates your message to your audience.

Prepare Helpful Notes

Notes are the written prompts used to help you effectively deliver your speech. When you prepare your notes, initially begin with the minimum content that you need to get through your speech. As you practice and become more and more confident, delete words, phrases, and entire sentences from your notes. The resulting set of notes you actually use for your presentation should be in the form of key words and phrases, with

● **FIGURE 2.3** Example of Initial Note Card for Introduction of First Presentation.

Introduction Note

<u>Motivate Audience:</u> Can you name the student in this room whose mother gave her father a pot-bellied pig for his birthday? Do you know which student in this room became best friends with the person who caused her to have a car accident while they were waiting for the police to arrive? Can you name a student in this class who on the first day of the semester decided not to come to school but instead to work on a cruise ship?

<u>Introduce Your Topic:</u> The student in all of these examples is me. My name is Karen. I'm from Chicago, and I am attending this university to study horticulture.

<u>Preview Major Points:</u> Today I'm going to tell you about my family, about my ability to make friends, and about my spontaneous personality.

● **FIGURE 2.4** Example of Note Card after Practicing.

Introduction Note

pot-bellied pig; car accident friend; cruise ship

name, major

today I'm going to tell you: family, friends, spontaneity

---

plenty of white space in between to allow you to focus your attention on your audience. Too many notes can be a hindrance, because you may find it difficult when you consult your notes to find exactly the word or point you need. If you are incorporating visual support into your presentation, consider depending on your visual support in place of notes and eliminating other forms of notes. Notice the difference in the two note card examples, in Figure 2.3 and Figure 2.4. Before practicing, the student speaker used a note card with the introduction written out almost entirely. Following practice sessions, the note card used for the speech contained only key words.

notes The written prompts you use to help yourself effectively deliver your speech.

Practice Your Presentation

Practicing your presentation should be approached similarly to the ideal way you would prepare yourself for an important exam. Rather than "cramming" for the exam the night before, you would ideally begin studying several days in advance. Your practice sessions for your presentation should be planned the same way, beginning several days before your scheduled speaking day. As you practice, concentrate on major points that you want to make and the order in which you will make them. Remember key words and transition phrases but do not memorize words or plan gestures. Think about relating an event to your friends or telling a joke to them. Each time you relate the event, or tell the joke, it's unlikely that you use the exact same words in the exact same order, yet the point of your story or joke is the same each time. Essentially, delivering a speech should be done the same way. The best way to ensure that you will be able to achieve this delivery is by using minimal notes and by practicing.

If you completed the visualization exercise in Act and Reflect 2.10, you probably feel totally confident about presenting your speech of introduction. However, just in case you are feeling some anxiety, the next section will suggest some ways to help you feel more confident.

Manage Speech Anxiety

How do you feel about giving a speech? On the one hand, as a speaker you wield a certain amount of power and ability to influence your audience as you deliver your message. On the other hand, sometimes it is difficult to focus on these positive

ACT&REFLECT

2.10: Visualize Your Best Delivery

ACT • Find a quiet place where you can make yourself comfortable. Close your eyes and picture yourself standing in front of your classroom audience giving your speech of introduction. Picture your classmates responding to you with interested expressions on their faces. When you say something humorous in your speech, picture them laughing at your comment. When you say something they agree with, picture them nodding to show their agreement. Picture yourself proceeding through your speech in a calm, capable manner. You seem to be enjoying yourself as much as your audience is enjoying listening to you. Now picture yourself concluding your speech and listen to your classroom audience clapping as you end your speech.

REFLECT • What did you see or hear yourself doing that resulted in a response from your audience that you wanted? What did you see or hear yourself doing that resulted in a response that was not what you intended? What can you do differently in these areas?

Everyday Example

"Dear Abby"

Dear Abby: I am a sophomore in high school and the class clown. I crave the spotlight. However, when it comes to giving an oral presentation in front of the class, I clam up, sweat, and get so scared I can hardly speak. It doesn't make sense because I sing in the choir and have taken large roles in school plays—all in front of huge audiences.

   Why is it I'm shy in front of my class, but not in front of a crowd?—*Shy Clown in California*

Dear Shy Clown: When you're singing lyrics or reciting lines written by someone else, you assume another personality. It's the mark of a talented performer. However, when you're making a presentation in front of the class, you are being yourself, and the ideas are your own. This makes you feel vulnerable. Consider this: The next time you do an oral presentation, pretend you're a strong, confident newscaster. I'll bet you ace the assignment.

Source: "Dear Abby," April 16, 2003, retrieved from Universal Press Syndicate Web site, at www.uexpress.com/dearabby. As seen in DEAR ABBY by Abigail Van Buren a.k.a. Jeanne Phillips and founded by her mother Pauline Phillips. © 2003 Universal Press Syndicate. Reprinted with permission. All rights reserved.

aspects if you are feeling anxious. Keep in mind that nervousness is energy and it can be channeled negatively or positively. Let's talk about positive or "good" energy first. If you have ever competed in athletics or acted in a play or performed in a music or dance recital, can you remember feeling keyed up before your performance or competition? It was important for you to feel that sense of exhilaration ahead of time because it helped you to focus and to perform better and more accurately. The audience also saw a better performance than would have been the case if you had not channeled your energy in a positive manner. The adrenalin rush helped you to give your best performance.

   Unfortunately, nervous energy can also work against us. Giving a speech or presentation is probably one of the most common times when people feel they are at the mercy of nonproductive nervousness. This counterproductive nervousness goes by several names: sometimes it is called speech anxiety, sometimes communication apprehension, sometimes speech fright, sometimes just "plain old" nervousness. If you feel nervous about the prospect of giving a speech, you have lots of company. The results of a study that originally appeared in the Sunday *London Times* on

October 7, 1973, listed the number one fear of the three thousand Americans surveyed as "speaking before a group."[8] Fear of heights was the second fear listed. The number three spot was tied among fear of insects and bugs, fear of financial problems, and fear of deep water. Although we are confident you will not be so terrified of presenting as the three thousand Americans surveyed in 1973, it is possible there will be times when your confidence could use a little boost. It is most important to keep in mind that you might feel nervous, but the right kind of nervousness is a good thing and will help you be in good form: that is, you will say what you want to say without having to correct yourself, you will feel better about your work, and your audience will feel better about listening to you. Here are some suggestions to help you channel your nervousness into energy that will work for you.

Be Yourself

Perhaps you are beginning to understand that "you are the message."[9] Just as a musician uses a piano or guitar or any other musical instrument to express a tune, you present your message to your audience through the instrument that is you. However, when you are presenting, it is really best not to focus on yourself but rather to focus on your message and on your audience. Through your delivery, you make connections with the audience. You use your voice, physical appearance, body, and space to make your audience care about your message as much as you do.

Some research suggests that audiences react to presenters on the basis of the consistency between their perceptions and knowledge of the presenter and the extent to which the presenter fulfills those expectations.[10] That means that if your listeners know you from a different environment from that of the presentation, they will expect you to "be yourself" as they know you while you are presenting. The more you differ from their expectations, the less positively they will respond to you. However, if you are presenting to listeners who do not know you, it becomes important to present yourself in the most positive light possible, and that still means "be yourself."[11] Being yourself is important because if you are being yourself, you are likely to be committed to what you are saying, you know what you are talking about, you are wrapped up in the moment, and your self-consciousness is gone.[12]

If your topic is one in which you are emotionally involved, let your audience know the nature of your involvement.[13] A presentation advocating that more federal dollars be spent on cancer research becomes more important to the audience if the presenter can give a personal example of a family member or loved one or even himself or herself as a cancer survivor. Appeals to the emotions not only reflect your true self but also may be a way to influence change in the audience's attitude.[14]

Breathe Smart

Nobody has to tell you to breathe. If you are a swimmer or deep-sea diver, you are probably conscious of times when you are not breathing, but how often at other times are you conscious of your breathing? Breathing is much like riding a bicycle. Unless something interferes, you don't think about it. However, when you are presenting, there is a difference between merely breathing and breathing smart. Breathing smart before and during your presentation can be a major asset to the confidence you display as you are presenting. Breathing smart can also help you to be in control. One of the ways you can increase your sense of confidence and control in presenting is to consciously consider your breathing before you present, as well as during your presentation.

How does this work? The next time you feel an emotion such as happiness, fear, or panic, try to be conscious of the way you are breathing. Depending on the emotion, you may have trouble catching your breath, your heart rate may speed up, you may tell yourself, "I'm panicking," and panic follows. In other instances, you may feel your breath is smooth, regular, and deep. The reason for this is the connection between your emotional state, your mind, and your nervous system.[15] When you experience emotions, you also experience a change in the way you typically breathe. If you control your breathing, you can also control your emotions.

An analogy can be made between the relationship of your breathing and your emotions and the relationship of a car's gears to its speed. In first gear, there is a limit to the

Yoga practitioners and effective speakers know that smart breathing can help control our emotions and manage our anxiety. ●

speeds you can reach; in third gear, your car can reach higher speeds. Similarly, if you breathe in shallow, fast breaths, you may experience a sense of panic or fear; if you are able to control your breathing through deep, even, slow breaths, the resulting emotion is calm and a sense of control and confidence: "Controlling the breath and calming the nerves is a prerequisite to controlling the mind."[16] How do you achieve powerful breathing that controls your mind? Take longer, deeper, slower breaths. As one expert notes, "Five to seven breaths per minute is . . . the measure of synchrony between the respiratory and cardiovascular systems" that "result[s] in a decreased heart rate and greater homeostasis in the autonomic nervous system, thereby reducing anxiety symptoms."[17]

How can you breathe correctly in preparation for a presentation so that you control your breath and your emotions, rather than your breath and emotions

A Question of **Ethics**

The Everyday Example: "Dear Abby" advises you, if you are nervous when you speak, to pretend you are someone else. Do you feel it is an ethical decision for you to pretend you are someone else when you are presenting if it is helpful to you in reducing your nervousness? What if your audience discovers the personality you projected when you spoke is not you? What are the possible implications?

controlling you? Deep, slow, and regular breathing, also called **diaphragmatic breathing,** is the way to achieve a sense of calm that will bring you confidence and control.[18] Again, think about your typical breathing technique. Place your hand on the front of your shirt. Is your chest moving in and out? Now place your hand just below your belt. Does your stomach rise and fall? Generally, it is in the chest area where you will feel movement. However, smart breathing involves that area below your belt.

To practice smart breathing, pretend your body is an empty glass. You are going to fill this glass with breath. The breath settles in the bottom of your glass; as you continue to breathe in more air, the glass slowly fills. When your glass is full, pause for a second to explore the way your body feels. Is your stomach extended? It should be, and if you have always thought you should keep your stomach "sucked in," you will probably feel that your extended stomach is grossly distended. Is your chest extended? It should also be slightly extended. Now, empty your glass. Beginning at the top of the glass, near the top of your chest, slowly begin to exhale as you are emptying the glass, all the way down to the lower parts of your stomach. When your glass is totally empty, take a second to explore your body. Is your chest flat? Is your stomach flat? Essentially all you have done is to take a very slow, deep, deliberate breath and then just as slowly and deliberately exhaled that breath. This is smart breathing. This is the way to breathe in a controlled manner rather than allowing your breath to control you. Through your controlled breathing you will also maintain control of your emotions and yourself. You are preparing yourself to present. Set aside five minutes daily for one week to practice smart breathing. Increase your practice time by a few minutes daily each week. Make a conscious effort to breathe smart whenever you need an extra boost of confidence, but especially right before you present.

Be Picky (PCCI)

Be picky (PCCI) about your presentation effect. There are four things an audience won't forgive: a presenter who is not Prepared, Committed, Comfortable, or Interesting.[19] These four points give a framework for suggesting other ways to prepare yourself for a presentation.

Be Prepared Know what you want to say and feel comfortable with what you say. Give yourself as much advance time to prepare as possible. If you need information from other sources, give yourself more time than you think you need to locate that information. If you are unable to locate information you initially need, you will have time to locate other information or make a decision about modifying your message. Give yourself time to arrange for visual support. Will a PowerPoint presentation enhance your message? If so, do you know how to create a PowerPoint presentation? Time is the best gift you can give yourself when preparing a presentation.

As you organize your presentation, begin with a list of the points you want to make and the pieces of information that will be necessary to make those points. Practice giving your presentation from this list. Occasionally students ask whether they should practice their presentations out loud. The answer is a resounding *yes!* If there are places where you get tongue-tied or you have diffi-

diaphragmatic breathing Breathing deeply, slowly, and regularly to achieve a sense of calm that will bring you confidence and control.

culty saying what you want to say, mark those areas on your notes. As you are practicing, always conclude your presentation as many times as you began it. If you practice your presentation up to the point where you begin to have difficulties, stop at that point, and start again, the front end of your message will have benefited from more practice sessions than the tail end. The audience should not be left with a weak ending. As you practice your presentation, make changes on your notes. Delete words and phrases you know. Your goal should be to reduce your notes to a key word outline on one piece of paper, a key word outline on one note card, or a key word outline on three note cards: one for key words for the introduction; one for key words for the body; and one for key words for the conclusion.

Be Committed Your listeners should not perceive a disconnect between you and your words. Your audience should not have the impression that you are saying something you don't believe or that you are insincere or that there is a discrepancy between what they know you to be and what you are espousing in your presentation. If you have never played golf and you decide to teach the class how to swing a golf club, your lack of expertise, enthusiasm, and commitment will be apparent to your audience. In rare instances you might find yourself speaking about a topic about which you are not totally clear yourself how you feel. Perhaps your professional position requires you to inform colleagues about a change in the company benefit policy, for instance, before you have a chance to know how you feel about it yourself. How can you display commitment in these instances? Take the time to create your own connection with the topic, as well as finding a connection for your audience.

Wearing comfortable yet neat clothing for your presentation can enhance your credibility and your confidence level. ●

Be Comfortable Practice in the environment where you will present. Know where everything is located. Know how to operate the equipment you will use and be sure you have keys to open cupboards to get to that equipment. Is there a tech crew present who can help if your equipment breaks down? Find out where they are located. Walk around. Sit in the chairs your listeners will use. As your audience arrives, greet individuals. Look into their eyes. These will become the faces you will speak to when you begin your presentation. Wear comfortable clothing that enhances your credibility. If your old, comfortable sweater still looks neat and clean, there is no reason to wear a new sweater that you haven't yet "broken in."

Be Interesting There is a reason you are presenting. You have expertise, you have experiences, you are committed to what you are saying. Be yourself, so these strengths will be visible to the audience and you will be a source of information and interest to them. Remember that listeners need to respond emotionally to your message. Don't hesitate to use examples to create an emotional response and to motivate your audience's interest. If you have several ways to express a point, select the one you feel will be of greatest interest to your audience. That may mean a set of statistics, an example, a joke, or all three.

Although we have discussed the four components of being PCCI, in practice it is difficult to attend to each of them individually because each influences the others. Your audience responds in a way that tells you your presentation is interesting, you feel comfortable with what you are doing, and you are also receiving feedback that tells you your commitment to the message is applauded. The only way you will attain these results is through your attention to preparation. Your PCCI-ness has paid off. Give yourself a pat on the back!

● GETTING TO WORK

Guidelines to Follow as You Prepare Your Presentation

1. Be conscientious about your preparation. As you read this book and attend class on a regular basis, apply what you are learning and discussing to your own work. Stay current in the preparation of your presentation.

2. When you have the choice of a topic, always choose topics that you are knowledgeable about, have experience with, and are committed to. Supplement your personal connection with information from other sources. If your instructor assigns a topic, select an aspect of the topic that interests you for your presentation.

3. Prepare a practice schedule and stick to it. Allow yourself several days of practice before you are scheduled to present, and plan to practice at least two to four times each day.

4. End your presentation as many times as you begin. As you are practicing, if you notice a rocky area, mark it quickly on your notes, but keep going and finish your presentation.

5. When you feel confident about what you are going to say and your practice sessions are going smoothly, audiotape or videotape yourself speaking. Listen or watch yourself as objectively as possible. What do you hear or see "that person" (yourself) do that you feel is effective? What do you hear or see that person do that you find distracting? Make notes and modify your work accordingly.

6. Before you give your presentation in class, rehearse in your classroom.

Guidelines to Follow on the Day of Your Presentation

1. Control your food intake. It is important to eat some nutritionally sound food before you speak because you might mistake hunger for nervousness. Avoid junk food and do not eat a large meal, because if your stomach is too full, you could feel lethargic.

2. Schedule a workout. If you can exercise, you will channel some of your counter-productive nerves into productive energy. If it is impossible for you to schedule a workout session, park further away from your class than usual so you have a chance for a brisk walk, or use the stairs instead of the elevator.

3. Choose clothing that looks professional but also allows you to feel confident. You don't necessarily need to wear an "interview suit," but at the other extreme, don't appear too casual. There is a relationship between your appearance and the credibility with which your audience absorbs your message. Avoid jewelry or other accessories that might cause you to fidget.

4. Before you leave home, check your notes, your visual support, and anything else you will need to speak. Do you have everything? Is everything in order?

5. As you sit in class waiting for your turn to speak, breathe in a controlled manner. If you can control your breath, you also control your anxiety. Neither has a chance to control you.

Guidelines to Follow as You Give Your Presentation

1. Before speaking, arrange the environment. Is media equipment convenient and focused? If you are using a microphone, is it adjusted for your height? Are your notes in order? Look at the audience and smile.

2. Take slow, deliberate breaths.

3. Carry a glass of water with you. If you begin to feel shaky or if you experience "cotton mouth," a short pause to sip water will break the shakiness and restore moisture to your mouth.

4. As you speak, make eye contact with audience members. Look at them; notice their facial expressions and their responses to you.

5. Take advantage of the fact that all attention is on you. Your audience is listening to you, considering what you are saying, viewing you as the expert.

Guidelines to Follow after Your Presentation

1. Schedule some time to relive your experience. What went well? Make a note to reinforce this in your next presentation. What do you wish you had done differently? Again, make a note so that you can modify this aspect in your next presentation.

2. What did you notice about the responses of your audience? What responses indicated to you that your presentation was effective? Again, make a note of this so you can reinforce this area next time. At what points were audience members' responses surprising to you? Consider what caused these responses. What have you learned that inspires you to make changes for your next presentation?

3. Celebrate your speaking skills. Reward yourself. Call some friends. Eat some ice cream. You deserve it!

SUMMARY

In this chapter we have worked through the entire process of preparing a presentation to assist you in developing your first classroom assignment. Although we cannot give you a "connect the dots" approach, here is a checklist of actions you should take in planning your first and your future presentations.

Checklist for Planning Presentations

_____	1. Identify a topic
_____	2. Know your audience
_____	3. Formulate your speaking goal
_____	4. Identify major points
_____	5. Select support material
_____	6. Organize major points
_____	7. Create an ear-catching introduction
_____	8. Construct a memorable conclusion
_____	9. Insert transitions
_____	10. Practice and prepare notes

If you are not assigned a topic, *identify a topic* about which you feel expert, experienced, and committed. Take some time to consider how well you *know your audience*. To what extent does the cultural composition of the audience or their demographic characteristics or the areas they are knowledgeable about or interested in help you to focus your speech? *Formulate your speaking goal* to help yourself remember what you want to accomplish through your presentation.

On the basis of your topic and what you know about your audience, *identify the major points* you will discuss in your presentation. *Select support materials* to help your audience understand your major points. Look to your personal experience, as well as other sources, and implement the results of cognitive research as you develop your support materials. Now you can *organize the major points* in a manner that will help your audience understand how they relate to each other and to your speaking goal.

After you have developed the body of your presentation, you are ready to *create an ear-catching introduction and construct a memorable conclusion*. The introduction should attract the audience's attention, introduce them to your topic, and preview your main points. The conclusion restates something you want your audience to remember and creates closure. Finally, you will *insert transitions* to connect the key parts of your speech.

When the content of your speech is complete, it is time to *practice your speech and prepare your notes*. Strive for a prepared yet conversational delivery using minimal notes. Finally, as you prepare your presentation, on the day of your presentation, and as you give your presentation, follow the tips given in this chapter to help yourself feel confident.

VIDEO EXPERIENCE

MSL

The two video clips for this chapter show Julie discussing her hobby of scrapbooking and Cindy describing the summers she and her family spent with a traveling circus.[20] Besides learning about Julie's scrapbooking hobby and Cindy's summers, what else do you learn about these two speakers? That is, how does each speaker use the framework of the hobby and the summer to divulge other information about herself? As you watch each introductory presentation, identify two ideas from each that you could implement in your own speech of introduction to relate information about yourself to your classroom audience.

THINKING BACK, THINKING AHEAD

1. After you have presented your introductory speech, spend some time thinking about your delivery: identify two areas of your delivery you felt were effective and two areas where you would like to become more effective for your next presentation. How can you modify those behaviors to become more effective? Practice them and identify ways you can turn your ineffective behaviors into speaking strengths.

2. Dedicate a page of your notebook to a topic inventory. Whenever you think of a topic that might make an interesting speech, record it in your topic inventory. Duplicate the brainstorming matrix at the beginning of the chapter and, on a regular basis, review newly added topics to determine whether you possess the expertise, experience, and commitment you need for them to be good topics for you to consider for future speeches.

3. Keep a journal in which you write down the messages you present in everyday presentations. What are your listeners' responses to you? Do listeners respond as you would like them to? Why or why not? What does listener response tell you about your communication skills?

4. Read the list of suggestions for before, during, and after presenting. Which of these behaviors will you practice in relation to the first presentation you will give to your classmates?

5. Create a schedule that you will follow to plan, organize, and practice your first presentation.

NOTES

1. Ilana Mainaga, speech to a positive audience, September 22, 2004.
2. Laura Johnson, speech to a positive audience, September 27, 2004.
3. Shannon Kirton, speech to a negative audience, November 10, 2004.
4. Maya Shariff, speech to a negative audience, November 19, 2004.
5. Ross Kelderman, speech to a neutral audience, October 15, 2004.
6. Scott Sturm, speech to a positive audience, September 27, 2004.
7. R. Caine and G. Caine, *Education on the Edge of Possibility* (Alexandria, VA: Association for Supervision and Curriculum Development, 1997).
8. D. Wallechinsky, I. Wallace, and A. Wallace, *The Book of Lists* (New York: Morrow, 1977).
9. R. Ailes, *You Are the Message: Secrets of the Master Communicators* (Homewood, IL: Dow Jones-Irwin, 1988), 90.
10. B. R. Schlenker, "Identity and Self-Identification," in *The Self and Social Life,* edited by B. R. Schlenker (New York: McGraw-Hill, 1985), 82–83.
11. Ailes, *You Are the Message,* 53.
12. Ailes, *You Are the Message,* 26.
13. N. Morgan, "The Kinesthetic Speaker: Putting Action into Words," *Harvard Business Review,* April 2001, 112–119.
14. R. P. Weiss, "Emotion and Learning," *Training and Development, 54* (2000): 45–48.
15. S. Rama, R. Ballentine, and A. Hymes, *Science of Breath: A Practical Guide* (Honesdale, PA: Himalayan Institute Press, 1998).
16. Rama, Ballentine, and Hymes, *Science of Breath,* 83.
17. B. Horowitz, *Communication Apprehension: Origins and Management* (Albany, NY: Singular, 2002), 90.
18. Horowitz, *Communication Apprehension,* 16.
19. Ailes, *You Are the Message,* 53.
20. Julie Spratt, speech to the Municipal Clerks' Institute, Ames, Iowa, July 13, 2005. Cindy Kai, speech to the Municipal Clerks' Institute, Ames, Iowa, July 13, 2005.

Chapter

3

Speaking Ethically

✓ To present an ethical framework to guide you in developing presentation ethics

✓ To discuss the relationship of rights guaranteed by the First Amendment and ethics

✓ To list qualities you can display to assist your listeners in determining your ethicality

✓ To suggest ethical considerations when you prepare your speech

✓ To identify ethical actions you can display when interacting with your audience

✓ To acknowledge areas of possible ethical differences that may come into play when you are speaking to a diverse audience

✓ To introduce an ethical framework for your audience members

"*Last week, amid increasing questions about the authenticity of documents used in support of a '60 Minutes Wednesday' story about President Bush's time in the Texas Air National Guard, CBS News vowed to reexamine the documents in question—and their source— vigorously. And we promised that we would let the American public know what this examination turned up, whatever the outcome.*

"*Now, after extensive additional interviews, I no longer have the confidence in these documents that would allow us to continue vouching for them journalistically. I find we have been misled on the key question of how our source for the documents came into possession of these papers. That, combined with some of the questions that have been raised in public and in the press, leads me to a point where—if I knew then what I know now—I would not have gone ahead with the story as it was aired, and I certainly would not have used the documents in question.*

"*But we did use the documents. We made a mistake in judgment, and for that I am sorry. It was an error that was made, however, in good faith and in the spirit of trying to carry on a CBS News tradition of investigative reporting without fear or favoritism.*

"*Please know that nothing is more important to us than people's trust in our ability and our commitment to report fairly and truthfully.*"

—*Dan Rather* ●

Dan Rather's statement was issued following a newscast airing memos alleging that President George Bush received preferential treatment while in the National Guard.[1] Why did this incident receive the attention it did and why did Rather issue the apology? Much of what is disseminated through the media is information that most of us are not in a position to experience firsthand, so we entrust journalists with the responsibility to create our view of the world. We make decisions about the way we live our lives on the basis of the information we receive from the media. If doubt is raised regarding the messages we receive from journalists, they lose their credibility and the ability to influence us. We begin to doubt the information we receive through the media, and we may no longer feel able to depend on the media as a source of information useful in our decision making. Ultimately our personal welfare comes to be in jeopardy. Questions about the source of information motivated Dan Rather to issue the statement. Like journalists, public speakers must also make ethical decisions regarding their speeches and their audiences.

Defining Ethics

We give presentations for the purpose of influencing our listeners. If that were not the case, we wouldn't be concerned about what is said during a presentation, how it is said, how audience members view the presenter, or whether they consider the presentation credible.[2] As a speaker, you have choices about the content of your message and the way you will make an impact on your listeners. You also make decisions about the topics of your presentations, and you choose the information you will present to your listeners. The decisions you make place you in a position to influence the individuals in your audience, and they, in turn, might pass your message along to countless others. The potential depth and breadth of your influence is huge. Think of the power with which your audience entrusts you when you speak to them; think of the power you have over your listeners to influence the way they think and act and live their lives. The choices you make when you speak are truly important, not only in regard to the perception your listeners have of you as a person and as a source of information but also to the extent that they trust the information you give them as a worthy basis for making their own decisions. Sometimes the choices speakers make about the information they present to an audience are easily made. Other times, the choices are less clear. The way one resolves these situations is based on one's **ethics**, a set of guidelines that are a result of one's values, culture, and personal experiences and that help one make decisions about what is "right" or "wrong" or "good" or "bad."[3]

To help yourself become aware of your personal ethics, consider these situations. In your communication class, would it be right or wrong to plan and present a speech on a topic that someone else has suggested to you? Would you make statements during a presentation that exclude or are offensive to some members of your audience? Is it honest or dishonest to present information to your audience if you are uncertain of its accuracy? Would you withhold information from your listeners that might influence them in a different direction from one consistent with your goals? Is it good or bad to imply that anyone who does not agree with your viewpoint is, in some

ethics A set of guidelines that help us make decisions about what is "right" or "wrong" or "good" or "bad."

way, inferior? You might be more certain about the answers to some of these questions than others, but in all cases, your responses are a result of your ethics. The "right" or "good" or "honest" or "fair" decision is not always obvious, nor is it easy, and that is where our ethics become important. Kenneth E. Andersen, who has spoken and written on the topic of communication ethics, believes that acting ethically means we must think through the implications of our actions and find the right path.[4]

What is the right path? Throughout history, philosophers have put forth their views of an ethical code intended to guide the choices people make as they go about living their lives. Aristotle's golden mean focuses on building strength of character and advises identifying the proper balance between excess and deficiency in the choices people make. John Stuart Mill, another philosopher, advocated a code of ethics called utilitarianism that called for making choices that would result in the greatest happiness for the greatest number of people. Immanuel Kant's categorical imperative stated that laws should exist that are enforced for all without regard for individual circumstances. Other philosophers have said that one should live a moral life, practice tolerance, and display strength of character.[5]

You can see through these examples that some of the common components of ethical perspectives are personal character, the nature of individual actions, and a consideration for the effect of one's choices on others. These three components are also important as you consider the ethical choices you make as a speaker. You might be asking why you would need to be concerned about making ethical choices. After all, doesn't the Bill of Rights guarantee our freedom of speech? Doesn't that mean one can say whatever one wishes to say?

Maintaining the proper balance between excess and deficiency, Aristotle's golden mean, remains relevant for us today. ●

Ethics and the First Amendment

Congress shall make no law respecting an establishment of religion, or prohibiting the free exercise thereof; or abridging freedom of speech, or of the press; or the right of the people peaceably to assemble, and to petition the Government for a redress of grievances.
—*First Amendment to the U.S. Constitution*

The First Amendment of the Constitution does, indeed, guarantee freedom of speech. Although there may be clauses in the legal code that prohibit some types of messages, such as threats against other persons, the First Amendment still provides for great latitude in what individuals can say. The right to freedom of speech allows us to speak out against those with whom we disagree; allows us to criticize our government and the actions of our elected officials; allows us to engage in public discourse about important, controversial issues. The right to freedom of speech allows Dan Rather to read any memo he wishes on his television broadcast. And that is why it is the responsibility of speakers—who have the ears of many, who are in a position to influence the thoughts and behaviors of others—to proceed ethically.

While the First Amendment does not censor the right to speak, it is up to individuals to determine what should and should not, what can and cannot, be said. Embracing an ethic that guides us in decisions about what can and should be said about whom and in what circumstances ultimately preserves that right to freedom of speech. When individuals do not rise to their ethical responsibilities, the right to freedom of speech becomes endangered.

While the First Amendment does not prohibit us from exercising our right to freedom of speech, it is up to us as speakers to carefully protect that right by making ethical decisions that preserve the dignity of those who listen to us, that preserve their right to agree or disagree with or even ignore our messages, and that cultivate a society in which the freedom of speech is allowed because we have made ethical choices about what we say when we speak.

The Role of Ethics in Presentations

Whether you are in the position of speaking to a large audience or giving an everyday presentation to five or six colleagues at a meeting, you are speaking in order to accomplish a goal. Your audience members agree to listen, and they assume that you have knowledge about your topic, that you are a reliable source, and that the knowledge you disseminate is accurate. A relationship has been constructed in which the audience trusts you. They might need the information you give them, or they might agree to a belief or action you are advocating through your speech. If your listeners discover that you are unworthy of their trust, you may never be able to regain it.

Another reason to present yourself and your message ethically to your audience has to do with a much larger picture. When you speak to an audience, you are communicating to the audience, and the audience is communicating back to you. One philosopher said, "Communication is not the transference of knowledge but a dialogic encounter of subjects creating it together."[6] This means that although you are the person who is doing most of the talking, your audience also has a role in contributing to the resulting

Speakers' words can result in a ripple effect through audience members' influence on others within and beyond the audience. ●

message. They are responding to you nonverbally—and possibly verbally—during your presentation, and they may also ask questions or make comments afterward. In addition, they may talk to each other later about the points you made, and they might repeat parts of your message to others. The information and opinions you choose to include will influence your listeners' actions and may have a ripple effect that touches others as well. If unethical ideas or actions become a part of this complex mix, everyone is diminished. The preamble to the code of ethics of the National Communication Association (Figure 3.1) describes the results of unethical actions and messages as a threat to individuals and to society.

What is the communication ethic to which you should subscribe? We will not prescribe a specific **code of ethics**—the set of ethics that guides your actions and your speaking decisions; it should be of your own design. However, being perceived as an ethical speaker by your audience and making ethical decisions about your message and interactions with your audience that confirm your ethicality involves a certain number of constants. When you read the ethical code of the National Communication Association, notice that the concepts in the code are not applicable solely to speaker, message, or audience but rather have relevance to all three. We will discuss ethics as it relates to you when you present, to decisions you make about your presentation, and to your perception and corresponding treatment of your audience.

Presenting Yourself as an Ethical Speaker

How do you become an ethical speaker? In fact, it is the audience who decide whether or not you are one. Audience members take into account a variety of factors, such as your credibility regarding a specific topic, your character, the extent to which they view you as a trustworthy person, or the degree to which they believe you have their best interests at heart. All of these perceptions contribute to the audience's judgment that you are ethical, a decision made by your audience as a result of your own actions. In other words, although your audience decides whether you are ethical, that decision is influenced by decisions in your life over which you have control. One aspect of your ethicality, your initial credibility, is created even before you speak.

Your Initial Credibility

To clarify the process by which listeners conclude whether a speaker is ethical before that person speaks, let's think about an experience that might be familiar to you. How did you decide which school to attend? Part of the process that led to your decision might have involved asking people for their advice. You might have decided who to consult on the basis of whether people knew or attended the schools you were considering; you might have consulted people you believed had a concern for your best interests; you might have also thought about whether you trusted or respected these individuals. Notice that in this hypothetical situation, your choices were based on how you felt about the individual's personal qualities and characteristics, on the basis of your

code of ethics The set of ethics that guides your actions and your speaking decisions.

● **FIGURE 3.1**   National Communication Association Credo for Ethical Communication.
Source: Retrieved from the National Communication Web site, at www.natcom.org/policies/
External/EthicalComm.htm. Used by permission of the National Communication Association.

Preamble

Questions of right and wrong arise whenever people communicate. Ethical communication is fundamental to responsible thinking, decision making, and the development of relationships and communities within and across contexts, cultures, channels, and media. Moreover, ethical communiation enhances human worth and dignity by fostering truthfulness, fairness, responsibility, personal integrity and respect for self and others. We believe that unethical communication threatens the quality of all communication and consequently the well-being of individuals and the society in which we live.

Principles

We advocate truthfulness, accuracy, honesty, and reason as essential to the integrity of communication.

We endorse freedom of expression, diversity of perspective, and tolerance of dissent to achieve the informed and responsible decision making fundamental to a civil society.

We strive to understand and respect other communicators before evaluating and responding to their messages.

We promote access to communication resources and opportunities as necessary to fulfill human potential and contribute to the well-being of families, communities, and society.

We promote communication climates of caring and mutual understanding that respect the unique needs and characteristics of individual communicators.

We condemn communication that degrades individuals and humanity through distortion, intimidation, coercion, and violence, and through the expression of intolerance and hatred.

We are committed to the courageous expression of personal convictions in pursuit of fairness and justice.

We advocate sharing information, opinions, and feelings when facing significant choices while also respecting privacy and confidentiality.

We accept responsibility for short- and long-term consequences for our own communication and expect the same of others.

prior relationship with that person. In other words, you identified individuals to consult on the basis of your perception of their initial credibility.[7]

Part of the audience's perception of you as an ethical speaker is based on your **initial credibility**. If the audience is aware of your reputation before you speak and they view you as an ethical individual, your initial credibility may contribute to that perception of ethicality. A former

initial credibility The audience's estimation of your credibility before you speak.

CEO of a large company who has been indicted for dishonest acts might not be viewed as ethical according to the audience's sense of initial credibility. What this means is that your life and the decisions you have made before a speaking event have some impact on the audience's perception of your ethicality—even though you might be well suited to present on a particular topic.

Audience members will also judge your ethicality during your presentation. There are a number of qualities audiences might look to when deciding whether you are an ethical person; among them are truthfulness and your perceived intentions.

Jimmy Carter brings credibility to the speaking situation based on what his audience already knows about him. ●

Truthfulness

Audiences need to be able to feel confident that you are telling the truth. At the beginning of this chapter, you read about a memo that had been presented as fact that was later discovered not to be so. Why is **truthfulness** a quality of an ethical individual? If you could not trust a speaker to be truthful, how could you make decisions on the basis of the knowledge conveyed in the presentation? If you felt you could not trust the speaker to be truthful, to what extent would you continue to listen to that person, and what power would that person have to influence you? When we believe we cannot depend on a source of information to be truthful, the speaker has lost a listener, and the listener has lost a source of information. The entire basis for communication becomes irrelevant.

A communication ethics textbook not only recommends that truthfulness should be the norm but also observes that speakers who are truthful do not have to remember what they said.[8] In other words, if you deviated from the truth, you would carry the additional burden of remembering to whom you told what.

It seems that it would be a simple thing to simply "tell the truth." But sometimes, as these examples indicate, telling the truth is not so simple:[9]

- Is it ethical to deviate from the truth to protect someone or to preserve another person's confidentiality? If you are giving a speech about the need for better lighting on your campus and you describe a friend who was raped when walking in a poorly lit campus area, is it acceptable to use a fictional name to protect your friend when describing her experience?

- Is it ethical to be deceitful in order to protect a larger truth? Should the president of the United States announce in a speech to the nation that troops will be sent into another country on a different day than is planned, in order to ensure that the military action is a success?

- Is it ethical to lie if a boss or supervisor asks you to? If your supervisor asks you to, is it ethical to reassure

truthfulness The speaker's presentation of information that the audience believes is factual or can be verified.

coworkers at the daily information meeting that the plant will continue to be open for the foreseeable future when you know the workers will be told the following week the plant is closing immediately?

- Is it ethical to avoid the truth to help a friend? If you agree to do your own work and your friend's work for your class presentation because your friend has personal problems, are you engaging in an ethical act?

- Is it ethical to lie when you believe someone does not want to know the truth? When you speak to the parents of new students at campus orientation and a parent asks you whether alcohol is allowed in the dorms, is it ethical for you to reassure the parent that alcohol is never allowed in the dorms, knowing that alcohol is sometimes smuggled in by students?

Did you find that the decisions you would make in some of these situations were more obvious than in others? For example, you might feel that it is all right to stray from the truth to protect your friend who was raped, but you believe the parents of new students have the right to know that alcohol is sometimes found in the dorms. You might find it degrading to withhold information about a plant closing from employees but understand that national security often requires the president to withhold information from citizens. The way you decide when it is imperative to tell the truth or when it is acceptable to take another approach is a part of your ethical code. Sometimes, however, despite your ethical code regarding truth telling, your intentions are not enough.

Your Perceived Intentions

What if you fully intend to tell the truth but discover later, as did Dan Rather, that you have unintentionally deceived your audience? Robert Johannesen, who writes on human communication ethics, says that people tend to be more willing to overlook an inaccuracy when they believe or discover it was unintentional, but an inaccuracy that is conveyed deliberately is not so easily forgiven. Johannesen poses these questions about **intentionality,** or the extent of the perceived trustworthiness of your intentions:[10]

1. Should speakers be responsible for the credibility of sources from which they gather their information as well as the information itself? CBS News used a memo from a source they initially viewed as credible, learning after it had been aired that the source was not dependable and the memo could not be authenticated. Is the network accountable? If you use a newspaper article in your speech, believing the content of the article to be factual, only to discover that the reporter who wrote the article was dismissed for fabricating his news stories, would you expect your audience to forgive you or to hold you accountable for your choice? What, if any, steps could or should you take to repair damage to your credibility?

    It's true that your listeners might forgive you for using unreliable information in a speech once or twice, but do not assume that you will be "off the hook" all of the time. You cannot know the character or credibility of every source from which you derive the information you use in your

intentionality The degree of the perceived trustworthiness of a speaker's intentions.

speeches; however, you can and should take steps to ensure that the sources from which you select your information are those you can trust. In addition, if you are willing to acknowledge that you divulged information that you now know cannot be verified, you are upholding your commitment to truthfulness.

2. How can a speaker know whether information is deliberately or unintentionally inaccurate? You may not be able to differentiate on the basis of one piece of evidence, but you can make a habit of checking other sources for agreement about the nature of the information. You can also check the credential(s) of the person(s) who is/are the original source(s) of the information and include those credentials in your presentation.

3. To what extent does the depth of your sincerity or passion about your message outweigh your ethical responsibilities? If it is tremendously important to you that your listeners take an action to ensure their own health or safety, are you released from ethical guidelines, if this will increase the chances that your audience will be persuaded to take the actions you suggest? A student in one of our classes once felt passionately opposed to gun control. In the middle of a presentation in which he stated that guns themselves were not dangerous but that the people who owned them were the danger, he reached into his pocket and pulled out a gun. You can imagine the terror felt by the audience; however, the speaker felt justified in displaying the gun as an illustration of his point. In this example, the speaker neglected to consider the safety and comfort of his audience. Speakers should feel commitment to their views, but that commitment must be reconciled with actions that do not result in the audience fearing for their personal safety, well-being, or comfort.

Johanessen's questions focus on the extent to which speakers are responsible and accountable to their audiences. You might be able to think of specific instances when speakers deserve audience forgiveness if they divulge inaccurate information, or if the credentials of sources are flawed, and specific instances when audience members should be challenged, but in a safe manner, in order to make a point. However, because it is your audience who decides whether you are an ethical person, because you may not know all of the members of your audience, and because the people who make up your audience are in a position to carry your message to others, we suggest that you err on the side of accuracy, virtuous intentions, and decisions that have as their highest priority the safety of your listeners.

Always take steps to ensure that you are presenting information you believe to be accurate, use sources you can authenticate, select methods for making memorable points that confirm your image as a responsible source of information. If there is any doubt in your mind about the veracity of information you present, inform your listeners of your lack of confidence and be prepared to explain why you have chosen to include that information, or omit it. Remember that if your audience begins to see you as an unethical source, their ability to use the information they receive from you is diminished, as is your ability to influence them. It is imperative that you preserve your relationship with your audience for the benefit of all.

The decisions you make about the content of your presentation should also be informed by your ethics and will continue to influence your audience perception of your ethics.

Preparing Your Speech Using Ethical Principles

Have you ever attended a speaking event where you simply did not understand what the speaker was saying? Perhaps the speaker used terminology that was unfamiliar to you, or you were unable to follow the logic of the presentation. Besides expecting a speaker's message to be accurate, listeners also believe that a message should be presented in a way that can be understood.[11] As an ethical speaker, what can you do to ensure that your message reflects ethical principles? As you prepare your presentation, there are ethical decisions you should make regarding clarity, accuracy, and the crediting of sources (see Act and Reflect 3.1, page 71).

Present Information Clearly

At the most basic level, when you are unable to understand a message, it is not useful to you. What are you supposed to think or do with a speech that isn't clear? Communication does not occur, and the goal of the interaction is not met for either the speaker or the audience. Another result of using unfamiliar or unclear wording is that people may view this as a strategy to distance or elevate the speaker. How would you feel if it seemed to you that the speaker was purposely working to confuse or disenfranchise the audience? You might be reluctant to ask questions, fearing the speaker's response, or you might feel offended that the speaker seems to be artifically enhancing his or her position, or you might conclude that the speaker is attempting to distract or manipulate the audience. Whether the results are intended or not, it is not to the benefit of a speaker to allow an audience to draw any of these conclusions.

Choose Accurate Language

Do your word choices reflect well on yourself, your ideas, and your audience? One discussion of ethics in human communication suggests that speakers should select words that accurately represent or describe the ideas they are conveying; in other words, your word choices truthfully reflect the ideas you present.[12] If, for example, you observe that "mobs" of people protested a decision of your school president and an

A Question of **Ethics**

To what extent do you believe that everyday presentations are ethical actions in themselves? When giving an everyday presentation, you are attempting to influence your listeners' actions and thoughts, and you may be doing so by aligning yourself and your message with issues you know are important to your listeners. Is an everyday presentation an ethical act? If so, how? If not, why not?

audience member challenges your use of the term "mob," insisting the protest was conducted peacefully, will your credibility suffer or will you be able to explain your choice of the term "mob"? Is it the habit of you and your friends to use casual language when you are together? If, during a presentation, you find yourself using words that could not be published in a newspaper, or in this textbook—while such word choices might be legal—they will influence the way your audience views you and your message and may also cause the audience to draw conclusions about your intentions toward them.

Avoid Plagiarism

Always give credit to the source when you use someone else's work. Speakers who use words, ideas, or information from another person or source, such as an organization or government agency, without giving credit to that person or source are guilty of **plagiarism.** Whether the failure to give the source is intentional or not doesn't matter; it is still considered plagiarism. Plagiarism is an unethical, dishonest act, and there are potential legal consequences for committing it.

What specifically constitutes plagiarism?

- Presenting someone else's speech as your own work
- Using parts of someone else's work without giving credit to that person
- Including information, such as statistics or a policy statement, generated by another source without naming the source
- Paraphrasing, that is, expressing someone else's ideas in your own words, but failing to name the source
- Converting into a different format information that has been generated by someone else, for example, creating a pie chart from a database without naming the source
- Representing someone else's idea as your own

Why should you work to avoid plagiarizing words, ideas, information, or anything else? The obvious reason to conscientiously avoid plagiarizing material for your presentations is that the consequences could be severe, ranging from failing the specific assignment on which the plagiarism occurred to failing the entire class or even worse, depending on the academic honesty policy of your school. As dire as those consequences are, however, we believe the possible academic consequences pale in comparison to the consequences of the unethical nature of the act.

At the beginning of this chapter, we spoke of the importance of establishing trust between an audience and presenter. How will your audiences, not only in your communication class but other audiences as well, perceive you if they know you have committed plagiarism? Will they be able to place their trust in you as a reliable source of information? Will you ever be able to regain their trust? If you are perceived as unethical in presentation situations, how will that image influence people's impressions of you in other circumstances? These repercussions are much more dire and long lasting then failing an

plagiarism The use of words, ideas, or information from another person or source without giving credit.

assignment or class. Besides the possible major consequences of failing to cite your sources, there are benefits that are even better reasons for citing them.

When you cite your sources, it adds to your credibility. When you use the names of experts or well-respected publications or well-thought-of organizations as the sources of information you include in your presentations, the prestige of those sources also benefits you. Your credibility is enhanced.

Citing your sources adds to the strength of your arguments and the value of the information you present. If you credit an expert in a particular area with an idea you present in your speech, your audience may feel confident that the knowledge you present was acquired by the expert through accepted research methods.

Finally, providing documentation of your information adds to the free will you want to accord your audience. You are providing the audience with all of the information they need, allowing them the freedom to respond to your presentation as they feel is warranted.

How can you avoid committing plagiarism? The best ways are to anticipate your presentation needs, keep good records, and allow yourself enough time to do your work.

Throughout this book, we encourage you to anticipate your speaking assignments by thinking and planning ahead. If you follow this advice, you will have an active list of possible topics for your speaking assignments, you will be in the continued process of compiling information about your classroom audience, and you will be collecting interesting and creative pieces of information as you come across them that might be useful support material for your speeches. When you anticipate future assignments and respond in an organized manner, your orderly planning will help you avoid making bad decisions that result from your not having access to useful information.

As you collect information for use in your speeches, maintain good records of the sources of that information. If you tear an article out of the campus paper, for example, be sure to jot reference information in the margin or attach a sticky note with the information. As you research your speech topics, take careful notes. Clearly mark your notes to indicate direct quotations, and include the page number of the quotation as well as the complete citation for the source. As you continue to work on your presentation, it will be easy to cite sources when you need to, because the necessary information will be right in front of you.

Finally, allow yourself plenty of time to complete your assignments. If you wait until the last minute, the chances of committing unintentional plagiarism increase simply because you may feel the need to cut corners. Remember that you are creating something that has not heretofore existed: a speech. The synthesis of information from a variety of sources, the preparation of visual aids, and the organization of your speech can be time-consuming. You will also need time to practice your speech. Begin to work as soon as your instructor gives you your assignment.

How should you cite your sources? We have noticed that sometimes students do not cite sources because they don't know how to insert that information into their speeches without interrupting the flow of ideas. Here are some suggestions for including your sources.

Guidelines to Help You Cite Your Sources

1. Think about the way you go about telling a friend something you heard from another friend ("I heard the strangest thing from Jane the other day. . .") or when you discuss an assignment with a classmate ("According to Professor Palermo, we are supposed to. . ."). The process you use to insert a source is exactly the same. Here is how Cindy cited her source in her speech on euthanasia and physician-assisted suicide:[13]

   > According to clinical psychologist Rob Neals, whom I quoted earlier, . . .

2. If you are using slide ware, such as PowerPoint or some other visual aid, write the source of the information directly on the visual. On her PowerPoint slide showing happiness ratings of home-schooled adults, notice how Katelyn provided the source of the data.[14]

3. When you directly quote a source, consider reading the quotation directly from the source. In other words, take the book, magazine, brochure, newspaper, etc. from which you plan to read to class with you. At the point where it fits into your speech, put down your notes, pick up the source, and read directly from it. Katelyn reads directly from a farming magazine when she discusses a particular point about life on a dairy farm.[15]

4. If your source is unknown to your audience, briefly establish the credentials of your source, as Crystal did when she discussed the food pyramid:[16]

   > Walter Willet, who is the chairman of the Nutrition Department for Harvard, is quoted as saying . . .

Decisions about your message convey sensitivity toward and regard for your audience, but there are other ethical decisions to be made that demonstrate a concern for the well-being of your audience.

ACT&REFLECT

3.1: Preparing a Speech Using Ethical Principles

ACT • Choose a speech you are currently working on that includes quotations. Prepare a second version of this speech in which you convert the quotations to paraphrases.

REFLECT • Which will be more effective when you give your presentation, the quotation or the paraphrase? Which of the two versions is more ethically principled? Why?

Interacting with Your Audience Ethically

The position taken in this book is that all presentations are a form of influence. When one presents to an audience, one is using the presentation as a means of achieving a goal. We want and expect to influence the manner in which our listeners think, believe, and act. However, an ethical speaker will not strive to meet his or her own goals without considering the well-being of the audience. Richard Weaver, a rhetorician, says, "The noble speaker glorifies and intensifies the worth of the audience and reflects an attitude of respect, concern, selflessness, involvement, and a desire to help the audience self-actualize."[17] What does this mean for your decisions as a speaker? Key ethical considerations that speakers take into account are promoting free will, avoiding control, and cultivating inclusiveness.

Promote Free Will

In a democracy, we believe that individuals have the right of **freedom of choice**, that is, the right to make their own decisions. This important democratic concept extends itself to the speaking environment as well. Even though as a speaker you wish to influence your audience, an ethical means to meet this goal is to provide your audience with sufficient information so that they can arrive at their own decisions. It might seem that we are advising you in a contradictory manner: you are speaking to influence your listeners, but you should allow them to make up their own minds. The information you present to your audience should be organized and presented in such a manner that your audience is able to consider an array of options and will understand why the option you suggest is the best in a given situation.

Eliminate Control

It should also be your goal as an ethical speaker not to attempt to exert your control but to present your message in a manner that allows your audience to exercise their right to freedom of choice. There are a number of ways you can influence without controlling your audience.

Guidelines for Influencing Your Audience without Controlling Them

1. Present your message in a manner that is understandable to your audience. We have discussed the importance of selecting words that your audience is able to understand, but consider also the organizational structure you use. If audience members are unable to follow your thinking as it is displayed in your presentation, they may feel that you are acting in a manipulative manner, hindering your ability to influence them.

2. Give your listeners enough information to enable them to make up their own minds. Although it is difficult to say

freedom of choice The right of the audience to make their own decisions.

what "enough information" entails, if you think about what your questions would be if you were an audience member listening to your presentation and then include the answers to those questions in your presentation, you are probably verging on developing a presentation that will fully inform your listeners.

3 If you are recommending a particular course of action that is applicable only to a very specific situation, say so. This is called the **condition of acceptability**.[18] For example, if you are advocating that an illegal drug should be made available to terminally ill patients to reduce their pain, be sure to indicate that this is the specific application you intend. If you are perceived as advocating an illegal act, your audience obviously may not wish to support you.

4 Allow your listeners to disagree with you. A challenging situation for any speaker is to influence an audience who disagrees with the speaker's goals. However, tolerating disagreement is a part of allowing freedom of choice. When you know your audience disagrees with you, acknowledge the specific areas of disagreement. You might say, for example, "The main area in which we disagree is the implementation timeline." Once you have identified the area(s) of disagreement, confirm that the difference of opinion is valid and offer your solution. You might also indicate that while you realize that there are areas on which you and your listeners disagree, there are many areas on which there is agreement and you intend to build on that. When you and your audience disagree, an important part of allowing your audience freedom of will is to acknowledge and tolerate the disagreement. Do not imply that those who disagree are less worthwhile individuals.

Cultivate Inclusiveness

For every member of your audience to feel that he or she is included in your message is imperative. You can cultivate inclusiveness in many ways, beginning with your choices of pronouns. Messages display **inclusiveness** when pronouns include rather than exclude and when examples demonstrate concern for the welfare and well-being of all audience members.[19] Selecting inclusive pronouns is not difficult: "we," "us," and "you" all include rather than exclude; however, you might need to plan the phrasing of sentences so these pronouns sound natural and sincere (see Act and Reflect 3.2).

Practicing inclusiveness also means that individuals have the right to feel they are entitled to their own views and to the presentation of those views, ensuring that you will maintain a dialogue with them. Here are some ways you can practice inclusiveness:[20]

1. Foster dialogue by presenting yourself authentically, develop a sense of equality with your audience, create a supportive climate; for example, it is not out of line to extend your sincere compliments to your audience, nor is it out of line to share a relevant personal experience with your audience.

condition of acceptability A particular course of action advocated by the speaker that applies only in a specific situation.

inclusiveness The speaker's involvement of the audience, by using, for example, inclusive pronouns or demonstrating a concern for the audience's welfare.

ACT&REFLECT

3.2: Practicing Inclusiveness with Your Audience

ACT • For the speech you are currently working on, identify the inclusive behaviors we have discussed here that you could extend to your audience.

REFLECT • How will you go about implementing these ethical actions in your speech?

2. Embrace a variety of discourses; that is, express yourself in several different ways; for example, you might make the same point with a quotation, a personal example, and a statistic to ensure that everyone in your audience will understand at least one of your approaches.

3. Empower everyone: allow listeners to contribute meaningful input during question-and-answer sessions and throughout your presentation, if appropriate.

4. Provide adequate information and options for your listeners; don't back them into a corner by making demands they may not be able to fulfill.

Although these suggestions for creating inclusiveness are important with every audience, there are some specific considerations when presenting to diverse audiences.

Ethical Considerations in a Diverse Environment

Julia Wood has written about sensitivities that communicators can observe when interacting with diverse individuals on an interpersonal basis. Some of her suggestions are also applicable when engaging in the everyday presentations we are discussing.[21] See also Act and Reflect 3.3.

Guidelines for Communicating with Diverse Audiences

1 Assertions: being "forthright" about presenting your views may be viewed differently in other cultures. Although some audiences may want to hear in a clear and straightforward manner what you want them to think, believe, or do, in some cultures, a straightforward approach may be too bold.

2 Individuality: individual rights or welfare are not always viewed in other cultures as more important in comparison to the welfare or rights of the family or a particular group. If you are advocating a benefit to individuals, you should also describe how the larger membership of the group will benefit from the view you espouse.

3 Disclosure: revealing personal thoughts or feelings may not be welcome to all audiences. In some cases, it might be more beneficial to use statistical representations or quotations from individuals your audience admires.

4 Involvement: the degree to which a speaker demonstrates commitment about his or her speaking goal may be acceptable to different degrees with different audiences. With some audiences, you may or may not want to show your emotional involvement with your message.

5 Feedback: in some instances, listening may signal agreement; in other instances, it may simply mean "I hear you." If you notice your diverse audience nodding, or making positive verbal responses or nonverbal utterances, do not assume that they are agreeing with you. They may simply be demonstrating that they are listening to your message.

ACT&REFLECT

3.3: Speaking Ethically to a Diverse Audience

ACT • Assume you are speaking to a diverse audience. Develop an action plan that demonstrates an ethical basis for speaking to this audience.

REFLECT • How will you reconcile the ethical information presented here with ethical approaches recommended for speaking to other audiences?

Ethical Considerations for Audience Members

When you become an audience member for a presentation, you are entering into an unspoken covenant with the speaker that both you and the speaker will both adhere to certain ethical principles—principles that dictate civil treatment and respect for one another. Regardless of whether your attendance is voluntary or mandatory, the very act of being in an audience imposes a certain set of responsibilities. Your behavior as a listener should be governed by a set of ethics that rests on the premise of respecting speakers and their right to speak even if one disagrees with their messages (see Act and Reflect 3.4 on page 78). We offer a set of ethics we believe audience members should follow:

1. Listeners should not engage in any behaviors that threaten the speaker's face (cause embarrassment or ridicule). This includes heckling, name calling, throwing things (like rotten tomatoes), or physical confrontations.

2. Listeners should avoid any behaviors that interfere with the flow of the speaker's message. This includes interrupting at inopportune times, asking questions at inopportune times, creating distractions that disrupt the speaker (talking to other listeners, leaving the room at an inopportune time, etc.). Inopportune times are those that are not invited or encouraged by the speaker or that prevent a speaker from completing an idea. When speakers are open to questions from the audience, you should find the least disruptive time to ask your question.

Peanuts: © United Feature Syndicate, Inc.

Everyday Example

"Disagreeing" Disagreeably at Cal State Sacramento

The following article is a commentary on the behaviors of students who disagreed with the keynote speaker at their college graduation. Which of the set of ethics for audience members do you see in violation in this commentary? What would have been a more ethical way for the students to register their disagreement? What ethical or unethical choices do you feel the speaker made?

Shouting down an unpopular campus speaker has a long, unfortunate history on our nation's campuses. Those of a certain age will remember the disruptions caused by student radicals during the late 1960s, and those who think of history in terms of archival research will know that what happened recently during commencement exercises at Cal State Sacramento is not particularly new. Nonetheless, the specter of students cat-calling a speaker off stage remains appalling, then and now.

What an admittedly small number of the 10,000 in attendance objected to were the questions raised by Janis Besler Heaphy, the president and publisher of *The Sacramento Bee*. She wondered, for example, if the delicate balance between national security and civil liberties has been put in jeopardy during the anxious days that followed the September 11th attacks. Heaphy made it clear that she was not questioning the war effort or the buildup of domestic security, but that she has problems with the suspension of certain civil liberties that, once conceded, may not be easily recovered.

The crowd, whether confined to the bleachers or more widespread, did not share her views—and more to the point, did not want to hear her rattling on about them. So, they made it impossible for her to finish what was to have been a nine-minute speech. Cal State Sacramento is not a distinguished university nor is *The Sacramento Bee* a major urban newspaper, but the disruption created national attention. For some, it was clear

evidence that this generation of college students, unlike many of their professors, is uncompromisingly patriotic. They do not care about the niceties of civil protection, especially if those being "protected" might well be terrorists. We are at war, and that alone justifies everything, absolutely everything, the government is now doing. In this regard, Cal State Sacramento students presumably echo what repeated national polling tells us is the majority view. Other students, interviewed after the ugly fact, were hardly rally-round-the-flag types.

This was their day, and what they had looked forward to was a short speech that would be light, upbeat, and focused on concerns that the bulk of the graduating class could relate to. Many, reporters learned, were suffering from September 11th exhaustion; they simply didn't want to hear about it. I'm not sure what to say to such students, other than to remind them that they will be living in a post September 11th world whether they like it or not. Moreover, commencement addresses (one thinks of Winston Churchill's "Iron Curtain" speech) often address important national issues. Apparently, their education had not equipped them to listen to nine minutes of moral gravitas, and to think about its implications.

Does this mean that I think they should simply have agreed with Heaphy and clapped until their hands were raw? Hardly. But a college graduate should know how to disagree without becoming disagreeable—and this apparently is a lesson many students had not learned in four years at Cal State Sacramento. Instead, they turned an academic ceremony into a version of "The Jerry Springer Show," one in which a chorus of angry boos are hurled at a speaker until he or she cannot continue. To his credit, Donald R. Gerth, Cal State Sacramento's president, urged the crowd to be civil; to his shame, he did not utter the two words that these boorish efforts at censorship required: "Shame, shame!" It never crossed his mind to ask campus security to remove the hooligans, although that is precisely what he should have done. Why so? Because those who would disrupt the speech of a person with an unpopular, controversial opinion have no place in an institution of higher learning. This, of course, did not happen, and the damage to free speech was done.

Afterward, and in the face of national security, the university put its PR wheels into motion: most of the students, we are told, had listened politely to Heaphy's remarks, and there were even those, such as Bob Buckley, the faculty president, who tried to make the case that the students at Cal State Sacramento were no different from students anywhere. "I think she [Heaphy] could have given the speech at any university in America," he said, "and the reaction would have been the

same. People in this country are hurt, angry, and vengeful. There's a lot of emotion out there."

However, I would remind Mr. Buckley that the Heaphy speech was not delivered in the first weeks after September 11th. Three months have passed and it is now appropriate to engage in the critical thinking—and, yes, even dissent—that struck me as unseemly when served up a few short days after the attack and against the backdrop of the still smoldering World Trade Center. Even more important, Mr. Buckley's efforts to mitigate the emotionalism of the crowd is a sad commentary on the place of reason in higher education.

Source: © Sanford Pinsker, "'Disagreeing' Disagreeably at Cal State Sacramento," a guest commentary, retrieved from M. Shapiro Web site, "The Irascible Professor: Irreverent Commentary on the State of Education in America Today," http://irascibleprofessor.com/comments-01-12-02-epr.htm.

3. Listeners are expected to listen objectively. Direct your attention to the speaker and the speaker's message. Ignoring the speaker, sleeping, or engaging in other activities during a speech are inappropriate. Be supportive by attending to the speaker as best you can by maintaining eye contact and positioning yourself to face the speaker as directly as you can, and be appropriately responsive.

4. While listeners have the right to their own beliefs and opinions, statements of disagreement should not interfere with the speaker's presentation and should

Audience members have a responsibility to disagree with a speaker in an ethical manner. ●

ACT&REFLECT

3.4: Develop a Listener Code of Ethics

ACT • Maintain a log of your own behaviors and the behaviors of your classmates when everyday presentations are being given in your communication class.

REFLECT • To what extent do your own behaviors reflect ethical actions? On the basis of what you observe in other audience members, what could you add to your listener code of ethics? How can you transfer your code of ethics into practice?

reflect respect for the speaker (you can challenge the ideas, but don't attack the messenger).

5. Don't plagiarize the content of a speech. Just as you need to cite any written source from which you draw information, you need to do so for oral sources. When repeating original content from other people's speeches, you need to appropriately cite them.

6. Don't create noise or distractions for other listeners. Respect the rights of others to listen without interference. This includes talking to others during the presentation, making noise, and bothering others.

● GETTING TO WORK

It is difficult to predict the role that ethics plays for a speaker attempting to achieve a speaking goal or for audience members' willingness to allow the speaker to influence them. However, surely if your audience views you as an unethical person or if you arouse suspicions as a result of your speech, or if your listeners perceive that you do not have their best interests at heart, to reach your speaking goal will become very difficult. If you are speaking to a group of individuals you interact with on a regular basis, your long-term effectiveness with them at all levels may be endangered. Conversely, it is also true that one of the highest displays of regard humans can confer on each other is the acknowledgement that "_____ is an ethical person." When you are viewed as an ethical person, your actions and opinions are viewed differently in all parts of your life compared to the opposite view. So how can you use the information we have presented in this chapter in your preparation as a speaker?

1 Although our perspective in this book is to prepare you to achieve your speaking goals in giving everyday presentations, it will not be a disadvantage if you live a virtuous life. President Bill Clinton was impeached for acts that many Americans felt were unbecoming, that is, unethical of the president of the United States. Did Clinton's actions effect his ability to carry out the responsibilities of the presidency? In some voters' minds, yes; in others, no. However, the reality and the ethical perceptions often become the same.

2 Identify ways you can walk the fine line between making it clear to your audience what it is you are trying to accomplish yet doing so in such a way that your listeners see that whatever you are advocating is the best choice. You can do this by preparing a message that seems clear and logical to your listeners, that presents a thorough discussion of the issues relevant to your goal, and that anticipates and responds to your listeners' concerns about your topic.

3 Decisions you make about the organization and content of your message do influence your relationship with your listeners, so you should make ethical decisions that reflect your esteem for your audience and your commitment to their welfare and safety. Every decision you make about your own conduct, the organization and content of your message, and your actions toward your audience contribute to the ultimate priority: creating and maintaining a relationship with those with whom you are constructing meaning.

4 Consider the ethical views of diverse audiences. Identify areas of your message that might be offensive to members of diverse groups. Show your respect for differing codes of ethics by making accommodations in your speech.

5 Audience members also agree to a code of ethics. Communication in everyday situations is a complex interaction in which a speaker presents ideas to audience members who agree to listen to and give thoughtful consideration to those ideas.

SUMMARY

"Ethics" refers to a set of guidelines that help people to determine what is "right" or "wrong," "good" or "bad." When giving everyday presentations, it is imperative that a speaker's message and actions be guided by ethical decisions. The relationship between speaker and listener is tentative and delicate. We speak with the intention of exerting an influence on listeners' thoughts or actions. Essentially, we are depending on the relationship and the goodwill we create with our audiences to achieve our own ends. Given that we are asking listeners to think or take action in certain ways, it is especially important for the speaker to make decisions with the highest ethical concern to avoid the actual or perceptual manipulation of the people we are attempting to influence. Speakers should strive to present an ethical image to their listeners, and they should strive to maintain the highest ethical principles when developing their messages and when interacting with their listeners.

Issues relating to the ethical image that a speaker presents include the speaker's initial credibility, truthfulness, and perceived intentionality. Initial credibility is the image the audience has of the speaker as a result of interaction with the speaker before the speech. Speakers should be committed to providing truthful and accurate information in their speeches, although the meaning of "truth" may be situational. Speakers should make every effort to ensure that the information and the sources of that information they present to their listeners is accurate. It is worthwhile to verify the authenticity of information. Although speakers should be committed to the ideas they espouse in their messages, their commitment should not endanger or cause discomfort to their listeners.

When constructing a speech, ethical decisions should be concerned with clarity, accuracy, and the crediting of sources. Ideas should be presented in such a manner that the audience can clearly understand them. Speakers should carefully choose words that reflect the ideas they intend to convey. Finally, giving credit to others for their words and ideas is not simply an ethical decision; it is illegal to use another person's work without giving credit.

Speakers should demonstrate the highest regard for their audiences by interacting with listeners in a manner that recognizes and promotes individuals' free will, avoids exerting control, and cultivates inclusiveness. Speakers should provide sufficient information to enable listeners to make their own decisions. Disagreement should be acknowledged and addressed. If the goal of the speaker is relevant only in specific circumstances, the nature of those circumstances should be clearly indicated in the speech. Inclusiveness with the audience can be cultivated by fostering dialogue with the audience, embracing a variety of discourses, empowering everyone, and providing adequate information and options for listeners.

The ethical speaker realizes that diverse audiences acknowledge ethics in diverse ways. Some of the considerations ethical speakers should thoughtfully address when speaking to diverse audiences include making assertions in an appropriate way; advocating for the individual as well as, not instead of, the group; proceeding cautiously when making personal disclosures; determining the proper degree of involvement to display with a topic; and realizing that with some audiences, when listeners say yes, they are not signalling agreement but simply indicating that they are listening.

In assuming the role of audience member, individuals also assume responsibilities for displaying ethical actions. Listeners should not attempt to defame the speaker or interrupt the speaker's messages. Listeners need not agree with the speaker but should strive to be thoughtful and objective listeners. They should respect the right of other listeners to hear the speaker and should not behave in distracting ways. And listeners are obligated to accurately represent the speaker's message when relating it to others.

VIDEO EXPERIENCE

The video clip for this experience shows Jessica's speech to a negative audience on gay marriages.[22] As you watch the speech, what, if any, instances are you able to identify where Jessica has adhered to the ethical guidelines we have discussed in this chapter? What, if any, violations of the ethical guidelines do you identify? What changes could you suggest to Jessica to eradicate the violations you have found?

THINKING BACK, THINKING AHEAD

1. Investigate the circumstances of public figures whose words or actions resulted in allegations of unethical acts. What were the immediate and long-term results of the allegations? In your judgment, was the individual guilty of unethical actions? What can you learn for your own use as a speaker from the ethical dilemmas of others?

2. Write your own personal code of ethics. To what extent do you believe that an ethical person is also an ethical speaker? On your calendar, write reminders to yourself to review and revise your ethical code as you are preparing each everyday presentation you give.

3. As you listen to others' everyday presentations, do you begin to see a common code of ethics that guides speakers' decisions, or do you believe that ethics are largely situational? From this exercise, how are you guided in decisions you make when planning an everyday presentation?

4. We have recommended different ethical considerations for diverse audiences. How will you reconcile your own ethical code with the suggestions we have made for speaking to diverse audiences when there are differences between your code and the codes of your listeners?

NOTES

1. D. Rather, *Statement on Memos*, retrieved from CBS News Web site, at www.cbsnews.com/stories/2004/09/20/politics/main644546.shtml. H. Kurtz, "CBS Apologizes for Using Disputed Memos," *Des Moines Register*, September 21, 2004, pp. 1A, 14A.

2. R. L. Johannesen, "Communication Ethics: Centrality, Trends, and Controversies," In *Communication Yearbook 25*, edited by William B. Gudykunst (Mahwah, NJ: Erlbaum, 2001), 200–235.

3. M. Timmons, *Conduct and Character: Readings in Moral Theory*, 4th ed. (Belmont, CA: Wadsworth, 2003).

4. K. E. Andersen, *Recovering the Civic Culture: The Imperative of Ethical Communication*, Carroll C. Arnold Distinguished Lecture, National Communication Association Convention, Miami Beach, Florida, November 20, 2003 (Boston: Pearson, 2005), 19.

5. Ethics Updates Web site, edited by L. Hinman, at http://ethics.acusd.edu.

6. C. G. Christians, "The *Ethics* and Its Relevance for Communication and Media Ethics," in *Communication Ethics and Universal Values*, edited by C. Christians and M. Traber (Thousand Oaks, CA: Sage, 1997), 46–67.

7. J. Devito, *The Communication Handbook: A Dictionary* (New York: Harper & Row, 1986), 83.

8. J. Jaksa and M. S. Pritchard, *Communication Ethics: Methods of Analysis* (Belmont, CA: Wadsworth, 1988).

9. Jaksa and Pritchard, *Communication Ethics*, 101.

10. R. L. Johannesen, *Ethics in Human Communication*, 5th ed. (Prospect Heights, IL: Waveland Press, 2002).

11. E. Arens, "Discourse Ethics and Its Relevance for Communication and Media Ethic," in Christians and Traber, *Communication Ethics and Universal Values*, 46–67.

12. Jaksa and Pritchard, *Communication Ethics*, 39–40.

13. Cindy Johnson, speech to a negative audience, November 8, 2004.

14. Katelyn Ver Hoef, speech to a negative audience, November 10, 2004.

15. Katelyn Ver Hoef, speech to a neutral audience, October 15, 2004.

16. Crystal Nord, speech to a neutral audience, October 18, 2004.

17. Richard Weaver, quoted in Johannesen, *Ethics in Human Communication*, 66.

18. Arens, "Discourse Ethics," 51.

19. J. Makau, "Embracing Diversity in the Classroom," in *Communicating Ethics in an Age of Diversity*, edited by J. Makau and R. C. Arnett (Urbana, IL: University of Illinois Press, 1997), 48–67.

20. L. P. Stewart, "Facilitating Connections: Issues of Gender, Culture, and Diversity," in Makau and Arnett, *Communicating Ethics in an Age of Diversity*, 110–125.

21. J. T. Wood, "Diversity in Dialogue: Commonalities and Differences between Friends," in Makau and Arnett, *Communication Ethics in an Age of Diversity*, 5–26.

22. Jessica Culhane, speech to a negative audience, November 10, 2004.

Chapter 4

Connecting with Your Audience

Delivering Your Message

Goals

✓ To illustrate for you the importance of building and maintaining a connection with the audience, creating immediacy, and establishing credibility through delivery

✓ To emphasize cultural influences that may exist in your audience that affect the sending and receiving of your nonverbal messages

✓ To identify nonverbal actions that will assist you in delivering a more meaningful presentation

✓ To suggest specific ways of managing proxemics, kinesics, physical appearance, and paralanguage to allow you to build a connection, appear credible, and create immediacy with your audience

In 1960, John Kennedy and Richard Nixon ran against each other for the office of president of the United States. In a series of televised debates, Kennedy was effective in making a connection with television viewers; Nixon, however, was not so comfortable on television. Eventually, Nixon's notes were placed directly above the television camera so that when he read his speech, he had to look at the camera, and it would look as though he was looking into the eyes of the television audience.[1]

Many factors led to Kennedy winning the election, but it is surely the case that at least partially to blame for Nixon's loss was his difficulty in making that crucial connection with his audience through the television. Because we feel that we have personal interactions with the people we watch on television, as well as the contacts we make through various other forms of technology, we have come to expect presenters who are in the same room with us to create a "personal" connection with us.[2] ●

The 1960 Nixon-Kennedy presidential debates demonstrate that a speaker's delivery and connection to the audience have an impact on the speech's outcome. ●

The Kennedy/Nixon debates illustrate the importance of delivery. It is through your delivery that you make a connection with your audience, as well as creating a sense of immediacy and establishing credibility. **Delivery** refers to the synthesis of everything about you that contributes to the meaning of your message and builds your relationship with your audience. Delivery includes your voice, your eyes and face, your gestures, your attire, and the way you use space in the environment in which you are presenting.

The Importance of Delivery

Oh body swayed to music, O brightening glance,
How can we know the dancer from the dance?[3]

No, you didn't pick up the wrong book; this is your communication text. The topic of this chapter is still delivery. The lines from the poem describing a dancer make an important point about delivery. You can probably identify those of your friends who like to dance. The expressions on their faces, their gestures and posture, the movements of their shoulders, their singing along with the music, and, of course, the steps they take with their feet all reveal their enjoyment. Those who love to dance, as the poem says, become the dance. You can't tell where the dancing ends and where your friend begins. You can also identify those of your friends who do not enjoy dancing. Their pained facial expressions, the stiffness of their posture, the lack of gestures and singing along—these dancers just aren't "into it," and it might be just as difficult for you to watch as it is for them to dance.

There are similarities between these dancing scenarios and the way people feel and look when giving presentations. Can you think of a time when you were trying to pay attention to a presentation but it was impossible because you were distracted by the presenter's mannerisms? Or maybe you felt embarrassed or nervous on behalf of a presenter who appeared completely ill at ease. At other times, you felt the presenter was speaking only to you, even though there were others in the room. How do some speakers make listeners feel involved and others create an uncomfortable experience for their listeners? Just as the good dancer "becomes the dance," the good presenter becomes the message he or she is presenting. Everything about the effective presenter is geared to the message and the audience: posture, facial expressions, eye contact, gestures, voice, and the management of the presentation space. These nonverbal elements called delivery fuse you with your message, creating a synergistic effect in which the result is greater than the parts, and your listeners cannot separate the presenter from the message.

During a presentation, delivery is a key force in assisting the presenter to reach his or her communication goal. If it is difficult to hear your voice or you do not maintain eye contact with your listeners, some listeners might not put forth the effort to overcome your delivery weaknesses, and even the most brilliant verbal message can be ignored. Some listeners might become "hooked" on your presentation not because of your

delivery The synthesis of everything about you that contributes to the meaning of your message and builds a relationship with your audience.

verbal message but because they were influenced by your very effective delivery. For most audiences, effective delivery will make it much easier to listen to your message.

Your delivery also influences whether listeners will be persuaded by your message. If listeners disagree with what you are saying, certain mannerisms might make them suspicious of your motivations or question your credibility. For example, if you are pacing aimlessly around the room, or your hands are drawing meaningless pictures in the air, your listeners might attribute your mannerisms to a character or credibility flaw, and it might be convenient for them to use your distracting delivery as a reason not to be persuaded by your message. On the other hand, if your delivery conveys the impression of an individual who sincerely believes in and is committed to his or her message, it is possible your delivery will influence your audience.

Distracting mannerisms may also work to keep your listeners from listening to what you are saying. Perhaps you are explaining a new customer service policy to servers you supervise at the pizza shop. You expect them to implement this policy immediately. However, if your delivery distracts them as you are explaining the new policy, it's possible they will not understand or even hear your verbal message, reducing the likelihood of their implementing the change. On the other hand, effective delivery can make your verbal message more meaningful and can help listeners retain what you are telling them.

Besides influencing your listeners' responses to you and your message, your delivery can also influence the way you yourself feel about the message and the presentation environment. If you thoughtfully consider your delivery, your presentation can make you feel exhilarated and confident. While you are presenting, these positive feelings will, in turn, make you even more effective as a presenter, increasing the chances you will achieve your presentation goal. You have a great deal of control in the construction and the outcomes of your presentation. Why not create a positive experience for yourself and your audience through your delivery?

Remember that we use presentations for the purpose of attaining a communication goal. By understanding the way your delivery influences your listeners and by considering the contribution each of the elements of delivery can make to your total presentation, you are simply increasing the chances that you will meet your communication goal. It is also through delivery that we initiate and maintain connections with our listeners.

Making Connections

Even though you are only one person making a presentation to many others, you should view the presentation as a time to create a **connection:** a relationship with each person to whom you are speaking, such that it feels as though only the two of you are in the room. Depending on the nature of your message and your audience's responses to you, your success in influencing the audience might be as simple, yet as complex, as the way they see you, first as a person, and second as a presenter. It is through this connection that you, in turn, receive valuable information from the audience that can help you create a more effective presentation as you are giving it. You might notice that your audience

connection A relationship with each person in your audience that feels as though only the two of you are in the room.

does not seem convinced about your advice to schedule an annual flu shot, for example. Their reactions to your message can help you make on-the-spot decisions about what you say and how you say it to change their responses as you are presenting. Or if your explanation of sales figures is met by puzzled looks, those facial expressions are important information from the audience informing you that you need to make changes in your presentation so the sales figures can be understood.

Making connections with your audience is important not only because it helps you influence your listeners, and vice versa, but also because your audience expects it.[4] Millions of viewers catch the late-night talk show monologue before calling it a day. Nonetheless, you, sitting in your living room, feel that your favorite talk show host is speaking to you alone. Because of our feeling that we have personal interactions with the people we watch on television, as well as the contacts we make through various other forms of communication technology, we have come to expect presenters who are in the same room with us to create the same type of "personal" connections with us that we enjoy with television personalities. This is the effect for you to aspire to with the audience who are in front of you as you present. The resulting connection creates a relationship, a sense of closeness, or immediacy, between presenter and listeners.

Creating Immediacy

Albert Mehrabian said, "People are drawn toward persons and things they like, evaluate highly, and prefer; and they avoid or move away from things they dislike, evaluate negatively, or do not prefer."[5] The psychological closeness Mehrabian was describing is known as **immediacy.** Those people in your life whom you refer to as "close" friends are those with whom you have created immediacy. People with whom you have experienced immediacy influence you and are influenced by your beliefs, actions, and thoughts.

When teachers are able to create immediacy with their students, research shows that not only do the students feel more positively toward the teacher and the subject compared to other classes, but also they learn more. In other words, when you feel a sense of closeness to your instructors, it results in positive feelings about the instructor, the class, and the subject, and this positive attitude seems to influence the extent to which you pay attention in class, interact with your instructor as well as your classmates, and eventually come to own and understand the knowledge that is disseminated in that class.[6] A sense of immediacy established between presenter and audience members should result in the same benefits. In the classroom, knowledge is imparted just as it is during a presentation; those who inhabit the classroom are influencing and being influenced by each other, just as during a presentation. Just as the teacher is a key individual in the classroom, the presenter is a key individual when presenting.

Constructing immediacy during a presentation should benefit the presenter and listeners in the same way it does the members of a class. When listeners feel a sense of immediacy with the presenter, they are more positively predisposed to the presenter, they are likely to pay more attention to the presentation, and they will become more actively involved in the presentation context, with the result that the

immediacy A sense of psychological closeness that results from eye contact, natural movements, and other verbal and nonverbal speaker choices.

You can create a sense of immediacy with your audience through strong eye contact, consistent facial expressions, and physical closeness. •

presenter has influence on them, increasing the possibility of reaching the communication goal. Essentially, nonverbal cues—such as maintaining open spaces with listeners rather than creating barriers with a lectern or table, maintaining eye contact with your audience rather than avoiding looking at them, using an expressive, varied voice, and moving your body naturally rather than displaying rigid movements—all contribute to bringing you both psychologically and physically closer to your listeners, resulting in a sense of immediacy.[7]

Establishing Credibility

Credibility is the perception of the audience that the presenter has trustworthy intentions and is conveying information that is accurate. When you present, credibility is a result of your delivery, as well as what you say. Your credibility is also based on the extent to which you yourself are committed to your message. This commitment is reflected in the way you present and in the message you present.

Your audience might have a sense of your **initial credibility,** that is, the credibility the audience perceives you to have before you present.[8] When your audience members know you or when they have had an opportunity to learn about you through other means, their view of you is established before you begin to speak. For example, when you present in your communication class, your classmates have a view of your initial credibility that is based on their experiences with you in class. In a professional environment, your conversations at the elevator or the drinking fountain influence your initial credibility when you speak up in meetings. If your initial credibility is not high, you may find yourself starting off on the wrong foot with your listeners, losing precious time as you overcome perceptions of low initial credibility held by your audience. If your

credibility The perception of the audience that the presenter has trustworthy intentions and is conveying information that is accurate.

initial credibility The audience's estimation of your credibility before you begin to present.

initial credibility is high, that can be advantageous to you in achieving your communication goal.

The extent to which your audience views you as credible as a result of your presentation your **terminal credibility.**[9] How can you present yourself in order to create a connection with the audience that allows establishing immediacy and that will allow you to create strong terminal credibility? The components of your delivery that will make a difference in your listeners' assessment of you and your message include the way you use space, the way you present your physical self, and your voice. On the following pages you will read about ways to manage these nonverbal areas. However, keep in mind that you cannot simply "try on" a facial expression or walk to a part of the room in which you are presenting or speak in a loud or soft voice and automatically attain any of the benefits of immediacy or credibility or connecting with your audience. Every presentation you give must be grounded in your own commitment to achieve your communication goal and the sincerity you feel about your message and toward your audience as you interact.

The Relationship of Culture and Delivery

Delivery differentiates itself from your speech in that delivery refers to the nonverbal means a speaker displays to give the speech its meaning. Nonverbal communication is heavily influenced by culture. In fact, "one of the most basic and obvious functions of nonverbal communication is to communicate one's culture."[10] The behaviors that are condoned by your culture are such an innate part of you that often you do not recognize the characteristics of your own culture until you are faced with an individual from another culture whose behaviors differ from your own. As you deliver your speech, you might find that behaviors that are a part of your culture are inconsistent with those condoned by the cultures represented in your audience.

As you continue reading about delivery, you will learn that space in the speaking environment should be managed in a certain way, that eye contact is important, that posture and facial expression will influence the audience. However, you should also keep in mind that the advice given here is largely for members of western cultures. Perhaps the members of your classroom audience, as well as other audiences to whom you speak, include individuals from other cultures. The western value of eye contact is not necessarily shared by other cultures; display of emotions through facial expression or gestures or other ways of communicating nonverbally may not be condoned. When audience responses differ from what you have expected, the influence of your delivery should be your first consideration. Thinking on your feet, is there a change that you can make to attain the desired response?

As you plan your presentation, consider the cultural composition of your audience. Are there certain behaviors that are part of your culture that are interpreted differently by members of your audience? Although we are not advocating that you abandon the behaviors of your own culture, without compromising yourself, are there changes you might make in your delivery or delivery behaviors from which you could

terminal credibility The extent to which your audience views you as credible as a result of your presentation.

refrain? Even as you seek to inform and to influence your listeners, be aware of the information you receive from the diverse members of your audience.

Guidelines for Speaking to Diverse Audiences

1 Consider your use of space and territory. Cultures differ in their uses of these. If you are presenting your speech on a raised platform or if you plan to move around, particularly throughout the audience, you might find members of other cultures responding differently from what you would expect of members of your own culture.

2 Consider your use of your face and body. Cultures differ regarding animation or responsiveness of facial expression and regarding eye contact. Gestures are not interpreted in the same way in every culture. If your audience does not respond in a particular manner to a joke or emotional story, their differing responses might reflect their diverse cultures.

3 Consider your physical appearance. Cultures differ regarding what is considered appropriate attire. You may discover that your expectations of appropriate attire for your presentation do not coincide with those of your diverse audience.

4 Consider your vocalics. Appropriate use of the voice differs in various cultures. The way you have been taught in your culture to use your voice to sound credible and knowledgeable may be interpreted differently by members of other cultures.

Elements of Delivery

Consider the way in which you manage proxemics, kinesics, paralanguage, and your physical appearance as a way to create connections, to attain credibility, and to achieve immediacy with your audience.

Proxemics: The Way You Manage Space

Ordinarily, we might not consciously manipulate space unless our sense of appropriate space in a particular situation is violated. When you are presenting, the way you manage the space within the presentation environment is a way to create an important connection with your audience.

Proxemics refers to the relationship of space and your interaction with others in that space. There are two ways to consider the space in which you are presenting. First, be aware of the environment within which the presentation will occur, second, consider ways that your movements within that environment can create relationships or connections with your listeners that will facilitate reaching your communication goal.

Managing Space in the Environment The environments where presentations occur range from the largest public arenas, where the audience might blend together as an almost indistinguishable mass, to the most personal of spaces, where you can see every blink

> **proxemics** The relationship of space and your interaction with others in that space.

A Question of **Ethics**

As you can see, delivery is an important means of making connections with your audience. In any speaking situation, your audience is likely to be made up of members from a variety of cultures, as well as having other diverse qualities. On the basis of what we have said about the things you should keep in mind when delivering your speech to a diverse audience, is it ethical to manage your delivery in order to create a connection with some members of your audience, knowing you will be excluding others? In instances where appealing to the interests of only one group will result in your meeting your speaking goal, how can you appeal to that group without excluding other groups? Is it ethical to manage your delivery to appeal to only one group? Why or why not?

and facial response of your listeners. We believe that most of your presentations will occur in smaller spaces, and this school term, perhaps most of your presentations will occur in your communication classroom. Occasionally you might find yourself speaking in an auditorium-like setting.

In large spaces, the characteristics and the challenges of the environment are that you will not easily be able to manipulate furniture or other objects within the area; you will need to be aware of points in your presentation when you must be close enough to technical equipment to be able to operate it; and any relationship you attempt to create with your listeners will need to be with small, easily accessible groups, such as those in the front row. The remainder of your audience will view your interactions with these few accessible individuals, and the relationship you make with them will be transferred to all of the other listeners you are unable to reach.[11]

Your communication classroom has its own characteristics. You might be tempted to stand behind a lectern, but when you feel comfortable doing so, consider moving out from behind that lectern to make connections with your classmates. You can move back and forth across the front of the classroom or use the center aisle of the room to make connections with your classmates who are sitting in all parts of the room.

Most often you will find yourself presenting in a smaller room such as a conference room or boardroom; these spaces have their challenges as well. The tables and chairs and other objects within the room often fill the available area so that movement becomes awkward. You may not be able to easily move throughout the room. Rather than taking the risk of tripping over a listener or getting yourself in some other awkward situation while you are presenting, consider whether it makes more sense for you to simply remain seated; if so, select your seating position strategically. If it is possible for you to sit on the side of a table that allows you eye contact with the majority of listeners, you can still make connections. If the seating arrangement makes it impossible to place a majority of your listeners within your vision, you are presented with an "advantageous challenge." Because you are sitting close enough to everyone that you can make the connection both personal and interpersonal, you can lean forward, gesture toward, and make eye contact with all of your listeners. With a small number of listeners who are close enough for you to see them, you can interact directly with each of them throughout your presentation.

In addition, there will be any number of "in-between" situations when the surroundings will allow you to move freely among your listeners. Maybe your professional organization holds events in a rented hotel meeting room, or your residence hall peers congregate in the comfortable dormitory lounge, or your service club meets in the banquet room of the local coffee shop. Any of these or similar settings gives you opportunity to work the space to establish special connections with your audience. Making those special connections with individual members of your audience brings forth another set of challenges regarding your management of space.

Managing Space with Your Listeners The anthropologist Edward T. Hall found that individuals who interact with each other tend to organize their interactions within four **"distance zones"** ranging from zero to more than twelve feet.[12] The distance zones one selects when interacting with others is dependent on a number of factors, such as one's relationship with the others and the topic being discussed.

Since you want to connect to each listener in your audience, you should modify the distance between yourself and your audience in accordance with what you are saying and what you want to accomplish. Perhaps you are speaking on behalf of a tax increase to build a new elementary school in your community. Move closer to your audience as you read comments written by the children who would attend the new school describing how much they are looking forward to their new facility. When you display a PowerPoint presentation depicting tax increases anticipated over the next few years, move away from the audience so you are in a position to include everyone as well as gesturing toward the PowerPoint presentation. As you move toward the conclusion of your presentation, again reduce the space between your audience and yourself as you appeal to them to vote in support of the tax increase.

This technique is particularly effective if you are presenting to a small audience when you know each person, as in your communication classroom or with another group of colleagues. If there are parts of your presentation when you refer to individuals by name, reduce the distance between yourself and the person you are referring to and then increase the distance between the two of you so as to include all of your listeners in the next part of your message.

When Matthew gave his presentation on snakes, he made use of the large room MSL in which he presented by moving around the room to enable all of his audience to hear him and to see the boa constrictors he used as visual aids. He also wanted his audience to be able to touch his visual aids (only if they wanted to) and to point out various characteristics of the boa constrictors. In order to achieve closeness with the audience for the interactive parts of his speech, Matthew varied the space between himself and individual audience members.[13]

Besides using space to connect with your audience, you can use your posture, facial expressions, eye contact, and gestures.

> **distance zones** Areas ranging from zero to more than twelve feet that can be managed to create a connection with the audience.

Kinesics: The Language of Your Body

The robins sang and sang and sang, but teacher you went right on.
The last bell sounded the end of the day, but teacher you went right on.
The geranium on the window sill just died, but teacher you went right on.[14]

No one likes to admit being responsible for a situation like the one in this classroom; however, we have probably all been present in such an environment. The purpose of this discussion of **kinesics,** or body language, is to alert you to the wonderful resource you have in your own person for creating a presentation in which the geranium on the windowsill will never die and your listeners will hang on to your every word. Perhaps the most important part of delivery refers to the way you use yourself as a means of conveying your message. Your posture, facial expression, gestures, and eye contact are valuable resources for creating a connection with your audience and enhancing the meaning of your message.

Your Posture Are you getting tired of reading this text? For a change of pace, close this book and try balancing it on your head. Do you feel natural with the book on your "noggin"?—that is, is this the way you usually feel when you are sitting or standing? If not, it could benefit you to practice both walking and sitting with this text on your head for a few minutes daily until you feel comfortable. Do you notice that with the book on your head, if you are too "uptight" or too relaxed, the book falls on the floor? When you are able to achieve that delicate balance of the book on your head while sitting and standing and feel natural doing it, that is your best posture. When you do achieve that delicate balance, what is the position of your body? The distance between your ears and your shoulders has increased, and your neck seems to have grown longer. The distance between your shoulder blades has narrowed, and your shoulders are positioned low on your back. Catching a glimpse of yourself in the mirror, you notice your stomach is pulled in, and it appears that you've lost a few pounds. These are certainly benefits of strong, straight posture; but what is the benefit to your presentation? (You can remove the book from your head now. Try retaining your new look without the book.)

MSL

When you enter a room, even before you speak, the audience draws conclusions about you on the basis of your posture, the only source of information they have about you at that point. Even if your audience knows you, their impression of you on that day, at that moment, is based on your posture. Your posture speaks for you before you begin to speak. After you begin to speak, your posture continues to represent you. Descriptions of good posture often include words such as "dignified," "strong," or "confident" (see Act and Reflect 4.1). Your posture will convey these impressions to your audience. As you move about the presentation space, maintain the distance between your shoulders and your ears; keep your shoulders lowered and together on your back. The resulting view to your listeners should be one of "relaxed alertness." Good posture should be similar to breathing: although it is not something you are conscious of, your practiced control of it will work to your advantage. Jessica maintained excellent posture for her entire presentation on sleep. Her posture appeared effortless and added to the image of a knowledgeable and confident presenter.[15]

kinesics The use of the eyes, facial expression, posture, and gestures that contribute to the speaker's delivery.

In some instances, you might find yourself standing behind a lectern. Occa-  sionally, in these circumstances, it is tempting to recline on the lectern, with the result that your posture says to your audience "I'm tired," "This is unimportant," or "I'm not committed to what I am telling you." Even though a large portion of your body might be hidden behind the lectern, continue to maintain your confident posture. Even when you lean forward toward various members of your audience, continue to retain your posture. Try lengthening the area between your waist and the bottom of your rib cage before leaning forward to maintain the confident line of your body. During her presentation on tanning pills, Chelsea moved from the Elmo to the lectern to a space in between, yet her upright posture did not change. She remained tall even though she had the opportunity to "recline" on the lectern or against the cart on which the Elmo was placed.[16]

Your Facial Expression Your face is also a primary source of information to your listeners; in fact, some researchers view the face as a source of information of importance second only to the presentation itself.[17] See Act and Reflect 4.2. When your audience perceives a conflict between your verbal messages and your nonverbal messages, they are likely to assume that your facial expression is the "real" representation of your message. A facial expression that does not mirror or emphasize or in any other way communicate the point of your presentation could cause the audience to question your sincerity or your credibility or to focus on your face and stop listening to your words. Your face is an important means for you to make a connection with your audience. If you were discussing a wave of vandalism on campus, your face would likely display a serious expression to match your feelings about this topic. As you describe a successful fundraising effort, your facial expression might reflect pride. Just as your face typically reflects the emotions you experience as you talk spontaneously, so should your facial expression reflect the various emotions you feel about your message as you move through your presentation. After encouraging her classmates to attend a rally to combat ignorance, Maya described the T-shirt they would receive in appreciation of their attendance. Upon concluding her speech, she invited the audience to ask questions. Her facial expression subtly changed to reflect her message as she progressed through her presentation.[18]

How can you be assured that your face not only reflects sincerity but also displays emotions that project your message? It is helpful if you know what your face feels like when you are displaying certain expressions. Knowing how the muscles feel around your eyes, the position of your eyebrows, and the shape of your mouth, and being aware of the way various feelings look to others, can help you make adjustments, ensuring that

What message does this speaker's posture tell you about her attitude toward the audience? ●

ACT&REFLECT

4.1: Checking Posture

ACT • Take a break from your reading and note the posture of the other individuals within your view. If you see people you know, is their posture consistent with what you know about their personalities? What does the posture of individuals you do not know lead you to conclude about them?

REFLECT • What have you learned about the importance of posture from your observation? What improvements can you make to your own posture? How will you go about making these changes?

your audience sees on your face the same message you want them to hear in your words. What can you do to ensure you will have this knowledge of your face so as to use it to your advantage?

You could go so far as to check a mirror from time to time when you are feeling particularly emotional. When you feel happy, what is the expression on your face? More important, what does it feel like? If you have access to a camera, ask a friend to film you as you practice a presentation. Watching yourself, does it seem you are presenting a "total" message—that is, does your face reflect what you are saying?

An even better way to determine what you look like as you present is to look around the room at your listeners. Their facial expressions will be reactions to your message. What do you see on the faces of your audience? Do their expressions appear to be appropriate responses to what you are saying to them? If so, your expressions are probably reflecting the emotion you yourself are feeling about your topic. Your hands can also help you to convey your message.

ACT&REFLECT

4.2: Faces

ACT • Again, put down your book. Look at the faces of individuals around you who are studying or working alone. What expressions do you see on their faces? What information about them do you receive from their facial expressions?

REFLECT • What have you learned from your observation that will be helpful to you as you present?

Your Gestures In a sports context, "follow-through" is an important concept; it means to carry a throw to its natural completion. The same idea is important in a presentation context: follow-through is needed to effectively display your gestures. Gestures without follow-through are distracting and look like signs of nervousness. Follow-through will give your gestures the power they need to make the point for which you are using them, just as in an athletic context, follow-through helps to ensure the ball will hit its mark.

Some people naturally use their hands a great deal when they talk; others do not. Whether you generally do or do not, it is unwise to identify gestures you will use at certain points in your presentation and practice those gestures in advance. You are apt to look exactly as if you have identified and practiced your gestures. It is just as unwise not to give some thought to your gestures. There is a fine line between rehearsing gestures and using your hands to add meaning to your message. If you know what you want to say and you are committed to what you are saying, your gestures are more likely to enhance your presentation in a natural, effective manner. As Jon discussed the advantages of participating in extracurricular activities, he described his misgivings about moving from a small to a large high school and the reasons he became motivated to become involved in extracurricular activities. His gestures illustrated what he was saying and involved his audience in his presentation.[19]

Guidelines to Ensure That Your Gestures Will Enhance Your Presentation

1. Use fewer rather than more gestures. Not every word or idea has an accompanying gesture. Save your gestures for areas of your presentation when your hands can help emphasize, repeat, clarify, or explain.

2. Gestures should be larger rather than smaller. Small gestures could go unnoticed or be mistaken for signs of nervousness. When your hands are far enough away from your body that your audience can see them, the gestures you make will be large, will look deliberate, and will not be mistaken for a nervous habit.

3. Gestures should be made slowly. A quick gesture can be overlooked. Slow gestures are more easily noticed; they give you the opportunity to think about their effect on the audience; and they give the audience time to acknowledge and derive meaning from them.

4. Gestures should be made toward the audience and away from you. This way you display inclusiveness, and you involve your listeners in your message.

5. Always follow through. The follow-through is the completion of the gesture. Allow your hand to linger in the air for a second.

Reaching that point between displaying natural-looking, effective gestures and displaying rehearsed, artificial-looking gestures requires a delicate balance of sincerity and commitment to your message. You can become more aware of your use of gestures by checking yourself in a mirror, practicing your presentation before a camera, and using gestures during presentations and checking your listeners' responses to them.

Eye Contact During a presentation, eye contact creates connections with the audience, as well as establishing a channel through which communication occurs. Maintaining eye contact also serves other important functions (see Act and Reflect 4.3).

Eye contact signals a willingness to communicate.[20] It is difficult to communicate when there is no eye contact. The simple act of looking at the audience allows communication to happen.

Eye contact increases the value of a message.[21] In an experiment involving surgical students taking oral exams, the surgical faculty gave higher scores to actors who used a more direct gaze, even though their responses were the same as those of the real surgical students.[22] Your listeners' estimation of the quality of the knowledge you impart, as well as your own credibility, could be enhanced as a result of your eye contact. Your lack of eye contact could result in a decrease in the perceived value of your message and your credibility.

Eye contact influences judgments about the characters of others. We tend to draw conclusions about the trustworthiness or credibility of people who cannot maintain eye contact with us. Eye contact says something about your desire to include your listeners. If, as the presenter, you are unable to make eye contact or "sustain gaze" with your listeners, they may feel their value is diminished. If your listeners feel that you do not respect or value them, it will be difficult for you to meet your communication goal.

Eye contact plays a role in sustaining and controlling relationships.[23] When you present, you may be speaking to many listeners; however, each should feel you are speaking directly to them as an individual. Eye contact can assist you in making a connection and maintaining a relationship with each listener. Eye contact promotes intimacy or the feeling of being personally involved.[24] Generally, we look at people we like, and we avoid eye contact with people we do not feel positively about. When someone avoids eye contact with you, you feel less highly regarded, and in turn, you might feel less regard for that person.[25] In many ways, a lack of eye contact makes us feel invisible. Katie introduced her speech on the value of studying abroad by first discussing her own misgivings about studying abroad followed by her friend's responses to them. She established eye contact with each member of the audience as she spoke, and it seemed she truly wanted her audience to understand her reluctance and why her friend's responses overcame that reluctance.[26]

Finally, eye contact controls turn-taking. When you are presenting, you need to be aware of your listeners' reactions to your message. Eye contact gives you access to that information.[27] When you are watching your audience, waiting for their reaction, you are allowing the audience their turn to communicate with

MSL

off the mark   by Mark Parisi

NEWSCAST 5

NEWSMAN SHEP OWEN HAD *EXTRA EYES* TATTOOED ON HIS HEAD SO HE WAS NEVER CAUGHT LOOKING AT THE WRONG CAMERA.

ATLANTIC FEATURE ©1993 MARK PARISI offthemark.com

Cartoon copyrighted by Mark Parisi, printed with permission.

ACT&REFLECT

4.3: The Eyes Have It

ACT • Are there situations in which you have difficulty maintaining eye contact or individuals with whom you have difficulty doing so? What is there about these situations or individuals that makes it difficult for you to maintain eye contact?

REFLECT • What can you do to overcome your difficulty?

you. Your gaze maintains a connection with the audience even when you stop speaking, to give time to listeners to think about what you have said.[28]

When you are in a meeting room or other small space, it should not be difficult to maintain eye contact with your audience. However, when your audience is too large for you to easily or practically make eye contact with everyone, what should you do? Select a few friendly faces at different points throughout the room and focus on them. Your eye contact with these individuals will be observed by others in your audience, and the benefit derived from your eye contact with the few will be extended to the many.

Besides considering the role of your posture, your face and hands, and your eye contact, your physical appearance will also contribute to the overall impression you make and will assist in constructing connections with your audience too.

Physical Appearance: The Way You Look

Dear Abby: I am a 17-year-old girl in high school. Recently I was required to make a presentation in my science class. Naturally I wanted to look my best. That morning I selected a denim skirt and black shirt—neither of which was too short or low-cut. Black nylons and chunky-heeled black shoes completed my ensemble. I headed off to school feeling confident about my appearance.

The minute I arrived on campus, I realized I had made a severe miscalculation. It was as though I had broken some unspoken, but well-known rule. Kids looked me up and down and stared at my legs. One astonished girl gasped, "Oh my god! She's wearing black stockings!"

I still think the black panty-hose were appropriate for my outfit. Could you shed some light on this?

—Dazed and Confused in the Midwest

Hopefully the clothing decisions of "Dazed and Confused" were more appropriate for her science presentation than they were in the estimation of her peers. Your clothing choices have an influence on the manner in which your audience views you as a presenter and their responses to your presentation.[29]

To select your attire for a presentation, consider the situation (see Act and Reflect 4.4). Who is your audience? Your peers? Children? Professional colleagues? What is the environment in which you are presenting? A classroom? A community setting? Why are you presenting? Whatever the situation and whomever your listeners are, wear clothing that is similar to theirs but is slightly dressier. If you are making a presentation to other renters in your apartment complex, for example, they may appear straight from the swimming pool or racquetball court. In such a situation, wear clean casual clothing. Perhaps you are giving a presentation to colleagues at the office. The culture of your business organization will help you identify appropriate attire; however, because you are presenting, lean toward being slightly more formal in your attire than your listeners. What about your classroom presentations? Dress as your peers dress, but avoid clothing with distracting visual depictions or distracting words unless they are relevant to your presentation.

Your clothing choices might also be influenced by the topic of your presentation. Is there a particular manner in which someone who is expert about your topic would be dressed? If the topic of your presentation is associated with a particular type of clothing, dress in that manner. If you are demonstrating a martial arts move, for example, wear your martial arts garb. When Irene demonstrated the use of the foam roller to a fitness class, she wore clothing that enabled her to clearly demonstrate the use of the roller and also allowed her to present herself as the expert in the use of the roller.[30]

Choose clothing that will be comfortable for you to wear. The way you look and what you are wearing can increase or reduce your confidence.[31] Women who do not regularly wear high-heeled shoes should not give a presentation wearing heels. Men who do not regularly wear a tie should avoid wearing a tie if at all possible. If you are someone who fidgets with jewelry, remove your jewelry before your presentation. Empty your pockets or avoid clothing with pockets if you are inclined to jingle the coins in your pockets. Consider the type of floor in the room where you will be presenting. If you are speaking on a tile floor, and if you are overcharged with energy, you might end up distracting your audience if you nervously tap your toes or stomp your feet.

Don't forget the importance of your overall physical appearance. Individuals who are considered physically attractive benefit from a variety of advantages. In a nonverbal communication class taught by the authors of this book, the class is asked to list two qualities they find attractive in the opposite sex and two qualities they believe are attractive in their own sex. After conducting this survey for almost a decade, the results consistently show that both men and women view good grooming, cleanliness, a nice smile, and a positive personality as physically attractive qualities. Accordingly, a pleasing physical appearance is available to everyone. As you prepare for a presentation, allow yourself time to tend to your personal grooming. In

ACT&REFLECT

4.4: Assess Yourself

ACT • List your best physical attributes. How could these attributes serve you advantageously in creating a memorable presentation?

REFLECT • Create an action plan to assist yourself to achieve that memorable presentation.

a nutshell, your appearance and attire should look like you, but "notched up" a bit. You will increase the chances of creating a more positive image with your audience, and knowing that you are well groomed will give you additional confidence.

Paralanguage: The Sound of Your Voice

MSL

Your partner informs you that he or she would like to take you out to the most expensive restaurant in town. You reply, "Great!" Your boss asks you to work on Saturday morning. You also reply, "Great!" The same word has two entirely different meanings. The ability of your voice to give meaning to words is called **paralanguage.** Another example of paralanguage is Jane's account of the challenges of owning Ruff Dog. Jane used her voice to create a kind of audio picture of Ruff Dog's encounters with guests, with the exotic chickens, and at the vet.[32] Without Jane's paralanguage, it would have been much more difficult to picture these scenarios.

Your paralanguage is important to your presentation for several reasons. First, the use of your voice to give meaning to words is related to an audience's attitude change and an increase in their retention of information.[33] Second, if it is easier for your audience to understand what you are saying, they are more likely to view you as a credible and competent speaker, resulting in the likelihood that they will be persuaded by your presentation.[34] It is not overstating it to say that the sound of your voice has a greater influence on your audience than they or you might realize.

If you wish to appear confident, trustworthy, and competent, if you want to have an influence on your audience, if you want to create a situation in which your audience is most likely to retain the knowledge you convey through your message, your voice should attain a style called "prepared conversational style." That means that your voice sounds conversational but that you have considered what you want to say in advance of your presentation and you have prepared the way you will convey attitudes and ideas. A voice that is fluent, that makes brief hesitations, that expresses variations in pitch; a voice slightly louder than what might be considered normal in the context;

paralanguage The ability of your voice to give meaning to words.

a voice slightly faster than would be considered normal in the context:[35] all of these qualities of the voice will help you to effectively convey your message (see Act and Reflect 4.5 on page 106).

Fluency When you speak, knowing what you are talking about is not enough. You must also sound like you know what you are talking about. If you are in the habit of sprinkling your conversations with "um's" and "uh's" and "you know's," all of these interrupt the flow of what you are saying, and your audience may conclude you lack competence, reducing the degree of influence you are able to exert on them. If you say "um" and "uh" too many times, your audience could give up trying to figure out what you are saying and stop listening entirely. Everyone says "um" or "uh" occasionally. These "nonverbal utterances," as they are called, help us to pause for a second as we organize our thoughts and also allow us to maintain control of the interaction, making it difficult for anyone else to speak. If the nonverbal utterances seem to make up the bulk of the speech, that is when the power of the speaker is reduced.

You might not realize that you use or, more important, overuse nonverbal utterances. To eliminate this habit, you must first determine whether you are an "overuser." How? Ask a trusted friend if he or she notices your repeated use of any nonverbal utterance. If you are in the habit of audiotaping or videotaping yourself when you practice your presentations, be sure to listen for nonverbal utterances. If there are areas of your speech when nonverbal utterances seem especially prevalent, consider whether you feel uncomfortable presenting this part of your speech. Are you expressing sensitive views or using potentially unfamiliar terms? Are you simply not familiar enough with that part of your speech? See if you can find another way to express your views, choose different terms that you feel more comfortable using, or practice that area of your speech enough to make it familiar.

Hesitations If "fluency" means that you are able to eliminate nonverbal utterances, hesitations are empty disfluencies—periods of silence that, as is the case with "um" and "uh," can also contribute to making a negative impression on the audience. Like nonverbal utterances, hesitations are a part of everyone's paralanguage habits. We pause because we are thinking of what we want to say or the way we want to say it. But too many hesitations or hesitations that are too long tend to work against the image of the speaker. "Why did the speaker hesitate for so long? What was going on there?" "Considering how long the speaker was silent he (or she) must have been caught off guard." "I wonder if the speaker was being straight with us since she (or he) faltered so often." These are the suspicions of audiences who witness either prolonged or repeated hesitations.

As is the case with nonverbal utterances, it is not the hesitation itself but rather the number and length of hesitations that is detrimental. A hesitation can be advantageous to a speaker when it is clear to the audience that the speaker is using the time to compose a response that is sensitive to the audience's needs. Brief hesitations in which it is obvious the speaker is thinking are also advantageous. But

fluency The extent to which the flow of your speech is uninterrupted by nonverbal utterances.

hesitation A pause to consider what you will say next.

Everyday Example

In Search of the Voice of the People
(Kerry may need to adjust his pitch, speech experts say.)

This excerpt from a Boston Globe *article discusses experts' opinions on the vocalics of John Kerry while he was campaigning for the presidency. To what extent do the experts credit Mr. Kerry's vocalics with his potential success as a presidential candidate? Do you believe your audiences are aware of your vocalics? What advice given in the article could you adopt and practice for your own vocalics?*

Over the course of a few whirlwind months, John F. Kerry has been transformed from front-runner to forgotten man to comeback kid to winner of the Democratic primaries.

But one crucial thing has not changed much: Kerry's speaking style. Only Kerry's most ardent supporters would call him a stirring orator, even when he's flush with a primary-night victory or on the attack against President Bush. At a time when voters seem to respond to the conversational style perfected by Bill Clinton and adopted by John Edwards, Kerry's discourse tends toward an old-fashioned sonorousness. Two decades in the US Senate will do that to a guy.

"Kerry's got that deep, deliberate voice," observes Geoffrey Nunberg, a Stanford University linguist and National Public Radio commentator. "He isn't the sort of person you want to sit down and have a drink with, necessarily. . . . He is somebody whose speech was formed in boarding schools."

To be sure, Bush's scrambled syntax, especially when he works without a script, can make him hard on the ears. But the wealthy, blueblood Republican has used what Nunberg calls "faux Bubba-isms" to create a regular-guy image that the wealthy, blueblood Democrat cannot yet match. As Kerry seeks to win over uncommitted voters between now and Election Day—and avoid the caricatures of wood-enness that dogged Al Gore in 2000—Kerry may need to loosen up and de-Brahminize his delivery. . . .

Yet Kerry's speeches can be encrusted with a formalism that seems to belong to a bygone political age. Even some Kerry supporters, such as actress Dossy Peabody, say his delivery needs work. "He gets into a sort of da-da-da, emphasizing every fifth or sixth word," said Peabody. "If there's a steady kind of pattern, that can make people kind of sleepy. You want to change up, find different colors, tempos, notes. Go up into a higher register; go into a lower register. Whisper. Go staccato. . . . You want to connect with the energy of the word."

Part of the challenge for Kerry is emotional, and part of it is technical. For one thing, a man whose candidacy has been marked by rise and fall and rise needs to have a lot more of that quality in his speeches.

"His voice seems to be pitched in a very narrow range," said Eda Roth, a former actress who advises business executives on how to communicate. "He doesn't have high pitches, so it begins to be"—she switched to a monotonous rhythm—"like this and like this and like this."

Some exercises Kerry could try, according to Peabody, are to imagine he is talking in a church, then imagine he is talking to someone over the noise of a subway car, then to an audience of children, then to an ailing patient. Kerry should also do breathing exercises to "uncover parts of the voice that may be unfamiliar or covered by habit," Roth said. In giving a speech, she added, he needs to be willing to go "off the page" in the manner of Clinton or Martin Luther King Jr., adjusting to the audience.

Source: Don Aucoin, "In Search of the Voice of the People: Kerry May Need to Adjust His Pitch, Speech Experts Say," Boston Globe, March 20, 2004, pp. C1, C7.

repeated hesitations, however brief, may cause a negative response from the audience. When Ashley instructed the audience in the organization of a resume, she inserted occasional nonverbal utterances and hesitations in her presentation. However, the resulting impression was that she was considering the best word choice or the most clear way to express a piece of advice about resume building. In addition, her hesitations allowed the audience time to consider or, in some cases, take notes about the information she was giving them.[36]

Pitch   Have you ever noticed that when you are frightened or nervous the pitch of your voice is raised? **Pitch** refers to how high or low the voice is. If you are nervous or frightened, your voice might raise to a high pitch, becoming a squeak. When you feel confident, you are likely to speak with a lower pitch than when you become uncertain or afraid. Your pitch is important when you are presenting because it contributes to your audience's impression. Generally, voices pitched lower are viewed as more credible than voices pitched higher; voices that use a variety of pitch relevant to the message maintain audience interest more than voices that are monotonic, remaining at one pitch.

Everyone has a pitch range—that is, the range of low to high pitch that one's voice is capable of. To create a credible image of yourself with your audience, try to maintain a speaking voice that is at the lower end of your pitch range. Your most credible voice might feel as though it is emerging from your throat at a point just above your collar. As you speak, if you feel your voice moving upward toward your chin, you are probably moving toward a more highly pitched voice, possibly because you are nervous. Unless your words merit a higher pitch, it is to your benefit to move your voice downward toward the lower end of your pitch range. In other words, move it back down your throat until it feels as though it is emerging from the point above your collar. To do so: Stop. Take a deep breath. Picture your voice moving downward. Begin to speak again, and you will be speaking in a lower voice.

A second reason to be aware of your pitch is that by varying it you are likely to maintain your audience attention as a result of the variations you introduce into your voice. Try to become aware of the way you use pitch in a natural conversation. When you ask questions, your pitch rises at the end of a question. When you make statements you feel confident about, your voice is pitched low. When you offer an opinion you are open to discussing, your voice might again be at a higher pitch. You should use the same natural fluctuations of your pitch in concurrence with what you are saying in your presentation.

Volume   The volume with which you speak—the loudness or softness of your voice—is important for three reasons. First, the audience needs to be able to hear you; second, your volume may help to build your image as a confident speaker; third, your volume contributes to the emotional dimension of your message. In some instances, you will speak with a microphone, and that helps your audience hear you. In the many other instances, when you do not have a microphone, if your listeners have to work to hear you because you are speaking too softly, they may not bother, and if you are speaking so

pitch How high or low the voice is.

loud that you seem to be hollering, they might feel that you are berating them. If you are uncertain whether you are speaking loudly enough, don't hesitate to ask, and then adjust your voice as is necessary so your listeners can hear it easily.

To come across as a confident speaker, you should speak slightly louder than you usually do. We tend to associate volume with confidence. If you can remember a time you were unsure of what you were saying, you probably spoke in a soft voice. You are using your confident voice if your voice feels as though it is originating from a spot right below your rib cage. To achieve this volume, you will need to take deep, slow breaths. As you speak, make sure that breath remains below your ribs and, in essence, the breath will push your voice outward at a louder volume.

Finally, adjust the volume of your voice to create an emotional dimension to your message. Will your message be more effective if delivered in a louder than normal voice? A softer than normal voice? A voice that fluctuates between loud and soft? As you practice your speech, consider the emotion you wish to create. Will a whisper convey that emotion? A shout? A combination of loud and soft? Adjust your voice to create the emotional dimension you wish.

As Karen discussed the dangers of floodwaters in her speech on hazardous weather, her strong voice naturally had sufficient volume to enable the audience to easily hear her and to allow her to portray an image of confidence. She did not vary the range of her pitch drastically, but the small changes were effective enough for her to make her point.[37]

Clarity "Youneedtospeakclearlysoyouraudiencecanunderstandyourwords."

"What did you say?"

"You need to speak clearly so your audience can understand your words."

"Oh. I couldn't understand what you were saying the first time."

Unfortunately, speakers often get lazy or are in a hurry to finish their speech, and some or all of the speech is delivered with the same lack of clarity demonstrated here. When speaking, **clarity** means to pronounce your words clearly by using your entire mouth so that your audience can identify each word, and it means speaking without using "verbal clutter."

To achieve clarity, you must use your entire mouth to pronounce your words: your tongue, your teeth and jaw, and your lips. You might feel that you already speak clearly, but check yourself by trying this quick experiment. The next time you visit with your parents, try singing to them a few bars of your current popular favorite song that would be unfamiliar to them. Sing the bars the first time without moving your tongue; next, sing the same bars without moving your lips; finally, sing the same bars without moving your teeth or jaw. If they are unable to identify any words of the song, it is because you were not using all the parts of your mouth. Now, ask yourself whether any of the parts to this experiment feel familiar. If so, there may be times when others have difficulty understanding what you are saying.

A speaking environment provides additional challenges to speaking with clarity: first, it is unlikely an audience member will ask you to repeat what you are saying if you are not speaking clearly, so your message may not reach your audience; second, there are

clarity Clear pronunciation and lack of "verbal clutter."

many opportunities for your voice to be lost. Audience members moving around, fidgeting, and other sounds within or outside the room can all make it more difficult for listeners to hear your voice. Not only is it necessary for you to use every part of your mouth but also it might be helpful for you to slightly exaggerate the use of your mouth to achieve clarity. Don't worry, the exaggeration will not be visible to your audience.

Another element of clarity is saying what needs to be said without verbal clutter. Verbal clutter includes nonverbal utterances, or it might mean the speaker is using twenty-five words when three will do. Verbal clutter may be interpreted by the audience as indecisiveness on the part of the speaker; they may wonder if the speaker is attempting to be deceitful or otherwise covering up; or they might not draw any of these conclusions because they have quit listening.

Rate Just as it is to your benefit to speak in a voice slightly louder than usual, it is also to your advantage to speak slightly faster than what might be typical for you. (Note that we said only *slightly* faster. Your audience still needs to understand what you are saying!) A good speech **rate** gives an impression of knowledge and commitment. How fast is slightly faster? One estimate puts the average presentation rate at about 125 words per minute with a range of 75–225 words per minute.[38] The trick is to vary your rate to match the intensity of what you are saying. If you are discussing the pros and cons of a balanced federal budget, your rate of speaking will be closer to the lower end of the range. If you are describing the closing seconds of a horse race, your speed will be at the faster end.

In her speech on euthanasia and physician-assisted suicide, Cindy integrated a fast rate of speaking while maintaining clarity. Her rate of speech revealed her passion and commitment about her views on her topic, yet the audience could still understand what she was saying. In addition, when she related that some persons faced with a terminal illness put off making a decision about euthanasia or physician-assisted suicide because they have hope that their lives might take a different turn, Cindy's rate and clarity maintained a feeling of seriousness, as she questioned whether hope is a realistic response of terminally ill patients.[39]

Pronunciation If you needed advice on diet and nutrition, how seriously would you view a presenter who advised you to eat "college cheese?" It is imperative that you use the correct word in the correct instance and with the correct pronunciation. **Pronunciation** means to say words in ways that are generally accepted or understood. If you use words incorrectly or pronounce them incorrectly, your credibility will be reduced. If you have any hesitancy or uncertainty about a word, spend a few minutes with a dictionary. If you feel uncomfortable using a particular word because you are unused to saying it, practice until you feel comfortable using it or choose another word. If your presentations are about topics related to the medical or technical fields, it is especially important that you pronounce medical or technical terms correctly as well as with confidence. Chelsea used the proper names of drugs and terms for the parts of the body those drugs affect, in her speech on tanning pills. She pre-

rate How fast you speak.

pronunciation To state words in ways that are generally accepted or understood.

sented the names of the drugs confidently and referred to the parts of the body correctly.[40]

Pauses According to a mid-nineteenth-century proverb, "Silence is golden." Silence can be golden when you use it judiciously during your presentation. Silence, or in a speech, a **pause,** or brief time when you do not speak, can be effective at the beginning, at the end, or throughout your presentation. Before you begin to speak, pause for a moment of silence to focus your listeners' attention on you. Enjoy the moment. Look around at your audience. Smile. Catch the eyes of friendly faces in your audience. When you have everyone's attention, begin. When you have finished your presentation, don't rush to get away too quickly. Remember the importance of follow-through with your gestures? It's also important to follow through with silence. After you have delivered your strong conclusion, take a deep breath, look at your audience, make eye contact one last time to allow your point to stay with the audience a bit longer. Invite questions, if that is your plan, or exit.

MSL

During your presentation, pauses can be used to give meaning to the words you speak. If you are relating an especially emotional example to your listeners, after you have presented the example, pause for a few seconds to give the audience time to consider the example, to let the emotional impact "sink in." You can also pause before making an important point, to give your audience a chance to focus their attention on you before you make the point. Think of silence as being the picture frame that sets off the art it surrounds. Silence is the space around words that gives meaning to the words. There are not many ways that you can contribute to the effectiveness of your presentation that are accomplished by doing nothing. But pauses that are well placed are indeed golden. Sherry used pauses very effectively to convey the grief she experienced at her son's death and to express her ability to grow from the tragic experience.[41]

If you thought that all you had to do to give a speech was to talk, after reading this chapter, you now understand there is a great deal more. The way you use space; the management of your body; your appearance and the way you sound—it would be difficult to rank in importance all of these aspects of speaking that we call delivery. And we are not yet finished—because the format of the notes you use also influences the speaking environment.

Ways to Present Your Message

Most presentations are given with at least a few minutes of advance preparation, and generally the presenter, to be sure of making all the necessary points accurately, uses notes. **Notes** are prompts that help you make the most effective connection with your audience and give them the most meaningful and accurate presentation. If your presentation is written out completely in a manuscript, it might be more difficult for you to connect with your audience if you are too intent on reading from your manuscript. But if you are speaking in an impromptu fashion without any advance preparation, you might find

pause A brief time in which you do not speak.

notes Written prompts that help you make the most effective connection with your audience and give them the most meaningful and accurate presentation.

ACT&REFLECT

4.5: "It's Not What You Say, It's How You Say It"

ACT • Using this checklist, assess the way you use your voice.

1. I am generally a fluent speaker. _____ Yes _____ No

2. When I know what I'm talking about, my response time to questions is brief. _____ Yes _____ No

3. I generally practice pitch variation to create meaningful messages. _____ Yes _____ No

4. I always speak so the audience can hear. _____ Yes _____ No

5. I speak clearly so the audience can understand my words. _____ Yes _____ No

6. In comparison to others, I speak slightly faster. _____ Yes _____ No

7. I generally use the correct word and pronounce it accurately. _____ Yes _____ No

8. I use pauses to add meaning to my message. _____ Yes _____ No

REFLECT • For every "no" you check, set one goal to help yourself change the "no" to "yes."

yourself deviating from the initial point of your message, and you might also convey inaccurate information because you do not have a chance to verify points you are not certain about. Along with your delivery, then, the format of the notes you use influences your connection with the audience and ultimately what you achieve through your presentation with them. In addition, the requirements of the speaking situation may in part determine the type of notes you choose to use. There are four presentation methods:

Impromptu

An **impromptu presentation** is given "off the top of your head," with little advance preparation. When you answer a question in class or present an opinion in a meeting, you are giving an impromptu presentation. Despite little or no preparation, such a presentation should still be given thoughtfully and logically.

A basic pattern for you to follow when you speak on this basis is the classic, three-part "First you tell them what you

impromptu presentation Presentation you give "off the top of your head" with little or no advance preparation.

are going to tell them, then you tell them, then you tell them what you told them." In other words, state your response; give an example to clarify your response, or tell why you believe your response is the best; then restate your response, using different words. You can even jot down a note or two to help you present your commentary in an organized fashion.

For example, your note reads: "Carwash. Financial reports: Carwash is success. Carwash boost treasury." Your impromptu speech goes like this:

> For our club fundraiser this year, I'd like to suggest we hold a car wash.
> The financial report from past years shows that a car wash has always been our most successful fundraiser.
> I hope you will consider the car wash as the best way we can give our treasury a much-needed boost.

The bottom line for impromptu presentations is to keep the verbal message simple so you sound confident and committed and underscore that confidence and commitment through the use of your voice and your body, creating a strong connection with your audience.

Memorized

The memorized presentation is exactly what it sounds like. The presenter has worked from a script or from very thorough notes and has memorized exactly what will be said. Because it is important to make a connection with the audience, there are several disadvantages to memorized presentations—the major disadvantage being that it is memorized and might result in a presentation that sounds insincere. A memorized presentation also makes it difficult to be responsive to the audience. Such a presentation is similar to a theater performance; however, in the theater, the audience expects the actors will have memorized their lines and behaves accordingly. When actors recite their lines, they are expected to become the characters they are playing, and it is part of their professional expertise to sound "natural." If you achieve a conversational mode of delivery while making a memorized presentation, that is to your credit. However, often, during a memorized presentation, the presenter is tempted to "get it over with." The important commitment to the message is more difficult to achieve and can be lost.

Is there ever a time when it is advisable to give a memorized presentation? Yes. If you are presenting in a carefully timed situation such as a radio or television broadcast, a memorized presentation will assist you in complying with the time limits. However, for most of us who find ourselves presenting in a variety of circumstances, it is best to know our message well but to stop short of memorization.

Manuscript

With a **manuscript presentation,** the presenter has the presentation written out word for word and reads it to the audience. Manuscript presentations are most useful in circumstances when an event is carefully timed or accuracy is of the essence. For example, the ten o' clock news is presented by manuscript to allow the news anchor to cover the events of the day, to include commercials, and to sign off as scheduled. When the president of the United States delivers a televised message, teleprompters display the words of the speech to assist the president in presenting his or her points without adding unintended meaning.

Under some circumstances delivering a speech from a manuscript is acceptable, possibly crucial. ●

These are occasions when a manuscript is essential. However, the downsides of presenting by manuscript are many: if the presenter is not careful, all contact with the audience is lost as the speaker becomes intent on the manuscript and forgets to maintain eye contact with the audience; perhaps the speaker wants to finish as quickly as possible, and all of the dimensions of the voice that make the speech meaningful are forgotten; pauses are mismanaged and, instead of adding to the emotion and meaning of the words, are inserted at strange points and cause different meanings. Finally, having all of the words of your speech in front of you is not necessarily an advantage. Speakers with manuscripts do lose their places and have difficulty finding them because they become lost in the sea of words.

If you find yourself in a situation that calls for you to speak from a manuscript, strive to write your words as you personally speak them to avoid creating a presentation that sounds canned. Stop from time to time to say out loud the words you have written. Do they sound as you wish for them to sound? Do they mean what you want them to mean? Do they sound like you? Mark pauses directly on the manuscript to remind yourself of the importance of silence at certain points. Finally, practice reading your manuscript until you know what it says so that you can focus on your audience as you give the scripted presentation.

manuscript presentation Presentation written out word for word and read it to the audience.

Extemporaneous

The word **extemporaneous** comes from two Latin words: *ex,* meaning "out of," and *tempus,* meaning "time." It almost sounds as if an extemporaneous presentation could be an impromptu presentation, and there are similarities between the two. The extemporaneous presenter wants to appear naturally committed and somewhat spontaneous in presenting the message. The connection of presenter and audience is of prime importance. Having the ability to use one's physical self to create a relationship with the audience and to give meaning to the message is imperative. All of these considerations apply to extemporaneous as well as impromptu presentations.

However, there is one major difference between the two. The extemporaneous presenter has thought out in advance what needs to be said, how the major points should be presented, and in what order. The presenter has given thought to examples and other support material, perhaps preparing a PowerPoint presentation or other visual support to clarify specific points. The presenter uses notes or an outline as reminders and guides to what is to be said when. The presenter has practiced the presentation in advance. However, many of the words used to convey ideas are a product "out of the time." And as the extemporaneous presenter makes the connection with the audience and notices their reaction to various points or word choices, even the decision whether to present an example or idea may arise "out of the time."

An extemporaneous presentation, then, is one that is prepared and practiced in advance, includes the use of notes or an outline, and allows the presenter to make that important connection with the audience but benefits from a flexibility allowing the presenter to be responsive to the reactions and needs of the audience. The extemporaneous presentation allows all of the benefits of all of the other modes of presentation. Most of your presentations will be presented extemporaneously; thus it is the extemporaneous presentation we discuss in this textbook.

● GETTING TO WORK

The delivery for you to strive toward as you present extemporaneously is a prepared yet conversational delivery style. Each person in your audience should have the sense that you are speaking to him or her. To achieve that impression, begin by taking an honest look at yourself. The best way to accomplish this assessment is to literally view yourself speaking. Ask a friend to tape you as you practice your presentation. Now the hard part: view yourself on tape, but pretend the person you are viewing is someone else. If you were in the audience while "that" person was presenting, would you feel that he or she was speaking to you? Why? Why not? What do you see in your delivery that is beneficial to making a connection with your listeners? Make a note of these behaviors, because it is important to know which behaviors you already display that are effective. But, even more important, take note of those behaviors that work against building relationships with the members of your audience. Make a list of those behaviors. Methodically, one by one, draw up a plan that will help you

extemporaneous presentation A presentation that sounds conversational and somewhat spontaneous but that has been given advance preparation and practice.

practice more effective delivery behaviors. Practice your planned behaviors as you interact with friends and family on a daily basis. Become aware of others' responses to you. When the responses of others in social situations are the way you would like them to be, videotape yourself again. You will probably notice improvements in some, if not all, of the behaviors you wanted to improve. If there are still areas in which you would like to become more "audience oriented," keep practicing.

Identify family and friends you can trust to give you objective feedback. Ask them to help you make changes in your nonverbal behaviors. Ask them to tell you when they notice you have made the changes you want to make. Much of the information you need to help yourself will be gained from the response and information you derive from others.

Don't forget to practice the changes you have made, so you will transfer them to the presentation environment and all the members of your audience will feel you are speaking directly to them. When you present, your priority should be the prepared conversation with your audience. Practicing your delivery in advance will allow you to focus on your listeners yet deliver your message with your most effective nonverbal behaviors.

SUMMARY

Now that you've read this chapter on delivery, you might have the impression that what you say in your presentation isn't nearly as important as the way you manage presentation space, the way you make use of the kinesic elements available to you, the decisions you make regarding your attire and appearance, and the way you use your voice. In other words, it might seem as though you should put forth more effort in developing an effective delivery than in thinking about what you will actually say. It isn't truly possible to say that your delivery exerts a certain percentage of influence on your audience and your words carry the remaining power and influence; both should be of concern to you. However, it is certainly the case that your delivery has the power to create and maintain an important relationship with the audience; it is through your delivery that you are able to develop that sense of immediacy with the audience; and it is in response to your delivery that the audience will often conclude that you are

a credible source of information or dismiss you and your message on the grounds that you are not credible. There is no doubt about it— what you say is important, but the way you "say it," that is, present your message, is very, very important.

The suggestions given here relate to members of western cultures. Since you will often find members of other cultures in your audiences, you should become alert to the ways other cultures manage their nonverbal behaviors. As you seek to inform and influence your listeners, be aware of the information you can receive from the diversity that is represented in your audiences.

As you prepare a presentation, consider how you might use to your advantage the space in which the presentation occurs. How can you involve that valuable resource, your body, to enhance the meaning and power of your presentation, while negotiating and maintaining a connection with your audience? What clothing and grooming decisions will you make to help your-self achieve credibility and a sense of immediacy with your audience? How will your voice stay with the audience after you have made your point? Without your careful consideration of the role all of these elements will play in your presentation, all you have is an essay.

It is through your management of yourself and your space that you bring that essay to life and it becomes a presentation and speaks to your audience. When you do well all the things we have discussed in this chapter, you are the ultimate beneficiary. You will have enhanced the possi-bility that you will achieve your communication goal, and you will feel strong and confident in yourself as a presenter.

Presentations are given in one of four different modes: impromptu, manuscript, memorized, and extemporaneous. Each method allows varying degrees of connection to the audience, and each method works best in a particular situation. Because the extemporaneous mode allows the speaker to prepare in advance and to present in a sincere manner while focusing on the audience, it is this mode of presentation that is the priority of this textbook.

VIDEO EXPERIENCE

The video clips for this experience include a num-ber of speeches that feature different aspects of delivery. Charles Bourland's speech relates to the audience his experiences working for NASA; Nancy's speech instructs the audience about important factors to consider when buying a puppy; Ross cautions people about the use of eBay.[42] Assume you are a speech coach. How would you critique each of the speakers in the areas of delivery we have discussed in this chapter? What do you notice in the delivery of these speakers that you would like to "borrow" to use in your own delivery? What do you observe that you would like to avoid in your own delivery?

THINKING BACK, THINKING AHEAD

1. Using the Act and Reflect opportunities in this chapter, prepare a profile of your delivery strengths and weaknesses. For each weak-ness you identify, create an action plan de-scribing how you will improve that weakness and the way you will recognize improvement. Example: You feel your inability to maintain eye contact is a weakness. How could you go about cultivating stronger eye contact and how will you know when you have attained the ability to maintain the confident eye contact you desire?

2. What nonverbal actions have you observed presenters displaying that you feel create a connection with the audience, develop a sense of immediacy, and establish presenter credibil-ity? Keep a record of the actions you observe others display and consider borrowing those you admire most when you give your own pre-sentations.

3. What nonverbal behaviors have you observed in presenters that you feel are detrimental in creating a connection with the audience, de-veloping a sense of immediacy, and estab-lishing presenter credibility? Add these actions to your record and strive to avoid them when you give your own presentations.

4. In circumstances where you often present—a campus organization, church group, or class-room environment, for example—make an effort to observe your listeners' responses to

your presentations. What cues do listeners give you that you find helpful in revising your delivery style as you are presenting? Are you able to notice these responses to you? What can you do to encourage listeners to respond to you?

5. For your next presentation, create a timeline for yourself that helps you make sure you have sufficient time to gather information, plan, organize, and practice your presentation. Adhere to your timeline.

NOTES

1. P. Webbink, *The Power of the Eyes* (New York: Springer, 1986).
2. N. Morgan, "The Kinesthetic Speaker: Putting Action into Words," *Harvard Business Review,* April 2001, 112–119.
3. W. B. Yeats, "Among School Children," in *The Collected Poems of W. B. Yeats,* rev. 2nd ed., edited by R. J. Finneran (New York: Simon & Schuster, 1996): 215–217.
4. Morgan, "The Kinesthetic Speaker."
5. A. Mehrabian, *Silent Messages* (Belmont, CA: Wadsworth, 1971), 1.
6. S. J. Messman and J. Jones-Corley, "Effects of Communication Environment, Immediacy, and Communication Apprehension on Cognitive and Affective Learning, *Communication Monographs, 68* (2001): 184–200.
7. P. L. Witt and L. R. Wheeless, "An Experimental Study of Teachers' Verbal and Nonverbal Immediacy and Students' Affective and Cognitive Learning, *Communication Education, 50* (2001): 332.
8. J. Devito, *The Communication Handbook: A Dictionary* (New York: Harper & Row, 1986), 84.
9. Devito, *Communication Handbook,* 84.
10. P. A. Anderson, *Nonverbal Communication: Forms and Functions* (Mountainview, CA: Mayfield, 1999), 75.
11. Morgan, "The Kinesthetic Speaker," 118.
12. E. T. Hall, *The Hidden Dimension* (Garden City, NY: Anchor, 1969), 116–125.
13. Matthew Graham, speech to Municipal Clerks' Institute, July 13, 2005.
14. A. Cullum, *The Geranium on the Windowsill Just Died but Teacher You Went Right On* (New York: Harlan Quist, 1971), 56.
15. Jessica Culhane, speech to a positive audience, September 22, 2004.
16. Chelsea DeSousa, speech to a neutral audience, October 18, 2004.
17. M. Knapp and J. Hall, *Nonverbal Communication in Human Interaction,* 4th ed. (Fort Worth, TX: Harcourt Brace, 1997), 305.
18. Maya Sharif, speech to a neutral audience, October 18, 2004.
19. Jon Sheller, speech to a positive audience, September 22, 2004.
20. Knapp and Hall, *Nonverbal Communication,* 351.
21. Webbink, *Power of the Eyes,* 1.
22. P. A. Rowland-Morin, K. W. Burchard, J. W. Garb, and N. R. Coe, "Influence of Effective Communication by Surgery Students on Their Oral Examination Scores," *Academic Medicine, 66* (1991): 169–171.
23. Knapp and Hall, *Nonverbal Communication,* 352.
24. Webbink, *Power of the Eyes,* 1.
25. Webbink, *Power of the Eyes,* 22.
26. Katie Dencklau, speech to a neutral audience, October 22, 2004.
27. A. Kendon, "Some Functions of Gaze Direction in Social Interaction," *ACTA Psychologica, 26* (1967): 22–63.
28. A. Kalma, "Gazing in Triads: A Powerful Signal in Floor Apportionment," *British Journal of Social Psychology, 31* (1992): 21–39.
29. S. Chaiken, "Physical Appearance and Social Influence," in *Physical Appearance, Stigmas and Social Behavior,* edited by C. P. Haman, M. P. Zanna, and E. T. Higgins, vol. 3 (Hillsdale, NJ: Erlbaum, 1986).
30. Irene Lewis-McCormick, presentation to Pilates class, July 27, 2005.
31. J. Gorham, S. H. Cohen, and T. L. Morris, "Fashion in the Classroom," *Communication Quarterly, 47* (1999): 281–299.
32. Jane Walters, speech to Municiple Clerks' Institute, July 13, 2005.
33. Knapp and Hall, *Nonverbal Communication,* 379, 402.
34. J. K. Burgoon, T. Birk, and M. Pfau, "Nonverbal Behaviors, Persuasion, and Credibility," *Human Communication Research, 17* (1990):140–169.
35. Burgoon, Birk, and Pfau, "Nonverbal Behavior," 140–169.
36. Ashley Osgood, speech to a positive audience, September 22, 2004.

37. Karen Tarara, speech to a neutral audience, October 22, 2004.
38. J. Wagstaffe, *Romancing the Room: How to Engage Your Audience, Court Your Crowd, and Speak Successfully in Public* (New York: Three Rivers Press, 2002), 173.
39. Cindy Johnson, speech to a negative audience, November 8, 2004.
40. Chelsea DeSousa, speech to a neutral audience, October 18, 2004.
41. Sherry Hohenadel, speech to the Municipal Clerks' Institute, July 13, 2005.
42. Dr. Charles Bourland, speech to NASA Food Technology Commercial Space Center, April 21, 2004. Nancy Baker, speech to Municipal Clerks' Institute, July 13, 2005. Ross Kelderman, speech to a positive audience, September 22, 2004.

Chapter 5

Listening

Being an Effective Audience Member

Goals

✓ To understand the components (perceiving, interpreting, evaluating, retaining and recalling, and responding) that make up listening

✓ To improve the skills that contribute to effective comprehensive listening

✓ To improve critical listening

✓ To improve recognition of logical fallacies

Here's a promo for a fictitious product we've created that is similar to some of the promos you actually encounter:

Our new Ab-Electro-Roller-Reducer is guaranteed to help you develop a six-pack abdomen when used in conjunction with the accompanying exercise and diet plan. It's fun, easy to use, and stores under your bed. One owner went from a thirty-eight-inch waist to a thirty-two-inch waist in just three weeks. Studies have shown that you can indeed create a more defined and attractive midsection. The Ab-Electro-Roller Reducer was designed by health professionals to strengthen the rectus abdominus without the need for expensive gym equipment or health club fees. In fact, sales of the AERR have been so strong, the money-grubbing Health Club Association of America seems afraid they'll lose memberships and, as you might have heard, are suing us to prevent further sales. Act now while there's still time. ●

Assuming you wanted a six-pack stomach, would you buy the Ab-Electro-Roller-Reducer on the basis of this message? Hopefully, your answer would be no, but thousands of people buy such products every day after watching a thirty-minute infomercial that is filled with "evidence" to support the claims about the product being sold. The AERR message is filled with deceptions, false logic, intentional ambiguity, and inferences that lead an uncritical listener to a false conclusion. Look at the message again and see if you can spot any. Here are a few fallacies we built into the example that we will discuss later in the chapter:

1. The "accompanying exercise and diet" plan is probably what produces any change and not the actual AERR. Failure to follow the plan allows the seller to disregard complaints.

2. The statement that one owner went from a thirty-eight- to thirty-two-inch waist makes no specific claim about the AERR. Owning is not the same as using—plus the lack of any other controls means the reduction could be for lots of other reasons. Perhaps the owner had liposuction during that time.

3. While the statement that begins "Studies have shown . . ." is valid, this actually has nothing to do with the AERR. The intention is for the listener to infer that the study was about the AERR.

4. The term "health professional" is ambiguous. The term includes nurse's aides, dental assistants, dieticians, even high school P.E. teachers.

5. Another ambiguous term is "designed." Just because something is "designed" for something doesn't mean it works.

6. The ad uses name-calling to demean the Health Club Association of America and implies that the reason they are being sued is because the organization "seems afraid."

While this book focuses on the development of effective presentations, it is also indirectly about being a better listener. Everything you learn about the development of presentations and various related strategies increases your preparation to be an effective audience member. Listeners who understand the process of developing and presenting speeches are better prepared to act on what they hear and be sensitive to covert attempts to influence them. Listening is an important and often neglected skill that can be improved. People generally spend a lot more time listening than they do speaking—look at your typical college day to confirm this. Yet how conscious are you of your listening strengths and weaknesses? One study found that students started the semester with an inflated perception of their listening skills, which dropped during the semester as they learned more about their own listening inadequacies.[1] This result parallels our own experiences in courses in which we teach listening skills. This chapter is specifically devoted to a discussion of how you can be a more effective audience member by improving your listening.

You can also become a better speaker by understanding the listening process. In essence, understanding how people listen and respond to information is part of audience analysis. Knowing the strengths and weaknesses of the listening process

Our level of attentiveness often reflects how well we are listening. ●

allows speakers to adapt their presentations to ensure effectiveness. For example, speakers can better control noise and distractions when they recognize how these can impair listening. People who develop promos like the one given here are keenly aware of people's failure to listen critically and exploit that. An ethical speaker does not exploit weaknesses in people's listening but rather tries to reduce listening failure. You need to know the logical fallacies and problems associated with listening to avoid using them inadvertently.

The Listening Process

The example that opened this chapter doesn't convey a full sense of what is involved in listening—after all, you read it! This means it was processed through the visual channel, and when you hear something, you process it through the aural channel. Most of us typically equate listening with hearing, but listening is much more. As a term, "hearing" really represents just the physical aspect of the ear drum being stimulated by sounds. When we talk about someone having a hearing problem, we are referring to physical problems. Listening, on the other hand, occurs when the mind meets the sounds, when we make sense of our senses. **Listening** is a set of processes that involves perceiving, interpreting, evaluating, retaining and recalling (memory), and reacting to oral messages and their accompanying cues. Listening is a set of processes because each of the elements that make up listening is a process in and of itself, involving an ongoing, dynamic activity. Understanding each of these processes is necessary to an understanding of how they all contribute to the cumulative process of listening.

listening A set of processes that involves perceiving, interpreting, evaluating, retaining and recalling (memory), and reacting to oral messages and their accompanying cues.

Perceiving

The first stage, **perceiving,** involves selecting and attending to particular stimuli. You've probably been to a party or sat in a classroom where many people were talking at the same time and been able to focus your attention on just one conversation. This ability to attend to specific oral messages exemplifies this first stage. In attending to the one conversation, however, you are also blocking out the others. Interestingly, this demonstrates the difference between "hearing" and "listening." The membranes in you eardrums are vibrating with the sounds of all the conversations around you, which is "hearing"; however, listening involves the additional steps of mentally processing the selected physical stimulations.

Interpreting

Interpreting occurs when we attribute meaning to what we perceive. In listening, interpretation involves combining the information acquired from several senses in the formation of some meaning. After a humorous exchange with a student, a student jokingly asks the teacher if their discussion will be on the exam, to which the teacher responds, in a whimsical tone of voice, "This will *definitely* be on the test," and winks and smiles. Your interpretation of this statement depends on your ability not only to decode the words that were used but also to understand what they mean within the context of the nonverbal cues and what is happening in the class. In this way, listening is paying attention not just to the spoken words but to all the factors that influence their meaning. Some individuals fail to recognize nonverbal cues, and thus their listening is impaired. The meanings you attribute to what you perceive are derived from your experiences—from what you have learned, observed, and remembered.

The meaning the speaker has in mind when expressing a particular message and the meaning listeners attribute to that message may or may not be the same. The degree to which individuals attribute the same meaning to a message is called **shared meaning,** as was briefly discussed in the first chapter. Suppose a speaker is telling the following story: "When I was ten, I was walking home from school when a dog I had not seen before came charging toward me barking wildly; needless to say, I was petrified." What image of a dog is evoked in your mind? You might have thought about a large dog like a Rottweiler, pit bull, or Doberman because those are dogs that are often viewed as frightening. Some people will think about a particular dog that might have attacked them in their own childhoods, perhaps even a poodle or terrier. How much shared meaning would occur if the speaker's experience had been with a Chihuahua? You both thought of dogs, but there was also a certain amount of discrepancy. Speakers and listeners both need to take the responsibility to ensure they have reached a high degree of shared meaning.

perceiving The first stage of listening that involves selecting and attending to particular stimuli.

interpreting The second stage of listening that occurs when we attribute meaning to what we perceive.

shared meaning The degree to which individuals attribute the same meaning to a message.

Evaluating

As you develop an understanding of the messages you perceive, you can begin **evaluating** those messages to determine what you should do with the information. Evaluation and interpretation may occur simultaneously, each contributing to the effectiveness of the other. This evaluation process is extremely important when you are being asked to make some decision on the basis of a presentation. The intensity of our evaluation varies among the positive, neutral, and negative audiences; negative audiences are more likely to scrutinize the speaker's message than positive audiences. Deciding whether to agree or disagree with a message involves evaluating the message against some criteria you hold in your head. What is your reaction to the statement "The money we spend on space exploration would be better spent on improving the education of our youth"? Your agreement or disagreement with this statement reflects your values—humans should reach for the stars, or education is underfunded. The evaluation process is often the focus of a type of listening called critical listening; we will discuss this in greater detail later in this chapter.

Retaining and Recalling

The part of the listening process in which information gets stored in and retrieved from memory is known as **retaining and recalling.** This stage demonstrates that we have actually listened. Perhaps you've had an interaction like this:

"Why didn't you show up at eight like I told you to?"
"I don't remember you ever telling me to come over at eight."
"You may not remember it but I told you. I wish you'd listen better."

The inability to retrieve information that we have perceived, interpreted, and evaluated demonstrates that we have not actually listened. Recalling doesn't require a word-for-word recitation; it is, rather, the ability to restate the general essence of the message that was sent. On the other hand, after listening to lectures, you are often called on in examinations to recall specific details. In this instance, you can make a concerted and conscious effort to "memorize" what you're listening to—or at least take notes so you can review the message and facilitate its memorization. This is a conscious attempt to retain information that is considered important as a result of interpreting and evaluating by moving the information from short-term to long-term memory. Unfortunately, we tend to forget information we have heard in lectures pretty quickly. Think about a lecture you heard last week. How much can you remember from it? Without studying or reviewing your notes, you probably have forgotten all but the most important or emphasized points (those committed to long-term memory). We provide suggestions throughout the text for speakers to help increase an audience's retention of information, and later in this chapter we will provide advice for listeners.

evaluating The third stage of listening, in which you determine what you should do with the information received.

retaining and recalling Fourth step of listening, in which information gets stored in and retrieved from memory.

We don't always have to make a concerted effort to memorize oral messages; we also remember what we've heard without consciously trying to do so. Throughout this book, we discuss a number of psychological factors, such as primacy and recency, that unconsciously influence the way people process and retain information. We are apt to remember the first things a speaker says (when we are most attentive). We remember things that are repeated, relevant, emphasized, and recent. We remember the most novel, familiar (make sense), emotional, and coherent (good stories).

Responding

By definition, for communication to occur, a message must evoke some response; that is, if a message is transmitted and nothing is affected, then communication has not occurred. The final process that makes up listening, **responding,** is any action a spoken message evokes from a listener. Responses vary from simple nonverbal cues that reflect attention and understanding (head nods, saying "uh-huh," or timely smiles) to detailed paraphrasing of the speaker's message or implementation of some requested action (such as following instructions).

Reasons for Listening

Speakers are at the mercy of listeners—speakers can't force people to listen (as many parents of teenagers will attest). That's why we emphasize the need for a speaker to motivate the audience to listen. As an audience member, you make a choice to listen or not listen. That decision is generally based on an assessment of whether any need will be met by listening. You must be convinced that there is something to be gained by attending to the speaker. Even in your interactions with friends, you need the sense that you will gain something by listening, even if it is simply preserving friendships. Speakers may not provide you with a reason for listening. (How often do your instructors start a lecture by telling you why the information is important to learn?) Without a reason being given, it might be easy to simply discard the presentation as irrelevant; however, you might be missing valuable information. You have to listen to determine whether you should continue listening—your motivation is to be sure that you are not missing vital information. Even in those instances when the information may not be very relevant to your needs, you should consider the impact of your behavior on the speaker. Your motive for listening might be to maintain your own image of being a nice person or to maintain a positive relationship with the speaker. Your supervisor might be making a presentation of information you've heard a hundred times before; your reason for listening (complete with positive nonverbal responses) is to maintain a good relationship and make your supervisor feel good about the presentation.

Your reason for listening is directly related to the type of speech being presented to you. If the speaker seeks to inspire or move you, then your goal as a listener is to empathize. If the speaker is attempting to convey an idea, then your goal in listening is to understand. (This doesn't mean you have to agree with the idea.) If the speaker is

responding The fifth and final stage of listening, representing any action evoked from a listener by a spoken message.

ACT&REFLECT

5.1: Barriers to Listening

ACT • Think about the last lecture you heard. See if you can generate an example of a moment listening broke down because of a problem with a component of listening. For example, you were talking to a classmate during the lecture and didn't hear some minutes of the lecture (perceiving), or you thought the instructor was talking about having babies when he was actually discussing rabies (interpreting).

REFLECT • How difficult or easy was it for you to come up with examples? What does this tell you about your own listening?

Which component seems to be the one in which you have the most difficulty? Why?

For each component, what types of things can you do to reduce the barriers or breakdowns?

attempting to teach you how to do something, then your goal for listening is to comprehend and retain (see Act and Reflect 5.1). If the speaker is attempting to persuade you, then your goal for listening is to critically evaluate what is said before making a decision. Our focus in this chapter will be on strategies for improving comprehensive (content) listening and critical listening.

Improving Comprehensive Listening

Listening with the goal of understanding, retaining, and recalling spoken messages is called **comprehensive listening.** Comprehensive listeners seek shared understanding with the speaker. They are trying to acquire knowledge that they can utilize in some way, such as performing a task. Most of the time in class lectures, you are engaged in comprehensive listening. Your goal may be to gain the necessary information you will need to perform well on an exam, to complete some assignment, or to conduct some activity (a lab experiment, an art project, or a musical performance).

You might already consider yourself competent at comprehensive listening; but have you ever gotten less than a perfect score on an exam or assignment? If so, part of the problem could be that you were not able to listen as well as you might. Improving comprehension involves working on skills and strategies that contribute to effective

Copyright 2004 by Randy Glasbergen,
www.glasbergen.com

"I gave a presentation today but I only pretended to know what I was talking about. Fortunately, my audience was only pretending to listen."

comprehensive listening Listening with the goal of understanding, retaining, and recalling spoken messages.

listening and overcoming barriers that interfere with the listening process. While this text includes things speakers can do to improve the audience's comprehension of a speech, not every speaker has read this text! As a listener, there are numerous strategies you can apply to help you retain information better in spite of a speaker's shortcomings. However, just as we have different styles of speaking, we also have different styles of listening. Some people are good at listening to lectures without taking any notes and remembering the information until the exam, while other people need to take copious notes if they are to learn anything from a lecture. For these reasons, not all of the strategies listed here will necessarily apply to you. You need to select those that best fit your listening style.

Prepare

Listening for content can be aided by a certain amount of preparation prior to actually hearing the presentation. In some instances, you might be provided with advanced materials to examine that are meant to prep you for the presentation. You know about classes in which the instructor expects you to read a chapter before the lecture. Usually that means the instructor is going to cover some of the material or expand on the material and wants the students to have a foundation for the lecture. Materials are often disseminated prior to meetings so that participants can better understand the issues that are discussed. Reading any advance materials enhances listening by increasing shared meaning with the speaker. Perhaps you've failed to read materials assigned before a class period and were lost during the lecture.

Another way to prepare for a presentation is to consider its purpose, reflect on the speaker's motivation, and determine what you want to gain from the presentation. Knowing the purpose and the speaker's motives provides a context for what you hear during the presentation. Knowing what you want to gain prepares you to listen for information that is most relevant to you. For example, suppose you read a chapter that was the focus of the next day's lecture and found one section particularly confusing. You know that when you listen to the lecture you have a goal of clarifying the confusing material.

Finally, you can prepare yourself mentally to be attentive and ready to learn information. Avoid trying to listen to a presentation when you have lots of other things on your mind. They will create internal noise that will prevent you from listening effectively. Put away things that might be a distraction to you—newspapers, cell phones, and so on. If you have the opportunity to select where to sit, choose a location that enhances your attentiveness—sitting in the back corner of a room increases the likelihood of becoming disengaged from the speaker. When you know the topic in advance, try to get in tune with your own perspectives, values, and beliefs. Recognize either when they are interfering with your openness to the speaker's message or when the speaker is conveying information contrary to your own position.

Take Notes

Taking good notes in classes directly relates to achievement; however, most students don't take very good notes.[2] Typical lecture notes capture only about 20 to 40 percent of the material presented.[3] One reason listeners might not take more notes is that writing notes competes with listening. Effective note taking is a skill that involves time, practice, and the use of specific strategies. For instance, writing notes in an outline format allows listeners to capture the relationships among the concepts presented, while the use of a matrix is an effective way to show comparisons among concepts.[4] Accuracy of note taking has been shown to be more important to test performance on tests than completeness or length of notes.[5] However, some note taking is apparently better than none. One study found that students had a 50 percent chance of recalling information from their notes but only a 15 percent chance of recalling information not in their notes.[6] The very act of note taking seems to improve recall, even if the notes are not studied.[7] While you might think of note taking as only a classroom activity, any time you are exposed to information that you are seeking to comprehend, keeping notes is an excellent way to enhance your retention and recall of that information. In other words, don't be shy about taking notes during meetings.

Use the Difference between Thought Rate and Speech Rate

The average speaking rate is between 125 and 175 words per minute; however, we are able to mentally process information four to five times faster than that. What often happens is that our mind engages in other activities while we listen to someone because of the extra time the mind has available for processing information. However, we sometimes become so wrapped up in our thoughts, we miss a lot of the spoken words. To overcome this barrier, focus your extra thinking time on the message itself rather than on other issues. Here are some ways to do this:

Guidelines for Using the Difference between Thought Rate and Speech Rate

1. Think about each concept or piece of information the speaker is sharing.
2. Think about the nonverbal cues that may provide additional meaning to the message.
3. Identify in your mind the key issues or main points.
4. Think about the relationships among the points.
5. Create your own "chunking" to organize information in the ways that work best for you.
6. Develop strategies in your mind to help you retain and recall the main points and subpoints.
7. Review and repeat in your head what has been said.
8. Ask yourself questions about the content, the meanings, the speaker, and yourself.

Maintain Attention and Minimize Noise

One of the dangers of having extra thought-time is a tendency to engage in thinking about issues tangential or unrelated to the speech (daydreaming), which is called **psychological noise** or **internal noise.** Internal noise occurs whenever we become pre-occupied by our own thoughts. A speech about a great vacation getaway might cause you to get lost in your own recollections of childhood vacations, or you might have a number of pressing matters that are occupying your thoughts. This is one of those so-lutions that is easier said than done: "concentrate." You have control over what you think about, but it isn't always easy to filter out distracting thoughts. You might have to continually remind yourself to "pay attention" during a presentation. Ask yourself what was the last point the speaker said and keep asking this as the speech progresses.

The ability to set aside personal issues or concerns and concentrate on a presen-tation has limits; sometimes skipping or leaving a presentation may be the appropriate course of action. The thoughts we have can also be a legitimate response to the pre-sentation but still interfere with continued attention. Your attention might get tied up considering several weaknesses that are apparent to you in the purchase plan being advocated by a colleague. One way to handle that is to make a brief note to yourself about the weakness as a reminder. In essence, you defer your extended thoughts until a more appropriate time.

External noise is anything around us that distracts us from listening to the intended message. Too many times to count, our lectures have been interrupted by cell phones ringing, garbage trucks beeping as they back up outside the classroom windows, hammering during remodeling, window washers, jets passing overhead, clanging steam pipes, laughter or applause from the next classroom, students' whispered conversations, or loud talking in the hallway. Each of these distractions usually causes students to turn their attention toward the noise, and if the noise is sustained, it becomes particularly challenging to regain and sustain the students' attention. These types of noise may go beyond simply being a distraction and actually drown out the speaker's words. However, external noise also may be more subtle and is not just limited to sound. The student next to you might be doodling in his notes, causing you to watch what he does; your attention might be broken by erratic flickering of the fluorescent lights; or you might get involved in reading the handout the speaker provided during the presentation. The first step to overcoming external noise is to recognize that it is occurring. Some external noises, like watching the doodler or reading the handout, can be easily tuned out if the noise isn't actually interfering with the reception of the oral message. Some external noise can be controlled, like turning off cell phones or finding a quieter room. Other times, the speaker has to either wait for the noise to subside or attempt to speak over the distraction, requiring more effort and concentration from the audience.

The speaker may be a source of external noise as well; perhaps the speaker talks too quietly, speaks with an accent, mispronounces certain words, speaks with a lisp or stutter, has

internal noise (psychological noise) Thinking about issues tangential or un-related to the speech (daydreaming); becoming preoccupied by your own thoughts.

external noise Anything that distracts you from listening to the intended message.

Do you think it is easier for a speaker to overcome internal or external noise? ●

a voice you find grating, paces back and forth, or says "um" frequently. If you focus on any of these aspects about the speaker, your attention to the spoken message may wane. Again, the first step is to recognize that you are failing to maintain your attention to the spoken message. You can increase your efforts to focus on the message and ignore the distraction. The specific strategies for offsetting the impact of speaker distractions depend on the nature of the distraction. For instance, if the speaker is too quiet, you can move closer or politely ask the speaker to talk more loudly.[8]

Have you ever been so tired you can hardly stay awake while listening to a lecture? Okay, so that was a silly question. Our ability to listen and comprehend a presentation can be affected by actual physical problems that constitute **physiological noise.** Besides fatigue, physiological noise can be caused by hearing loss, hunger, illness, or other physical conditions. Obviously, overcoming fatigue depends on another way to prepare for a presentation—a good night's sleep. Other physical problems may need specific treatments, for example, the use of hearing aids or medications for illness. What you eat can affect how you think. Obviously, caffeine and sugars may provide a boost of energy and enable you to listen more effectively for a short time. Sometimes a number of factors may interact to distract you from listening. For example, you face a particular challenge to maintaining your attention if after having just lunched on a large plate of pasta you attend a presentation in an overly warm room listening to a monotone speaker talking about a topic you find of little interest.

physiological noise Actual physical problems (fatigue, hearing loss, hunger, illness) that impair the ability to listen and comprehend.

Become an Engaged, Connected, and Active Listener

Listening to presentations for content often makes us feel like we are simply receptacles of information sitting passively, waiting to be fed information by the speaker. Adopting such an attitude is apt to increase the likelihood of becoming bored, drifting off, and feeling disconnected from the presentation. Adopting an active listener perspective means that you see yourself sharing with the speaker the responsibility for achieving comprehension. Rather than sitting passively, you engage yourself in the presentation. Engagement means demonstrating your involvement and responsiveness to speakers and their message. Engagement is reflected in good eye contact with the speaker, positioning yourself so you directly face the speaker, nodding in agreement, and laughing or smiling when appropriate.

Devote some of your extra thinking time to finding personal relevance and connection to the speaker's material. While the speaker might fail to show how her discussion of the expense associated with solar energy is important to you, you can generate the reason yourself. Think about how you can use the information, what implications the information has for you or others, or the connection of this issue to issues that are important to you. The more you can make connections with what the speaker is saying, the more likely it is that you will be able to retain and recall it. You can also improve retention by connecting the information you are hearing with information you already know.[9]

Active listeners ask questions to seek clarification or gain further explanations; they paraphrase or repeat to themselves or other people what they heard, as appropriate to the situation. Many speaking situations lend themselves to interactions between the speaker and the audience members. Take advantage of those opportunities. Some instructors try to foster this skill in students by requiring certain students to ask a question at the end of a lecture. This helps the students adopt a more active listening style in which they are thinking about the material and deciding what information is confusing or incomplete. This process can be adopted even if there is not an opportunity to directly ask questions, by writing the questions down to either ask the speaker after the presentation or research on your own.

Understanding Critical Listening

Comprehensive listening involves taking in information, essentially without regard to its quality, legitimacy, or accuracy. In essence, the goal of comprehensive listening is simply to learn the information. However, such unbridled acceptance of information can be detrimental, and we need to develop and apply a critical perspective. The saying "Caveat emptor," or "Buyer beware," can be modified as an appropriate dictum for audience members as well: "Listeners beware." This is one reason critical listening is often identified as a core educational goal. The state of Hawaii requires twelfth-grade students to have two critical listening skills: the ability to evaluate evidence and the ability to recognize weaknesses in reasoning. For eleventh-graders, Indiana established an academic standard that students must be able to critique a speaker's use of words and language, while recognizing the impact on an audience; in addition, students should be able to identify logical fallacies used in speeches. Other states have similar requirements, and during your education you have probably been exposed to efforts to improve your critical listening skills; that effort continues here. See also Act and Reflect 5.2.

Critical listening is really critical thinking applied to what you hear. **Critical thinking** is the ability to analyze and evaluate information, reasoning, and evidence. The critical thinker is able to distinguish sound arguments from unsound, valid evidence from invalid, and logical reasoning from illogical (truth from fiction). Critical thinking allows us to make effective decisions. When we apply critical thinking to the information we acquired while listening to a speech, we are engaging in critical listening. Unfortunately, most of us seem to be pretty lazy about running our critical thinking engine and accept a lot of what we hear without adequate assessment. Think about how much information you learn from what other people tell you and the degree to which you readily accept that information without really questioning it. How often during a lecture do you think, "The evidence being presented doesn't warrant the conclusions being claimed by the instructor?" (Okay, maybe not articulated quite like that, but at least something similar.)

Improving Critical Listening

Improvement of your critical listening skills will not happen overnight, because you have to develop your critical thinking skills. The ability to analyze and evaluate information represents the highest level of human cognitive processing and develops in the final stages of our cognitive development. Nonetheless, here are some suggestions that apply specifically to the listening process and to your development as an effective critical listener.

Be Aware of the Reasons Underlying Your Reactions and Decisions After many presentations you've probably thought to yourself, "I didn't like that presentation" or "I don't agree with what the speaker was saying." But do you know why you thought those things? Critical listeners are aware of why they reached their conclusions about an oral message. To reach this point, critical listeners are able to evaluate the speaker's reasoning, evidence, arguments, and so on, in determining the legitimacy of the speaker's claims.[10]

Assess the Credibility of the Speaker and Speaker's Evidence Critical listeners should try to determine the speaker's biases and be sensitive to their own biases. Part of this process also involves assessing the credibility of the speaker and of the evidence presented, such as quotations and statistics. In previous chapters you read about how to establish credibility as a speaker and for your evidence. As a listener, you need to ask the same types of questions. Is the

critical listening Critical thinking applied to what you hear.

critical thinking The ability to analyze and evaluate information, reasoning, and evidence.

ACT&REFLECT

5.2: Assessing Your Cognitive Listening Skills

ACT • Analyze your ability to think about the messages you hear. On a scale of 1 to 5 (with 1 being low and 5 being high) indicate the degree to which each statement accurately describes your typical behavior when listening to a presentation.

_____ 1. I actively concentrate on what the speaker is saying.

_____ 2. I try to remember the speaker's main ideas so I can share them with others.

_____ 3. I mentally try to summarize the speaker's important points as I listen.

_____ 4. I recognize and evaluate a speaker's biases.

_____ 5. I think about what the speaker is saying.

_____ 6. I "catch myself" when I stop focusing on the speaker's message, and I make a genuine effort to refocus on the message.

_____ 7. I listen to only one message at a time.

_____ 8. I listen "between the lines" to what is not said.

_____ 9. When I am not interested in the speaker's topic of discussion, I do not stop listening; rather, I continue to listen for something of value to me.

_____ 10. When listening, I ignore distractions that I cannot eliminate.

_____ 11. I actively try to remember the speaker's important points, concepts, ideas.

_____ 12. I concentrate on what the speaker is saying rather than waiting for an opening in the conversation so that I can express my ideas.

_____ 13. I work hard when I listen.

_____ 14. I am aware of why I am listening.

_____ 15. While and after listening to a persuasive speaker, I use established criteria to evaluate the speaker's evidence, logic, reasoning, and motivational appeals.

_____ 16. While listening, I determine the speaker's purpose as quickly as possible.

_____ 17. I differentiate between a speaker's relevant and irrelevant points.

_____ 18. I continue to listen to the speaker even when I think I have previously heard what he or she has to say.

_____ 19. Rather than relying on the speaker to motivate me to listen, I motivate myself to listen.

_____ 20. While listening, I mentally anticipate the speaker's next point.

REFLECT • What commonalities are there among the items that you scored highest on? Lowest on?

What are some of the possible reasons for your lower-scored items? Higher-scored items?

To what degree were you previously aware of these listening behaviors in yourself?

Source: K. K. Halone, T. M. Cunconan, C. G. Coakley, and A. D. Wolvin, "Toward the Establishment of General Dimensions Underlying the Listening Process," *International Journal of Listening, 12* (1998): 18–19. Reprinted by permission from the International Listening Association.

evidence valid? Has it been taken out of context? How relevant is the evidence to the situation to which it is being applied? How credible is the source of the quotation or statistics?

Use Qualifiers as Warning Signs You need to develop your own Spiderman spider-sense, or listener-sense, to warn you of information that is not be trusted. For example, you should be cautious in accepting conclusions advocated by a speaker who fails to provide specific references and instead says things like "My sources have told me," "I have it on good authority that," or "From what I've read." Another trigger for your "listener-sense" would be a speaker's use of qualifiers such as "perhaps," "apparently," "maybe," "I think," "should," "would," "may," "might," or "could be."[11]

Be Sensitive to Ambiguity Related to qualifiers is the use of ambiguous language, which should also arouse your listener-sense. "Most of the people surveyed," "Many of our customers," "There are a few concerns," "Occasionally it fails," and "We have frequently found" all use ambiguous words in relation to some notion of frequency. How many is "most" or "a few"? Such terms vary greatly in meaning and thus must be viewed with caution. Ideally, speakers will provide more specific details and the exact numbers, percentages, or statistics.

Major Logical Fallacies That Undermine Critical Listening

Many of the claims made in the advertisement for the Ab-Electro-Roller-Reducer involved the use of logical fallacies. Logical fallacies involve the assertion of some claim based upon faulty logic or diversion from logic. There is an extensive number of such fallacies; we present only a few of the more common and apparent ones, in hopes of raising your "listener-sense."

Everyday Example

Calling for Civility among Audience Members

The following editorial reflects an audience's responsibility to listen objectively, to evaluate the message, to assess the credibility of the speaker, and to recognize what underlies their reactions to a speaker.

Listening to Ward Churchill speak must be a lot like watching a train wreck—horrifying yet riveting.

So we can't fault anyone for wanting to hear the Native American activist and critic of U.S. policies when he speaks tonight at UW-Whitewater. And we hope that any protest of his lecture is respectful and peaceful.

We may disagree with almost everything Churchill says, but to deny him the freedom to say it, and deny others the freedom to hear, would diminish the liberty we all enjoy as Americans.

Moreover, denying him an opportunity to speak would be to forgo a chance to judge just how recklessly wrongheaded he is.

Churchill, a University of Colorado professor, came to the nation's attention earlier this year at the center of a controversy. After he booked a lecture tour, the colleges on the tour learned of an essay he had written following the Sept. 11, 2001, terrorist attack on America. In the essay, Churchill blamed the United States for provoking the attack. He also called the victims in the World Trade Center "little Eichmanns," a reference to Nazi war criminal Adolf Eichmann. Protests followed. At least one college canceled Churchill's speech.

Two student groups at UW-Whitewater had invited Churchill to speak there on racism against Native Americans, a subject on which Churchill has conducted much research. Chancellor Jack Miller decided to permit the lecture to go ahead as scheduled.

The essay in response to Sept. 11 may have been shocking, but it was vintage Churchill. He has made a reputation and a career out of spewing highly charged criticisms of mainstream America and its European heritage.

His essay on Sept. 11 was not the first time he employed Nazi comparisons. He once likened Christopher Columbus to Heinrich Himmler, the Third Reich official who orchestrated the extermination of Jews. In fact, Columbus is one of his favorite targets. Last fall he tried to stop a Columbus Day parade in Denver, claiming it constituted hate speech against Native Americans. Apparently, he has a rather one-sided view of freedom of speech.

Last week he spoke at the University of Hawaii–Manoa. Here is a sample of what he said:

He called the American people "a willfully ignorant, self-deceiving public that celebrates the obliteration and carnage of others because they devalue them to the point of being not human."

He declared the United States "has never had 15 minutes of its history when it was not butchering some people for its perceived interests somewhere."

He said, "White is a state of mind. It's not a gene code, by the way. You've got to choose to act white in order to be white."

If his aim is to be thought-provoking, he obviously emphasizes provoking at the expense of thought. It's not your average scholarly approach. Indeed, there is some doubt about whether he is a scholar at all. Denver newspapers have questioned his credentials and how he got tenure. They have also questioned his claim to being one-sixteenth Cherokee.

Many Native Americans have their own questions. Suzan Harjo, president of the Morningstar Institute, a national Native American rights organization, has said Churchill "tells these huge lies. He's notorious, and he's not an Indian."

Vernon Bellecourt, an American Indian Movement activist in Minneapolis, has called Churchill a fraud.

Tonight we in Wisconsin can judge Churchill for ourselves. We should welcome the opportunity.

Source: Wisconsin State Journal, March 1, 2005. Reprinted with the permission of *Wisconsin State Journal*.

Ad Hominem An **ad hominem attack** is a diversion, rather than a form of logic, in which a speaker attacks the character of the proponent(s) of the opposing position. Speakers might use this strategy when they feel they cannot present sufficient arguments to counter another person's position. Name calling is one of the oldest ways of diverting attention from the issue and attempting to win an argument. Be wary of a speaker who shifts from discussing an issue to ridiculing the other side. Discussion of the actual issues may get lost as a debate about character escalates. In the Ab-Electro-Roller-Reducer ad, the Health Club Association of America was labeled "money grubbing" as an attempt to undermine the credibility of their suit. In the classic movie *Mr. Smith Goes to Washington,* a junior senator who has been framed and is discussing impending legislation before the U.S. Senate is rebuked by an ad hominem attack by another senator: "The gentleman stands guilty as charged. And I believe I speak for every member when I say that no one cares to hear what a man of his condemned character has to say about any section of any legislation before this House."

Red Herring Similar to using an ad hominem attack to create a diversion, a **red herring** is a contention or assertion that really is not relevant to the issue, intended to divert attention from the real issue. An example would be employees coming to hear about their company's plans for lay offs and hearing the following: "We are committed to maintaining adequate health care for employees, which is becoming more and more expensive. I'm sure you're concerned about your health care benefits, too . . ." In this way, the speaker has chosen to focus on an issue that is of concern to the listeners, using it to distract them from other issues.

Hasty Generalization When speakers make all-encompassing statements based on too limited a sample, they are making **hasty generalizations.** For example, a speaker might say, "Tuesday night I turned on the TV to a major network, and the show was filled with sex and violence. Thursday night I turned on the TV to another network, and again the show was

ad hominem attack When a speaker attacks the character of the proponent of the opposing position.

red herring A contention or assertion that is not relevant to the issue and that is intended to divert attention from the real issue.

hasty generalization When speakers make all-encompassing statements based on too limited a sample.

A Question of **Ethics**

1. You decide that the speaker you are listening to lacks credibility and is attempting to present false arguments and invalid evidence. To what degree is it ethical for you to (a) take a nap; (b) interrupt and challenge the speaker; or (c) whisper your misgivings to other members of the audience.

2. After listening to a speech, you think you understand the information pretty well, but you aren't sure of a couple of points. To what degree do you have a responsibility to get all the information before you start telling other people about what you heard? To what degree is it unethical for you to convey information you have heard in a presentation even though you know you're missing some points?

filled with sex and violence. Obviously, television is filled with nothing but sex and violence." A sample of two shows on two nights doesn't really warrant the conclusion that all TV is filled with sex and violence. Listen carefully to how broad the support is for any claims a speaker makes—is the sample sufficient to warrant the general claim?

False Cause and Effect "He studied hard for the exam, so he got an A." Do you believe this is true? Have you ever studied hard and not gotten an A or not studied hard and still gotten an A? The statement implies that studying caused the good grade; but the exam might have been particularly easy, or the student might have taken good notes, and so on. This is an example of **false cause and effect,** in which two events are presented as though one is the cause and the other is a direct effect, usually because one precedes the other in time. Here's another example you might find disheartening: "Getting a college degree leads to a higher income." Do college graduates get higher salaries because they have a degree, because they've learned important skills, because companies are biased toward college graduates, or because they have demonstrated the ability to work hard and put up with the demands of academia? The degree itself doesn't cause people to get higher salaries.

Non Sequitur This involves presenting a premise and conclusion as though they are connected when they may not be. For example, "Going to graduate school increases your chances of developing a meaningful romantic relationship." Huh? One reaction to **non sequiturs** is to say to yourself, "That doesn't make sense" or "That's not logical." Such reactions are right on point; non sequiturs are not logical but pretend to be. Sometimes they take a negative form, claiming an interdependence that may be false, such as "Well, if I can't go, you can't go, either."

Straw Man If you were to forced into a boxing match with someone, but you could choose your opponent, you'd probably choose someone you knew you could defeat. That's the

false cause and effect A logical fallacy in which two events are presented as though one is the cause and the other a direct effect, usually because one precedes the other in time.

non sequiturs Presenting a premise and conclusion as though they are connected when they may not be.

underlying logic of the straw man fallacy. **Straw man fallacies** occur when the speaker connects a person or plan to issues that are vulnerable, overemphasizes and attacks the less critical issues, or misrepresents or simplifies the opposing position so it can be more easily challenged. In general, you should be cautious in accepting any characterization of a plan for which you lack firsthand knowledge. A person may distort (intentionally or not) a description of another person's plan. This is particularly problematic when you haven't had a chance to actually hear the originators describe their own plans. Such characterizations are heard often during political campaigns, as candidates try to discredit each other's programs. Then-governor George Bush used the following straw man attack against Senator Al Gore during their October 3, 2000, debate when talking about the impending budget surplus: "There's a difference of opinion. My opponent thinks the government—the surplus is the government's money. That's not what I think. I think it's the hard-working people of America's money."

How does getting emotionally aroused by a speaker affect listening? ●

Circular Argument, Reasoning, Definition "School is good for you because you need an education." Think about that statement for a minute—it's really circular but uses synonyms that make it look like a logical argument. Another way of saying the same thing that makes its circularity more apparent is "Education is good for you because you need an education." Of course, you might think we're using another form of false logic by assuming that education and school are synonymous. You might counterargue that you've known lots of people who've gone to school and never learned a thing! **Circular arguments, circular reasoning,** and **circular definitions** all involve a support and a claim that are really the same. Circular arguments are hard to spot, but substituting similar words can help flush them out. See if you can make the following a more obvious example of circular reasoning: "Switching from an income tax to a national sales tax will help improve the economy by putting taxes on what we buy instead of what we earn." (Could you tell that this is also a non sequitur?)

Emotional Appeals: Fallacy or Not? Some advocates of critical listening are strongly committed to the notion that decisions should be made only on the basis of sound logic and reasoning; however, as we'll discuss later, people respond to stories and act on their emotions. Such actions are frowned on by critical listening purists. Our position is that you should be aware of a speaker's attempt to influence you with emotional appeals or narratives, but you should not automatically reject the speaker's claims. Why regard acting on compassion as less worthy than acting on reason? Narratives and emotional appeals can be critically evaluated and accepted or rejected not because of their logical

straw man fallacies When the speaker connects a person or plan to issues that are vulnerable; overemphasizes and attacks the less critical issues; or misrepresents or simplifies the opposing position so it can be more easily challenged.

circular arguments, circular reasoning, and circular definitions Forms of logical fallacy in which the support and the claim are really the same.

ACT&REFLECT

5.3: Watching for Logical Fallacies

ACT • Watch at least ten minutes of a political presentation on C-Span or some other channel, with a paper and pen in hand. Make a list of the types of fallacy discussed in this section and briefly note any instance of fallacies in the speech. You can get transcripts and clips from the following Web sites: www.americanrhetoric.com/ or www.historychannel.com/speeches.

REFLECT • How difficult was it for you to listen and identify possible logical fallacies? To what degree do you feel confident that you identified all the fallacies that occurred? Why or why not?

What types of fallacies were most prevalent? To what degree do you think the fallacies were intentional? Why or why not?

forms but because they meet other criteria. Narratives can be evaluated by listeners using the following criteria:[12]

Fidelity: Is the story true?

Coherence: Does it make sense? Does it fit with my experiences and knowledge?

Inclusion: Has the story included everything it should (characters, events, actions)?

Sequence: Does the narrative accurately and completely reflect the order of events?

Meaning: Does the story really support the point the speaker is making?

Intent: What is the speaker's purpose for telling the story? Am I being manipulated?

● GETTING TO WORK

Here are some general listening suggestions:

- Work to develop an awareness of your abilities in each of the stages of listening.
- Expand your focus of perception as you listen to speakers; listen to the words and the way the words are delivered and notice the mannerisms of the speaker.
- Expand your perceptions to include verbal, nonverbal, and contextual cues as you interpret the meaning of what you are listening to.
- If you are concerned about whether you have understood the speaker, make a mental note to ask for clarification at the appropriate time.
- Recognize your initial reaction to and evaluation of the message and use critical thinking skills to develop an objective evaluation.
- Develop ways to increase your retention and recall of the messages you hear. What are the main points of the presentation? What support is used to back up any claims made by the speaker?
- Mentally summarize what you hear the speaker saying from time to time during a presentation.

When listening for comprehension:

- Be sure you are prepared to listen both in terms of any information you need to have in advance and in terms of your own knowledge.

- Take notes to help you get information into your memory.
- Use the extra time that your thought rate provides to review elements of the speech rather than drifting off onto other thoughts.
- Recognize and minimize the impact of internal, external, and physiological noise. You should make efforts to address such noise problems as thinking about other things, being surrounded by bothersome audience members, or being fatigued.
- Take an active role in listening—think about the personal application of what you are listening to, seek clarification when needed, challenge yourself to listen more attentively.

When listening critically:

- Analyze and evaluate the information being presented.
- Examine the validity of the evidence.
- Evaluate the soundness of the reasoning and arguments the speaker advances.
- When you act on the basis of what you have heard from a speaker, reexamine the foundations for your decision. What evidence or arguments are you basing the decision on? How confident are you of that information?
- Question the credibility of the speaker and the evidence—be skeptical of who and what you listen to.
- Recognize that the presence of qualifiers and ambiguous language may signal weaknesses in the speaker's arguments and reasoning.

When listening for logical fallacies (see also Act and Reflect 5.3 on page 134):

- While you probably won't remember the names of all the different fallacies presented in this chapter, you should work to recognize the underlying elements that lead you as a listener to make false assumptions.
- Recognize when a speaker intentionally or unintentionally makes statements that result in an erroneous conclusion.
- You should be able to tell when a speaker is attempting to divert attention from the issue either through ad hominem attacks or red herrings.
- Recognize that speakers will offer false conclusions that are based on hasty generalizations from small samples, on invalid cause-and-effect relationships, and on irrelevant premises as non sequiturs.
- Listen for inaccurate portrayals of opposing positions or presentations of counterarguments that are weak and easily dismissed; the speaker may be using a straw man approach.
- Develop sensitivity to the use of synonyms to create circular statements, in which the premise and conclusion actually mean the same thing.
- Evaluate stories and emotional appeals just as conscientiously as you would a logical argument.

SUMMARY

Listening is a set of processes involving perceiving, interpreting, evaluating, retaining and recalling (memory), and reacting to oral messages and their accompanying cues. Perceiving involves selecting and attending to particular stimuli, which are then interpreted by attributing meaning to them. In making sense of these stimuli, we engage in an evaluation to determine what we should do with the information. This information gets stored in our memory and recalled as necessary. Some reaction or response occurs after we have moved through the previous stages. Listening occurs because we believe we will gain something by listening; we listen for a reason, for example, to empathize, to understand, to comprehend and retain, or to make a decision.

Comprehensive listening has the goal of understanding, retaining, and recalling information. A number of strategies can help you improve your ability to listen comprehensively. You can prepare for a presentation by considering the speaker's motives and your motives and by examining advance information. Taking notes can help the recollection of information but can hamper your attention to the speaker. Because one can think faster than people talk, one's mind has time to reflect on what is being heard and thus enhance one's listening effectiveness. A number of distractions—psychological noise, external noise, and physiological noise—can interfere with your ability to maintain attention to the message. Recognizing and controlling these distractions will help to ensure better comprehensive listening. Finally, taking a position of being engaged and connected while actively listening to a presentation will help increase your attentiveness and acquisition of information. Take on the attitude that you as a listener are as responsible as the speaker for achieving shared understanding.

Critical listening is the ability to evaluate and analyze information, reasoning, and evidence. Critical listeners are aware of the reasons underlying their reactions to presentations. Critical listeners need a "listener-sense" that cautions them about accepting a speaker's conclusions. You need to listen more critically when you hear a lack of specific references, the use of qualifiers, or use of ambiguous language. A number of specific logical fallacies have been identified in which speakers attempt to influence listeners, under the guise of logical argument. These include the ad hominem attack (attacking character), the hasty generalization (generalizing from a small sample), the red herring (a diversionary issue), the straw man argument (presenting an easily defeated stance as that of an opponent), the non sequitur (a conclusion that doesn't really follow from the premise), circular argument (the support and claim are really the same), and false cause and effect (claiming one event causes another simply because it precedes it). Critical listening to narratives requires that you apply the following criteria: fidelity, coherence, inclusion, sequence, meaning, and intent.

VIDEO EXPERIENCE

Citizens from communities outside Boston, Massachusetts, attended a meeting with various officials regarding the future of a planned extension of the current subway system to their community. This video clip focuses on audience members who are listening to a panel member explaining the decision criteria.

Observe the audience's behaviors during the presentation. To what degree are they displaying good listening skills? What does various members' behavior tell you about how well they are listening? What impact might their behaviors have on the speakers? What recommendations would you make to the audience members on how to improve their listening?

THINKING BACK, THINKING AHEAD

1. Find a half-hour TV comedy show to watch. As the show progresses, see if you can identify each humorous event that revolves around a problem that can be linked to one of the components of listening. Ideally, select a show that involves some presentation or classroom situation (like *Saved by the Bell*). How difficult was it to spot the problem? Why do you suppose the problem was used as a comic tool? How could the characters have avoided the problem?

2. Challenge yourself to listen as comprehensively as possible to a lecture. Decide to test yourself to see if you can really listen well. Prepare in advance by reading any relevant materials. Take complete notes—perhaps using an outline format and then filling the notes out more completely after the lecture is over. Focus your attention on the lecturer and avoid distractions. Think about what the lecturer is saying, ask yourself questions, ask questions of the lecturer, if appropriate, to gain clarification, and so on. Afterward, complete the following reflection.

On a percentage basis, how different was this from your normal listening behavior in a lecture? On a percentage basis, how much difference do you think there was on the amount of information you acquired in this activity compared to your normal behavior? What was the most difficult part about engaging in this listening activity? What prevents you from continuing to listen comprehensively?

3. Listen to an infomercial. Write down the product name and your answer to the following questions. In what ways do they use ambiguous language, add subtle qualifiers, or fail to provide sufficient credible references to influence viewers? What forms of logical fallacies do they employ to entice viewers to buy the product? In what other ways are they misrepresentative or deceptive? Bring your responses to classes and share them with classmates. Which forms of logical fallacies were used most? What forms of deception or misrepresentation were commonly used?

NOTES

1. W. S. Zabava Ford, A. D. Wolvin, and S. Chung, "Students' Self-Perceived Listening Competencies in the Basic Speech Communication Course," *International Journal of Listening, 14* (2000): 1–13.
2. B. Armbruster, "Taking Notes from Lectures," in *Handbook of College Reading and Study Strategy Research,* edited by R. F. Flippo and D. C. Caverly (Mahwah, NJ: Erlbaum, 2000), 175–199.
3. K. A. Kiewra, "How Classroom Teachers Can Help Students Learn and Teach Them How to Learn," *Theory into Practice, 41* (2002): 71–80.
4. Kiewra, "How Classroom Teachers Can Help."
5. R. L. Williams and A. Eggert, "Notetaking Predictors of Test Performance," *Teaching of Psychology, 29* (2002): 234–237.
6. E. G. Aiken, G. S. Thomas, and W. A. Shennum, "Memory for Lecture: Effects of Notes, Lecture Rate, and Informational Density," *Journal of Educational Psychology, 67* (1975): 439–444.
7. Kiewra, "How Classroom Teachers Can Help."
8. A. Wolvin and C. G. Coakley, *Listening,* 5th ed. (Dubuque, IA: Brown and Benchmark, 1996).
9. Keiwra, "How Classroom Teachers Can Help."
10. R. A. Hunsaker, "Critical Listening—A Neglected Skill," paper presented at the annual meeting of the National Communication Association, 1991, Atlanta, Georgia. Retrieved from ERIC: ED347578.
11. B. Bohlken, "Training Citizens in a Democratic Society," paper presented at the annual meeting of the International Listening Association, 2000, Virginia Beach. Retrieved from ERIC: ED438584.
12. P. G. Friedman, "Listening for Narrative," in *Perspectives on Listening,* edited by A. W. Wolvin and C. G. Coakley (Norwood, NJ: Ablex, 1993), 201–216.

Chapter

6

Getting to Know Your Audience

Goals

✓ To show you the importance of establishing immediacy with your audience through audience analysis

✓ To help you become familiar with the operating procedures of the brain and ways you can use this information when planning presentations

✓ To show you how to create an audience analysis framework that facilitates your tailoring a message to a specific group of listeners

✓ To identify ways you can gather information about the audience and learn how to use it when composing your message

✓ To become alert to the times when you can gather information from the audience

His first public speech was as a 4-year-old, opening a Christmas pageant in a little prairie town in his native South Dakota. That talk earned him a silver dollar.

For the past twenty years, he has been talking as the nightly news anchor on NBC-TV, earning multimillions of dollars a year.[1]

The person about whom this story is told is NBC news anchor Tom Brokaw, a man who has clearly benefited from his presentation skills. Although you may never receive even a silver dollar, let alone "multimillions of dollars," for any presentation you give in your lifetime, what you will receive is a response from the listeners to whom you present.

As a sender or presenter of important messages in everyday presentations and in public speaking events, at the very least, you want the receivers of your message to listen to you and to remember what you say. Whether you are in a meeting, in class, or at a family reunion, in order for your message to have an influence on your listeners, you need to build your message with your audience in mind. That means engaging in audience analysis to identify who your listeners are, as well as how they are similar to and how they differ from each other.

What is the purpose of this? In just about every instance we can think of, when you express your opinion, when you provide information, when you speak to make people laugh, you are communicating to achieve a speaking goal, and that means influencing the audience. The way to achieve that speaking goal is to create a sense of closeness, or immediacy, with your audience. ●

Achieving Immediacy through Audience Analysis

In Chapter four we discussed ways to achieve immediacy with the audience through the use of nonverbal communication. In this chapter, we will discuss the dimensions of your audience that will help you to create immediacy.

Immediacy is what you experience when you feel understood, when you feel the person with whom you are communicating is speaking directly to you. Close friends or relatives are persons with whom you experience immediacy because it has flourished as a result of your relationships with them. Without the time to develop the kind of relationship you might enjoy with a relative or close friend, as a speaker you must find other ways to establish immediacy.

Audience analysis is the means to this end. Audience analysis allows you to construct a profile of your audience and focus your message to its specific qualities. The more you know about your audience, the better you are able to tailor your presentation to its specific qualities, and the more likely you are to reach your speaking goal. In your communication class, you may find it somewhat easier to systematically build a profile of your audience because of the time you spend with them. However, whether you are interacting with your class audience or speaking in a professional environment, in a community group, socially, or in some other setting, you should consider the same dimensions of audiences. With your class you have the opportunity to practice on a repeated basis using these dimensions of audience analysis in planning your presentations. That practice will serve you in one-time opportunities with other audiences.

Although there are an endless number of qualities and characteristics that differentiate audience members from each other, there are also similarities. First we will discuss how audience members are alike and then how they are different. It is to your benefit to consider both of these aspects of your listeners when you are preparing a presentation.

Gathering Information about Your Listeners before Your Speech

There are four ways you can gather information about your audience to assist in building your audience profile: by observing the members of your audience; by asking them questions; by surveying them; and by drawing conclusions about what you do not know on the basis of what you have been able to learn through the other methods.

Observing

In this text devoted to everyday presentations, we assume you will usually find yourself presenting to small groups that you are a member of, professional or community organizations, say, or small groups of people you are already somewhat acquainted with, as with a campus group. By simply keeping your eyes and ears open, you can acquire large amounts of valuable information about any of these groups that will help you in planning your presentations. In your communication class, you are in a position to observe your audience from your very first class meeting. Visit with individuals before and after class, becoming more mindful of everyone. Listen to the questions asked and comments given by your classmates during class discussions. Pay attention to classmates' presentations. As you listen to their speeches, you will be able to identify the topics your classmates are interested in and knowledgeable about; to acquire insights about their attitudes, beliefs, and values; to learn about the cultures represented in your classroom; and to accumulate demographic information.

As you listen to your classmates' speeches, keep notes on what you see and hear—to be incorporated into your audience profile. Don't forget that with each day of class and each round of speeches you will learn additional information about your classroom audience, so keep your profile updated.

Asking

To learn information about your audience that would be of advantage to you in planning your speech, you can always ask. If it is important to you to know what percentage of your audience is working to pay college costs, ask them. If you need to know how familiar your audience is with United States involvement during the Vietnam conflict, ask them. Remember that when you ask groups of people for information, you are somewhat limited in the type of information they will give you. Questions whose responses are in the form of yes or no answers are easier to administer than those requiring a more complex response. Questions about impersonal topics are better handled in class than questions about personal issues.

Before you ask your classroom audience questions, check with your instructor first to arrange the best time. Give your audience a brief background on why you are asking these questions and the type of response you would like from them; for example, "I'm thinking about giving my next speech on the importance of staying in this state after graduation. I would like to know how many of you currently plan to stay in the state when you graduate. May I see a show of hands, please?"

If you have follow-up questions, you might gather the follow-up information this way: "If you did not raise your hand in response to my question and you plan to leave the state after graduation, I am going to read a few reasons why you might have decided to leave. When I read the reason that most closely corresponds to the reason you have decided to leave, please raise your hand."

When you are planning a presentation to a group of which you are a member, you can use the same method at a gathering of the group before you present. If you are planning a presentation for a group of which you are not a member, you can send an e-mail to members in advance of your presentation, or you can attend a gathering of the group prior to your presentation.

Surveying

A more refined method of "asking" is to develop a paper-and-pencil or online survey for your audience to complete (see Figures 6.1 and 6.2). When you have several questions to ask, or when your questions require more than a yes or no response, or when they are about a sensitive topic, a survey is a quick, easy, and confidential way to gather information (see Act and Reflect 6.1). As you develop your survey, keep in mind that the questions you ask need to be clearly and briefly stated.

Guidelines for Developing and Administering Surveys

1 Ask a friend to take your survey before you distribute it to your audience, to check the clarity of your questions.

2 Keep your list of questions as short as possible.

3 When asking questions about a sensitive subject, make a statement at the beginning of your survey indicating that responses will be treated confidentially.

4 If you are surveying your classroom audience, remember to check with your instructor for permission and a time to distribute the survey.

5 If you are surveying a group you are a member of, be considerate of other activities that occur in the group.

6 If you are surveying a group you are not a member of, check with a contact person from the group about protocol for distributing the survey.

Always preface your survey questions with a brief description of the purpose and use of your survey: "I look forward to being the guest speaker at your next meeting. To assist me in planning my program on business etiquette in the age of technology, I would appreciate your responses to the questions on this brief survey."

If you have questions of a sensitive nature, how do you reassure your respondents their privacy will be protected? You can ask your respondents to reply to an objective or trusted third party who would agree to forward them to you. You can

ACT & REFLECT

MSL

6.1: Choosing the Best Survey Format

ACT • Read the sample surveys (Figures 6.1 and 6.2) that Katelyn and Jessica developed to gather information from their audiences for their speeches on home schooling and gay marriages. How are the two surveys similar? Different? What do you see as the potential advantages and disadvantages of the surveys in gathering the information the speakers want?

REFLECT • From the list of guidelines for developing and administering surveys, what suggestions or feedback would you give to Katelyn and Jessica for their surveys?

Katelyn's Survey

1. Do you think home schooling is a good form of education? Why or why not?

2. What are your past experiences with home schoolers and/or home schooling?

● **FIGURE 6.1 Sample Survey 1.** *Source:* Katelyn Ver Hoef, survey to gather information for a speech to a negative audience, November 10, 2004.

also include a statement in the survey reassuring the respondents that their right to confidentiality will be preserved. You can also reassure them that although you might use examples from their surveys in your presentation, you will not identify them. Also point out that their participation in responding to the survey is totally voluntary. Of course, it should go without saying that whenever you use a survey to gather

● **FIGURE 6.2 Sample Survey 2.**   *Source:* Jessica Culhane, survey to gather information for a speech to a negative audience, November 10, 2004.

Jessica's Survey

1. Are you opposed to the idea of gay marriage? Yes/No

2. If yes, do you oppose gay marriage for religious reasons? Yes/No

3. If you feel comfortable sharing, what is your religion (including denomination)?
   _____

4. Check the statements you agree with:
   _____ Homosexuality is "just not natural"
   _____ Gays have a choice of their sexuality
   _____ The goal or purpose of marriage is to reproduce
   _____ Gay couples should not be allowed to adopt or keep custody of children from previous marriages
   _____ Gays should not be allowed other rights associated with marriage (hospital visitation, property rights, etc.)
   _____ Gays cannot commit in a monogamous relationship and therefore will increase the divorce rate
   _____ Marriage is a tradition in America that should remain unchanged
   _____ Gay marriage will lead to a demoralization of American values

5. If you would like to further explain any of the statements above, I would very much appreciate your input:

   _____

   _____

---

sensitive information, you must be true to your word and preserve your respondents' privacy.

Drawing Conclusions

You will often find yourself in the position of having to draw conclusions about things you don't know about your audience based on information you do know. Sometimes you learn too late that you do not have information that would be helpful to you. There might be instances when a topic is so delicate that even if you were to ask a question, you would not receive an answer. At other times, it might not be possible to make contact with an audience in advance. Finally, there are occasions when you simply cannot ask an audience everything you would like to. When you are left to your own deductive abilities, be cautious. Base your conclusions on more than one piece of information: "On the basis of my observations of our last three meetings, I believe . . ." When you reveal information to your audience that is the product of a deduction, explain the thinking process that led to your conclusion: "I arrived at this conclusion in this manner: . . ." Be tentative in presenting your conclusions, recognizing that they are not necessarily facts. "Although this might not be totally accurate, I believe . . ." Finally, give yourself and your audience a way to save face: "I see other members of the committee in the room and they are welcome to add to my comments." You might find yourself using this last method of gathering information more often than you would think. Just be sure that you are able to justify your conclusion for your audience and be open to their responses in the event your conclusion is inaccurate or does not sufficiently represent the topic you are discussing.

How Listeners Are Similar

One very important characteristic audience members share is that they each possess a brain that helps them evaluate knowledge and decide what information is important enough to pay attention to and what is important enough to remember. What does this mean to you as you analyze your audience in preparation for your presentation?

Consider a typical day in your communication classroom when your class is in the midst of giving a round of speeches. Although many of your classmates appear to be listening attentively to the speaker, others are not. Some are reading the school newspaper; a few quietly whisper to each other, despite the disapproving glances of the teacher; others appear to be working on assignments for other classes; one or two have their eyes closed; the other scheduled speakers for the day are shuffling through their speech notes. Your classroom situation is not unusual: presenters are often faced with distracted, inattentive audience members. Keep in mind also, this scenario focuses only on visible behaviors; we have no way of knowing all of the distractions occupying audience members' minds. The speaker's goal of getting through to the audience, making an impression on them, and having an influence on their thoughts or actions seems an impossibility. In order to be successful as a speaker, you must think about what you know about your audience and show them you know them as you speak to them.

Speakers draw conclusions about their audience using information they already know and information they glean through observation. What useful information do you know about these individuals? What do you believe you would be able to conclude about them? ●

Getting to know your audience begins with an awareness of how the brain works. Essentially, the brain is in a constant process of prioritizing and assessing the information a person is bombarded with every second of every day. This is also the case as you are speaking: the brains of your audience members will prioritize and assess the information you divulge in your speech, not just once but many times before you finish speaking. If you understand that this constant prioritizing and assessing is occurring, you can plan your speech to respond to it. Taking the way the brain operates into account, there are four key ideas for you to keep in mind.

Attract the Attention of the Audience

Some researchers estimate that our brains are capable of processing up to forty thousand bits of information each second.[2] It is impossible for anyone to deliberately consider whether each of those pieces of information is really important. Happily for us, the brain screens out all of the clutter, or unimportant information, and allows us to be aware only of the important information. Your concern as a presenter is to attract the attention of your audience so your message is one of the bits of information singled out over all of the thousands of other bits they receive each second. There are two ways you can facilitate this process:

- Emphasize issues of high priority to your listeners as soon as you begin to speak. If your audience will not realize why or how your topic is important, establish a connection to something that is a priority.

- Appeal to the emotions of your listeners. Emotional appeals in presentations are often viewed as secondary in importance compared to factual information. However, in his book *Emotional Intelligence*, Daniel Goleman says: "When it

You can attract an audience's attention by appealing to their emotions and personally involving them. What do you suppose this speaker is saying to involve his listeners? ●

comes to shaping our decisions and our actions, feeling counts every bit as much—and often more—than thought."[3]

Personally Involve the Audience

Remember that the brain is constantly assessing and reassessing the importance of information. Even though you have been successful in attracting the attention of your listeners, you now have about thirty seconds for them to decide if they will continue to pay attention.[4] You can maintain their attention in two ways:

- Link audience members' names to your topic.
- Establish common ground with your audience by referring to an incident of which they share common experience or common knowledge, or refer to an issue about which they share agreement. Make your references as personal as possible for your audience.

Peanuts: © United Features Syndicate, Inc.

A speaker can provide an opportunity for an audience member to learn. How could the leader of this nature group provide opportunities for the hikers to learn? ●

Provide Opportunities for the Audience to Process Your Information

The adage "practice makes perfect" comes into play at this point. You can offer listeners an opportunity to process the information you give them in two ways:

- Keep key points limited, with a minimum of two and a maximum of five, so listeners don't feel overloaded with information.
- Build in opportunities for listeners to think about or practice the information: express your key ideas in different ways to appeal to different priorities or, if possible, allow your audience to become actively involved by giving them a chance to practice skills or to briefly discuss an issue with each other or to share an opinion with everyone.

Show Your Audience the Relevance of Your Information

It is possible that, up to this point, you have been able to attract and maintain your listeners' attention and provide them with sufficient opportunities to process the information you are giving them. You don't want them to think, "This has been interesting, and I understand what the speaker is saying, but this has nothing to do with me." In order to avoid this response, you must build into your speech answers to these two questions:

- "Does this information make sense in terms of what I know and how I view the world?"
- "What does this information have to do with me?"

As you consider the four points given here in regard to the constant assessing and prioritizing of the brain, a pattern emerges. You are making connections between the information you have to give your audience and what your audience members know and who they are. For every piece of information you give them, attach it to something that exists in their worlds and their frames of reference. Now let's consider how you can identify what is in their worlds and their frames of reference.

How Listeners Differ

Just as your listeners are similar in the way their brains process information, they are different as a result of the ways they have lived their lives. The interests, careers, cultures, and other differing qualities are also areas you must consider in your analysis of your audience. What dimensions of your audience should you consider? Everything.

The challenge to you is to identify characteristics of your audience that are relevant to your speech topic and to show your audience they will benefit from receiving the information you have to give them. In other words, tailor your message to the

Everyday Example

Romancing the Points

The four key ideas we have discussed about the brain involve appealing to audience members' emotions. Here is how Brian Tracy, a creator of audiotape programs to develop personal effectiveness, describes the way he applies this knowledge when he speaks.

"I resolved that I would be the opposite of speakers that are only jokes, only humor, and only emotion. Insincere emotion, what I call gush, gush, puke, puke emotion, stories that will work the emotions of the crowd. But my weakness is that I don't give enough emotion and too much content.

"Now I am working my way back to the center. I 'romance the points' I want to make. I have developed what I call the windshield wiper method of speaking, it goes: left brain, right brain. Left brain, right brain. Left brain, right brain. Left brain, right brain. Fact, story/anecdote. Fact, story/anecdote. Fact, story/anecdote. Fact, story/anecdote. So it's practical, with the fact for the left brain, then the story or anecdote that illustrates it for the right brain. If you have too much content, it's like pouring water on the ground. It forms a pool. If you keep pouring water in the water, it doesn't get a chance to soak in. It just evaporates or spills over. If you pour content into the mind, and then you go to the right brain, it gives the material a chance to sink in.

"The danger with stories is that they are so well received that they are like a narcotic. The audience laughs and smiles and 'likes' the speaker. And all speakers want to be liked."

Source: L. Walters, *Secrets of Superstar Speakers: Wisdom from the Greatest Motivators of Our Time and With Those Superstars Inspired to Dramatic and Lasting Change* (New York: McGraw-Hill, 2000), 181. Reproduced with permission of The McGraw-Hill Companies.

characteristics of your audience that are relevant to your speaking goal and use these characteristics to make your message relevant to them.

If you strive to find the answers to these questions, you will have much of the information you need about your audience to make the decisions necessary to result in a presentation that speaks to them:

- What are your listeners' demographic characteristics?
- What are your listeners' motivational characteristics; are they attending your speech voluntarily or are they a captive audience?
- What do your listeners know about and what are their interests? To what extent are they knowledgeable about and interested in your topic?
- What are the attitudes, beliefs, and values embraced by your listeners?
- What is the cultural context in which you are presenting?

Demographic Characteristics

Every time you register for classes, you provide information about yourself to your school. What is your major? Your hometown? Your age? These are examples of **demographic characteristics:** factual characteristics about you. Knowing your audience's demographic characteristics can be helpful because they can point to other qualities of the audience. If you are to give your presentation to several different audiences, identifying relevant demographic characteristics of each audience will help you adjust the basic message to make it relevant to each group. For example, let's say you are speaking on the topic of physical fitness to a group of senior citizens one day and a group of grade school children the next day. What you choose to tell each audience about ways to become physically fit, as well as the examples and other materials you use to support or clarify major points, will change simply according to the demographic characteristic of the average age of each audience (see Act and Reflect 6.2).

Are there specific demographic qualities you should always look for? That is, should you always know the average age of the members of your audience? Their yearly income or marital status? Not necessarily. It is more helpful to be able to identify demographic qualities that are of special importance to your audience and your speaking goal. For example, if you know the major of each member of your classroom audience, would that help you plan a presentation on little-known sources of financial aid? It might, but of even greater relevance would be the number of students in your audience who are receiving financial aid, as well as the number of students who were declared ineligible for it.

What if you have more than one group of individuals in your audience who share common demographics? For example, some members of your classroom audience are job-hunting seniors, and a presentation on preparing for job interviews might be just what they want to hear. Would this topic also interest a group of first-semester freshmen? Possibly, because your information could pertain to finding summer employment or employment

demographic characteristics Factual characteristics about individuals.

ACT&REFLECT

6.2: Creating and Using a Demographic Profile

ACT • The survey in Figure 6.3 contains the basis for you to develop a demographic profile of your classroom audience. Modify the survey so it will be useful to you for developing a demographic profile of your classroom audience by adding or deleting any items necessary. Reproduce the survey and ask your classmates to complete it. When your classmates have completed the survey, compile the results on another copy.

REFLECT • On the basis of information you have received from the completed surveys, how would you describe your classroom audience? What does this information tell you that will be important for you to consider as you plan and develop your next classroom presentation?

while attending classes. Knowing the demographic characteristics of your audience will help you identify clusters of individuals with similar demographics, to help you choose a variety of examples to clarify your points and establish relevancy for each group.

Knowing the demographic composition of your audience can help you to select a focus for your topic. A seemingly simple fact, knowing whether your listeners are present because they want to be or because they have to be, will give you important insights into your listeners' attitudes about you and your message.

Motivational Characteristics

Knowing why your audience is present can also help you make decisions about the content of your presentation. Are you speaking to a **voluntary audience**—they chose to attend? Are your audience members required to attend your presentation, making them a **captive audience**? Knowing what motivated your audience to attend will tell you about their attitudes, give you some idea of their knowledge about your topic, and provide some additional clues about their demographic characteristics.

Audience Disposition You should expect that an audience whose attendance is mandatory will be less positively predisposed toward you or your speech than the voluntary audience.

- To counteract the potentially negative response of the mandatory audience, emphasize the benefits available to them as a result of their attendance. Let's say that, having received one too many speeding tickets, you are required to attend a four-hour safety presentation held on a Saturday morning in order to retain your drivers' license.

voluntary audience Audience who has chosen to attend a presentation.

captive audience Audience who has been required to attend a presentation.

● **FIGURE 6.3** Audience Demographic Profile.

To assist me in planning my speeches this term, I would appreciate your taking a few minutes to tell me about yourself. Please respond to the survey by selecting the choice for each item that most closely describes you. If there are items that are not relevant to you or to which you prefer not to respond, you may leave them blank. Thank you.

1. My current classification is
   _____ freshman
   _____ sophomore
   _____ junior
   _____ senior

2. My age is
   _____ 18–19 years
   _____ 20–21 years
   _____ 22–23 years
   _____ older than 23 years

3. My marital status is
   _____ single
   _____ married
   _____ divorced

4. I have
   _____ no children
   _____ one child
   _____ more than one child

5. My college expenses are paid by (check all that apply)
   _____ my parents
   _____ my part-time employment
   _____ my full-time employment
   _____ financial aid
   _____ scholarships
   _____ loans
   _____ other

6. My cumulative grade point is
   _____ 3.5–4.0
   _____ 3.0–3.49
   _____ 2.5–2.99
   _____ 2.0–2.49
   _____ below 2.0

7. Besides attending classes, I am employed the following number of hours per week
   _____ more than 40
   _____ 30–40
   _____ 20–29
   _____ 10–19
   _____ less than 10

8. Before attending college I lived in
   _____ a rural setting
   _____ a small town setting
   _____ a suburban setting
   _____ a city

9. I currently live
   _____ in a residence hall
   _____ at my parents' home
   _____ off campus

10. I currently _____ am _____ am not affiliated with a fraternity or sorority.

11. I _____ have _____ have not served in the military.

12. I _____ am _____ am not active in campus organizations.

13. I _____ have _____ have not received instruction in public speaking before this class.

14. Politically I would describe myself as
    _____ a liberal
    _____ a moderate
    _____ a conservative

The officer in charge says that your attendance means you are a good citizen who wants to make a contribution to your community by changing your driving habits. The officer also indicates that you will be given a number of safe driving tips that will help you retain your driver's license and lower your auto insurance rates. Although you had no choice about attending the safety presentation, hearing the benefits of attendance pointed out to you might help to make the requirement more palatable.

- When you speak to a voluntary audience, it is still wise to reaffirm the audience's goodwill toward you. You may not need to work so hard to ensure this audience will be glad they attended, but you do want to cultivate and retain their goodwill.

Audience Knowledge Knowing what motivated your audience to attend will also help you draw conclusions about their knowledge of your topic and you.

- Generally you should assume that a captive audience will be less knowledgeable about you and your topic than the voluntary audience. You might need to provide the captive audience with background information or definitions of terms you will use in your presentation. They might also be unaware of who you are or why you are speaking to them. What are your credentials? Why are you speaking on this topic or on this particular occasion? In order for you to meet your speaking goal, you must tell them.

- A voluntary audience is likely to have a more thorough grasp of technical terms or background material. To go into the same amount of detail with a voluntary audience as you would with a captive audience might be perceived as insulting or "talking down" to them. However, it is still worthwhile to consider whether a brief summary of the current status of your topic, as well as a brief reminder of your credentials, would serve as a helpful reminder to the voluntary audience of their reasons for attending.

Demographic Characteristics We have already discussed audience demographic characteristics; knowing why your audience is in attendance may help you add to their demographic profile.

- You might find that with a captive audience, listeners will have fewer demographic characteristics in common than is likely with a voluntary audience. If you are speaking at the local public library about bird watching, for example, and your presentation is open to the public, you can probably be confident that the one thing your audience is sure to have in common is their love of birds. If you give your bird-watching presentation to a captive audience, you do not have even that one commonality to feel confident about, but you can work to build **common ground** by acknowledging other areas that audience members have in common with each other and with your topic. Even if you have an audience whose ages, education, majors, or other qualities are diverse, they have some commonalities. Identify the common quality, demonstrate its relevance to your topic, and emphasize it throughout your

common ground Commonalities that audience members share.

speech. In a previous example about financial aid, the speaker might emphasize the shared need of all audience members to attain sufficient financial aid to continue and complete their education.

- The voluntary audience at least has in common that they wanted to hear you speak or they wanted to hear your speech. Depending on your topic, you might be able to conclude that other areas of commonality exist. If you are speaking to an inline skating club, for example, does that tell you something about other interests or concerns your audience might share? Does it give you information about the economic status or average age of your audience? Drawing these conclusions can tell you something about the types of examples or other information that will help you meet your speaking goal.

As you can see, simply knowing why your audience is in attendance provides you with a great deal of guidance in planning the extent to which you will have to sell yourself and your topic to them, the extent to which you will have to provide relevant background material, and the effort you must exert to establish common ground (see Act and Reflect 6.3).

Listeners' Knowledge and Interests

How do you estimate the general knowledge and interests of the audience and the specific knowledge and interests in relation to the topic of your presentation? A sense of the areas the audience is already knowledgeable about and interested in can provide you with helpful information about what or what not to include.

- On the basis of what you know about your audience, make assumptions about what you don't know. For example, if the majority of members of your audience are education majors, you may be able to assume that they are aware of teacher

An audience member with knowledge about the speaker's topic will be motivated to learn even more. What would you guess is the level of expertise of these kayakers? What details are you using to identify their expertise? ●

ACT&REFLECT

6.3: Captive or Voluntary Audience?

ACT • Your classroom presents an unusual challenge. Although technically your classroom audience is a captive audience, it is possible that audience members may also have some of the characteristics of a voluntary audience. Answering these questions will help you identify which of the strategies for speaking to captive and voluntary audiences will benefit you and your audience in your next speech:

1. The topic of my next speech is:
2. I believe the **disposition** of my audience in relation to my topic is:
3. My audience most likely has this current **knowledge** about my topic:
4. The **demographic characteristics** my audience shares that are relevant to my topic are:

REFLECT • After responding to these questions, which of the suggestions given in this section will you implement in your speech to help you meet your speaking goal?

certification requirements. If you also know that they are specializing in physical education, you might conclude that they are aware of the differences in physical coordination between children in first grade and those in third grade.

- Knowing the general areas of audience knowledge and interest assists you in determining whether background material is necessary, whether it will be important to define terms, and whether you will be able to use technical language in developing your speech. For example, if you plan to speak on the benefits of investing in solar power as an energy source, knowing that the majority of your audience members are engineering majors will help you draw conclusions about the technical nature of the material you could present. If you are able to conclude that some or all of your audience are not so technically inclined, you may have to devote time to defining key terms or concepts or providing background information.

- A sense of your audience's knowledge and interest areas will help you determine whether it is more appropriate to give a general overview of a topic or to discuss a controversy or other topic of current concern in a particular field. For example, if your audience members are mostly food science majors, you might be able to discuss new developments regarding genetically modified foods. If your audience is a mixture of majors, a better route might be to discuss ways that ideas for new foods on the market have been developed.

ACT&REFLECT

6.4: Are They Interested? Knowledgeable?

ACT • How interested do you believe your audience will be in the topic of your next speech? How knowledgeable do you believe they are about your topic?

REFLECT • How can you plan your presentation to increase their interest? What can you do to retain the attention of those who are already interested? What steps can you take to ensure that audience members who have differing kinds of knowledge about your topic will understand and appreciate your presentation?

Identifying the motivations of audience members, demographic characteristics, and general areas of knowledge and interest are all necessary and helpful in planning your presentation (see Act and Reflect 6.4). Of equal importance is to become as familiar as you can with your audience attitudes, beliefs, and values.

Listeners' Attitudes, Beliefs, and Values

Do you like Brussels sprouts? Do you believe you can ward off cancer and other diseases with diet? Is good health important to you? These three questions focus on related issues that designate the next general area of the audience profile you are building. Your feelings about Brussels sprouts might seem relatively unimportant in comparison to questions about diet or health. Your feelings, whether positive or negative, are what we call **attitudes.** Given the right evidence, attitudes can sometimes be changed. For example, your feelings about Brussels sprouts might be easily changed if you were to taste a particularly wonderful or horrid dish containing Brussels sprouts. Your sense of confidence of the truth or falseness of an entity is what we call a **belief.** If you believe that by watching your diet, you will be less likely to fall victim to a life-threatening illness, you are expressing confidence that it is true that health is dependent on diet. Now think about the decisions you make regarding your health—decisions to smoke cigarettes or drink alcohol, your physical activity, medical care. If these decisions are made with the welfare of your body in mind, you are indicating a part of your value system. **Values** are those principles or standards by which we live our lives.

One theory explains that attitudes, beliefs, and values are interrelated, similar to the layers on an onion (see Figure 6.4).[5] Our attitudes and beliefs reside at the outer layers of the onion, and both are influenced by the value system at the core of the onion. Because people act consistently as a result of their attitudes, beliefs, and values, a knowledge of the areas your audience embraces can assist you in preparing your presentation in several ways.

attitudes Positive or negative feelings about an issue.

belief Confidence in the truth or falseness of an entity.

values Principles or standards that guide us in the ways we live our lives.

If the goal of your speech is to change an attitude, you will need to demonstrate that the network of beliefs resulting in that attitude is false or in error. You might do this by presenting recent research that demonstrates a belief that is no longer valid. I might feel my current weight is unhealthy because I believe there is an ideal weight for my height. If you can introduce information that changes my belief regarding ideal weight–height ratios, you might persuade me to change my attitude about my weight.

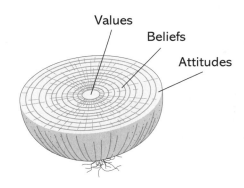

Values
Beliefs
Attitudes

● **FIGURE 6.4** An Onion Showing the Relationship of Attitudes, Beliefs, and Values.

If you wish to change the belief system of the audience, build consistency with the value system. Because values are a part of our self-concept and because they are condoned by our culture, they are not easily changed. A focus on values may be helpful to change beliefs and attitudes. With the Brussels sprouts example, let's say recent research indicates that a common method of raising Brussels sprouts requires large amounts of hazardous chemicals. By appealing to the health value of your audience, you can create an argument that says, "Because you value your health, you should know that the use of agricultural chemicals in raising Brussels sprouts is hazardous to your health." Although values are difficult, if not impossible, to change, they tend to be somewhat general and may be interpreted in a variety of ways.

Here is another example: Your audience values education. You want to persuade them to support a proposed double-digit increase in tuition. By appealing to the audience's value of education, you can demonstrate that their education is worth the increase in tuition. In contrast, if you want your audience to protest the proposed tuition increase, you can indicate to them that because they value education, they

ACT&REFLECT

6.5: The Values of Your Audience

ACT • What value is relevant to the next topic of your speech? Do you know the beliefs and attitudes of your audience that correspond to this value? To help clarify these issues, respond to these questions:

1. The topic of my next speech is:
2. A **value** that relates to this topic is:
3. A **belief** my audience holds about my topic that is a result of this value is:
4. An **attitude** my audience has about my topic based on this belief is:

REFLECT • Will your speech attempt to change a belief or attitude? What strategies should you build into your speech that will help you to accomplish this goal?

A Question of **Ethics**

You have analyzed your audience along the dimensions of their demographics; motivation for attending; knowledge about and interest in your topic; and attitudes, beliefs, and values. You have information about your topic that will appeal to your audience and will help you to meet your speaking goal. However, there is other information about your topic that you know will influence your audience in a different direction from your goal. Is it ethical to simply neglect to include this information in your speech? Should you include both pieces of information? How should you proceed?

should protest to ensure that they will still be able to afford their education. See Act and Reflect 6.5.

A final area that will be important in developing your audience profile is the cultural context of your audience.

Cultural Composition

We don't have to flip on the television or surf the Net to experience people and events that our parents and grandparents did not even dream of. Happily, members of other cultures can be found right in front of you in your audience. The speaker who wishes to meet his or her speaking goal must acknowledge the cultural context of the audience.

Culture has been defined as "beliefs, values, and norms, which affect the behaviors of a relatively large group of people."[6] Your culture influences who you are, what decisions you make about appropriate actions in a variety of circumstances, and how you perceive and interpret events.

In our discussions of demographics, motivation, knowledge and interest areas, and attitudes, beliefs, and values, we have considered the reasons that knowledge of these areas can assist you in presenting your thoughts. Culture is the umbrella under which most of the other elements can be found. Rather than caution you about why you should be aware of cultural considerations, we will present ideas for ways you can become acquainted with the diverse cultures that are sure to be present in your audience (see Act and Reflect 6.6). William Gudykunst, a noted intercultural researcher, suggests a number of skills that are relevant to communicating with members of other cultures. Three of these skills, in particular, seem most helpful for speakers who wish to become better acquainted with diverse audiences:[7]

Become Mindful To be mindful means you are actively seeking information about the people with whom you are communicating. By engaging members of your classroom audience in conversation before and after class, you are becoming mindful. Becoming mindful assists you in developing an awareness of the ways people are similar and the ways they are different.

culture A group of individuals who condone a common set of beliefs, values, norms, and behaviors.

Establish Empathy This means that you can demonstrate your total understanding of another person's thoughts or feelings. How can you establish empathy with a diverse audience? As you become more mindful, seek an understanding of others' experiences from their perspectives. During a presentation in one of our speech classes, a member of another culture pulled a thick stack of bills from his pocket to emphasize a point about the use of cash versus charge cards. Members of the audience were horrified that this person carried such a large amount of money with him. The speaker insisted that it was typical of him and other members of his culture to carry cash rather than credit cards. It was necessary for both speaker and audience to understand each other's dependence on a particular form of currency.

Demonstrate Behavioral Flexibility Having become mindful of the special qualities of other groups and attempting to understand and appreciate these differences, you can put your awareness into action by demonstrating behavioral flexibility. In learning about other cultures and understanding how others might differ from the culture with which you identify, you may adjust your own habits to honor other groups. You might wonder why you should adjust your behaviors, and of course you have the choice to do that or refrain. Think for a second about entertaining guests. If you know that a guest does not eat a certain food, do you insist that that particular food be served? As a considerate host, you would probably provide an alternative. Similarly, in your communication repertoire, you might consider acknowledging the verbal or nonverbal behaviors of individuals in your audience. Can you greet the audience in their language? Is there a particular path to logic that you might incorporate in an example or other part of your presentation in recognition of another culture? By incorporating these or other demonstrations of flexibility into your speech, you are also encouraging members of other cultures to recognize special qualities of your culture and possibly reciprocate.

Relating the Differences

We have shown that the audience characteristics the speaker must consider can be organized into two main areas: those audience members share and those they do not.

6.6: Cultural Communication Skills

A C T • What cultures are represented in your classroom audience? What is your current knowledge about each of the cultures of your audience members?

R E F L E C T • How could you practice the three cultural skills to learn about your classroom audience: (1) becoming mindful; (2) establishing empathy; (3) demonstrating behavioral flexibility?

As you read these pages, you may have observed that none of these areas is totally independent of the others. In some way, they are all related to each other. In order to meet your presentation goal, you cannot focus solely on one without considering the others. For example, if you know that the audience is voluntarily attending a presentation discussing the best way to gain entrance into graduate school, do you feel able to estimate the demographic quality of your listeners' average grade points? If you have a sense of average grade point, you probably know something, too, about the type of knowledge that is stored in the minds of your listeners. You will probably guess that such an audience will be made up largely of individuals who had been successful in their undergraduate careers. If you know that your audience has been successful in their undergraduate careers, what will you assume will be their area of knowledge and interest? Becoming more specialized in their majors might be a good guess. If you know they are interested in continuing and increasing their area of specialization, what will you expect will be a value they will share? Education might be a good guess. Are there clues here that might allow you to guess about cultural issues? Perhaps. Notice the use of the word "guess." Although you would be guessing, your guesses would be educated. But aside from guessing, how can you know your audience?

Gathering Information about Your Listeners during and after Your Speech

Q: "When should I gather information about my audience?"

A: "Before your presentation, during your presentation, and after your presentation."

Earlier we discussed ways to gather information about your listeners before your presentation. The information-gathering process does not stop when you give your speech, however. You will continue to gather valuable information during and after your presentation.

During Your Presentation

An effective speaker will be aware of audience responses to what is said during the speech and will make necessary adjustments whenever possible. Perhaps, judging by the puzzled looks on the faces of your audience, you believe you have misjudged how familiar your audience is with your topic. Judging by the fidgeting and general lack of attention, you know they are uninterested in what you are saying. What can you do about these unanticipated responses? You could state information in different ways to help your audience understand. If you believe your audience has lost interest, check your delivery. Perhaps you are not presenting yourself in a way that makes the audience want to listen. Or you could involve them in a short exercise or ask a question to restore their interest and attention to you and your message. Be alert to the valuable information your audience gives you as you are speaking and make as many adjustments as you can.

Everyday Example

Reprinted from *Successful Meetings* Magazine, December 2004.

Teen Talk

The following discussion illustrates the character-istics a speaker is sensitive to when presenting to teenage audiences and the ways he modifies his presentations accordingly.

Have you ever seen your attendees act like a bunch of high-school kids when a meeting session misses the mark? Eric Chester can sympathize. The president of Lakewood, CO based youth consulting firm Generation Why has not only spoken at many corporate and associ-ation meetings, but has also addressed gym-nasiums full of teenagers on more than 1,500 occasions. "And believe me, none of those kids asked to be there," he quips. "They're just happy to not be in class so they can hang out with their friends or take a nap." Such crowds practically dare Chester to say something that piques their interest, so "if I don't have my act together from the first five seconds, I'm dead to them, and it becomes the longest hour of my life."

Out of necessity, then, Chester is constantly reshaping his presentation. "I do not speak today, in content or style, the way I spoke yesterday," he says. "I need to think about reinventing every time. To be an effective keynoter, a speaker must know his own material cold, and must know the circumstances of the particular audience, and must solidly connect his material to that day's audience."

With his teenage audiences, Chester researches who the students are at that particular school, what they are facing (Was there a suicide recently? Is the football team doing especially well or badly?), what their feelings are this week, and what is coming up in their collective life that could make those feelings change. "This audience demands validity," he says, "and I'm going to know what they are thinking in order to win credibility from them."

Chester does this the old-fashioned way: He gets in their faces. Besides interviewing a sampling of kids well before the event, he'll also stand at the venue's entrance immediately prior to speaking, approaching kids to get up-to-the-minute details on the buzz and the mood among different segments of the student body. "I show them out in the open that I am gather-ing information specific to them," he says. "I interact with as many kids as I can and collect a few great anecdotes. From that, they see that you've made yourself a part of their situation. And as the session unfolds, I'll bring other kids up with me and create a dialogue with them on the spot. I know my stuff well enough, and I know that particular audience well enough, that I have no worries about doing that."[9]

Source: "Teen Talk," *Successful Meetings* (VNU Business Media, Inc., December 1, 2004).

After Your Presentation

Now that you have finished your presentation, you can forget about it, right? Wrong. Get into the habit of spending some time following each presentation to reflect on what happened, and use this valuable information to plan your next presentation, as well as to help yourself to become a better speaker. After your presentation, you can analyze your audience in several ways. If your audience has had the opportunity to ask questions, what does the nature of those questions tell you about your speech?

- Did the questions indicate a lack of understanding of various aspects of your speech?
- Did the questions indicate a lack of interest?
- Did the questions indicate that your audience was challenged or stimulated by what you said?

Another way to gather information from your audience is through audience feedback. In your communication class, your instructor might ask audience members to provide immediate feedback to you. Listen carefully to the feedback you receive, and take the opportunity to ask your classmates questions about your presentation. For example, sometimes presenters want to know if a particular example has been helpful in clarifying a point. If you have specific questions about your presentation, take advantage of the opportunity to ask them. If you are presenting to a group outside of your classroom, ask a trusted member of the group for feedback. If you don't know anyone in the group, after you have completed your presentation, look for a chance to initiate a conversation with one of your listeners who might be willing to share an impression of your presentation with you.

Another type of "afterward" information is written feedback from your audience. In your communication classroom, your instructor might assign certain members of your audience to write feedback. When you speak to outside groups, a feedback form is often distributed to attendees. When you receive written feedback, read it carefully to identify areas the audience viewed positively so you can reinforce these areas in the future. You will also want to identify those general areas the audience felt might be changed in some way and consider whether you can incorporate those suggested changes into your next presentation.

● GETTING TO WORK

This audience analysis planning sheet (Figure 6.5) will help you to centralize all of the information you know about your audience that is important regarding the topic of one speech. As you work through the planning sheet, you will soon notice that you are inserting pieces of information in more than one location on the planning sheet. Although we can't say this unequivocally, the information you find yourself repeating might be important to you in developing your speech. We urge you to carefully consider whether this is the case.

Notice also that, ideally, the information you could know about your audience is rather extensive. Make it your business to gather as much as you possibly can. It will be to your advantage to begin gathering information about your classroom audience at the very first class meeting. Perhaps you are an observant individual and you have already done that, and you have an initial, if vague, impression of your classmates. If not, begin to observe your communication classmates today. Be mindful, empathetic, and flexible, not only to learn more about diverse members but to learn more about everyone. You can practice these skills with any group you belong to, and the resulting information will help you in presentations you give to those groups, too.

● **FIGURE 6.5** Audience Analysis Planning Sheet.

1. My speech topic is:

2. These audience demographics are relevant to my topic:

   a.

   b.

   c.

   d.

   e.

3. My audience has these qualities of "captive" versus "voluntary" in relation to my topic:

	Captive audience	Voluntary audience
Disposition to my topic	_____	_____
Knowledge about my topic	_____	_____
Emerging demographics	_____	_____

4. Regarding my topic, my audience already knows:

   My audience is interested in my topic because:

5. Regarding my topic, my listeners' attitudes, beliefs, and values are:

   Values:

   Beliefs:

   Attitudes:

6. My audience's cultural composition is:

   Given my analysis:

1. I will attract the attention of my audience by:

2. I will involve my audience through:

3. I will provide opportunities for my audience to process my information by integrating these activities at relevant points in my speech:

4. I will show my audience my topic is relevant to them by:

When you plan to discuss a topic with your communication class and you aren't sure how to develop the presentation, you will need to resort to other methods of gathering the information we have discussed. On the basis of what you do know from your observations, what can you deduce that will be helpful to you? Will your instructor allow you to ask your audience a question or two or will you need to construct a survey?

If you have the opportunity to speak to an audience you are unfamiliar with, you will need to be more deliberate in learning about them. First, if you are invited to make a presentation to an unfamiliar group, get as much information about them as you can from the contact person who invited you. What are their relevant demographic characteristics that will help you construct your presentation? What is the group's purpose? Why have they invited you to speak? How does your area of expertise relate to their group or organization? These are some of the questions you should ask the contact person. See Act and Reflect 6.7.

Consider whether you need to make arrangements to receive feedback. If you do not automatically receive either written or oral feedback, after your presentation, request it. If you have questions about various aspects of your presentation, ask your listeners.

ACT&REFLECT

6.7: Analyze This!

ACT • For your next presentation, draft a plan of action for acquiring information about your audience before, during, and after your presentation. To facilitate this plan, complete the audience demographic profile before you speak; mark your notes at the points when you want to be sure to observe your audience's reactions to your commentary; afterward, schedule time to review the audience questions and to reflect on the total experience. In addition, consider interviewing individuals who were in your audience about how they think things went during your presentation.

REFLECT • What does the information you gained and the feedback you received tell you about areas of your presentation that worked well and areas in which you will want to make changes next time? How will you use this information for your next presentation?

SUMMARY

Audience members differ from each other but also share similar characteristics. If you have a good sense of the characteristics of your audience and the ways its members differ from each other and are similar, you are in a position to "tailor your speech" to fit their characteristics.

Before a presentation, you can gather information in a planned manner, through observations, questions, and surveys. You should assume that you are on an information-gathering mission with your audience. Simply observing what members of your audience do and say, as well as the way they present their own speeches, is an excellent way to learn about the audience. If there is a specific piece of information you need to know about your audience, ask. If you have several questions, or if they are questions that require more than a yes or no response, or if there are questions of a sensitive nature you need to ask, consider constructing a survey. Your survey might be in hard copy format distributed during a class OR group meeting, or you might do a survey via e-mail. Use the information you gather from your audience to draw conclusions about those areas for which you do not have information. When you deduce information about your audience, proceed carefully in drawing your conclusions.

The major similarity you will discover in your audience is the ways listeners' minds process knowledge. In order to ensure that your message will "get through" to the audience, make an impression on them, and influence their thoughts and actions, there are four actions you can take. Initially, you must attract their attention; next, you must find some way to personally involve them; third, provide them with opportunities to process your information; finally, make sure your speech has made clear to your listeners how the information you are giving them makes sense in the context of their knowledge.

In many other ways, your listeners will differ from each other. Although they may share some demographic characteristics, they may differ in regard to others. If they are attending your presentation voluntarily, you may assume they feel more positive about you or your presentation, may be more knowledgeable about you or your topic, and may share more demographic characteristics than if they were a captive attendance. Knowing the attitudes, beliefs, and values of your listeners will assist you in identifying support material for your presentation that will help you meet your communication goal. A sensitivity to the cultures represented in your audience will enable you to make good decisions about your content and delivery.

During your presentation, the members of your audience are constantly giving you information about themselves through their nonverbal behaviors and the questions they ask. You can take advantage of that information and make "on the spot" modifications in your presentation. After your presentation, you may have access to written or oral feedback. Take some time to reflect on all of the information your listeners have given you about themselves and their responses to your presentation. Don't overlook the value of this feedback in planning your next presentation.

VIDEO EXPERIENCE

MSL

In the clips for this experience, Katelyn speaks to a negative audience about the benefits of home schooling, and Jessica, also speaking to a negative audience, compares gay marriage with traditional marriage.[8] Earlier in this chapter you had an opportunity to read the surveys Katelyn and Jessica gave to their audiences in preparation for their speeches. As you watch each speech, notice how the speakers demonstrate to their audiences that they are knowledgeable about the audience views of their topics. How do they use their knowledge of their audiences' opinions on their topics to develop speeches that support their own viewpoints?

THINKING BACK, THINKING AHEAD

1. Using the demographic audience profile exercise at the beginning of this chapter, prepare a profile of your communication class and a profile of another group of which you are a member. Assume you are going to speak to both groups on the same topic. Select a topic from the brainstorming list you began in Chapter 2. How would you go about planning a presentation on the topic you selected for the two different audiences?

2. Continue to consider your two audiences from the previous exercise. How are the audiences similar and different in their motivations for attending your presentation? What would be the knowledge and interest of each audience regarding your presentation? Their attitudes, beliefs, and values? Their cultural composition? In each instance, how would you adjust your presentation to make it relevant to each audience? How do the resulting two speeches differ? In what ways are they similar?

3. Continuing to consider the two audiences you worked with in exercises 1 and 2, how will you initially attract the attention of each audience? How will you personally involve each audience and provide opportunities for them to process your information? Why is your topic relevant to each audience? How will you demonstrate its relevance? As you modify your two speeches to answer these questions, do you find the modifications you make for each speech are similar or different when compared?

4. How aware are you of other speakers' attempts to tailor messages with the specificities of their audiences in mind? Listen to speakers and identify strategies they use to focus on their specific listeners. Identify strategies you could adopt for your own use.

5. With whom do you communicate on a regular basis? Each time you interact with these persons, identify what you have learned about them. Set a goal to use that information in some way the next time you interact. What are the results?

NOTES

1. A. Neuharth, "Plain Talk," *USA Today,* November 23, 2002.
2. D. A. Sousa, *How the Brain Learns* (Reston, VA: National Association of Secondary School Principals, 1995), 10.
3. D. Goleman, *Emotional Intelligence* (New York: Bantam Books, 1995), 4.
4. Sousa, *How the Brain Learns,* 12.
5. M. Rokeach, *The Nature of Human Values* (New York: Free Press, 1973).
6. M. Lustig and J. Koester, *Intercultural Competence: Interpersonal Communication across Cultures,* 3rd ed. (New York: Longman, 1999), 30.
7. W. Gudykunst, *Bridging Differences: Effective Intergroup Communication,* 2nd ed. (Thousand Oaks, CA: Sage, 1994).
8. Katelyn Ver Hoef, speech to a negative audience, November 10, 2004. Jessica Culhane, speech to a negative audience, November 10, 2004.

Chapter

7

Researching and Outlining Skills

Goals

 To understand and implement various strategies for researching a topic

 To successfully use the full complement of library resources for researching a topic

 To locate and critically evaluate information retrieved via the Internet

To understand and apply the basic principles underlying information-getting interviews

To write coherent and complete full-sentence and key-word outlines

To convert outlines to effective speaking notes

To learn and apply strategies for conveying presentational structure to listeners

You notice in the papers from your hometown that the school board is meeting to deal with budget short-falls, and among the areas for potential cuts is the music program in the elementary schools. You decide this would be a good topic to present to the class: trying to arouse student support for music education. You know that you enjoyed your band and chorus experiences and believe they helped you develop discipline, self-confidence, and a lifelong love of music. You also know that simply talking about your own experiences probably won't be enough to motivate other students to support music education. You realize you need evidence that shows music programs make a valuable contribution to students such as yourself, but you don't know if such evidence exists.

Where do you go to find information about the value of music education in elementary schools? How do you go about searching for relevant and credible support for your topic? This chapter covers strategies for finding potential sources and information. After you find evidence and support, you will then need to create an outline that adequately reflects the structure of your speech—an outline that reflects your organizational and strategic decisions. Finally, you will need to convert your research and outline into a set of speaking notes that allows you to maintain a conversational, extemporaneous presentational style. ●

Researching the Issue

In Chapter 2 we discussed using your expertise, experience, and commitment to help you choose a topic. Your expertise, your experience, the audience's knowledge, and the situation determine the type and amount of information you should include in your presentation. Most presentations require some degree of research, even if you are an expert. Some of the information you discover is incorporated into your presentation, but some simply increases your expertise and prepares you to knowledgeably answer audience questions. The type of research you conduct depends on the nature of your presentation. For workplace presentations, your research is likely to include analyses of data, reviews of reports, and personal discussions with colleagues or experts. For class presentations, you might collect information from books, journals, newspapers, magazines, and the Internet, and by directly interviewing experts. Certain principles for researching a topic are applicable to both presentations.

Work out a plan to "navigate" your way through the research process. ●

Computers play dual roles when it comes to the research process: as a tool for conducting the search, and as a source of actual information. As a tool, you can use the computer to search bibliographic repositories, such as library catalogs for books or electronic indexes and abstracts for articles. As a source for information, you can access articles, opinions, data, and other information that is posted directly on websites, usually by searching the Internet. This section focuses on using the computer as a tool for conducting your search; the Internet, as a source, is covered later. All research material should be evaluated for its credibility, relevance, and reliability (these are discussed specifically in the next chapter on support materials).

Using the Research Process to Identify and Refine the Topic

The focus of many everyday presentations is often dictated by the situation and your role: for example, giving a weekly project update to your boss, making a proposal for changing a company policy, or addressing the local school board about impending cuts. In some ways, those situations are easier to prepare for than times when you are empowered to decide the topic. The very process of researching topics can help you decide which topic to address, as well as what aspects of it to emphasize. As you search for supportive materials, some topics might be devoid of significant support materials, making it difficult to develop an effective presentation. At other times, the research process results in learning new things about a topic, leading to a reconsideration of your focus or approach. The availability of support for various aspects of a topic inherently influences the direction and structure of your final presentation.

Synonym Topic List

Suppose you wanted to give a presentation to your classmates on how best to end a personal relationship. Looking up "ending relationships" on the Internet or a library database generates a lot of irrelevant results dealing with such things as ending a marketing relationship, ending international contracts, and so on. Adding "personal" to the search narrows down the list, but still includes lots of topics that might not be relevant, such as ending abusive relationships or divorce. Before you even begin searching for support, you should develop a list of synonyms for your topic. Instead of entering the term "ending," use terms like "deescalation," "termination," "dissolution," and "disengagement," combined with "relationship" or "relational," "strategy," "strategies," "options," or "methods." The right combination of key words will help you locate the most germane support (see Act and Reflect 7.1). Use a thesaurus to help find synonyms or examine the first articles you find to see what other terms are used by the authors of those articles. Generating this list often involves some good language skills, creativity, and dumb luck. Don't get discouraged if you can't find support or find too much. Either situation can usually be resolved by using alternative terms, more detailed terms, or one of the other methods covered in this chapter.

ACT&REFLECT

7.1: Generating Synonyms

ACT • For the following key terms that might be part of a presentation you are researching, try to generate as many synonyms as you can. See what you can do on your own first before using a thesaurus.

Topic Concept	Synonyms
Volunteering	
Relationship problems	
Censorship	
_____ (your next topic)	

REFLECT • How easy was it for you to generate synonyms? What could you do to help you generate more? In what ways might the synonyms change the focus of each of the possible presentations?

Convergence and Divergence

The presentation research process resembles an old-fashioned hourglass, starting out broadly, capturing as many pieces of supportive material as you can find, then narrowing to the specific focus, then broadening again as you look for research on that specific focus (see Figure 7.1). You will find a lot of information on ending personal relationships in your initial, diverging broad search, and as you review it, you will start weeding out the irrelevant, illegitimate, or tangential information. This broad spectrum of information also helps you gain a better sense of the direction to pursue in your presentation. As a result of this screening process, you converge to a narrow and refined focus; next you search specifically for information related to this more narrow and defined focus. As you search this focus, you find more and more evidence and support, resulting in an expansion of the points to be covered in the presentation; thus your research diverges again. Divergence occurs concurrently with your selection of strategies and development of a presentational organization. As you begin to put the pieces of evidence in place, you will discover areas for which you might be missing support, which will necessitate targeted searches.

Targeted Searches

One of the more challenging and sometimes frustrating aspects of presentational research occurs when you are seeking one specific piece of information to support a point you wish to make. Unfortunately, the discovery of this need usually comes toward the end of your preparation as you put all the final pieces together. One solution is to avoid the issue so you don't need the information, but choosing that option usually means you have compromised the strength of your presentation. In work situations, such a choice is often unwise, because inevitably someone will request that information, and your failure to have it can undermine your credibility. Sometimes the piece of information is readily accessible, for example, if you wanted to find out the current population of the United States or South Dakota. However, finding out the number of people in the United States or South Dakota with master's degrees is more challenging. Finding the number of people in the United States or South Dakota with master's degrees from 1953 is even harder. All this information exists, but accessing it requires time and sometimes expense (you might have to fly to Pierre, South Dakota, to search the state library).

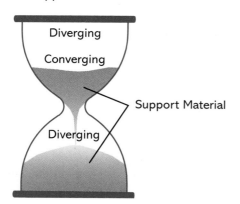

● **FIGURE 7.1** Convergence and Divergence of Support Material.

Snowballing

Articles usually include the sources on which they are based. Those references can be valuable sources of support for your presentation, even if the original article is not. You should peruse the first articles you find, looking for content that addresses issues of interest, and then review the sources used in those sections. In reviewing the second source, you might find additional sources of interest, thus producing a **snowball effect.** One problem in following up sources within sources is that after each iteration, the information is more and more dated. However, you can do a **reverse search,** wherein you use the older source to track down more contemporary articles. Here's an example of use of snowballing and a reverse search using Google™.

> **Topic and first search phrase:** "The Value of Music Education in Elementary Schools"
>
> **Found:** A statement of principles for the National Association for Music Education, which includes a reference to a study in *Neurological Research,* February 1997, that found increased temporal-spatial ability in students who received keyboard instruction.
>
> **Follow-up search:** "Neurological Research, February 1997"
>
> **Found:** The research was done by Drs. Frances Rauscher and Gordon Shaw.
>
> **Reverse search:** "Frances Rauscher"
>
> **Found:** A 2003 article by Dr. Frances Rauscher, available online from the Education Resource Clearinghouse (ERIC), which summarizes numerous studies showing the value of music education.

Boolean Logic

Many of the search tools available through your library or on the Internet utilize what is called Boolean logic to aid in the search process. Boolean logic is primarily concerned with defining "shared" space between and among concepts or terms. You have three stacks of articles in front of you; one is a stack of articles in which the word "value" appears, another has articles where "elementary schools" is mentioned, and the third has articles with "music education" in them. Some of the same articles might actually appear in two or three of the piles. These articles that occur in two or three of the stacks are likely to be the most relevant to your presentation. The three stacks of articles and how they might overlap can be visualized in Figure 7.2 on page 172 (this is called a Venn diagram).

Space A reflects any articles that are in both the "value" stack AND the "elementary schools" stack but NOT the "music education" stack. Space B reflects articles found in all three; space C those in both "value" and "music education," and space D those in both "elementary schools" and "music education." These shared and excluded spaces are found by using what are called **operators:** "AND" or plus (+) and "NOT" or minus (−). Some search engines automatically assume there is "AND" between any words you list together but won't necessarily search for the terms as a phrase. An exact phrase needs to be put in quotation marks if you want

snowball effect Research technique in which you use articles that address your issues of interest to find additional sources.

reverse search Research technique wherein you use an older source to track down more contemporary articles.

operators Symbols used to limit and define a Boolean Internet search.

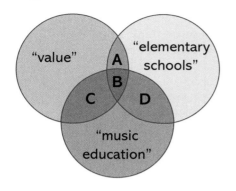

● **FIGURE 7.2** A Venn Diagram
Illustrating Boolean Logic.

to search for it as a unit. Thus, if you type *value of music education in elementary schools* it treats this as "value" AND "music" AND "education" AND "elementary" AND "schools"; however, if you enter "value of music education in elementary schools" (note the quotation marks around the phrase), it will show only those sites where that exact phrase appears. Sometimes a library or Internet search engine may have variations or additions to the ways you can apply Boolean logic, so do a quick review of their help page.

Table 7.1 shows how the use of various combinations of terms and operators results in a narrowing of the search results.

The overlap of the three terms results in over twenty-four thousand hits, which is too many pages to individually check. To help narrow the list further, you can combine the terms into other logical phrases; for example, using the phrases "value of music education" AND "elementary school" results in 161 hits. However, using all the terms as one phrase "value of music education in elementary schools" results in no sites; the phrase was too specific.

Adding other terms of interest to create more complex Boolean arguments is another strategy you can employ. Adding "child development" to the other three base search terms produced 646 hits. You can also use the "not" (−) to eliminate some unwanted results. Adding "− community" (not community) to the list of three terms reduces the hits to 684; however, there is a risk of eliminating relevant pages for which the appearance of the term "community" is unrelated to your topic. Remember that any Boolean-based search is dependent on the words and phrases you enter; thus, your ability to incorporate appropriate synonyms may determine the success of your searches. See Act and Reflect 7.2.

● **TABLE 7.1** Applying Boolean Logic. *Source:* www.google.com, July 25, 2005.

Terms and operators	Google hits	Location on Figure 7.2
Value	272,000,000	Value circle
"Elementary school" (entered as a phrase)	12,100,000	School circle
"Music education" (entered as a phrase)	1,810,000	Music education circle
Value AND "elementary school"	904,000	A & B
Value AND "music education"	183,000	B & C
"Music education" AND "elementary school"	94,700	B & D
Value AND "music education" AND "elementary school"	24,700	B

ACT&REFLECT

7.2: Applying Boolean Logic

A C T • Identify three different concepts that might be part of your next presentation that you can use in conducting a Google search. For example, if you wanted to talk about how important communication skills are in the workplace, you might enter such terms as "employment," "interpersonal communication skills," and "written communication skills." Use Google to conduct a search, going through each of the following steps.

1. Begin with each term or phrase individually (put phrases in quotation marks to specify the whole phrase).

2. Search by pairs of the terms (this produces three different searches).

3. Search using all three terms.

4. Combine all three in a phrase or sentence within quotation marks, for example, "Value of interpersonal communication skills and written communication skills for employment."

5. Enter the phrase or sentence you wrote in step 4 but without quotation marks.

6. Finally, enter two of the terms, then put a negative sign (hyphen) in front of the third term or phrase (to exclude it from the search). For example: employment and interpersonal skills–written communication skills.

R E F L E C T • Which concepts or phrases produced the largest number of hits? How many hits did all three terms produce? If it was too large, how might you narrow the results? What happened with the full sentence entry? How can you improve your success at finding specific and relevant results?

Using the Library

So far, we've been discussing strategies for finding information; now we will focus on the specific sources of that information. You are probably already experienced at finding information in the library, so for most readers this will be just a quick review. The primary information accessed in libraries is found in books, journals and magazines, newspapers, and documents and artifacts. Of these, books are the most challenging sources to research because they contain so much information, with much of it buried within pages and pages of text. Google's Book Search is attempting to overcome this challenge.

Books

Finding books that touch on your general topic of interest may not be difficult, but after finding them, you must review the table of contents, search the index, skim them, or actually read them in an attempt to find specific information relevant to your topic. The general search strategies discussed earlier can help direct you to a relevant book rather then depending on a shot-in-the-dark technique. As you continue to develop your own personal and professional areas of expertise, you are likely to acquire a library of both professional and personal books that will often act as a source of support materials for your presentations. See Act and Reflect 7.3.

The use of library search engines is an effective way to locate relevant books (even Google searches can turn up relevant bibliographies of books). Another way to locate potential books is to apply the snowballing effect— seek out and examine books mentioned in the first articles or books you have located. The discussion in these primary sources provides enough information on which to assess the relevance of these secondary/follow-up sources. If the authors in your primary source quote from the secondary source, the referenced page numbers accompanying the quotation provide a starting point for perusing the secondary/follow-up source. After reviewing the quoted pages, you can review the contents and index to determine the overall relevance of the secondary/ follow-up source to your presentation.

Students who rely exclusively on the Internet as their research source might overlook other information sources. ●

Journals, Magazines, and Newspapers

Journals are usually created by professional organizations for dissemination of information relevant to a select audience. Some journals, such as the *New England Journal of Medicine, Science, Nature, Psychological Bulletin,* and *Journal of Economic Literature,* include refereed articles (those evaluated by several expert reviewers rather than being commissioned by the editor) that report the results of research. Trade journals, such as *Advertising Age, Aviation Week and Space Technology, Computer World, Restaurant Business,* and *Variety,* typically have more anecdotal reports from professionals about their experiences or opinions. Popular magazines such as *Time, Newsweek, Better Homes and Gardens, Ebony, Rolling Stone,* and *Sports Illustrated,* are typically published for profit and are aimed at larger audiences (though innumerable specialty magazines exist that target a specific set of readers). Popular magazines usually pay authors to write articles that can range from news reports to creative writing. You need to be familiar with the editorial policy and intent of any magazine you use for support. Some magazines are biased and advocate a particular position, which might undermine their credibility. Even traditional news magazines like *Time* or *U.S. News and World Report* are often attacked by critics as having a biased political agenda. Newspapers typically provide the most current and up-to-date infor-

ACT&REFLECT

7.3: Finding Books

ACT • Choose two potential topics for a presentation and access your library's catalog. Enter some keywords and see how many relevant books you can locate. Play around with variations (synonym method) in the terms you enter and see how this affects your search. Get the most promising books from the shelves in the library and determine their usefulness.

REFLECT • What factors lead to the most successful sources? How helpful do you think the books you identified would be to your presentation? Why?

mation, but sometimes the information is not as complete as you might need. National newspapers, such as the *Wall Street Journal* and the *Christian Science Monitor,* and other major newspapers like the *New York Times,* the *Washington Post,* and the *Los Angeles Times,* provide very extensive articles on a variety of issues. Regional and local papers are good sources for community-based issues. Besides daily news, newspapers often include personal interest stories or other articles that might prove to be beneficial sources of support. The topic you are researching dictates whether journals, magazines, or newspapers will serve you best.

The computer age has revolutionized the methods of locating and reading journal and magazine articles. This has both an upside and a downside. On the upside, you usually can do the search from the comfort of your own room without going to the library. In addition, the full text of the articles is often available directly online. When the full text is not online, you will need to locate the journal in your library and either make notes about the article or make a photocopy for future reference. If your library doesn't carry that particular journal, you should enquire about interlibrary loans or check other libraries in your area. The downside of the computer searches is that, depending on how you conduct the search, you are likely to be overwhelmed with information, most of which is irrelevant to your research topic.

The availability of various academic search engines varies from school to school, since they require a subscription, so some of the specific indexes and abstracts discussed here might not be available to you. Your librarians should be able to help you find alternatives if necessary. The procedures discussed here will apply to most citation indexes and abstracts (see Act and Reflect 7.4). Many journals are abstracted according to disciplines; for example:

For psychology: *PsychINFO*
For sociology: *Sociological Abstracts*
For engineering: *CSA Engineering Research Database*

For business: *Business and Industry Database*

For agriculture: *AGRIS*

For education: *ERIC*

For general science: *Web of Science*

Access to trade journals and magazines can be found using

Business and Company ASAP

Expanded Academic ASAP

FirstSearch

Masterfile Premier

Lexis-Nexis Academic

Reader's Guide

Lexis-Nexis and *Newspaper Abstracts* provide searching and article recovery from a large number of newspapers.

Each of these electronic indexes and abstracts has different page setups and search parameters. Almost all have the capacity to search for specific key words or phrases. Some can be narrowed to specific time frames and or specific journals and newspapers. An important method to use with all of these search engines is the application of a variety of key words (the synonym method) to generate various lists. Be careful about which elements you use. Some have "topic" searches, which are different than "key-word" searches. The topic search will typically require the use of a select topic term (usually available by clicking the appropriate button). The key-word search allows for a more targeted search. Some search engines offer the choice of quick searches, which require the least amount of specificity on your part, while advanced searches allow you to control date, journal title, category, and so on.

Guidelines for Searching

1. Determine which index or abstract will be the best source for articles related to your topic.

2. Access the index or abstract and examine the available search options.

3. Enter the most complete key-word phrase you can.

   a. Remove some words if the results were too limited or empty.

   b. Add more words if the results were too large.

4. Peruse the list of articles, examining titles that seem most relevant.

5. Examine the abstracts of the most relevant titles and eliminate the less relevant.

6. Review the full article online, if available, or go to the library to locate and review the articles of interest.

ACT&REFLECT

7.4: Journal Index and Abstract Searches

ACT • Access one of the journal indexes or abstracts available online from your library. (Try *Expanded Academic ASAP/InfoTrac, Masterfile Premier,* or *FirstSearch,* if available.) Enter the same terms and synonyms you used for the book search earlier. Try entering various combinations to see how many articles are identified and how many are relevant. Use the best article you find and do a search using the names of that article's authors. Peruse the articles for other terms you might use in the search process that you might not have considered in your first search. Enter those new terms. Examine the search resource for ways to vary the search—by date, topic, terms, and so on.

REFLECT • To what degree was your search successful? Did you find too many articles or not enough? How relevant were the articles you found? How could you improve the quality of your search? How easy was the search resource you used? How can you go about reviewing the articles without consuming a lot of time?

7 Decide which articles have the most potential use as references in your presentation and copy them.

8 Read the articles and use them to guide the development of the presentation.

9 Identify elements from the articles that will be referenced as support during your presentation.

Librarians

© 1999 Ted Goff

Librarians are specialists in finding information. (That's why many of the degree programs are called Library and Information Science or Information Studies.) Librarians can help you in using the various indexes and search tools available at your school. Typically, the librarians won't do the work for you but will teach you how to use the reference tools. The clearer you are about your topic and what information you would like to find, the more the librarians can help you. However, since the search process may help you clarify your topic, don't let your confusion deter you from asking for help. Librarians are generally trained and experienced at helping patrons work through such uncertainties. If you are in doubt about what type of help your librarians provide, ask.

A Question of **Ethics**

1. You have located information from the Internet that cites another source as the basis for the facts and data. To what degree is it okay to cite the original source (the one not on the Internet) even though you didn't personally read or access that original source?

2. Your research uncovers information that contradicts the position you are advocating. To what degree are you obligated to share this information with your audience?

3. In preparing for a speech in this class, you decide to use a paper you did in high school as the foundation of the speech and simply to use the sources you cited there three years ago. How ethical would your decision be if (a) the instructor gave no specific instructions about the sources for your presentation, (b) the instructor specifically instructed students to go out and collect information using the techniques covered in the text; or (c) the instructor indicated that this was to be an original speech not based on any previous work you have done?

The Internet as a Source of Information

The previous discussion focused on the first role of computers in searching for sources of information. This section focuses on the second role that the computer plays as a source of information (primarily the Internet). A significant problem with the Internet as a source is judging the credibility of the retrieved information. Anyone can create a web page and put whatever information on that page that he or she wishes. You must

Everyday Example

Parody of the Digital Literacy Text

This column gives a tongue-in-cheek perspective on the looming notion that students will be tested in the future for their ability to display "computer literacy" and "information literacy."

Last month, the Educational Testing Service (ETS) rolled out a new test, the Information and Communication Technology Literacy Assessment, which it says is designed to measure students' "ability to use digital technology, communication tools and/or networks appropriately to solve information problems in order to function in

an information society." Some 10,000 college students from as many as three dozen schools around the country are expected to have taken the "pilot" test this spring.

And yet, as the *New York Times* noted in January, "just what is meant by 'information' or even 'technological' literacy remains a hotly debated topic in academic circles, and there is no widespread agreement on whether such skills can be taught, much less measured in a test." Herewith is an attempt at what a true test of digital literacy might look like:

1. You have been assigned a paper on Thomas Jefferson's presidency. What is likely to be the most reliable source of information?
   a. "Hero No More: The Lies of Thomas Jefferson," www.anarchyintheus.org
   b. "President Thomas Jefferson named after elementary school," www.theonion.com
   c. Jefferson Digital Archive, etext.lib.virginia.edu/Jefferson
   d. "The Presidency of Thomas Jefferson: Continuity and Upheaval," www.termpapers4sale.com

2. Please sort the following e-mails, by subject line, into their appropriate folders:
   1. Personal; 2. Junk; 3. Work; 4. Financial
   a. A message from John Kerry
   b. Hello from Mom!
   c. BIG $AVING$ ON PRINTER CARTRIDGE$!!
   d. Savings account_0504

3. Stephen receives an e-mail marked "IMPORTANT" and offering an attachment that will "increase his computer speed." He thinks this may contain a virus. What should he do?
   a. Reply to the sender, asking for more information about the offered systems upgrade
   b. Open the attachment, and see what it does to his hard drive
   c. Delete the e-mail
   d. Forward the e-mail to a friend, ask them to open the attachment, and see what it does to their hard drive

4. Jeanne downloads the new Arcade Fire album from an unauthorized fan site for $12.00. Which of the following is true:
   a. Jeanne paid too much.
   b. Jeanne violated the Copyright Law of the United States.
   c. Jeanne enjoys '80s-inflected emo/post-punk.
   d. All of the above.

5. Blogs are to Thomas Paine as
   a. Wikipedia.org is to the Library of Alexandria
   b. E-greeting cards are to Elizabeth Barrett Browning
   c. E-mail is to the Pony Express
   d. iTunes is to a wandering bard

6. While reviewing pirated video clips of yet-to-be-released movies, you receive an instant message that reads: "ht. yt? im j/c. uhoh MoS. bbl8r!" Choose the correct translation:
   a. "Policy makers in Washington, including Paul Wolfowitz, are greatly influenced by the writings of Leo Strauss."
   b. "Hi there. Where are you? I'm just chillin'. Uh oh, my mother is over my shoulder. I will be back later!"
   c. "Hello youth, I am Jesus Christ. Uh oh, it's Moses. Be back later!"
   d. "Hit the yeti, it may be John Cheever. Underhand overhand moshpit. Basketball obliterator!"

7. Brett receives an e-mail with the message "Lonely housewives want to meet local men." The message also includes a Web link. This message is:
   a. A cry for help from lonely housewives
   b. Publicizing a sociological study of deteriorating family structures
   c. A porn site solicitation
   d. A John Updike story collection

8. Computer literacy will be essential for many careers in the twenty-first century. The following represents a task many college graduates will likely be required to perform on the job. Please identify the hamburger:
   a.
   b.
   c.
   d.

Source: Nick Poppy, "Digital Literacy Test," *Boston Globe,* March 20, 2005, p. D5.

determine the legitimacy of the source and information. The domain name, particularly the top-level domain (TLD: the three letters after the "dot"), is one way of determining the credibility of a document. Web sites with the domains ".gov," for government sites, ".edu," for educational sites (when institutionally sponsored), and ".org," for organizational sites, should be credible. To judge the credibility of the information on the Internet, you generally have to research the research!

In our earlier example of searching for support on music education for children, we found an article attributed to a Diane C. Persellin, located at a Web site maintained by the International Foundation for Music Research. Is this a valid and legitimate source? In examining the web page, we see that the very end of the article provides information about the author, indicating she is a professor at Trinity University. Searching Trinity's home page reveals that Diane Persellin is a professor in music education. A closer look at the Web site sponsor also seems to indicate that it is a legitimate organization that publishes music research. Therefore, we are confident the results of this site are credible and can be used as presentational support. On the other hand, a number of statements can be found on the Internet that we probably should not use, including personal blogs, comments on bulletin boards, or other nonexpert postings. One source we found online for this topic was a letter to the editor from a nine-year-old girl in Holbrook, Massachusetts, proclaiming her support for the music program in her school. Would this be a good source? While lacking expertise, her perspective could have some emotional impact on the audience. Whatever sources you incorporate in your presentation, you will need to provide enough information so the audience can judge the source's credibility for themselves. (As an audience member, you should listen for such evidence.)

You can apply the various search strategies covered earlier in this chapter in searching the Internet. In addition, you should use the questions listed in Chapter 8 for assessing the validity, reliability, credibility, and relevance of information. Look for other cues as to the legitimacy of the site, such as the presence of e-mail addresses for contacting people involved with the site or the date when the page was last updated (many pages are out of date but are still posted). Be careful about secondary sources (someone posting information attributed to another source). Whenever possible, you should locate and quote from the primary source.

Here's a list of some of the search engines you might try:

Google	www.google.com
MSN search	search.msn.com
Yahoo	www.search.yahoo.com or www.yahoo.com
About.com	www.about.com
Ask.com	www.ask.com
Hotbot	www.hotbot.com
Metacrawler	www.metacrawler.com (searches other search engines)
Infomine	infomine.ucr.edu (academic sources for college students)

The personal interview is often an effective way to collect important information. ●

Interviewing

Looking for information on the Internet in the comfort of your own home or by wandering around the library is pretty stress free when compared to the prospect of having to actually talk to someone to gain information. Most of us would be a bit uncomfortable calling the music department on our campus and talking to a faculty member who specializes in music education. Nonetheless, interviews can be a valuable asset in the preparation of a presentation. An interview can provide firsthand expert testimony for use in your presentation; in addition, the interviewee might provide leads to other sources of information. For example, during an interview with a music professor, she tells you that more and more elementary schools are cutting back on their music programs because of budget cuts, and this is going to have a dramatic impact on the learning skills of children. Her comments can be used either as direct quotations or in a paraphrased format to support your presentation. When referring to your interview, you need to provide background about the source to the audience and how you collected the information. Besides specific comments gained in the interview, the professor tells you of a good book on the topic as well as the references for two recent research articles—thus providing you with leads for additional support.

Interviewing is a formal process of collecting information from a source. Interviews are usually best when conducted face to face but may also be done over the telephone or even through e-mail. Sometimes your interviews take the form of informal conversations with people within an organization. These might involve a quick phone call to ask a specific question, or more extended conversations about a given topic. Regardless of the formality, it is important to ask people's permission to cite them and the information they have shared. For example, "Thanks for the information on company turnover. Is it okay if I use this information and cite you as its source in my upcoming presentation?" Formal interviews usually involve requesting appointments with the interviewees while explaining the reason you'd like to speak with them. The following are some of the key guidelines for conducting a formal information-gaining interview:

1. Determine who has the information you need and arrange for the interview.
2. Establish your purpose—what you want from this person.
3. Develop a set of questions in advance, but be flexible as the interview progresses. Use open-ended questions that seek extended responses; they begin with such words as "How," "Why," and "What."
4. Begin the interview by explaining your purpose (tell the interviewee what you're going to do with the information), building rapport, and getting the person's background (so you can establish the person's credibility with the audience).
5. Decide how you are going to record the responses. If possible, use a tape recorder, but you need to ask permission to tape the interview. If you are taking notes during the interview, be as discreet as possible, to avoid distraction or interference with the flow of the interview. Review your notes as soon as possible, so you can fill in any gaps you failed to note at the time. If you wait until after the interview to record what you heard, write out your recollections immediately after the interview to reduce memory loss and errors.
6. As you ask your prepared questions, use follow-up questions to gain more detail and clarification.
7. Ask for any suggestions of sources you should read or people you should contact for additional support or answers to questions the respondents couldn't answer.
8. Paraphrase or summarize what you hear and ask for confirmation from the interviewees to ensure accuracy.
9. Thank the interviewees for their time and responses. Ask permission to call them again if you need any clarification as you prepare the presentation.

Outlining

You've got a topic, you did your research and found support for the points you think you're going to include, you've analyzed your audience, and you have some ideas about how to organize the information (specific organizational strategies are discussed in detail in Chapter 9). Now it's time to develop your presentational outline. While there are some general principles to guide outlining, individual teachers often have preferences for what they'd like their students to produce, so find out if that's the case in your class. This section provides suggestions to help you develop an effective presentation, but we encourage you to develop the approach that works best for you. Outlining is meant to be a tool to improve the quality of what you produce. The process of outlining can help you organize your thoughts, examine and better understand the relationships among your points, determine the most effective order and structure, and deliver a coherent presentation.

Preparing Full-Sentence and Key-Word Outlines

Two typical approaches to outlining are the full-sentence outline, and the key word outline. A **full-sentence outline** is a series of complete sentences that reflect the most significant points you are going to make in your presentation; it also includes statements connecting issues or linking evidence to your claims. Each component of the full-sentence outline is a full, coherent sentence that captures the essence of the point you are making. Developing full-sentence outlines can help you better understand the direction you are taking in your presentation and the value of the various points you are considering. In general, the sentences should be kept as simple as possible, typically including one concept that is being explained or connected to another concept. Full-sentence outlines are most helpful in the initial development of a presentation. Because they can be easily understood by others, they allow you to show the outline to others for their feedback. However, it is not usually a good idea to deliver the presentation from a full-sentence outline because there is a tendency to read your notes—tying your eyes to the notes while ignoring the audience.

A **key-word outline,** on the other hand, contains only key words or phrases designed to trigger your memory—evoking the thoughts you wish to convey to the audience. A key-word outline is difficult for another person to examine and respond to because the terms don't trigger the same thoughts for the reviewer. Key-word outlines are excellent tools for use in delivering presentations because they help you maintain an extemporaneous, conversational, and interactional style with your listeners. You can quickly scan the key words as you are speaking, allowing for continued focus on the audience. See Act and Reflect 7.5 on page 186 for an outline practice.

The general format of your outline includes the introduction, the body, and the conclusion. The two samples illustrate optional ways to structure and format a key-word outline. Version 1 applies strict numbering to each component of the speech. This allows you to see the relationships among the elements easily. Version 2 is a looser application of numbering each component that emphasizes the enumeration of the points in each section of the speech, which reflects what you are likely to be saying—the first major point is Roman numeral I.

Guidelines for Creating the Outline

The two sample key-word outline frameworks reflect a number of guidelines that underlie both full-sentence and key-word outlining as well as creating a strong presentation:

1 Keep the number of major points covered in the presentation to a minimum—two or three may be sufficient.

2 Keep the number of subpoints covered to the minimum. Too many subpoints will lose your audience and undermine the major point.

> **full-sentence outline** A working outline composed of a series of complete sentences that reflect the most significant points you are going to make in your presentation and the related connecting issues and evidence.
>
> **key-word outline** A delivery outline composed of key words or phrases designed to trigger your memory during your presentation.

Sample Full-Sentence Outline

I.   Music education in U.S. elementary, middle, and high schools is threatened.
     A. According to the Music Education Coalition, 28 million students are not receiving adequate music education.
     B. In my hometown, which has 4,500 students, the school board has proposed cutting back from five music teachers to three.
II. There are three significant reasons you should support music education in your hometowns.
     A. The first reason is that music education nurtures thinking.
         1. Research shows that music education improves spatial and abstract reasoning.
         2. There is a "Mozart Effect" in which music education results in improvement of other skill areas, particularly math and science.
             a. Students who had music education scored 57 points higher on their verbal SATs and 41 points higher on their math scores.
             b. Second-grade students who had piano keyboard training scored better on proportional math and fractions than those who did not.
     B. The second reason is that music education nurtures interest in music and the arts.
         1. Introducing music through performance to young children helps develop a lifelong appreciation of music and an ability to enjoy all types of music.
         2. Music education helps students develop an aesthetic sensitivity and appreciate diversity that is reflected in the international spectrum of music styles.
     C. The third reason to support music education is that it nurtures self-esteem.
         1. Music education confirms students' self-value because of their participation in a shared event with other students.
         2. Performing music develops students' pride in their accomplishments and in their observable skill development.
         3. Music education helps students develop creative skills and see themselves as creative.

3 Recognize and maintain the underlying logic and order of your outline to reflect the nature of the relationships among all the components of the presentation.

   a. Make the major points more critical and important than the subpoints.

   b. Select major points that are equivalent in importance.

   c. Coverage of each major point should be as equivalent as possible.

   d. Each subpoint should be of the same relative importance.

   e. Each subpoint should be logically and easily connected to its major point.

4 Organize your major points according to the organizational pattern that has the best strategic advantage.

5 Avoid citing just one subpoint, since that probably means you are just duplicating the major point.

6 Create parallel phrasing and use repeated terminology of major points and subpoints when possible. For example, "The main points I will be discussing today are: one, music education nurtures thinking; two, music education nurtures interest; and three, music education nurtures self-esteem."

Sample Key-Word Outline

Version 1

I. (Introduction) Greeting and acknowledgments
II. (Introduction) Introducing yourself
III. (Introduction) About the topic and reason for listening
IV. (Introduction) Preview of the presentation
V. (Body) First major point
   A. First subpoint
      1. Research support
      2. Quotation
   B. Second subpoint
V. (Body) Second major point
   A. First subpoint
   B. Second subpoint
VI. (Conclusion) Summary
VII. (Conclusion) Request for final action

Sample Key-Word Outline

Version 2

Introduction
   I. Greetings and acknowledgments
   II. Introduction of yourself
   III. The topic and reason for listening
   IV. Preview of the presentation
Body
   I. First major point
      A. First subpoint
         1. Research support
         2. Quotation
      B. Second subpoint
   II. Second major point
      A. First subpoint
      B. Second subpoint
Conclusion
   I. Summary
   II. Request for final action

ACT&REFLECT

7.5: Outline Practice

ACT • The following are a set of key words and phrases that represent the BODY of a presentation. See if you can identify which points are major points and which are subpoints by organizing them to fit the framework provided.

Interpersonal communication skills   Support conflict management

Persuasive writing   Enhance client communication

Strategic organization   Effective writing of memos

Enhance coworker communication   Clear and concise

Support effective listening   Written communication skills

Correct grammar   Communication skills important for jobs

Adaptation to readers' interests

(Hint: The first section provides a rationale for listening—creates a need. The second and third sections explain two major parallel concepts.) Answers can be found on page 192.

Framework:

I.

   A.

   B.

II.

   A.

   B.

III.

   A.

      1.

      2.

   B.

      1.

      2.

REFLECT • To what degree do you feel confident that you have identified the major points? How easily do the subpoints you've selected link to the major point? While some subpoints could be used in more than one place, how did you decide where they fit best? To what degree does your organization flow logically and reflect the various strengths and relationships among the issues?

Sample Key-Word Outline and Resulting Elaboration

Key-Word Outline Excerpt

> III. Music ed. nurtures self-esteem
>
>   A. Discover music skills—pride
>
>   B. Learn discipline, hard work
>
>   C. Develop teamworking skills—my H.S. band experience

Actual Speaker Comments

The third advantage of music education is that it nurtures children's self-esteem. Not every child is athletic, nor is every child musical, but many students are. Allowing children to explore music and discover their musical skills gives them a source for pride and achievement—boosting their self-esteem. Learning to play an instrument takes hard work and dedication, which are important qualities for success in life. Students develop discipline through music and find immediate reward when they play a song well. Finally, self-esteem is enhanced when children feel like they are part of a team. I can remember from my own experience in high school band how proud I felt when we'd play a piece well—the sound we'd create, the emotion, the feeling of accomplishment—especially when we nailed a particularly difficult number.

Converting the Outline to Speaking Notes

In Chapter 4 you read about the different ways of making a presentation: impromptu, memorized, manuscript, and extemporaneous. The impromptu speech might include a few brief notes that are composed on the spur of the moment, but it is the extemporaneous presentation that relies most heavily on speaking notes. Key-word speaking notes are generally the most effective for extemporaneous speeches. Your key-word speaking notes have the same purpose as Post-it notes—to remind you. You should use your speaking notes to provide you with several reminders. Obviously, you want reminders of the major points and subpoints that you have decided are important to share with your audience. You want reminders about the evidence such as statistics, source names, and dates of your sources. In addition, any direct quotations you are giving can be written out in your speaking notes. Speaking notes are a good place to put reminders to yourself about your delivery. For example, you could

● **FIGURE 7.3** Sample Speaking Notes on Cards.

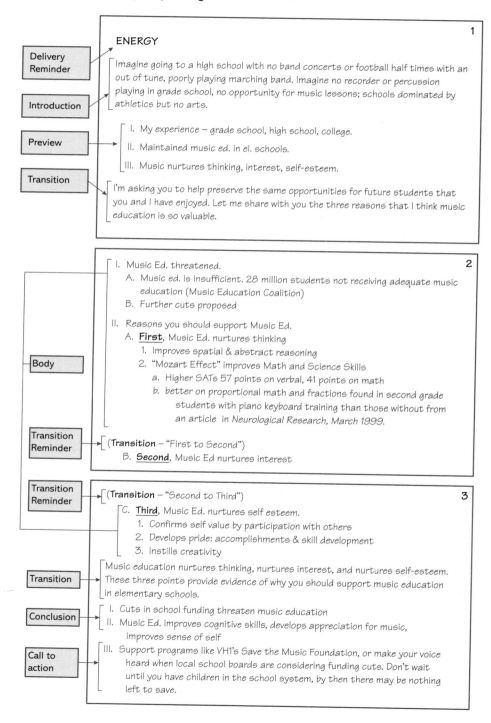

write "ENERGY" on the top of the speaking notes as a reminder to be enthusiastic during the presentation. You might want to include such reminders as "EYE CONTACT," "GET AWAY FROM LECTERN," "HANDS OUT OF POCKETS," "SLOW DOWN," "SPEED UP," or "RELAX AND BREATHE." Usually you want to be sure you see these reminders, so making them large, using a different color of ink, or highlighting them can help.

In developing your key-word speaking notes, write out the words or phrases that work best to remind you of the point you want to make. As you continue developing the presentation in your mind, you will discover that you are able to make complete and coherent statements simply by having the key-words as prompts, as illustrated in the sample excerpt from a key-word outline and a speaker's elaboration from it.

Not everything in your speaking notes will be in the form of key words. As mentioned above, you will want to write out the quotations you use, word for word. Reading quotations from your speaking notes is perfectly acceptable, though you still should maintain as much eye contact with your audience as possible (perhaps looking up midway through the quotation). Reading the quotation helps assure the audience that you are accurately reciting the words of your source. You may also want to write out the most

important parts of the presentation—those that you know need to be conveyed exactly or that you are worried about remembering. Speakers often write out the very first two or three lines of their presentations to help them feel confident that they know how they are going to begin. Getting started on the right foot often makes the rest of the presentation a cakewalk. Other aspects you might write out more completely include the major points and transitions between major parts of the presentations. See Act and Reflect 7.6.

The more you practice with the key-word speaking notes, the more confidence you gain in your ability to generate complete segments of your presentation. Don't try to remember word for word what you say each time you practice, but focus on the core idea. Use the same skills you use in everyday conversations to fill ideas out.

ACT & REFLECT

7.6: Key-Word Speaking Note Practice

ACT • Write down key words about some major point on any topic you know about. Then write key words for three subpoints that elaborate or support the main point. Now (make sure nobody's around) talk out loud about the main point, moving from subpoint to subpoint.

Go back and modify, edit, or add to the subpoints any variation that you discovered was important as you spoke. Now, talk out the points again.

REFLECT • How well were you able to talk about the major point and the three subpoints?

How was the flow and coherence the second time?

To what degree do you talk too much off topic or not elaborate a point adequately?

Enumerating your points helps the audience know where you are in your presentation. ●

Conveying the Presentational Structure to the Audience

You've probably tried to follow a car driven by someone who tended not to use turn signals or used them at the last moment. This might have caused you to miss a turn and lose the other car. In a similar way, your listeners depend on you to signal them when you are making a turn so they don't get lost. Once you have developed an outline, *you* can see how your presentation is organized and will flow; however, the audience can't see this, so you must use various presentational techniques to help convey the organization to them. Ideally, when you are done, the audience would be able to recreate an outline of your presentation that reflects the relationships among your points—which ones are major points, which are subpoints, which are supportive. Sometimes speakers display their outlines to the audience using PowerPoint or overhead projections. We don't recommend this technique, because it takes attention away from the speaker, can undermine effective delivery, and diminishes the importance of what you say. Following are some ways you can help convey the structure, organization, and relationships to your audience.

Use Enumeration Enumeration means numbering your points—"first," "second," "third," and so on, or "one," "two," "three." You can indicate to your audience that you have three major points and then recite the number associated with each as you cover it. The use of enumeration makes it easier for the audience to know where you are in your presentation and to see the relationships among the points. (Plus they know how close you are to being done!) You can also enumerate your subpoints, but you need to be careful about confusing your audience with too much use of enumeration; for example, "The second point of my third major reason for supporting music education is . . ." Usually it's best to use enumeration only for the main points or the subpoints but not both. Instead of enumerating all your points, you can use key words or phrases.

Create Key Words for Main Points and Repeat Them Throughout Key words help the audience grasp your structure by providing an easily recalled hitching post. "Nurtures thinking," "Nurtures interest," "Nurtures self-esteem" are key words that can be repeated many times so your audience will easily recall the phrases and the information associated with each one. You can use these key words first in your introduction, repeat them as you discuss each one, and repeat them in your conclusion. The same approach can be used for subpoints.

Repeat the Main Point When Discussing Each Subpoint Sometimes when you are involved in developing and discussing subpoints, particularly those that may involve lots of supportive material, the audience can forget the point of the discussion. You need to continue to refer to the main point as you discuss the subpoints to help guide the audience through your presentation. Key words are an effective way to reconnect the subpoint to the main point.

Example: "A research study by two music educators, Drs. Rauscher and Shaw, in 1997, found that keyboard instruction related to increased temporal-spatial ability in students, providing support for my first claim that music education nurtures thinking. Another study that shows how music education nurtures thinking was conducted in . . ."

Use Clear and Complete Transitions Make it clear when you are moving from one point to another by making statements to this effect; you need to signal to those following you that you are about to make a turn. Besides warning the audience that you are changing to another point, transitions can connect the point you have just discussed with the point you are about to discuss. Avoid incomplete or inane transitions like "My next point is" or "That was my third point, now here's my fourth." There are lots of variations in what you can use for transitions, for example, a brief summary of the subpoints you just discussed, along with a preview of the next point; a repetition of an ongoing theme you are using; or some logical statement that shows the connection.

Example: "Nurturing thinking and nurturing interest are valuable benefits to music education, but the third and final reason for supporting music education, nurturing self-esteem, might be the most important."

● GETTING TO WORK

Preparing a presentation begins with identifying a topic and developing a plan for finding support materials. Start with an open mind about the final focus your presentation. Let the research process help you refine the topic, determine the issues, and structure your speech. Do some brainstorming on a piece of paper: write down the key concepts or terms related to the topic you are considering. Next, write down as many synonyms for these various terms as you can. You can follow the guidelines we have given for conducting an Internet search, entering the various terms and examining the resulting sites.

Find out what online indexes and abstracts are available through your college or university library. Go to the most appropriate ones and enter the various terms related to your topic. Identify some of the most current, relevant, and credible articles and browse those articles. What kinds of information do they contain? Examine the references in these articles for additional sources. Use the information you accumulate to think further about your topic, refining it and narrowing its focus.

As you learn more about your topic and acquire support materials, play around with various ways you might best organize this information. Begin organizing the information in some systematic way that reflects the way your presentation might progress. Examine the areas for which you have sufficient support and identify the areas where more is needed (converging). Conduct additional research to find information to support these other areas.

The way you create an outline for your presentation may be prescribed by your instructor. If not, you have lots of choices about the best way to create a framework for an effective presentation. We suggest starting with a simple full-sentence outline that includes a statement of your overall speaking goal and major points. This outline should help you in seeing the overall direction and scope of your presentation. Next, add subpoints to flesh out the major points, using either full sentences or key words. As you develop the subpoints, consider where the research material you have located might be included as support. At this point, you should have a pretty good outline of your presentation. Your outline will need to be revised and refined as you learn about and incorporate information covered in the coming chapters on specific forms of support material, organizational choices, introductions, conclusions, and transitions.

Framework:

One Outline Solution to the Outline Practice found on page 186.

I. Communication skills important for jobs
   A. Enhance coworker communication
   B. Enhance client communication

II. Interpersonal communication skills
   A. Support effective listening
   B. Support conflict management

III. Written communication skills
   A. Effective writing of memos
      1. Clear and concise
      2. Correct grammar
   B. Persuasive writing
      1. Strategic organization
      2. Adaptation to readers' interests

SUMMARY

Besides providing materials that can be used to support the points you are making in a presentation, researching a topic can help you refine and define the topic itself. The process of conducting research is highly dependent on the terms and their synonyms used in the search. Initially you start with a wide, divergent set of information and continue to narrow your focus, converging on the particular topic and issues you are going to discuss. At that point, you begin to diverge again as you look for more and more information related to your focus. This second divergence usually entails a targeted search for information to answer a specific question. In the snowballing technique for finding information, you find an initial source of information and then look up the sources listed there for additional support. Searches often involve thinking about how various terms and concepts overlap with one another in a process that uses Boolean logic. You locate supportive material as identified in the overlaps of various terms. Much of this can be done by using computers as search tools.

Research conducted in or through a library will focus primarily on books, journals, magazines, and newspapers. Books can be sources of both specific technical support as well as more inspirational or metaphorical support. You can use various abstracts and indexes to find articles in journals, magazines, and newspapers, and you should familiarize yourself with which ones are available at your library. Librarians are also helpful resources not to be forgotten.

Your computer, besides being the tool for finding sources, can itself be a source. The Internet is an overwhelming source of information—information that must be cautiously and critically evaluated before being utilized in your presentation. Information obtained from the Internet needs to be scrutinized for its credibility.

Interviews are also part of the research process; direct interactions with experts can provide relevant quotations to incorporate in your presentation, as well as direction as to where you might find additional information.

Outlining is a way of sketching out your presentation so that you can look at it and easily see the relationships among the issues you are discussing. Full-sentence outlines use complete sentences to state major points, while key-word outlines use selected words or phrases to jog your memory about the complete idea. Among the principles to follow in creating an outline are keeping the number of major points and subpoints to a minimum (two or three); keeping the points parallel in strength, importance, and style; and using subpoints that are easily connected to the major points. Your outline can be converted to speaking notes by using a combination of key words and full sentences for important parts, such as the beginning and transitions. Speaking notes can also include helpful reminders to yourself about your speaking style. Finally, you need to help your audience understand the structure of your presentation by using such techniques as enumeration, repeating key words, repeating main points while discussing subpoints, and using good transitions.

THINKING BACK, THINKING AHEAD

1. The following activity involves creating a concept or issue genealogy, where one concept begets another concept, which begets another concept, and so on. Use an Internet search engine and enter a two- or three-word phrase associated with a topic you're considering (for example, "interpersonal communication skills"). Examine one of the resulting sites that includes some discussion of your concept. Find another concept or phrase that appears in that discussion related to your first concept (our search found "active listening"). Enter that new phrase in the search engine. Again, review the results for a discussion of the new phrase, and find another phrase to research (we found "conflict resolution"). Enter this third phrase and again review articles for another new term or phrase (we chose "mediator"). Continue this process at least one more time, or see if you can continue until you come full circle and your original phrase or concept is found again. How can you use this process in developing a presentation? What impact would adding other terms at the same time have (applying Boolean logic)?

2. Think of two possible topics you might be interested in presenting. Do a quick search of your library for books on each topic and write down the number found (exclude those that aren't relevant or recent enough). Do a quick search of potential journal articles using one of the indexes available through your library; again, count how many relevant articles there are for each topic. Finally, do a quick search of the Internet for reliable and relevant articles related to your topics. Just look at the first twenty-five results, decide how many of those would actually be useful, and write down that number for each topic. Now, review the results. Which topic seems to have the most support available? Setting aside the issue of quantity, for which topic does there appear to be the best quality of support?

3. Find a transcript of a brief speech (many are available online, or you can visit MySpeechLab page for links). Create a key-word outline based on this speech. How well did it convert to an outline? How easy was it to see the major points and the subpoints? What principles did the speaker follow to help make the outline more visible to the audience? What principles might the speaker have employed that would have improved the visibility of the outline to the audience?

Chapter 8

Supporting Your Presentation

Language, Reasoning, and Argument

Goals

- ✓ To understand the value and components of a good story
- ✓ To develop and incorporate imagery and comparisons
- ✓ To create appropriate illustrations and examples
- ✓ To apply reasoning and argument as support

 magine that the following is an excerpt from a speech given by a student in your class. Be aware of your thoughts and reactions as you read through the transcript.

Making friends isn't easy, and seems to get harder as you get older. In college we have lots of other students around us who are similar, and thus it's easier to start friendships. Having friends is important. Research has shown strong support for the value of friendships to mental and physical health. A noted British social psychologist, Michael Argyle, wrote, and I quote, "Friendship produces strong positive moods, happiness, health and mental health, and prevents loneliness."[1] [The speaker displays the accompanying PowerPoint slide.] ⟶

Developing friendships is ultimately up to each of us. I can remember feeling sorry for myself my first year in college because I didn't have any friends. What did I do about it? I spent most nights in my dorm room by myself, reading, listening to music, playing video games, and watching TV. Guess what? There's no way I had the chance to make friends because I had isolated myself from others. We should all heed the words of Winnie the Pooh, "You can't stay in your corner of the forest waiting for others to come to you. You have to go to them sometimes."

> *"Friendship produces strong positive moods, happiness, health and mental health, and prevents loneliness."*
>
> Michael Argyle, Emeritus Reader in Social Psychology, Oxford University

Do you agree or disagree with the content of this hypothetical speech? Do you believe it? Do you agree with and believe each of the points raised? You probably didn't question the claims if they matched your own experiences and insights. On the other hand, you probably disregarded the claims that lacked sufficient proof or support if you didn't agree with the speaker's position. The speaker's goals and perceived expertise, the audience's disposition, and the nature of the issue under discussion dictate the type and amount of support material required. ●

Support Materials Defined

While this may sound circular, "support material" is any material that supports your speech; but there's more to it than that. In general, **support material** is anything offered by the speaker that expands, enhances, proves, demonstrates, illustrates, justifies, or clarifies an idea or contention to an audience. From the audience's perspective, it's anything that is said that increases the believability, understandability, and/or acceptability of a speaker's position/idea/contention. Another way to think of support material is that it is essentially everything a speaker says about a main point. In the example, the speaker asserts: "Developing friendships is ultimately up to each of us." Everything that is said about that assertion becomes supportive material—the personal story and the quotation from Winnie the Pooh.

Support material can be classified according to its form. The form can be language-based (verbal/words), derivation-based, or visual. The **language form** includes the way messages are crafted—the way words are used to paint mental pictures and create impact through the use of specific phrasings, imagery, examples, illustrations, and stories. The **derivative form** depends on the creation of logical and intermingled ideas that build upon each other and lead to certain claims or conclusions. In the opening example, the speaker indicates that following the assertion of staying in her room there is an obvious, and unspoken conclusion: she wasn't going to make friends. The **visual form** is anything besides the message itself that stimulates audience's interest or aids in the retention of the message, or benefits a presentation in some manner. In essence, visual support material is anything a speaker "shows" the audience as a way of conveying information. The PowerPoint slide in this presentation is a visual form of support material.

Sometimes evidence is presented to help prove the validity of a story or to support an argument. **Evidence** is a particular type of support generally consisting of verifiable information, such as known facts or data. Evidence adds to the credibility and likelihood of acceptance of the other forms of support. Evidence includes documented experiences shared in stories, reliable statistics or testimonies used in arguments, and visual artifacts that audience members see for themselves. Evidence differs from other forms of support in that it is grounded in observable, verifiable, and/or referenced sources. We discuss how to identify and incorporate evidence in presentations in Chapter 9.

support material Anything offered by the speaker that expands, enhances, proves, demonstrates, illustrates, justifies, or clarifies an idea or contention to an audience.

language form of support material The use of words to paint mental pictures and create impact through the use of specific phrasings, imagery, examples, illustrations, and stories.

derivative form of support material The use of logical and intermingled ideas that build upon each other and lead to certain claims or conclusions.

visual form of support material Anything besides the message itself that stimulates an audience's interest or aids in their retention of the message, or benefits a presentation in some manner.

evidence Particular type of support generally consisting of verifiable information, such as known facts or data.

Consider the Audience to Determine the Type of Support Material

How did you react to the story the speaker told about the dorm experience? Generally, the use of stories or emotional imagery is an effective tool to use when speaking to a positive audience.[2] You might have been able to identify with the speaker or recognize such behavior in other people you have known. The story evokes a certain emotional response that aids the speaker in accomplishing her goal. Language can be used in a variety of ways to affect the audience through images and emotion. You must answer a number of questions as you decide what support strategies to use when talking to a positive, neutral, or negative audience.

A positive audience doesn't really need proofs to convince them if they already accept your position; however, they may need information. Sometimes speakers waste time presenting support material and arguing for the merits of some plan or the importance of some issue to an audience that is already on board. During the first years of teaching, one of the authors of this book was teaching a night class in public speaking. Previously this author had been teaching the typical class of eighteen- to nineteen-year-old students, in which he spent the first class period trying to convince them of their need for this required public speaking course. Unfortunately, your humble author failed to adapt to this new audience and started to give the same motivational speech about the importance of public speaking. The average age of this class was about thirty, and all of them were working during the day, many in professional jobs. They literally interrupted your author and asked why this pitch was being made. They had enrolled in the course because their life experiences had convinced them of the need to be able to give effective presentations if they were to move ahead in their careers. They didn't need the motivational presentation—they were a supportive audience ready for new information.

Neutral audiences are responsive to the same types of support material that are used with a positive audience. For example, just as storytelling can be used to engage and inspire the positive audience, storytelling is a useful tool for gaining the interest of the neutral audience. Just as you use referenced material and statistics to further educate a positive audience, you can use such material with unknowledgeable neutral audiences.

Imagine trying to convey information about the earth and constellations without visual support. ●

However, unlike positive audiences, the ambivalent neutral audiences (those with knowledge and interest but no formed attitude) will need to hear material to counter the opposing arguments they have already heard. Therefore, you will need to select specific supportive material to offset the information already known to these audiences.

Negative audiences are critical of opposing views and those who hold them. In addressing negative audiences, one of the first challenges is getting them to listen to you and then to present a message that will have some impact. Negative audiences will be defensive about attacks against their positions, which can prevent any openness to hearing opposing perspectives. Speaking to negative audiences involves establishing credibility, incorporating effective metaphors and stories, using evidence that they will actually evaluate, and presenting arguments that they will actually consider.

Language Forms of Support

One of the most powerful aspects of language is the ability to evoke emotional responses. The way we say things can inspire, disgust, frighten, soothe, energize, calm, provoke, and reassure. Words are the tools that the most effective speakers wield with skill and intelligence. We can take our audience on a magical ride and transport them into scenes reflecting the issues. Stories are one way we can engage the audience and smoothly guide their thoughts in a captivating manner. When the purpose of your presentation is to inspire, then the main type of support you will need is figurative language: imagery, metaphors, examples, and illustrations. Positive audiences are more affected by the emotional images you can create through figurative language than by logical arguments.[3] Figurative language can also be used as a tool for persuading or changing audiences.

Telling a Good Story

Positive and neutral audiences may be looking for inspiration and entertainment. They want to hear a good story. Think about the last good story you heard. Think about a time one of your instructors spent a couple of minutes in class telling you a story you found enjoyable. What was it about the story that you found pleasing? Walter Fisher, a communication scholar, argued for a **narrative paradigm,** which asserts that humans are storytellers who judge stories on the basis of their coherence and fidelity.[4] As you read on, consider whether you judge the stories you hear in these ways. You should develop stories for support that reflect these principles.

Coherence is the way a story hangs together. We judge how well the story flows, whether parts are missing, if it makes any sense. The way the parts of a story fit together and flow is referred to as **structural coherence.** We also judge stories in terms of how well they relate to other stories we've heard; this is called **material coherence. Character-ological coherence** is the degree to which the characters are believable—the degree to which they act consistently with

narrative paradigm Perspective that humans are storytellers that judge stories on their coherence and fidelity.

coherence The way a story hangs together.

structural coherence The way the parts of a story fit together and flow.

material coherence The way a story relates to other stories one has heard.

characterological coherence The degree to which the characters in a story are believable—the way they act consistently with how they have been characterized.

how they have been characterized. You've probably seen "bad" movies in which a wimpy character suddenly becomes instilled with bravery or where a strong female character turns into a screaming maniac when confronted by bad guys. These movies fail to meet the criteria of strong characterological coherence. The people in your stories need to be believable, to act according to the characteristics you have ascribed to them. Since we often tell stories about ourselves, the audience will weigh what you have to tell them against their impression of you, in deciding whether to believe your story.

Fidelity is the consistency of the elements of a story with our own worldviews and observations. We assess the degree to which a story seems to be "true," to accurately reflect reality—though there are times when listeners appreciate novelty, fantasy, and deviance from reality. If someone is presenting a story as "real," we assess its validity.

Audiences respond more to cohesion than fidelity.[5] In considering the use of a story in a speech, carefully and objectively evaluate its coherence and fidelity. Consider the audience's possible responses to your story choices. You might have to provide more explanation and support when your story lacks coherence (has a character who acts against expectation) or lacks fidelity (contradicts held beliefs or known facts).

Good stories also can be effective ways to influence audiences. Some research shows that telling a story can have more influence than presenting statistical evidence.[6] Former president Bill Clinton was famous for his use of stories to illustrate and make his points, as he did in a speech on working women he delivered at the White House on April 10, 1995:

> Then, there are a lot of people who just have circumstances that are down right almost unimaginable. I never will forget the last race I made for governor of my state. I always made a habit of going to a factory in the northern part of Arkansas, because they had the earliest factory gate in the state; everybody had to show up between 4:00 a.m. and 4:45 a.m. Everybody. And I was there at 4:30 a.m. one morning, and a pickup truck pulled up and in this pickup truck with one seat, there was a husband, a wife and three little kids.
>
> And I saw the mother get out and go to work at 4:30 a.m. in the morning. And I asked the father—I went over to the father and I said, how do you deal with this? He said, well, I don't have to be at work until 6:30 a.m. But, he said, my kids can't go to school until 7:30 a.m. or even to day care. So I had to find someone else to take my kids between 6:00 a.m. in the morning when I have to leave and the rest of the time. And we have to get them all up every day so we can drop their mother off, because we can't have anybody coming to our house.
>
> This sounds like an extreme example, but a lot you sitting in this audience have other examples that are just as difficult. This is the fact of life in America today.[7]

So is Clinton's story a good one? It is coherent and flows well, and it probably fits within most people's observations, so it would probably be judged as having fidelity. There is something else about the story that makes it a powerful tool and is one reason stories can be persuasive: it is very humanizing; it puts a face to otherwise cold statistics. In addition, the audience can visualize and perhaps identify with the characters in the story. See Act and Reflect 8.1.

fidelity The consistency of the elements of a story with our own worldviews and observations.

ACT&REFLECT

8.1: Recalling and Analyzing One of Your Stories

ACT • Think about a story from your life that you often tell other people. This can be anything from "How I spent my summer vacation" to "My most embarrassing moment," "A personal catastrophe I've had to work through," "An eventful work experience," and so on. Write down a few brief points that you would typically include.

REFLECT • Is this a good story?

How well does it meet the criteria of structural, material, and characterological coherence?

How well does it meet the criterion of fidelity?

Guidelines for Telling a Good Story

1 Make your story flow; it should progress in a way that can be easily followed.

2 Present detail, but make sure that your primary focus is on the story line.

3 If you present the story as real, make it believable and provide support for the less-believable elements.

4 Explain how you came to know the story (your source or your own experience).

5 Those in the story should act according to their characters.

6 Use stories to which the audience can identify or relate.

7 Keep stories concise.

8 Use stories to support your claims.

9 Make the point of the story clear to your audience.

Figurative Language: Imagery

While good stories have coherence and fidelity, the best stories also utilize the full range of available figurative language devices that give color to otherwise drab presentations. **Imagery** is word images or verbal pictures. The speaker's objective is to form an image in the minds of the audience; an image that evokes emotion, identification, connection, and confirmation (see Act and Reflect 8.2). Besides imagery, other figures of speech speakers use to add color to a presentation include alliteration (two or more successive words starting with the same letter or sound), onomatopoeia (the word sounds like the thing it is describing), hyperbole (use of exaggeration for effect), and irony (saying one thing while meaning the opposite). Our focus will be on the use of imagery, metaphors, similes, illustrations, and examples. As you read the following excerpt from a speech given by the Reverend Jesse Jackson to the 1988 Democratic National Convention, see how his use of figurative language enhances his presentation:

> We've come to Atlanta, the cradle of the old South, the crucible of the new South. Tonight, there is a sense of celebration, because we are moved, fundamentally moved from racial battlegrounds by law, to economic common ground. Tomorrow we will challenge to move to higher ground.

imagery Word images or verbal pictures.

ACT&REFLECT

8.2: Imagery Practice

ACT • Take each of the following situations and describe them using imagery.

1. College life
2. Your worst date or job
3. Your best date or job
4. Friendship
5. Current U.S. foreign policy

6. Your family
7. Celebrating a birthday
8. Rap music
9. A campus issue
10. An issue in the news

REFLECT • Which topics were easiest to describe? Which were most difficult? Why?

Common ground! Think of Jerusalem, the intersection where many trails met. A small village that became the birthplace for three religions—Judaism, Christianity and Islam. Why was this village so blessed? Because it provided a crossroads where different people met, different cultures, different civilizations could meet and find common ground. When people come together, flowers always flourish—the air is rich with the aroma of a new spring.[8]

One group of researchers have argued that words that create pictures in the minds of listeners (imagery) help presentations by increasing attention, comprehension, emotional arousal, and retention/recall.[9] Their research found correlations between charisma and the use of imagery in inaugural presidential addresses. In pivotal presidential speeches, they found both charisma and greatness correlated with the use of imagery. Another study that examined decision making by top managers in two hospitals found that their discussions were filled with imagery.[10] In addition, certain **reigning images** (images associated with a central issue that get adopted by others) were shared among the managers and affected subsequent decision making. With the creation of a dominant image, other people repeat and utilize that image so that it becomes an implicit criterion. For example, in a discussion of how to cover a college's rising deficits, a speaker opposed to raising tuition uses the imagery of "another attempt to bleed students dry." If other speakers adopt the phrase "bleed students dry," tuition raises may indeed be perceived as unfair without further detailed analysis.

reigning images Images associated with a central issue that get adopted by others.

You can use imagery or storytelling to create a mental picture in the minds of your audience. ●

Figurative Language: Comparisons

One way we can create images is by using comparisons—explaining or illustrating one thing by relating it to something else. Comparative figurative language includes **metaphors** (an implied comparison of two things that might otherwise seem unrelated), **similes** (a stated comparison between two things using such language as "like" or "as"), and **analogies** (a comparison of similarities between two things). Here's an example of a famous metaphor:

A house divided against itself cannot stand. I believe this government cannot endure permanently half slave and half free. I do not expect the Union to be dissolved—I do not expect the house to fall—but I do expect it will cease to be divided. It will become all one thing, or all the other. Either the opponents of slavery will arrest the further spread of it, and place it where the public mind shall rest in the belief that it is in the course of ultimate extinction; or its advocates will push it forward till it shall become alike lawful in all the States, old as well as new, North as well as South.[11]

Abraham Lincoln adapted a metaphor from the Bible and used that metaphor as a theme throughout this speech. The metaphor was extremely effective because it was both memorable and applicable to the issues he was discussing. We use comparisons such as metaphors as a way of explaining something new by connecting it to something familiar.[12] A metaphor is presented in the form of "A is B": A is the thing you are discussing, and B is another thing to which you are comparing or equating the original thing. Comparisons provide a transference of information from something the audience already knows, B, to your issue, A, in a manner that is thought provoking, stimulating, and memorable. Comparisons such as metaphors are intrinsically appealing to humans because they make information more accessible. Some scholars even believe that humans primarily think in terms of metaphors.[13]

Metaphors can create themes that organize information and make the information manageable, thus increasing the persuasive impact of the information on the audience.[14]

One review of research concluded that it is best to use a single metaphor, to place the metaphor toward the beginning of the presentation, and to extend the metaphor (use it as a basis for several different points).[15] Lincoln's speech did exactly this.

To be effective, speakers must select comparisons that tap into a base of knowledge possessed by the speakers. To

metaphor An implied comparison of two things that might otherwise seem unrelated.

simile A stated comparison between two things using such language as "like" or "as."

analogy A comparison of similarities between two things.

say "Studying for final exams requires cramming so much garbage into your brain that it oozes from your ears" will have the most impact with those who can readily identify and understand the nature of cramming for finals. Advertisers frequently utilize comparisons in attempting to tap into existing audience knowledge to explain their products. One famous campaign sponsored by the National Advertising Council used the phrase "Take a bite out of crime," which is both memorable and suggestive (though literally, it wouldn't taste too good). Chevrolet used the simile for its truck ads: "Like a rock." What metaphors can you think of that are used in advertising? You often hear instructors employing comparisons as a way of tapping into your existing knowledge to explain new concepts. See Act and Reflect 8.3.

Guidelines for Adding Imagery and Comparative Language

1. Use powerful, active, emotional words throughout your presentation.

2. Provide enough description to paint the picture in the mind's eye of the audience.

3. Be creative. Think of imaginative ways to explain the topic and issues.

4. Use images and comparisons to which the audience can relate.

5. Consider using a single image or comparison as a theme throughout your presentation.

6. Control the imagery and comparisons so that they don't become the focus of the presentation and undermine attention to the issues.

"What's this, Dawkins—another of your 'visual metaphors'?"

© www.CartoonStock.com

ACT&REFLECT

8.3: Figurative Language

Comparison Practice

ACT • For each item listed, identify a metaphor, simile, or analogy you could use to explain it:

1. College life
2. Your worst date or job
3. Your best date or job
4. Friendship
5. Current U.S. foreign policy

6. Your family
7. Celebrating a birthday
8. Rap music
9. A campus issue
10. An issue in the news

REFLECT • Select the three metaphors, similes, or analogies you think work best. How might they help you to explain the issue more clearly? How might they create confusion?

Figurative Language: Illustrations and Examples

Good illustrations and examples are part of telling a good story. We use illustrations and examples throughout this text for explanation and support. We use the speech excerpts as **illustrations** of the points we are making, that is, as descriptions that make something clearer, often by describing what happens when some concept or principle is put into action. On the other hand, we often conclude the discussion of a concept by giving you an **example** of it, that is, a sample that is representative of a larger group. Examples are a form of proof or evidence. Examples are persuasive because they show the actual occurrence of what you are talking about. Maybe you've had an argument with your parents or friends in which they challenged a claim you made by asking for an example. Failure to provide an example when asked leaves you defeated.

Illustrations and examples help audiences understand what you are talking about, make it easier for them to visualize the information, and can help them retain information. Such figurative language is particularly helpful in making abstract information more concrete. There's probably not a lecture you have attended that hasn't included some illustration or example to help you understand the material (okay, maybe you've had a lecture that didn't, but it probably wasn't a very good one).

illustration A description presented to make something clearer, often by describing what happens when some concept or principle is put into action.

example A representative sample of a larger group.

Here's an excerpt from a commencement address by the late Christopher Reeve (paralyzed in a horse-riding accident). See if you can identify the examples he uses and the function they serve:

> At OSU, students and faculty understand the importance of public service on both a local and global scale. Some focus on the environment, others on community outreach among many other programs. Students in the College of Engineering recently achieved a speed of 241 mph in the Buckeye Bullet Electric Car. (Can I put in a request for them to work on my wheelchair?) Students in the Civil Engineering program placed first in a national competition to design a better road pavement using recycled materials. Participants in the Learning Bridge bring the educational resources of Ohio State to meet the needs of public schools that serve the university neighborhoods.[16]

The examples used include the electric car, the road pavement, and educational resources. These examples provide proof of Reeve's opening claim that Ohio State University is committed to public service. See Act and Reflect 8.4.

ACT&REFLECT

8.4: Illustration and Example Practice

ACT • What illustration could you present for each of the following?

1. What would happen to students at your college or university if they had to pay a 20 percent tuition increase
2. How a theory or concept you have learned works (e.g., evolution, supply-side economics, autocratic leadership, stimulus-response, dialectics, or symbolic interaction)
3. A plan being proposed by your university, community, or other organization

Give an example from your own knowledge to support the following statements:

1. College life can be very hard.
2. A career in . . . (your choice) can be very rewarding.
3. Movies often provide us with windows on social problems.

REFLECT • How difficult or easy was it for you to generate illustrations and examples? What skills do you think you have or don't have that help or hinder your ability to generate these?

Guidelines for Adding Illustrations and Examples

1 Recognize where an illustration or example is needed in your presentation.

2 Conduct research, as needed, to find additional examples to support points.

3 Link the illustrations and examples clearly to the issue you are seeking to clarify or support.

4 Provide detail and proceed logically when using illustrations.

5 Compare what you are talking about to something the audience understands.

6 Incorporate examples relevant to the audience's experiences, interests, needs, and so on.

7 Connect the abstract with the concrete.

Derivative Forms of Support: Reasoning and Arguments

Language forms of support involve using language to create images and emotion; derivative forms of support depend on logic and reasoning. These language forms reflect a narrative approach to public speaking. You can also take a rational approach that involves the application of basic principles of reasoning, argumentation, and the scientific method to convince an audience to accept your claims. Derivative forms of support usually are a set of statements, premises, or assertions that meld together in support of a conclusion or claim.

The types of arguments you present to audiences depends on what knowledge the audiences already possess. Research has confirmed a somewhat obvious conclusion: informed audiences respond to strong arguments, whereas uninformed audiences do not.[17] Thus, such informed audiences as the positive supportive audience, the detached and ambivalent neutral audiences, and the negative audiences should be expected to respond to strong arguments. Unknowledgeable audiences cannot process complex arguments if they lack the foundation on which to understand them. Uninformed audiences, which would include the open positive audience and the detached neutral audience, appear to be more affected by such association strategies as

- citing support from sources the audience members regard highly
- showing a similarity to an existing audience belief
- or showing how audience members can feel good about themselves by supporting your position[18]

Elaboration Likelihood Model

Understanding how audiences vary in response to reasoning and arguments is important for making effective presentational decisions. In searching for ways to explain

The elaboration likelihood model tells us that once our audience is interested and engaged, they will listen critically. ●

variations in how audiences respond to persuasion, social psychologists Richard Petty and John Cacioppo created the **elaboration likelihood model**.[19] They found that an audience's level of involvement with an issue had an impact on how they responded to different messages. Essentially, the elaboration likelihood model asserts that audiences who are not involved or interested in an issue are more affected by what Petty and Cacioppo call peripheral factors, such as emotions and style, while involved audiences focus on the content and message. Those who are less involved are less likely to engage in strong cognitive analysis of what they hear; they are more affected by peripheral cues such as emotional appeals, speaker credibility, and message length. This has two implications for your presentation of evidence and arguments: first, their use may be inappropriate for a particular audience; second, for some audiences, you may need to start your presentation by arousing the interest and involvement of your listeners. Once their interest is evoked, they are more likely to differentiate between strong and weak arguments.[20] However, once you have gotten your audience members interested in your topic, they will listen more critically to your arguments.

According to Petty and Cacioppo, a motivated, objective listener wants to determine the validity of a message and thus is affected more by strong arguments than weak ones.[21] However, there is debate and uncertainty as to what makes a strong argument—which is understandable, since some audience members respond to peripheral dimensions instead of attending to the logically developed central arguments in a speech. Research is inconclusive as to whether presenting logical arguments can actually increase persuasiveness.[22] However, using evidence and logical arguments seems to build the credibility of the speaker—another peripheral influence. The validity of the arguments may not have an effect, but the very presence of arguments may. How an argument "sounds" to audiences, particularly unknowledgeable audiences, may be more important that its actual validity. (Otherwise, why would infomercials be so successful?)

elaboration likelihood model Model that asserts that audiences who are not emotionally involved in an issue are more likely to be affected by peripheral cues and that involved audiences focus more on content and message.

Reasoning

One way a speaker might support a given claim or proposal is to use reasoning and logic. You might take an audience step by step through various points that build a case in support of your position. This process is often dramatized in the closing statements prosecution and defense attorneys make to juries in TV dramas. **Reasoning** involves the use of accepted or provable premises that are logically interrelated as the foundation for a conclusion. The most basic approach to reasoning uses a **syllogism,** consisting of three parts: a major premise, a minor premise, and a conclusion.

The **major premise** posits a relationship between a global term and an intermediate term. Example: "All seniors have taken a communication course." ("All seniors" is the global term and "communication course" is the intermediate.)

The **minor premise** posits a relationship between a specific term and a global term. Example: "Rene is a senior." ("Rene" is the specific term; "senior" is the global term.)

The **logical conclusion** is the logical extension of the major and minor premises and connects the specific term to the intermediate term. Example: "Rene has taken a communication course." ("Rene" is the specific term; "communication course" is the intermediate term.)

Assuming one has evidence to support the major and minor premises, the conclusion is irrefutable. Now, reflect on your experiences as an audience member. How often have you ever heard anyone present such a logically developed argument? Probably not often, because to influence their audiences, speakers present only parts of a logical argument or even present fallacies that appear to be reasonable.[23] A number of fallacies audiences should be attuned to are covered in Chapter 5. Sometimes speakers present only two parts of the syllogism, which is called an **enthymeme,** because the audience members already know one of the points or can draw the conclusion themselves. If your audience knows that all seniors have taken a communication course, you need to state only the minor premise and conclusion, or maybe even just the minor premise. If you are discussing whether Rene took a communications course, you might simply say, "Well, Rene is a senior," leaving your audience to put the pieces together. Various factors, such as the audience's intelligence and their predisposition toward the issue, affect whether a speaker needs to explicitly state all the parts of their arguments. In the following discussion, we will review some of the principles of reasoning and argumentation as they apply to everyday presentations.

Formal reasoning is often categorized as deductive or inductive reasoning. **Deductive reasoning** begins with a

reasoning Using accepted or provable premises that are logically interrelated as the foundation for a conclusion.

syllogism A form of reasoning consisting of a major premise, a minor premise, and a conclusion.

major premise A statement that posits a relationship between a global term and an intermediate term.

minor premise A statement that posits a relationship between a specific term and a global term.

logical conclusion The logical extension of the major and minor premises, connecting the specific term to the intermediate term.

enthymeme An abbreviated form of syllogism in which only two of the three parts are specifically identified.

deductive reasoning Begins with a statement of a known generalization and applies it to a specific instance to prove the specific instance.

statement of a known generalization and applies it to a specific instance to prove the specific instance. In essence, a known law or principle is applied to a specific situation governed by the law. For example:

> College graduates have a higher annual average income than non–college graduates. Christie will be graduating from college in May. Christie can expect to earn a better income than non–college graduates.

Inductive reasoning begins with a piece of specific information or observation (usually several pieces), which is used to produce a general principle, which may then be applied to another specific instance. Conclusions reached by induction often are couched in terms of the probability of being true, because you are usually limited in terms of how many observations you can make. In the following example, an observation about five people is used as the basis for a general principle that is applied to a sixth person:

> Communication majors Christie, Rusty, Miguel, Frank, and Mona got well-paying jobs after they graduated. Obviously, communication graduates get well-paying jobs. Debbie will be graduating this spring in communication and can expect to get a well-paying job.

Keep in mind that you usually need strong evidence (discussed in detail in Chapter 9) to support claims and conclusions like those listed in these examples. For example, in the deductive reasoning example, you could add, "According to the 2000 U.S. census, people with bachelor's degrees averaged earnings of $45,400 a year, while high school graduates averaged earnings of $25,900."[24] To strengthen the inductive reasoning example, you might cite the specific salaries of your examples.

Arguments

Besides the use of logical reasoning, you can also create an **argument,** which typically consists of a claim, reasons for that claim, and support for the validity of the reasons. (See a more complex example in Stephen Toulmin's model of argumentation.)[25] The basis of such models is that one makes a claim and then provides some explanation and evidence as to the validity of the explanation and claim. The following is an example of a typical argument that might be included in an everyday presentation:

> **Claim:** "You should plan on going to college after you graduate from high school."
> **Reasoning/Grounds:** "You can get a better-paying job if you have a college degree."
> **Support/Backing:** "According to the 2000 U.S. Census, college graduates averaged earnings of over $45,400 a year, while high school graduates averaged only $25,900."

Underlying this argument is the presumption that a person would find making more money appealing. Underlying most arguments are the values, beliefs, and needs we associate with our listeners. If you make an inaccurate assumption about these qualities, then your argument will not be very effective. Years ago, for fun, one of your authors was listening to a door-to-door

inductive reasoning Begins with a piece of specific information or observation (usually several pieces), which is used to produce a general principle, which may then be applied to another specific instance.

argument Consists of a claim, reasons for that claim, and support for the validity of the reasons.

encyclopedia salesman. The salesman was using a technique in which he wanted agreement on several principles that he believed would be accepted beyond doubt (the idea being that if you get someone to agree to a series of no-brainer propositions, you get them in an "agreeable" mood). He said, "I'm sure you want your children do well in school, right?" He was trying to assert a basic value that would lead to the logical conclusion that buying an encyclopedia would ensure a child's good education. However, your author challenged his initial assertion with the comment "I don't believe school is necessarily a good thing for children." Since the salesman was working from a script, he was unable to respond to the challenge and eventually left without selling his product. This example illustrates several principles you should consider in presenting arguments in your speeches. First, be careful about what you assume are the values of your audience. Be aware of what values and needs you are appealing to, and try to ensure that they are valid. Second, people's resistance is increased if they suspect you are trying to be cleverly strategic. Third, you need to be flexible. If your audience doesn't respond to a particular argument, you should be prepared with additional evidence and arguments. This will be particularly helpful in situations where you might be responding to audience feedback and questions. Many of

Everyday Example

Faulty Reasoning

The following list has circulated on the Internet for several years, claiming that these are actual newspaper headlines; however, they have apparently been fabricated simply for their amusement value. Nonetheless, most of these are enthymemes in which the humor depends on making a logical conclusion based on the listener/ reader supplying the missing element of the argument. The humor of these lines depends on the absurdity involved in connecting the two points in each headline. See if you can identify the missing syllogistic elements.

Enraged Cow Injures Farmer with Ax

Lung Cancer in Women Mushrooms

Dealers Will Hear Car Talk at Noon

Two Soviet Ships Collide, One Dies

Lawmen from Mexico Barbecue Guests

Juvenile Court to Try Shooting Defendant

Stolen Painting Found by Tree

Hershey Bars Protest

Squad Helps Dog Bite Victim

Red Tape Holds up New Bridge

Police Begin Campaign to Run Down Jaywalkers

Killer Sentenced to Die for Second Time in 10 Years

Two Sisters Reunited after Eighteen Years at Checkout Counter

Milk Drinkers Are Turning to Powder

Queen Mary Having Bottom Scraped

Miners Refuse to Work after Death

Hospitals Are Sued by 7 Foot Doctors

Grandmother of Eight Makes Hole in One

Quarter of a Million Chinese Live on Water

Include Your Children When Baking Cookies

Astronaut Takes Blame for Gas in Spacecraft

Complaints about NBA Referees Growing Ugly

Man Eating Piranha Mistakenly Sold as Pet Fish

your everyday presentations will involve an interactive style in which you are expected to be able to provide more detail when requested. See Act and Reflect 8.5.

In preparing a presentation, you should identify the claims you are making and ask yourself if you can adequately explain the reason for each claim and if you have sufficient evidence to support your reasoning. Any unsupported claim you make can be rejected simply with the use of an unsupported refutation. Unfortunately, one of the most common errors of presenters is to make unsubstantiated claims. They often sound very appealing, but if the audience members listen critically, they will recognize the speaker's failure. More unfortunate, audiences often fail to listen critically. Nonetheless, there is an ethical and a moral code that suggests that speakers be able to back up their claims.

● GETTING TO WORK

Storytelling involves the use of language to paint pictures that an audience can visualize. Such visualization has an impact on listeners, and you can use it to effectively accomplish your presentational goals. Your stories and narratives need to have coherence and fidelity. Does your story progress in a manner that makes sense to the audience? Does the story ring true to the audience? Your presentation and stories can be enhanced if you use figurative language: imagery, comparisons (metaphors, similes, and analogies), and illustrations or examples. As you prepare your next presentation, think of figurative ways to describe the concepts and issues you are discussing. Develop metaphors or similes for the points you are making: ". . . is like . . ."

In deciding what support material to use, you need to think about how your

ACT & REFLECT

8.5: Reasoning and Arguments

ACT • Identify the major premise, minor premise, and conclusion, or the claim, reasoning, and evidence for each of the following statements.

1. All the top teams in the conference this year had a lot of returning starters and experienced players. We will have four starters coming back next year and a lot of experienced players coming off the bench, so our basketball team should be really good next year.

   Claim:

   Reasoning:

   Evidence:

2. Winter Park is a beautiful ski resort in Colorado that is actually owned by the city of Denver. Skiing at Winter Park would be a lot of fun, but it's going to be expensive. Ski resorts in Colorado charge a lot for lift tickets.

   Major premise:

   Minor premise:

   Logical conclusion:

3. Employee turnover has reached an all-time high. In the last six months, we've had almost 25 percent of our workers leave, which has meant a lot of money spent on hiring and training their replacements. We need to conduct a study to find out why our turnover rate is so high.

   Claim:

   Reasoning:

   Evidence:

REFLECT • Analyze the arguments in each case. To what degree do they follow the principles of good logic and argument? To what degree are the claims or conclusions logical?

audience thinks. Audiences don't always think logically but are often influenced by their emotions and biases. How can you apply that awareness to your use of reasoning and present arguments that are effective? Think about how you can best convey your arguments to an audience. Talk your audience through arguments, clearly identifying your claims, presenting strong support, and demonstrating how the two connect.

SUMMARY

The narrative paradigm asserts that people are storytellers and are affected by the stories of others. People judge stories on the basis of their coherence and fidelity. Coherence means how well a story hangs together, in terms of structure, relationship to other stories, and the consistency of the characters. Fidelity is the degree to which a story rings true—is consistent with our own views and observations.

Speeches can be supported by the use of figurative language that creates images (verbal pictures) in the minds of the audience members. Such imagery can increase attention, understanding, and retention of information. Metaphors and similes involve comparing something you are discussing with something else, usually something the audience is already familiar with. Illustrations are used in speeches to explain what will happen, while an example is a description of a sample drawn from a larger group.

You can support a presentation with sound reasoning and logical arguments. The elaboration likelihood model says that people who are involved in a given issue will listen more critically to arguments, and those who are less involved will be more affected by peripheral cues than by reasoning. You need to adapt your approach accordingly. Reasoning involves some variation of a form that includes a major premise, a minor premise, and a conclusion based on these two premises. An argument consists of a claim, the reasons for that claim, and support for those reasons.

VIDEO EXPERIENCE

1. Stories can be used both to support the speaker's claims and to create a structure around which to organize a presentation. The speech in the video clip, "Tales of the Grandmothers," by Dr. Anita Taylor of George Mason University, was originally presented as part of a Woman of the Year celebration but was recorded later when Dr. Taylor delivered it again to students at her university. As you watch and listen, evaluate the impact of the stories.

How effective are the stories in accomplishing the speaker's goal?

2. In the clips from student presentations, you see a variety of ways that logic and reasoning can be incorporated into a presentation. Listen to each clip and identify the premises, claims, evidence, and conclusions. How effective are they? What changes could be made to strengthen them?

THINKING BACK, THINKING AHEAD

1. You have been asked to talk about college to a group of graduating seniors in your old high school who are intending to go to college. Briefly consider two stories you could tell from your own experiences that might help inform them. How coherent are these two stories? To what degree will the audience feel your stories have fidelity?

2. Think about the most recent good lectures you've heard. Identify any imagery, metaphors, illustrations, or examples the instructors used. How helpful were these in learning the material?

How much information can you recall that was not linked to any figurative language? Consider a presentation you might be working on or might deliver in the future. Try to generate imagery, metaphors, illustrations, and examples that you could incorporate in your presentation.

3. You are giving a presentation to your class on a topic (you decide on one that is appropriate) in which they have no initial knowledge or interest. Your talk is limited to five minutes. What two pieces of evidence would you use that would be most effective in developing their interest? What two pieces of evidence would you provide that would be most effective in increasing their knowledge?

4. Look through a magazine or a newspaper and find an article on a topic you find of interest (for example, best athlete of the year, a report on a cancer-causing substance, tips for buying a DVD player, cooking with less fat, or a new diet trend). Examine the article for the following types of arguments or reasoning:

a. Syllogism: b. Argument:
   Major Premise: Claim:
   Minor Premise: Reasons:
   Conclusion: Evidence:

NOTES

1. M. Argyle, *The Psychology of Happiness,* 2nd ed. (London: Routledge, 2001).
2. T. Clevenger, *Audience Analysis* (Indianapolis: Bobbs-Merrill, 1966).
3. Clevenger, *Audience Analysis.*
4. W. Fisher, "Narration as a Human Communication Paradigm: The Case of Public Moral Argument," *Communication Monographs, 51* (1984): 1–22.
5. E. J. Baesler, "Construction and Test of an Empirical Measure for Narrative Coherence and Fidelity," *Communication Reports, 8* (1995): 97–101.
6. E. J. Baesler, "Persuasive Effects of Story and Statistical Evidence," *Argumentation and Advocacy, 33* (1997): 170–175 (online version from Gale Group).
7. The White House, Office of the Press Secretary, Remarks by the President at Working Women Count Event, retrieved online, at http://clinton6.nara. gov/1995.
8. Jesse L. Jackson, "Keep Hope Alive," Address to the 1988 Democratic National Convention, Atlanta, GA, July 19, 1988.
9. C. G. Emrich, H. H. Brower, J. M. Feldman, and H. Garland, "Images in Words: Presidential Rhetoric, Charisma, and Greatness," *Administrative Science Quarterly, 46* (2001): 527–557.
10. A. Sapienza, "Imagery and Strategy," *Journal of Management, 13* (1987): 543–555.
11. Abraham Lincoln, Senate race nomination speech, Springfield, Illinois, June 17, 1858.
12. S. Glucksberg and B. Keysar, "How Metaphors Work," in *Metaphor and Thought,* 2nd ed., edited by A. Ortony (New York: Cambridge University Press, 1993), 401–424.
13. G. Lakoff and M. Johnson, *Metaphors We Live By* (Chicago: University of Chicago Press, 1980).
14. P. Sopory and J. P. Dillard, "The Persuasive Effects of Metaphor," *Human Communication Research, 28* (2002): 382–419.
15. Sopory and Dillard, "The Persuasive Effects of Metaphor."
16. Retrieved from Christopher Reeve Paralysis Foundation Web site, at www.christopherreeve.org/ChristopherReeve/ChristopherReeve.cfm?ID=559&c=10.
17. W. Wood, C. A. Kallgren, and R. M. Preisler, "Access to Attitude-Relevant Information in Memory as a Determinant of Persuasion: The Role of Message Attributes," *Journal of Experimental Social Psychology, 21* (1985): 73–85.
18. D. Roskos-Ewoldson, "Implicit Theories of Persuasion," *Human Communication Research 24* (1997): 31–63.
19. R. E. Petty and J. T. Cacioppo, *Communication and Persuasion: Central and Peripheral Routes to Attitude Change* (New York: Springer-Verlag, 1986).
20. Petty and Cacioppo, *Communication and Persuasion.*
21. Petty and Cacioppo, *Communication and Persuasion.*
22. W. Thompson, *Quantitative Research in Public Address and Communication* (New York: Random House, 1967).
23. M. Burgoon and E. P. Bettinghaus, "Persuasive Message Strategies," in *Persuasion: New Directions in Theory and Research,* edited by M. L. Roloff and G. R. Miller (Thousand Oaks, CA: Sage, 1980), 141–169.
24. *United States Department of Commerce News,* July 18, 2002, retrieved from U.S. Census Web site, at www.census.gov/Press-Release/www/2002/cb02-95.html.
25. S. Toulmin, R. Rieke, and A. Janik, *An Introduction to Reasoning* (New York: Macmillin, 1979).

Chapter 9

Supporting Your Presentation

Evidence, Argument, and Support Strategies

Goals

✓ To understand how to present evidence effectively

✓ To learn how to appropriately paraphrase and directly quote outside sources

✓ To learn strategies associated with the use of statistical support

✓ To evaluate the credibility of outside sources

✓ To understand the strategies for effectively incorporating support and evidence

Read the following two hypothetical speech excerpts:

Speaker A: "Community colleges may be the route for you to consider when making your college plans. A lot of students go to community college and then transfer to a four-year school for their bachelor's degrees. There are lots of advantages to doing this, like saving money. Of course, community colleges are a lot less expensive than four-year schools. You can save a lot of money by going to a community college for two years and then transferring to a four-year school for your bachelor's degree."

Speaker B: "Community colleges may be the route for you to consider when making your college plans, but you need to carefully consider your needs. The number of students using community college as a stepping stone to four-year schools decreased from 43 percent in 1973, to 30 percent in 1980, to an estimated 15 to 20 percent today, according to a report published on the American Association of Communication Colleges' Web site.[1] If you are serious about starting at a community college and transferring, there is a substantial savings. The College Board reported tuition and fees for two-year schools averaged $2,076 in 2004, compared to $5,132 for four-year schools.[2] Bonnie Campbell, former Iowa attorney general and member of the U.S. Department of Justice, began her college career at a community college, about which she wrote, and I quote, 'for those people who know they are likely to continue their studies, the community colleges are an affordable and well-qualified place for them to launch their college education.'"[3]

How do these two excerpts compare? Both talked about the same topic, but the speakers' approaches were very different. Obviously, Speaker B talked more, so you might be inclined to appreciate the brevity of Speaker A. On the other hand, Speaker B has backed up claims and assertions with statistics and quotes. The referencing done by Speaker B should have led you to feel more confident in believing what Speaker B was saying. The sources Speaker B cites seem to be credible and trustworthy, again giving you confidence in accepting Speaker B's claims. Speaker B's use of statistics and quotations represents the incorporation of evidence. The evidence is used to support the claims and arguments the speaker is making; this speech is one example of how to strategically use evidence and support. ●

Providing Evidence: Testimony and Statistics

In the previous chapter, **evidence** was defined as particular type of support, generally consisting of verifiable information that sometimes reinforces other forms of support, such as stories, illustrations, reasoning, or argument. Among the types of evidence speakers can use are paraphrased statements and quotations from other people (usually experts); numerical references, including statistics; and "hands-on" visuals—including actual objects or demonstrations (discussed in Chapter 10). A speaker may need to establish the authenticity or credibility of the evidence for it to have an impact on the audience. Evidence is effective when it results in the audience accepting the claim you are asserting. In general, the more controversial the issue or claim, the more need there is for evidence. However, simply providing evidence does not ensure acceptance of your claim; certain conditions must be meet.

Making Evidence Effective

To be effective, evidence must meet four conditions: it must (1) be heard; (2) be thought about; (3) be evaluated as legitimate; and (4) be accepted as relevant, consistent, and supportive of the claim you are making.[4]

Evidence Must Be Heard First, the evidence will have little impact if the audience doesn't even realize that evidence was presented. This is one reason that providing full oral citation of your sources is helpful—it signals to the audience that you are presenting evidence.[5] An **oral citation** is the information the speaker provides that accompanies evidence and includes the source of the information (name of the author or speaker), where the information was found (newspaper or magazine), and the date the information was published. In reading written text, quotation marks show that a quotation is being presented. To signal listeners that you are using evidence, you should provide an oral citation. An oral citation for a quotation also includes "oral quotation marks" to indicate the beginning and end of the quotation. Here's a sample transcript of what a speaker might say:

> Professor Stephen Hawking is a noted theoretical physicist and cosmologist known for his work on black holes and as the author of a popular book entitled *A Brief History of Time*. In an interview in 1999 that appeared on the *Larry King Show*, Professor Hawking said, and I quote, "Life appeared on earth fairly soon after the earth was formed, 4.5 billion years ago. That suggests that primitive life will appear spontaneously on any suitable planet. On the other hand, intelligent life seems very rare. It has yet to be detected on earth" unquote.

Evidence Must Be Processed The mere fact that an audience realizes you are presenting quotations or statistics

evidence A particular type of support, generally consisting of verifiable information that sometimes reinforces other forms of support.

oral citation Information the speaker provides that accompanies evidence and includes the source of the information (name of the author or speaker), where the information was found (newspaper or magazine), and the date the information was published.

Do you think strong evidence would have an impact on these listeners? ●

doesn't mean they will really think about it. What did the Hawking quotation in this passage really mean? Did you think about it? Having audiences reflect on evidence can be particularly problematic in speeches where speakers quickly move from one piece of information to another and the audiences do not have the luxury readers have to stop to consider the meaning or significance of the evidence. A constant barrage of quotes and statistics is likely to undermine the speaker's intentions; rather than being impressed by the evidence, the audience is likely to ignore it.[6] As a speaker, you need to provide either help in processing the information or time for your audience to consider it, or both. Here's what a speaker might say after having just finished that quotation:

> Think for a moment about what Professor Hawking means when saying that life appeared early in earth's history and that primitive life could be expected on any suitable planet. Professor Hawking's comment suggests that it is reasonable to assume there is life on other planets because it happened so quickly and easily here on earth. His tongue-in-cheek comment that there still isn't intelligent life here on earth also reveals that while there may be life on other planets, how that life has evolved and what its current state might be is uncertain, which might be why he refers to it as primitive life.

The lack of adequate time to process evidence presented might be one reason that research has found audiences changing their attitudes several weeks after a presentation.[7] This potential impact can be a distinct advantage in those instances where you speak to an audience about the issue on more than one occasion. If the audience reflects on the evidence and arguments from your first presentation, their negative attitude may soften, thus allowing you an opportunity to make additional headway.

Evidence Must Be Accepted as Legitimate Any positive impact associated with consideration of your evidence depends on the audience accepting the evidence as legitimate. What factors influence that acceptance? One factor obviously is the credibility of the source. Negative audiences will be particularly critical in evaluating the expertise, objectivity, honesty, and accuracy of speakers' sources. The use of evidence with low credibility and low relevance by highly credible speakers can actually undermine their efforts to influence the audience.[8] On the other hand, speakers with moderate credibility can enhance their persuasiveness by using relevant and highly credible evidence or even highly credible evidence that is not relevant.[9]

Even when a source is seen as credible, like Stephen Hawking, listeners might still discard the evidence. Audience members might feel Hawking erred in his conclusion, especially when no details are provided about how he reached it. Giving such detail often involves providing the reasoning and logic used in reaching conclusions. The legitimacy of your evidence may be rejected not because it lacks merit but because it challenges deeply held audience values. People tend to hold more firmly to basic values and fundamental beliefs, even when the evidence shows those values or beliefs are in error. History is filled with examples where evidence was rejected because it conflicted with beliefs—the world is flat, not round; the earth is the center of the universe (not the sun); AIDS is inflicted on gays as punishment from God; smoking cigarettes is not harmful to your health.

One way to reduce rejection of your evidence and bolster its legitimacy is to piggyback it on the statistics and evidence the audience already accepts as legitimate. Citing sources and facts familiar to the audience not only helps your credibility but also creates an entree for introducing new evidence and arguments. Here's an example from a speech designed to reduce alcoholic drinking:

> You've probably seen friends or family members get really drunk and do stupid things. Alcohol impairs our judgment. You know that excessive drinking impairs driving and is a leading cause of automobile accidents. You may know many states consider you to be driving under the influence if you have a .08 blood/alcohol level. But did you know that, according to the National Institute on Alcohol Abuse and Alcoholism, some

NON SEQUITUR © 2004 Wiley Miller. Dist. by Universal Press Syndicate. Reprinted with permission. All rights reserved.

ACT&REFLECT

9.1: Evaluating Conditions That Determine the Effectiveness of Evidence

ACT • Our daily interactions are filled with examples in which our failure to meet one of the four conditions necessary for evidence to be effective undermines our efforts to get others to agree with us. Recall instances in your everyday interactions where your attempts to persuade someone failed for each of the four specific conditions.

Condition	Example
Listener failed to hear the evidence:	
Listener failed to processes the evidence:	
Listener did not view the evidence as legitimate:	
Listener rejected the connection of evidence to conclusion:	

REFLECT • For each of your examples, what might you have done differently to meet the condition?

---

driving skills are affected with only a .02 blood alcohol level? That's the level found in a 160-pound man one hour after having a single beer. Now imagine having a couple of beers or a hard drink.

Evidence Must Be Accepted as Supporting the Conclusion The audience may hear the evidence, process the evidence, and judge the evidence as legitimate but still not be influenced by it. The audience must see the evidence as relevant, consistent, and supportive of the claim. In essence, the audience must see and accept a clear link between the data you provide and the claim you say the evidence supports. There is always a gap between the evidence and the claim that must be filled by the speaker and the listener. The larger that gap, the more likely the audience is to reject the connection. Listeners would reject a claim by a speaker that drinking increases the likelihood of a car accident if the evidence consists of irrelevant statistics on alcoholism and alcohol-related diseases—the gap is too large between the evidence and the claim. Don't assume an audience automatically makes the connection between your evidence and your claims; you need to explain the connection. Making connections is a question of argumentation—supporting a claim with valid evidence, which is discussed later in this chapter. The principles of reasoning and argument dictate whether your evidence will ultimately have an impact on persuading your audiences. Many TV courtroom dramas demonstrate this principle, as lawyers spend considerable amount of time trying to build a case that connects the evidence to some claim of innocence or guilt. The jury then decides whether the evidence is legitimate, is sufficient, and supports the claim of one lawyer more than the other.

Anything that interferes with any of these four conditions undermines the effectiveness of providing support (see Act and Reflect 9.1). Interference can include a failure to recognize evidence, distractions that prevent the audience from processing what you've said, or bias that prevents objective evaluation. On the other hand, too much evidence will overwhelm the listeners and cause them to tune out. You've probably listened to lectures in which the instructor pummeled you with evidence, quotations, and statistics to the point that you quit listening. Given the number of factors that can interfere with the effectiveness of your evidence, the best strategy is often a concise and focused presentation that relies on a small number of very strong pieces of evidence. One good argument backed up with strong evidence is better than several wimpy ones.

Use of Referenced Materials

Our knowledge of the world comes either from our own observations or by learning it from other people. When you have expertise and credibility, then some audiences accept your observations on face value. Whenever you lack personal knowledge of an issue, then you need to conduct research. Referenced materials presented in a speech should include an oral citation (source and date) like the one provided earlier for the information from Stephen Hawking. Providing an oral citation is not just a matter of choice; you are ethically bound to provide clear referencing any time you use information from a source other than yourself. Clear referencing of material adds credibility to the presentation, lets the audience judge the information's value and importance, and assures the audience that the information is valid and reliable. Typically, referenced ideas and concepts are presented in either a paraphrased or direct quote format.

Paraphrasing   When you take information you learned and put into your own words—words your audience can easily understand—you are **paraphrasing.** The following is an example of a direct statement and how a speaker might have presented it in a paraphrased manner:

Printed Text
"O can accept (confirm) P's definition of self. As far as we can see, this confirmation of P's view of himself by O is probably the greatest single factor ensuring mental development and stability that has so far emerged from our study of communication."[10]

Sample Paraphrasing
"Three therapists, Watzlawick, Beavin, and Jackson, searching for alternatives to traditional psychiatry, wrote about their conclusions in a 1967 book entitled *Pragmatics of Human Communication.* The most important factor leading to mental growth and stability that they found in their communication studies occurs when people accept the way a person defines himself or herself."

Paraphrasing lets you take complex material and simplify it. You can reword a passage so that the audience can more readily understand it. The direct text in the example is difficult to understand, even when you can reread it. In spoken mes-

paraphrasing Taking information you learned and putting into your own words—words the audience can easily understand.

sages, the audience gets one chance to understand what you say. They probably would not understand the first passage above as a direct quotation (test this by reading the passage to a friend or roommate and see what he or she thinks it says). The paraphrased statement captures the essence of the direct text but makes it easier to comprehend. A significant danger in paraphrasing is misrepresentation and inaccuracy. Positive audiences are more forgiving and less likely to question the accuracy of either your paraphrasing or quotations. However, negative audiences will be skeptical of such messages. The best practice is to develop skills to accurately paraphrase referenced material.

Guidelines for Paraphrasing

1 Make sure you understand what the original material means.

2 Restate the material two or three times after reading it while preparing for the presentation to ensure you have a grasp of it.

3 When in doubt about your understanding, have someone else read the material and listen to your paraphrased statement.

4 Include sufficient referencing such as the authors' names, the title, and the year of publication. A complete reference should be available to anyone who requests it.

5 If the audience is unfamiliar with the source, you may need to provide background information about the source.

6 If you present an extended discussion of material from another source, you need to mention the main reference periodically as a reminder.

7 Your delivery (tone of voice, pausing, etc.) needs to clearly convey that you are paraphrasing information and not quoting it.

Direct Quotations There are times when it is more effective and appropriate to directly recite the words of others through **direct quotations** or **testimony.** Direct quotations are used for two different reasons. The first is to act as a figurative language device. Quoting famous people adds color to your presentation. Quoting from sources that are revered by your audience is another way of inspiring and uplifting them. Democratic Party candidates love to include quotations from John F. Kennedy when talking to supporters, while Republicans often quote Ronald Reagan. This use of direct quotations is often found in more formal addresses. Commencement addresses often include quotations from some "famous old dead white guys" (which may also indicate the failure to adapt to diverse audiences). The use of such quotations creates an aura of sophistication and intelligence around the speaker. In essence, it sounds impressive to quote Aristotle, Einstein, Kennedy, Lincoln, Reagan, Thoreau, Truman, or Shakespeare. This type of quotation is often more philosophical and tangential to your issue. For example, when talking about the importance of confirming another person's sense of self, a speaker might say, "The poet Emily Dickinson once wrote, 'I felt it shelter to speak to you.'" The connection between the quotation and the point you are making may need to be explained to your listeners.

direct quotations (testimony) Directly recited words of others.

The second use of direct quotations is to add legitimacy to information. Quoting a well-known expert legitimizes your point. Reciting direct quotations allows the audience to judge the applicability and reliability of the quotation themselves. Underlying this point is the belief that speakers are ethical and that they quote accurately. This is an ethical responsibility you should embrace. You need to consider the use of quotations as part of your presentational strategy. How do they help your presentation? What information do they convey? How effectively do they convey the information? How will the audience respond to them? Your ability to satisfactorily answer these questions will determine whether the quotations are an asset or a liability.

Guidelines to Consider when Selecting Quotations

1. Quote well-known people, or at least those known to the audience.
2. Quote people whom the audience admires and reveres.
3. Quote experts (provide their credentials when they are not well known).
4. Quote people who are personally affected by the issue (to humanize the issue).
5. Consider quotations that are provocative (to increase audience's interest).
6. Consider the information value of the quotation (does it really convey anything?).
7. Use quotations that are well phrased and use figurative language.
8. Consider the interest value of the quotation (will the audience find it interesing?).
9. Choose quotations that are most relevant and pertinent to the issue.
10. Have quotations written out on note cards so you can accurately present them.

Use of Numbers and Statistics

Your company is changing to a new health care insurance plan that will expand the coverage for all the employees, and you have been assigned to explain it. Obviously, you will include an explanation of what is covered, how the plan different from what

A quote from which of these former presidents about the challenges of peace in the Middle East would you find most credible? ●

was provided before, and what it will cost. You know that while everyone wanted better coverage, there is a concern about the cost. One way to address these concerns is to provide a statistical analysis of how much it will be costing the company and how much it will cost each individual.

You are making a presentation in a class in your major in which you are discussing certain trends in your field. Your classmates are interested in your presentation because the information is relevant to their careers (and because the instructor is testing them on the material). You describe some basic statistics that you have found relevant to the topic.

In both these presentations, you are incorporating statistics as another supportive device. Statistics can be an efficient and influential way to present data. However, statistics are also sometimes hard to convey verbally. Statistical presentations are often accompanied by charts, graphs, handouts, and overheads. The specifics of such visuals aids are covered in detail in Chapter 14. Here, we will focus on simple statistical information that might be included within your commentary. **Statistics** are numerical reductions and analyses of larger pools of data or observations. Instead of saying that 423 people out of 900 surveyed in September 2003 disapproved of downloading music over the Internet, you could more efficiently report that 47 percent of those surveyed felt that way.[11] The statistical simplification of the raw data makes the information more accessible to the listeners and is more powerful. It's hard to quickly get a sense of whether 423 out of 900 is a significant portion, but 47 percent makes it clear. Now the troublesome part of statistics in presentations is that speakers add commentary to influence audience perception. One speaker might say, "Only 47 percent of those surveyed found it objectionable," while another speaker says, "Downloading music was disapproved by a whopping 47 percent of those surveyed." As a speaker, you have choices about how you present numerical data; those choices often involve making an ethical decision about how to characterize the information fairly for the audience's consumption.

Numbers are incorporated in various forms within presentations, and those forms serve different functions, as shown in Table 9.1. This list is far from complete, because specific professional presentations often include statistical analysis of data in the form of correlations, t-tests, regression analyses, market analyses, profit analyses, and so on. The presentation of technical reports follows the same guidelines that are discussed here, except that in such professional presentations, the audience wants to hear the results of the statistical analysis.

Understanding numbers usually is easier when you read them than when you just hear them. You need to think carefully about the statistics you present and consider how well the audience will be able to follow what you say. For example, consider the following statement: "According to the 2000 census, the racial makeup of the United States was 211,460,626 White; 34,658,190 Black; 10,242,998 Asian; 2,475,956 American Indian and Alaska Native; 35,305,818 Hispanic/Latino; and 398,835 Native Hawaiian and Other Pacific Islander." Reading this statement allows you to glance at the numbers, round them off in your head, and compare them as you examine them. Listeners can't do that (unless you've put the numbers up on a PowerPoint slide or overhead). So what should you do? The first question is "Why do you want the audience to hear these

statistics Numerical reductions and analyses of larger pools of data or observations.

● **TABLE 9.1** Types and Functions of Statistical Information

Raw numbers: the actual number associated with the item. "This method is being used in 329 hospitals and 533 clinics throughout the United States."

Percentages and ratios: numbers indicating proportions or relative strength. "In 2001, 41 percent of traffic accident deaths were alcohol related." "Four out of five students surveyed on campus were in favor of changing the length of each term."

Central tendencies: numbers that reflect averages (means), midpoints (median), and most frequently occurring (mode). "The average score on the test was 83 percent." "*Trading Spaces* was the most popular TV show among college women."

Probabilities: numbers that reflect likelihood of occurrence. "Your chances of winning the lottery are usually less than one out of 250 million." "There is a 40 percent chance of rain tomorrow."

Trends: the numbers used to show changes. "In each of the last five years, the number of students participating in intramural sports has increased by at least 5 percent a year." "The market fell another 125 points this week, marking the twelfth week in a row the market has fallen."

Comparisons: presenting numbers for two or more issues in order to facilitate evaluation. "Plan A was supported by 46 percent of the students, plan B by 20 percent, and plan C by 10 percent, with 14 percent having no opinion."

Relationships: numbers used to show a connection between two or more events. "Men who smoke are 22 times more likely to get lung cancer than men who don't."* "High school students who participate in sports are 1.7 times less likely to drop out of school."**

Sources: *Centers for Disease Control and Prevention, "Smoking-Attributable Mortality and Years of Potential Life Lost—United States, 1990," Morbidity and Mortality Weekly Report, 43 (1993): 645–648; **R. McNeal, "Extracurricular Activities and High School Dropouts," Sociology of Education, 68 (1995): 62–81.

numbers?" Your intended use of statistics dictates the format you should use. If your intention in listing the racial makeup of the United States is to show the significant size of certain minority groups, then you might want to present those groups only as percentages of the overall population. Thus, "African Americans made up 12.3 percent of the U.S. population in the 2000 census, while Hispanics/Latinos made up 12.5 percent. These two groups now comprise one-fourth of the U.S. population." This statement is easier to understand when spoken than the first statement. In addition, saying "one-fourth" rather than "24.8 percent" makes the number more comprehensible.

Here's an excellent example of making statistics accessible to an audience.

"If we can shrink the world's population to a village of only 100 people, keeping all existing ratios the same, that village would look like this: there would be 57 Asians, 21 Europeans, 14 from the Western Hemisphere—north and south—and 21 Africans; 52 would be female; 70 would be nonwhite and 30 white; 70 would be non-Christian and 30 would be Christian.

"Six of the 100 people would own 59 percent of all the wealth in the world, and all 6 of those people would be from the United States. Eighty of the 100 people would live in substandard housing. Seventy would be unable to read and write. Fifty would suffer from malnutrition. One would have a college education."[12]

In this example, the raw numbers of millions and billions are converted to proportions of one hundred, which are easier to grasp. Julian Bond used proportions and percentages to effectively convey the inequities that exist in the world and hopefully sensitize his audience to where they fit in the world picture.

Guidelines for Using Statistics

1. Keep them simple. Use round numbers when appropriate.

2. Don't overwhelm your audience with numbers.

3. Explain what the numbers mean; statistics don't have meaning without context.

4. Tie statistics to stories in order to personalize the numbers and increase retention.

5. Repeat numbers to help the audience grasp them.

6. Look for alternative and creative ways of conveying the statistics.

7. Present statistics in an ethical and objective manner.

Source Credibility

Which of the following would convince you that there are aliens from other planets living here on earth (assuming you don't believe they are)?

1. A quotation from Mr. Michael Peterson, a trucker from New Mexico, who claims to have met an alien at a rest stop one night.
2. A quotation from Dr. Shelly Fredonia, an astrophysicist from UCLA, who claims to have taped interviews with three aliens, but their voices didn't record.
3. An actual alien from another planet (who looks just like a human), who claims to be from the planet K-PAX.
4. A graph showing a dramatic increase over the last twenty years of people reporting discussions with aliens living on Earth.
5. A copy of a top-secret Air Force report that details several conversations between Air Force personnel and aliens.
6. An actual alien from another planet, which has three eyes, four arms, three legs; has no hair, is silver metallic in color, and produces high-pitched sounds.
7. None of the above.

These sources are listed roughly in order of increasing believability or credibility. You are most likely to believe what you can see for yourself and least likely to believe an unknown man or woman on the street who has no specific evidence. If you believe there is no possibility of an alien on earth, you might even reject the silver alien you see for yourself as a hoax or fabrication. Your level of skepticism (a form of resistance) will dictate what evidence and how much evidence is sufficient to alter your view.

In more "down-to-earth," everyday presentations, you might listen as a manager advocates the adoption of a flexible hours proposal that she claims will increase sales by

Everyday Example

Speaker Effectively Uses Statistics in Presentation on AIDS to Baylor University Students

The following article from the Baylor University student newspaper, the Lariat, describes a speaker's effective use of statistics in seeking support for the Christian relief and development organization World Vision.

Rich Stearns, president of World Vision, stunned Chapel audiences Wednesday with his staggering statistics on HIV and AIDS.

"Thirteen million kids have lost their parents in sub-Saharan Africa," Stearns said. "If they were all to join hands they would stretch from New York to Seattle to Philadelphia to San Francisco to Washington, D.C., to Los Angeles and end in Albuquerque, New Mexico."

World Vision, which was started by Dr. Bob Pierce as a relief fund for children orphaned during the Korean War, has grown into one of the largest humanitarian groups in the world.

Stearns said his concern for the AIDS "pandemic" stems from the increase of victims in Africa and around the world. Stearns said within a few years the life expectancy of a person living in sub-Saharan Africa will be approximately 29 years and a person will hit middle age by the age of 14 or 15 years. An even bigger concern Stearns has is the lack of Christian involvement in helping fight the AIDS epidemic. Stearns said he has found the willingness of the Christian community to help

support children with AIDS could not even compare with the support given by the non-Christian community. Stearns said he also has been surprised at the communities that have reached out to this cause. "In my opinion, Bono of U2 has done more to support and fight AIDS than any other person in this world," Stearns said.

World Vision expanded from aiding only orphaned children in 1953 to its first child sponsorship program in Korea. The expansion continued and soon included other Asian countries, Latin America and Africa.

"AIDS is the greatest humanitarian crisis of our time," Stearns said. "It's unlike any other problem ever before. It's the single issue that would define the Christian church in the 21st century."

Stearns emphasized that it is up to the generations to come to keep fighting this global crisis. "I was shocked and disturbed at the AIDS statistics," Jenny Kinslow, a Lebanon, Tenn., junior said. "I can't even imagine living in those circumstances with all of the odds against you."

Stearns ended his lecture with encouraging words to students and a reminder that "right thinking must be followed by right doing."

Source: Natalia Angelo, "Thirteen Million Reasons to Fight an Epidemic," *The Baylor Lariat*, October 10, 2002, Baylor University, Waco, Texas.

30 percent. How do you know this statistic is true? The manager should provide more information about its source. Perhaps she has information about another branch of the company that adopted the flex plan and increased their sales, or maybe she has an article from a credible trade publication in which the results of a controlled study support her claim. But can you trust those sources? Being skeptical of sources is probably safer than being totally accepting. **Source credibility** is the degree to which a source is believable and trustworthy. Sources vary in terms of their credibility. The sources listed earlier vary in their credibility. When you collect information to include in a presentation, you need to evaluate the credibility of the sources, and at times you might need to convey that evaluation to the audience. A few questions you might ask will help you in determining the credibility of the source, both in developing the presentation and as a critical listener:

source credibility A source's believability and trustworthiness.

Ascertaining the Credibility of Quotations

1. What is the source's expertise, training, education, and knowledge?
2. To what degree is the source serving his or her own self-interest?
3. How is the source regarded by other credible sources?
4. Under what circumstances did the source make the comment? Is the comment taken out of context?
5. Was the source in a position to know?

Ascertaining the Credibility of Statistics or Study Results

1. How valid (actually testing what it claimed to test) is the statistic or study on which the statistics are based?
2. Who were the participants? Were they randomly chosen to participate?
3. How generalizable are the results? Just because a survey is true for one group of people doesn't necessarily mean it is true for another group.
4. How large and how representative was the sample that participated?
5. Who conducted the study? To what degree might the statistics be skewed?
6. What other interpretations might be drawn from those statistics?

Speakers need to feel confident in the credibility of their statistical support. ●

Ascertaining the Credibility of Quotations and Statistics

1. What is the date of the source? Is it outdated (have things changed since the source appeared)?
2. To whom does the information pertain? Is it really relevant and applicable to this audience?
3. To what degree is the quotation or statistic atypical? Are there other sources that make the same claim or have the same finding?

Strategic Use of Support and Evidence

Understanding the types of support, such as stories, figurative language, reasoning, arguments, and evidence, is the first step in the process of strengthening a speech. The next step involves being strategic in how you use support. Simply providing a cavalcade of stories, quotations, statistics, and arguments doesn't make for an effective speech. Strategic use of supportive materials can increase speaker credibility, but this depends on selecting material that is appealing and connected to the audience's needs, values, and motives. This is facilitated by helping your audience visualize the support, limiting the amount of support, keeping the support simple, and selecting relevant material.

A Question of Ethics

1. Twilla has a quotation from a Dr. Jones that she wrote down while doing research at the library, but she forgot to write down the journal and date and hasn't been able to relocate the article. Should she just make a best guess as to the journal and date, present the quotation without the other information, or skip the quotation altogether? What is the rationale for your choice?

2. While describing the credibility of one of the experts Terrance quoted, he explained that the source had been a doctor for thirty years, had worked at the National Center for Disease Control, and had published over twenty research articles. Terrance also discovered but did not share with his audience the fact that his source's medical license had recently been taken away for unethical medical practices. To what degree is Terrance's omission unethical?

Use Support and Evidence to Increase Your Speaker Credibility

Speaker credibility is the degree to which an audience believes and trusts the speaker. Ultimately, your credibility determines whether the audience accepts any of your claims or evidence. If you have low speaker-credibility (or, worse yet, negative speaker-credibility), they will also judge your evidence with incredulity. The more negative the audiences are toward speakers, the more speakers must build their credibility and incorporate highly credible information. Positive and supportive audiences view speakers as highly credible and need little evidence to be persuaded—they accept the speaker's word. College students rarely challenge the information instructors provide because they view them as credible (we hope). Occasionally students who have a negative attitude toward an instructor may challege the instructor's claims. Figure 9.1 shows the balance between speaker credibility and the need for evidence.

One factor that might not be obvious from this continuum is that by citing evidence the audience views as credible, the speaker's own credibility may be increased.[13] The degree to which source credibility carries over to the speaker will depend on the perceived expertise and trustworthiness of your sources and the relevance of the evidence.[14] Which of the following two statements would you trust more in listening to a speech seeking to discourage college students from binge drinking?

Studies show that two out of five college students participated in binge drinking and that this behavior was associated with academic problems, antisocial behavior, automobile accidents, and other health and psychological problems.

Researchers from the Harvard School of Public Health published an article in the *Journal of American College Health* in 2002 in which

speaker credibility The degree to which an audience believes and trusts the speaker.

● **FIGURE 9.1** Speaker Credibility and the Need for Evidence.

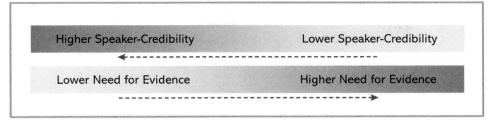

they reported that two out of five college students participated in binge drinking and that this behavior was associated with academic problems, antisocial behavior, automobile accidents, and other health and psychological problems.[15]

Assuming these two statements were made by different speakers, you should be inclined to see the second speaker as more credible for citing a specific source. In your presentations to negative audiences, you should include the names of the sources, their credentials (if not already known by the audience), the year of the publication, and the location where the information was found.

Select Evidence That Is Appealing

Remember that the Elaboration Likelihood Model suggests that uninvolved or uninterested audiences are less critical of and more affected by peripheral factors, such as stories and style of delivery, than are involved or interested audiences. This doesn't mean that you shouldn't provide any information; just that your information does not have to be particularly detailed. Look at the following two examples:

Example 1:
    In 1993 coach Ruthann Vilder started the women's soccer program. She left coaching in 1997, and our current coach, Michelle Foster, was hired at that time. The first season the team had two wins, thirteen losses, and one tie. Last year the team had its best season and went 10, 8, and 2, losing in the first round of the conference tournament. Our spring season starts next week, and we're excited by the experience we bring back and the new players, such as Jenny Fragle, a freshman all-state player who was a highly recruited midfielder with incredible speed, and Mary Winston, who was a nationally ranked junior college goalkeeper.

Example 2:
    The score is tied, time is running out; the team is moving the ball quickly down the field, passing the ball with great efficiency, dodging the defense; finally, from ten yards out, our midfielder kicked a high, arching ball that hit the bottom of the crossbar and bounded into the goal, giving the women's soccer team a final winning score of 2 to 1. This was how last year's game against our archrivals, Northeast State ended. Our team is off to a great start this year with a record of 3 and 1, and we play

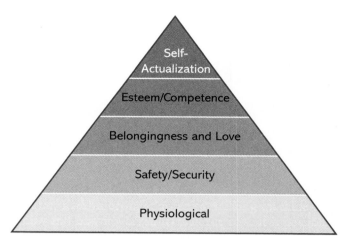

● **FIGURE 9.2** Maslow's Hierarchy of Needs. *Source:* Abraham Maslow, *Motivation and Personality* (New York: Harper & Row, 1970).

Northeast State next week. It will be a great opportunity for you to bring your family to see exciting sports action.

Both of these examples contain various pieces of information previously unknown to the audience. Which example do you think would generate more interest from the alumni audience? The first example provides factual data about the team's history and its potential for this year. The second example combines the use of storytelling with less factual information that was chosen because of its potential appeal to the listeners. Some audiences, like the positive or neutral audiences, won't be challenging the facts or information, though you have an ethical responsibility to be honest.

Connect Support to Audience Needs

You've probably heard the phrase "Sometimes people just don't realize what they're missing." That phrase applies to some of the audiences you will be facing. This means raising the awareness of audiences about an unrecognized need they have. Life insurance salespeople face this situation all the time. Before they can sell a policy, they have to convince people of their need for insurance—they have to generate interest. Not all needs are self-apparent, and certainly the connection of an audience's needs to your topic may not be readily apparent. So what are some of the needs you can identify and utilize for the audience?

Abraham Maslow created a **hierarchy of needs,** which can be drawn as a pyramid, depicting ascending levels of human needs (see Figure 9.2). In this widely accepted model, Maslow presents needs relative to one another, beginning at the bottom with the most basic needs. We are moti-

hierarchy of needs A model developed by Abraham Maslow that ranks ascending levels of human needs in the shape of a pyramid.

ACT&REFLECT

9.2: Appealing to Needs

ACT • Assume you are speaking to your current class on each of the following topics. Identify a need to which you could appeal if you had evidence and explain the connection.

Topic	Need	How It Connects
1. Medicare		
2. Owning a pet		
3. Hybrid autos		
4. Learning a second language		
5. Your own topic		

REFLECT • Which of these would probably be the most effective connection? Why? To what degree would your fellow students accept the connections you claim without evidence?

vated to satisfy these needs; in general, we first seek to meet the needs at the lower levels before moving to the next higher level. As you read about each of the levels, consider how you might show an audience how listening to a topic you are considering for your next presentation will meet one or more of their needs. Physiological needs are just that—the needs we have for our physical being to survive, including food and water, shelter, clothing, sex, and so on. Safety and security represent our need to feel protected and free from threat or harm. Next are our needs to belong to groups or families, to be accepted, and to be loved. The fourth level, esteem and competence, reflects our needs for approval, to be valued, to have abilities and skills. When you have no worries about meeting your basic needs, love, or esteem, you then find yourself able to explore such issues as your own nature, religion, spiritual life, aesthetics, or peace. This occurs when we seek to satisfy the final level of needs, self-actualization, which includes our need to meet our potential, and to feel fulfilled.

Let's try to apply these needs to an analysis of your classmates to determine the type of supportive material you could use to attain their interest. Choose a hobby you have or would like to pursue and think about its application to this example. Suppose you are a quilter and are planning to talk to the class about some of the traditional designs, techniques, and fabrics. Quilting probably doesn't seem like anything that can be connected to Maslow's hierarchy. Making such connections requires an open mind and creative thinking (see Act and Reflect 9.2). Here's what you might consider:

Physiological Needs (Acquiring money is a significant way we fulfill these needs)

- Old quilts can be very valuable.
- Quilts often turn up at garage sales and flea markets.
- Knowing what makes a quilt valuable might mean your listeners could make a profitable purchase.

Need for Belonging

- Talk about the number of people who are involved in quilting or who own quilts.
- You should support the appeals to your audience's needs by supplying specific evidence. For example, belonging to a large, active group could be supported by citing a survey from the *Quilter's Newsletter Magazine* that found almost 20 million quilters in the United States in 2000 spending over $1.8 billion a year on quilting products in an industry that has increased in value by over 50 percent in three years.

Need for Competence and Aesthetics

- A knowledge of quilting helps one to appreciate the art, history, and effort that are involved in the creation of quilts.

Appeal to the Audience's Values and Motives

In his 1935 public speaking text, Alan Monroe recognized that Maslow's hierarchy could be expanded to include a larger set of factors he called "motive appeals" that speakers could use as a basis for influencing the audience.[16] Other researchers have developed similar lists identifying values associated with a given culture that can serve

What needs are this audience likely to have? ●

● **TABLE 9.2**   Values Held by Citizens of the United States.

Achievement	Economy	Popularity
Acquisition/Saving	Endurance	Power/Authority
Adventure, Change	Family	Pride (reputation, self-respect)
Beauty	Fear	Quality
Collectivism (group work)	Fighting and Aggression	Reverence, Worship
Companionship/Affiliation	Health	Sexual Attraction/Sex
Competition	Individualism	Social Status
Convenience	Independence	Sympathy/Generosity
Courtesy	Imitation/Conformity	Technology
Creativity	Leisure/Recreation	Tradition
Curiosity	Loyalty (to family, friends, etc.)	Uniqueness
Deference	Modernity/Newness	Wealth
Dependence	Nurturance	Wisdom
Destructiveness	Patriotism	Work
	Personal Enjoyment (comfort, pleasantness, freedom from restraint)	Youth

Source: List drawn from A. H. Monroe and D. Ehninger, Principles of Speech Communication, 7th brief ed. (Glenview, IL: Scott, Foresman, 1975); H. Cheng and J. C. Schweitzer, "Cultural Values Reflected in Chinese and U.S. Television Commercials," Journal of Advertising Research, 36, (1996): 27–45.

as the basis for formulating persuasive and advertising appeals. The majority of research that has looked at appeals to the audience has focused on commercials and advertisements rather than presentations. Table 9.2 shows some of the values typically identified as important to citizens of the United States.

Monroe pointed out in his original discussion that while several of the values are contradictory, that is part of the nature of humans. We like both tradition and modernity, we like individualism and collectivism, and we like both authority and independence. One study of the United States found that appeals to enjoyment, modernity, individualism, economy, youth, effectiveness, competition, and sex were those most used in TV commercials.[17] Advertisers obviously believe these values are important to consumers, and appeals to such values by speakers are likely to met with similar success. When you are planning your presentation, appeal to the values that are most closely aligned with your topic, audience, evidence, and goals.

The values that are associated with the United States are different from those for other cultures. More important, for you, even within the United States, the groups you speak to may reflect a different set of value priorities. For example, organizations and

ACT&REFLECT

9.3: Appealing to Audience Values

ACT • Examine the list of values/appeals. Write down the five you think are most important to your classmates. Think about a topic you are developing or might develop. Write down how each of the values you identified could be linked to your topic.

Value	Link to Your Topic
Example: Individualism	Each quilt is unique and reflects a quilter's personality and culture.
1.	
2.	
3.	
4.	
5.	

REFLECT • Why did you pick the five values you did? How well would these values apply if you were talking to a group of first-year high school students or a group of employees at Wal-Mart?

their members can be described by the values they hold that make them unique.[18] You can probably identify differences in the values held by the various companies or stores in which you have worked. You need to be sensitive to what values your listeners have and then appeal to those values.

As with needs, you will need evidence to connect your topic to the audience's values (see Act and Reflect 9.3). The stronger the connections you can make for the neutral audience, the more likely you are to arouse their interest. For example, values such as tradition and patriotism might be linked to quilting in our sample speech:

> Quilting in America was initially only done by those who had free time because they had household help, and even then, only for special occasions such as weddings or births. Not until the American textile industry blossomed and started producing affordable fabrics in the 1840s did quilting became a more common practice, according to the book *Quiltmaking in America: Beyond the Myths*. Quilts are part of the American tradition. They were made and sold to raise funds to support the Civil War, and signature quilts can be found that capture a moment in time of entire communities. Similarly, there is now an AIDS quilt that emotionally reflects the lives of many who have been infected.

Show the Impact through Visualization

You can also help the audience see the impact of your position through a technique known as **visualization,** by which you seek to generate an image in the mind of your audience members. Visualization can be used anywhere in your presentation when you want the audience to visualize the impact on them. (Visualization is one of the steps Alan Monroe identified in his organizational pattern called the Motivated Sequence, which we discuss in the next chapter.) It is a way you can convert information that is abstract or removed from the audience's experience into something more relevant and tangible. The use of storytelling is an effective way to help your audience visualize something. For example, rather than discussing how the recent tax increase has hurt people in general, a speaker might use visualization in a story that describes the Grover family of four, whose father was forced to take a second job at night working at a 7-Eleven convenience store because the tax increase had reduced the annual family income by $3,000, just as one of his children was headed off to college. Audience members might identify with the example.

When seeking the interest of the neutral audience, you can use visualization to show your audience how listening to your presentation can have an impact on them. Using the quilting speech example again, you might say the following (notice the various values that are included):

> You've graduated and are now working at a great job, but money is a little tight as you pay back your loans. Saturday rolls around, and you find yourself with nothing to do. Your spouse suggests going on a little adventure to yard sales to find some bargains. You agree, and pretty soon you find yourself looking at what appears to be an antique quilt. The design is very striking and appealing to you. The price is just fifty dollars. You decide to buy it and take it home, where you display it on the back of your couch. One day a friend is visiting who knows a lot about quilts and proclaims that your quilt is worth at least one thousand dollars. You were lucky, but by knowing a little more about quilts, you might increase your chances of such a fortunate outcome.

Would you be inclined to listen to this speech? You might be if you could visualize yourself in the story. The effectiveness of the visualization depends on your ability to identify the needs and motives of your listeners and to use those in creating a visualization with which they can identify. One problem with this visualization is that most of us realize we're not ever going to find the $1,000 quilt, and thus we might tune out the speaker. The visualization needs to be believable, and to have fidelity and coherence.

Simplify and Limit Support Material

Again, your audiences' backgrounds are going to determine how complex or simple the evidence and support materials are

visualization Showing the impact of your position by generating an image in the mind of your audience members.

that you incorporate in your presentations. When your audience is primarily unknowl-edgeable; they don't have the background knowledge to understand detailed and complex information, so you have to keep it simple.[19] In discussing the use of argu-ments, we made the point that unknowledgeable audiences are less likely than knowl-edgeable audiences to critically analyze what you say.[20] This means you should avoid complex and sophisticated support material. Your own classroom experiences may reflect this principle. You've probably understood complex and detailed information in courses where you had taken the necessary prerequisites or related courses better than in courses for which you lacked the prerequites. Fortunately, most instructors have a good sense of the students' academic backgrounds and adapt the information accord-ingly, just as we are suggesting you do.

As mentioned earlier, unknowledgeable audiences are more affected by pe-ripheral factors, such as emotions and speaker credibility, than by the content. This means you don't need to overwhelm these audiences with evidence. In general, you want to carefully select a few of the strongest, simplest, and most relevant pieces of evidence. However, selecting the choicest material can be more challenging than presenting a plethora of data. What follows is a set of different support mate-rials you could use in a presentation to your classmates about the value of caucuses in the presidential primaries. As you read, try to imagine hearing someone say these lines, because there is a difference in how well we digest spoken versus written in-formation.

Party caucuses were the most common means of selecting presidential candidates until 1968, when, according to a 2000 article in the journal *Social Education*, Democrats dis-satisfied because they thought caucuses gave too much control of their party to too few people, pushed for more use of primaries. In 1968, for the Democratic Party, seven-teen states used primaries. In 2004, forty-one states used primaries.

A quotation from the January 21, 2004, *Omaha World Herald* illustrates the advantage the Iowa caucus has over later primaries: "Still, many observers have correctly noted that in Iowa, at least everyday citizens get face-to-face exposure to the candidates—an opportunity to look them in the eyes and shake their hand and actually talk with them." In addition, the article said, "After that, the campaign morphs relentlessly into simplistic TV sound bites and 'debates' that typically aren't true debates at all. There's not much substance there for the average citizen."

The caucuses allow people to get an in-depth look at the potential candidates and to be kind of a test run for the actual presidential race. One reporter for the *New York Times* wrote after the 2004 Iowa Caucuses that it "tested the candidates, over many months, first in small settings and then in a media glare, and revealed weaknesses that were not initially clear and strengths that only gradually became apparent."[21] Such an intense evaluation doesn't seem as likely to occur when only primaries are used for the selection of candidates.

Assuming you have a neutral attitude about caucuses versus primaries, the third example probably has enough information in it to influence you. The other two examples have more than you need. That doesn't make them necessarily bad, just inefficient. Here's a little follow-up activity related to those three examples. Without looking up at the example, look away from the book and see what facts you can recall. Most neutral listeners remember only the gist of the evidence and are more likely to remember the more simple information. You should be selective in what evidence you provide and keep it simple.

While neutral audiences may not fully comprehend support material that is over their heads and complex, that apparently doesn't mean you have to be concise. Research shows that longer messages change unknowledgeable audience's attitudes more than shorter messages, but this is not true for knowledgeable audiences.[22] As we mentioned before, unknowledgeable listeners are affected by peripheral cues, including message length. Apparently, these audiences equate the length of the message to its importance, because they are not critically processing a lot of the information or arguments, only assessing their general impression—"It was long; it must have been important."

Select Relevant Information

The final factor to consider about support material is the degree to which it is important for your audience to remember and recall that information. When you want the audience to remember your evidence and support material, you need to make it relevant. Studies indicate that the brain looks for familiar, interesting, and important information.[23] Providing your listeners with such information increases the likelihood that they will hear and remember what you've said. Information is relevant when we see it having some value for us. As audiences listen to your speech content, they are making decisions about whether to retain the information you provide. As listeners, we try to reduce the amount of information we have to process and retain; otherwise, we are overwhelmed. So we retain only the information we regard as important and relevant and discard the rest. That's one reason students often ask instructors, "Will this be on the exam?" For students, lecture material is relevant because it is needed to pass exams and the course. Students have an amazing capacity to forget everything they "learned" the moment they have completed an exam. Other audiences are no different; they will remember information and be positively influenced by you when they see the information as relevant, and only for as long as it is useful.

What makes something relevant or important to us? One model (Table 9.3) identifies five factors that determine the amount of vested interest a person has in an issue. Each of these five can be related to the kinds of questions you should ask yourself when deciding which pieces of support or evidence to incorporate.

● **TABLE 9.3** Determining the Relevance of Your Support.

Factors	Questions
Personal consequence: Gain or loss for the listeners	How well does the support show the personal impact on your listeners?
Salience: Degree of obviousness or importance	How obvious is it that the support is important to listeners?
Certainty: How sure listeners are that the issue affects them	To what degree does the support make it clear that the listeners are definitely affected?
Immediacy: How soon the issue is likely to have an impact	How well does the support demonstrate an immediate impact on the listeners?
Self-Efficacy: Ability of the listeners to do anything about it	To what degree are you providing evidence that the listeners' actions will make a difference?

Source: W. Crano, "Attitude Strength and Vested Interest," in Petty and Krosnick, *Attitude Strength: Antecedents and Consequences,* 131–158.

● GETTING TO WORK

Chapter 7 provides guidance on how to locate testimony and statistics that can be utilized in your speeches. One part of the process involves deciding which parts of your presentation need support. As you locate potential support material, you will have to evaluate its credibility and decide how to best convey that information to the audience. In some instances, you might decide that the statistics are too complicated to describe and instead incorporate the use of a visual aid, as discussed in the next chapter.

In developing your presentation, there are a number of decisions you must make about the need for quotations or statistics and what types of these to incorporate. Those decisions, again, will depend on the type of audience you have and their attitude toward you. Negative audiences will require strong evidence that they view as credible, while positive audiences require little, particularly when you are presenting claims they already endorse.

Be strategic in your selection and inclusion of support materials by addressing the following questions:

- Which points are most in need of support (which will the audience question the most)?
- What types of evidence will your specific audience be most responsive to?
- How will the audience react to each source (is the source credible to them)?
- How can you connect your support and evidence to the audience's needs, values, and motives?
- Is the support material relevant to the audience and your issues?

- In what ways can you make the support and evidence easier for the audience to visualize and understand?
- Are you presenting enough or too much support and evidence?

The inclusion of relevant and powerful evidence and support often makes the difference between an effective and an ineffective presentation. However, the key is balancing between too much and too little evidence. You don't want to overwhelm your audience with so many facts and figures that they miss the big picture. On the other hand, a speech devoid of support is not only dry but easier for listeners to discard.

SUMMARY

Evidence is anything a speaker uses to back up claims and assertions that is typically verifiable. Evidence includes reference to information from outside sources (using quotations or paraphrasing), statistics, or actual "hands-on" visual support. Simply adding evidence in the form of testimony or statistics will not ensure that it has an effect on your audience. Evidence must be heard, thought about, and evaluated as legitimate, and the connection between evidence and your conclusion must be accepted. You can reference material to support your speech by paraphrasing it or directly quoting the words of your source. There are a number of guidelines to follow in deciding whether a source is appropriate to use and how to use it.

Numbers and statistics can be used as evidence in support of your presentation. Speakers need to be careful about not confusing the audience with

numbers by keeping them simple, using more concise ways of conveying information, such as percentages, and personalizing the information. Source credibility is the believability and trustworthiness of your sources. The audience needs to believe that the source is trustworthy, has relevant expertise, and is not being misquoted or misrepresented. Statistics need to be reliable, based on sound research, and correctly interpreted.

Support and evidence should be used strategically. Use them to increase your speaker credibility; select evidence that is appealing; connect support to audience needs, such as those reflected in Maslow's hierarchy of needs; appeal to the audience's values and motives; show the impact of the evidence by using visualization; keep the evidence limited and simple; and, finally, select evidence that is relevant to the audience.

VIDEO EXPERIENCE

1. Dr. Jon Oberlander, a faculty member in social medicine at the University of North Carolina, Chapel Hill, addresses health reform and the uninsured at a state conference in North Carolina. He provides statistical information in both a visual and oral manner to support his contentions.

2. Bill Gates is well known as a cofounder of Microsoft. One of the directives of his foun-

dation is the improvement of education. In this address to a national conference of governors and educators, he uses a prepared manuscript to ensure the accuracy of his comments. He uses a variety of support materials and follows a number of the strategies discussed in Chapters 8 and 9.

THINKING BACK, THINKING AHEAD

1. Find a recent article in the newspaper or a magazine that includes quotations and statistics. To what degree does that evidence effect your reaction to the article? Does it make the article more believable? Does it make the article more persuasive? In what ways might the support materials undermine the purpose of the article? Reading an article is not the same as listening to a speech. If you were developing a speech based on this article, what would you change in the presentation of the evidence?

2. How credible are the following sources?

   a. A tobacco executive quoted as saying smoking is not addictive.

   b. A mother talking about the death of her child from Sudden Infant Death Syndrome.

   c. A college English professor talking about how great her new SUV is.

   d. 1990 statistics from the Labor Department about minority employment in the United States.

   e. Survey results by *Rolling Stone* magazine showing support for legalizing marijuana.

   For each of these five issues, what sources would be more credible? For your next presentation, what sources could you look for that would have strong credibility?

3. Look through a magazine or newspaper and find an article on a topic you find of interest (for example, best athlete of the year, a report on a cancer-causing substance, tips for buying a DVD player, cooking with less fat, or a new diet trend). Examine the content of the article for evidence and support that you might be able to use for a speech on the topic. Assume you are speaking to your classmates and that they are uninterested and unknowledgeable about the topic.

   a. What evidence from the article would be appealing?

   b. What evidence is there that relates to your classmates' needs, values, or motives?

   c. What evidence is there that you can use to help the audience visualize the issue?

   d. Find another piece of evidence in the article. What does your audience already know to which you can relate the evidence?

   e. Find a piece of complicated information in the article. How could you simplify it?

   f. What evidence is there that will help you demonstrate the relevance of the issue to your classmates?

NOTES

1. Amaury Nora, "Reexamining the Community College Mission," retrieved from the American Association of Community Colleges Web site, at www.aacc.nche.edu.

2. *Trends in College Pricing 2004*, retrieved from College Board Web site, at www.collegeboard.com.

3. Retrieved from College Board Web site, at www.collegeboard.com/article/0,3868,4-21-0-8169,00.html.

4. The first three factors are drawn from R. A. Reynolds and J. L. Reynolds, "Evidence," in *The Persuasion Handbook: Developments in Theory and Practice*, edited by J. P. Dillard and M. Pfau (Thousand Oaks, CA: Sage, 2002), 427–444.

5. Reynolds and Reynolds, "Evidence."

6. Reynolds and Reynolds, "Evidence."

7. T. B. Harte, "The Effects of Evidence in Persuasive Communication," *Central States Speech Journal, 27* (1976): 42–46.

8. J. A. Luchok and J. C. McCroskey, "The Effect of Quality of Evidence on Attitude Change and Source Credibility," *Southern Speech Communication Journal, 43* (1978): 371–383.

9. Luchok and McCroskey, "The Effect of Quality of Evidence."

10. P. Watzlawick, J. H. Beavin, and D. D. Jackson, *Pragmatics of Human Communication* (New York: Norton, 1967), p. 84

11. FOX News/Opinion Dynamics Poll, September 9–10, 2003, Retrieved from Polling Report.com Web site, at www.pollingreport.com/computer.htm.
12. Julian Bond, commencement address, Washington University, St. Louis, May 19, 2003. Retrieved online from the *Record* on March 23, 2006 at http://record.wustl.edu.
13. R. M. Perloff, *The Dynamics of Persuasion: Communication and Attitudes in the 21st Century,* 2nd ed. (Mahwah, NJ: Erlbaum, 2003).
14. D. J. O'Keefe, *Persuasion: Theory and Research,* 2nd ed. (Thousand Oaks, CA: Sage, 2002).
15. H. Weschler, J. E. Lee, T. F. Nelson, and M. Kuo, "Underage College Students' Drinking Behavior: Access to Alcohol, and the Influence of Deterrence Policies," *Journal of American College Health, 50* (2002): 223–236.
16. A. Monroe, *Principles and Types of Speech* (New York: Scott, Foresman, 1935).
17. Cheng and Schweitzer, "Cultural Values."
18. M. E. Panakowsky and N. O'Donnell-Trujillo, "Organizational Communication as Cultural Performance," *Communication Monographs, 50* (1983): 126–147.
19. W. Wood, N. Rhodes, and M. Biek, "Working Knowledge and Attitude Strength: An Information-Processing Analysis," in *Attitude Strength: Antecedents and Consequences,* edited by R. Petty and J. Krosnick (Mahwah, NJ: Erlbaum, 1995), 283–314.
20. Wood, Rhodes, and Biek, "Working Knowledge and Attitude Strength."
21. T. S. Purdum, "Shattering Iowa Myths," *New York Times,* January 20, 2004 (retrieved online through Lexis-Nexis).
22. Wood, Rhodes, and Biek, "Working Knowledge and Attitude Strength."
23. R. Sylwester, *A Celebration of Neurons: An Educators' Guide to the Human Brain.* (Alexandria, VA: Association for Supervision and Curriculum Development, 1995).

Chapter 10

Supporting Your Presentation

Visual Support

Goals

✓ To show you how visual support differs from other forms of support

✓ To help you realize how visual support can benefit your presentation and you as you present

✓ To familiarize you with various types of visuals, how to use them, and their pros and cons

✓ To lead you through the basics for designing viewing visuals

✓ To develop in you an awareness of general do's and don'ts when you use visual support

The Columbia Accident Investigation Board at NASA released Volume 1 of its report on why the space shuttle crashed. As expected, the ship's foam insulation was the main cause of the disaster. But the board also fingered another unusual culprit: PowerPoint, Microsoft's well-known "slideware" program.

NASA, the board argued, had become too reliant on presenting complex information via PowerPoint, instead of by means of traditional ink-and-paper technical reports. When NASA engineers assessed possible wing damage during the mission, they presented the findings in a confusing PowerPoint slide—so crammed with nested bullet points and irregular short forms that it was nearly impossible to untangle. "It is easy to understand how a senior manager might read this PowerPoint slide and not realize that it addresses a life-threatening situation," the board sternly noted.[1]

The last time you viewed a PowerPoint presentation was probably very recent, and you might even have seen more than one recently. Perhaps you have instructors who depend on PowerPoint presentations for dissemination of course material during lectures; maybe you have viewed a PowerPoint presentation in a motorcycle showroom or other store to learn about a new product; possibly you have seen a classmate's PowerPoint presentation or even created one yourself for a speech. Did you notice we are using the term "PowerPoint presentation," as if the point of the presentation is to view a series of PowerPoint slides, with the presenter being superfluous? Apparently NASA relied on PowerPoint for that very reason, that is, to transmit critical information without other explanation or supplement.

The reason we bring these PowerPoint examples to your attention is to remind you that PowerPoint plays a major role in the dissemination of information. However, PowerPoint is not the message itself; PowerPoint is a visual aid. The role of PowerPoint is to provide visual support for a presentation. Rather than PowerPoint, or any other visual aid, for that matter, becoming the message, this chapter subscribes to the viewpoint that visual support or visual aids do just that: they "aid" a presenter in the delivery of a presentation, and they "aid" the audience in receiving the content of the presentation in a number of ways. ●

Defining Visual Support

When we use the terms **visual support** or **visual aid,** we are referring to anything besides the message itself that stimulates audience interest, aids in their comprehension or retention of the message, or benefits a presentation in some other manner. Visual aids include information from the presentation that is displayed to the audience in a different format; for example, you might display a bar chart to demonstrate height and weight gains of Americans over a period of years. Visual aids are also objects that replicate the content of the presentation, as when you are explaining the uses of different golf clubs and you display an example of each type of club as you are discussing it. In addition, people also serve as visual aids, as when a presenter demonstrates ways to protect against an attacker or dances a few steps of the latest dance.

Although we will devote most of this discussion to visual support, there might be instances when you will choose audio support. If you are discussing the evolution of the work of the music group U2, a series of cuts of their releases, with key examples, might be the most effective way to show the audience how the group's music has changed.

Improving Your Presentation Using Visual Support

"Presentations using visual aids were found to be 43% more persuasive than unaided presentations."[2] "Curves and bar charts . . . can increase comprehension by as much as 500 per cent."[3] We can't confirm that incorporating visual support results in such drastic changes as these two studies claim, but we do believe using visual support results in a number of advantages for audience members and for the presenter.

Positive Perceptions of the Presenter

How do you view presenters who use visual support in comparison to those who do not? Does it seem to you that a presenter who takes the time to plan, develop, and implement visual support is more professional? Do you believe that presenters who use visual support are probably better presenters? That is the case with audiences who are listening to a speaker who uses visual support.

The inclusion of visual support appears to enhance the listeners' perceptions of the presenter in a number of ways. Presenters who incorporate visual aids are viewed as more credible by their listeners than those who do not.[4] Presenters who incorporated visual aids into their presentations were also viewed as being more professional, as giving a more concise message, and as being more interactive with their audiences than those who did not do so.[5]

Increased Attention

If you had the choice of attending a history class with an instructor who was in business attire lecturing on the Revolutionary War campaigns of George Washington or attending a

visual support Anything besides the message itself that stimulates audience interest or aids in comprehension or retention of the message or benefits a presentation in some other way.

visual aid Same as visual support.

history class with the instructor wearing clothing authentic to the time, which would you prefer? If you chose the authentically-clad lecturer, it was for a reason that you are likely to be already aware of: the use of visual aids increases listener attention.[6] The more distinctive the visual aid, the more likely it is to retain your attention. If your instructor lectured while wearing the usual attire, the effect of the lecture might be reduced; if the authentic attire is worn, attention-getting value would be increased. A neutral audience would be motivated to "sit up and listen" to a presentation that included such striking or distinctive visual support.

Improved Comprehension

You might believe that you yourself are a "visual learner." That is, it is easier for you to understand knowledge that is disseminated visually than through other methods, such as lectures or reading textbooks. Clearly, for audience members who are visual learners, it would be advantageous to present certain pieces of knowledge this way. Nonetheless, there are also some kinds of knowledge that are simply more easily understood or comprehended if presented visually. For example, if you were listening to a presenter discussing changes in temperature as an influence on various food crop yields, it might be easier for you to understand the point if the presenter provided a line graph showing temperature fluctuations and food production within a given time frame, rather than giving you a verbal account spanning several years of average temperatures and average food crop yields.[7]

Would your attention be attracted to this speaker if he wore a traditional business suit? Visual support, including speaker attire, helps to attract and maintain audience attention. ●

What information about educational attainment is available to you at a glance at the line graph in Figure 10.1? Using a visual aid such as this graphic allows you to present information that your audience will be able to comprehend more easily than if they were to listen to a verbal explanation that would have to contain references to the twenty-five-year period illustrated and the age range indicated. And there is another advantage to using this type of graphic. When you indicate areas on the graphic that you want the audience to focus on, you are guided by the visual aid to provide more clear commentary (see Act and Reflect 10.1).

Greater Agreement

"Show me," says the Missouri license plate. Because they have the power to show your audience what you, the presenter, can only tell them, visual aids also influence agreement and general attitude change among audience members.[8] Since securing listeners' agreement is often a reason for giving a presentation in the first place, the "agreement" function of visual support is especially important. Have you ever said, "If I

● **FIGURE 10.1** A Sample Line Graph: Educational Attainment of the Population 25 Years and Over by Age: 1947 to 2003.
Source: U.S. Census Bureau, Current Population Survey and the 1950 Census of Population. From N. Stoops, "Educational Attainment of the Population Twenty-five Years and Over by Age: 1947 to 2003," retrieved from U.S. Census Bureau Web site, at http://www.census.gov/.

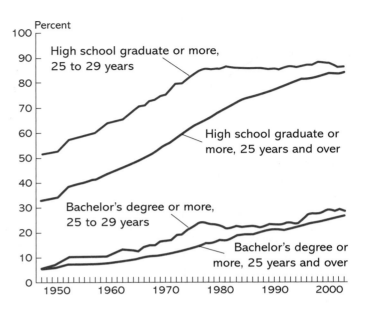

ACT & REFLECT

10.1: Conduct an Experiment with Pie Charts

ACT • Ross gave a speech urging his audience to vote.[9] He demonstrated that low voter turnout occurred in a variety of elections, by showing pie charts of voter turnout in campus, state, and national elections. As he displayed each pie chart, he verbally interpreted the point displayed by each chart, that is, the percentage of those who voted compared to those who did not. Watch this brief clip of Ross's speech three times: the first time with the volume turned up, but with your eyes averted from the clip; the second time with the volume turned off, watching the visual representation; the third time with the volume turned up, watching the clip.

REFLECT • How effective would this segment of Ross's speech have been for you if the visuals had not been included? Would his point have been clear to you with only the verbal message? To what extent would the point have been clear if Ross had not interpreted the results and you had only the visuals to depend on? What does this experiment tell you about the value of visual support in helping an audience to comprehend a speaker's message?

hadn't seen it, I wouldn't have believed it?" This might be the way audience members respond when you are able to demonstrate that a person of very small stature could protect himself or herself against a much larger person by using various martial arts moves. Or it could explain why individuals pull out their wallets in response to a video showing disaster victims. Visual aids make words come to life; visual aids create a feeling of reality, and they are a powerful means to influence attitudes and elicit agreement from the audience. The "ability to influence" dimension of visual support is certainly one of the most powerful reasons to incorporate visual aids into a presentation; however, because of this, choosing and incorporating visual aids is also one of the more difficult and important decisions a speaker can make. When you are presenting to a negative audience, it will help you reach your communication goal if you present evidence to support your viewpoint visually as well as through your own effective delivery. When your audience is neutral, you will want to choose visual support that stimulates their interest. When your audience is positive, visuals that inform and add to their existing knowledge should be your choice.

To demonstrate the relationship of the amount of tip given to servers as a result of their attire and responsiveness to diners, Kelley chose to display the results on the bar graph shown in Figure 10.2. Could a line graph or pie chart be used instead to display this type of information? Probably not, because Kelley is comparing several variables that were measured at several points in time. What other advantages do you see in Kelley's choice of bar graph as a visual aid for the information that is displayed on it?

Better Retention

Besides the power of visual support to influence listeners, visuals also help the audience retain information longer than if they were not included. In one study, faculty in a psychology department investigated whether visual support incorporated in lectures

A Question of **Ethics**

We hope you are beginning to see the power that visual support brings to your presentation. Along with that power, however, comes responsibility. When you select a visual aid, at what point do you conclude that some visual representations should not be displayed within the environment of your presentation? If you are trying to influence your audience to donate to the Red Cross following a natural disaster, for example, is it ethical to show victims of the disaster to illustrate who will benefit from their donations? Is it ethical to show families grieving over family members who did not survive the disaster? To show individuals as they arrive at their destroyed homes for the first time following the disaster? At what point does a visual aid illustrate a situation you are trying to make "real" for your audience and at what point does the visual aid become an invasion of the privacy of suffering human beings?

● **FIGURE 10.2** A Sample Bar Graph: Comparing Attire of Server and Tips Received.
Source: Kelley Kunz, bar graph developed to illustrate relationships of servers' attire, responsiveness to diners, and amount of tips, October 25, 2005.

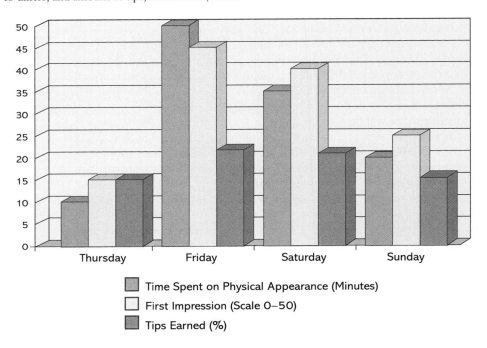

■ Time Spent on Physical Appearance (Minutes)
□ First Impression (Scale 0–50)
■ Tips Earned (%)

and other classroom activities influenced the extent to which students were able to retain information from classes at the end of the semester. The researchers concluded that aids that were especially vivid, such as videotapes and demonstrations, were most likely to be recalled by students at the end of the semester.[10] See Act and Reflect 10.2. In addition, it could be that visual aids help us to remember because we are receiving information through two channels: visual and audio.

Advantages for the Presenter

Besides the fact that visual aids present a number of advantages for audience members, our work with students in public speaking classes indicates that such aids also help presenters.

Reduced Nervousness

Just as you warm up before running five miles, you can also "warm up" before you begin your presentation if you are using visual aids. When you place a transparency on

ACT&REFLECT

10.2: When Would You Use a Matrix?

ACT • Table 10.1 is intended to illustrate that integrating visuals enhances an audience's retention of information. If you were to use this table to illustrate your speech, what would you say as you displayed it to your audience and which, if any, parts of it would you point out to your audience?

● **TABLE 10.1** A Sample Matrix: Retention of Information When Visuals Are Integrated into Presentation.

	Retention after	
	3 hours	*3 days*
Tell only	70%	10%
Show only	72%	20%
Show and tell	85%	65%

Source: Copyright 1984 by T. C. Smith, *Making Successful Presentations* (New York: Wiley, first published 1984), p. 52.

REFLECT • What does this exercise tell you about the use of a table? Are there certain applications that make tables more useful than other visual aids? What considerations would a speaker need to keep in mind to effectively use a table?

the overhead projector to ensure it is focused, when you check to make sure the objects you will need are all in front of you and in the correct position, when you log on to the computer for your PowerPoint presentation, you are, in effect, warming up before you actually begin. You are working in front of the audience in the physical space in which you will be presenting, and you are "psyching yourself" to begin your presentation. This advantage alone is reason enough to consider ways you can incorporate visual support.

Increased Clarity of Explanations

Referring to your visual support can help you present clear explanations. When you project a map of a newly opened city park to inform your audience of the trails, fishing spots, and other amenities, you might use a laser pointer to indicate these features. You could easily organize your presentation with a major point corresponding to each type of feature. As you focus on each area with the laser printer—for example, fishing spots are all on the north side of the park, beaches are to the west, and the trails connect all of the features, your explanations or descriptions are anchored to each area. If you are explaining a complex process, perhaps the path of a bill on its way to becoming a law, or describing the operation of a new piece of machinery in a training session, referring to various areas of the visual while you are disclosing information helps you to organize your own thoughts in a clear manner.

Reduced Dependence on Notes

With the use of a visual aid, you might also be able to reduce or totally eliminate your notes. In the case of the map of the new city park, you could reduce your notes to a few key words and phrases that lead you through your introduction and conclusion. During the body of your presentation, you could refer to the map and totally dispense with notes. If you are using a transparency that identifies key points you intend to

Everyday Example

Visual Aids Benefit the Presenter

The photo shows Professor James Pease during his weekly radio show. Even though his listening audience is unable to appreciate his visual aids, Dr. Pease routinely includes them during his show on animal ecology because they help him organize his comments. In the speech you are currently preparing, are there areas where visual aids might help you present your message with greater clarity? With better organization?

Even though this person is speaking on radio, the use of taxidermal animals as visual aids assists him in organizing his thoughts. ●

Visual aids benefit the speaker by serving as reminders of what comes next. ●

convey to your audience, if you are able to feel relatively confident of your introduction and conclusion, as you reveal each point that is on a transparency to your audience, you are also reminded of what you wish to say next. In this instance, you might be able to work without any notes at all.

MSL

When Amy explained the differences in four types of athletic footwear, she used an Elmo, a machine similar to an overhead projector, to display information and illustrations of the four types of footwear for her audience. She also used the visuals as her notes. From time to time she glanced at the information where it was resting on the Elmo to guide herself through her presentation.[11]

Greater Confidence

The act of determining which pieces of information in your presentation require visual support will surely require you to carefully consider the points you plan to convey. The additional scrutiny you give your presentation as you do so should have the added benefit of helping you own your message.

Types of Visual Support

We have already mentioned a few of the options you have available to you in selecting visual support. Now we'll talk about them in a more systematic and inclusive manner. We will also give some suggestions for choosing and preparing "hands-on" visuals, and finally we will discuss ways to use people as visual aids.

"Viewing" Visuals

Slide Ware (like PowerPoint) This is any computer software that is used for creating slides (the formatted panels that are

slide ware Computer software used for creating slides.

displayed using a computer and projector). PowerPoint is by far the most dominant of these programs, because it is usually part of the Microsoft software bundle, but others exist as well. You may already be skilled in developing your own slide ware; however, if you believe you need some additional information, or a review, we have included basic principles to understanding slide ware and an introduction to the basics of creating materials in Appendix B.

MSL

When Crystal wanted to show her audience how levels of obesity had risen in the United States over a period of several years, she used color-coded maps of the country to demonstrate the increasing percentage of adults who were considered obese throughout her time frame. Her slide ware allowed her to present several facts about each year she discussed over a time frame of several years in a relatively concise manner.[12]

Advantages There are many advantages to using slide ware in your presentation. If you have a computer, generating your own slide ware is cost effective. Slide ware can result in professional-quality graphics that are sharply defined and attractive and include a variety of media, such as photos, graphics, and text. With slide ware, you are only limited by your imagination as you create. Presenting with slide ware is clean and uncluttered. The range of information and visuals available to you and your audience, with the press of a button, is limitless. Depending on the facilities, slide ware is easily visible to audiences of all sizes. Slide ware is an ideal medium for presenting information visually; however, there are several important disadvantages to using it.

"This PowerPoint slide has a dynamic layout comparing reading scores throughout the district, which you would have seen if I remembered to bring a spare projection bulb."

Disadvantages The major disadvantage of slide ware is the temptation to make it the presentation rather than an aid to the presentation. There are other important disadvantages for you to be aware of as well before you decide to use slide ware. Although it is fine for speakers to use their visual aids in place of notes, often speakers maintain eye contact with the projection screen, ignoring the audience. Slide ware comes with many special effects, but when their inclusion on a slide is irrelevant to the content of the slide, they are distracting and confusing. There may be problems of compatibility between your own equipment and the equipment available in the presentation environment. Slide ware is not always flexible, especially for presenters who tend to "move around" or think on their feet; you might find it confining to present information the way you have it organized on slide ware. Finally, there are times when slide ware just doesn't work due to technical glitches.

Presenting with Slide Ware

- As you consider incorporating slide ware into your presentation, think about the benefits to your audience and yourself. What ideas do you want to convey that would be enhanced with visual support, particularly with slide ware? If you can't come up with a benefit for using slide ware, don't.

- As with all of the types of visual support we discuss here, the information you display on slide ware should enhance your presentation. This means that you should not project a manuscript of your presentation and proceed to read it to your audience verbatim. It does mean that you should consider ideas or other pieces of information that can be presented more clearly when displayed graphically.

- As you create your slides, limit the number of special effects you place on each slide, and be sure they are relevant to your presentation. A background chosen from the slide ware offerings can be distracting if you are displaying a graph showing yearly earnings, for example.

- Besides limiting special effects, limit to one the number of ideas or pieces of information you place on one slide.

- Consider whether the equipment available to you in the presentation environment will be compatible with your own equipment. Test the equipment available in advance. Better yet, take your own laptop.

- As you present using your slide ware, overcome the temptation to look at the screen where your visuals are displayed. You should still work to make a connection with the audience. If you are depending on the content of your slide ware for your notes, glance at the screen on your laptop instead. If you are not controlling the projection of each slide yourself, be sure that you have practiced with your assistant so that your slides and your message are coordinated.

- Finally, be sure you have a backup plan. There are all sorts of technical reasons that slide ware chooses not to work during your presentation. Be prepared for this eventuality. There are three things you can be ready to do if your slide ware does not work:

  1. Be prepared to make your presentation without visual support. That means you will have to think about ways that words will convey the ideas the slide ware was supposed to.

  2. Take a set of transparencies with you that contain your most important visual points.

  3. Take photocopies of your slideshow to distribute to your audience.

Overhead Transparencies These are transparent pieces of a synthetic material that are projected on a screen by an **overhead projector.** You have probably seen instructors use overheads in classes countless times. Overhead transparencies can be printed with a computer printer, and they can be made with most copy machines. You can also make a transparency by

overhead transparencies Transparent pieces of a synthetic material that are projected on a screen by an overhead projector.

overhead projector A special projector used to project transparencies onto a screen.

writing on it with special pens that come with both washable and permanent ink. Presenters who are concerned about the image they create with the audience will probably want to create visuals on a computer and then either print the resulting graphic directly on a transparency or print out the graphic and make a transparency at a copy machine. Either way works, and using the copy machine does not compromise the quality of the printing.

Should you ever use a hand-written transparency? Generally, no. Remember that the visual aids you use reflect on your credibility and general image as a presenter. Handwritten transparencies may not present a positive image of you, nor are they always legible. There are a few instances when you could use them. One is when you solicit the input of the audience in a common activity such a brainstorming or generating a list of ideas. If you are responding to audience questions and comments in an environment where there is an overhead projector, creating a spontaneous sketch or visual representation by hand to answer an audience member might be the best way to respond.

In some speaking environments you might have access to a projector called an **Elmo.** An Elmo works in much the same way as an overhead projector, except that you can project a piece of paper or book or photograph or any other graphic on a screen with the Elmo without having to transfer the graphic to a transparency. An Elmo also has more refined projection capabilities: you may be able to project a much smaller item or piece with a smaller font than you can on an overhead projector.

Ilana illustrated her guided tour of Hawaii with several transparencies that she projected with the overhead. She interspersed transparencies of fish, plants, and other attractions with a map of Hawaii. Each time she showed the map, she stepped back to the screen and pointed to the location of the attraction she was about to discuss. Although she usually turned off the overhead projector between transparencies, there were one or two occasions when she showed several transparencies in fast succession; at those points, she left the projector turned on.[13]

Advantages Transparencies allow you flexibility, in that if you are thinking on your feet and need to change your presentation, all you need to do is set the unused transparencies aside. Transparencies are relatively inexpensive, costing only a few cents apiece, and can be purchased individually or by the box in office supply stores and at many copy centers. In addition, overhead projectors are widely available. Once you know what you want to include on a transparency, they are relatively easy to produce, and it is easy for you to control what is included. Overhead projectors are useful in all but the largest spaces. Finally, the only skills involved in using transparencies are to know where the "on" and "off" buttons are located on the projector and to remember when and when not to display a transparency.

Disadvantages The major disadvantage is giving in to the temptation to place an entire presentation on an overhead. Remember that all visuals are an aid to your presentation, not the totality of it. A second disadvantage is the way some pre-

Elmo A projector that does not require transferring information to a transparency but that can project a piece of paper or book or photograph or any other graphic onto a screen.

senters look over their shoulders at the displayed transparency and talk with their backs to the audience. You are able to see the content of your transparency where it lies on the overhead projector. You should be able to look at the contents of the overhead and continue to focus your attention on the audience simultaneously. Finally, overhead projectors sometimes suffer from burnt-out bulbs. If you are in the habit of presenting in different environments using an overhead projector, you might consider taking your own bulb with you in case this happens.

Presenting with Overhead and Elmo Projectors

- Before your audience arrives, learn where the on and off buttons are located and practice focusing the projector you will be using. Turn on the projector and, using one of your transparencies, determine whether you will have to adjust the distance of the projector from the screen. Using your practice slide, focus the projector. Turn the projector off.

- When you begin your presentation, do not turn on the projector until you show your first transparency. Keep parts of the transparency that you do not initially discuss covered until they become relevant to your message.

- As you continue through your presentation, place transparencies you no longer need in an orderly pile—you might need to refer to one during the question-and-answer session.

- Do not at any point turn toward the screen and talk to it with your back to your audience. Instead, keep a pen near you and point to specific areas on the transparency.

- If you are showing several transparencies in a series, there is no need to turn off the projector. If there is a lag of several minutes between transparencies, turn off the projector after the first transparency or transparencies have been shown, and turn it on when you are ready to show the next group. For situations somewhere in between these two examples, rather than turning the projector off and on, consider placing a dark piece of paper over the light platform of the projector.

- When you have displayed all of your transparencies, turn off the projector.

Posters Recipe for a poster: assemble items from different media, such as photographs, tables, or graphs; blocks of text; 3-D items. Arrange on a piece of poster board or large sheet of paper. Write captions for each item, and add a title that summarizes the items. Arrange items in an order that would tell a story or give viewers insights or knowledge about the topic. Perhaps you are making a poster presentation of a project you designed and carried out for a class. You might display photos of various phases or highlights of the project; blocks of text displaying key pieces of information, and graphic representations of other related information, such as line or bar graphs showing results; photos or illustrations of products, and quotations from other people who are involved in the project. A poster allows you to be both creative and informative. If it is attractive and well organized, it can gain the attention of the audience and reflect positively on the presenter.

Advantages Cost and accessibility are key advantages of posters. They can be relatively inexpensive to create. If you are skilled with a computer, you can create a very professional and attractive poster. Even for someone who is not so skilled, posters can be assembled with scissors and paste on a sheet of poster board purchased from a stationery store and still be effective. The finished product can be laminated or copied on a poster printer at a copy center or left as is.

Disadvantages Disadvantages relate to the logistics of displaying the poster during the presentation. Posters are only useful in a relatively small environment or in a presentation context where the audience is able to move close to the poster itself. And although it seems rather elementary, supporting a poster can be challenging, depending on how large it is. An easel is one way to display a poster; in a classroom the chalk tray is a possibility; or you might place the poster on a table and lean it against a wall.

Presenting with Posters

- Posters have a number of focal points, all of which are visible at the same time to listeners. When you use a poster, it is important that you devise a way to focus the audience attention on the part of the poster that is relevant to what you are saying at any one time.
- A wooden pointer or laser pointer is helpful for creating focus. When you use a laser pointer, hold the light still on the item you are illuminating; don't jiggle the pointer.
- An alternative to a pointer when you are speaking to a small audience is to stand close to the poster and gesture with your hand at the areas you are discussing. Keep your eyes on your audience, though.

Flip Charts A **flip chart** is similar to a giant spiral notebook standing on its end with the spiral running across the top. Flip charts are generally not used to prepare visual support in advance, but they are used for interactive areas of the presentation. For example, you might spend a few minutes at the beginning of the presentation to identify questions or concerns the audience has about the topic. Flip charts can also be used for recording various ideas presented by the audience or for brainstorming sessions.

Advantages Flip charts are helpful for encouraging audience participation. They are also easy to use—if the speaker prefers not to record the feedback from the audience, an assistant can be the recorder.

Disadvantages These are similar to those of the poster. The positioning of the flip chart might present a challenge. If the chart is to be used to record audience responses, finding a stable place to display it might be difficult. Although an easel is a logical choice, they aren't particularly sturdy. Visibility is also a possible challenge. Considering that the flip chart is best used as a recording device for information from the audience, it is most useful if everyone present can see it; therefore, it is best used with small audiences or presentations held in small

flip chart A giant spiral notebook standing on its end with the spiral running across the top; generally used not to prepare visual support in advance but for interactive areas of the presentation.

rooms. In comparison to other visual support, flip charts are rather expensive, particularly if you plan to use one for only one or two presentations.

Presenting with a Flip Chart

- The flip chart should remain visible to the audience during the presentation. When you use a flip chart, you need to remember to refer to it at the points during the presentation when the items on the chart are relevant to what you are saying.

- Using a flip chart requires you to be confident enough that you can deviate from a prepared message. You might place the notes you need on Post-it notes so you can arrange them in the order of items on the flip chart; you can also use regular note cards with one idea to a card, so you can shuffle the cards to correspond to the ideas on the flip chart.

- When you act as the recorder as well as the presenter, you need to be able to write legibly on the flip chart without prolonged breaks in contact with the audience. It might be easier, depending on the nature of the items being recorded, to ask a volunteer to record items, enabling the presenter to maintain audience contact.

Chalk and Dry Boards   A chalk board is exactly what you have experienced in classrooms throughout your education. A **dry board** is similar, except that one writes on a dry board with a special type of marker that wipes off, similarly to the way chalk is erased. Dry boards tend to be cleaner to work with than chalk boards due to the absence of chalk dust. Chalk boards or dry boards are used in much the same way as flip charts, that is, during interactive moments when it is important to record audience input. You can also use chalk or dry boards to record key terms or terms that might be unfamiliar to the audience, important facts, or statistics or to draw a quick, spontaneous sketch during a presentation.

Advantages   Chalk and, in professional environments, dry boards are readily available. They are a cost-effective method of presenting information. There is on-site control by the presenter: if an error occurs, all the presenter needs to do is erase the board.

Disadvantages   A major disadvantage is writing on the board. A certain amount of time will be spent with the recorder's back to the audience. Necessary supplies might not be available. Check the markers ahead of time to ensure that they are usable. Similarly, if you are going to be working in a room with a traditional chalk board, you will need chalk and erasers. A final disadvantage relates to the act of writing on the board. If the presenter is also the recorder, it can be difficult to juggle both roles simultaneously.

Presenting with a Chalk or Dry Board

- We've discussed the challenges to the presenter in writing and speaking. When the writing time is over is the moment the fun really begins for the presenter. You cannot and should not ignore the content that was generated by your audience.

- If the content is relevant to your presentation, you need to remain alert to what the board says and integrate that

> **dry board** A board similar to a chalk board on which one writes with a special type of marker that wipes off.

Everyday Example

Health Hazards of Chalk

Is the chalk board an archaic form of visual aid? Read the dry board/chalk board debate reported in this news story. If you have the choice of using either a dry board or chalk board for a presentation, do you feel, as does Professor Wygant in the story, that using a board allows your audience to observe your thinking process? If you were to use a dry board or chalk board as visual support for your speech, what steps would you have to take to feel confident allowing your audience to observe your thinking process?

For a glimpse of the latest split between tradition and technology on campus, watch professor Tom Walsh illustrate his lecture with a jumbo piece of chalk on a blackboard while students take notes on laptops and hand-held computers.

Circles, arrows and formulas unwind beneath the chalk as Walsh teaches his honors physics class at the University of Minnesota. He quickly fills half the board, then erases some of the formulas, leaving a trail of white dust.

It's the dust that has officials at the university, and other colleges and universities across the nation, gradually replacing blackboards with a cleaner alternative—markers and white boards.

It's another sign of progress—to some professors' dismay.

"Chalkboards were a simple, brilliant invention," Walsh said. "Whiteboards are not an advance."

Not so, argues Steve Fitzgerald, director of classroom management at the university's Twin Cities campus. Electronic equipment in classes with blackboards has to be cleaned twice as often, and rooms with chalk dust cost more to clean.

"Dust gets sucked into electronics, causing them to overheat and then fail," Fitzgerald said. "After 10 or 12 hours of use with chalk and blackboards, a room can get coated—literally—with white powder."

Fizgerald said he is trying, little by little, to educate faculty members on the benefits of using whiteboards. About 60 percent of the university's 300 classrooms still have blackboards, but the percentage will drop as buildings are renovated.

Ken Heller, associate head of the university's physics department, said not all faculty members back the blackboards—some call it a health hazard. For him, the debate is silly.

"It doesn't have anything to do with education," he said.

Physics professor John Wygant prefers old-fashioned chalk to glorified slide shows. "With blackboard, students are watching you solve (a problem) in your head," he said.

Source: E. Dunbar, Associated Press, "Chalk One Up for Technology: Blackboards Fall out of Favor," as printed in the *Des Moines Sunday Register,* October 3, 2004, P. GC.

content into your presentation. When you had planned to discuss a topic that is also a result of your audience interaction, you can simply insert a transition: "Judging by your response, I see you have the same concerns that I have . . ."

- If there are ideas on the board that you have chosen not to discuss or when something you hadn't thought of appears, then what? If you can think on your feet, do so. Otherwise, quickly write on your notes a reminder to bring up a topic when it seems most relevant to your prepared comments.

- When you have completed your presentation, refer back to the board. Are there items you have not acknowledged? If so, now is the time to do it. "There are some important points left here. Let's talk about them." Do not ignore any issues your listeners have raised.

Videotape or DVD According to one study, videos used in the classroom were the primary items that students were able to recall at the end of the semester.[14] Videotapes and their more recent relative, the DVD, are excellent media with which to present action, bring examples to life, attract attention, establish credibility, and take your listeners to the scene. Videos and DVD are also effective because of the abundance and variety of material that is available. Movies, documentaries, "how-to's," interviews, training films, everything you could ask for is available, and if something is not, you can always make your own. Adam, Corey, Kyle, and Patrick did just that. When their class assignment required them to inform the class about research related to the way people observe space, they wandered around campus with a camera and filmed examples of people managing space, to illustrate the conclusions they found in their research articles. As they showed their film, they referred to the relevant research, so the audience was able to see the example in concurrence with the research summaries.[15]

Advantages The major advantage of using videos or DVDs is the availability, flexibility, and cost-effectiveness of these types of visuals. Depending on the point you wish to make in your presentation, you can find a clip from a motion picture, or you can tape a segment of a television program. You can also make your own video or DVD to illustrate any point you wish. The cost of any of these is relatively minimal. We caution you that if you are using a clip from a motion picture or other commercially produced video, or if you are incorporating a taping from television, you must familiarize yourself with federal laws that might regulate your use of these visuals. And, of course, if you are making your own videotapes, consider permissions that might be required from the people who appear in your tapes.

Disadvantages Arranging for playback equipment might be a disadvantage. If you plan on using either format, you will need to make arrangements in advance to ensure that the proper system will be available to you. As is the case with any projection equipment, if you are expected to run it yourself, will you be able to do so? If you are presenting in a different environment than usual, allow yourself some time to make sure that you know where the start and stop buttons are located. Depending on the speaking event, you might need to secure permission to use some videos or DVDs as well. Will the equipment allow you to project on a screen large enough for everyone to view? If the only screen available to you is a twelve-inch TV monitor, and only the first row of viewers will be able to see it, is your video or DVD going to aid your message? If the audio does not allow everyone to hear, does your audience benefit? Check these ahead of time, and if the video is not visible, or if either the visual or audio is not accessible to your entire audience, consider something else.

Presenting with Videos and DVDs

- Select a "clip" from a video or DVD carefully. Make sure that whatever you are showing has a point that relates to your presentation.

- Briefly introduce the clip you will be showing: "Conflict management skills are necessary in a variety of situations, as this video clip will show you . . ."

- If you are using a motion picture clip, you might also need to briefly summarize what is occurring in the clip or even the whole plot, so your audience will be able to appreciate the point of the clip: "In this clip we see the parent and child in conflict in a public place. You should be aware that this is the fourth time that day the parent feels the child has misbehaved."

- Remember that a visual aid should enhance or contribute to the message rather than becoming the message. With videos or DVDs, it is easy to "give in to temptation" to use more of the story than is necessary. Keep in mind that your listeners have not come to see a movie.

- Be careful that the clip you select is not too long. It is difficult to say what is "too long," but if you are giving a ten-minute presentation and your clip is five minutes long, that is too long. Strive instead to make your video clips total not more than 10 percent of your total speaking time. If your presentation is five minutes, the total length of the video clips you include should not exceed one minute.

Audiotape and CDs An audiotape is not a "viewing" visual, but many of the considerations the presenter needs to take into account with audio aids are similar to "viewing" visuals. To capture the sounds of a car exhibiting various mechanical maladies, a student used an audiotape on which he had recorded the sounds of the various mechanical problems he planned to discuss. The use of audiotape in this case was probably the very best way for him to use to "illustrate" the points of his presentation; however, each example was rather long. After his classmates had heard thirty seconds or so of the example he was playing, they tended to become restless and started whispering to their friends. The speaker was faced with having to deal repeatedly with an audience whose attention wandered several times throughout his otherwise thoughtful and informative presentation. Although audiotapes are the best choice for illustrating some types of information, there are also challenges for a presenter who uses them.

Advantages There are some types of information that cannot be effectively presented to an audience in any way other than with audiotapes or CDs. They can be cost effective and easily available. As with videotapes and DVDs, if the examples you need are unavailable, you can easily make your own audio aids.

Disadvantages These relate to quality of sound and volume capabilities. If you do not have access to a speaking environment with a good sound system for that environment, it might be best to identify some other means of demonstrating what you want your audience to hear or understand as a result of your audio aids.

Presenting with Audio Aids

- Check the sound system in your speaking environment in advance to ensure that your audio aids can be easily heard by your listeners.
- Be sure that your audio aids are cued properly.
- Just before playing an example, preview what your audience will hear so they can appreciate the example.
- After playing the audio example, briefly review the features you want your listeners to remember.
- Your audio examples should not be too long. The 10 percent rule of thumb we suggested should be strictly adhered to. How long an audio example should be depends on the idea it presents, as well as the length of your presentation and the total number of audio examples you plan to use.
- Particularly with audio aids, your examples should be distinct from each other and limited in number.
- Help your listeners differentiate examples through the use of thoughtful previews and reviews of each example.

"Hands-On" Visuals

Besides "viewing" visuals, another type of visual aid is the three-dimensional "hands-on" visual. Individual objects or models and demonstrations make up this category of visual support.

ACT & REFLECT

10.3: Planning Your Visuals

ACT • As you prepare your next presentation, identify points where showing visuals will benefit your audience and also benefit you in presenting your message.

REFLECT • What specific types of visuals will be most beneficial to use to display this information? What arrangements will you need to make in advance, such as reserving equipment, to ensure that everything will go smoothly when you make your presentation?

Objects   The speaker used her collection of teddy bears to illustrate a particular historical period. With each historical event she discussed, she selected a teddy bear that displayed a costume or style or accessory illustrating some aspect of the historical event she was discussing. Another presenter placed what appeared to be a mound of dirt on the overhead projector. As she continued her presentation, it became evident the "mound" was alive, as worms and many-legged creatures crawled around on the overhead and were projected on the screen behind the speaker.

In each case, the speakers selected objects to enhance and illustrate their presentations. During the teddy bear speech, the audience learned about the influence of historical events on the design of teddy bears. While the crawling insects caught the attention of the audience, that visual was so distracting that no one listened to the message. For one of her classroom speeches, Katelyn invited her audience to tour an imaginary dairy farm. Katelyn brought an actual milking machine to show how it is attached to the cow and how it worked to milk the cow. It is possible that if she had simply explained the process, it would not have been so clear or so interesting as it was with the addition of the milking machine. For listeners who had never seen a dairy farm, to be able to see the machine was also informative.[16]

Advantages   The object is the real thing. That is the major advantage of using objects as visual aids. You can show a real flower, a real bicycle. The three-dimensional quality of objects increases interest. Comprehension is enhanced. When objects are the possessions of the speaker, the audience's perception of the speaker's expertise may be greater.

Disadvantages   The main challenge with objects is making them visible, organizing them, and managing them. Objects should not be visible to your audience until they are discussed in the presentation. You will need to find a way to organize them and keep them out of sight until you need them. For speakers who depend heavily on notes, managing notes and objects can be awkward at best and impossible at worst. Objects should not be distributed among the audience. One speaker brought a collection of pottery made by a local artist. As the speaker began to pass around pieces of pottery, the audience began to discuss among themselves the qualities of each piece rather than listening to the speaker. When a piece of the pottery hit the floor and shattered, the presenter realized that passing around the collection was an unwise move.

Presenting with Objects

- The objects must be accessible to the speaker but at the same time not be easily visible to the audience until they are relevant to the presentation. The teddy bear speaker, for example, placed her bears under a table away from the gaze of the audience. She also arranged them in the order in which she planned to discuss them in her presentation.

- If you are using a number of objects, your presentation needs to include enough description so that it is clear why you are displaying a particular object and how it is different from those before and after it.

- While you are discussing them, objects must be visible to the audience. That means that when you are displaying an object, you might need to "wade into" the audience so that everyone has an opportunity to view the object easily. If you are speaking in a room with a center aisle, you might end up walking the length of the aisle, pausing to display an object so listeners on either side of the aisle can see it.

- You can't afford long periods of silence while you walk around the room showing your audience your visual aids. As you are walking around displaying your objects, you will need to be able to keep talking. It can be awkward for you to juggle your objects and your notes while you are talking, so be sure to spend time in advance preparing what you will say and how you will handle these points in your presentation so you can do so with confidence.

As Matthew informed the audience about snakes, he walked the center aisle of the large room where he was presenting, to allow his listeners to view the boa constrictors he was holding. During this time he continued to speak in a confident manner without notes.[17]

Demonstrations The goal of the presenter was to show three wall-painting techniques the audience could use to decorate their apartments in a cost-effective manner. The presenter displayed finished examples of each of the three paint techniques on pieces of cardboard large enough to be viewed by everyone in the audience. Each example was discussed individually as the presenter displayed the tools, paint, and other supplies needed to create the effect. At the close of the presentation, the speaker distributed handouts containing illustrated directions for achieving the paint techniques. Although no actual painting occurred, the demonstration was so clear the audience members felt they would be able to go home and duplicate the paint technique they liked the best.

Although we have emphasized that visual aids are not the point of the presentation but rather enhance it, when one is conducting a demonstration, the visual is the point of the presentation. A demonstration is a type of "how-to" speech. A demonstration speech might display how to perform a first aid procedure, how to change a tire, how to greet a customer, or any other procedure the audience needs or wants to learn.

The demonstration speech is a common way to convey information that listeners need or want. Demonstration speeches are used in professional environments and are referred to as training sessions. Demonstration speeches are also available on a variety of topics through community, private, and commercial venues for anyone who wishes to attend. Irene demonstrated the use of an object called a foam roller to a fitness class. As she instructed the class in the use of the foam roller, her own actions illustrated what she was saying. The class was able to model Irene's actions because of her ability to select informative ways to explain the use of the foam roller and her clear demonstration of the way to use it.[18]

Advantages A major advantage of a demonstration is that, if it is done well, a large number of people can learn a new technique or skill or other process in a relatively cost-effective manner. Sometimes demonstration speeches allow the attendees to have a hands-on opportunity to work along with the presenter. When that is the case, audience members can help each other learn the particular skills or procedures being demonstrated and might also add to the information that is being disseminated by recounting their personal experiences with the topic.

Disadvantages These relate mainly to the logistics of organizing the necessary supplies and ensuring that the demonstration will be visible to everyone. And the presenter needs to be knowledgeable, because the hands-on nature of the event often draws audience members who have some expertise and/or knowledge about the topic and are in attendance because they have questions or problems related to it. If the presenter is unable to help them, they may be disappointed, and they may question the presenter's expertise.

Presenting during a Demonstration

- Visibility should be a major concern to the presenter who is planning a demonstration. If you are attending an Italian cooking class at a local kitchen-equipment store and you are unable to see how the vegetables should be cut or how the dish should be assembled, you would be just as well off reading a cookbook. Try to speak from a platform or rearrange audience seating so everyone can easily see your demonstration.

- Practice your demonstration at the same time as your presentation so you become adept at integrating them. As you practice, you might find that some steps of the demonstration will require a helper or that you will need duplicate tools or other equipment.

- When some of the parts of the demonstration are longer or more complex than others, how will you ensure that your audience will understand the complex parts and remain attentive to the longer parts? Is there some way you can repeat the complex parts and perhaps supplement them with handouts? Is there a way you can include audience participation during the long parts to help retain their attention?

Handouts These include a multitude of items: lists of resources that are relevant to the topic of the presentation; additional information the speaker did not include in the presentation; brochures; anything the audience is given to take home.

We've already discussed the hazards of passing objects among the audience. Similar challenges occur when using handouts: listeners become engrossed in reading handouts rather than listening to the presenter; with multipage handouts or brochures, perusing them can be noisy as audience members turn pages and shuffle papers.

Advantages Handouts are useful for disseminating additional information that you might not have time to discuss in your presentation or information that is related but not strictly necessary. You can provide the audience with additional sources of information that you could not easily state verbally or place on a visual—for example, a list of resources such as books or people who are knowledgeable about your topic. In addition, if you want to become known as an expert in the area of your presentation, a handout allows you to include contact information about yourself so interested persons can follow up.

Disadvantages If handouts are not distributed until the end of your presentation, the disadvantages are minimal. The actual distribution can be awkward, but if you give some thought to the best way to accomplish "handing out the handouts," that challenge can be overcome. Copying costs might escalate, but if you are an invited speaker, it is possible your host will cover the task of copying and its cost.

Presenting with Handouts

- Generally, handouts should be distributed at the latest possible moment in a presentation. (If there is a need to distribute handouts during your presentation, you might be planning a demonstration speech.)
- When you have any type of handout for your audience, build the distribution of it into your presentation. For example, if you are distributing brochures about recreation equipment that can be rented on campus, say something like "The next time you want to rent a canoe, or cross-country skies, this guide to the campus rec center will help you go about doing that." Always provide a brief transition to the distribution of your handouts that lets the audience know what they are receiving.
- If you have several handouts, you will need to plan their distribution so audience members will know what they have and have not received.
- Color-coding copies is useful for multiple handouts. With color-coded handouts you can say, "Let's take a look at the green handout." Or "You should all have three handouts: one yellow, one blue, and one green. Who still needs handouts?"
- If you are presenting to a large audience or if the audience is distributed over a large room, you might want to place handouts in a convenient location near the exits so people can receive them as they leave; or you may need assistants to help you with the handout distribution.

People as Visuals

As the speaker discussed his experiences as a children's T-ball coach, he briefly demonstrated the technique he used to determine which hand very young children would use for pitching, catching, and batting. Although his hand gestures could have been helpful, because the speaker was standing behind a tall lectern, they were not visible to most of the audience. Another speaker discussed appropriate attire to wear to a job interview. As she modeled the attire she recommended, she walked before the audience so quickly that no one had a chance to see the characteristics she told them to look for. Two volunteers showed martial arts moves that could be used for self-protection. However, the demonstration was not coordinated with the presenter's message, and the audience didn't understand what they were seeing. These examples show that you should consider people as possible visual aids for your presentation—and that you must ensure that their use will be effective. See Act and Reflect 10.4.

Advantages The greatest advantage to using people is their flexibility. People can repeat their movements, move around the room, and modify their movements, all to ensure that the audience understands what is happening. People bring with them the three-dimensional advantage of being objects and the wealth of information that "viewing" visuals can provide; they can repeat their visual information as often as needed; and they can answer questions, too.

ACT&REFLECT

10.4: Analyzing a Demonstration

ACT • Irene's presentation on how to use the foam roller was not only a demonstration; she used herself as the visual support for her demonstration. Watch Irene's speech.[19] Try to follow Irene's instructions as she gives them and as you watch her conducting the demonstration. If you have access to a foam roller, use it. If you do not, you can substitute a similar object such as a rolling pin or any other item that resembles the roller.

REFLECT • Referring to the guidelines we give for using people as visual aids, identify the points in Irene's presentation where her implementation of the guidelines helps you to follow the instructions she is giving.

Disadvantages The disadvantages of using people as visuals relate to the fact that people visuals really need to be actors, and often they are not. Using people visuals involves some risks. People have to stand in front of the audience, sometimes for prolonged periods; they need to be skilled in what they are displaying; and often the human visual and the message are not coordinated.

Presenting with People

- When you use people as visual aids, whether it is yourself or a helpful assistant, the area of focus needs to be visible, emphasized, and coordinated with the presentation.

- When the topic the person is illustrating is relevant to your presentation, place the person in a location where the audience can see the visual. The T-ball coach we discussed earlier, for example, moved away from the lectern and repeated the part of his presentation the audience had been unable to see.

- A people visual needs to be slow and emphasized. The speaker modeling professional attire, for example, should have paused in front of the audience and gestured toward all of the items she was wearing that characterized proper attire.

- The people visual needs to be practiced with the presenter to coordinate the message and the actions so the audience will gain the benefits of the visual. That means the presenter will need to adjust his or her speaking rate as well.

- If you plan to use a person as a visual, you could be that visual yourself, but you might consider whether the value of the person visual would be enhanced and if the content of the message would be better understood by your audience if you asked a friend to assist you.

Suggestions for Using Visual Aids

Without regard to the type of visual support you have chosen, there are a number of tips that can guide you in planning and displaying visual support (see Act and Reflect 10.5).

Make Your Visual Aids Visible

Your visual aids must be visible from all over the room. We have discussed the display of objects and people; here are some pointers for making "viewing" visuals visible:

1. On individual slides or poster boards, use lots of white space to make sure words are visible.

2. Give each individual visual a title that summarizes its content.

3. Sources differ on the number of words that should be placed on one piece: some advocate the "**6 x 6 rule**" that states you should have no more than six lines of text with a limit of six words per line on any one slide.[20] Other sources suggest simply limiting the number of items you place on a slide. The most useful piece of advice is that you should have a limit of one idea or thought to each slide.[21]

Negative Aspects of Pain
- ☹ Pain
- ☹ Immobilization
- ☹ Restricted Activity
- ☹ Unrelated Pain
- ☹ Sudden Popularity

● **FIGURE 10.3** A Sample Slide: Got Pain? Get the Right Attitude. *Source:* Shannon Kirton, PowerPoint presentation slide for speech to a neutral audience, October 20, 2004.

Which of the visual "do's" and "don'ts" do you see reflected in Figure 10.3? Does this visual adhere to the 6 × 6 rule? What advantages, if any, would using this slide have for the audience? For the speaker?

4. Align your visuals with the world: on maps, north should be at the top of your visual. Horizontally formatted slides are easier for people to read than vertically formatted slides.[22]

5. Limit the number of verbal visuals, you display to two or three; then insert a different type of visual, such as a picture.

6 x 6 Rule Rule that states you should have no more than six lines of text with a limit of six words per line on any one slide.

Make Your Visuals Aid Your Presentation

We have discussed several advantages to incorporating visual aids in your presentation. Consider which advantage you and your audience will get from each visual aid you plan to use.

1. Ask yourself "Why am I using this visual with my presentation?" Be sure you have a reason for each visual you use.
2. Identify points you want your audience to understand or remember from your presentation. Do you have visual support for these important points?
3. Are you using font sizes so that the relationship of titles to content is clear? Use larger font sizes to show titles and subtitles, smaller font sizes for text. Limit the number of font styles you use to two or three.
4. Use color to show relationships of ideas. Lighter colors on darker backgrounds work best for projected slides.

Do's and Don'ts of Visual Support

Do ask your audience to move to areas of the room where it will be easier for them to see your visuals, if necessary.

Do maintain eye contact with your audience, even if the visual is projected behind you.

Do practice your presentation with your visual aids in the room where you will be presenting.

Do make sure you will have necessary equipment and other supplies and that you know how to use all the equipment.

Do check spelling on visual aids (do you mean "to" or "too" or "two"?); also check to make sure information is accurate.

Do give the source of information on each visual.

Do use a laser pointer or wooden pointer to focus on the screen.

Do consider the cultural norms regarding use of visual aids. In some business organizations, for example, if PowerPoint is not used, the presenter is not perceived as credible.

Don't say, "You probably can't see this but . . ." or "The last time I used this it didn't work . . ."

Don't look over your shoulder at your visuals as you talk to the audience.

Don't display your visuals until you are talking about them in your presentation.

Don't leave projector lights on after you have finished using the equipment.

Don't read your visuals to your audience.

Don't bring controlled substances, alcohol, firearms, or anything potentially hazardous to use as visuals unless you are certain they are necessary to your presentation and legal in the presentation environment.

Don't use animals, reptiles, amphibians, or insects unless their use has been arranged in advance.

Don't make your visuals the point of your presentation.

Figure 10.4, showing the number of people who did and did not vote in an election, was one of the visual aids Ross used for his speech on voter turnout. What advantages are there for the audience and the speaker to use this pie chart instead of a bar graph or a line graph or some other representation of the information? What do's and don'ts do you see on the pie chart?

● **FIGURE 10.4   A Sample Pie Chart: Ames Election Turnout.** *Source:* Ross Kelderman, PowerPoint slide for speech to a neutral audience, October 15, 2004.

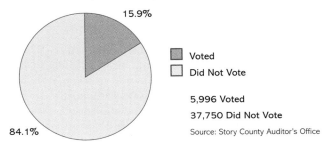

● **GETTING TO WORK**

It is tremendously important that your visual aids are not the reason for your presentation but rather that they enhance your presentation in the ways they should. In order to ensure that your visuals serve in this "supplementary" manner, first, complete your presentation. When you feel confident that the content of your presentation is unlikely to change, take some time to think through which areas would benefit from visual support. Look for areas in which it would be beneficial for your audience to be able to remember parts of your presentation. Those are parts that would benefit from visual support. Then look for areas that, depending on your knowledge of your audience, might be difficult for them to comprehend. In particular, check areas for which you find it necessary to present statistics or other information numerically. All of these are types of information that might be best understood with visual support.

Once you have identified information that would benefit your audience if presented visually, your next concern is to consider what type of visual support would be the best way to present this information. Some information simply does not lend itself well to human or object visuals. Other information does not lend itself to viewing visuals. When you have a sense of the types of visual that would work, you are ready to convert the information from your presentation to the suitable visual formats.

Your visuals should be a part of your presentation rehearsals. If you discover any difficulties with any of your visuals, don't assume that the difficulties will take care of themselves. You might need to re-create something. You might discover that equipment is not available in the room where you are scheduled to present. Can you arrange for the necessary equipment from another source? If not, you probably need to make plans to incorporate other visuals.

On the day of your presentation, arrive early enough to test all of the equipment you will be using. If you find that something is not working, you can make alternative arrangements. Finally, if during your presentation a bulb burns out or equipment malfunctions, do you have an alternative plan? Can you talk your audience through a visual that has malfunctioned? Remember, your visuals are aids; they are not your support system. Although an audience will view a speaker who has visuals more positively than a speaker who does not incorporate visuals, a speaker who is able to overcome an unplanned event will benefit from continued audience support.

SUMMARY

We have discussed the selection and implementation of visual support—anything besides the message that enhances your presentation in some way. The advantages of implementing visual support are many. Visual support enhances the audience's image of the presenter and can increase their attention; the audience's comprehension, agreement, and retention can also benefit. In addition, visual support can help you, as the presenter, depend less on your notes, clarify your points, and have more confidence.

The three major formats of visual support are what we have called "viewing visuals"; these include slide ware such as PowerPoint, overhead transparencies, videotapes and DVDs, posters, and flip charts; "hands-on" visuals such as objects, demonstrations, and handouts; and the use of people as visual aids. In addition, there may be instances when using an audio example will benefit your particular presentation. We discussed advantages and disadvantages for each of these and made suggestions for you to follow as you incorporate them into your presentations.

"Viewing" visuals such as overhead transparencies require certain design considerations, such as the sheer amount of information that should be placed on one overhead. We have listed some other design considerations as well for you to take into account as you design overheads.

Finally, no matter what type of visual aid you choose for your presentation, there are many basic "do's" and "don'ts" to keep in mind. We have listed the major ones for you to consider as you identify, design, and implement visual aids into your presentation.

VIDEO EXPERIENCE

The four speeches for this experience show more about the value of visual aids: Cindy's speech is on subliminal advertising, Karen discusses the weather, Mandy tells you about her hometown of Chicago, and Scott informs you about the X-Prize.[23] Although the first three speakers use slide ware, the materials they are projecting differ somewhat from speech to speech. Scott uses the Elmo projector. Using the information we have discussed in this chapter, identify the advantages to both the audience and the speaker that you see inherent in the visual aids for these speeches. Which of the "do's" of visual support do you see illustrated by the speakers? If you were to advise each of the speakers on ways to make their visuals more effective, what would you suggest?

THINKING BACK, THINKING AHEAD

1. To help yourself get a sense of how to use objects or demonstrations in a presentation, watch one of the cooking shows, or home project shows, or any other of the many TV "how-to" shows. When the host is discussing why a piece of furniture is considered an

antique, displaying the qualities of a flower arrangement, or demonstrating how to install a new sink, what do you see that person do and what do you hear that person say so that the object or demonstration is visible and makes sense to the viewer? What tips do you learn that you can incorporate into a presentation using objects or demonstrations?

2. Watch your favorite news show or your local news broadcast. When video clips are used, about how long are they, and what is their content? Do you identify any information in a video clip that you feel is unnecessary? How is the announcer's message geared to the clip so that you understand the significance of what you are seeing? Which of the journalists' techniques could you use when you incorporate a video or DVD clip in a speech?

3. We have discussed the use of the computer to make PowerPoint-like slides and the use of overhead projectors, videos and DVDs, and audio tapes. Do you know how to operate all of these? If not, select one that you are unfamiliar with and learn to use it. Become confident enough that you could use it in your next presentation.

4. The next time you are tempted to prepare a PowerPoint-like presentation, stop yourself. Which of the other visual aids available to you might make a more effective presentation and why?

NOTES

1. C. Thompson, "PowerPoint Makes You Dumb," *New York Times,* December 14, 2003, retrieved from *New York Times* Web site, at www.nytimes.com.
2. Douglas R. Vogel, Gary W. Dickson, and John A. Lehman, *Persuasion and the Role of Visual Presentation Support: The UM/3M Study,* working paper, June 1986, retrieved from Web site, at http://misrc.umn.edu/ working papers/fullpapers/1986/861.1pdf.
3. T. C. Smith, *Making Successful Presentations: A Self-Teaching Guide* (New York: Wiley, 1984).
4. W. J. Seiler, "The Effects of Visual Material on Attitude, Credibility, and Retention," *Speech Monograph, 38* (1971): 331–334.
5. Vogel, Dickson, and Lehman, *Persuasion,* 10, fig. 4.
6. S. W. Vanderstoep, A. Fagerlin, and J. S. Feenstra, "What Do Students Remember from Introductory Psychology?" *Teaching of Psychology, 27* (2000): 89–92.
7. K. A. Kiewra, "How Classroom Teachers Can Help Students Learn and Teach Them How to Learn," *Theory into Practice, 41* (2002): 71–80.
8. Seilor, "Effects of Visual Material."
9. Ross Kelderman, speech to a neutral audience, October 15, 2004.
10. Vanderstoep, Fagerlin, and Feenstra, "What Do Students Remember."
11. Amy Diekevers, speech to a neutral audience, October 29, 2004.
12. Crystal Nord, speech to a negative audience, November 19, 2004.
13. Ilana Mainaga, speech to a positive audience, September 22, 2004.
14. Vanderstoep, Fagerlin, and Feenstra, "What Do Students Remember."
15. Patrick Boberg, Adam Bosman, Kyle Gragert, and Corey Orehek, DVD to illustrate proxemics presentation, October 6, 2005.
16. Katelyn Ver Hoef, speech to a neutral audience, October 15, 2004.
17. Matthew Graham, speech to Municipal Clerks' Institute, July 13, 2003.
18. Irene McCormick-Lewis, demonstration speech, July 27, 2005.
19. McCormick-Lewis, demonstration speech.
20. T. Leech, *How to Prepare, Stage, and Deliver Winning Presentations,* 3rd ed. (New York: AMACOM, 2004).
21. Anonymous, *Presentations, 18* (February 2004): 38, retrieved from Web site, at http://proquest.umi.com/.
22. Smith, *Making Successful Presentations,* 72.
23. Cindy Johnson, speech to a neutral audience, October 20, 2004. Karen Tarara, speech to a neutral audience, October 22, 2004. Mandy Sadoski, speech to a neutral audience, October 20, 2004. Scott Sturm, speech to a neutral audience, October 22, 2004.

Chapter 11

Organizing Presentations

Goals

✓ To list for you the benefits of a well-organized presentation

✓ To guide you in the formulation of purpose and thesis statements

✓ To identify, describe, and recommend to you organizational frameworks useful for positive audiences

✓ To identify, describe, and recommend to you organizational frameworks intended for neutral audiences

✓ To identify, describe, and recommend to you organizational frameworks recommended for negative audiences

For their spring service project, the members of a residence hall planned to deliver flowering plants to local elderly care facilities. The residents asked a horticulture major to conduct a workshop for them on the care of the plants before the deliveries could be made. The horticulture major presented a long list of complicated and confusing instructions, as well as information on a number of other plants that were not a part of the service project. When the residence hall members began to ask questions, the horticulture major became flustered and impatient. The residence hall members, in turn, became frustrated with the presenter, the workshop, and the entire project.

The example illustrates what can happen if a speaker does not carefully consider in advance the purpose of a presentation and the needs of the audience. The workshop would have been more successful if the presenter had thought beforehand about the reason that the plant care workshop was being given and what the residence hall members expected or wanted to learn about plants. The results of that thinking would have been channeled into the formulation of two important statements: a purpose statement and a thesis. These statements would have helped the horticulture major more clearly define the presentation and organize the necessary information. The resulting workshop would more likely have contained a set of instructions on the care of the plants to be distributed in the service project, without the unnecessary information. In addition, the residence hall members would have learned exactly what they wanted and needed to know about the care of the plants and retained their goodwill. ●

Selecting the proper organizational framework for a presentation can benefit both presenter and audience members in several ways. In this textbook we recognize that you might find yourself speaking to an audience who feel positive, neutral, or negative about your topic. The residence hall members were not knowledgeable about the care of the plants for their service project, but because they were open to and interested in learning, they began as a positive audience. Knowing how your audience is likely to respond to your topic will assist you in the selection of an organizational framework.

Selecting an organizational framework will also help you to clarify what you should include and how you should arrange it, as well as what should not be included. In the example, the horticulture major organized the information in a way that was difficult for the interested but unknowledgeable residence hall members to understand and included information that only confused the audience. Selecting the proper organizational framework provides an important guide to the speaker for planning the content and arrangement of that content.

Formulating Your Speech Purpose and Thesis

Selecting the appropriate organizational framework begins with the formulation of a purpose statement and a thesis. Before you consider the best choice of organizational framework, you will need to determine what you wish to accomplish through your speech and what your audience needs or wants to know.

Your Purpose Statement

What is it that you want your audience to know, do, or believe as a result of your speech? Do you want to familiarize them with the way tuition rates are determined at your university? Do you want them to learn a few steps of the latest salsa dance? Do you want them to agree with your views on a proposed new speed limit? Whatever it is that you want to achieve as a result of your presentation is your speech purpose (see Act and Reflect 11.1). Your **purpose statement** is a brief, preferably one-sentence statement of what you want to accomplish through giving your speech. For example:

> "My positive audience will understand how our tuition rates are determined."
>
> "I want my neutral audience to become interested in learning salsa dancing."
>
> "My negative audience will agree that the proposed new speed limit should not be voted into law."

Notice that each of these purpose statements includes a reference to the type of audience, the topic of the speech, and a brief description of the information about the topic that will be discussed. Taking the time to plan a purpose statement is a valuable investment for a speaker. Doing so requires you to consider the type of audience you will be speaking to, and that directs you to possible organizational

purpose statement A brief, preferably one-sentence statement of what you want to accomplish as a result of your speech.

ACT&REFLECT

11.1: Formulating Your Purpose Statement

ACT • Complete this exercise:

The topic of the speech I am currently preparing is:

I want my audience to (choose one) **know/do/believe** _____ about this topic.

I believe my audience is (choose one) **positive/neutral/negative** about this topic.

Write one sentence that includes the information you provided in this exercise as well as the terms you chose about your topic and your audience. This is the purpose statement for the speech you are currently preparing.

REFLECT • On the basis of what you have written in your purpose statement, what pieces of information do you believe should be included in this speech? That is, what do you need to present to your audience in order to accomplish your purpose?

frameworks. In addition, as you determine your topic and what you want your audience to know, do, or believe about it as a result of your speech, you are considering what must be included as well as what should not be included. The purpose statement serves to guide you, the speaker, to what you want to accomplish through your presentation.

Your Thesis Statement

Your **thesis statement** identifies the necessary information your audience wants or needs to hear in order for you to accomplish your speech's purpose. Formulating a thesis statement is important because the information you include in it will become the main points of the body of your speech. Limit the information you include in your thesis to a minimum of two and a maximum of five pieces. This will help your audience more easily understand and remember what you are saying. In the following examples, how many pieces of information do you find that will become main points of a speech?

If you want your audience to understand the process by which tuition rates are determined at your university, what information would your audience need to know? Your thesis statement might read like this: "To understand how our tuition rates are set on this campus, it is necessary to know how the budget is determined, who sets the budget, and the key sources of income." See Act and Reflect 11.2.

If you want your audience to become more interested in learning the salsa, this might be your thesis: "You will learn about the origins of the fun dance the salsa, and why it is currently popular; you will see a demonstration of an easy

thesis statement A summary of the necessary information your audience wants or needs to hear in your presentation in order for you to accomplish your speech's purpose.

ACT&REFLECT

11.2: Formulating Your Thesis Statement

ACT • Use the purpose statement you formulated in the previous **Act and Reflect 11.1.** In order for you to meet the purpose of your speech, what key pieces of information will your audience need or expect to hear? List these key pieces of information. Now write a one-sentence thesis that includes all of these pieces of information.

REFLECT • How many total pieces of information does your thesis contain? If you have more than five pieces of information, what can you combine or eliminate?

salsa step; you will learn the places on and around campus where you can receive free or inexpensive salsa lessons."

If you are attempting to persuade your negative audience that the proposed new speed limit should not become law, what should they hear in order for them to agree with you? "If the speed limit is raised, fatal accidents will increase, gas prices will go up, and the number of speeding tickets issued will rise dramatically."

•

Your Main Points

We have indicated the importance of carefully considering the thesis statement because it will help you identify the specific pieces of information you must include in your presentation. In fact, if your thesis statement is well-thought-out, it is possible that the major points of the body of your presentation are already stated within the thesis, as the following examples demonstrate.

EXAMPLE 1

Your purpose statement is: My positive audience will understand how our tuition rates are determined.

Your thesis statement is: To understand how our tuition rates are set on this campus, it is necessary to know how the budget is determined, who sets the budget, and the key sources of income.

Your main points will be:

I. The budget is determined as a result of the state revenue available to our institution and the priorities and needs of the campus.

II. The budget is set by the president of our school with assistance from campus budgetary advisors and input from all of the department chairs on campus.

III. There are several key sources of income, including state revenues and the tuition we all pay to attend our school.

EXAMPLE 2

Your purpose statement is: I want my neutral audience to become interested in learning salsa dancing.

Your thesis statement is: You will learn about the origins of the fun dance the salsa, and why it is currently popular; you will see a demonstration of an easy salsa step; you will learn the places on and around campus where you can receive free or inexpensive salsa lessons.

Your main points will be:

I. The origins of salsa dancing span two continents and influence several cultures.

II. The current popularity of salsa can be traced to the proliferation in our culture of musicians and music from Mexico.

III. I have enjoyed salsa dancing for several years and would like to demonstrate some easy salsa steps for you.

IV. If you would like to learn to dance the salsa yourself, there are locations on and around campus that teach salsa very inexpensively, and sometimes for free.

EXAMPLE 3

Your purpose statement is: My negative audience will agree that the proposed new speed limit should not be voted into law.

Your thesis statement is: If the speed limit is raised, fatal accidents will increase, gas prices will go up, and the number of speeding tickets issued will raise dramatically.

Your main points will be:

I. In other states, data from highway departments shows a direct relationship between the speed limit and the number of fatal accidents.

II. Driving at higher speeds requires our cars to use more fuel, and that results in the possibility that gas prices will increase.

III. The state highway patrol has indicated that increases in the speed limit generally result in motorists driving even faster than the speed limit, thus anticipating an increase in the number of speeding tickets.

Notice in the three examples that the main points in the bodies of each speech are already indicated in the thesis statements. Investing the time to carefully compose a thesis

"**What do you want to mention first, the senior defections, the profits warning or the aborted takeover talks?**"

These kids are an example of an open audience—they don't know much about sea turtles, but they certainly are interested. ●

statement will benefit you in determining the points you should include and, perhaps even more important, will help you decide what to omit.

After determining your purpose statement, thesis statement, and the resulting main points, the next step is to determine the type of audience you will be speaking to. Having a sense of your audience's attitude will help you determine the order of your main points.

Organizing Presentations for Positive Audiences

Positive audiences are interested audiences. Some positive audiences became interested as they acquired more knowledge about a topic. As a result of their initial knowledge, they want to learn more. We call this type of positive audience the **supportive audience.** Another type of positive audience, the **open audience,** are interested, but they have little or no knowledge about the topic. There is simply something about the topic that makes them think "Hmmm . . . I'd like to hear more about this."

The speaker who presents to a positive audience has an advantage: the audience is interested in what the speaker has to say before he or she even begins to speak! However, as we showed in the example at the beginning of this chapter, a positive audience will not necessarily remain positive. One of the ways a speaker can make sure the audience retains its positive quality is by considering the needs of the audience and selecting an organizational framework that will meet those needs.

Organizing to Inform: The Open Audience

The residence hall members who attended the workshop on the care of spring flowering plants were an open audience. They had little knowledge about plant care, but they were interested in learning about it for their service project. When you are presenting to an open audience, your major concern is to provide information about your topic (while retaining the interest the audience members bring with them to the event). Three organizational frameworks that will allow you to focus on providing information are topical, spatial, and chronological organizational frameworks.

supportive audience A positive audience that, as a result of their initial knowledge, wants to learn more about a topic.

open audience A type of positive audience that is interested in a topic but has little or no knowledge about it.

Topical Organization **Topical organization** identifies patterns, themes, or other relationships that exist between major points. The ways to organize speeches topically are endless. Some common patterns used with topical organization are as follows.

Prioritizing To **prioritize** major points means to arrange them in order of importance. Prioritizing allows you to indicate the advantages and disadvantages of some points over others: you can discuss the special characteristic of each point that makes it more or less valuable than the others. Jon arranged his presentation on the benefits of extra curricular activities by prioritizing in order of immediate to long-term benefits:[1]

EXAMPLE: The Benefits of Extracurricular Activities

Purpose statement: To show my positive audience the benefits of participating in extracurricular activities.

Thesis statement: Participating in extracurricular activities enables us to share interests, meet people, have fun, and learn skills that will be important in the future.

    I. Of initial importance: participation in extracurricular activities allows you to meet people who share your interests

   II. Meeting people will benefit your social life.

  III. Next, we cannot overlook that participating in extracurricular activities is fun.

  IV. Of greatest importance, extracurricular activities will help you learn skills that can be used in your career.

Stock Categories Organizing by **stock categories** is sorting your information into groups according to shared commonalities. We maintain our own mental inventories of categories to help us organize many things, from physical items, such as shoes or cars, to relationships: "He is a friend," "She is an acquaintance." You can organize your presentation according to known stock categories, or you can create your own categories. Ross categorized his advice about using eBay into two stock categories:[2]

EXAMPLE: How to Use eBay

Purpose statement: To instruct a positive audience in the use of eBay.

Thesis statement: Whether you are a buyer or a seller, you should proceed with caution when using eBay.

    I. There are several precautions that buyers should take when purchasing on eBay.

   II. If you are selling on eBay, there are also precautions you should take.

topical organization A type of organizational framework that identifies patterns, themes, or other relationships that exist between major points.

prioritize Arrange major points in order of their importance.

stock categories An organizational framework that sorts information into groups according to shared commonalities.

Typology A **typology** is a systematic framework for organizing knowledge. The plant and animal worlds are organized according to typologies that include areas such as family, species, and cultivar. A well-known typology is the journalists' Six Questions of five Ws and an H: "Who?" "What?" "Where?" "When?" "Why?" and "How?" Using a typology gives you a "ready-made" organizational structure, and each area gives you a topic sentence to help you move from point to point. Katie chose a part of the five Ws and an H to discuss her senior honors project:[3]

EXAMPLE: Getting Started on Your Senior Honors Project

Purpose statement: To inform members of a positive audience of freshmen and sophomores about the senior honors project.

Thesis statement: The basics for freshman and sophomore honors students to begin thinking about now for the senior honors project are what it is, why do it, and how to do it.

   I. *What* is a senior honors project?

  II. *Why* should you complete a senior honors project?

 III. *How* should you go about planning your project?

Complexity When organizing by **complexity,** you arrange your presentation by explaining a basic point or component of your topic and then building on it to become increasingly more complex.

EXAMPLE: A Statistics Tutorial

Purpose statement: To demonstrate to a positive audience the calculation of the statistical test regression.

Thesis statement: Knowing how to calculate regression depends on understanding the calculation of other statistical tests.

   I. First, the most simple test is calculating a mean.

  II. Next, a slightly more complicated statistical test is calculating t-tests.

 III. An even more complex test that incorporates the t-test is ANOVA.

 IV. Finally, the most complex test is the calculation of regression.

Comparison or Contrast Organizing by **comparison** or **contrast** informs the audience of the similarities or differences between two points. A **Venn diagram** facilitates identifying similarities and differences between two items, as is illustrated in Figure 11.1. Once you have the similarities and differences

typology A systematic framework for organizing knowledge.

complexity Explaining a basic point or component of the topic and then building on it in order to present increasingly more complex information.

comparison Identifying the similarities of two or more points.

contrast Identifying the differences between two or more points.

Venn diagram A structure of overlapping circles that readily displays similarities and differences between two items.

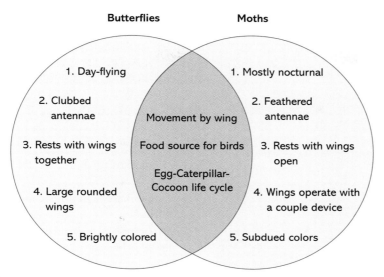

Butterflies   **Moths**

1. Day-flying   1. Mostly nocturnal

2. Clubbed   Movement by wing   2. Feathered
   antennae   antennae

                        Food source for birds
3. Rests with wings   3. Rests with wings
   together   open
                        Egg-Caterpillar-
4. Large rounded   Cocoon life cycle   4. Wings operate with
   wings   a couple device

5. Brightly colored   5. Subdued colors

● **FIGURE 11.1** Venn Diagram: Similarities and Differences of Butterflies and Moths. *Source:* Carter, D. (2002) *Butterflies and Moths: A Smithsonian Handbook* (New York: Dorling Kindersley, Inc.), pp 70–71.

clearly diagrammed, choose the qualities of the similarities or the differences your audience wants or needs to hear about.

EXAMPLE: How Butterflies and Moths Differ

Purpose statement: My positive audience will learn how butterflies and moths are different insects.

Thesis statement: The main differences between butterflies and moths is most apparent in three areas of their physical structure.

   I. The design and appearance of the antennae of butterflies and moths differ.

  II. The wing structure of butterflies and moths is different.

 III. The coloring of butterflies is more vivid than that of moths.

Repetition *"Come, Dick. Come and see. Come, come. Come and see. Come and see Spot. Look, Spot. Oh, look. Look and see. Oh, see. Run, Spot. Run, run, run. Oh, oh, oh. Funny, funny Spot."*[4]

MSL

Just as the creators of the *Fun with Dick and Jane* books used repetition to teach children reading skills, you can also use repetition of a key word or phrase to help your audience learn and remember information in your presentation. Amy used repetition in her speech about the benefits of music.[5]

ACT & REFLECT

11.3: Merging Themes

ACT • As you prepare your next presentation, write each bit of information that you would like to include on a sticky note. Now attach the sticky notes to a section of wall space where you can see all of them at one time. Move them around until individual notes are grouped with other notes that refer to similar topics. Give a title to each category that emerges.

REFLECT • What patterns result as you merge these topics into categories? What organizational option(s) discussed here would be useful for your presentation?

EXAMPLE: Success through Music Participation

Purpose statement: I will demonstrate to a positive audience the ways that participation in musical events can result in benefits to you and to society.

Thesis statement: Participating in musical events results in benefits to society, in school, and in other areas of our lives.

 I. Participating in music benefits all of society.
 II. Participating in music benefits us in school.
 III. Participating in music benefits us in many other ways.

Logical Patterns Emerging from Your Topic The patterns discussed here are not a complete inventory of all the possible topical organizational patterns that exist. The most effective topical pattern is the one that emerges as a result of the pieces of information you present to your audience. As you formulate your purpose and thesis statements, be alert to the patterns that emerge. As Jessica prepared her speech on sleep deprivation, she realized that the information she planned to present grouped itself into three areas.[6]

EXAMPLE: How to Overcome Sleep Loss

Purpose statement: My positive student audience will understand that sleep deprivation is a widespread problem.

Thesis statement: Students are a special group of people who experience sleep deprivation; however, there are ways for us to overcome sleep loss.

 I. Most people are sleep deprived.
 II. There are some special reasons sleep deprivation occurs in students.
 III. There are steps you can take to help you to overcome sleep deprivation.

Spatial or Geographical Organization Sometimes it is easier to present information and easier for your audience to understand and remember your information when you organize your points according to the ways they relate to each other physically; this is **spatial or geographical organization.** Katelyn used this method to demonstrate the benefits of laughter.[7]

EXAMPLE: Laughter Is Good for You

Purpose statement: To encourage my positive audience to laugh their way to a better life.

spatial or geographical organization
Organizing points according to physical relationships.

Thesis statement: Laughter results in emotional, physical, and social benefits.

I. Laughter causes the brain to create endorphins.
II. The immune systems of people who laugh are stronger than of those people who do not laugh.
III. People who laugh are more physically fit than those who do not laugh.
IV. Besides the health benefits, laughter also benefits people socially.

Chronological Order When you organize points in the order of time, you are using **chronological organization.** This is useful when a series of steps needs to occur in a specific order to achieve a desired result or when understanding an event is possible only if the events that lead up to it are presented in the order of their occurrence. Robyn chose chronological order to describe a tragedy that destroyed a town and its rebuilding.[8]

Storytelling is a key element in Garrison Keillor's radio monologues.

EXAMPLE: The Day Our Town Burned Down

Purpose statement: To show my positive audience how tragedy can bring people together and cause good things to happen.

Thesis statement: Our town was destroyed by fire, but the rebuilt town is now on the Historical Register, and the tragedy was the motivation for antifireworks laws.

I. On June 27, 1931, at 3:30 in the afternoon two small boys looking at fireworks in the drugstore ignited a sparkler.
II. Within fifteen minutes the street began to burn, and seventy businesses were wiped out in one day.
III. Plans to rebuild began immediately, and less than six months after the fire, the city held a grand opening to show off the new business district.
IV. Today we have a beautiful downtown district that is on the Historic Register.
V. Our tragedy resulted in a statewide ban on the sale of fireworks.

Organizing to Inspire: The Supportive Audience

Like the open audience, the supportive audience is also a positive audience. The supportive audience differs from the open audience in that it is more knowledgeable about the topic. One goal of the speaker who is presenting to a supportive audience is to inspire the members to recommit their positive feelings toward the topic. A second goal is to give the audience new information about the topic while

chronological organization Organizing points in the order of time.

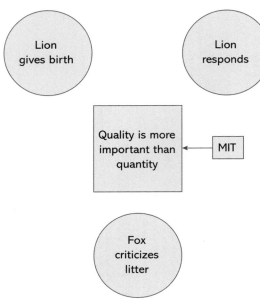

● **FIGURE 11.2** Storytelling Example: Most Important Thing (MIT).

maintaining their interest. Two organizational possibilities present themselves to attain these goals: you can tell a story; or you can arrange the key points according to a "familiar-unfamiliar" organizational pattern.

Telling Stories *A fox referred disparagingly to the fact that the Lioness gave birth to only one cub at a time. "Only one," replied the Lioness, "but a lion."*[9]
—*Aesop*

What does this brief fable say to you? Hearing the story and interpreting the meaning is likely to be more interesting than if the point were stated literally. Such is the power of a story. Stories encourage an emotional response from the audience by causing them to feel uplifted, to feel hope—in other words, to feel inspired.[10] In Chapter 8 we discussed the use of stories to support key points of your presentation. You can also present your entire speech as a story if your goal is to inspire your audience.

A good place to begin when preparing a story for presentation is to decide what the one point is that you want your audience to get from your story. That is, as D. Lipman asks, what is "the most important thing, or the **MIT**"?[11] After you know the MIT, look at your own experiences for a story that illustrates that point. The key incidents in your story should be limited to two or three. Tamara described her son's dedication to car racing by telling a series of family stories:[12]

MSL

EXAMPLE: Don't Ever Give Up on Your Kids
_____

Purpose statement: To motivate my positive audience to always be supportive of their children's ambitions.

Thesis statement: My son realized his dream of getting into NASCAR Tech.

   I. Our experience began when we came home one night and found the race car in the garage.

  II. Soon we started going to the track to watch our son, and we soon realized all of our time was being spent at the track.

 III. Only one in five thousand kids ever gets accepted at NASCAR Tech. Our son was one of them.

    IV. MIT: Don't ever give up on your kids.

MIT The "most important thing" a storyteller wants the audience to understand from the story.

A Question of **Ethics**

What if you have a "sort of" story, but the way the event actually occurred doesn't quite create the type of impact you would like it to? Storytellers generally agree that "storytelling transcends life and facts."[13] They mean that although you should not fabricate a story, you have a storyteller's license to embellish events in order to make your MIT the MIT to the audience.

An international student whose home country was run by a dictator told the story of a typical day in his country. He told of soldiers patrolling the streets; he related the difficulties and dangers of traveling around the country and around his town; he described changes in the quality of life and the stressful effects felt by his family. When asked if he had actually experienced everything he stated in his speech, he admitted he had not personally, but that the details he provided were realistically descriptive of life under the dictator. His story horrified his classmates and impressed upon them the advantages of living in a democracy, and that was his goal.

Was the storyteller being ethical in presenting the events he had not personally experienced as though they were reality? To what extent do you feel a speaker has license to insert details or entire incidents into a story in order to make a strong point?

Guidelines to Assist in Becoming an Inspirational Storyteller

1. Draw a square in the middle of a piece of paper surrounded by no more than three circles.[14] In the square, write the MIT, or the point of the story. In the three circles, write key words representing the major incidents leading up to the MIT (see Figure 11.2). You do not need as many as three incidents in your story, but you should not have more than three. Your job as storyteller is to make the incidents come alive for your audience and connect the incidents to each other to create a story.

2. Alternate the key incidents with the point you want the audience to understand. When you move back and forth between the theme and the key incidents, you are reminding the audience that the story is the vehicle by which the point is made.

3. Not all stories are funny; however, if a story is supposed to be funny, make it so. If a main character has an unusual posture or gesture that is key to the story, rather than describing this mannerism verbally, adopt it nonverbally.

4. Consider the point of view from which you are telling the story. If you want to make the story very personal, use the first person—"I"; if you want your listeners to become the main character, use the second person— "you"; if you are telling a story about a well-known person or historical figure, use the third person—"he" or "she."[15]

ACT&REFLECT

11.4: Telling Stories

A C T • Identify one experience you had today. Based on that experience, create a story. Identify the MIT, select the key incidents. Plan the details and other information you will present to describe the key incidents. Practice your story out loud. Include physical mannerisms and point of view that make the story come alive. Tell your story to a friend.

R E F L E C T • What do you learn about yourself as a storyteller? What are your strengths? In what areas might you make changes?

5 Tell your story to elicit the emotions of your listeners, but do not become too emotional yourself. A student speaker related an account of the brave death from cancer of his girlfriend's mother. The narration was intended to impress upon the audience the importance of regular cancer checkups, but the speaker began to cry, was unable to stop, and had to leave the room without completing his presentation. The audience was so distressed that many of them said they stopped listening to his words and tried instead to think of ways to comfort him. The point of the story was lost. See Act and Reflect 11.4.

MSL **Familiar-Unfamiliar Organization** This type of organization recognizes the knowledge the supportive audience already has and then adds to that knowledge. This pattern works to keep the supportive audience positive by complimenting their expertise and/or experience and maintains their interest by adding to their existing knowledge. Scott used the familiar-unfamiliar pattern to encourage his audience to attend sporting events besides football and basketball.[16]

EXAMPLE: "Lesser" Sports

Purpose statement: To encourage positive sports fans to attend a variety of sporting events.

Thesis statement: There are many sports on this campus deserving of our support in addition to football and basketball.

    I. Almost everyone follows football and basketball.

   II. There are other sports that need our support.

Organizing Presentations for Neutral Audiences

Not every audience is a positive audience. You might find yourself presenting to an audience whose members are neutral. Although "neutral" sounds about as exciting as vanilla ice cream, a neutral audience is the result of a complex interaction of varying degrees of members' knowledge and interest. Presenting to a neutral audience is indeed a challenge for a speaker, due to the "I don't care" attitudes of neutral audiences. As a presenter, you want your audience to experience an "aha moment" as a result of your presentation. Thus, the organizational options offered here are concerned with "hooking" the interest of the audience first and then transferring knowledge to them as a result of that hook. We recognize three types of neutral audiences: the **apathetic neutral audience** is knowledgeable about the presentation topic but has little or no interest in it; the **detached neutral audience** has neither knowledge of nor interest in the topic; the **ambivalent neutral audience** has knowledge and interest, but, as the term "ambivalent" indicates, audience members aren't sure which direction to go with their interest.

Organizing to Interest: The Apathetic Audience

Although at first glance it might seem inaccurate to say so, the apathetic neutral audience and the supportive positive audience are similar. Both are knowledgeable about the presentation topic; the supportive positive audience is interested, whereas the apathetic neutral audience is uninterested. The goal with the supportive positive audience is to inspire them to recommit their interest. The goal with the apathetic neutral audience is to motivate them to become interested. The speaker's goal with both audiences is the same, but the two audiences begin at different points of interest. For the supportive audience, we recommended the familiar-unfamiliar organizational framework to inspire interest; we recommend the same framework for the apathetic neutral audience to motivate interest.

Familiar-Unfamiliar Organization With the apathetic neutral audience, the familiar-unfamiliar framework begins by discussing an aspect of the topic that is familiar to the audience and of interest to them, as a means to motivate their interest and connect them to a topic about which they have no interest. Because the apathetic audience is knowledgeable about the topic, this framework enables the presenter to add to the foundation of knowledge that already exists within the audience.

For example, you begin your workshop on conflict management for the Young Scientists Organization on your campus with a brief discussion of the scientific method and then move on to discuss the conflict management process, drawing parallels to the scientific method. As you discuss the scientific method, the mention of the issue familiar to your audience should spark their interest as you demonstrate the parallels to conflict management, an issue in which they have some knowledge and need to polish their skills but about which they are uninterested.

apathetic neutral audience Audience who are knowledgeable about the presentation topic but have little or no interest in it.

detached neutral audience Audience who have neither knowledge nor interest in a topic.

ambivalent neutral audience Audience who have knowledge and interest in a topic but aren't sure in which direction to focus their interest.

The apathetic audience is knowledgeable but needs to be motivated to get them interested. If you were speaking to this audience, what are some steps you could take to stimulate their interest? ●

EXAMPLE: Conflict Management Skills

Purpose statement: To interest a neutral audience of young scientists in the use of conflict management skills.

Thesis statement: Conflict management skills parallel the scientific method and are useful in managing your professional and personal lives.

I. The scientific method plays an important role in your current academic work and in your future career goals.

II. Conflict management skills follow a process similar to the scientific method and are useful in maintaining professional and personal relationships.

Organizing to Interest and Inform: The Detached Audience

Surely the most challenging audience a presenter will ever face is the detached neutral audience, an audience without interest and without knowledge regarding the presentation topic. For this neutral audience, we recommend an organizational framework called **Monroe's motivated sequence.**[17] The motivated sequence (as it is sometimes called) is a framework that can be applied to many speaking situations with a variety of types of audience. We recommend using the motivated sequence with the detached neutral audience for two reasons. First, the motivated sequence is organized to elicit specific responses from audiences, making it helpful in getting the detached neutral audience interested and involved; second, because the detached neutral audience is not knowledgeable about the topic, the complexity of this organizational framework allows you flexibility both in the range of

Monroe's motivated sequence An organizational framework that is patterned after the manner in which individuals think when they are attempting to make a decision.

knowledge you might include and in the way you choose to deliver that knowledge. You do not have to include all five components of the motivated sequence. You can rearrange or omit any of the steps as your presentation context requires. However, when you are speaking to the detached neutral audience, it is probably to your best advantage to use the entire sequence. The combination of opportunities to involve and inform your detached neutral audience make the sequence a powerful framework for your message.

Monroe's motivated sequence contains five parts (see Figure 11.3, page 291):

Part 1 The **attention step** serves as the introduction and draws audience attention to the topic being discussed. Once your detached neutral audience has heard your attention step, their response should be "I didn't realize that. Tell me more," or even "That's awful. How can this be happening?"

Part 2 The **problem or need step** presents a problem in need of a solution, or an unsatisfied need. There are three areas to address in this step:

- Present information that shows the problematic nature or the unmet need of the issue.
- Create **psychological discomfort,** or the feeling of an unmet need; that is, your listeners should feel a sense of inconsistency or imbalance when comparing what does exist with what they feel should exist.
- Develop ownership of the problem by showing the audience they have a responsibility or an opportunity to take action to resolve the problem or satisfy the need.

Having heard the problem or need step, the response of your audience should be "What can be done about this?"

Part 3 The **solution or satisfaction step** offers a solution to the problem or a means to satisfy the unmet need. When you offer the solution, it is important that you demonstrate that the solution you are advocating is the most likely or best solution or way to satisfy the need. Audience response to your proposed solution should be "If this solution is implemented, what will be the benefit?"

Part 4 The **visualization step** creates a mental picture to help your audience visualize the positive results of implementing the solution you have proposed. Include as many benefits as you can in this step to influence your detached audience; if there are both immediate and long-term benefits that will result from your solution, include both.

Should you develop the visualization step by focusing only on positive results of accepting the solution you advocate or focusing on negative consequences of not accepting it or both? Which will be of greater importance or have a greater influence on your detached audience? Perhaps it will be more

attention step Serves as the introduction for Monroe's motivated sequence and draws audience attention to the topic being discussed

problem or need step The part of Monroe's motivated sequence that presents a problem in need of a solution, or an unsatisfied need that must be resolved.

psychological discomfort The sense of inconsistency or imbalance that motivates an audience to seek a solution or resolution to an undesirable situation.

solution or satisfaction step The part of Monroe's motivated sequence that offers a solution to the problem or a means to satisfy an unmet need.

visualization step The part of Monroe's motivated sequence that creates a mental picture to help the audience "see" the positive results of implementing the solution.

ACT&REFLECT

11.5: Practicing
Monroe's Motivated Sequence

ACT • Watch Laura's speech on eyewitness identi-fication or Crystal's speech on the food pyramid.[18] Both are organized according to the motivated sequence.

REFLECT • If either of these speeches were given to your communication class, how would you recommend developing the psychological discomfort in the problem/need step for your particular class? What benefits or consequences in the visualization step would appeal to your communication class audience? How can you use this experience to help yourself develop a speech organized according to Monroe's motivated sequence for your class?

powerful to discuss both the benefits and the consequences. You must decide. When you have completed the visualization step, the internal response of your audience should be "I like those benefits! What can I do?" or "Those consequences must be avoided. What can I do?"

Part 5 The **action step:** the "What can I do?" response carries you into the last step of the motivated sequence. As its name suggests, the action step identifies actions your audience can take to actualize your suggested solution. This step also acts as the conclusion for the motivated sequence. See Act and Reflect 11.5.

EXAMPLE: The Parthenon Marbles

Purpose statement: My neutral audience of art majors needs to become informed about and act on the tragedy of the Parthenon Marbles.

Thesis statement: The Parthenon Marbles have been wrongly removed from their home in Greece, and they must be returned.

Attention step: Ask the audience how they would feel if the English ambassador to the United States decided to take the Statue of Liberty to England for safe-keeping. Compare to the case of the Parthenon Marbles.

Problem/need step: Describe the Parthenon Marbles and give a historic per-spective. Develop the problem that many people in the art world believe that Lord Elgin stole the Parthenon Marbles from Greece.

Solution/satisfaction step: Call for returning the marbles to Greece, where a new museum is being built for them.

Visualization step: State the benefits of returning the marbles: (1) the new museum is climate controlled and will preserve them better than their current home in the British museum; (2) justice will be served. State the consequence of not returning the marbles: it creates a precedent, placing the national treasures of any country at risk.

Action step: Urge audience members to send an e-mail to the United Nations committee responsible for returning cultural properties to countries of origin.[19]

action step The part of Monroe's moti-vated sequence that suggests actions the audience can take to make sure the solution is implemented.

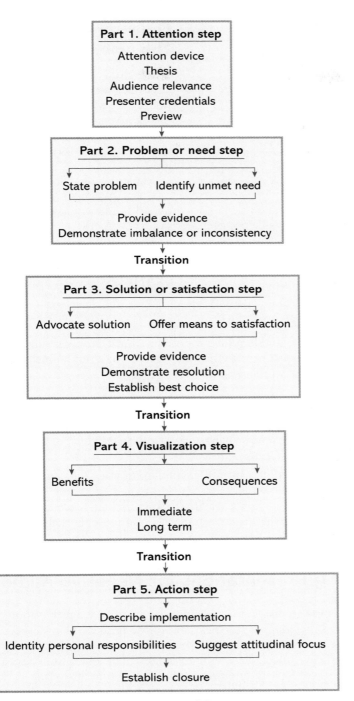

Part 1. Attention step

Attention device
Thesis
Audience relevance
Presenter credentials
Preview

Part 2. Problem or need step

State problem   Identify unmet need

Provide evidence
Demonstrate imbalance or inconsistency

Transition

Part 3. Solution or satisfaction step

Advocate solution   Offer means to satisfaction

Provide evidence
Demonstrate resolution
Establish best choice

Transition

Part 4. Visualization step

Benefits   Consequences

Immediate
Long term

Transition

Part 5. Action step

Describe implementation

Identity personal responsibilities   Suggest attitudinal focus

Establish closure

● **FIGURE 11.3** Monroe's Motivated Sequence.

ACT&REFLECT

11.6: Practicing Organizational Frameworks for Neutral Audiences

ACT • Select a topic you are considering for a future presentation or the topic of a presentation you have already given. Create outlines of the content of the presentation using all of the organizational frameworks discussed for the neutral audience.

REFLECT • What advantages and disadvantages do you see in each of the frameworks?

Organizing to Influence: The Ambivalent Audience

The neutral ambivalent audience is knowledgeable and interested in the topic, but is not certain what to think about it; they are unable to make up their minds, and their neutrality is the result of their ambivalence. The ambivalent audience needs guidance, and the one-sided framework provides that guidance.

The **one-sided organizational framework** simply presents a list of reasons to support your thesis. The framework looks like this:

EXAMPLE: No New Mall!

Purpose statement: To guide my ambivalent audience to the conclusion that the new mall should not be built.

Thesis statement: Building the proposed new mall would result in an abundance of consequences that would effect the local ecology, our municipal economy, and an increase in the working poor.

I. The proposed new mall would endanger the nearby wetland.

II. The proposed new mall would divert business from locally owned stores.

III. A cost-effectiveness analysis has not been conducted, but our area already has enough big box stores.

IV. The proposed new mall offers minimum-wage jobs only.

Perhaps you now see how speaking to a neutral audience challenges a speaker. The last audience type, the negative audience, also presents challenges, but of a different variety. See Act and Reflect 11.6.

Organizing Presentations for Negative Audiences

Negative audiences are made up of people who are knowledgeable about the presentation topic, and they oppose the viewpoint of the speaker. The prospect of speaking to an audience that is opposed to you before you even begin speaking can be off-putting. Nonetheless, the audience's knowledge can be a benefit to a speaker because it means you needn't spend time providing background information or defining terms. The audience's knowledge can also serve you as a starting point for advocating your own viewpoint. Negative audiences can be sorted into two groups:

one-sided organizational framework Organizational framework that presents a list of reasons in support of the thesis.

Everyday Example

Seminar on "Art of Presentation"

You might be wondering to what extent the information you are reading in this chapter has any relevance outside your own communication classroom. The following article taken from Global News Wire emphasizes the importance of organizing a presentation in another culture. How is the information given here applicable to your classroom environment? To other circumstances in which you might find yourself presenting?

The speakers at a seminar organized by Defence School of Business Education in DHA termed the "Art of Presentation" as the most essential and decisive factor for success in any venture. The key note speaker Syed Mumtaz Saeed, an eminent expert and writer on management maintained that the art of making successful presentation was a God-gifted quality but could be refined and developed to an optimum level through proper training and guidance. He said that the effectiveness of presentation depended on putting across one's ideas in a logical and simplified manner so that the audience could easily comprehend them. The speaker unfolding the mechanics of presentation said that gathering and organizing the material, in-

depth research and formulation of concrete ideas was an essential requirement for making a presentation. He said that relevance of topic, logical outflow of ideas, thoughts and critical analysis of the subject were essential ingredients of a good presentation. He said that presentation was the final outcome of intellectual efforts. He maintained that the presentation must be based on facts and statistics and punctuated with quotations, unusual ideas, special experiences, humor and relevant stories to make it interesting, entertaining and informative in its real essence. Brig (R) Muzaffar-ul-Hasan, director [of] Education DHA, advised the participants to intricately learn the delicate art of presentation which he said was a stepping stone that would open new vistas of success and opportunity in their careers. A very lively, thought-provoking and intellectually stimulating question-answer session was the hallmark of the seminar.

Source: © Pakistani Press International "Seminar on 'Art of Presentation,'" Pakistan Press International Information Services Limited, Global News Wire, November 1, 2004, retrieved from Lexis-Nexis Web site, at http://web.lexis-nexis.com/universe/document?_m.

those that are knowledgeable about the presentation topic and oppose the speaker or the speaker's viewpoint but have lost interest will be referred to as **passive negative audience;** and those that are knowledgeable about the presentation topic and oppose the speaker or the speaker's viewpoint but retain their interest—the **active negative audience.**

Organizing to Rekindle Interest: The Passive Audience

The passive negative audience has given up. Passive negative audience members are knowledgeable individuals, and they are opposed to the views of the speaker, but they are no longer interested in the issue. Why? Perhaps they believe that

passive negative audience An audience who is knowledgeable about the presentation topic but, despite having lost interest, still opposes the speaker or the speaker's viewpoint.

active negative audience An audience who is knowledgeable about the presentation topic, retains interest, and opposes the speaker or the speaker's viewpoint.

ACT&REFLECT

11.7: Practicing with Organizational Frameworks

ACT • In anticipation of the organizational frameworks discussed here, select a controversial topic from the list or identify a current topic that is controversial on your campus or in your town. Identify an audience. It might be your communication classmates, a campus organization of which you are a member, your religious group, or some other group. Suggested topics:

Controlling globally emerging diseases

Search engines and privacy

The fast food industry and animal rights

Legalizing gay marriages

Budget allocations for space exploration

Your choice of topic

REFLECT • As you read about each organizational framework, consider your controversial topic and your audience. To what extent would each organizational framework be the best choice for a presentation of your controversial topic to your audience? How effective would each be as an organizational framework for your particular topic and audience?

an active involvement in issues would result in negative consequences for them from the presenter, or they might have been led to believe they "don't count," or they might feel they haven't been heard. Their knowledge is current, and they feel anger or have other negative attitudes toward the speaker, but they have given up. The speaker to a passive negative audience must organize a message in ways that rekindle the spark—that revive and direct their interest. There are two organizational frameworks that make this possible. See also Act and Reflect 11.7.

Agree/Disagree Organizational Framework When the audience is less opposed to the speaker's position than they are to the speaker, Michael Sproule, a public speaking professor, suggests the **agree/disagree organizational framework.** This framework allows you to establish common ground with the audience by introducing an aspect of the topic they agree with before introducing an area of the topic they disagree with. In particular, Sproule suggests that "establishing common ground early in a speech is useful because it helps the audience see the speaker as 'one of us,'" and so may deflect negative attitudes toward the speaker.[20]

Agree/disagree has two major points in the body: first, the presenter establishes common ground to demonstrate

agree/disagree framework Organizational framework that establishes common ground with the audience by introducing an aspect of the topic the audience agrees with before introducing an area of the topic they disagree with.

that, despite the attitude of the audience, an area of agreement exists between them. After the speaker establishes common ground, the area of disagreement is presented in the second point.

Shannon organized her speech on competitive athletics according to the agree/disagree organizational framework.[21]

EXAMPLE: Children Shouldn't Compete

Purpose statement: To show my negative audience how competing in athletics is damaging to children.

Thesis statement: When children compete in athletics, the consequences for self-esteem and health can be costly.

    I. We all agree that participation in competitive sports is beneficial to children.

   II. Despite the benefits of children participating in competitive sports, I want to tell you about the costs of participation, specifically focusing on damage to self-esteem and injuries due to overuse.

Two-Sided Refutational Framework This framework is similar to an op-ed page in a newspaper. It allows the presenter to acknowledge the viewpoints held by the audience, to refute or identify weaknesses in these viewpoints, and to emphasize the view the presenter wishes the audience to adopt. One study found that if your listeners are well informed about the issue and have a viewpoint that is in disagreement with yours, it is more advantageous to you to acknowledge the opposing views as well as presenting your own view.[22] By acknowledging the opposing views, you are also demonstrating to your audience that their opinions have been heard. However, it is not enough to merely mention that you are aware that the audience has other viewpoints; you must also indicate the weaknesses in those other viewpoints and state your own view.[23]

Katelyn organized her speech on home-schooling according to the two-sided refutational framework.[24] Notice how for each point she gave research to refute the point and then concluded the point by summarizing the research.

EXAMPLE: Benefits of Home-Schooling

Purpose statement: To show my negative audience that home-schooling is beneficial to students.

Thesis statement: Home-schooling benefits students educationally, socially, and as adults.

    I. Many of you are concerned about parents educating kids; you feel parents aren't certified or qualified.

        • Research shows home-schooled children score higher on basic battery tests and on ACT tests than public-schooled children.

> **two-sided refutational framework**
> Framework that allows the presenter to acknowledge viewpoints held by the audience, to refute or identify weaknesses in these viewpoints, and to emphasize the view the presenter wishes the audience to adopt.

- Educational results for home schooled students tend to be a little above average compared to those for public-schooled students.

II. There was huge concern among you about socialization of home-schooled students.
- Research shows home-schooled children have contact with people who aren't their age and are more involved in organized activities than public-schooled children of their age.
- The research shows that it is the contact with adults that is advantageous to home-schooled children. Also there are fewer behavior problems.

III. The real test is how do home-schooled students turn out as adults?
- Research shows the home-schooled students went on to complete higher levels of education than the public-schooled students and then tended to vote in higher numbers than the public-schooled. They are also happier.
- Home-schooling makes students pretty good adults.

The negative audience is knowledgeable, but they oppose the speaker's viewpoint. What are some approaches a speaker could take with an active negative audience to address the opposition? ●

Organizing to Redirect Interest: The Active Audience

The **active negative audience** shares with the passive negative audience an opposition to the speaker's viewpoint and knowledge about the presentation topic. However it is the most harsh of the audiences a speaker is likely to encounter. Unlike the passive negative audience, active negative audiences are still interested and involved in the topic. Figuratively and perhaps literally, they are still fighting for their views. The challenge to the speaker who presents to the active negative audience is to demonstrate a respect for the often vast knowledge embodied in this group while presenting new knowledge in such a way that it will withstand the challenge of their strong views. The three organizational frameworks suggested for use with the active negative audience allow you to present a thorough examination of the audience's viewpoints while affording presentation of your own viewpoints.

The Scientific Problem-Solving Organizational Framework This framework is based on the scientific method and is useful for active negative audiences, because it allows the presenter to provide information the audience might not have considered and explore the strength of various solutions, including those advocated by the audience. An additional strength of this organizational framework is the inclusion of a discussion of criteria by which to identify the best solution. The scientific problem-solving method contains these major parts:

scientific problem-solving organizational framework Organizational framework based on the scientific method that allows the presenter to provide information the audience might not have considered and explore the strength of various solutions, including those advocated by the audience.

I. Inform the audience that a problem or issue exists.

II. Identify the causes and effects of the problem.

III. Present criteria or a criterion that will resolve the issue or problem.

IV. List possible solutions and tell why they do or do not meet the criteria.

V. Select the solution that best matches the criteria or criterion and tell how it will resolve the problem.

Collin chose the scientific problem-solving method to discuss Title IX:[25]

EXAMPLE: Problems Caused by Title IX

Purpose statement: To convince my negative audience that Title IX has not been interpreted as was originally intended.

Thesis statement: Title IX must be amended to allow men and women to participate in athletic programs.

I. Four hundred men's athletic programs have been cut over the last thirty years.

II. Title IX has to take responsibility for the loss of programs, loss of profits, and negative effects on everyday people.

III. The best solution must be the one that lets men and women play.

IV. Possible solutions are to eliminate the statute, do nothing, or amend the statute.

V. The best solution is to amend the statute to allow private boosters and to penalize schools that eliminate programs.

Elimination of Alternatives (Method of Residues) When audience members oppose not only the speaker's views but also other audience members' views, this framework is an effective one to choose.[26] It acknowledges all of the possible courses of action that could be considered and eliminates all but the one advocated by the speaker. In the example, a student leader tries to convince a student audience to agree to a specific solution to quell student riots that occurred during a student-run festival. The "best" course of action advocated by the speaker is presented last, hence the name "method of residues."

EXAMPLE: What to Do about Our Student-Run Festival

Purpose statement: My negative audience needs to understand that most of the proposed solutions to the problems related to our student-run annual festival will not effectively resolve them.

Thesis statement: We should cancel the student festival for one year and take the time to explore other options.

I. First possible solution: do nothing. This is not acceptable because the reputations of all students who have participated in this festival are at stake.

elimination of alternatives Acknowledges all of the possible courses of action that could be considered and eliminates all but the one advocated by the speaker.

method of residues Same as **elimination of alternatives.**

    II. Second possible solution: cancel the event forever. No one wants to cancel a tradition.

   III. Third possible solution: ask bar owners to close early during the event. This violates owners' rights.

   IV. Fourth possible solution: hold the event in the middle of winter. Travel difficulties would reduce attendance.

   V. Fifth possible solution, advocated by the presenter: cancel the event for one year and appoint a task force to investigate causes of rioting to determine best course of action.

Although we present the negative audience as being in opposition to the speaker's views, the active negative audience might also oppose the speaker's views without knowing what those views are, as a result of their strong opposition to the speaker.

Reflective Thought Organizational Framework **Dewey's reflective thought pattern** allows you to demonstrate the undesirable nature of a current situation by providing new information unknown to the audience, to evaluate pros and cons of potential solutions resulting from the new information, and to focus on the solution you advocate, which is not divulged until the end of the speech.[27] An advantage of this framework is that it allows the speaker to provide information that could influence audience thinking about the problem or issues without categorically opposing the new information because of their attitudes toward the speaker. The reflective thought organizational framework is organized like this:

   I. Review the current undesirable situation. What makes it undesirable?

   II. Present additional information that is unknown to the audience.

  III. List all the possible solutions to resolve the undesirable situation and give the pros and cons of each.

  IV. Identify the solution you want the audience to support and give benefits of supporting this solution.

MSL Mandy choose this framework to inform her audience about a proposed tax to eliminate obesity.[28]

EXAMPLE: The Twinkie Tax

Dewey's reflective thought pattern
Allows the presenter to demonstrate the undesirable nature of a situation by providing new information unknown to the audience, to evaluate pros and cons of potential solutions resulting from the new information, and to focus on the solution the presenter advocates.

Purpose statement: To persuade my negative audience of the need for a solution to the problem of obesity.

Thesis statement: The Twinkie Tax is a possible solution to the national problem of obesity.

   I. Obesity is a national problem rivaled in seriousness only by smoking.

II. I would like to inform you of national standards used to determine obesity.

III. Possible solutions to the obesity problem are to encourage healthy eating, to encourage an increase in daily exercise, and to mandate healthy eating among the obese through tax incentives.

IV. The best solution would be implementation of the Twinkie Tax to facilitate the process for Americans to make better food choices and reduce the obesity problem.

● GETTING TO WORK

You have learned about many different organizational frameworks in this chapter. Selecting the best framework for your presentation might seem like an overwhelming task. We have tried to help you focus on the best organizational frameworks for your presentation, based on what you want to accomplish and on the type of audience you will face. The first step is to make sure you know your purpose in speaking and decide what your audience wants or needs in order for you to meet that purpose. The process of writing the purpose and thesis statements should serve as a way for you to check that you know what you want to do, as well as being the first step in your planning.

By writing your purpose statement you are also thinking about the type of audience you will be speaking to: are they likely to be a positive, neutral, or negative audience? For the purpose of writing this chapter, we have treated each audience as though all the members will be similar in their attitudes toward your topic and the extent to which they are informed. However, remember that you will probably never have an audience composed solely of one type of person. What do you do, then? Identify the individuals in your audience whom you want to reach with your message. For example, if you are giving a sales presentation, are there one or two persons in the room who will actually make the decision to buy your product, with the remaining persons being present as spectators? If so, tailor your message to the one or two who are the decision makers. At other times, when you are presenting to an audience of whom you believe most members share a common attitude toward your topic, as well as being similarly informed, focus your presentation on the majority.

After you have formulated your purpose and a thesis statement and you know the type of audience toward which your message is focused, you are ready to consider the organizational framework. Here is a quick look at the organizational frameworks we have discussed in this chapter.

Organizational Patterns for Positive Audiences

The Open Audience

The speaker's goal is to inform and retain interest.

1. Topical organizational patterns identify themes, patterns, and relationships that exist between major points. Examples are:

- Prioritizing: arrange points in order of importance
- Stock categories: sort information into groups according to shared commonalities
- Typology: a systematic framework for organizing information
- Complexity: begin with a basic point and build on it with each succeeding point
- Comparison or contrast: show the similarities or differences between two entities
- Repetition: begin each main point with the same key word or phrase
- Logical patterns that emerge from your topic: arrange points according to a pattern that is specific to your topic and points

2. Spatial or geographical organization: organize main points to demonstrate physical or spatial relationships
3. Chronological order: arrange points in order of time

The Supportive Audience

The speaker's goal is to convey new information and inspire the audience to recommit to the issue.

1. Storytelling: develop the speech as a story with each main point becoming a scene in the story
2. Familiar-unfamiliar organization: Recognize knowledge the audience already possesses and then add to or build on that knowledge

Organizational Patterns for Neutral Audiences

ACT & REFLECT

11.8: Practicing Audience Empathy

ACT • Select a topic you feel strongly about. Put yourself in the shoes of persons who are hostile but might not be well informed. With what attitude would these persons listen to your presentation?

REFLECT • Besides selecting the most appropriate organizational framework for your presentation, what other strategies could you incorporate into your presentation?

The Apathetic Audience

The speaker's goal is to create interest. Familiar-unfamiliar organization: discuss an aspect of the topic they are already interested in and then develop a related area where they do not have interest. See Act and Reflect 11.8.

The Detached Audience

The speaker's goal is to inform and create interest. Monroe's motivated sequence is a method for organizing information that helps you inform and develop interest. It contains these steps:

Attention step: introduces topic

Problem or need step: informs about an undesirable situation or unmet need

Solution or satisfaction step: presents a solution to resolve the problem or satisfy the unmet need

Visualization step: creates a mental picture to allow the audience to see advantages of implementing the proposed solution or to consider consequences of not supporting it

Action step: describes actions the audience can support to facilitate implementation of the proposed solution

The Ambivalent Audience

The speaker's goal is to direct the audience to support a specific aspect of an issue. The one-sided organizational framework presents a list of reasons in support of the thesis.

Organizational Patterns for Negative Audiences

The Passive Audience

The speaker's goal is to build goodwill, persuade the audience to agree with the speaker's viewpoint, and rekindle interest in the topic.

1. Agree-disagree framework: establishes common ground by introducing an aspect of the topic the audience agrees with before introducing the issue they disagree with
2. Two-sided refutational framework: acknowledges viewpoints of the audience, refutes or identifies weaknesses of each viewpoint, concludes with the view the speaker supports

The Active Audience

The speaker's goal is to build goodwill and persuade the audience to agree with the speaker's view.

1. Scientific problem solving method: Allows presentation of unfamiliar information and assessment of all viable options; contains these steps:

    Inform the audience a problem exists

    Identify causes and effects of the problem

    Present criteria or a criterion that will resolve the problem

    List possible solutions; show how they do or do not meet the criteria

Select the solution that best matches the criteria and demonstrate how it will resolve the problem

2. Elimination of alternatives (method of residues): acknowledges all possible solutions and eliminates all but the solution the speaker proposes.

3. Reflective thought: Presents new information, assesses each possible solution, and allows the audience to consider new information without opposing it because of negative attitudes toward the speaker; contains these steps:

Review a current undesirable situation

Present additional information that is unknown to the audience

List all viable solutions and assess each

Identify the solution the speaker advocates; give benefits of the solution

You might find one of the options will work perfectly for what you want to accomplish with your particular audience. When nothing we have discussed here seems to work, what should you do? You can design your own organizational framework. Borrow parts of frameworks we have discussed here that you feel will work to help you achieve your speaking goals. Choose one part from one framework, two parts from another framework, something else from a third framework. Assemble them in an order that you believe will give your audience what they want or need in such a way that helps you to meet your purpose.

SUMMARY

This chapter has focused on organizational frameworks that are useful for a variety of types of audience. Before selecting one, you must know your purpose in speaking and identify the pieces of information the audience will need or want to hear in order for the purpose to be met. Constructing a speech purpose statement involves identifying the type of audience to whom the speech will be given, knowing the topic of the speech, and considering what the specific audience will need or want to hear. The thesis statement takes the purpose to a more specific level by listing the individual pieces of information the audience will hear. These individual pieces of

information become instrumental in designating the main points of the body of the speech.

We discussed three major types of audience: the positive, neutral, and negative audiences. Each of the major types of audience can be further refined, depending on the audience's attitude and the amount of knowledge they have about the topic.

There are two types of positive audiences. The open positive audience is interested but not knowledgeable about the speech topic. When presenting to the open positive audience, you might arrange the content of the presentation topically, geographically, or chronologically. Supportive positive audiences are already knowledgeable and interested in hearing more about the topic. Telling stories and a familiar-unfamiliar organizational framework are good ways to present information to the supportive audience.

Neutral audiences are characterized by an "I don't care" attitude. We discussed three types of neutral audiences. The apathetic audience has knowledge about the topic but is uninterested. For this audience, the familiar-unfamiliar organizational framework was also recommended. The detached neutral audience is one of the more challenging groups to whom a speaker can present, because detached audiences are without knowledge and without interest. We recommend Monroe's motivated sequence as an organizational framework that provides opportunities for speakers to inform and stimulate interest in the detached audience. The ambivalent neutral audience is the most knowledgeable of the three neutral audiences, but they cannot decide what to think about the topic. For this audience, a speaker should be prepared to direct the audience's thinking, and the one-sided organizational framework allows a speaker to present one viewpoint.

There are two types of negative audiences. The passive negative audience are knowledgeable about the topic and disagree with the speaker's views but are apathetic. Passive negative audiences may not care, because they believe they haven't been heard or they in turn are not cared about. When speaking to this type of audience, you could use the agree-disagree framework or the two-sided refutation framework. Both allow

you to acknowledge your audience's view and present your own view.

Active negative audiences are knowledgeable about the topic and are actively involved in furthering their own views but are opposed to the speaker's views. With this type of audience, you need organizational frameworks that provide an analysis of the often vast knowledge and strong opinions of this group but still give you an opportunity to present your views. To accomplish this formidable challenge, we recommend three organizational frameworks: the scientific problem-solving framework presents a criterion for the most desirable resolution and builds in an opportunity for the speaker to apply the criterion to each possible solution; the elimination of alternatives framework includes an exploration of views—useful when audience members not only oppose the speaker but also may be in disagreement with each other; the reflective thought organizational framework is useful when the audience's opposition to the speaker is so great as to overshadow any recommendation the speaker might present.

Although we discussed the three audience types as though all members of an audience might be consistent in their knowledge and interest, the reality is that most audiences are mixed. The choice of organizational framework should be based on the needs of the audience members it is most important for the speaker to reach.

Finally, speakers are encouraged to create their own organizational frameworks to meet specific needs.

VIDEO EXPERIENCE

The following additional speeches are available to you.[29] (1) As you listen to each speech, try to identify the organizational framework the speaker has chosen. (2) On the basis of the framework you have identified, for which type of audience do you believe the speech is intended? (3) If these speakers were to appear as guest speakers in your communication classroom, what advice would you give them about your classroom audience and how would you suggest they organize their speeches to meet the interest and knowledge of your audience?

Chelsea's speech on cell-phone etiquette

Kasey's speech on procrastination.

Karen's speech on harmful weather.

Scott's speech on the X-Prize.

Ilana's speech on the Peace Corps and Ameri-Corps.

Amy's speech in support of mandatory school uniforms.

THINKING BACK, THINKING AHEAD

1. Remember the brainstorming list of possible topics you created in Chapter 2? Select any topic from your list and assume you are going to prepare a presentation on that topic for an audience outside your classroom. What organizational frameworks suggest themselves?

2. Listen to one of the do-it-yourself television programs: a cooking show; a show featuring home owners' projects; a craft or gardening program; other how-to shows. How are instructions for the projects presented to viewers? Can you list the key points as you listen? If you were to follow the instructions yourself, what unanswered questions would you have about the project? What did the program teach you about organizing presentations for positive audiences?

3. Listen to Garrison Keillor on *Prairie Home Companion*. What do you notice about the way Keillor tells a captivating story? What techniques do you notice that you could adapt for your own use when telling a story?

4. Observe your favorite television advertisements. How does an advertisement that attracts and maintains your attention do so? Are there any strategies you notice that you might use to involve a neutral audience in a presentation? Do you notice that advertisements are organized similarly to any of the organizational frameworks presented in this chapter?

5. Compare a class that is important to you with a class you attend merely because you believe it is expected. What causes the difference in your attitude? Is the reason you feel the one class is important related to something about the course content or the instructor, or both? If you were to advise the instructor of the "neutral" class of ways he or she could help you feel the class is more important, what would you say?

6. When you find yourself hanging on to a presenter's words, identify the methods the presenter uses to elicit your involvement. Does the presenter include stories? Does the presenter make miniassignments for you to consider? Are there opportunities for you to become involved? Which of these methods could you incorporate into your next presentation to a neutral audience?

7. Keep a log of the presentations you have attended or seen on television where a negative audience has been in attendance. How do presenters respond to the negativity? Have you witnessed a presentation in which the speaker responded to the negative audience in a similarly negative manner? What was the result? What do you learn about ways presenters can and should respond to negative audiences?

8. Attend an event where a controversial issue is being discussed and anyone can voice an opinion. You might attend a student government meeting on your campus or a school board or town council meeting off campus. What is your assessment of the effectiveness of those individuals who speak up? Do you feel they are successful in influencing their listeners? Why or why not?

9. Think about your presenting strengths. What qualities do you possess, both personal qualities and presentation qualities, that could be beneficial to you when interacting with negative audiences? Neutral audiences? Positive audiences?

NOTES

1. Jon Sheller, speech to a positive audience, September 22, 2004.
2. Ross Kellerman, speech to a positive audience, September 24, 2004.
3. Katie Denklau, speech to a positive audience, September 22, 2004.
4. "A. Sterl Artley, Last Surviving Author of Dick & Jane Dies," *History of Reading News, 22* (fall 1998), retrieved from Web site, at www.historyliteracy.org/scripts.
5. Amy Diekevers, speech to a positive audience, September 29, 2004.
6. Jessica Culhane, speech to a positive audience, September 24, 2004.
7. Katelyn Ver Hoef, speech to a positive audience, September 29, 2004.
8. Robyn Larsen, speech to Municipal Clerks' Institute, July 13, 2005.
9. "The Lioness and the Fox," in *The Fables of Aesop*, translated by Patrick and Justina Gregory (Boston: Gambit, 1975), 96.
10. A. Wylie, "Storytelling: A Powerful Form of Communication," *Communication World, 15* (1998): 30–33.
11. D. Lipman. *Improving Your Storytelling: Beyond the Basics for All Who Tell Stories in Work or Play* (Little Rock, AR: August Houser, 1999), 90.
12. Tamara Coleman, speech to Municipal Clerks' Institute, July 13, 2005.
13. J. G. Robinson, *Did I Ever Tell You about the Time . . . How to Develop and Deliver a Speech Using Stories That Get Your Message Across* (New York: McGraw-Hill, 2000), 159.
14. Taken from D. Lipman, *Improving Your Storytelling*, J. G. Robinson, *Did I Ever Tell You About the Time . . .*, and J. Maguire, *The Power of Personal Storytelling: Spinning Tales to Connect with Others* (New York: Putnam, 1998).
15. M. Wacker and L. Sullivan, *Stories Trainers Tell: 55 Ready-to-Use Stories to Make Training Stick* (San Francisco: Jossey-Bass, 2003), 88–89.
16. Scott Sturm, speech given to a positive audience, September 27, 2004.
17. A. Monroe, *Principles and Types of Speech* (New York: Scott, Foresman, 1935).
18. Laura Johnson, speech to a neutral audience, October 18, 2004. Crystal Nord, speech to a neutral audience, October 18, 2004.
19. L. Rosenbaum, "Meeting of the Marbles?" *Art in America, 91* (2003): 41–44. (The Monroe's motivated sequence outline was based on information found in this article.)
20. J. M. Sproule, *Speechmaking: An Introduction to Rhetorical Competence* (Dubuque, IA: Brown, 1991), 411.
21. Shannon Kirton, speech to a negative audience, November 10, 2004.
22. A. A. Lumsdaine and I. L. Janis, "Resistance to 'Counterpropaganda' Produced by One-Sided and Two-Sided 'Propaganda' Presentations," *Public Opinion Quarterly, 17* (1953): 311–318.
23. D. J. O'Keefe, "How to Handle Opposing Arguments in Persuasive Messages: A Meta-Analytic Review of the Effects of One-Sided and Two-Sided Messages," in *Communication Yearbook 22,* edited by Michael E. Roloff (Thousand Oaks, CA: Sage, 1999), 241.
24. Katelyn Ver Hoef, speech to a negative audience, November 10, 2004.
25. Collin Schmidt, speech to a negative audience, November 17, 2004.
26. D. Bridges and J. C. Reinard, "The Effects of Refutational Techniques on Attitude Change," *Journal of the American Forensic Association, 10* (1974): 203–212.
27. J. Dewey, *How We Think* (Boston: Heath, 1910).
28. Mandu Sadowski, speech to a negative audience, November 17, 2004.
29. Chelsea de Sousa, speech to a positive audience, September 29, 2004. Kasey Pfabb, speech to a positive audience, September 29, 2004. Karen Tarara, speech to a neutral audience, October 22, 2004. Scott Sturm, speech to a neutral audience, October 22, 2004. Ilana Mainaga, speech to a negative audience, November 10, 2004. Amy Diekevers, speech to a negative audience, November 19, 2004.

Chapter 12

Managing the Organization

Introductions, Conclusions, and Transitions

Goals

- ✓ To help you understand the functions of the introduction and conclusion

- ✓ To help you learn to identify the components of introductions and conclusions

- ✓ To show you different guidelines for developing introductions and conclusions when presenting to positive, negative, and neutral audiences

- ✓ To clarify for you the function of transitions and when to insert them in a presentation

- ✓ To show you guidelines for selecting transitions in presentations for positive, negative, and neutral audiences

The cheetah's survival is in jeopardy due to declining numbers of prey species; conversion of land to agriculture and livestock farming; conflict with livestock farming; and poaching and illegal trade. The estimated population of less than 15,000 animals are found in fragmented and small groups in perhaps 26 African countries with a remnant population of less than 200 in Iran, and viable populations maybe found in fewer than half of the countries where cheetah still live. Neither protected reserves (due to conflict with larger predators), nor captive management (due to limited breeding success), can be relied on to support the survival of the cheetah. Today the cheetah's survival is in humans' hands. Therefore, developing strategies for maintaining free-ranging cheetah populations and habitats outside of protected areas are critical for the long-term survival of the species. In order to develop long-term conservation programs, we must think critically about the needs of humans and the needs of the cheetah and find ways for both to live together. . . .

I began working with cheetahs over 25 years ago at the Wildlife Safari in Oregon. As the Curator for Cheetahs for 16 years, I helped develop North America's most successful cheetah breeding center.[1] ●

If these were the first words of a presentation that you heard, would they be interesting enough to influence you to want to listen to the remainder of the presentation? When the speaker describes her experiences working with cheetahs, you might feel confident about the value of the information presented in the speech, knowing that she has expertise with these animals. You also have a sense of the additional information she will discuss, because she has indicated some of the strategies she feels need to be implemented to resolve the cheetah problem. Any of these points might attract your attention and influence you to continue listening. In these few lines, you have acquired background about the presentation topic, you have been informed about the credentials of the speaker, and you have an idea of the direction the speech will go. If you had not heard this information, would you want to continue listening? Maybe not. Would you understand why this was a topic worthy of your attention? Again, maybe not. Would you view the speaker as someone who was knowledgeable about her topic? Again, you might not. These pieces of information you have learned about cheetahs and about the speaker who is discussing them are a part of the area of the speech we call the **introduction**.

Does it seem strange to you to read eleven chapters of information on the various aspects of planning, organizing, and presenting a speech before you learn about how to begin and how to end it? The reason we have ordered the topics this way is that you should devote your attention to the body first, because that is the substance of your message, and you need to know what you will say to your audience. Your introduction and conclusion frame the body of your presentation just as a picture frame surrounds a photo. Just as you would want to select a frame that sets off the photo you plan to display within it, you plan the introduction and conclusion to "set off" your message after you have organized the body of your presentation.

In this chapter we are going to discuss the kinds of information you will need to divulge to your audience as soon as you begin to speak, or rather, why and how you should introduce your presentation. We will also discuss the importance of developing a memorable ending, or **conclusion.** Finally, we will identify points during your presentation when you will need to insert words, phrases, or sentences to create connections. These connections are called **transitions.**

introduction The beginning of your presentation, which attracts the attention of your audience and prepares them to listen.

conclusion The last part of your presentation, which summarizes what you want your audience to recall from your message.

transitions Words, phrases, and sentences that connect parts of your presentation while allowing you to move from point to point.

Introductions

Think about all of the decisions you have made about your presentation: you have a sense of the positive, negative, or neutral attitudes of your audience; you know what you want to say to them and approximately how you will say it; you have gathered and developed support material for your key points; you have designed visual support. Now that you have considered all of these aspects of your presentation and made the necessary accompanying decisions, it is time to think about introducing your presentation to your audience.

Why Does Your Presentation Need an Introduction?

Your presentation needs an introduction for several reasons. Even though your audience is sitting in their chairs, waiting for you to speak, their attention is probably elsewhere. They might be thinking about experiences they had before arriving at your presentation or about what they will do later, after they hear you speak. Maybe they are visiting with other audience members. As you give your introduction, your listeners have an opportunity to clear their minds of other distractions and prepare themselves to hear your presentation. In an earlier discussion, we indicated that people receive thousands of bits of stimulation from their environments at any one time. In order for your presentation to provide useful information to your listeners, your first challenge as a speaker is to motivate listeners to ignore the other thousands of bits of stimulation they are receiving and focus on you and your message. The introduction gives you the opportunity to do that.

Although your audience might have some general knowledge about your topic, the members of your audience may have varying degrees of knowledge, and they might not know exactly what to expect from your presentation. An introduction will help to lay the groundwork for what you will say in the body of your presentation, so your

The introduction gives audience members a chance to make a transition from their own thoughts and activities to attend to the speaker. ●

audience has a sense of the path you will take. If you've ever gone on a road trip and depended on the road signs to get to your destination, you might have taken a wrong turn or two before your arrival, using more time and fuel than was necessary. If you had taken the time to check a map beforehand, your trip was probably more efficient in terms of time and less costly as far as fuel consumption. The introduction to your presentation works in much the same way for your audience by helping them anticipate the path of your message and enabling them to follow that path more efficiently.

Your audience might not be totally certain why they should listen to you discuss your topic. They might be in attendance because they are interested in your topic but not familiar with you or your experiences or expertise regarding it. The introduction gives you an opportunity to introduce yourself and to describe your relationship with your topic, and it informs your audience of why you have the right to discuss the topic. In turn, your audience may feel more confidence about the value or accuracy of the information you give them in your presentation.

Finally, for various reasons, it is possible that not all of the members of your audience understand how they might benefit from hearing your presentation or realize its relevance to them. Such individuals are asking themselves, "Why should I listen to this? What does this have to do with me?" In your introduction, you have the opportunity to answer these questions so your audience will understand why your message should matter to them.

As you can see, your introduction carries a heavy burden, in that if you do not attract your listeners' attention, they might continue to be preoccupied with their own thoughts; if you do not present a clear picture of what you plan to discuss, they might become confused or even "vote with their feet," by walking out; if your audience doesn't understand how your presentation relates to them or if they don't understand why they should listen to you discuss your topic, the value of your message and the magnitude of your influence will be minimized.

Despite the important role the introduction plays in your overall presentation, it is only a part of your speech and is not the entirety of your presentation. Therefore, it must be concise. As a rule of thumb, assume that your introduction is going to consume no more than 20 percent of your presentation. In other words, if your presentation lasts for thirty minutes, your introduction should last for no more than six of those minutes. Most presentations are not nearly that long, so you will have to find ways to state all of the important information you need to include in your introduction within a very brief period of time. That means it is important for you to do some thinking and planning about how you will accomplish this.

As with every decision you make regarding your presentation, the content of your introduction is dependent on your audience. Knowing that your audience is generally negative or neutral or positive toward you or your topic will help you craft an introduction that is tailored to their specific qualities.

Components of the Introduction

There are five functions the introduction fulfills, depending on the nature of the speaking situation. We will look at ways to develop each of the five functions first and then discuss how to construct introductions for specific audiences. These are the five functions of an introduction:

- Gain audience attention
- Establish your credibility
- Generate relevance to your audience
- State your thesis
- Preview your main points

Gain Audience Attention As soon as you begin to speak, your audience is deciding whether or not they want to listen to you. Those first few words you utter make or break the opportunity you have to attract and maintain the attention of your audience. If you do not say something that makes them want to listen to you, you might find that you have to work to attract their attention for the rest of your presentation, and you might never be successful. You must also select the best means of attracting their attention, depending on who you are, who they are, and what the nature of your topic is. There are a number of methods for attracting audience attention; depending on the circumstances of your presentation, some work better than others.

State the Topic You Will Discuss This method means that you simply come right out and state the topic you will be discussing in your presentation. Both the advantage and the disadvantage to this approach is that it is obvious and to the point.

This works best in two situations:

- When you know the topic has some value or interest to your audience, such as "Today I will discuss the predicted double-digit tuition increase"
- When there is attention value in the topic itself: topics such as sex, money, death, and love are examples of topics that are inherently interesting to most people

MSL

Cindy's approach to attracting the audience attention was simply to say, "I decided to talk about my backyard."[2] The audience knew that Cindy lived adjacent to a state park, so the simple approach attracted their interest, yet seemed mysterious.

Extend a Personal Greeting to Your Audience A personal greeting at the beginning of a speech works exactly the same as a personal greeting when you meet a friend. This works best in two situations:

- If you have a personal relationship with your audience, as when you are speaking to an organization of which you are a member
- If you are able to connect your greeting to the topic of your presentation

MSL

Jessica greeted her audience with an intensely personal greeting that allowed her to explore the importance of gay marriages:

Today I'm in a great mood because I am in love. I'm sure many of you have significant others and you feel the same way. Maybe some day you're thinking about marrying that person. But imagine what it would feel like to be told by everyone that love was wrong and to want to marry that person was something evil and was hated as much as gay marriages today.[3]

Refer to the Occasion   Use this approach to bring the audience's attention to a special event or "official" special occasion at which you are speaking. The reference to the occasion could be selected in these circumstances:

- When the event at which you are speaking observes a special occasion
- When the topic of your speech is a result of the occasion or is related to the occasion

MSL

Ross's speech on affirmative action referred to the observation of Martin Luther King's birthday. Although his speech was not given on that day, the reference gave him a basis for introducing his topic:

> How many of you remember where you were the morning of January 15 of this year? None of you? I remember the morning very vividly because I woke up at my normal time. Took my shower. I noticed, "Hey there's nobody in the bathroom, that's kind of odd . . ." And then I walked across campus to class. There was nobody on campus and I thought "this is really strange." Then I got to my classroom right across the hall from this one. The lights were off, nobody's in there, so I flipped the lights on. I sat down. I waited about fifteen minutes. Nobody shows up. Okay, joke's on me. Turns out it's Martin Luther King, Jr., day and there's no class. So I turned around and walked back home and I figured I've got all day now and nothing going on so I should do some research now and find out the history on it.[4]

Make a Startling Statement   A **startling statement** includes statistics or other facts that give your audience unusual or unexpected information. When a startling statement includes statistics or other data that someone has generated, or when the statement is the result of someone else's opinion or work, you will need to include documentation that verifies the accuracy of the information. Avoid using this approach simply to attract audience attention. We have heard students introduce their classroom speeches by promising to discuss one topic while intending to discuss a completely different topic: "Today I'm going to tell you everything you always wanted to know about sex but were afraid to ask. Now that I've got your attention, let's talk about why you should donate blood in the next campus blood drive." Although you might initially attract the attention of your audience, they could feel let down by your real topic and even begin to distrust you. Begin your speech with a startling statement when in these situations:

- You know the audience will view your statement as unusual
- You can relate your startling statement to the topic of your presentation
- You are able to document the source or otherwise verify the content

startling statement An approach to attracting your audience's attention that includes statistics or other facts that give your audience unusual or unexpected information about your topic.

Collin integrated two types of approach in his introduction. After initially asking the audience a question, he connected their responses to his startling statement:

> Let's see a show of hands here: how many of you use SPF sunscreen of fifteen or stronger when you go outside more than thirty minutes? (He paused, looked around the room.) Wow! That's really good because according to melanoma.com, fifteen out of a hundred thousand people are diagnosed with melanoma every year, and it's the most deadly form of skin cancer. Closer to home, narrow that down to Iowa State's population, four of us will be diagnosed with melanoma this year.[5]

Begin with a Quotation This can be an effective way to attract your audience's attention. Your quotation can be an opinion, or you can quote any relevant passage from literature, music, or any other source. Before you begin your speech with a quotation, consider these points:

- Is the source of the quotation someone your audience would find credible or a source that would be familiar and of interest to them?
- Will the source of the quotation or the quotation itself have the greatest attention value?
- Is the content of your quotation relevant to your topic, and will it interest your audience?
- Will the quotation serve as a foundation for the content of your speech?

Jessica began her presentation on sleep deprivation with a quotation:

> Two hundred and fifty years ago, Benjamin Franklin wrote in *Poor Richard's Almanac:* "Early to bed, early to rise makes a man healthy, wealthy, and wise." I'm sure all of you have heard of this proverb and most of you agree with it.[6]

Ask a Question A question directs your audience's thinking toward a particular aspect of your topic. There are two kinds of questions you can use: a **direct question** requires the audience to respond to it; a **rhetorical question** does not require an overt response but is used to focus and encourage audience thinking. Direct or rhetorical questions are useful in specific situations.

Choose a direct question in these situations:

- When the range of possible responses from your audience is limited
- When you can integrate audience members' responses into your speech
- When your audience is uninterested in your topic or unaware of how your topic relates to them

direct question A question you ask your audience to which you expect a response.

rhetorical question A question you ask your audience that does not require a response but is used to focus and encourage the audience's thinking.

Choose rhetorical questions in these situations:

- When the range of possible responses to your question is large
- When the question is of a sensitive nature
- When you are asking your audience to think about a hypothetical situation

For both kinds of question, you can use these guidelines:

- Clearly state the type of response you want from your audience
- Manage your voice so your question sounds like a question, and maintain eye contact with your audience
- Give your audience time to respond to a direct question, or a moment to think about a rhetorical question
- Prepare a transition to connect your audience response to your presentation
- Throughout your presentation, whenever you are able, refer to the audience response to your question

MSL

Maya introduced her speech on the benefits of exercise by asking a direct question:

Can I see a show of hands: how many of you were involved in high school sports or high school extracurricular activities that involved physical activities of any kind? (She pauses and raises her hand to demonstrate what she is asking.) A lot of you. And you did this not just because you knew the benefits of exercise but because it was fun. A lot of times when we get to be college students, we forget that exercise can be fun.[7]

Copyright 2002 by Randy Glasbergen.
www.glasbergen.com

GLASBERGEN

"Always start your presentation with a joke,
but be careful not to offend anyone! Don't mention
religion, politics, race, money, disease, technology,
men, women, children, plants, animals, food..."

Tell a Joke. It is no joke that people like to laugh. Telling a joke as your attention-grabber can start your speech off on the right foot, or, unfortunately, it can be a disaster from which you might not recover. It is not an overstatement to say that joke telling is a serious matter. When do jokes not work well? Some speakers tell jokes better than others. Avoid telling jokes if you are generally ineffective at telling jokes or if you are not familiar with your audience and you don't know whether they will find your joke funny. Never tell a joke that is sexist or racist or in any way minimizes or devalues a person or group of people or belittles issues of importance to an audience. If it is possible that a joke you are considering fits even peripherally in any of these categories, don't tell it.

As you see, telling a joke is risky. You risk offending all or part of your audience, and in the process, you risk damaging your own character, reputation, and relationship with them. Despite all the risks, if you do choose to tell a joke to attract the attention of your audience, there are several points to keep in mind:

- Practice the joke so that you can tell all the necessary details and give the punch line effectively and accurately
- Devise a plan that allows you to respond appropriately to your audience's response to your joke before you continue with your speech. If your audience laughs, give them a few seconds to enjoy themselves and then tentatively continue on with your speech
- Devise a plan for when your audience doesn't laugh
- Refer to your joke throughout your speech, if possible

MSL

Ashley introduced her speech on gas prices using a visual aid of a sign at a fuel station that showed the prices of the different kinds of fuel as "an arm," "a leg," and "first-born child." She integrated the sign into her approach:

> Let's start out today by looking at this picture, because most of you feel like this: high gas prices cost quite a bit. A lot of us feel like it's an arm and a leg and eventually, if it keeps going, it's going to end up costing us our first-born child.[8]

Tell a Story Story is defined here to mean an account of an event or a series of events that might or might not be humorous, might or might not be true, might or might not conclude with a lesson or a point. Telling a story enables you to create a connection with your audience; and it allows you to convey information. If you do not have a personal experience on which to build your story, you can fabricate a story, but be sure to let your audience know that you have done so. One of our former students told the story of his childhood experiences following the divorce of his parents. When a member of the audience expressed her regrets for the childhood he described, he replied, "Oh, I made all that up for my speech. My parents live in town. I see them every weekend." The audience was furious. They had trusted and believed his story, and he betrayed them. While his story was very effective in setting the scene for his topic, a simple "I'd like you to imagine a situation with me for a minute" before he launched into his story would have saved the day.

If you use a story to attract your audience's attention, here are guidelines for preparing your story:

- Focus on necessary details and information; cut unnecessary details and information so you can say a lot in a few words

story An account of an event or a series of events used to attract your audience's attention.

A joke or story is an effective way to introduce a speech. ●

- If you fabricate a story, clearly inform your audience
- Practice your story so you can tell it to your audience without consulting your notes
- Make the point of your story clearly and effectively
- Provide a transition from your story to the next sentence in your introduction
- Throughout your speech, make reference to your story

Ross introduced his speech on the use of eBay by telling a story about his own experiences trying to save money and comparing it with Christopher Columbus:

> When Christopher Columbus went to the queen of Spain and said "I wanna go travel," it wasn't to find North America; it was to find a cheaper way to get goods from western Europe to eastern Asia, or maybe I have that backward. It doesn't matter, you know what I mean. That was because it was so expensive to get goods from overland that way. And so, like Christopher Columbus, I'm always looking for ways to save money. Also like Christopher Columbus, once I decided I'm going to try to save money on textbooks, the way I thought I would save it isn't the way I ended up saving it. Originally I thought I'd call up some publishers; I'll look at some of those big national bookstore chains and see if they have lower prices than the university bookstore. It turns out publishers won't send books to students unless they claim to be professors, and national chains aren't any cheaper. But what I did find is eBay. And I kinda compare it to Christopher Columbus's North America. It's not what I expected, but it's way better than what I was looking for.[9]

We have discussed eight different ways to attract your audience's attention. How do you decide which of these options to use? First, the best choice serves the nature of your audience, the occasion, and yourself. What would make your audience want

ACT&REFLECT

12.1: Trying Out Attention Approaches

ACT • Select a topic from the list, or if you are working on a presentation for your classroom audience or some other audience, use the topic of that presentation.

cell phone ring tones	wind power	geo-cache
eyebrow waxing	blogging	avian flu
iPods	body piercing	owning versus leasing cars
Internet dating	50 Cent (the rapper)	organic foods

Practice developing an attention approach for your topic, using all of the approaches we have discussed here. Begin with the first, stating your topic, and proceed in the order in which we have discussed the approaches, building each new approach on the previous ones.

REFLECT • Which of the approaches do you think would result in the most effective approach if you were using it to introduce a speech to your classroom audience? Choose another audience outside your classroom. Would the same approach be useful for that audience? Why or why not?

to listen to you? What is the purpose of your presentation? What will you feel most confident about delivering? Second, inherent in each approach are advantages and disadvantages regarding their "attention-grabbing value." The eight options are organized from generally least effective to generally most effective. An effective attention-grabber is a must-have for your introduction. Without it, it is possible that nothing else you say will matter. See Act and Reflect 12.1.

Present Your Credentials If your audience does not personally know you, your introduction is also the part of your speech in which you will present your credentials. Why should your audience be willing to listen to your message and view you as a credible source? They may be looking to you for information they will use to make important decisions. To assure your audience that your message contains information they have the right to feel confident applying to various aspects of their lives, to reassure them that they can base their thinking on the information you tell them, you will need to establish your **credentials.**

We suggested earlier that you should speak only about topics about which you have expertise, experience, and commitment. The introduction is the first point in your presentation at which you need to divulge your expertise, experience,

> **credentials** The experience, expertise, or commitment of the speaker in relation to the topic that allows the speaker the right to discuss the speech topic.

and commitment to your audience to enable them to conclude you are a credible source of information on the topic you are discussing. If there are several dimensions to your credentials, if you have expertise, experience, and commitment to your topic, reveal all of them to your audience as concisely as possible. If you have not had experience in all of the areas, however, emphasize your experiences in the areas that apply to you.

Ashley informed her classmates about multiple sclerosis. She developed her credentials in this manner: "I've had experience with MS for eight years now. My dad was diagnosed in '96. So I've researched the topic for personal interest, and because of my knowledge I want to share with you today."[10] Which of the methods—to establish expertise, experience, or showing commitment—does Ashley use to establish her credentials?

Establish Audience Relevance Even though you might have the attention of your audience and they view you as a credible source, they might wonder why they should spend time listening to you. If your audience wonders what your presentation has to do with them, the influence you have on their way of thinking, feeling, and behaving is limited. Essentially what you are doing is entertaining them while you speak, but the extent to which they might retain your message will be minimal.

When you establish **audience relevance,** you are helping your audience understand what a topic has to do with them. Why should your audience care about your presentation? How will they benefit from hearing what you have to say? The connection might be perfectly obvious to you, but you must tell the audience why and/or how your message is relevant to them. You have some choices in the way you establish relevance:

- First, identify immediate benefits to your audience. As a result of your speech, will they save money, live healthier lives, do their jobs better, or acquire some other information or skill that will benefit them? If so, tell them.
- Second, if your audience will not personally benefit, will others benefit? Will your presentation give the audience information that will help them make choices that will make the world a better place, environmentally, politically, or some other way? If so, say it.
- Third, will your presentation provide important information to your listeners for their future benefit? Will the content of your presentation equip them to respond to future situations? If so, show them.
- Finally, use all of these approaches if your topic and information allow you to show relevance in all three ways.

Cindy's speech on subliminal advertising established relevance with her audience in this way:

audience relevance Reasons the topic is applicable to the audience's needs or interests.

I'm gonna go ahead today and show you some examples today that I feel represent subliminal advertising and I'm gonna let you decide for yourself whether or not companies possibly use subliminal advertising to get you to buy their products. Hopefully when I'm done, you'll be able to think about that; the next time you see advertising, see behind what you are registering consciously in your mind and think whether or not there are things going subconsciously in your mind that are influencing you to buy certain products.[11]

State Your Thesis You don't want your audience to listen to your message and wonder afterward what you were trying to accomplish. What is it you want your audience to understand or believe, or what actions do you want them to take as a result of your presentation? The statement that describes the effect you would like your speech to have on your audience as a result of your presentation is your **thesis.**

You might find that within your introduction you state your thesis several times in a number of ways: your attention approach might imply a certain thesis; your credentials, your topic, and the specific nature of your knowledge about your topic might point to your thesis; in establishing audience relevance, the relationship of your audience to your topic is clarified, and your audience might grasp what you intend to discuss. It is possible that you indicate your thesis in some or all of these areas of your introduction. To be certain your audience hears your thesis once, identify a place in your introduction where you can state your thesis clearly, strongly, and unequivocally, in case your listeners are still not quite certain what it is you plan to discuss. Along with stating your thesis, you can also help your audience listen to your presentation by previewing the key points you will discuss in the body.

Preview Your Main Points The final component that is necessary in order to prepare your audience for your message is a preview of the major points you will make in the body of your presentation.

Doing this makes it easier for your audience to follow your presentation, because they are able to anticipate the order in which you will present your points. When you preview your main points, you need to walk a fine line between telling your listeners enough about your major points so they can follow you but not so much that you seem to be giving your presentation before you give your presentation. Earlier we discussed the importance of writing out a specific purpose statement. If you drafted a statement of specific purpose for your speech, that statement might serve as your preview of main points.

To introduce her speech on fighting ignorance, Maya stated her thesis and previewed the main points she will discuss:

> Homo! White trash! Fag! Nigger! Jap! These are all derogatory terms that we sometimes hear. Not always do we act out against them. So what I would like to talk about to you today is the "Got Ignorance" campaign. So I will talk about what "Got Ignorance" is; the reasons for having the campaign. I'll give examples of different acts of ignorance, ways the campaign wishes to eradicate these acts and ways that you can participate in the campaign because that is what I'd really like for you to do.[12]

Now we have discussed all five functions of the introductions and given you suggestions for developing each of the functions. Does every introduction for every speech you

thesis A statement that describes the effect you would like your speech to have on your audience as a result of your presentation.

give need to include all five areas? Not necessarily. The five areas can be modified according to the type of audience.

Developing Introductions for Positive, Negative, and Neutral Audiences

You will need to modify your introduction to meet the varying qualities of different audiences. The introduction allows you to build or rekindle a connection with a negative audience, spark the interest of a neutral audience, reinforce the interest of a positive audience.

Positive audiences are interested audiences whose members differ in the amount of knowledge they possess regarding the speaker's topic. Your introduction to the positive audience acknowledges their existing interest and knowledge and extends their knowledge while retaining their interest.

Guidelines for Developing an Introduction for a Positive Audience

1 Attract the audience's attention with one of the more complex approaches, using a quotation, startling statement, joke, or story to maintain their interest.

2 Establish your credentials by relating personal experiences that reflect your expertise, experience, and commitment to the topic, allowing them to draw their own conclusions about your credibility. They are more likely to be impressed by what you show them regarding your experiences than by what you tell them about your expertise.

Everyday Example

Find What You Love

This is the introduction to a commencement address that Steve Jobs, the CEO of Apple Computer, gave at Stanford University on June 12, 2004. As you read the introduction, what do you notice about the approach with which Mr. Jobs introduces his presentation? Is this approach the one you would recommend? Can you identify the other components of the introduction that we have discussed? To what extent does the fact that Mr. Jobs did not graduate from college enhance or detract from his credentials? For what type of audience do you believe this speech is intended? After you have read this introduction, would you want to read the remainder of his speech? Why or why not?

I am honored to be with you today at your commencement from one of the finest universities in the world. I never graduated from college. Truth be told, this is the closest I've ever gotten to a college graduation. Today I want to tell you three stories from my life. That's it. No big deal. Just three stories.

Source: S. Jobs, "Find What You Love," Stanford University commencement, June 12, 2005, retrieved from the Web site, at www.humanity.org.

3 Concentrate on creating strong relevance. Use inclusive pronouns: "you," "we." Treat very knowledgeable positive audiences as colleagues, complimenting them on their knowledge. For less knowledgeable audiences, compliment them on their interest and willingness to learn a new skill or subject area.

4 The thesis should demonstrate that you plan to build on the audience's existing foundation of expertise or interest. Begin by describing your audience's current knowledge or interest and state how you will build on that in your speech.

5 A preview is necessary for any of the recommended organizational patterns for positive audiences except storytelling. When you tell a story, briefly state what the story is about, but do not preview the key events you will relate.

Negative audiences vary in the degree of active involvement or commitment they feel for the topic. Your key goal is to build common ground with your audience to use as a basis for the rest of your speech and to demonstrate respect for them and their knowledge.

Guidelines for Developing an Introduction for a Negative Audience

1 Attract your negative audience's attention by acknowledging valuable or important aspects of their opinions or viewpoints; if areas of agreement exist between you and them, use one of the attention approaches that allows you to acknowledge these areas of agreement.

2 Establish your credentials minimally. Negative audiences already know who you are, and that's why they are opposed to you. Describe your actions or responses regarding experiences, expertise, or commitment consistent with their viewpoints.

3 Establish audience relevance in a sincere, complimentary manner. If you admire or respect their opinions or the cause for which they stand, say so. Negative audiences can be very knowledgeable audiences. Construct a connection between their existing, potentially vast knowledge and the content of your presentation.

4 Most of the organizational frameworks recommended for negative audiences advise not stating the thesis at the outset but rather leading your audience through the organizational structure that will eventually conclude with your thesis. For the other organizational frameworks recommended for negative audiences, state your thesis in somewhat general terms: "Let's explore the nature of (the topic)."

5 Describe how you will proceed through your presentation but do so in an imprecise manner: "First I'd like to acknowledge your views on this issue; then I'd like to tell you some of mine . . ."

Your challenge with the neutral audience is to inspire them to become interested and to direct their interest to support your thesis. When you speak to a neutral audience, do not forget the importance of delivery. Because emotions can be contagious, make sure that you are interested in your topic and that your delivery reflects this interest. Work to sustain this delivery for your entire presentation.

Guidelines for Developing an Introduction for a Neutral Audience

1 Attract the attention of your neutral audience by making a startling statement, choosing an unusual quotation (the content is unusual or the source of the quotation makes the content unexpected), or telling a joke or story about your topic to pique their interest.

2 The remainder of your introduction should be as concise as possible to allow you to get to the body of your speech while maintaining their interest. Your next task is to establish relevance. Is there an unusual connection between the audience and your topic that will allow you to reinforce their interest?

3 Establishing your credentials should be peripheral at best. Your neutral audience may not care about your credentials or be impressed by them.

4 State your thesis with as much passion as you can manage.

5 Consider eliminating the preview of points you will discuss in your presentation, or state them as briefly as possible. Although a neutral audience isn't necessarily an audience with a brief attention span, if you have been able to attract and

ACT&REFLECT

12.2: Modifying Introductions for Different Audiences

ACT • Choose one or use both examples on MySpeechLab: Katie's speech on developing a senior honors project and/or Chelsea's speech on cell phones.[13] Listen to the introduction and try to identify the five components. For what type of speech is the introduction you have chosen intended? Does the speaker modify the introduction according to the guidelines for specific audiences that we have discussed here?

REFLECT • How would you suggest the introduction be modified if the speech were to be given to a different kind of audience? What specifically would you suggest be changed? Now take a look at the presentation you are preparing for your classroom audience. What type of audience do you believe your classroom audience will be regarding your topic? How will you develop your introduction to attract their attention and fulfill the other functions of the introduction?

maintain their interest, move on into the body of your presentation rather than spending time previewing your main points. See Act and Reflect 12.2.

Conclusions

We won't use nearly so much space discussing conclusions as we have introductions. A conclusion isn't as complex in its construction as an introduction, and a conclusion is typically more brief than an introduction. However, don't be fooled! On the basis of our experiences as both speakers and teachers of speech, we think the conclusion is a much more challenging area of a speech to develop than the introduction. It seems that it is easier for people to start talking than it is for them to strongly and gracefully stop talking. Just as it is necessary for you to spend time developing an "ear-catching" introduction, it is equally necessary for you to devote thought to developing a memorable conclusion.

Why Does Your Presentation Need a Conclusion?

The first impression you create in your introduction is important, but so is the last impression you make. Of the following examples, which impression would you rather leave with your audience?

Would you prefer to be the speaker who takes a breath and says in a voice that dies away, "Um, uh, that's about it, I guess . . ."?

Would you rather be the speaker after whose speech there is a long moment of silence, because the audience doesn't realize you are done talking?

Do you aspire to be the speaker whose speech "goes out with a bang," with the audience responding with thundering applause?

We hope you selected the last choice. Your conclusion is the last impression your audience has of you. While you might have given a flawless speech, your conclusion must sustain the strong impression you have created. A weaker conclusion will stay with your audience. If your audience doesn't realize you are finished, that element of surprise and confusion as they catch on to the fact that you are done talking might be what sticks in their minds. However, if you can sustain the climate, concluding in the same commanding way you presented the rest of your speech, the audience will be more likely to leave your presentation with you and your message on

A function of the conclusion is to say "the end." ●

A Question of Ethics

On January 28, 1986, the spaceship *Challenger*, with seven astronauts on board, exploded seconds after liftoff. All on board were lost. One of the seven was a civilian schoolteacher; her participation in the event was highly publicized, and schoolchildren all over the country watched the launch. President Ronald Reagan had originally intended to deliver his State of the Union address that evening; however, in its place he delivered a eulogy to the astronauts. The eulogy concluded with these lines: "The crew of the space shuttle *Challenger* honored us by the manner in which they lived their lives. We will never forget them, nor the last time we saw them, this morning, as they prepared for their journey and waved goodbye and 'slipped the surly bonds of earth' to 'touch the face of God.'"[14]

The phrases "slipped the surly bonds of earth" and "touch the face of God" create a memorable conclusion to Mr. Reagan's eulogy and serve as fitting tributes to the deceased astronauts. However, while the phrases sounded in the eulogy as though they had been composed by Mr. Reagan or his speechwriters, they are lines taken from a poem written by John J. MaGee, a nineteen-year-old volunteer member of the Royal Canadian Air Force who died in 1941 in the Battle of the Bulge.[15] MaGee's name was not divulged when Mr. Reagan presented the eulogy on national television.

Throughout this book we have advocated citing sources of others' ideas and words as a part of every speaker's ethical code. In this eulogy, Mr. Reagan did not cite the source. To what extent do you believe it is ethical to refrain from citing sources if the sentiment or the effect of the sentiment might be interrupted or destroyed by a citation? Do you see a way that Mr. Reagan could have inserted a citation without interrupting the memorable conclusion to his eulogy?

their minds. That's what you want. Let's talk about how you can achieve this kind of ending.

Components of the Conclusion

The conclusion of your speech serves only two functions, but as we have indicated, they are very important. They are:

- To influence your audience one last time
- To establish closure

Influence Your Audience One Last Time The conclusion is your last opportunity to influence your audience. What do you want your audience to know or believe or do as a result of your presentation? What is it you want your audience to remember from your presentation? It could be your thesis statement, a summary of your main points, one of your main points, or perhaps an action you are advocating. Once you have selected the point or points you want your audience to remember, decide what is the most effective way to repeat this point or points. You could repeat it **verbatim,** that is, word for word exactly as you stated it in your speech. You could paraphrase. Remember that to **paraphrase** means to state the same idea but in different words. How do you decide which method works best?

If the idea that you want to leave your audience with was stated in a catchy way in your speech, you can probably repeat it verbatim, because your audience will recognize it. If the idea you want to leave your audience with is somewhat lengthy—for example, if you intend to review all the main points of the body of your speech—it will probably be best for you to paraphrase these main points in one or two concise sentences. Why should you repeat or paraphrase an idea from your speech? There are two reasons.

First, it is true that your audience has already had the chance to hear what you are saying at least once, perhaps several times. Restating what you want your audience to remember in your conclusion affords you the very practical opportunity to give your audience one last chance to hear what you wanted them to acquire from your speech. And just in case they became distracted during your speech, they have a chance to hear that point at least once.

The second reason to repeat or paraphrase what you want your audience to remember is based on the **recency effect.** You might remember that the recency effect means that the last thing your audience hears is likely to be what they will remember. If you are attempting to inspire your audience members to take a specific action, if you want your audience to change their opinions to agree with yours, if you want to interest your audience in your topic, the recency effect means that what you say in your conclusion is likely to be the part of your presentation that remains with your audience long after you have finished talking. While your audience might forget details or even key points of your presentation, it is likely to be the conclusion that lingers with them like the line of a song they can't get out of their minds.

After you have repeated or paraphrased that one point you want to leave with your audience, you will still need to say something that lets your audience know you have come to the end of your speech; you need to establish closure.

Establish Closure Before you end your cell phone call, you establish **closure:** you say something that informs the person you are interacting with that you are about to end your phone call. You need to do the same thing as you end your speech—to say "The End" in a graceful and memorable manner. Closure is to the conclusion as the strategy to attract attention is to the introduction. In fact, the strategies we discussed for you to use to attract attention can be used to establish closure, sometimes with some slight modifications. Here are ways to use these strategies to establish closure.

verbatim To repeat a statement word for word exactly as it was originally stated.

paraphrase To restate an idea in different words from those in which it was originally stated.

recency effect A concept that says the audience will remember the last thing they heard in a speech.

closure The very last words of the speaker that signal the speech is finished.

MSL **State the Topic You Have Discussed** If the topic of your presentation has had interest value, you can establish closure by naming the topic and referring to it in the past tense. Cindy concluded her speech by referring one last time to her backyard: "I'd just like to invite any one of you or all of you to come stay in my backyard.[16]

MSL **End with a Personal Comment** If you were honored to be asked to speak, close your presentation with a comment that expresses your appreciation at having been invited. Cindy established closure by stating the topic she discussed in her speech and also ending with a personal comment, an invitation. Karen also concludes her speech with a personal comment that is an invitation:

> You know, life can't be all studying, can it? You have to have fun. That's what we're really about, to tell you the truth. Hopefully I've been able to shed some light on the mysteries of living in an honors house. You guys can feel free to stop by third and fourth floor Freeman anytime. You can come over and visit or maybe even move in since we have a few empty spots on the house. And whatever you do when you come to see us, I guarantee you will receive a warm welcome.[17]

MSL **Refer to the Occasion** If you are speaking on a special occasion, reaffirm the special nature of the event. As an example of using an occasion as a means to attract attention, we quoted Ross's description of Martin Luther King Day. Ross established closure in that speech in this manner:

> I'd like to close with an excerpt from Martin Luther King's "I Have a Dream" speech, which he did in 1963 in Washington, D.C.: "I have a dream that my four children will one day live in a nation where they will not be judged by the color of their skin, but by the content of their character." It's been forty years, and if his kids were applying to a university today, they'd still be evaluated by their race.[18]

MSL **Make a Startling Statement** If you began your speech with a startling statement, refer to that statement when you create closure. Collin introduced his speech on melanoma with a startling statement about the high incidence of melanoma on his campus. He concluded his melanoma speech with these words:

> Hopefully if you paid attention to what I've said today, you'll keep an eye out for these suspicious moles or [suspicious] looking skin formations. You'll live a life free of melanoma, [with] healthy skin, and hopefully you won't be one of those four Iowa State students that I've talked about that unfortunately will get melanoma this year.[19]

End with a Quotation Quotations are often more effective for creating closure than as attention grabbers. As you are preparing your presentation, if you encounter a passage in your research that captures the essence of what you are saying in your presentation, save it for your closure. You could use a quotation from one of the sources that provides information for your speech, or you could use a passage from poetry or other literature. Remember that when you use someone else's words, you need to give credit to the source. The challenge to ending your presentation with a quotation is determining where you will cite your source: before or after you present the quotation. Usually you should cite the source before you present the quotation, so that the very last words your audience hears are those in your quotation.

MSL

Crystal spoke on the importance of volunteering. She established closure in her speech with a quotation:

> Whenever you are questioning whether or not you have time to volunteer or whether your volunteering will make a difference, I want you to consider a quote by Gandhi who was actually a famous leader who helped bring independence to India through his small movements: 'Whatever you do will be insignificant but it is very important that you do it.[20]

MSL

Ask a Question When you ask a question during your closure you should pose the question as a challenge. Closing with a question requires you to draw on your delivery to make the question sound challenging and like the ending of your speech. Maya established closure for her speech on ignorance by asking the audience a question:

> This year our theme for Got Ignorance is "Exercise Your Right." So not only . . . you should act out against acts of ignorance. Don't just let them pass. If you see something that's unjust, go ahead and stand up and say something about it. For the few people who commit acts of ignorance an entire crowd stands and watches. What will you do?[21]

Tell a Joke This can be done for closure if the joke contains an obvious point that is relevant to the speech. The cautions about telling jokes as closure are the same as those for telling a joke to attract attention. An alternative to ending your speech with a joke is to make a reference to one you've told earlier when you establish closure. If you chose not to end with a joke but you introduced your speech with a joke, try to establish closure in a lighthearted, humorous manner like that with which you introduced your speech.

Tell a Story Closure may not lend itself to telling an entire story. If your story is short and has a very clear point that reinforces whatever it is you want your audience to remember, this will work. Another approach would be, if you attracted your audience's attention with a story, to refer to it again during closure. If you prefer not to refer to your story when you establish closure, an additional option would be to simply end with a comment that is in the same mood as your story.

MSL

Ross told a story at the beginning of his speech on eBay. When he established closure, he did not refer to Christopher Columbus again or to his attempts to save money as he purchased textbooks. Instead, his commentary involved the audience:

So, to sort of wrap things up, the reason eBay works is because so many people use it. And I think you guys should use it too to help them and help yourselves so you can save money for things like chess, or gymnastics, or country music.[22]

Which of these strategies to establish closure is the best? Notice how often we have advised you to tie your closure approach to your attention-grabbing approach in the list of options. We suggest you select your approach to closure by looking at the method you used to attract your audience's attention (see Act and Reflect 12.3).

Besides devoting attention to selecting the best approach to establishing closure for your conclusion, there are also some delivery considerations for developing an effective conclusion:

- Do not begin to conclude your presentation until you are ready to deliver the conclusion. If you say, "Just one more thing and then I'd be happy to entertain your questions" but instead you continue talking, you may lose the audience's attention.

- Once you move into your conclusion, it should be brief, to the point, and strongly and confidently delivered. Your conclusion should probably not be more than 10 percent of your presentation. For a thirty-minute presentation, the conclusion would be approximately three minutes.

- To some degree, the effectiveness of your conclusion depends not so much on what you say as on your delivery. Just before you conclude, pause for a moment, allowing your audience a few seconds to consider the points you have made in the body of your message; then conclude.

- Do not thank your audience for listening to you. If you want to show appreciation for their attention, focus on their interest in your topic or generate another means to display your appreciation.

- As you begin to conclude your presentation, pay attention to the sound of your voice and the pace at which you speak. Speak slightly more slowly and deliberately than you did during the body of your presentation. The change of pace and the emphasis on each word will signal to your audience that you are concluding your presentation. Don't memorize your conclusion, but have a high degree of familiarity with what you will say, to enable you to focus your attention on your audience. When you are finished, pause for two or three seconds.

ACT&REFLECT

12.3 Practice Establishing Closure

ACT • This exercise is a continuation of the first Act and Reflect exercise in this chapter. Use the topic you selected for that exercise. Practice establishing closure for a speech on your topic using all of the approaches we have discussed here. Begin with the first, stating your topic, and proceed in the order in which we have discussed the approaches, building each new approach on the previous ones.

REFLECT • Which approach do you think would result in the most effective closure if you were using it to conclude a speech for your classroom audience? Choose another audience outside your classroom. Would the same approach be useful for that audience? Why or why not?

Count to yourself, "Mississippi-one . . . Mississippi-two . . ." Maintain eye contact with your audience, and then say, in a sincere voice, "I'd be happy to answer your questions."

Developing Conclusions for Positive, Negative, and Neutral Audiences

Because your conclusion is shorter than your introduction, because you need to end your presentation on a note that sustains the message you want your audience to remember and the image of yourself that you created during your presentation, and because you want to maintain the relationship you have built with your audience as a result of your presentation, it will be worthwhile to spend some time thinking about what you want to say during this important part of your speech with the characteristics of your particular audience in mind (see Act and Reflect 12.4).

You want to retain the interest and support of the positive audience.

Guidelines for Developing Conclusions for Positive Audiences

1. Use "you" pronouns to demonstrate your admiration for their interest and knowledge in your subject.
2. Because the positive audience views your presentation as an opportunity to learn something new about a topic of interest to them, concisely and clearly summarize the key points presented in your speech that are most likely to be new.
3. Establish closure with a strategy that commends your audience for their ongoing interest and expertise in your topic.

You will want to reaffirm the common ground you have established with your negative audience while encouraging them to be accepting of the position or action you have advocated.

Guidelines for Developing Conclusions for Negative Audiences

1. Use "we" and "us" pronouns to emphasize your common ground.
2. Repeat or paraphrase the position or action you advocated in your presentation.
3. Establish closure by describing the benefit or positive outcome that will result from your negative audience accepting your position or action.

The challenge in concluding your presentation to the neutral audience is to retain the directed interest in your topic that you established throughout your presentation.

Guidelines for Developing Conclusions for Neutral Audiences

1. Use "you" pronouns to help neutral audience members understand the relevance of the topic to themselves or the difference the topic might make in their lives.

Everyday Example

Address at Digital Hollywood Online Entertainment Conference—Conclusion

This conclusion is from a speech Courtney Love gave on music piracy. The speech can be found in its entirety at http://gos.sbc.edu/l/ love2.html. Before you read the speech, read the conclusion. What would you expect to find as the main points in the speech? What does Ms. Love want you to believe or know, or what actions does she want you to take regarding music piracy? How effective are the methods she uses for establishing closure? For what type of audience—positive, negative, or neutral— do you think Ms. Love prepared her conclusion?

I'm looking for people to help connect me to more fans, because I believe fans will leave a tip based on the enjoyment and service I provide. I'm not scared of them getting a preview. It really is going to be a global village where a billion people have access to one artist and a billion people can leave a tip if they want to.

It's a radical democratization. Every artist has access to every fan and every fan has access to every artist, and the people who direct fans to those artists. People that give advice and technical value are the people we need. People crowding the distribution pipe and trying to ignore fans and artists have no value. This is a perfect system.

If you're going to start a company that deals with musicians, please do it because you like music. Offer some control and equity to the artists and try to give us some creative guidance. If music and art and passion are important to you, there are hundreds of artists who are ready to rewrite the rules.

In the last few years, business pulled our culture away from the idea that music is important and emotional and sacred. But new technology has brought a real opportunity for change; we can break down the old system and give musicians real freedom and choice.

A great writer named Neal Stephenson said that America does four things better than any other country in the world: rock music, movies, software and high-speed pizza delivery. All of these are sacred American art forms. Let's return to our purity and our idealism while we have this shot.

Warren Beatty once said: "The greatest gift God gives us is to enjoy the sound of our own voice. And the second greatest gift is to get somebody to listen to it."

And for that, I humbly thank you.

Source: C. Love, speech given at the Online Entertainment Conference, New York City, May 16, 2000, retrieved from the Gifts of Speech Web site, at http://gos.sbc. edu/l/love2.html.

2 Repeat or paraphrase the one or two most striking differences or major benefits your information will bring to your audience.

3 Establish closure by issuing a personal challenge to your audience that emphasizes their personal accountability regarding the point of your presentation.

ACT&REFLECT

12.4: Developing Conclusions for Different Audiences

ACT • Choose one or use both of the two examples on MySpeechLab: Jessica's conclusion to her speech in favor of gay marriage or the conclusion to Cindy's speech on physician-assisted suicide and euthanasia.[23] Listen to the conclusion and try to identify its components. For which audience do you believe this conclusion is intended? Does the speaker develop the conclusion according to the guidelines for specific audiences that we have discussed here?

REFLECT • How would you suggest the conclusion be modified if the speech were given to a different audience? What specifically would you suggest be changed to make the conclusion a memorable ending for that type of audience? Now consider the presentation you are currently preparing for your classroom audience. What type of audience do you believe your classroom audience to be regarding your topic? How will you develop your conclusion to create a memorable ending for your audience as well as fulfilling the functions of the conclusion?

Your presentation is now made up of an ear-catching introduction, a clearly organized and strongly supported body, and a memorable conclusion. Your presentation is complete, right? Not quite. The last decision you need to make about the content of your presentation concerns the insertion of transitions.

Transitions

Words, phrases, and sentences that connect parts of your presentation and allow you to move from point to point are called **transitions.** You add them to your presentation after you have developed all the other parts of it.

Why Does Your Presentation Need Transitions?

Transitions provide two very important functions. They show relationships between points and ideas, helping the audience to follow your presentation; and they allow you to move through your presentation and so are beneficial to you in a number of ways.

Transitions Help the Audience Listen You have selected a particular organizational framework and arranged the information you included in each of the parts of the framework in a way that makes sense to you. However, it is quite possible that without some assistance, the clarity with which you see the ideas you have included is not so apparent to your audience. Transitions show the relationships of the

transitions Words, phrases, and sentences that connect parts of your presentation and allow you to move from point to point.

MSL

ideas you present by prioritizing them, by justifying your decision to include or exclude information, and by providing directions for your listeners.

- Transitions show the relationships of the ideas you present. Amy proceeded to explain her attention to elementary school students in her speech to her communication classroom in this manner: "Now you're probably wondering why I'm telling you how elementary kids benefited from music in their education."[24]

MSL

- Transitions prioritize ideas. When you are presenting ideas hierarchically, transitions let your audience know which are most important.
- Transitions provide directions for your listeners. If you have several ideas, number them to help your listeners know how many they have yet to hear. We call this type of transition a **signpost.** In her speech on cell phone etiquette, Chelsea used transitions to prioritize and provide signposts for her audience. As she presented a list of etiquette guides, she placed these transitions between her points: "First of all, location . . ." "Also, you shouldn't use them in your vehicle . . ." "Another place you can't use cell-phones is in a hospital . . ." "Now I don't know about you guys, but . . ."[25]
- Transitions provide **internal summaries** and **internal previews** by reviewing what you just said and previewing what you plan to say next. In her speech on sleep deprivation, Jessica inserted transitions that served as internal summaries. She used transitions to preview the next point: "What motivates us to put off the sleep we need and miss so much the next morning?" She used transitions to summarize several pieces of information before moving on to another point: "Most of us know we need to get more sleep, but it's kind of hard to do when college life is so exhausting." She also used transitions to review information and preview what she would discuss next: "You already know that you're tired. What can you do about it?"[26]

Transitions Help You Move through Your Presentation Just as transitions can help your audience, they can also help you.

- The simple act of inserting transitions that show relationships, prioritize points, and provide directions and internal summaries gives you the spur to move from point to point. You need to give point 2 because you just gave point 1, and so on.
- If you are familiar with your transitions, you may not need to depend on notes: "There are three points you should remember . . ."
- If you are familiar with your transitions, you will gracefully move from point to point: "We've looked at the problem; now let's look at some possible solutions."

Types of Transition

Transitions assume the form of words, phrases, or complete sentences. As a rule of thumb, the larger the parts of your presentation you are connecting, the longer your transitions should be; the shorter or smaller the parts you wish to connect, the shorter your transitions should be.

Word transitions allow you to connect phrases and sen-

signpost A transition that helps the audience know how many points they have yet to hear.

internal summary A transition that reviews a point a speaker has just made and previews the next point.

internal preview A transition that previews what the speaker will say next.

tences: "*First,* summer school classes allow you more attention from the instructor; *second,* summer school classes allow you to take classes of different term lengths."

Phrase transitions help you to connect parts of sentences and sentences and to make topic changes. "*On the one hand,* receiving individualized attention from the instructor can be an advantage; *on the other hand,* sometimes you don't want to attract the attention of the instructor."

Sentence transitions facilitate moving from main point to main point within the body of your speech and moving from one part of your speech to another part. "We've seen some of the problems associated with attending summer school. Are there any solutions to these problems? Let's discuss those."

Developing Transitions for Positive, Negative, and Neutral Audiences

Here are a few brief suggestions for selecting transitions in presentations intended for specific audiences.

Guidelines for Developing Transitions for Positive Audiences

1. Select transitions that allow you to connect information the audience knows to information they do not know.

2. Select transitions to demonstrate that you are building on information they already know.

Guidelines for Developing Transitions for Negative Audiences

1. Select transitions that allow you to state information the audience agrees with first, and then move on to information you believe they may not agree with.

2. Insert transitions that allow you to demonstrate your appreciation for the negative audience and their ideas whenever you are able to fit them into your message.

Guidelines for Developing Transitions for Neutral Audiences

1. Select transitions that allow you to connect a point that will be interesting to your audience to a point about which you want them to be interested.

2. Use your voice to emphasize transitions so as to highlight interesting or unusual relationships of points.

● GETTING TO WORK

Have you ever heard the saying "The devil is in the details"? That is exactly what this chapter is about: details, important details. If the details of your introduction do not prepare your audience for the main points in the body of your presentation, they may not hear or pay attention to or understand those main points. If you do not prepare a memorable conclusion, they may not remember the main points. And if you do not select effective transitions, they may not understand why you are presenting your points or how they relate to each other.

After you have the body of your presentation planned, you can move on to either the introduction or the conclusion. Whichever one you choose, follow these checklists:

To plan the introduction:

_____ 1. You should have done this already: state in one sentence what it is that you want your audience to think, believe, or do as a result of having heard your presentation. This is your thesis statement, and you need to say it in your introduction.

_____ 2. As succinctly as possible, summarize the main points of the body of your presentation, with an action verb and no more than one or two words for each point: "Today I will show you, I will tell you how to; I will help you understand."

_____ 3. Select an approach for attracting your audience's attention. From the list of eight approaches we discussed in this chapter, which will be most effective for your particular speaking situation?

_____ 4. Identify reasons that your audience should listen to you. Why do you have the right to discuss your topic? Summarize your expertise, experience, and commitment in not more than three phrases: one each to describe expertise, experience, commitment.

_____ 5. Generate reasons your audience should care about your topic. How will they benefit from hearing your speech? Group your reasons into no more than three sentences: the first, on ways your audience will benefit immediately; the second, on ways others will benefit; the third, on ways your audience will benefit in the future.

_____ 6. Reorganize your points in this order:
  a. Your approach to attracting your audience's attention
  b. Your credentials
  c. Your audience relevance
  d. Your thesis statement
  e. Your preview of main points

_____ 7. Practice your introduction out loud until you feel comfortable "talking it."

_____ 8. Time your introduction. Remember it should take up no more than 20 percent of your total time. Make adjustments as needed.

To plan the conclusion:

_____ 1. What is the last thing you want your audience to hear you say? That is, how will you establish closure, choosing from the eight approaches we have discussed in this chapter? If you have planned your introduction, how did you attract your audience's attention? See if you can coordinate the two.

_____ 2. What is it you want your audience to remember from your presentation? Here is a way to decide what you would like to say: pretend your best friend is late arriving for your speech. Your friend rushes in and says breathlessly "What did you say?" What is your answer? Whatever you would say to your friend is what you will repeat in your conclusion.

___ 3. Reorganize the two pieces of information you have just developed so that you review what you want your audience to remember first and then establish your closure.

___ 4. Practice talking through your conclusion so you can maintain eye contact with your audience as you deliver it and your voice sounds confident. Practice holding a moment of silence when you are finished talking. Count to yourself: "Mississippi-one . . ."

___ 5. After you feel certain of what you will say, time yourself. Your conclusion should take up no more than 10 percent of your total time.

After your introduction and conclusion are planned, insert transitions:

___ 1. Begin with the main points of the body of your presentation.
    a. Are there complex sentences that require word or phrase transitions within them for clarification?
    b. Are there sentences to be connected with signposts or word or phrase transitions?
    c. Do your main points require internal summaries or other transitions?

___ 2. Proceed to the major parts of your presentation.

    a. You should already have a transition between your introduction and body: the preview of your main points. If the preview doesn't do "transition duty," insert another transition.
    b. Between the last point of your body and your conclusion you will need a transition other than "in conclusion;" or become comfortable with a pause.

Your speech is now complete. Practice the entire speech until you feel comfortable presenting it and you are ready to face your audience.

SUMMARY

In this chapter we have discussed the finishing touches you will need to put on your presentation: the introduction, the conclusion, the transitions.

Your presentation needs an introduction to prepare your audience to listen to what you have to say. The introduction must serve five functions: attract the attention of your audience, present your credentials, establish audience relevance, state your thesis, preview your main points. There are eight approaches available to you to attract your audience attention: you can simply announce your topic, extend a personal greeting, refer to the occasion, ask your audience a question, begin with a quotation, develop a startling statement, tell a joke, or tell a story. Your credentials are the evidence your audience is seeking to reassure them that you have the right to discuss your topic. To develop your credentials, look to your expertise, experience, and commitment. When you establish audience relevance, you are telling your audience how they will benefit from the information you will give them in your speech. To establish audience relevance, assume your audience is asking, "What's in this for me? Why should I listen to this?" The answers to these questions will help you to establish audience relevance. Remember that your audience relevance might involve benefits or consequences to your audience immediately or in the future or benefits or consequences to others. Your introduction also includes a statement of your thesis and a preview of the major points you will discuss.

After you have developed your introduction, your next step is to develop your conclusion. Allow yourself some extra time to develop a conclusion that says "The End." Your conclusion should first summarize what you said in your speech that you want your audience to remember. This could be your thesis statement, a summary of your major points, an action you want your audience to take, or all of these. Whatever you want your audience to remember, you will need to find a way to state it concisely and clearly. Now establish closure. Closure is to your conclusion what your attention approach is to your introduction. Your attention approach was the first thing your audience heard; closure is the last thing your audience hears. The strategies we suggested for attracting audience attention can all be used to establish closure.

The last step is to insert transitions. Between major parts of your speech and between the main points of the body of your speech, insert sentence transitions that both preview and review major points. These are called internal summaries. Within major parts and major points, insert transitions that connect sentences and ideas. These transitions are often called signposts and may be phrases or key words.

VIDEO EXPERIENCE

The video clips for this chapter include four very different speeches: Sherri's thoughtful presentation on lessons learned from the death of her son; Chelsea's speech on cell phone etiquette; Nancy's suggestions for buying a new dog; and Linda's experiences as the mother of a fourteen-year-old son.[27] Select one of these. As you listen to the introduction, does the attention approach motivate you to listen to the speech? If not, select another speech. When you find one of the four speeches that you would like to listen to, pay special attention to the introduction. Does the introduction prepare you to listen to the remainder of the speech? Do you feel that you know what key points the speaker will discuss as a result of the introduction? As you continue to listen, start to make a list of the transitions you hear. How do the transitions help you to understand the relationships between the points the speaker makes? Is it clear to you what the speaker wants you to think or believe or what action the speaker wants you to take as a result of the conclusion? Is the conclusion memorable? Does the closure method say "The End"? Does the speech seem to you to be prepared for a positive, negative, or neutral audience? What are the clues that lead you to your conclusion about the audience? From watching these speeches, choose one idea you have learned about developing introductions, one idea about developing transitions, and one idea about developing conclusions and use these ideas in your next classroom speech.

THINKING BACK, THINKING AHEAD

1. Begin to build a resource file of quotations, jokes, newspaper clippings, stories, and other items you can turn to for ideas to attract audience attention and establish closure as you develop future speeches.

2. Listen between the lines. When people talk—not just speakers but anyone talking in any situation—what transitions do they use? Do you hear the same single word transition repeatedly? Do the transitions people use seem to make

sense in relation to the ideas they present? What ideas do you derive from listening for inserting meaningful transitions into your speeches?

3. Go through the dictionary and compile a list of twenty-six word and phrase transitions, so you have a resource file for your next speech. Add to your list when you hear other speakers use effective transitions.

4. What are some ways that speakers establish audience relevance? Do you notice a connection between the speaker's and/or audience's value system and the way relevance is established? In general, is relevance established only in the introduction or throughout the speech?

5. What techniques do you notice that speakers use to establish their own credibility? Do they tell stories or cite their experiences or accomplishments? Or do they depend on someone else to establish their credibility? What method do you think works best?

6. Listen to the ways that people stop talking. Not just speakers but anyone. When you hear a strong conclusion, try to identify what makes it effective. What do you learn about preparing more effective conclusions for speeches?

NOTES

1. L. Marker, "The Cheetah's Race for Survival," speech to the Cincinnati Zoo, September 21, 2000, Barrows Conservation Lecture Series, retrieved on from Gifts of Speech Web site, at http://gos.sbc.edu/m/marker.html.
2. Cindy Sleep, speech to the Municipal Clerks' Institute, July 13, 2004.
3. Jessica Culhane, speech to a negative audience, November 10, 2004.
4. Ross Kelderman, speech to a negative audience, November 15, 2004.
5. Collin Schmidt, speech to a neutral audience, October 15, 2004.
6. Jessica Culhane, speech to a positive audience, September 22, 2004.
7. Maya Sharif, speech to a positive audience, September 27, 2004.
8. Ashley Osgood, speech to a neutral audience, October 25, 2004.
9. Ross Kelderman, speech to a positive audience, September 22, 2004.
10. Ashley Osgood, speech to a neutral audience, October 25, 2004.
11. Cindy Johnson, speech to a neutral audience, October 20, 2004.
12. Maya Sharif, speech to a neutral audience, October 18, 2004.
13. Katie Dencklau, speech to a positive audience, September 22, 2004. Chelsea DeSousa, speech to a positive audience, September 27, 2004.
14. R. Reagan, White House Address to the Nation, January 28, 1986, in *Great Speeches for Criticism and Analysis,* edited by Lloyd Rohler and Roger Cook (Greenwood, IN: Alistair Press, 1988), 309–310.
15. R. Bytwerk, "Ronald Reagan's Eulogy of the Challenger," in Rohler and Cook, *Great Speeches for Criticism and Analysis,* 311–319.
16. Sleep, speech.
17. Karen Tarara, speech to a positive audience, September 22, 2004.
18. Kelderman, speech.
19. Schmidt, speech.
20. Crystal Nord, speech to a positive audience, September 22, 2004.
21. Sharif, speech.
22. Ross Kelderman, speech to a positive audience, September 22, 2004.
23. Culhane, speech. Cindy Johnson, speech given to a negative audience, November 8, 2004.
24. Amy Diekevers, speech to a positive audience, September 27, 2004.
25. DeSousa, speech.
26. Jessica Culhane, speech to a positive audience, September 22, 2004.
27. Sherri Hohenadel, speech given at the Municipal Clerks' Institute, July 13, 2005. DeSousa, speech. Nancy Baker, speech to Municipal Clerks' Institute, July 13, 2005. Linda Klopping, speech to Municipal Clerks' Institute, July 13, 2005.

Chapter

13 Responding to Audiences

- ✓ To provide you with a general plan for responding to questions from audience members

- ✓ To identify challenges and suggest response methods when you entertain questions and comments during a presentation

- ✓ To recommend methods for you to respond to questions and comments following a presentation

- ✓ To guide you in ways to respond when the answer is known

- ✓ To suggest approaches for you when you do not know the answer to a question

- ✓ To list approaches for you when the audience has no questions

- ✓ To offer response methods you can use when dealing with challenging questions and questioners

The dynamic speaker concluded the speech to thundering applause. Listeners strained toward the speaker vying to be called upon to ask their questions about the provocative speech.

The speaker responded to the questions in a bored manner. The responses were vague and at several points contradicted ideas that were presented in the speech.

The question-and-answer session was a marked change from the excellent speech. One by one the disappointed listeners left, wondering what they had just experienced.

The way presenters interact with audience members is every bit as important, perhaps even more important, for the purpose of reaching the communication goal, as the presentation itself. In his advice on preparing professional presentations to managers, Tom Leech indicates that it is the interaction with the audience that can make or break a presentation.[1]

In our roles as instructors, it is common to watch a student heave a sigh of relief after concluding an in-class speech, apparently feeling that "the real" or "the important" part of the assignment is over. However, during the question-and-answer part of the presentation, it is still important that you be on your toes, because that is when the audience has their opportunity to participate. Wise presenters anticipate audience comments and questions and may even practice responding to them. Despite the best efforts of presenters, it is also possible that a listener will ask a question or make a comment that is totally unanticipated. To avoid damaging your relationship with your audience, it is equally important that you retain your alertness and energy when your presentation is over and you announce to your listeners, "I'd be happy to answer your questions." ●

Suggestions for Responding to Questions

How one responds to audience questions is heavily dependent on what seems "right" in a specific instance. Who the questioner is, the nature of the question, and the general attitude of the audience are all aspects that will influence your responses. However, here are some general guidelines for responding to questions:

1. *Focus your attention on the questioner as the questioner is speaking, but when responding, focus your attention on the entire audience.* When an audience member is asking a question, there are only two people in the room: the questioner and you. By focusing your attention on the questioner, you demonstrate that the question and the questioner are important. You are also giving yourself every opportunity to be a good listener and to understand the question. However, as you respond, assume the presentation mode you used when speaking so that you include your entire audience in your answer.

   Crystal demonstrated this procedure clearly when Scott asked her a question after her speech on required physical education. As Scott asked the question, Crystal maintained eye contact with him, but when she responded to the question, she spoke to the entire room.[2]

2. *Repeat simple questions and paraphrase more complex questions before you respond.* When you were presenting, you occupied a central location in the speaking environment or used a microphone or stood behind a lectern. During your presentation, the chances are good that everyone could see and hear you. Repeating or paraphrasing questions gives everyone the same chance to hear the question. In addition, if you have the least doubt about your understanding of the question, repeating or paraphrasing will provide a check with the questioner to ensure that you both agree on the question. Finally, if you aren't certain of the answer or a way to approach answering, the act of repeating or paraphrasing can buy you some thinking time.

3. *Shape your responses.* Just as you organized your presentation with an introduction, body, and conclusion, practice organizing your responses to audience members in the same way. Keep your response brief, but give it three parts:
   1. A brief response to the question
   2. Support or clarification by way of an example or explanation
   3. A restatement of your position in a way that supports your speaking goal.

   Suppose you are asked if the United States should continue to fund its space program. A response constructed in the three-part manner would look like this: "Yes, the United States should continue to fund the space program. History shows that in space we find solutions to many of the dilemmas we face on earth. While funding the space program will benefit our space exploration, it will also benefit our life on earth."

When you respond to the question of one member of a group, focus your answer on the entire group. ●

4. *Practice equality.* Try to call on individuals in the order in which they indicated their interest in speaking. Enlist another person to help you keep track of the order so as to free yourself to focus on the questions. If you are addressing a particularly involved or talkative audience, you may need to follow a procedure in which no one can ask a second question until everyone who wishes to do so has asked a first question. You might also request that the audience ask only questions that have not been asked before. (Sometimes, in waiting their turn, individuals are not listening to the other questions but are concentrating on the question they plan to ask.) Finally, if a small but vocal minority threatens to consume all of the questioning time, be courteous to them by indicating there are others who would like to pose questions.

5. *Keep your cool.* Just as there are positive, neutral, and negative audiences, you can encounter positive, neutral, and negative individuals within those audiences. Even in a generally positive audience, you may have one individual who disagrees with you, who is annoyed at having to attend your presentation, or who may be just plain angry, and you may become the logical target for this person to vent his or her frustrations. Keep your cool when dealing with audience members who are obnoxious, frustrating, angry, hostile, and so on. E. J. Natalle and F. R. Bodenheimer have advice for women speakers that applies to everyone: "If you appear irritated or crack under the pressure of an insult, you may wind up compromising the intended effects of the speech."[3]

When you do respond to negative individuals, do so in a positive, courteous manner. Your audience might be just as annoyed as you are by difficult individuals; however, even if the audience is on your side, they may also believe that the challenging audience member deserves to be heard. And, of course, that is true. On one occasion, an angry audience member went on at length about unfair treatment he believed he had received. The presenter waited patiently for the individual to conclude the heated narration. When it was over, the presenter said quietly but playfully, "That wasn't a question." The audience exploded with laughter. The angry individual grudgingly smiled, and the presenter maintained rapport with everyone. Humor may work for some speakers in some situations; however, generally, the best response to an angry audience member is to respond to the individual's question and then move on to the next question.

These general tips will help you be responsive whether you agree to interact with individuals during your presentation or prefer to wait until you have completed it.

Responding during the Presentation

Sometimes audience members will wait until you have completed the planned part of your presentation before they ask their questions or present their comments. However, there may be times when listeners who want to ask a question or make a comment will spontaneously interrupt your planned presentation. If you are making a budget report to your campus organization, for example, your report could be interrupted by other members with questions for additional information regarding the points you are making. If you are running a workshop on the new software your company is buying, you might be interrupted by participants asking you to repeat points or give examples of how to use the software. In these instances, you could expect to be interrupted, because of either the small size of the audience or participants' need to be able to apply or practice the information you are giving them.

When the audience is small or when the culture encourages doing so, before beginning your presentation, you might invite your listeners to ask questions or comment whenever something occurs to them: "If you have questions or comments, don't be shy! Let me know what's on your mind." When you invite your listeners to speak up during your presentation, be sure to help them plan their questions in a timely way by providing a thorough preview of your presentation before beginning.[4]

By agreeing to respond to questions or comments during your presentation, you have not only agreed to monitor your audience for signs they want to speak but also opened yourself up to several challenges. As you are speaking, be aware of the posture and facial expressions of your audience, as well as gestures or raised hands that might signal individuals would like to speak.[5] Responding to questions or comments during a presentation places you at risk of (1) having to reorganize your presentation to respond to listeners; (2) finding yourself in the position of discussing issues you had not intended to discuss; (3) losing audience attention; and (4), if you are operating

Responding to one audience member's question during a presentation carries with it the peril of losing other audience members' attention. ●

within a time frame, not having the time to discuss everything you needed to, wanted to, or promised you would cover. See Act and Reflect 13.1.

Taking Points Out of Order

Your message is organized and prepared, and you have thought carefully about what you want to say and how and when you want to say it. Maybe your message is organized chronologically, or you have chosen an organizational framework that requires you to make certain points at certain places in your presentation. A hand goes up, and an audience member asks a question about an issue you intend to bring up later. What to do? After all, the listener is simply responding to your invitation. This is one of the difficulties that arise when a presenter generously offers to respond to audience members during the presentation. There are a couple of options available to you in this situation.

If the order in which you give information is not important, go ahead and respond to the question. If you prefer to proceed in the order originally intended, thank the questioner for reminding you to discuss this important point and indicate you will speak to the point later in your presentation. When you arrive at that point, be sure to introduce it by saying something like "Now, about the point the interested listener (refer to the person by name if you know it) asked to be discussed . . ." Remember that when you introduce your presentation, if you provide a clear preview of the issues you intend to cover, prematurely asked questions might be reduced or totally avoided.

Discussing Unplanned Issues

When an issue is raised that is either not relevant or that you have decided not to discuss, how do you respond? You can say that although the issue is important, it was not a part of what you had planned to discuss in the current presentation. You can also indicate that, although important, the topic is related to some other issue or is tangential to your topic. You can agree to discuss the topic after your presentation if time allows. Finally, you can offer to discuss the point with the individual after the presentation is over or at his or her convenience. If you make this offer, be sure to honor it.

Losing Listeners' Attention

Remember that your audience is in attendance to hear you speak or to hear your message, or both. By entertaining questions during your presentation, you are running the risk of listeners introducing their own agendas or questions that might compromise the advertised goals of the presentation. If you devote too much time to one interested audience member, you risk losing the interest or attention of the majority of the audience. When you take questions or comments during your presentation, do so sincerely and cordially but with brevity.

Operating within a Time Frame

Presentations always occur within a time frame, either explicitly or implicitly stated. On some occasions, you are presenting an item that is part of a meeting agenda and is intended to last a specific period of time to allow time for other business. Sometimes you are invited to present as part of a program for an agreed-on period of time. Remember, also, that the natural attention span of your audience will be limited not only by expectations based on the topic and occasion of your presentation but

ACT&REFLECT

13.1: Responding to the Classroom Audience

ACT • What events do you commonly attend where the presenter responds to questions or comments during a presentation? Classes, of course! Your teachers probably expect and, most likely, welcome the questions and comments of students in their classes. Keep a record for one week of the ways your teachers respond to these questions. Also note the manner in which they proceed with their lectures after responding.

REFLECT • What do you learn from your teachers that you could apply to situations in which you respond to your listeners during your presentations?

also by their own commitments. To give you an idea of the proportion of audience interaction to expect in relation to your message, for a thirty-minute presentation, a rule of thumb is to plan on five to ten minutes for interaction.[6]

Sometimes you will not entertain questions or receive comments during the presentation, nor will your audience expect it. Rather, both you and your audience anticipate your willingness to respond to audience questions and concerns following the presentation.

Responding after the Presentation

As we mentioned earlier, the conclusion of your presentation isn't the end of your responsibility. It is only one more point in a series of events. When you have completed your presentation, take a deep breath, take a sip of water, smile, and invite your audience to ask questions. You can do this in a number of ways. "I'd be happy to answer your questions" is one way to phrase the invitation. If you are pressed for time, you can say, "I see we have a few minutes remaining. I'd be happy to answer your questions." However you say it, it should be clear to the audience that it is their turn to speak and that you look forward to their questions and comments.

Cindy and Chelsea responded in different manners, but they both conveyed the invitation to their audiences to ask questions.

Cindy crisply stated, "Are there any questions about subliminal advertising?"[7] Chelsea presented her invitation differently: "I'd be happy to answer any questions or if you guys have comments, I'd love to answer them . . ."[8]

MSL

Responding to questions after a presentation also brings with it a set of challenges for you to consider.

When You Know the Answer

Easy. When you know the answer to a question, phrase it according to the three-part structure of response, example or other support, and conclusion. Respond briefly but thoroughly. If you have anticipated questions and practiced responses to them, this is the moment you will benefit from your advance planning.

When You Don't Know the Answer

Repeat to yourself ten times: "There is no shame in not knowing the answer to *every* question." The key word in that sentence is "every." There are some questions that reveal issues you should have discussed in your presentation. It is also the case that you cannot be expected to know the response to every question your audience might come up with. The key is to retain your composure and not to allow the fact that you do not know an answer to diminish the relationship you have worked to build with the audience. How can you respond to those puzzling questions in a way that allows you to retain your credibility as well as maintain your relationship with the audience?

First, use the time as you are repeating or paraphrasing the question to think. Listen to yourself as you state the question to ensure that you understand what the questioner is asking.

Second, admit that you don't know the answer before responding further. But find a way to do so that does not minimize your credibility. If the question is truly "off the wall," you might say, "That's an interesting question, and I don't believe I've ever thought of it before . . ." or "No one has ever posed that question before." Or you could indicate that you are not familiar with the topic area of the question.

Having given yourself some time to understand and think and having then indicated that the questioner has been so creative or thoughtful that you are unfamiliar with the question, you have some final alternatives.

Make an educated guess. "On the basis of my experiences, I would say . . ."

When Scott was asked "How long can a spaceship stay up there—forever?" following his speech on the X-Prize, he was not certain of the answer. His response included an admission that he did not know the answer and an educated guess that satisfied the questioner: "I'm not exactly sure but I know the website, I don't know if I have it on here, there was a time line. From the time it disconnected from White Night to the time it landed was about twenty minutes. It's not up there for very long, but it's up there long enough to win . . ."[9]

Refer to knowledge that comes from another source. "There is a recent article in the *Journal of the American Mechanics Association* that might provide the answer to your question about diesel engines."

Ask if anyone else in the audience has knowledge about the question. "I haven't experienced that personally, but maybe someone here could help us out." Karen was asked a question about the number of students who lived on honors floors in dormitories who received midterm grade slips. She was uncertain of the response and called on Ross for assistance: "I'm actually not sure how they computed that . . . Ross, can you expand?"[10]

Return the question to the questioner. "How would you handle that situation?"

Offer to check on the response and get in touch with the individual. "We do have an expert on that topic in the office. If you'd like to leave your name and contact information, I'd be glad to have our office expert get in touch with you." When you make such an offer, be sure to do it.

However you choose to respond, always maintain confident nonverbal behaviors. Don't allow your voice to die away. Be just as confident in your uncertainty as you are in your certainty. Treat these instances as times to learn more about the topic, more about interacting with audiences, and more about your own ability to deal with challenging situations.

When No One Asks

If you felt the least bit uncertain at any point during your presentation, you might feel comforted to know that you have lots of company: all of the members of your audience may feel a similar sense of unease at the prospect of asking you a question. Remember that you are the person who, in effect, is getting paid to speak. To ask a question of you, the very confident presenter, could be viewed as a risk by some members of your audience. Audience feelings are similar to the way you might feel about asking a question in class when you're afraid the class will laugh or the instructor will become impatient with your question. Audience members can have the same misgivings about raising questions. Another reason you might not have an immediate response to your invitation is that the audience is still thinking about your presentation and is trying to figure out what they want to ask you. Be patient, smile, and wait for them to formulate their questions while you are counting to yourself "Mississippi-one . . . Mississippi-two . . ." Cindy remained calm and retained eye contact following her speech on subliminal advertising when the audience had few questions, yet her facial expression was encouraging and receptive.[11]

If you believe the audience has had enough time to formulate questions, and still there is no response, what can you do?

- If you presented information that you believe is new to your audience, ask them a question about it: "Of the pointers I gave you about preparing for a presentation, which would work best for you?" or "Genetically modified seed corn is quite new, as I indicated. Has anyone here planted it? How did it work out?" Asking the audience questions about issues that they are likely to have experience with might stimulate them to talk and come up with their own questions.

- If there is information you omitted from your presentation due to time or other considerations, this is the point to present it: "One of the things I didn't discuss in my presentation was . . ."

- You can tell a story or give an example: "As I was talking about Spain, I remembered an experience my fellow travelers and I had one morning . . ."

Everyday Example

Mrs. Bush Responds to Questions Following Her Remarks during a Visit with Families Affected by Hurricane Katrina

Following the devastation resulting from Hurricane Katrina in the Gulf states, First Lady Laura Bush toured the area and spoke to families at an elementary school in Southaven, Mississippi. After her remarks, she responded to questions from the audience. Which of the guidelines we have suggested here do you see her observing as she responds to the questions?

Mrs. Bush: Any questions?

Q: How did you pick out DeSoto County to come to this school district?

Mrs. Bush: Well, I wanted to come here because this is a school district that has kids in it from Mississippi and from the New Orleans area that couldn't go to school in their home school districts. I wanted—I'm going to later visit, as you know, a shelter that's here. I wanted to visit another shelter. I've visited several so far. All of them have been organized and run very, very well for the benefit of the people who are having to be sheltered, who are choosing that. So that's why I really picked DeSoto County to come to.

Q: How will the government help these districts in the long term, taking all these—

Mrs. Bush: That's a very good question for Secretary Spellings. (Laughter.) But the government will. I happened to sit in on a meeting with the President and Secretary Spellings, talking about the ways to get money right away to school districts that have a larger population because of the hurricane.

Secretary Spellings: Another reason we came here is because this is a great school district with a great superintendent, and they met all their AYP targets down here. (Laughter.) And so I—(applause)—before I answer that question.

But we're helping in a number of ways. Resources, the President asked me to put together a plan so that we can ask for adequate compensation for the affected school districts, those who are taking in students as well as those who have been devastated. And I expect to get that to the Congress and to him, obviously, very shortly.

In the short run, we're allowing lots of flexibility on resources, letting people move funds around and do things. They're waiving various aspects of the law and so forth. We're providing flexibility for various provisions of No Child Left Behind so that people can get about their business as quickly as possible.

And then we're trying to engage the education community so that we can—we've launched a website called www.ed.gov, "Hurricane help for schools," where we're matching people in the education community and around the country with the needs of schools.

So just a number of things. Resources will be forthcoming. We know they're needed, and we can't wait to get them here.

Q: —families that you're giving—(inaudible)— what do you want them to know? What's the message you're trying to send to them?

Mrs. Bush: Well, I want them to know that they're doing really the right thing by putting their children in school. A lot of families who are displaced are not sure they're going to stay where they are for very long or how long they're going to be where they are. But it's really important to go ahead and put your children in school, even if you move them in a few weeks because you decide to make other plans or move to another site or move to get an apartment or whatever— however it works out.

But I want families to know how important it is to make sure their children are taken care of. A lot of children will suffer, they'll be afraid, they'll be afraid to leave their parents. There are probably parents who are afraid to let their children leave them. And it's really important to try to get your child, as soon as possible, into as normal a situation as you can. And that includes what all of us know children need, which is a caring adult with them, water, food, sleep. Children need to be able to go to bed early and not be so fatigued they have a hard time controlling their emotions, which they're likely to do anyway under such circumstances.

Q: Is there one child or one story you've heard that is sticking with you?

Mrs. Bush: Well, I've heard a lot of stories in shelters, and all of them are stories that make me know how important schools are in the life of a child. One mother told me—I told Secretary Spellings this earlier; I think this was when I was in Lafayette—and she was with her little boy, and she said, you know, he was going to go off to his first year in preschool, his first time in school, and he was so excited about it. And so not only was their life upended because of the hurricane and the flood, but also his plans and his—what he expected to go to school was.

And then I told this story before in another town, but my assistant's dad is a football coach at a big football powerhouse school in Texas, and they got their first student earlier in the week from Louisiana. They said sort of a thin, small high school student, and two great big football players stood on either side of him and took him to his

class and said, "You're in the right school," and met him after his class to take him to his next one.

And I know that's what will happen across the United States as children go into school districts, new schools for them, new school districts for them. The districts will be very welcoming, the children will be very welcoming, and it's a real learning experience for all children to have this opportunity to get to meet people from another part of the country, to get to figure out what ways they can help them. And it's a real American experience, I think.

Q: Mrs. Bush, how do you feel the federal government has responded to Hurricane Katrina just across the board?

Mrs. Bush: Well, I think across the board very, very well. That's what I would say. I think we've seen a lot of the same footage over and over that isn't necessarily representative of what really happened in both—in a lot of ways. And we know now that New Orleans is pretty much totally evacuated. There was a huge number of people who were rescued, especially considering that a lot of people were rescued one at a time by helicopter.

Shelters have set up around the country very, very well. You read every day anecdotal stories in the papers about families who are so—their hearts are so warmed by the response of the people who come to the shelter, to volunteer there, to play with their babies so they can get some sleep, or to help them in whatever way they can.

This was a huge storm, and it was an unbelievably devastating storm, the largest, probably, our country has ever seen. And when you consider that, and you consider the numbers of communities, particularly in this state that were literally wiped out, then you have to know that—I think overall, it was a very good response.

Source: L. Bush, "Remarks during a Visit with Families Affected by Hurricane Katrina at Greenbrook Elementary School, Southhaven, Mississippi," retrieved from White House Web site, at www.whitehouse.gov.

It's possible your audience honestly does not have questions. If so, how do you gracefully end your presentation? Invite them to ask their questions two or three times, and if they still do not come up with questions or comments, thank them for being good listeners, and tell them you enjoyed your time with them and you hope you were able to provide them with helpful information. If you wish to do so, offer to remain for a few minutes in the event that anyone would like to talk to you after the presentation. See Act and Reflect 13.2.

Responding to Challenges

When interacting with audience members, challenges present themselves through the questions that audience members ask and through the motivations of the audience members themselves.

Challenging Questions

Challenging questions wear two faces. First, there are those that are challenging simply because of the degree of difficulty of responding to them. Second, questions may be challenging because in responding to them, you are placing yourself in a position that could minimize gains you made during the presentation and end the presentation event on a negative note. You can anticipate difficult questions and practice responses to them. Of course, you might also fold the responses into your presentation so that questioners will not have those issues to question you about.

You might also need to "buy some time" to organize your thoughts for your responses. Don't be afraid to jot down a note or two to yourself immediately after the question is asked to ensure that you understand the question. And, of course, be sure

13.2: Responding to Classroom Questions

ACT • Listen carefully to the way your classmates respond to questions your instructors pose. When instructors ask questions in class and no one knows the answer, or everyone is uncertain about the answer, how do your classmates respond? How do classmates respond to questions when they know the answer? Considering the ways your classmates respond, what conclusions do you reach about their credibility?

REFLECT • What do you learn from these observations that will be useful when you are responding to audience members' questions?

to repeat or paraphrase the question to check with the questioner that you have accurately heard the question.

Steven Rafe has written a book on the art of thinking on your feet. He suggests that to buy "think" time, you should remain silent. He estimates that you can gain two seconds as you silently collect your thoughts. If you use the questioner's name, you pick up another second or two, and you can generate an additional three seconds for thinking by repeating the question or by asking the questioner to repeat the question.[12]

Besides being intellectually challenging, questions can also be challenging when the obvious responses to them risk backing the presenter into a corner where something is said that works against the goal of the presentation. Five common types of these questions are what Rafe calls "the A-B question," "the irrelevant question," "the absent party question," "the inconsistency trap," and "the loaded question."[13]

The "Do you still commit academic dishonesty or have you stopped doing that?" question is an example of the **A-B question.** This type of question asks the presenter to choose among two or more choices, both of which might cause negative repercussions. If selecting one of the choices will negatively reflect on the speaker, such as "Who do you support for the next president of the student body? Mary Jones or John Smith?" a reasonable response would be "Either one would make an excellent student body president," followed by a brief summary of the strengths of each candidate. If the A-B question is one such as "Which would be the better way to deal with the budget crisis? Raise student tuition or limit student enrollment?" The response could be to say "Neither. I would like to propose instead . . ." and then to briefly describe a third possibility.

Following his speech on affirmative action, Shannon asked Ross a question that itself was not an A-B question but that forced Ross to give an A-B answer. He handled it this way:

MSL

> Thanks for asking that. Shannon asked if Iowa State had any like those programs that I've been talking about this morning. My answer is yes and no. For admission, pretty much if you meet the minimum requirements, you can come to Iowa State. I think they'll take anyone they can get. On the other hand, they do have programs for, for instance in their hiring program, where they will give preference to minority applicants, and for financial aid and scholarships they have programs that are only available to minority students. I think there are also programs like Carver programs that are only open to those who are minorities and they aren't open to white students.[14]

The **irrelevant question** asks about a topic that is related to the presentation but is irrelevant to the presenter's goal. At an open forum focusing on whether campus security officers should be allowed to carry firearms, an audience member challenged the sponsors of the forum by criticizing the credentials of the presenters and the organization of the events that occurred during the forum. In such an instance, a

A-B question A question that asks the presenter to choose between two or more answers.

irrelevant question A question that asks about a topic that is related to the topic of the presentation but is irrelevant to the presenter's goal.

presenter might simply thank the listener for the information or suggestion and agree to take it into account for future presentations. A second response is to point out the differences between the questioner's and the presenter's goals, by saying for example, "The purpose of the forum was to solicit input from members of the campus community, rather than to be an informative presentation." Scott asked Ashley a question that, while related to her topic of fuel prices, was tangential to her purpose. She responded:

The question is why do gas prices vary from place to place. I did find some information but that wasn't exactly what I was researching, but different states have different regulations they have to meet. I know that California is a lot stricter on its regulation because of the pollution problem so that gas has to be designed to meet those regulations.[15]

A third type of challenging question is the **absent party question**. This type of question asks about the opinion of someone other than the speaker. "How do you think the faculty feels about increases in class enrollment?" You can handle this type of question by pointing out that you don't know what the absent party thinks: "Since I'm not a faculty member, I'm really not qualified to respond to your question." Or you can turn the question back to the questioner: "How do you believe the faculty would feel?" Or you can make a statement of support about the absent party: "I know my instructors go to great efforts to handle the challenges of larger classes without compromising student learning."

The fourth challenging question is the **inconsistency trap,** in which a questioner points out an inconsistent action or view of the presenter. "Previously you indicated you were supportive of child care facilities on campus; now you are saying it is a bad idea. How do you account for your flip-flop on this topic?" Your best response in this instance is to indicate that upon giving this important issue additional thought, you realize that there are other issues that needed to be taken into account. Or you might say that you have received new information that you did not have previously. Barring additional information, you believe your current view is the best position for you to take at this point.

A fifth type of challenging question is the **loaded question,** designed to put the presenter on the spot. "You have said you would support tuition increases. Why should we vote for a student body president who appears to be working against the student body?" There are a couple of possible responses to this type of question. First, observe that you and the questioner seem to have a misunderstanding: "I understand you believe I am supportive of tuition increases; however, that is not an accurate portrayal of my position." Another possible response is to acknowledge that you and the questioner have a difference of opinion. In both cases, conclude your response with a positive statement that reaffirms your com-

absent party question A question that focuses on the opinion of someone other than the presenter.

inconsistency trap A questioner points out an inconsistent action or view of the presenter.

loaded question A question that places the presenter in a potentially awkward personal or professional situation.

A Question of **Ethics**

Sometimes the specific situation and details about which a question is asked require the speaker to give a response that seems contradictory or is potentially contradictory to what was said during the speech. If the audience is a negative audience, any connection the speaker has been able to make during the speech may have been somewhat tenuous, so that the speaker's response could damage it.

If you found yourself in a situation like this, how could you ethically respond to the question while retaining whatever connection you have been able to make with your negative audience?

munication goal: "I will work to support the student body if I am elected as its president."

Finally, when the challenge lies in responding to a question stated negatively, repeat or paraphrase the question without using the negative terms.[17] Although your audience has had the opportunity to hear the entire question, chances are they will recall the negative terms rather than the point of the question. By restating it in a way that avoids those terms, you leave the audience with the most recent statement of the question in positive terms. If the question is "How do you account for the decrease of sales this year?" your restatement before responding could be "You are asking me to discuss our annual sales." And then you proceed to do so.

Challenging Questioners

Sometimes the challenge comes not so much from the content of a question as from the person who is asking it. Questioners ask challenging questions because they are annoyed at having to attend your presentation, because they disagree with your position or harbor negative feelings about you personally, or because they are in a bad mood. Whatever the reason, you become the focus of their negative energy. See Act and Reflect 13.3.

Generally, there is a four-step process you can follow when dealing with negative or challenging questioners:

1. Separate the question from the questioner. Listen to the question, and do not allow yourself to respond to the emotion of the questioner. In some instances, you might say, "I understand your feelings about this very important issue; however . . ." and then proceed with your response.
2. State points that you want the audience to hear.
3. Retain control of your emotions so that the audience hears the voice and response of a courteous, confident speaker.
4. Be brief.

ACT&REFLECT

13.3: Challenging Questioners and Challenged Respondents

ACT • Attend an event where a public issue will be discussed: a school board meeting, a town council meeting, a political candidate speech—all of these are possibilities. Make a list of the questions that are asked and the way they are answered.

REFLECT • Which, if any, responses did you feel worked best to satisfy the questioner and retain the credibility of the respondent? Which of the types of responses could you file away for your own use during a presentation?

In addition to this general process for responding, there are ways to respond to specific types of challenges. First, some questioners don't have a question. When they have finished talking, you can say, "I didn't hear the question in your commentary. Would you repeat the question please?" If there is no question, simply express thanks for the comment and recognize another individual. Second, when a questioner seems to be going on and on, asking a question and then giving several examples and asking the question again, wait for the person to take a breath, state the question you believe

What can you do to get your presentation back on track after a challenging question? ●

they are asking, briefly respond, and recognize another individual. Third, when a questioner gets off target, you can say, "Your experiences are interesting; thank you for telling us about that." Then recognize another questioner.

Finally, when a questioner asks a personal question, that is, a question that is of specific interest to the questioner rather than of general interest to the audience, briefly respond to the question but conclude with a comment that has value or interest to the entire audience. "I'm sorry to hear about your college loan debt; you are an excellent example why we all need to work to reduce tuition."

When questions or questioners threaten to change the impact you have made through your presentation, take a few minutes to briefly summarize the points you made during your presentation to remind your listeners of your view and to reaffirm your position with them.

Any questions?

● GETTING TO WORK

Now that you have read about interactions with your audience, we hope you agree that anticipating questions your audience will ask is every bit as deserving of your thought and attention as the actual preparation of your presentation. Your thought and attention to the questions on your listeners' minds should begin with the initial steps of preparing your presentation. What does your audience already know and what will they want to hear in your presentation? What is your communication goal? You will probably find that your goal does not interface perfectly with what your audience will want to hear. The points at which the interface does not occur are the points where you should anticipate audience questions.

Once you have determined what those questions are likely to be, consider whether it will be advantageous to answer those questions as part of your presentation. Is an issue so volatile that you would prefer to address it in your own way in your presentation? Or do you prefer to ignore it in your presentation and take the chance that no one will bring it up? Which of these approaches will allow you to build or maintain rapport with your audience?

If you decide not to address certain issues within the text of your presentation, be prepared to be questioned about them anyway. These are the issues about which you should anticipate questions and practice your responses to them. Ideally, you can videotape yourself responding to challenging questions to identify areas where you need to work on stronger responses.

Make a list of the points you want to make that you want your audience to remember. Be sure you know what those points are, so you can repeat them often as part of your responses to listeners' questions.

Finally, work on maintaining consistent and confident nonverbal displays so that you present a consistent image when you know the answers and are confident about them, as well as when you do not know the answers or when you are challenged.

SUMMARY

Generally, when responding to audience members' questions, the presenter maintains contact with the questioner as the question is asked and then responds to the entire audience when answering the question. Responses to questions should follow the organizational pattern of speeches: you should give a brief answer to the question, then give an example or explanation, and conclude with a statement that supports your communication goal.

Speakers will sometimes respond to listeners during the presentation if the audience is small, if the culture supports such interaction, or if the presentation is instructional. In this instance, you will need to consider responses to questioners who "jump ahead," responses to questioners who wish to discuss issues you had not intended to bring up, ways to keep everyone interested, and ways to maintain a reasonable time frame.

Sometimes, presenters will entertain audience questions and comments after the conclusion of the presentation. When the speaker knows the answer to a question, the challenge is to respond briefly but thoroughly. When the presenter does not know the answer some options for responding are to paraphrase the question to buy thinking time, to admit you don't know the answer, to make an educated guess or refer the questioner to a source that contains the answer, to ask the audience for assistance. If no one asks a question, the presenter can ask a question of the audience or can use the time to discuss information that was not included in the speech.

Finally, when presenters are faced with challenging questions or challenging questioners, the best approach is to determine the exact nature of the question and respond to it in such a way as to provide a response without compromising the communication goal of the presenter while allowing the questioner to save face. When challenging questions are asked, it is advisable to conclude the question-and-answer period with a summary of the points made in the presentation.

VIDEO EXPERIENCE

The video clips for this experience show three speakers responding to their audience's questions. Shannon responds to her audience after her speech on pain; Maya after her speech on ignorance; Crystal after her speech on required physical education.[17] Each speaker is faced with a different question-and-answer situation. Identify what you believe are the special circumstances in each situation. To what extent do you feel the speakers were able to maintain their connections with their audiences by the way they chose to respond? Would you suggest that the speakers handle their question-and-answer sessions differently? If so, how?

THINKING BACK, THINKING AHEAD

1. Practice repeating or paraphrasing questions before you respond to them. When you converse with your friends and family, as well as when an instructor asks you a question, before you respond to the question, try your hand at repeating simple questions as well as paraphrasing more complex questions. If the person who asks you the question indicates that you have not accurately paraphrased a question, try again until the questioner feels you

have accurately stated it in your own words. Practice repeating simple questions with friends and family so that you will remember to do so when you are responding to questions during or after a presentation.

2. As you are preparing for a presentation, brainstorm a list of all of the questions audience members could possibly ask you. Refine your list: delete all of the questions that seem so "far out" they would probably not be asked. Of the remaining questions, delete all of the questions that you will discuss as part of your presentation. Of the remaining questions, check those that would be the most challenging for you, either because of the nature of the question or because of the person who would most likely ask the question. Write responses for all of these questions. Ask a friend to pose as an audience member and to ask you these questions so you can practice responding to them. Videotape yourself and review the videotape. Where were you able to "rise to the challenge" and which questions do you need to continue to work with to prepare yourself?

3. Put yourself in the role of questioner. When you watch the evening news or any of the news programs on TV, become aware of the behaviors of the news anchors or the reporters. How do they present particularly difficult or challenging questions? What could you learn about asking questions from these professionals? How will your knowledge help you to answer questions?

4. As you watch the evening news or any of the news programs on TV, pay attention to the way individuals being interviewed respond to difficult questions. Are they able to "keep their cool"? How do they manage? If they are unable to remain calm, what could you suggest they try? What have you learned from this experience that will help you respond to audience questions during your next presentation?

5. After your next presentation, review the questions you were asked, as well as your responses to them. In what ways were your responses strong? In what ways would you like to improve your ability to respond to questions?

NOTES

1. T. Leech, *How to Prepare, Stage, and Deliver Winning Presentations,* 3rd ed. (New York: Amacom, 2004).
2. Crystal Nord, speech to a negative audience, November 19, 2004.
3. E. J. Natalle and F. R. Bodenheimer, *The Woman's Public Speaking Handbook* (Belmont, CA: Wadsworth, 2004), 71.
4. Leech, *How to Prepare,* 264.
5. T. C. Smith, *Making Successful Presentations: A Self-Teaching Guide* (New York: Wiley, 1984), 162.
6. Leech, *How to Prepare,* 261.
7. Cindy Johnson, speech to a neutral audience, October 20, 2004.
8. Chelsea DeSousa, speech to a neutral audience, October 18, 2004.
9. Scott Sturm, speech to a neutral audience, October 22, 2004.
10. Karen Tarara, speech to a negative audience, November 10, 2004.
11. Cindy Johnson, speech to a neutral audience, October 20, 2004.
12. S. C. Rafe, *How to Be Prepared to Think on Your Feet* (Grand Rapids, MI: Harper Business, 1990), 146.
13. Smith, *Making Successful Presentations,* 163–165.
14. Ross Kederman, speech to a negative audience, November 15, 2004.
15. Ashley Osgood, speech to a negative audience, November 15, 2004.
16. Rafe, *How to Be Prepared,* 139–140.
17. Shannon Kirton, speech to a neutral audience, October 20, 2004. Maya Sharif, speech to a neutral audience, October 18, 2004. Nord, speech.

Chapter 14

Making Presentations to Positive Audiences

To Inspire and Inform

Scenario 1. A member of a local church administrative council is addressing the other members about the upcoming annual rummage sale, which has been advertised for a month.

Scenario 2. A student in a design course is explaining to the other students how she applied the principles they had been studying to her project.

Scenario 3. A manager is explaining how to use the new e-mail program that contains a number of features the staff has been asking for.

Scenario 4. On the first day of a senior-level elective class, the instructor begins teaching the students some of the fundamental concepts on which the course will build. ●

A song on *Sesame Street* had lyrics that can be modified to describe these scenarios: "Two of these are not like the others, two of these just don't belong" and "Two of these things belong together, two of these things are kind of the same." Scenarios 1 and 2 are similar, as are 3 and 4; however, both pairs differ from each other, and all four share something in common. Can you figure it all out? All four have positive audiences, because they are interested or involved in the topic; they have a curiosity and concern that creates attentiveness. Involvement can also be thought of in terms of commitment—how much effort a person is willing to expend. The more involved or committed audience members are, the more effort they will put into listening and evaluating information relative to the issue.

Now for the differences. The two pairs of audiences differ in terms of their knowledge and attitude toward the topic. The first two audiences have a certain knowledge base about the issue on which the speaker can build. The second two audiences lack knowledge of the issue, but because of their interest, they want to acquire information. When an audience has knowledge, they are able to evaluate an issue and therefore develop an attitude (liking or disliking) toward it.

Speakers need to adapt their goals to the underlying qualities of the positive audience. For some audiences, the goal may be to inspire or confirm their position, while for others the goal is to inform and educate. This chapter also includes a discussion of presentational strategies that can be adapted to both types of positive audiences to accomplish these goals.

Positive Audiences: Supportive and Open

Positive audiences are interested in what you have to say and are open to learning information and are often in agreement with your own positions on issues. Scenarios 1 and 2 represent a type of positive audience called a supportive audience. A **supportive audience** is a type of positive audience that is interested in the topic or issue, has a positive attitude toward it, and is knowledgeable about it. What do you suppose the speaker's goal might be with these audiences? One goal might be to simply get them excited about an upcoming event—to inspire them, as with the church group. Another might be to get the members to participate or contribute to the sale. Another might be to build on the audience's existing knowledge—to provide information they don't already know—to inform them, as with the design students.

Scenarios 3 and 4 represent a type of positive audience who are interested in the topic or issue, have no established attitude toward it, and have little or no knowledge about it: the **open audience.** These audience members want to learn, and thus the focus will primarily be to inform them. In meeting this goal, the speaker probably also has the goal of producing a positive attitude. The manager hopes the employees will learn the information about the e-mail program and develop a positive attitude toward it.

The open audience potentially could develop a negative reaction to your topic after you have completed your presentation. Employment interviews demonstrate how this can

supportive audience A type of positive audience that is interested in the topic, has a positive attitude toward it, and is knowledgeable about it.

open audience A type of positive audience that is interested in the topic, has no established attitude toward it, and has little or no knowledge about it.

ACT&REFLECT

14.1: Identifying Supportive or Open Audiences

ACT • Identify two topics you could talk about toward which your classmates are likely to be positive (ask around if you aren't sure).

REFLECT • On a scale of 1 to 10, consider how interested they are in the topic, with 1 being a little positive to 10 being very positive, and how knowledgeable they are about the topic (1 to 10). (Again, you could ask your classmates for verification of your assessment.) Given these numbers for each topic, to what degree are the students a supportive or open audience? In what ways might you have to change your focus to increase their supportiveness?

happen. An employer invites a job candidate for an interview (interested but unknowledgeable), but after visiting with the candidate (who is doing his or her best to present positive information), the employer decides against hiring that person (makes a negative evaluation). In speaking to an open audience, your goal is for them to "hire" you: to adopt the position or attitude you are advocating. For that reason, this chapter discusses strategies not only for informing an audience but also for creating a positive attitude.

The open audience is a more common audience type than you might think, for example, sales presentations of new products, class lectures (hopefully, you're interested some of the time), and business briefings (see Act and Reflect 14.1). In all of these situations, the audiences have an interest in what is being presented, and because they lack knowledge, they are particularly susceptible to influence. The amount of new information needs to be sufficient without being overwhelming. The audience needs enough information with which to form their initial opinions, but too much information too soon could turn them off. You've undoubtedly experienced this phenomenon in some of the classes you've taken, in which you started out eagerly only to become disenchanted by an onslaught of information. You also need to adapt the information to your audience's background. Too often, speakers speak in jargon and terms only understood by those in the know. You've probably heard the scientists at NASA news briefings sometimes forget to make such adaptations in their daily updates on a mission.

Goal Setting for Positive Audiences

What you can accomplish as a speaker is different for supportive than for open audiences. Both audience types have different reasons for listening, different motivations and goals. Effective presentations usually represent a melding of the speaker's goals with the audience's goals. One of the most important questions you need to answer if you are to be an effective presenter was discussed in Chapter 1: "What do I want from

ACT&REFLECT

14.2: Preparing for Positive Audiences

ACT • Recall a presentation for which you were a supportive audience member (interested, positive attitude, knowledgeable). Now recall a presentation for which you were an open audience member (interested but lacking knowledge).

REFLECT • In what ways do you think the speakers adapted to your qualities as a supportive or an open audience member? In what ways do you think the speakers failed to adapt to your qualities? What do these observations tell you about how you might behave in giving a speech to your classmates on a topic toward which they are supportive? Open?

my audience?" Speeches are ineffective when speakers fail to clearly identify their goals and their audiences's goals. You might find yourself inclined to move straight to selecting a topic without regard to what you want to actually accomplish in your presentation. The goal and the topic are interdependent—you can't have one without the other, and each defines the other. There is a reason for giving a presentation; that is the goal. What the presentation is about is the topic (see Act and Reflect 14.2).

In the third scenario, the speaker might have decided to focus on the benefits of the new e-mail software. This goal ignores the employees' need to learn how to actually use the software. A more effective speaking goal is to focus on developing the employees' skills in using the new program. In addition, the speaker should recognize that the employees' goal is to learn what they need to know but to minimize the time they spend on training. Regretfully, the authors of this book have sat through too many long training sessions in order to learn the five minutes of information they really wanted. The key in this situation is to blend the speaker's goals and audience's goals in creating an efficient presentation that conveys the information succinctly.

Informing

Presentations to positive audiences usually have some combination of one or more of the three goals shown in Table 14.1: to convey information; to inspire; and to change commitment, behavior, or actions. The goal of conveying information means that you want your audience to hear and retain information you think is important for them to have. Underlying this goal is a belief that the information is valuable and necessary for your audience to know. In classrooms, instructors often get frustrated when students ask, "Will this be on the test?" even though such a question reflects an attempt by the audience to determine the utility and value of the lecture material. Slightly more insightful students might ask "How will this information be of value to me?" While the question might seem facetious, the instructor should be able to

● **TABLE 14.1**   Presentation Goals with Positive Audiences.

Goals	Examples
To convey information; to teach	Training sessions, classroom lectures, how-to work-shops, company orientations, briefings and updates, committee reports.
To inspire; to maintain commitment	Half-time locker room speeches, rallies in support of a candidate or a cause, sermons, motivational speeches.
To change the audience's commitment, behavior, or actions (to move to act)	Motivational speeches, sales staff meetings, proposals, speeches to move supporters to action, presentations to get donors to give money in support of a cause.

answer that question, just as you should be able to answer the same question for any presentation you make when your goal is to convey information. Another way of phrasing the question is "What can your audience do with the information you provide?" Suppose you had the goal of informing your fellow students about the following topics; what value would there be for them in listening?

Topics	Value to Audience
Interpersonal conflict management techniques	?
My spring vacation in Orlando	?
The value of leasing a new car	?
Paraguay	?
History of tennis	?

The value of learning about each of these topics might not be readily apparent to the audience. Establishing this value often occurs in the introductory portion of the presentation, as we discussed in Chapter 6. On the other hand, maybe there isn't any real reason for the audience to learn the information, in which case the presentation becomes superfluous and unnecessary. Understanding *why* you want and what you want your audience to learn will help you decide what information to include and exclude. See Act and Reflect 14.3.

Inspiring

Presentations that seek to inspire seek to arouse or reawaken the audience's commitment to their beliefs and values. Two methods that can be used in this type of speech are (1) increasing the sense of belonging to a group and (2) increasing the sense of common goals and values.[1] You can inspire audiences by emphasizing their membership and pride in the group that shares the values or beliefs about which you are speaking. You often hear about athletic teams adopting some motto for their season to reflect their shared vision. This motto is repeated during coaches' speeches as

For what classes have you been an open positive audience member? ●

a way of creating cohesion and inspiration. Mottoes also serve to increase a sense of a common goal by simplifying the goal in one succinct concept. Focusing on a few core values and goals is another strategy for arousing and sustaining audience motivation.[2] Speeches to inspire are usually laden with emotions often aroused by figurative language support, such as imagery (discussed in Chapter 5).

Maintaining Commitment and Resistance to Detractors

In addition to inspiring supportive audience members, you might have the goal of simply maintaining their commitment. This might involve preparing your audience to respond to other people's attempts to influence them. The primary method for doing this is to provide the audience with facts and counterarguments. The director, actor, and activist Robert Redford delivered the annual Nancy Hanks Lecture on Arts and Public Policy in 2003, to an organization called Americans for Arts, in which he provided information to support the audience's predispositions:

> Government support for the arts is not the frivolous give-away that some would have you believe. It's a good investment and it is a sound economic development. Art and public policy is good business. Let's look at the financial stake that the government has in the arts. The nonprofit arts world is roughly a $134 billion a year industry, employing millions. It generates nearly $81 billion in spending by those who participate in its cultural offerings and is responsible for some $24 billion in taxes going back to federal, state, and local governments annually. And this doesn't take into consideration the impact the nonprofit sector has as the training ground for writers, musicians, actors, dancers, painters, photographers, filmmakers, and the like. It doesn't take into

consideration the ultimate effect these people and their work have on a thriving multi-billion dollar private sector. So supporting the arts is good business and the numbers bear this out.[3]

As another example, suppose you are speaking to a group dedicated to preventing the rezoning of part of their community from residential to commercial use. You know that the developers are planning to argue that their efforts will increase jobs, which might be appealing to your audience members. Your presentation seeks to bolster the listeners' opposition to development by arguing that jobs are created even if the project is placed in another area of town. This argument prepares your supporters to fend off the developer's claim of job growth in the area they want rezoned.

There are several other ways to prepare audiences to resist detractors.[4] Sometimes people forget their values, and thus a speaker might remind the audience of their values and beliefs. You have probably heard more than one courtroom drama in which the attorneys reminded the jurors of values such as "justice," "fairness," or "rights" in their closing remarks. Having audience members verbalize, either privately or publicly, their beliefs about the issue reinforces their commitment. Fundraising drives push hard to have people sign pledge cards as a way of securing their commitment. Having an audience act on the issue rather than simply confirm their support helps to sustain commitment.

ACT&REFLECT

14.3: Goal Setting with Positive Audiences

ACT • Use the two topics you identified in the first exercise in this chapter to answer the following questions. Which goal fits each topic best?

To convey information: What do your classmates already know about the topic? What additional information do they need to know? Why is that important for them to know?

To maintain or change their commitment—to inspire them: What would you like your listeners' commitment to be? What forces are acting to diminish their commitment? What is preventing greater commitment? What issues about this topic might inspire them?

To alter their behavior: What is the audience's current behavior in regard to your topic? What would you like them to do that they aren't doing? Are you asking for too much? What is the minimum behavior you could change? What is the maximum?

REFLECT • How can you use the above analysis to assist you in preparing your next presentation?

Increasing Commitment or Motivating to Act

When attempting to motivate a positive audience to action or to increase their commitment, you need to know what's holding them back. What are their reservations? Their concerns? Their questions? This information is critical in developing an effective presentation. Once you have it, you can aim your presentation at addressing the issues that are impeding your audience's commitment or action. Suppose you are trying to get students to donate blood during a campus drive. Most students think donating blood is a good idea, but they are reluctant to do it. Why? What do you think their reservations are? Maybe it's a belief they don't have blood to spare; if so, you need to provide information about how much blood the human body has and how quickly the body replaces it. Sometimes the resistance to act is so great that you are really giving a speech to a negative audience, that is, one that opposes what you propose. We discuss strategies for addressing strong resistance in detail in Chapter 16.

Identifying Supportive and Open Audiences

How do you know if you are speaking to an audience that has interest and or a positive attitude toward your topic? Fortunately, many everyday presentations are given to audiences of people you already know (coworkers, managers, students, fellow volunteers, etc.). Your interactions and observations of these listeners provide you with a strong foundation for assessing their support for and openness to some of the issues you might be called upon to address. Deciding their reaction to a given topic can be easy if the topic is part of previous discussions or presentations. Audience members might have expressed strong feelings one way or another about the issues. Determining audience reactions to unfamiliar topics requires making deductions based on how they have reacted to related issues and your own audience analysis. Overestimating their regard for the issue can lead you to undersupport your positions; underestimating their support can cause you to spend time presenting unnecessary arguments.

Determining whether the audience is supportive or open means you need to determine how knowledgeable they are about the issue. What do they already know? What don't they know? What terms might be unfamiliar and need to be defined? How complex can you make your presentation? Audiences often have interest in issues about which they know little. You've probably enrolled in courses because the titles sounded interesting, even though you knew little or nothing about the topics. Many issues hold intrinsic interest for people, which means they are open to hearing what the speaker has to say. The primary goal with open audiences is to increase their knowledge. For supportive audiences, the speaker may choose to expand on the knowledge the audience already has or to use their knowledge as the foundation for discussing other issues. Building on listeners' existing knowledge reflects the goal of informing; however, speakers often seek to inspire or motivate supportive audiences to action.

In deciding what information to convey, you need to determine what the audience already knows. You have undoubtedly sat in a class where the instructor gave a lecture on information you and the rest of the class already knew. How did you react? What did you gain? What goal did the instructor achieve? To avoid this, some instructors give students

Everyday Example

Conservative Group Lauds Tax Foe Owens

The following article appeared in the Denver Post *on January 19, 2001. It describes an event in which Governor Bill Owens of Colorado, who is known for pushing hard for tax cuts, addressed a group in Washington, D.C., known for its opposition to taxes. Consider the speaker and the audience goals as you read. What impact do you suppose the governor's speech had?*

The Republican governor went before a dinner meeting of The Club for Growth, a political organization that supports only what its president, Stephen Moore, called "true conservatives" and vows to "keep the heat on moderate Republicans." Moore, who works at the Libertarian Cato Institute, said the Washington think tank had decided to give Owens a "B-plus" in its annual ratings for his efforts to reduce state taxes.

"I love this guy because he hates taxes as much as I do," Moore told the crowd of about 60.

Owens responded by telling the group he is pressing for a third round of tax cuts from the state legislature. He also said his earlier cuts had laid the foundation for Colorado's rapid economic growth.

"Colorado is doing very, very well economically, so much so that one of our challenges this year is how to better manage the growth," he said.

"My point is this: Lower taxes have helped increase and improve Colorado's economy," he said. "Tax rate cuts really do provide incentives for growth and development."

The governor, a friend of George W. Bush, was in the nation's capital to attend the president-elect's inauguration and to promote the nomination of Gale Norton, a former Colorado state attorney general who's been tapped as the Bush administration's interior secretary.

The Club for Growth raises money for conservative Republican congressional candidates.

a quiz at the beginning of a course to determine their knowledge level and then adapt the course accordingly. By knowing what your audience knows, you can build upon that base and provide them with additional information. Your audience's level of knowledge is one of the factors that determines the goals you can set for your presentation.

Giving a quiz to your audience isn't usually the most effective way to determine their level of knowledge. Your own observations and interactions with the audience can

serve as one basis for assessing their knowledge. You can talk with audience members in advance of the presentation to find out what they already know and what they would like to learn. You can also make assumptions on the basis of what you know of the audience's background—their age, education, sex, professional positions, and so on. Finally, you can adjust presentations as you speak in response to audience feedback. The audience provides a number of nonverbal (and sometimes verbal) cues that sometimes reveal their level of understanding. The most effective presenters remain flexible while delivering their speeches, editing out material in response to audience reactions. Less-effective presenters are either oblivious to the cues or too tied to their structured presentation to adapt, which usually results in a bored and disenchanted audience.

Speaking to Supportive Audiences: Strategies to Inspire and Enhance Interest

Generally, your goal with positive audiences that are already supportive, is to inspire, enhance interest, or motivate to act. The supportive audience is already in agreement with you on the position; your goal is to reinforce their position and make them feel excited about that position. In general, presentations to supportive audiences will be emotional, uplifting, inspirational, motivating, energizing, confirming, and exciting. Anything you can do to evoke such responses from the supportive audience will help you accomplish your goal.

Adopt a Style That Complements Your Content

Positive audiences want to hear a "good" presentation. In Chapter 1 we discussed the importance of speaking thoughtfully and with sincerity, that is, with eloquence. With positive audiences, you need a style that does not interfere with your message. Positive audiences are usually a little more forgiving than other audiences in terms of a speaker's style; nonetheless, you need a style that does not hamper the ability of the audience to fulfill their need, such as gaining information. In Chapter 3, you read about developing your own style, but there may be selective aspects of your style that fit best with a supportive audience. As you give a presentation, try to monitor your style. If there are problems, develop a plan of action for responding to any distractions.

Related to your style is your credibility. If the audience already knows you or knows about you and has a positive impression of you, you can move directly into discussing the issue or topic. If they don't know much about you and it is important for them to trust you, then you might have to explain your background and expertise. Whether or not to discuss your credentials depends on the impact it would have on your ability to accomplish your goals. We give suggestions for improving your credibility later in this chapter.

Expand On or Present Old Information in New, Interesting Ways

As mentioned earlier, sitting through a presentation that simply covers information you already know tends to be boring and unrewarding. We don't mind hearing some information we already know, but we like to hear it expanded or treated in a novel or entertaining way. For example:

"Drinking and driving is a dumb thing to do" doesn't really inform you of anything new.

"Forty-one percent of all traffic deaths involve alcohol" or "Fifty-nine people every hour of every day in the United States are injured in alcohol-related accidents" expands beyond the more general statement and provides specific information of interest to the audience.[5]

Use the Familiar as the Foundation for the New

While you don't want to rehash what the audience already knows, audiences cannot absorb a presentation of totally new information. This would be like someone talking to you in a foreign language you didn't understand, in which every word is new and unfamiliar. On the other hand, we often pick up the meaning of a foreign phrase when it is used within the context of what we do know. *"Verstehen sie?"* Can you figure out what the German phrase means? It's "Do you understand?" If you figured it out, it shows how we can learn new information as long as it's grounded in the familiar. If you didn't figure it out, then it's probably a poor example.

How might the presentation be affected if the speaker stood behind the podium instead of sitting? ●

Emphasize and Confirm Existing Audience Values, Beliefs, and Attitudes

In Chapter 6, you learned about the need to analyze the audience and assess their values, beliefs, and attitudes. This information is helpful because, as simple as it might seem, audiences like to hear speakers praise and confirm these qualities. At political conventions, speakers receive loud applause and cheers when they unabashedly reiterate the values held by the members. People like to hear support and endorsement for their ideas, decisions, and beliefs. Have you ever spent a lot of money to buy something like a new car, computer, or stereo? If you have, you probably noticed that after you finally decided on what to buy and bought it, you experience some doubt about having spent all that money. This uncertainty creates a condition called cognitive dissonance.

Cognitive dissonance is a tension that exists when people hold contradictory beliefs or when their beliefs and actions are contradictory. The belief that you should save your money is in conflict with your belief that you deserve the new item. Researchers have found that to reduce this dissonance ("Did I make the right decision?"), we tend to seek information that validates our decision.[6] To reduce your dissonance, you might talk to other people who have bought the same product who will tell you how great it is. You might notice newspaper articles or reviews that sing the praises of the item you purchased. This phenomenon of seeking validation probably holds true for most of our attitudes and beliefs. We like to hear them supported and endorsed by others. The more difficult the decision, the more we seem to need this support. In making a presentation to a positive audience, provide added information that validates their decisions, confirms their attitudes, and supports their beliefs.

Use Support Materials That Inspire: Illustrations, Examples, and Stories

Supportive audiences share the same positive attitude toward the topic as the speaker, thus reducing their need for cited sources of support—they are already convinced. This audience is receptive to information, so your main goal is present information in the most palatable form. How can you present additional information in a way that will facilitate learning it? The use of examples and illustrations is one way to make information easier to understand. Using figurative language (metaphors, examples, and illustrations) increases the audience's attention and interest, which should lead to better retention. Remember that information can be more easily recalled when it is presented as a well-organized and coherent story. Emotional images also have a stronger impact on positive audiences than logical arguments.[7] Telling stories that personalize the audience's beliefs raises their emotional investment and inspires them. Such arousal can be used to evoke action from your audience as well.

Focus on Action, Recommendations, and Conclusions

When you are seeking some specific action from a positive audience, you don't need to direct a lot of additional argument or evidence toward changing their attitudes. What they need is to know what you are asking for, what your recommendations are, what conclusions you have reached. Say you are giving a presentation to a group of managers in your company. Everyone is concerned about the recent high employee turnover. You don't need to spend much time trying to convince them there is a problem. The managers want to solve the problem. They want to know what should be done; they want suggestions, a plan of action. Your presentation should focus on addressing these issues. More will be covered on strategies to motivate the audience in Chapter 16.

Adapt the Introduction and Conclusion

We have discussed the stock introduction and stock conclusion in Chapter 12. You know that the components of a stock introduction are an attention-grabber, your credentials, a

cognitive dissonance A tension that exists when one holds contradictory beliefs or when one's beliefs and actions are contradictory.

statement of audience need, your thesis, and a preview of your major points. The stock conclusion should have a statement of the point or points you want your audience to remember and a device to establish closure. For your presentation to a supportive audience, you cannot go wrong if your introduction and conclusion contain all of these stock components. However, you might also consider developing your introduction and conclusion somewhat differently.

The supportive audience might already be aware of your credentials; you might not need to remind them of the reason you are speaking on a particular topic or of their need to hear your message. If you are telling a story, the most important point of your story might also serve as your attention-grabber. If you are asking for action from a group of listeners who are hungry for a means of overcoming a problem they all share, rather than following the stock introduction, you might only need to state your speaking goal as your introduction. The audience will be changing their attention from their thoughts to your topic during your introduction. Effective instructors know that you should never make announcements in the first couple of minutes of a class because the students are still making this transition; similarly, your introduction should allow for this transition.

If your presentation has primarily been one long story, or if you are using a story to conclude your presentation, you may not need to review the major points in your conclusion. You do want to emphasize your most important point—say it one more time to establish closure. The audience should be able to easily tell when you have reached the end of your story and thus the end of your presentation. You might reflect on a story shared in the body of the speech as a final reminder of an important issue. If you are recommending a particular action, you may need to repeat the procedure needed to complete the action and then remind the audience of the benefits they will gain by taking this action. Seeking some form of immediate action by the audience at the conclusion of your speech is a good way to reinforce their commitment and take advantage of any emotional energy you have generated. Asking for them to sign pledge cards, to sign a petition, to vote in favor of a motion, or to storm the Bastille are ways of concluding your presentation.

Speaking to Open Audiences: Strategies to Inform

"I took a speed reading course and read 'War and Peace' in twenty minutes. It involves Russia."

—*Woody Allen*

Open audiences attend presentations because they want to know what the speaker will say—because they are interested in the issue and they believe that the presentation will include knowledge they need or want. You might attend a class at the local Y to hear a presentation on belly dancing because you are interested in learning this ancient art, or you might attend a presentation on different types of insurance policies because you believe the information presented will be important to you in future decision making. In both cases, you hope to take away skills or knowledge that will

Everyday Example

Arousing and Inspiring a Supportive Audience

The following article describes a situation in which the speaker was able to inspire her listeners with a message adapted to their specific needs and circumstances. What goals does the speaker appear to have? What techniques does she use to accomplish her goals?

In Houston's first celebration of National Black Nurses Day on Feb. 1, Mary Holt Ashley, Ph.D., RN, encouraged her audience of more than 200 African-American nurses to adopt "Ashley's B-Attitudes": to believe in themselves, to break the mold, to blaze their own trails, to bring passion to the table and to boost their inner spirits. In a rousing speech, "Leadership: What It Is to Be a Black Nurse in 2002," Ashley outlined the steps for the African-American nurse's professional journey and suggested methods for coping with racial disparity.

As associate administrator and chief nursing officer of Ben Taub General Hospital in Houston, Ashley is specially qualified to point the way to success for other African-American nurses. She challenged her audience to seek advanced degrees and higher-level positions in nursing. Stressing the need for passion, commitment and spiritual stamina, she advised aspiring nurses to maintain a clear vision of their desired destinations, evaluating what tools they will require and how long the journey will take. Careful planning and scheduling are essential, as is an awareness of how to cope with possible roadblocks.

Because they are a minority in the nursing profession, African-American nurses need to be active and self-confident. Ashley stressed the need to ASK (ask, seek, keep). Nurses should ask for what they want, ask for extra projects, ask to join professional groups, ask for a seat at the table and ask others how they are doing. They need to seek out people at higher levels, seek higher education and certification, seek African-American mentors, seek to be team players and seek advice from others. Finally, they need to keep up with the latest trends, keep their résumés updated, keep a can-do attitude, keep spiritually and physically fit, and keep their eyes on the prize.

To combat racial disparity, she said, African-American nurses need to aid in the recruitment of other African Americans, mentor new nurses in the workforce, tutor students in order to foster academic success, and publicize the activities and successes of other African-American nurses. She emphasized the importance of joining professional organizations and inspiring one's peers to do so.

As a finale to her speech, Ashley asked the audience to stand and join her in a chorus: "Say it loud, I'm black and I'm proud. Say it loud, I'm black and I'm proud to be an RN in 2002." Lola Denise Jefferson, RN, founder and president of the Fort Bend County (Texas) chapter of the Black Nurses Association, said her group sponsored the event to celebrate African-American nurses and encourage them to stay in the nursing profession. Given the enthusiastic responses from attendees, she is convinced that the association accomplished these goals.

make a difference in your life. You don't want to be the person who responds to the experience as Woody Allen did, by saying, "The presenter talked about dancing with veils" or "The presentation involved numbers." You want more from your experience; you want skills or knowledge, and you want to be able to retain the skills or knowledge for future use whenever a need presents itself. Your goal in speaking to an open audience is to sustain their interest while providing them with information and possibly influencing them to develop a positive attitude toward the issue.

Establish Your Speaker Credibility (Ethos)

You read in Chapter 4 about the effect of your delivery on your credibility and in Chapter 9 about source credibility. We'll explore the concept of speaker credibility further here, including how the content of your message affects it. We tend to believe information provided by people we trust and to be skeptical of that from people we distrust. This means that if you simply provide good information, it doesn't necessarily mean your audience will embrace that information. You need to establish yourself as a credible source of information—as believable. Aristotle referred to a person's credibility as *ethos*, and it has endured through the millennia as a crucial element of making effective presentations.

For over fifty years, speaker credibility has been the subject of research for over fifty years, examining how audiences are affected by a speaker's credibility, and how speakers can improve their credibility. Research has found that speaker credibility is best thought of as multidimensional, with expertise and trustworthiness being the most prevalent dimensions.[8] **Expertise** is the degree to which audiences feel speakers are particularly knowledgeable and informed about the issue on which they speak because of the speaker's education or experience. The research findings show that when an audience is told about the speaker's credibility before they read or hear the message, they respond more positively to it. We don't know much about what happens when the speakers discuss their own expertise within the context of their presentation, but despite this limitation, the general recommendation is that speakers should explain their expertise: tell the audience how you know what you know. Obviously, you don't want to appear boastful or conceited, but you do want to appear well informed. When you talk to people who already know you (when you have initial speaker credibility), they know your expertise, and you won't need to restate your credentials.

There are experts, however, whom we don't trust, which is why trustworthiness is another dimension of speaker credibility. How many people can you think of who are experts but whom you dislike or believe are dishonest? There are also a lot of people we trust who are not necessarily experts. You frequently accept the word of trusted friends without concern for their level of expertise. **Trustworthiness** refers to an audience's perception of a speaker's honesty, integrity, sincerity, and character. Trust often requires some amount of time to establish; however, the speaker's sincerity and character are judged to some extent by the speaker's nonverbal behaviors, as discussed in Chapter 4, and by the speaker's verbal messages. One study that examined this effect used two groups of college students who listened to a three-and-a-half-minute speech on breeding qualities of Himalayan cats (considered a noninvolving topic).[9] For one group, the speaker engaged in the immediacy behaviors of continuous eye contact, occasional movement toward the

expertise A dimension of credibility; the degree to which audiences feel speakers are particularly knowledgeable and informed about the issue on which they speak because of the speaker's education or experience.

trustworthiness A dimension of credibility; an audience's perception of a speaker's honesty, integrity, sincerity, and character.

audience, gesturing, and vocal expressiveness. For the other group, the same speaker was nonimmediate, by standing behind a podium, not making eye contact or gesturing, and using a nonexpressive voice. The listeners reported greater trustworthiness in response to the immediacy behaviors. They also indicated that they liked the first speaker more and saw the speaker as more attractive and more competent.

Some of the other dimensions of speaker credibility are goodwill (caring or concern for the listener), fairness, dynamism, character, extroversion, sociability, composure, and prestige.[10] While the research that identifies each of these qualities as part of speaker credibility has not been overwhelming, the fact that such qualities can affect an audience's perception of you as a speaker is worth noting. Displaying these qualities will not hurt your effectiveness as a speaker, and is most likely going to at least create a positive impression on the audience, even if it doesn't directly affect your credibility.

Your credibility will be affected by information the audience knows about you (either provided by others or by yourself) and by the audience's perception of you. You will want to tell your audience the basis of your knowledge. This can be anything from your academic or professional background related to the topic to explaining the research you have conducted on it. While having expertise directly related to the topic is best, being an expert in one area can help create credibility in other areas. You've watched lots of commercials where athletes or actors are selling you hamburgers, cars, or clothes. See Act and Reflect 14.4.

ACT & REFLECT

14.4: Assessing Your Speaker Credibility

ACT • For each of the following topics and audiences, rate your credibility on a ten-point scale, with 1 being "no credibility" and 10 being "absolutely credible."

Credibility	Topic	Audience
_____	Life as a college student	Seniors at your former high school
_____	Destruction of the rain forests	Your classmates in this course
_____	Best places to eat and hang out in town	Incoming college students during orientation
_____	The importance of a well-balanced diet	Senior citizens in a retirement community
_____	Your next speech topic for this class	Students in this class

REFLECT • How could you establish or increase the audiences' perception of your credibility in each of these situations?

Use Memorable Techniques

What helps you to remember new information? Most of us remember information that is repeated, patterned, novel, and enumerated. We also remember information attached to keywords or key phrases that are easy to remember and recall. Think about the most significant pieces of information that you want your audience to remember. You can help the audience remember information by previewing it in the introduction, repeating it several times in the body, and reviewing it in the conclusion. Using enumeration or lists helps us remember how many things we should try to recall. For example: "There are three advantages. The first advantage is . . ." Repeating "three advantages" several times in your speech will help the audience remember there are three advantages, and then they will know how many advantages they should recall. If each advantage has a key term attached to it, that also aids in recollection. "The first advantage is 'profitability.' The second advantage is 'affordability,' and the third advantage is 'easy implementation.'"

You can also help an audience remember information by using your delivery to emphasize and highlight key pieces of information. Pausing, raising or lowering your voice, changing your tone, body movement, and so on can be used to ensure audience attention and emphasize the importance of the information. Information that you present visually through such means as models, PowerPoint projection, overheads, or posters can also help the audience understand and retain information by using another communication channel. More information on the use of visual aids is presented in Chapter 10 and Appendix B. Handouts are particularly helpful when you have complex information that is not easily conveyed in a presentation. Your presentation serves to highlight important points with the expectation that listeners will turn to the written text to learn the details.

Consider Information from the Audience's Perspective

The material you present needs to be consistent with the audience's existing values, beliefs, and attitudes if you are to convert them to your position. They will generally be dependent on the facts you provide, and unless the facts are incongruent with what they already know, your facts will form the basis of their impression. However, as you read in Chapter 8, people judge facts for their *fidelity* (the degree to which something is consistent with what they already know). Think about your own experiences in classes. You generally accept the new information your instructors provide without much hesitation, unless the instructor says something that seems out

An enumerated list can help your audience remember key information. ●

of left field. For example, we teach interpersonal communication classes in which we discuss differences between men and women in developing intimate relationships. The differences that we lecture on are readily accepted until we report on a study that men report that their romantic relationships move toward marriage earlier in a relationship than do those of women. The women in our classes usually challenge this finding because it lacks fidelity for them—it doesn't match their own experiences and observations.

Organize with the Brain in Mind

As a presenter, you want to ensure that the content of your presentation is useful to your listeners. The following features can help your open audience store information in their long-term memory so it can be accessed and used again:

1. Attract your listeners' attention and focus it on your topic.
2. Limit the number of new pieces of knowledge in your presentation.
3. Present the knowledge in a way that makes sense to your audience.
4. Allow your audience the opportunity for active involvement.
5. Show your audience why your message is relevant to them.

There is no specific formula for including these requirements in your presentation, but at some point in your presentation, it will be beneficial to your audience and yourself if you are able to apply these recommendations.

Use Information Transfer and Build on the Familiar

As you watch cooking shows like Martha Stewart's, you get ideas for special dinners you would like to prepare. You don't have Martha's cooking equipment, food budget, or ability to carve fancy vegetables, but you easily modify her tips to fit your own kitchen equipment, food budget, and culinary skills. Although you are usually able to transfer the cooking information from Martha's show to your own kitchen, it might be helpful if Martha would offer suggestions such as: "To whip airy eggs, if you don't own a wire whisk, you can get the same airy effect by using a fork," or "Many people bake their salmon uncovered, but that tends to dry the fish. Instead, the fish retains its flavorful juices if you cover the pan with foil." Applying knowledge from one context or environment to another is called **transfer.**[11] Martha could facilitate transfer in her cooking show by assisting you in these ways:[12]

- First, suggest ways the knowledge presented for one context can be modified for use in another context. In the scenario, Martha suggested a fork if a wire whisk was unavailable.
- Second, acknowledge possible misconceptions of listeners and correct them. If new knowledge is added to incorrect knowledge, the result is still incorrect. In the scenario, Martha mentioned a common misconception about cooking salmon and corrected it.

transfer Applying knowledge from one context or environment to another.

- Third, transfer works better if the information is not presented too specifically but rather in more general or conceptual terms. Regarding the suggestion about using a fork if a wire whisk was unavailable, the key concept was whipping airy eggs.

Transferring information from one context to another often depends on building on information already familiar to the audience. Imagine you were trying to explain some complex game rules to someone for the first time. You would probably try to incorporate references to rules from other games the person might know. By using the familiar, the person is better able to understand your information. Failing to use any familiar information would be akin to speaking a foreign language. In this text, we intentionally use words you are familiar with in order to explain new concepts with which you aren't familiar. We use examples that are familiar to you to illustrate new principles.

Adapt the Introduction and Conclusion

Previewing the information you are about to convey in an organized and logical fashion can help in the retention of the information as it is repeated in the body and conclusion. Keywords should be used in the introduction to begin building a framework to which the listeners can attach the information you are going to provide. While audience members have an interest in the topic, you may still need to explain the reasons they should learn the information you are about to provide.

For the open audience, you should take the last opportunity in your conclusion to summarize the major points you have presented—this can help reinforce the information and help the audience retain it. Again, repeating keywords or key phrases provides one last reinforcement of what they have been listening to.

Speaking to Open Audiences: Strategies to Evoke a Positive Attitude

Besides providing information to open audiences, another goal is to develop a positive attitude toward the issue. Indeed, your goal may be more about creating a positive attitude even without informing the audience, even though this might be counter to the audience's goal. We are often exposed to brief previews of upcoming movies or TV shows that are intended to produce a positive attitude about them without really giving us much information on the shows' content. There are some interesting tendencies in people who lack knowledge that you can utilize in building support for your position. Here's a test for you to take (don't worry, it's not graded); don't use a dictionary or look online before you answer the questions.

1. If you had the time, would you accept an all-expenses-paid trip abroad to visit Delemarto?
2. You are meeting for the first time with an unpropitious person. Do you think you'll like him or her?
3. Someone has offered to give you a "Redback" from Australia; would you be inclined to accept it?

Use Positivity Offset

Without understanding what these questions are really asking, most people would probably respond somewhat positively to these three offers. However, there is no such place as Delemarto, so you wouldn't be traveling very far. The word "unpropitious" means unfavorable or unkindly, and if you knew that, you probably predicted disliking the other person. Finally, Redback (which is not someone who is even more conservative than a redneck) is a type of poisonous spider, which would lead most of us to reject the offer. If you answered yes to any of the questions, you displayed **positivity offset,** which is the slight tendency to view something as positive when there is a no other information available.[13] In essence, people tend to view things slightly in a positive light if they have no other information. However, finding issues on which people have no information or aren't influenced by other biases is difficult.

Use an Audience's Positive Attitude toward You

Social psychologists Richard Petty and John Cacioppo examined people's responses to variations in advertisements and gained insight into how to create a positive attitude toward an issue.[14] They found that people who had little involvement with the product developed a more positive attitude when they felt positive about the spokesperson. Audiences with little knowledge of an issue could be expected to respond positively to an unfamiliar topic when it is presented by credible and charismatic speakers. Similarly, a halo effect often occurs whereby people see things in a positive light when they are associated with people they like. As a presentation strategy, you want to get the audience to like you as a speaker. The more they like you, the more they are likely to also accept your attitude toward an issue. You can probably think of lots of instances in your own life when a friend's attitude toward an issue you know nothing about has led you to adopt the same attitude.

Use Group Identification

People's attitudes are influenced by **group identification:** a person will adopt a given attitude when he or she believes it is the attitude held by a group with which the person either associates or wishes to associate. This means that if a specific issue or attitude is linked to a group we identify with or would like to join, then we are more likely to adopt their attitude. This is somewhat akin to peer pressure; you agree to something because it makes you a member of the group. Many of our attitudes are affected by group identification— our religious groups, schools, majors, teams we support, and so on. Group identification was used repeatedly over the years in advertisements for the United States Marines that declared, "We're looking for a few good men" and "The Few, The Proud, The Marines." These messages were accompanied by positive images of select individuals, of an exclusive group that viewers were challenged to join.

positivity offset The slight tendency to view something as positive when there is no other information available.

group identification The tendency to adopt a given attitude when one believes it is the attitude held by a group with which one either associates or wishes to associate.

Use the Bandwagon Effect

Similarly, there is a **bandwagon effect,** in which people agree to something because everyone else is agreeing to it—they want to be on the wagon with everyone else. The bandwagon effect has been seen most prominently in politics when a candidate's rising popularity entices undecided voters to jump on the wagon. People who are undecided often want to know what other people are thinking and, once they find out, appear to place their faith in the majority. This doesn't always happen, because some people pride themselves on being independent and can actually reject an issue simply because everyone else is supporting it. Nonetheless, if you are talking about an issue that your audience is interested in but is lacking knowledge, providing evidence of the way the bandwagon is moving can influence your listeners to think more positively about the issue. You might say something like the following:

The bandwagon effect can be seen when people stand up because other audience members have. ●

> Changes in the academic calendar next year are obviously of interest to you because it impacts your entire plans for the year. This new proposal calls for expanding the break between winter and spring terms. This idea has been supported overwhelmingly by the school faculty, by the student body government, and the results of a recent poll also show strong student support.

Use Emotional Appeals

People who are uninformed and uninvolved can be more influenced by emotional appeals than informed people.[15] According to the elaboration likelihood model that we discussed in Chapter 8, those who are less involved are less likely to engage in strong cognitive analysis of what they hear. They are affected by what is referred to as peripheral processing, including emotional appeals. Here is where the use of storytelling can be used to evoke emotions in support of your position. In an episode of the TV show *West Wing*, a White House staff member was indifferent about supporting a manned mission to Mars. However, her mind was changed after hearing a story (which is true) about the NASA *Voyager 1* traveling beyond our solar system with a disk of music selections, including a song by a blind gospel-blues singer named Blind Willie Johnson. The staff member was told that

bandwagon effect When people agree to something because everyone else is agreeing to it—they want to be on the wagon with everyone else.

A Question of **Ethics**

1. To what degree is it ethical to get people to support your position not because of its merits but because of group identification or the bandwagon effect?

2. Under what circumstances is it okay for a speaker to get an audience riled up in order to get them to act when their reasoning tells them not to?

this little-known man, blinded as a child by lye thrown by his stepmother, died after his church was burnt down, but nonetheless, his song is sailing beyond the solar system. The spirit and emotion of this story led the staff member to be view the information about the value of the mission more positively. While the example is from a TV show, it nonetheless illustrates well the impact a good story can have on a listener.

The unknowledgeable audience's emotional state can also affect their openness to information. In essence, when people are in a good mood, they are more likely to have a positive reaction on issues about which they are uninformed than if they are in a bad mood. Maybe speakers know this intuitively, and that's why speakers often begin with jokes or lighthearted stories and why so many TV commercials use humor. While the research on humor in presentations has produced mixed results, humor does seem to create a positive reaction toward the speaker and to have some impact on the retention of material.[16] See Act and Reflect 14.5.

ACT&REFLECT

14.5: Applying Psychological Tendencies and Emotional Appeals

ACT ·

1. Identify two issues or topics about which you believe the other students in this class would have no knowledge. Ask two or three students to indicate whether they have a positive or negative "gut" reaction to the topics.

2. Consider two topics about which your classmates are probably unknowledgeable. What could you say about this topic that would encourage them to jump on the "bandwagon"?

Topic A:

Topic B:

REFLECT · Which psychological tendencies do you think would have the most impact on your classmates? Why? Which would have the least impact? Why?

Overcoming Threats to Positive Audience Attitudes

You've probably experienced the following: you sign up for a class that sounds interesting, and you look forward to going; but once you're in the class, you become very disappointed. You started out as a positive open audience member, ready for a positive experience. What happened? There are lots of things that cause audience members to start out positively and then become disenchanted. Here are five problems speakers encounter that diminish a positive audience's attitude, along with recommendations for overcoming the problem. See which ones explain what happened in situations in which you started as a positive audience member but didn't end up that way. See also Act and Reflect 14.6.

- **Problem:** *Weak Presentational Style.* In the above example, the speaker or teacher may have done such a poor job of conveying information that you lost interest. Perhaps the speaker's style was dull, disorganized, even insulting. **Solution:** *Maintain an Enthusiastic and Sincere Presentational Style.* Obviously, the speaker's enthusiasm can have a great deal of influence on an individual's enthusiasm for a topic. If you are talking about a topic you care about, let that enthu-

ACT&REFLECT

14.6: Selecting Strategies

ACT • Decide which of these six strategies applies to the topic(s) you are considering for your next presentation. Explain how those strategies can be applied to your presentation.

Strategy	How does it apply to your presentation?
1. As the speaker, you need to adopt a style that complements your content.	1.
2. Don't spend time elaborating on your credentials if they already know and trust you.	2.
3. Don't rehash what they already know.	3.
4. Use the familiar as the foundation for the new.	4.
5. Give information that supports or furthers the audiences' existing beliefs.	5.
6. Focus on action, recommendations, and conclusions.	6.

REFLECT • How would you actually go about applying each of these strategies to your next presentation?

siasm shine through. Carry on an energized "conversation" with your listeners. Apply the delivery suggestions from Chapter 4 to help you achieve this goal.

- **Problem:** *Repeating Only Known Information.* You might have lost interest because you already knew almost everything covered in the course; thus, you became bored and restless. **Solution:** *Use Known Information as a Foundation to Present New Information.* The effective speaker builds on what the listeners know while introducing new information.

- **Problem:** *Exceeding the Audience's Capability.* Besides being bored by old information, you can become bored by information that is over your head. One of your authors, who had a strong conceptual background on statistics, decided to audit a graduate-level statistics class called "Regression Analysis." However, the entire course involved doing matrix algebra far beyond the mathematical skill of your author, and this author couldn't wait to get out of the class, never to return! **Solution:** *Match or Adapt the Complexity of Information to the Audience.* Effective speakers either simplify where needed or provide the necessary foundations for comprehending the information.

- **Problem:** *Failure to Meet the Audience's Expectations.* A class might prove disappointing if your expectation was very different from how the course turned out. In essence, you were expecting something different from what was taught (like the heavy math component of the statistics course). Regrettably, course descriptions are sometimes works of creative writing and might not reflect the actual content. This difference in expectation is probably one of the most common reasons that initially positive audiences become disappointed. **Solution:** *Identify and Adapt to Audience Expectations.* Audiences enter presentations with various expectations, and the degree to which you meet those expectations often means the difference between success and failure.

- **Problem:** *Including Information That Evokes a Negative Attitude.* The information provided by the instructor could evoke a negative attitude toward the issue if the instructor takes a position that contradicts your values or beliefs. For example, "Technology and Social Change" might sound like an interesting course, but after a few lectures you develop the attitude that technology is the bane of humanity. **Solution:** *Be Sensitive to the Audience's Developing Attitude.* The speaker needed to be sensitive to how the audience reacts and engage them in such a way as to develop a positive attitude.

● GETTING TO WORK

As in all speaking situations, you can improve your effectiveness by understanding and adapting to your audience. The following sets of questions will guide you through an analysis of the positive audience and help you to select the best strategies to accomplish your goals.

Questions about the Positive Audience

How interested is the audience in your topic?

Is the audience supportive or open?

How much knowledge do they have on the topic?

What information do they need?

What do they want to learn?

What is your goal? Do you want to inspire, inform, maintain commitment, or motivate to action?

Questions of Audience Interest

To what degree will your delivery style affect audience interest?

Are you providing new information that the audience will find interesting and supportive of their position?

What is the audience's expectation of you? Can you fulfill their expectations, and if so, how?

Questions about Inspiring and Motivating

How can you present information the audience already knows in "interesting" ways?

What new information do you want the audience to retain when you're done?

How can you connect the new information to what the audience already knows?

How can you connect what you say to the listeners' values, beliefs, and attitudes?

What opportunities are there for you to incorporate inspirational support materials and good storytelling? (What stories, examples, or illustrations can you present that enhance the knowledge the audience holds?)

When seeking action, what are the recommendations you have for the audience?

What audience values should you emphasize as a foundation for action?

What will work to gain the audience's attention in the introduction?

Is a preview necessary?

What main points do you need to review in your conclusion?

Questions about Informing Open Audiences

How can you establish your credibility—your expertise and trustworthiness?

How does your delivery help or hinder your credibility with the audience?

What techniques can you incorporate that will help the audience learn the information?

What keywords or key phrases can you use for organizing new information?

Can you enumerate your points?

What information needs to be repeated to increase its retention?

In what ways can you use your delivery to emphasize important points?

To what degree is the information you provide consistent with the audience's values, beliefs, and attitudes?

Do your stories have fidelity and will the audience believe, accept, and retain them?

What techniques can you use to get information into the audience's long-term memory?

What can you say that will result in transferring information from one context to another that is relevant to the audience?

What information should you preview to increase audience retention?

What key words (reflecting the main concepts and information) can you introduce in the introduction, repeat throughout the presentation, and review in the conclusion to increase retention?

Questions to Create a Positive Attitude

What is your relationship with the audience?

What can you say that will strengthen your relationship with the audience?

What groups with whom the audience identifies can you discuss that support your position?

What emotional appeals can you make to this audience, and are they appropriate?

Questions to Help Avoid Threats to Positive Attitudes

What can you do to enhance your delivery to reflect enthusiasm and sincerity?

To what degree are you repeating information the audience already knows?

How well does the level of complexity of your presentation match the audience's capabilities?

Why are the audience members listening? What are their expectations? Are you prepared to meet those expectations?

How prepared are you to monitor and adapt to audience reactions as you speak?

SUMMARY

Positive audiences are interested in what you have to say and are open to learning information, and are often in agreement with your own positions on issues. There are two major types of positive audiences: supportive audiences and open audiences. A supportive audience is interested in the topic, has a positive attitude toward it, and has knowledge of it. The open audience is interested in the topic, has little or no knowledge of it, and has no fixed attitude. Speeches to positive audiences can have several goals, among them are: conveying information (informing and teaching), inspiring or seeking to maintain listeners' commitment (thus increasing resistance to detractors), and altering behavior in some way, such as increasing commitment or motivating action. Determining whether your audience is positive involves assessing both their attitude and knowledge on the basis of your knowledge and your ability to make inferences from what you know about them. There are many strategies you can employ to inspire and enhance a supportive audience:

- Adopt a style that complements your content.
- Expand on or present old information in new, interesting ways.
- Use the familiar as the foundation for the new.
- Emphasize and confirm existing audience values, beliefs, and attitudes.
- Use support materials that inspire, such as illustrations, examples, and stories.
- Focus on action, recommendations, and conclusions.
- Adapt the introduction and conclusion to inspire.

In speaking to open audiences, the goal is often to inform—to create a presentation in which the audience learns and retains desired information. The following strategies are geared toward accomplishing these goals:

- Establish your speaker credibility (your ethos)—your expertise and trustworthiness.
- Use memorable techniques such as repetition, patterns, novelty, and enumeration.
- Consider information from the audience's perspective—match their values, beliefs, and attitudes.
- Organize with the brain in mind—use techniques that move information to long-term memory.

- Use information transfer and build on the familiar.
- Adapt the introduction and conclusion to increase learning and retention.

While audiences might have an interest and be open to your presentation, they might not yet have a positive attitude. Recognizing that you are speaking to this type of listener means you need to incorporate some of the following strategies to evoke a positive attitude:

- Use positivity offset—draw on people's tendency to think positively about the unknown.
- Use an audience's positive attitude toward you as a basis for being positive about the issue.
- Use group identification—identify other desirable groups who support the issue.
- Use the bandwagon effect: "Everyone else is joining in—shouldn't you?"
- Use emotional appeals—less informed audiences are often affected by their emotions.

The speaker needs to recognize and avoid actions that can actually diminish an audience's positive attitude. Among these are using a style that turns off the listeners, sharing only information the audience already knows, exceeding the audience's capabilities, not meeting the audience's expectations; and including information that evokes a negative attitude.

VIDEO EXPERIENCE

1. "What Digital Reference Isn't" is a presentation on using Google that was given at a meeting of the Online Computer Library Center (OCLC). While this audience is mainly people interested in the topic area, see if you can identify techniques the speaker uses to convey memorable information.

2. We include a video copy of the sample student presentation at the end of this chapter. In this

presentation the student is talking to inform a positive audience about things to see and do when visiting Maui, Hawaii. Consider reading the transcription before you watch the video. Listen to the way in which the speaker affects audience interest and conveys information. In what ways did your reaction from reading the transcript change after watching the presentation?

THINKING BACK, THINKING AHEAD

1. Brainstorm as many situations as you can think up in which a speaker is usually speaking to an audience who have an interest in and positive attitude toward the topic. For example, presidential candidates at a support rally, a coach at a student rally for her team, or an instructor to students enrolled in their first driver's education course. Examine your list and decide which goals each speaker has set: to convey information (to teach), to inspire or maintain commitment, or to move to action. What do the various speakers do to achieve their goals? What lessons can you apply from these to developing a presentation to a positive student audience on the topics you identified earlier?

2. You have been asked to talk about college to a group of graduating seniors in your old high school who intend to go to college. What do you think they already know? What do you think they don't know? Think about the most unusual aspect of college you have discovered; how could you explain this by applying it to something which the students are already familiar with?

3. Sometimes speakers make presentations conveying information to an audience that already knows the information. For example, an employee meeting where the manager spends a half hour covering news items already distributed during the week by email. Why do you think a speaker would do this? What is the likely audience reaction? What should the speaker do? How should the presentation have been changed? What would you do if you started a presentation and found out as you were proceeding that the audience already knew the information you intended to convey?

4. The following is our "Topic Select-O-Matic." Completing each of the steps will help you in developing a presentation that is appropriate to a classroom, supportive audience.

Step 1. Brainstorm six items under each category that reflect your interests:

Your hobbies, activities, pastimes, interests, etc.:

1.	4.
2.	5.
3.	6.

Local, state, national, or international issues that interest you:

1.	4.
2.	5.
3.	6.

Things you know a lot about or things you'd like to know more about:

1.	4.
2.	5.
3.	6.

Step 2. Select the two items from each group that you like to talk about most.

Step 3. Will the class be a supportive audience on this topic?

Hobbies, activities, pastimes, interests:

1.
2.

1. Yes   No
2. Yes   No

Local, state, national, international issues:

1.
2.

1. Yes   No
2. Yes   No

Things you know or want to know:

1.
2.

1. Yes   No
2. Yes   No

Step 4. Select two of the topics the audience supports and write down as many ideas as you can about related issues you could talk about on this topic:

Topic 1   **Topic 2**

Step 5. Select from the list in step 4 the topic to begin exploring as your presentation.

Sample Speech

Presentation to a Positive Audience

Most "mainlanders" look favorably on the idea of taking a trip to Hawaii, and that consideration serves as the foundation for treating the students listening to this presentation as a positive audience. While the attitude toward a Hawaiian vacation is positive, the audience members probably don't have a clear idea of what to do in Hawaii. How should you spend your time? The speaker in this presentation answers this question, drawing from her personal knowledge.

Review the suggestions given in Chapter 12 about developing an introduction and conclusion for a positive audience. Identify the ways the speaker follows those suggestions. What are some other ways the speaker could effectively begin and conclude her presentation?

Identify transitions throughout the body of the speech. How do the transitions fulfill the function required of transitions? Would you use any different transitions? Where? Why?

Review the strategies covered in this chapter and identify those reflected in this presentation. What other strategies for speaking to a positive audience might have been applied?

Five Things Tourists Should Experience If They Visit Hawaii
Ilana Mainaga, student, Iowa State University, fall 2004

As you read this introduction consider these additional questions. How does Ilana attract her audience's attention? Would you look forward to hearing this speech? What strategies does she use to establish her credibility? Would you consider her credible? Why or why not? Identify the point at which audience relevance is established. What advice would you give the speaker to strengthen the relevance to you?

Imagine a place where there is no daylight-saving time, there is no snow, and people around you are saying "Maui no ka oi." Well, if you can imagine a place like this, then you're imagining Maui, my birthplace, and since I lived in Maui for about thirteen years, I can pretty much say "Maui no ka oi" as well. "Maui no ka oi" means "Maui is the best," and I can pretty much vouch for that. There are five things that I would recommend a tourist do if they were to travel to Hawaii. Those would be: experience the culture, impress the locals and natives, go on a whale watch or snorkel cruise, and travel to Hana, and Haleakala.

Introduction

◄ What is the thesis statement? Is it clearly established?

◄ What does the speaker gain by limiting the number of new pieces of information to five?

◄ What advice would you give the speaker regarding the preview of key points? Does the preview serve as a transition to the body of the speech?

Body

◄ How credible is her father as a source of support?

◄ How effective is this use of example and illustration?

◄ What is the impact of this early focus on action?

Experiencing the culture isn't that hard, because once you arrive you're immersed in the culture, but I would highly recommend that you attend workshops that are at the hotel that you're staying at and they're free. For instance, my dad works at a resort called the Four Seasons on Maui, and they have workshops for learning the Hula, learning some of the Hawaiian language, lei making, Hawaiian storytelling. But where else in the world can you do something like that but Hawaii? So I would definitely take advantage of that.

(continued)

Sample Speech for a Positive Audience continued

Here, the speaker demonstrates another goal of speaking to positive audiences. What is it? ➤

How motivated would you be to learn the information? ➤

To what degree is the speaker using emotional appeals here? For what purpose? ➤

How effectively does the speaker use emotion here? ➤

What assumptions does the speaker make about audience values here? ➤

How do the description, sincerity, and emotion impact you as a listener? ➤

What is the impact of repeating the name of the triggerfish? ➤

While you might never have heard of Hana, are you affected by positivity offset here? ➤

What does the speaker do to help the audience make sense of this information? ➤

What audience values are confirmed in the speaker's statements here? ➤

How well does the emotional appeal work here? ➤

Another reason why it would be good to visit Hawaii would be to impress the locals. Not many tourists can do this. But if you, for instance, know some Hawaiian connotations before you go, it would be a good idea. So I'm going to give you a little lesson on the Hawaiian language. Okay, this is a fish [shows overhead of a fish]. It is the Hawaiian triggerfish. It is the official, well actually unofficial, state fish of Hawaii. It has not been made official yet, but it will be. Does anyone offhand happen to know the name? All right, no? Okay (laughs), this is the Humuhumunukunuku apua'a. And if you can get that down, you're set to go to Hawaii and impress those locals, I'm telling you. Seriously, it's a good thing to know some Hawaiian pronunciations. It will get you far when you're in Hawaii. It's appreciated. The locals really like it when you know what you're pronouncing. They can help out a lot more, and they might be a little bit insulted if you don't know how to say the things. So it's generally good.

Next I think we should start our Maui journey. Here is Maui [shows an overhead of a map of Maui]. There, now you can see all of Maui, and we should start at Maalaea Bay and here is where you should go if you are in Hawaii, Maui specifically, during the winter months of December to March. You can go on a whale watch during this time, and it's really awesome because the humpback whales come down from Alaska and use Maui as a breeding grounds. If you can't make it to Maui during the months from December to March, I highly recommend going on a Molokini snorkel cruise. Molokini is an island right off Maui, and here it is [points to location on the map]. No one lives here. It is actually the tip of an extinct volcano. You can only get there by boat, and you can go there to snorkel, and it's really awesome because you have 150 feet of visibility. It's a once in a lifetime experience and you might even see Humuhumunukunuku apua'a.

Next on our journey, you should take a trip to Hana. And Hana is an awesome place to go for many reasons. It is right here on the other side of the island [shows location on map]. To get here you travel along the coast. It's at least a two- to three-hour drive, depending on how fast you go. The average speed limit in Hana is twenty miles per hour. The reason for this is that there are 617 winding turns, and there are fifty-six one-lane bridges, meaning if there's oncoming traffic, you have to wait. You just have to share turns crossing the bridge, so it takes a long time to get to Hana. You're right on a cliff, so if you drive off, you don't get to see Hana. It's really awesome if you get there, because you can see some of the natural pools which are considered sacred by Hawaiians. And if you make it to Hana, you just have to go to Hasegawa General Store. It's basically an old shack that's been there for basically forever, but you can get the obligatory "I Survived the Road to Hana" T-shirt and I highly recommend it.

Next on our trip is Haleakala—this is a great way to wrap up a trip on Maui. Haleakala is right here [shows location on map]. Haleakala is the world's largest dormant volcano. It's at a 10,023-feet elevation, and there are two reasons why you should visit Haleakala. It literally means "House of the Sun," and the reason for this is because you can see some awesome sunrises. You're above the clouds and you're pretty much immersed and you're taking part in the sunrise. You may have seen a sunrise from a plane before, but this is something totally different. And another reason why you should go is to see the silversword.

The silversword can only be found on Haleakala, and it's really pretty when it blooms, as you can see right here [displays photo of the flower] and it's a once-in-a-lifetime experience because you can only find it on Maui.

This concludes our trip to Maui, and if you guys ever get a chance to go to Maui, I really recommend that you guys keep in mind my suggestions because I think you'll have a lot more fun this way, and as we say in Hawaii, "Maui no ka oi."

Conclusion

◄ What audience values is the speaker appealing to here?

◄ What would the speaker like you to remember from the speech?

◄ What strategy is used to establish closure? Is it effective or would you suggest another approach?
The speaker prepared her presentation for a positive audience. Would the audience remain positive throughout the speech? Why or why not?

NOTES

1. R. P. Hart, G. W. Friedrich, & W. D. Brooks, *Public Communication* (New York: Harper & Row, 1975).

2. Hart, Friedrich, and Brooks, *Public Communication.*

3. Robert Redford, "The Sixteenth Annual Nancy Hanks Lecture," September 9, 2003, Washington, D.C., retrieved from Americans for the Arts Web site, at www.americansforthearts.org/global/print.asp?id=1297.

4. Adapted from Hart, Friedrich, and Brooks, *Public Communication.*

5. Data from the National Highway Traffic Administration, retrieved from Mothers Against Drunk Driving Web site, at www.madd.org/stats/.

6. L. Festinger, *A Theory of Cognitive Dissonance* (Stanford, CA: Stanford University Press, 1962). S. Oshikawa, "Can Cognitive Dissonance Theory Explain Consumer Behavior?" *Journal of Marketing, 33* (1969): 44–49.

7. T. Clevenger, *Audience Analysis* (Indianapolis: Bobbs-Merrill, 1966).

8. R. M. Perloff, *The Dynamics of Persuasion: Communication and Attitudes in the Twenty-first Century,* 2nd ed. (Mahwah, NJ: Erlbaum, 2003).

9. T. A. Buhr, T. I. Clifton, and B. Pryor, "Effects of Speaker's Immediacy on Receivers' Information Processing," *Perceptual and Motor Skills, 79* (1994): 779–783.

10. Perloff, *Dynamics of Persuasion.* S. B. Kenton, "Speaker Credibility in Persuasive Business Communication: A Model Which Explains Gender Differences," *Journal of Business Communication, 26* (1989): 143–157.

11. National Research Council, *How People Learn: Brain, Mind, Experience, and School* (Washington, D.C.: National Academy Press, 2000), 9.

12. National Research Council, *How People Learn,* 9–20.

13. J. T. Cacioppo & G. G. Berntson, "Relationship between Attitudes and Evaluative Space: A Critical Review, with Emphasis on the Separability of Positive and Negative Substrates," *Psychological Bulletin, 115* (1994): 401–423. T. A. Ito and J. T. Cacioppo, "Variations on a Human Universal: Individual Differences in Positivity Offset and Negativity Bias," *Cognition and Emotion, 19* (2005): 1–26.

14. R. E. Petty and J. Cacioppo, *Communication and Persuasion: Central and Peripheral Routes to Attitude Change* (New York: Springer-Verlag, 1986).

15. Petty and Cacioppo, *Communication and Persuasion.*

16. R. Zemke, "Humor in Training: Laugh and the World Laughs with You—Maybe," *Training, 26* (1991), retrieved from Expanded Academic, 2/16/04.

Chapter  15

Making Presentations to Neutral Audiences
To Interest and Inform

Goals

 To understand how neutral audiences differ in terms of interest and knowledge

 To distinguish among the three types of neutral audiences: detached, apathetic, and ambivalent

 To appreciate the underlying causes for a lack of interest

 To learn strategies for increasing a neutral audience's interest

 To learn strategies for increasing a neutral audience's knowledge

To learn strategies for addressing knowledgeable neutral audiences

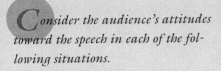

Consider the audience's attitudes toward the speech in each of the following situations.

Scenario 1. *As part of an ongoing company safety training program, every six months the employees listen to a presentation about the need for and proper use of safety equipment.*

Scenario 2. *A group of college students who are just beginning an internship with a large manufacturing company listen to a presentation on the company's retirement plan.*

Scenario 3. *A group of undecided voters is listening to a presidential candidate debate. They find certain things they like about both the Democrat and Republican candidates but also quite a few things they dislike.*

The audiences in these scenarios all have a neutral attitude toward the issue that is being discussed; however, they also differ in important ways. They vary in terms of audience interest and audience knowledge on the topic. In this chapter, we will examine the nature of neutral audiences and suggest possible strategies you can use with them to accomplish your presentation goals. ●

Neutral Audiences: Apathetic, Detached, and Ambivalent

The most defining characteristic of **neutral audiences** is that they hold no positive or negative attitudes toward the issues or topics—they neither support nor oppose the issue a speaker is discussing. As you read in Chapter 1, communication scholar Theodore Clevenger typed neutral audiences according to two dimensions: their interest in the issue and their knowledge of the issue.[1] Just as we used these two dimensions to distinguish between the two types of positive audiences, they can be used to distinguish neutral audiences. We will address three types of neutral audiences in this chapter: the *apathetic,* the *detached,* and the *ambivalent.* The first two, apathetic and detached, both lack interest in the issue; the apathetic audience has knowledge of the topic, while the detached audience does not. Ambivalent audiences differ from both of these, in that ambivalent audiences have an interest in the issue but are unable to decide whether to support or oppose it. Here is a summary of the qualities associated with each of these three:

> **Apathetic audience:** has a neutral attitude toward the topic or issue and has little or no interest in it but is knowledgeable about it.
>
> **Detached audience:** has a neutral attitude toward the topic or issue, has little or no interest in it, and has little or no knowledge about it.
>
> **Ambivalent audience:** has a neutral attitude toward the topic or issue but has both interest and knowledge of it.

In the first scenario, the employees have already learned the information that is being conveyed, and while they are certainly concerned about safety, they probably have little interest in hearing the same information they've heard before. This apathetic audience is likely to immediately tune out the speaker, which means they might very well miss any new information the speaker has to share. Again, the listeners need a reason for listening—some need must be met attending to the speech. The speaker needs to build on the knowledge the audience has rather than simply repeat it.

The internship students in scenario 2 are probably not very interested in hearing about the company's retirement plan and probably haven't acquired much knowledge about retirement plans either; thus, they represent a detached audience. In this situation, the speaker needs to recognize the lack of interest and knowledge in the audience and either modify the topic to match the audience's needs or identify ways to increase the audience's interest. Simply providing information without creating interest will have essentially no impact on the audience. The speaker needs to be clear about his or her goals for giving the presentation on this topic.

neutral audience An audience that holds no positive or negative attitudes toward the issues or topics—they neither support nor oppose the issue a speaker is discussing.

apathetic audience A type of neutral audience that has a neutral attitude toward the topic and has little or no interest in it, but is knowledgeable about it.

detached audience A type of neutral audience that has a neutral attitude toward the topic or issue, has little or no interest in it, and has little or no knowledge about it.

ambivalent audience A type of neutral audience that has a neutral attitude toward the topic or issue, but has both interest and knowledge of it.

Perhaps the goal is to provide a positive picture about being employed by this company, in hopes that the interns will consider applying for full-time positions in the future. While a good retirement package might provide some positive spin, college graduates probably have more concern about other aspects of the company that should be the focus of the presentation.

Scenario 3 represents an ambivalent audience, in which the voters find things they like and dislike about both candidates. They are stuck in neutral because of contradictory information. To help them get unstuck, a speaker needs to provide additional positive information and attempt to discount the negative information to which they have been exposed. Within ambivalent audiences, there can still be a range of neutrality. It is almost impossible to have information about an issue and be truly neutral. People usually have some inclination one way or the other, but because they don't feel strongly about that inclination, they consider themselves neutral. If possible, knowing which way the audience is leaning will improve your ability to adapt your presentation. Obviously, as a speaker, you will have less resistance to overcome if the audience is leaning in your direction.

Clevenger also refers to an audience's "commitment" to their position. We can understand someone being committed to supporting or opposing a particular issue, but it is also possible to be committed to remaining neutral. Uncommitted neutral audiences are indifferent to the issue, making it possible for a speaker to move them to a committed support by speaking to their indifference. Committed neutrals have examined the issue and decided not to take a side. Sometimes this is motivated by what Clevenger refers to as extrinsic grounds. Suppose you are in a conference meeting where your colleagues are split about a particular issue. Rather than risk alienating members of either side, you commit to remaining neutral by abstaining in any vote taken. The neutral audience might also have intrinsic grounds for being committed to neutrality. Clevenger felt that those who are committed to neutrality are similar in nature to audiences who are committed to a positive or negative position and just as difficult to change.[2] Our attention in this chapter will be on the audience that is not committed to remaining neutral but is simply indecisive. When you face a committed neutral audience, you will need to draw on relevant strategies from the three audience chapters, particularly the persuasive strategies discussed in Chapter 16.

Goal Setting for Neutral Audiences

The overall goal in speaking to neutral audiences is to essentially convert them to positive audiences. This conversion involves three specific goals: increasing interest, creating a positive attitude, and providing information. Comparing the different types of neutral audiences to the different types of positive audiences highlights the specific goals. Both the supportive and apathetic audiences have knowledge, but the apathetic audience lacks interest and has a neutral attitude. To convert the apathetic audience to a supportive audience requires increasing their interest and fostering a positive attitude. Both the open audience and the detached audience lack knowledge, but the detached audience, unlike the open audience, also lacks interest. To convert the

This speaker is confronted with a neutral audience, uninterested in what he has to say. •

detached audience to an open audience establishes the presentation goal—generating interest. Once a detached audience's interest is aroused, you are essentially addressing an open audience, one that wants to learn more, whose attitude you can potentially move toward the positive. Both the ambivalent and supportive audiences have knowledge and interest, but the ambivalent audience lacks the positive attitude. Thus, the goal with an ambivalent audience is to create a positive attitude toward the issue.

The same goals and strategies used with positive audiences can be applied to neutral audiences once you convert them to positive audiences. Thus, you might have a secondary goal of inspiring, increasing commitment, or calling to action the apathetic audience. Once interest is aroused in the detached audience, your goal will be to inform them and foster a positive attitude. Once you have developed the positive attitude in the ambivalent audience, you can then work on inspiring, attaining commitment, and motivating to act.

Identifying Apathetic, Detached, and Ambivalent Audiences

The processes for identifying the type of neutral audience are essentially the same as those discussed for the supportive audience and in Chapter 6. In determining the attitude, interest, and knowledge of your audience, you can rely on your own observations of the audience members and discussions with representatives of the audience. For situations in which you have an ongoing relationship with audience members, as with coworkers, you can generally tell when the members are apathetic because of the history you share with them. The manager explaining safety to the employees knows the employees have heard the information before. The manager will notice audience

Everyday Example
Creating Interest in a Neutral Audience

While serving as the chief executive of the Mille Lacs Band of Ojibwe Indians in Minnesota, Marge Anderson spoke at a monthly forum sponsored by the University of St. Thomas in St. Paul, Minnesota. This excerpt is from the beginning of her presentation. See if you can identify her efforts to generate interest in her presentation.

Aaniin. Thank you for inviting me here today. When I was asked to speak to you, I was told you are interested in hearing about the improvements we are making on the Mille Lacs Reservation, and about our investment of casino dollars back into our community through schools, health care facilities, and other services. And I do want to talk to you about these things, because they are tremendously important, and I am very proud of them.

But before I do, I want to take a few minutes to talk to you about something else, something I'm not asked about very often. I want to talk to you about what it means to be Indian. About how my people experience the world. About the fundamental way in which our culture differs from yours. And about why you should care about all this.

The differences between Indians and non-Indians have created a lot of controversy lately. Casinos, treaty rights, tribal sovereignty—these issues have stirred such anger and bitterness.

I believe the accusations against us are made out of ignorance. The vast majority of non-Indians do not understand how my people view the world, what we value, what motivates us.

They do not know these things for one simple reason: they've never heard us talk about them. For many years, the only stories that non-Indians heard about my people came from other non-Indians. As a result, the picture you got of us was fanciful, or distorted, or so shadowy, it hardly existed at all.

It's time for Indian voices to tell Indian stories.

Now, I'm sure at least a few of you are wondering, "Why do I need to hear these stories? Why should I care about what Indian people think, and feel, and believe?"

I think the most eloquent answer I can give you comes from the namesake of this university, St. Thomas Aquinas. St. Thomas wrote that dialogue is the struggle to learn from each other. This struggle, he said, is like Jacob wrestling the angel—it leaves one wounded and blessed at the same time.

Source: Marge Anderson, "The Value of Indian Culture," speech delivered at the First Friday club of the Twin Cities, March 5, 1999.

nonverbal cues that reflect their apathy, such as talking among themselves, poor eye contact, and lack of responsiveness. Any audience that lacks interest in a presentation is likely to display these cues. You've probably seen situations in which an audience doesn't laugh at a stand-up comic's jokes, eliciting the comment from the comic: "Is anybody out there?" The lack of laughter cues the comic that the audience is unresponsive to his or her humor—in essence, the audience lacks interest. Unlike the comic, you want to anticipate the level of interest as much as possible in advance of your presentation, rather than discovering it as you begin your talk.

Assessing what the audience already knows is probably easier than assessing their level of interest. The background of the audience members and your subsequent interactions with them provide the basis for determining their level of knowledge and understanding. What you must develop is an ability to determine what an audience doesn't know. What information will be new to them? What information do they need that they don't already have? This can be particularly important when addressing an ambivalent audience that you are trying to move toward being positive. Imagine a political candidate seeking his or her party's endorsement. Audience members may already know about the candidate but be unsure of whom they wish to support. The candidate needs to provide that audience with information they don't know that will help remove their ambivalence. See Act and Reflect 15.1.

In identifying a neutral audience, you have to be careful about assuming that other people are as interested in a topic as you. Such egocentric tendencies inevitably lead to weak and unsuccessful presentations. On the other hand, you have to be careful about assuming the audience won't be interested. Some topics hold intrinsic interest, in which case the audience is more like a positive audience than a truly neutral one. Discussions with selected audience members in preparation for a presentation can help you determine the audience's interest. However, the authors of this book have both been the victim of talking to representatives of some group only to discover that those representatives' interests differed from those of the audience members to whom we actually spoke. This happens when arrangements are made through a manager or committee and they have a particular agenda behind the topic on which they invite us to speak.

You should appreciate now that all neutral audiences are not the same, and therefore you cannot treat them in the same way when giving a presentation. You must adapt your presentation to the type of neutrality your audience represents and adopt strategies that will allow you to accomplish your goals. Effectively addressing neutral audiences requires correctly gauging the amount of effort to spend on changing their level of interest and the amount of effort to spend providing information. In the following sections, we will first deal with the general issues of lack of audience interest and lack of knowledge, and then look specifically at the three types of neutral audiences.

Detached and Apathetic Audiences: Strategies for Addressing Lack of Interest

Why would people not care about an issue? There are lots of reasons, and you need to try your best to determine the factors influencing your audience. Try to identify the reason an audience lacks interest and direct your presentation toward resolving that reason. Here are some general reasons:

1. **Perceived irrelevance:** the issue may not seem relevant to the audience members. Communication is need based; that is, we communicate for a reason, and that includes listening. We listen to others to meet our needs. If the audience does not believe your presentation will meet any of their needs, they may adopt a neutral attitude.

2. **Burned out:** audiences can get burned out on an issue to the point that they don't care anymore. Sometimes when people spend an enormous amount of time and energy on an issue without any success or change, they may just quit caring.

ACT&REFLECT

15.1: Determining the Type of Negative Audience

ACT • Identify two possible topics you could talk about toward which your classmates are likely to be neutral (ask around if you aren't sure). Ask them if they find the topics interesting. Next, ask them how knowledgeable they are about each topic. If they are knowledgeable, ask them if their attitude toward the topic is positive or negative, or if they are uncertain.

REFLECT • On a scale of 1 to 10, consider how interested they are in the topic, with 1 being not at all and 10 being strongly, and how knowledgeable they are about the topic (1, no knowledge, to 10, a lot of knowledge). Given these numbers for each topic and their attitudes, to what degree can the students be classified as apathetic, detached, or ambivalent? How would this affect your goal? How does this affect your focus?

For instance, sometimes parents repeat the same "lecture" to their children (on such topics as driving, drinking, or sexual activity) to the point that the children don't care and don't listen. (Did this ever happen to you?) Sometimes issues evoke such controversy that they are continually debated without resolution, thus producing despondency.

3. **Fear:** audiences might be afraid to care. Caring for something produces a certain amount of vulnerability and commitment. Remaining aloof is a form of protection. Suppose a colleague has a proposal for reorganizing the office staff. At first you might be inclined to be supportive, but then you remember that the last time you supported a similar proposal it never went anywhere. If you invested a lot of time and energy for naught, you might restrain yourself from caring about this new proposal.

4. **Inability:** audiences may be unable to care. They may not have the emotional or psychological strength to invest in an issue because of other factors in their lives. You've probably been in situations in which you were so overwhelmed with the things happening in your own life that it was difficult to turn any energy toward someone else's problems. The same phenomenon can happen to audiences. On 9/11, most of our students still showed up for class, but it was obvious we could not give that day's intended lectures; the students would have been unable to listen. Perhaps that happened to you, too, on 9/11. Recognizing the condition of our students led us to change the day's lecture into a discussion and sharing of feelings of what was transpiring that day.

After identifying the potential reasons the audience might not have interest or has lost interest in your topic, you can then decide which strategies to employ to help overcome them. Each strategy involves some adaptation to the audience members through such means as appealing to their needs, arousing their emotions, helping them connect to the issue, and developing an interesting and involving organization.

Appealing to Needs

Generally, the most powerful way to overcome lack of interest is to show how the topic is important to the audience, which directly addresses the issue of relevance. Consider explicitly telling the audience how listening to your presentation will benefit them, will meet their needs. To effectively do this, you must know the audience's needs. Chapter 8 presents some basic notions about human needs, including Maslow's hierarchy of needs, that can be applied to arousing the audience's interest. You may have to be creative in terms of what needs might be fulfilled by listening to your presentation. For example, why should interns listen to a speech on retirement benefits? Here's what a speaker might say:

> After your internships, many of you will be looking forward to securing permanent jobs. We all want jobs because they help us pay for the things we want in life. One thing jobs provide is a secure income when you finish your career—retire. When you're only twenty-one or twenty-two, retirement isn't usually something you even consider, but when you decide to take a job, you really owe it to yourself to examine how well you will be protected after devoting your life to a given company. I'm going to describe our company's retirement program, not so you can learn about our policies but so you can learn what is typical in a retirement package. After all, how many of you know about substitute annuity convertibility or phased retirement options?

This speaker focuses on issues such as security and protection to gain the audience's interest. Besides appealing to needs, you can also appeal to an audience's values and motives. You can increase a neutral audience's interest by selecting evidence that is directly related to their values and motives. Cite evidence that demonstrates to the audience how some of their needs will be met by listening to your presentation. Tell the audience why they should be interested. Try to find and include in your presentation evidence that supports your claim that they will benefit by listening.

If you have to stretch too far, however, the audience is unlikely to buy the connection you are trying to make. You shouldn't give a speech if there really isn't any reason for the audience to listen. There are often connections to audience needs that we're not even aware of, and the challenge is identifying those in order to explicitly state them. Even in your public speaking class, you should choose a topic for which there are real reasons the other students should listen other than just because they are a captive audience. Use the Act and

"Please don't make me use another water balloon to keep your attention."

© Ted Goff

ACT&REFLECT

15.2: Audience Needs

ACT • List three needs that are generally shared by the students in this class.

1.

2.

3.

REFLECT • How could each of these needs be connected to each of the following topics?

1. My hometown
2. Taking a course in _____ (use an unusual course you've taken or heard about)
3. A hobby or activity you know about

If you couldn't connect the needs and the topics, what other needs can you think of that would be fulfilled by listening to each of these topics?

1. My hometown
2. Taking a course in _____ (use an unusual course you've taken or heard about)
3. A hobby or activity you know about

Reflect: 15.2: Audience Needs, to consider what needs affect your classmates. As you complete that activity, think broadly about what constitutes needs and benefits. Sometimes the inability to link to an audience need means you are giving the wrong speech to the wrong audience. In this instance, consider changing your focus so that you can relate to audience needs.

Arousing Emotions

You've read about creating speeches to inspire; similarly, part of your presentation to a detached audience might focus on inspiring them—arousing their emotions. One way to accomplish this is by linking the audience's beliefs or values to specific emotional outcomes: "Your children's welfare is threatened by the failure of the school system to provide adequate security." "Your college has led you to believe that your degree will improve your career opportunities, but you've been duped." "Your efforts on behalf of this organization have resulted in the most productive quarter we've ever had." If the audience believes each of these statements, their emotions will be aroused. Concern for children's welfare will evoke fear; being duped raises anger; and success raises pride and positive self-esteem. In addition, each of these statements

AIDS activist Mary Fisher successfully aroused the emotions of a neutral audience of convention-goers. ●

MSL

raises the emotion of curiosity. Aroused emotions are likely to increase an audience's interest in finding out more information. Stories and figurative language are an effective way of arousing emotions and interest. Some speakers continually balance the evocation of emotion through figurative language with the presentation of information. The following excerpt from a speech that AIDS activist Mary Fisher gave at the 1992 National Republican Convention involves arousing emotions and providing facts.

The reality of AIDS is brutally clear. Two hundred thousand Americans are dead or dying; a million more are infected. Worldwide forty million, or sixty million or a hundred million infections will be counted in the coming few years. But despite science and research, White House meetings and congressional hearings, despite good intentions and bold initiatives, campaign slogans and hopeful promises—despite it all, it's the epidemic which is winning tonight.

In the context of an election year, I ask you—here, in this great hall, or listening in the quiet of your home—to recognize that the AIDS virus is not a political creature. It does not care whether you are Democrat or Republican. It does not ask whether you are black or white, male or female, gay or straight, young or old.

Tonight, I represent an AIDS community whose members have been reluctantly drafted from every segment of American society. Though I am white and a mother, I am one with a black infant struggling with tubes in a Philadelphia hospital. Though I am female and contracted this disease in marriage, and enjoy the warm support of my family, I am one with the lonely gay man sheltering a flickering candle from the cold wind of his family's rejection.[3]

A Question of **Ethics**

In using strong emotional imagery to arouse an audience's interest in unwed teenage mothers, a speaker made up stories about fictitious teens. While the stories were not based on real people, the events they reflected were not that uncommon and probably have happened more than one time. However, the impact of the story would not have been as great if the speaker had told the audience the situations were fictitious.

1. To what degree is the speaker's action ethical?

2. To what degree do the ends (arousing the audience's interest over a real problem) justify the means (presenting fictitious stories as real)?

Involving and Connecting the Topic to the Audience

We are more inclined to listen to things we personally identify with. When you give a presentation, select examples and evidence that are relevant to your listeners. Ultimately you want to "put your audience in the driver's seat" so they get the feeling of being immersed in the topic. You can apply this principle anywhere in your presentation, but here's an example of how you might apply it in an introduction on the topic of health care reform to your classmates.

> Workers contribute to the costs of health care insurance through policies offered in their workplace. The continuing escalation of health care costs has resulted in greater expense for the companies and their employees. In 1988 the average employee spent $52 a month on their health care premiums. In 2003 that cost escalated to an average of $201 a month, and the costs are likely to continue rising. There are many reasons why health care costs have escalated. Let me explain some of the reasons.

Now look at another introduction of the same topic that is intended to relate to students in your class:

> Right now, as students, many of you don't have to worry too much about your health care costs or access because you are covered by your parents' policies or by the policy provided through school. Others are working in jobs where you may already know about the cost of your health care insurance. For those of you who haven't participated in an employer's health care program, you're in for a rude awakening. You might not realize it, but the cost to employees, to you, the amount taken out of each month's take home pay for premiums, has escalated from an average of $52 in 1988 to $201 in 2003, and by the time you graduate it will be worse.[4] So why will your health care premiums be so much when your graduate? Let me tell you some of the reasons.

While both introductions essentially cover the same information, the second one makes the topic more personal, thus increasing the likelihood that the students will listen. Putting the audience into the presentation is one of the best ways to illustrate how their needs are affected. You both create a need for them to learn and make the topic relevant to them. You remove their neutrality.

Even evidence can be made more personal by putting the audience in the picture rather than presenting the information in an abstract form. Putting your audience in the picture when you share statistics and quotations helps make them more tangible and visceral. For example, a speaker might say, "Look around you at the other audience members. As you look around, realize that almost one out of every three people you see here will die from heart disease—the number one cause of death in the United States." In a similar manner, presenting support in a narrative format that places the audience in the situation can increase their interest and move them from their neutrality. See Act and Reflect 15.3.

Organizing to Enhance Interest

You need to consider which of the organizational patterns discussed in Chapter 9 works best with the information you have to generate interest. If you are additionally going to provide information to the audience, then a general organizational pattern that first focuses on creating interest and then focuses on providing information should be adopted, such as Monroe's motivated sequence. The complexity of Monroe's motivated sequence allows the speaker to connect to the detached audience by appealing to their needs and emotions while informing them about the issue. In speaking to an apathetic audience, the familiar-unfamiliar organizational framework may be best. It strives to create interest and confirm knowledge by building common ground with the audience; this allows the speaker to then move to the presentation of a message that both informs the audience and supports the communication goal. The specific organizational framework you choose will depend on which strategies you employ to generate interest. For example, if you decide your best strategy is to present three reasons you believe the audience should care about your topic, then you might organize those reasons according to some topical pattern or prioritize them according to their relative importance.

Besides matching your organizational choice to the strategies you are adopting, consider the ways you can organize the points within that framework. For example, if

15.3: Connecting with and Involving the Audience

ACT • For the following topics, think about what you could tell each of the designated audiences to increase their sense of involvement or connection with the topic.

Topic	Audience
1. Your major	Middle school children, grades seven and eight
2. A proposal to provide flexible hours to hourly workers	Senior managers and company executives
3. Highlights of your last vacation	A travel club that meets at the local library
4. A topic of your choosing for your next presentation	Your classmates

REFLECT • For which topic would it be easiest to generate audience involvement? Why? Which would be the hardest? Why?

With which audience would it be the easiest to connect? Why? Which would be the hardest? Why?

you have selected Monroe's motivated sequence, you have made a commitment to present a rather complex message to your neutral audience. Although you can "sort" the knowledge you wish to convey to your audience so that the five points contain the information intended, you are still in a position to organize the information deposited in each step to create the greatest impact. For example, could the problem step be constructed chronologically or spatially or according to cause/effect reasoning? Could the solution step be structured topically? Could you tell a story to develop the visualization step?

With the one-sided and familiar-unfamiliar frameworks, also think about how you can develop each of their major parts. If you are using the one-sided argument, what order will have the greatest impact? Do the points vary in their priority? Would chronological or geographical order work best? Is there a mnemonic device or key phrase you could repeat? The familiar-unfamiliar framework also requires you to make decisions about the organization of each step. Could the familiar points be developed through a story, for example, or through an additional organizational framework?

Hook the Audience's Attention For an audience to learn new information, they have to first hear it (or perceive it) before they can retain it (put it into memory). In Chapter 6 you read about how the brain uses filters in processing information before moving it to memory. Remember that it is the job of the reticular activating system (RAS) of the brain to prioritize all of the sensory information your listeners will receive. With all audience types, the RAS should be of concern to the speaker, but when presenting to the neutral audience, appeals to interests are especially important. Your neutral audience is being bombarded with all sorts of stimuli at the same time you are speaking to them. Beginning with your first words, you will have to "hook"

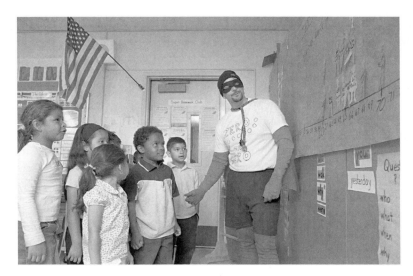

Wearing a costume while speaking to young audience works to hook their attention. ●

them, or attract their attention, so that all of the other stimuli are ignored and the focus becomes you and your message. If this initial contact does not occur, your chances of delivering the rest of your message to your neutral audience and reaching your own communication goals are greatly reduced. What can you say or do that is relevant to your topic that will hook your neutral audience so that other stimuli are minimized, and you and your message become their focus?

Use the Introduction as the First Step in Generating Interest With all organizational frameworks and all neutral audiences, it will be to your advantage to give some careful thought to beginning your presentation with an attention-grabber that does just that—grabs your audience and motivates them to want to hear your presentation. Surprise your audience; startle your listeners; knock that neutral audience off of its neutral fence as soon as you begin to speak. However, make sure that your attention-grabber is relevant to the topic of your presentation and stays within the bounds of good taste. As we already mentioned, students in a public speaking classes of one of the authors of this book were in the habit of beginning their speeches with an attention-grabber that went like this: "Today I'm going to tell you everything you've always wanted to know about sex but were afraid to ask. Now that I have your attention, let's talk about student financial aid." Aside from the fact that repeated uses of this strategy caused it to become less and less effective, there was also the troublesome fact that the actual topic of the presentation was a let-down, at least in comparison to what was promised in the attention-grabber! Also, sometimes the listeners were confused about the actual topic of the speech. So what is the moral of this example? Be sure to select an effective attention-grabber that relates to your topic and initially presents your topic as worthy of your listeners' attention.

A second component in the introduction to neutral audiences is to establish the "you," or to establish the relevance of the presentation. Remember that the neutral audience may be playing a tape in their minds that says over and over "Why do I have to be here?" Take some time to think about the important reasons and valuable results that will answer this question to their satisfaction, and change that tape to "I'm glad I'm here." If there are several ways you can demonstrate the relevance of your topic to the neutral audience, all the better. In the earlier excerpt, Marge Anderson provided an explanation in her introduction of why the forum attendees should listen to her presentation.

What about your credentials? Will it be important to inform or remind your audience of your credentials? With this component, the answer is maybe. Does your neutral audience already know you? Are you speaking to a group of professional colleagues? Are you making a student presentation at a national professional organization? Are your listeners peers in a campus organization with whom you have worked on numerous service projects? Is there some aspect of your credentials that, if known to your audience, would add to your hook? In instances when you believe your neutral audience does not know you, your credentials must be included. However, even when presenting to an audience whose members do know you, consider presenting your credentials in a surprising way.

You might be able to attach your credentials to another component of your introduction. Perhaps you are advocating legislation that prohibits talking on cell phones in cars, except in emergencies. You establish relevance by citing statistics about the number of accidents in your state that are believed to be caused by drivers talking on cell phones and remark, "I caused a car accident recently while talking on a cell phone. My experience led me to talk with law enforcement officers about the number of incidents they are experiencing where the cell phone is the cause of the accident." Your credentials become a part of the topic relevance. You might also be able to grab the audience's attention by beginning your presentation with a first-person account of your accident: "As I moved closer to the intersection, I vaguely noticed the other driver and planned to stop. But, the person on the phone asked a question and . . ." You would continue to describe details of the event that ended in an accident.

The thesis and preview of major points are necessary with all audiences, simply because supplying these two important pieces of information makes the responsibility of the audience, that is, to listen, easier. With an organizational framework such as the one-sided argument, however, it is probably unnecessary to preview each point you will discuss in the introduction, but you can summarize the nature of the content of your presentation. For example: "Today I will show you three ways you can fly to your spring break vacation and have the airlines pay you!"

Use the Conclusion to Reinforce Their Interest The conclusion of your presentation is important not only because it establishes closure but also because you want to end in such a way that the neutral audience remains positive about having attended your presentation. If you are using Monroe's motivated sequence, you can end with an action step that inspires the audience to some degree of involvement with your topic, or you can move from the visualization step directly to a stock conclusion. However, in both cases, after you have indicated the action(s) you want your audience to take or the point(s) you would like them to remember, establish closure in a manner that speaks directly to them. For ideas for your closure, look at your attention step or introduction. Do you begin your presentation with a brief story or question or startling statement that you could also use to establish closure? If so, refer to the story or question or statement again one last time.

For the familiar-unfamiliar organizational framework, the conclusion could be developed by looking to the common ground that was established in the "familiar" point. After establishing common ground with your audience, you moved into an area that was unfamiliar. Lead your audience back to the familiar in your conclusion by reminding them about the common ground you share.

For the one-sided organizational framework, if your points are arranged in order of least to most important, your last point might serve as a conclusion: "And finally, you should be aware that . . ." However, if it does not seem that any particular arrangement of major points will be more beneficial than any other, it is wise to add a conclusion. The conclusion could repeat the thesis, or a reference to the attention-grabber could create a sense of cohesion.

Detached Audience: Strategies for Addressing Lack of Knowledge

Once you've gained the interest of a detached audience, you have created a positive audience, the open audience—one that has interest, a desire to listen and learn, but lacks knowledge. Essentially, this means that the remainder of your presentation to the detached audience should draw on the strategies and discussion in Chapter 14. Realize that in just one presentation you have an opportunity to significantly affect and change an audience that started with no interest and no knowledge on your topic. Here is a quick review of the information from Chapter 14 followed by some additional strategies *not* covered in Chapter 14.

- When necessary, establish your credibility (ethos). Audiences must be convinced that you know what you are talking about if they are going to learn the information you are conveying. The audience needs to trust your expertise.
- Use memorable techniques. Your audience will remember the information better when you repeat key words and important information, use easily recalled patterns, connect the information to something memorable or novel, and enumerate the main points.
- Present information that is consistent with the audience's predispositions and that has fidelity. People believe and accept information that is consistent with their existing beliefs and knowledge.
- Organize with the brain in mind. Keep the information simple, relevant, and involving, and present it in a way that makes sense to the audience. We present more on this later.
- Use information transfer and build on the familiar. Use general or conceptual terms and help the audience relate that information to their own circumstance. Correct misconceptions and build on what the audience already knows.
- Adapt the introduction and conclusion. Preview and review the main points you want the audience to learn.

Creating a Foundation for Understanding

In the beginning of your presentation, you may need to orient the audience to the topic and provide some fundamental concepts and definitions. You need to explain relevant but unfamiliar terms. The audience will be in a better position to understand the rest of your presentation once they understand key terms and fundamental concepts. In addition, you might provide additional background information to make sure they are confident of their ability to follow the rest of your speech (see Act and Reflect 15.4).

Using Supportive Materials Strategically

You need to also be strategic in your use of evidence and supportive materials. Why should the audience believe the information you are sharing with them is true? You need to consider how much evidence is needed to support the information you are presenting. Incorporate evidence that makes an issue relevant to an audience. Use evidence that demonstrates the importance of the issue to the specific audience. Use evidence that is clear and credible. In those instances when your expertise has been established, you might have less need to provide additional evidence beyond your own word. (Think about your openness to what your instructors tell you without their citing supportive material.) More evidence is probably needed the less the audience is aware of your expertise.

ACT & REFLECT

15.4: Strategies for Increasing Interest and Knowledge

ACT • Reexamine each of the three scenarios at the beginning of this chapter and identify appropriate strategies for increasing the audiences' interest and knowledge.

	Strategies to Increase Interest	Strategies to Increase Knowledge
Employees hearing about safety training		
Interns hearing about retirement		
Undecided voters		

Identify two topics toward which your classmates are probably neutral and that you're considering for a presentation. Identify a strategy for each that you could use in increase interest and knowledge.

	Strategies to Increase Interest	Strategies to Increase Knowledge
Topic 1: _____		
Topic 2: _____		

REFLECT • Which of these five topics will require the strongest support material and most strategic use of that material? Why?
   Which strategies will be the most difficult to accomplish? Why?
   What organizational patterns work best for each scenario?

Presenting Memorable Reasoning and Arguments

You can use reasoning and argument strategically to help convey information. The development of logical arguments in the form of syllogisms or enthymemes is another way of conveying knowledge. If you are attempting to convey derivative knowledge (knowledge based on deduction or on reasoning rather than observation), then you will need to present evidence, explain your premises, and help direct the audience to the conclusions. In some instances, your goal is for the audience to remember your argument. This means presenting each point clearly, repeating the points, and reviewing them as a way to ensure their retention.

Ambivalent Audiences: Strategies for Removing Indecision

People who have knowledge about a topic but who have no strong feelings either in favor of or opposition to it are more critical when listening to additional information than those who lack knowledge or who have strong feelings on the issue.[6] This means that while your audience has no strong attitudes toward the issues, they will be critical of the arguments and information you provide. Their evaluation will be relatively unbiased, which means they should respond well to strong, well-supported arguments. This creates a bit of a paradox, in that you have an audience that isn't very interested in listening, but when they do, they listen objectively and critically.

Overcoming the indecision of an ambivalent audience would seem to be an easy task; just find out what's causing the hang-up and eliminate it. This strategy has merit, but is not so easy to accomplish. Remember, an ambivalent audience has information on both sides of the issue and has interest in the issue. As you read earlier, it's hard to find anyone who has information on both sides of an issue and not have some inclination toward one side. It's almost impossible to have that much balance of information on two opposing issues. For these people, the underlying issue is probably lack of confidence in their choice or decision. Try to think about some issue on which you are ambivalent—a choice of two candidates for an office, best movie of the year, favorite class, whether to study or go out (okay, so maybe there's no ambivalence on that one). You probably are leaning toward one candidate, or one movie, or one class, but there's enough doubt in your mind to prevent you from totally committing. As a speaker, you need to remove doubts and provide sufficient information to help increase confidence. The following sections detail spe-

Uncertainty motivates listeners (and readers) to seek information. In this case it is an open book. ●

ACT&REFLECT

15:5 Adapting to the Three Types of Neutral Audiences

A C T • Identify a topic and a particular audience that fit each of the three neutral audience types. Identify two strategies you could use in developing a positive audience attitude.

Audience Type	Topic	Who	Two Strategies
Detached			1.
			2.
Apathetic			1.
			2.
Ambivalent			1.
			2.

R E F L E C T • In which of these situations do you think you would be most successful? Why?
Which would be the most difficult? Why?

cific strategies you can use when speaking to ambivalent and apathetic audiences. See Act and Reflect 15.5.

Utilizing the Desire to Remove Uncertainty

Fortunately, most of us don't like to be in a state of indecision; we want to settle on a choice. According to **uncertainty reduction theory,** which was developed initially to explain people's interpersonal behavior when first meeting, people dislike uncertainty and are motivated to obtain information to remove it.[6] As there are a number of exceptions to this principle, others modified it when applying it to other contexts like organizations.[7] The theory essentially claims that people are motivated to seek information when the uncertainty concerns things that have a direct effect on them and when the reward associated with gaining information outweighs the cost. You are more likely to press an instructor for clarity about an assignment's requirements when the assignment and course grade are critical to completing your degree than if you're taking the course pass–no pass. On the other hand, if the instructor intimidates you and you are concerned that questioning the requirements will have a negative impact on you, then you are less inclined to reduce uncertainty. Similarly, ambivalent audiences face uncertainty about something for which they care. Such audiences are likely to want information that will help them

uncertainty reduction theory A theory that was developed initially to explain people's interpersonal behavior when first meeting; people dislike uncertainty and are motivated to obtain information to remove that uncertainty.

remove their uncertainties. Directly discuss the audience's uncertainty, let them know you have information to reduce it, and then present that information. This is another way of creating a need to listen. For example, a speaker might make a statement such as "There appear to be equal benefits to both proposals; however, comparing the costs of one proposal to another shows that proposal B is the better choice. Let me explain the comparisons." The audience should be open to listening to the speaker's information because it will help them remove uncertainty.

The more important an issue is to an ambivalent audience, the more you can expect them to want information. As a speaker, you need to have some sense of how important your topic is to your audience. The less important it is, the less likely they will be to listen. You might need to spend part of your presentation making the issue more important to the audience—making it more relevant. There might also be other issues that restrict their openness to reducing uncertainty. At the end of a lecture, instructors often ask students if there are any questions (this is a check for uncertainty), and most of the time nobody asks any questions. Does this mean that the students have understood everything from the lecture? Probably not. Students weigh the importance of finding out the answers to their questions to the costs involved in speaking out in class or delaying the end of class. There also might be times where people don't want their uncertainty reduced for fear of what the certainty might be (hearing unwanted news).[8] Imagine working someplace where there are rumors of the plant closing. Workers might not want to reduce their uncertainty if they fear the rumors are true. You must adapt your presentation to address factors that have led to and are sustaining your audience's ambivalence.

While he was the president of the accounting and consulting company Price Waterhouse World Firm, Dominic A. Tarantino delivered the 1995 commencement address at his alma mater, the University of San Francisco. The new graduates were probably a neutral audience, ambivalent about their career choices; he created uncertainty by telling them they need to become knowledge-based products and then proceeded to offer an explanation and information to reduce the very uncertainty he had created:

> I recently read a fascinating article that says the future will belong to those who can combine brainpower, technology, and information to create knowledge-based-products. A knowledge-based product is one which—to quote—"filters and interprets information to enable the user to act more effectively." If you want a piece of the future, you—yes, you—have to become a knowledge-based product.
>
> You have to be a self-contained, self-motivating, totally unique, continually improving package of technology, information and brainpower that makes your users more effective, whether they be employers, colleagues, customers or clients.
>
> Let's look at the key characteristics of the business world you are about to enter. And then let's talk about how you mold yourself into a knowledge-based product that will succeed in that world.[9]

Expanding the Positives While Diminishing the Negatives

A presentation to an ambivalent audience should affirm what the audience already knows and then provide additional arguments they may not have considered. Expand on the advantages and positive aspects of the side of the issue you are advocating.

However, you can't ignore the opposing information the audience already knows. Remember, ambivalent audiences have information that is both supportive and contrary to your position. You should openly discuss the contrary aspects of the topic—shaping the discussion in favor of your perspective; acknowledge the contrary arguments; and provide evidence to refute them or minimize their relevance and impact. However, if you are unable to refute the opposing arguments, then you are better off ignoring them.[10] To accomplish this balance, Monroe's motivated sequence is useful because you can introduce new information and recognize and refute negative views as well as emphasizing the viewpoint you wish the audience to embrace.

● GETTING TO WORK

Neutral audiences may lack interest, lack knowledge, be apathetic, or be ambivalent. To be successful, you will need to identify and address the particular factors underlying your audience's neutrality. The following guidelines are meant to help you assess the audience and select relevant strategies.

Preliminaries

Decide how much interest the audience members have in your topic.

Determine how much knowledge they have on the topic.

Your overall goal is to create a positive audience. Set your goals according to the audience type: detached audience—needs to become interested and informed; apathetic audience—needs to become interested; ambivalent audience—needs to move toward a supportive position.

Creating Audience Interest

Why do the audience members lack interest? Perceived irrelevance? Burnout? Fear? Inability? Some other reason?

Identify and discuss audience member needs that are relevant to your topic.

Arouse the audience member's emotions—use figurative language and stories.

Talk in a way that involves and connects the topic to the audience.

Select an organizational framework that contributes to building interest.

Hook your audience member's attention on you and your topic.

Capture the audience's attention in your introduction and begin to explain the relevance of the topic.

Use the conclusion to reinforce the audience interest and review important information.

Detached Audiences: Addressing the Lack of Knowledge

Use the strategies appropriate for an open audience: establish credibility, use memorable techniques, present information consistent with audience predispositions, organize with the brain in mind, use information transfer, and adopt an appropriate introduction and conclusion.

Include an explanation of relevant terms, concepts, and history to create a foundation for understanding.

Include evidence that is relevant, important, clear, and credible.

Present reasoning and arguments that each audience member can remember. State each point clearly, repeat important points, and review them as necessary.

Ambivalent Audiences: Removing Indecision

Identify and address the reasons for the audience members' ambivalence.

Arouse their interest and be prepared for critical listening.

Identify what information the audience members lack that will help to reduce their ambivalence.

Identify what issues the audience members are unaware of that are relevant.

Discuss the audience members' uncertainty and explain how your information can reduce it—then do so.

Discuss the positive aspects of your position while diminishing the negatives or the importance of alternatives.

SUMMARY

Neutral audiences can be classified according to their interest and their knowledge of an issue, producing three types of audiences: detached, apathetic, and ambivalent. Detached audiences have no interest in and no knowledge of the topic. Apathetic audiences have knowledge about the issue but lack interest. Ambivalent audiences have knowledge and interest but are not inclined to be either positive or negative toward the issue. The overall goal is to convert the neutral audience to a positive audience by increasing interest, creating a positive attitude, and providing information.

Among the reasons an audience member might lack interest are perceived irrelevance, burnout, fear, and inability. Understanding why an audience lacks interest in a topic will help you develop appropriate strategies to generate interest. Among the strategies

you can employ are appealing to needs, arousing the audience's emotions, involving the audience and connecting the topic to them, and organizing the presentation to enhance interest. You should try to hook their initial interest in your introduction and reinforce that interest in the conclusion. Once interest is aroused in the detached audience, they essentially become an open audience (interested, but lacking knowledge), strategies on this audience type were covered in Chapter 14. Additional strategies we covered in this chapter for addressing the lack of knowledge include: creating a foundation for understanding, using supportive materials, and using memorable reasoning and arguments.

Ambivalent audiences already have knowledge on the topic, and therefore, the focus has to be addressing the underlying causes ambivalence.

One strategy to use with these audiences is to utilize people's desire to remove or reduce uncertainties. Expanding on the positives and diminishing the negatives is another.

VIDEO EXPERIENCE

1. Those invited to deliver commencement addresses often face audiences who are more anxious to be done with the experience than to listen to the speaker's comments. Speakers are challenged with gaining and holding their listeners' interest. You can find many examples of commencement addresses on the Internet; we've included one in MySpeechLab in which the speaker, Dr. Steven Wood, a lecturer in the Haas School of Business at Berkeley, addresses the 2005 graduating class. Listen to how he engages students who might otherwise be apathetic.

2. We include another video copy of the sample student presentation at the end of this chapter. You may choose to follow along with the transcription as you watch. The speaker is talking about voting in campus elections; students are typically apathetic about participating. Listen to his attempts to generate interest and create a positive attitude.

THINKING BACK, THINKING AHEAD

1. Create a list by brainstorming as many situations as you can think of in which the audience was neutral at the beginning of a presentation. Next to your item for each audience, identify where they stood in terms of the two dimensions of interest/lack of interest and knowledgeable/unknowledgeable. Label each audience detached, apathetic, or ambivalent. For each situation, indicate whether at the end of the presentation the audience was still neutral, became positive, or became negative toward the issue. For those that became positive, indicate what the speaker did to accomplish this.

2. For each of the following situations, decide what strategies you could apply to move the audience from neutrality:

   a. As part of a course, you are required to make a presentation covering the reading that all the students were assigned to read. The topic is not something the students find very interesting. (You can decide what the class and topic might be for this scenario, e.g., an English class discussing Shakespeare's sonnets, an engineering class covering principles of design, or a psychology class covering research articles on learning theory.)

   b. You are speaking to a group of high school seniors who are visiting your campus. They have also visited the campus of another school similar to yours (could be an in-state rival if you have one). They are ambivalent about which school to attend. They have interest and knowledge of both schools.

   c. You are giving a report about the past year's activities in your office to the annual meeting of company managers and executives from across the country.

3. You are giving a presentation to this class on a topic (you decide one that is appropriate) in which they have no initial knowledge or interest. You are limited to five minutes to talk about this topic. What would be the first thing you would tell your audience? What information would be the best to convey? Why?

Sample Speech:

Presentation to a Neutral Audience

The speaker attempted to generate a positive attitude in his student audience toward voting in campus and noncampus elections. The listeners were treated as an apathetic audience, having a neutral attitude toward voting, having knowledge about elections, but lacking interest.

Review the strategies covered in this chapter and identify those reflected in this presentation. What other strategies for speaking to a neutral audience might have been applied? Identify the suggestions from Chapter 12 about introductions and conclusions for a neutral audience the speaker followed. What other ways could the speaker effectively begin and conclude his presentation?

The Importance of Your Vote

Ross Kelderman, student, Iowa State University, fall 2004

Which approach does Ross use to attract attention? What other approach from Chapter 12 could be used here to motivate you?

What strategies does the speaker use to gain audience interest? How well do they work?

What impact does the speaker's ambiguity in identifying his topic have on a neutral audience?
Where does Ross establish audience relevance? What methods for establishing audience relevance does Ross implement in his speech? To what degree do these two sections connect the topic and the audience? How does that impact interest?

How well does the introduction observe the guidelines suggested for addressing neutral audiences?

What type of visual support might be used in the following sections of this speech?

To what degree does Ross acknowledge members of the audience who might not be neutral?

When I was in eighth grade I was at the Christian School, and it was so important that I could go to Valley High School with all my friends. I argued with my parents non-stop for seven months about this. Come the end of the eighth-grade year, I was still registered at Des Moines Christian for high school, and I did not win; I had to go to the Christian High School, because it was their decision. Fast-forward a few years, and you get to my senior year of high school. I really wanted to go to Iowa State, and my parents wanted me to go to Dordt College in Sioux Center, Iowa, or Central College in Pella, Iowa, and neither one appealed to me at all, especially Dordt. It smells terrible up there, and I didn't like the small campus and stuff like that

So I guess what my speech is on is kind of the difference between that, as we get older, we get to make more decisions in life. I know this morning if I wanted to sleep until two in the afternoon, nobody's going to stop me.

There are a lot of decisions like that we need to make now, since we're on our own. There are other decisions that affect more than just ourselves; so, we elect officials to make these decisions for us. Together those people make a lot of decisions on the national level, they'll do like taxes, and speeding limits, and who can get married and who can't and things of that nature.

On the more local level, maybe your Greek house cabinet or your residence house cabinet will make decisions on what social events are going to be done with our house dues, or, will incense be allowed on our floor, something like that. I know that's one we voted on. So as Iowa State students, most of us are eighteen I think, and even if you aren't, you still get to vote in a number of Iowa State elections. I've done research on voter turnout at various venues and I'll just go over those real quick

The first one we'll talk about—IRHA [Inter-Residence Hall Association]. This is a group that represents just residence hall students, so if you live in Greek or off campus, this really doesn't apply to you. But about half the class that does live in the residence hall, so bear with me on this. Last spring we had our elections and there's five thousand students who lived in the residence halls at the time. [Displays pie graph] Of those about five hundred actually voted, that's about 9 percent. Those numbers are pretty low.

Now those of you that don't live in the residence halls, you would have been able to vote in the GSB [Government of the Student Body] elections, which was also in the spring, and that affects all students. You paid about thirty dollars to them per semester in dues, and then with that, they support things like Cy-Ride [local bus service] and they make other decisions like which campus groups get money and which ones don't—decisions like that. [Displays pie graph] For that there were about twenty seven thousand students who could have voted, and of that about five thousand did. As you can see, it's about 18 percent of all of the voters voting.

Now in contrast with these two, I'd like to show you the percentage of Iowans who voted in the 2000 presidential election [displays pie graph]—49 percent. It's much higher as you can see; it's still only half the people who can vote, voting. It's still a larger number. And then compared to the national election we were a little bit below average [displays pie graph]—51 percent of national voters over the age of eighteen voted, whereas in Iowa it was 49 percent. My point in all this is that many people fail to exercise their right to vote. I feel there are several downsides to this.

Noted essayist and critic George Nathan would agree with me on this. He's quoted as saying, "Bad officials are voted by good people who don't vote." I think this is so true. That may seem odd to some of you, since you only get one vote in each election and very rarely is an election won by one vote. But there are some things to remember on that. First off, if you use that excuse, you're not the only one using the excuse. I think, like on this [displays last pie graph again], these 49 percent of people, I bet like half of those are using that excuse as a reason not to vote. Let's say we get together and vote. They could rule any election. They're close enough. These people matter. I'd also like to compare it to littering. Sure if you throw one pop can out your window it's not going to destroy the environment. But if everybody did that, we'd live in a landfill, it would be terrible. I think it's a lot like that. Another example has to do with the student government

I ran for UDA [Union Drive Association—a residence hall association] president last year, only 8 percent of the residents voted and I got almost all the votes, but that's still only like one hundred votes for three thousand people. So when I go to administrators and say "This is something they'd like to see done," I'm not taken as seriously as if, say, I'd gotten like a thousand votes or two thousand votes. So it's not really so much voting for a particular person, because the person I ran against probably didn't disagree on any of the issues. My opponent probably wasn't any less qualified than me. I feel I won because my name was higher on the ballot. That's okay, but I'd like to see more voters actually voting for, not necessarily one person, but just more voters voting. It's sort of the same in national elections.

I think our age group is vastly underrepresented in the numbers of people who vote. Because of this politicians tend to represent the older groups. If you watched the debates, you probably noticed Medicare and Social Security come up a lot, and we don't have a whole lot of interest in this. We'd be more interested in more money going to education to lower tuition. I've heard some students talk about the legalization of marijuana and stuff like that. These are issues we want to hear about, and I think if more people in our age group would vote, we'd be more represented by them. For those people who vote already, I applaud you. I remember I had you raise your hand in the GSB [campus-wide student body] election. I was so amazed by the amount of you that did. It seemed like the only people who didn't raise their hands were the people who were in high school last year, so that's awesome.

(continued)

◄ How well does the discussion of student fees appeal to their needs?

◄ What could be done to increase the emotional impact of these statistics?

◄ Here the speaker develops a logical argument. To what degree is it clear? How effective is it?

◄ How effective is this outside source? What could make it stronger?

◄ How effective is the speaker in this section in addressing apathy caused by perceived irrelevance?

◄ To what degree is this argument effective? What could make it stronger?

◄ How well does this metaphor help the speaker's goal?

◄ How credible is Ross so far regarding this topic? How does the disclosure of his run for residence hall president affect his credibility?

◄ How well does this personal story support the speaker's claims?

◄ How well does this work as a logical argument?

◄ Here the speaker makes a logical argument while connecting the topic to the audience. How effective is this?

◄ What impact is created by the speaker displaying a knowledge and understanding of the audience?

Sample Speech for a Neutral Audience continued

Here the speaker connects the topic to the audience, but what impact is there by his pointing out their failure to vote?

➤

What does Ross want the audience members to remember as a result of his speech?

➤

The speaker is providing new information for the audience members to know. What strategies are used to help the students remember the information?

➤

How effective is this appeal to action? Why?

➤

What types of appeals does the speaker use in this segment of his speech?

➤

How does Ross establish closure?

➤

How credible is this source? How effective is effort to arouse emotions?

➤

How well did Ross implement the guidelines for concluding a speech to neutral audiences?

➤

Which of the organizational frameworks for neutral audiences has Ross implemented? What feedback would you give Ross about his choice?

To what degree do you believe this speech would move the audience from their position of neutrality? Why?

But I did some research and in the IRHA [residence hall] election. There are nine of you who could have voted last year. Karen [a student in the class] and I were the only ones who did. So that was a little disappointing. But if you do vote, keep in mind that you probably have friends who don't. And if you can get maybe two or three other students to vote, you change your vote to four or five or ten.

You can also get involved with campus organizations like the New Voter's Project. This is a group that I'm very impressed with. Nationally they set a goal of registering 265,000 people to vote by the deadline for registering voters. They already have 330,000, so they've blown that goal out of the water. Here's a flyer [displays actual flyer in overhead] that's been going up around Iowa State and it's pretty clear. Basically at the top they have their little line, it says, "Your right to vote won't exercise itself." I think that's kind of catchy. They also realize that people our age maybe haven't voted before. I know I haven't voted in a presidential election yet because I'm only twenty [wasn't eighteen during the last presidential election]. They have a lot of information that is valuable to people who might vote, or who maybe don't understand the process or the deadlines or even when to vote. So you'll probably be seeing these up a lot over campus, and I really think these guys are great. You can get involved in groups like that to encourage others to vote and also talking to your own friends

The final reason you should vote is its low cost. When I was in Econ 101, I learned there's a cost-benefit analysis that we perform on everything we do. The cost is very low for voting. For the campus elections, it takes thirty seconds to log in and then you're done. In national elections it takes a little bit more time but it's, like ten minutes if you vote by absentee, and it's very easy.

Speaking of the cost of voting, we aren't all this lucky. People in China and North Korea—they can't vote at all. They're run by one person who isn't held accountable to anyone except himself and in some cases the United Nations. Thanks to the war on terror, Afghanistan was able to have its first open election last Saturday. There were still a lot of people nervous and apprehensive that maybe they'd get punished if they tried to vote. But despite that, many did anyway. Swailla Noorstani, a schoolteacher out there, told a *USA Today* reporter that despite the fact that she could get punished for voting, she was going to vote anyway. She said, "If I lost my life for the honor of my country I would be proud." I think we could all learn a lesson from Swailla. We should try to make a harder effort to get involved. Now if any of you have questions, I would be so happy to answer them right now.

NOTES:

1. T. Clevenger, *Audience Analysis* (Indianapolis: Bobbs-Merrill, 1966).
2. Clevenger, *Audience Analysis.*
3. Mary Fisher, "A Whisper of AIDS," speech presented at the Republican National Convention, August 19, 1992.
4. *Kaiser/HRET Survey of Employer-Sponsored Health Benefits: 2003.* Retrieved Kaiser Family Foundation Web site, at http://d.kff.org/insurance/ehbs2003-8-chart.cfm.
5. W. Wood, N. Rhodes, and M. Biek, "Working Knowledge and Attitude Strength: An Information-Processing Analysis," in *Attitude Strength: Antecedents and Consequences,* edited by R. E. Petty and J. A. Krosnick (Mahwah, NJ: Erlbaum, 1995), 283–313.
6. C. R. Berger & J. J. Bradac, *Language and Social Thought: Uncertainty in Interpersonal Relations* (Baltimore: Edward Arnold, 1982). J. J. Bradac, "Theory Comparision: Uncertainty Reduction, Problematic Integration, Uncertainty Management, and Other Curious Constructs," *Journal of Communication, 51* (2001): 456–476.
7. M. Kramer, "Motivation to Reduce Uncertainty: A Reconceptualization of Uncertainty Reduction Theory," *Management Communication Quarterly, 13* (1999): 305–316.
8. Bradac, "Theory Comparison."
9. Dominic A. Taratino, "The Ultimate Knowledge-Based-Product—You," Commencement address, McLaren School of Business, University of San Francisco, May 19, 1995.
10. D. J. Okeefe, *Persuasion: Theory and Research,* 2nd ed. (Thousand Oaks, CA: Sage, 2002).

Chapter

16

Making Presentations to Negative Audiences

To Placate and Persuade

Goals

 To develop an understanding of negative audiences

 To understand how knowledge, attitude, and interest affect a negative audience

 To clarify reasons why negative audiences attend presentations

 To understand appropriate goals for negative audiences, including setting realistic goals for change, changing attitudes and behaviors, and identifying immediate and long-term goals

 To appreciate the variety of strategies available in designing a presentation to negative audiences, including foothold, psychological, support, and organizational strategies

 To become adept at developing ways to gain interest and gain an initial foothold

 To learn the psychological strategies for increasing support for your issue, including: appealing to values and needs, responding to concerns and objections, using group identification and membership, creating a favorable frame for the message, and using fear appeals

 To understand and use the various support strategies, including: narratives, metaphors, statistics; reluctant testimony; effective logic and arguments

 To adopt effective organizational strategies for use with negative audiences, including selection of the most effective structure, narrowing the presentation focus, adapting introductions, and adapting conclusions

Consider the audience members' interests, attitudes, and knowledge of the topic in each of the following scenarios.

Scenario 1. After an increase in employee accidents, a supervisor is making a presentation to employees about the need to follow the safety guidelines they were taught when they were hired.

Scenario 2. For three years, Jack, a member of the social planning group, makes his pitch during the winter holidays for holding a formal dinner at a local restaurant, and the other members vote it down.

Scenario 3. A representative for a developer who is planning a mall on the outskirts of a small town faces a citizen forum of those who are strongly opposed.

Scenario 4. A member of a student organization that is sponsoring a blood drive is addressing fellow students in her sociology class to encourage them to donate blood.

What is similar and what is different among these four scenarios? ●

Negative Audiences: Passive and Active

Scenarios 1 and 2 represent knowledgeable audiences that oppose what the speakers are advocating and have little or no interest in what the speaker is discussing; these are **passive negative audiences.** The employees in scenario 1 are probably not aggressively opposed but more likely don't like to be bothered with making an effort to follow safety guidelines. Scenario 2 is not a particularly significant issue, and thus the process may be rather perfunctory. Scenarios 3 and 4 represent audiences who are also knowledgeable and opposed to what the speaker is advocating, but they have a much stronger interest in the issue than the audiences in the first two scenarios; these are **active negative audiences.** To review the qualities of each, see Table 16.1.

Audiences who have a negative attitude toward a topic usually base that attitude on their knowledge of the issue. Only infrequently will you face audiences who hold negative attitudes even though they lack information. More often, you will face audiences who hold a negative attitude but have lost interest in the issue, making them passive negative audiences. You may also face audiences that have a negative attitude toward you as the speaker, requiring you to engage in relationship building.

- **Knowledge of the Topic** People can have strong feelings about an issue without actually having much knowledge. Their attitude is affectively based rather than cognitively based. You can probably think of several things you have strong feelings about but not lots of information. Perhaps there's a political figure, musician, or actor whom you really like, but about whom you know little. Audiences that have strong attitudes based on little knowledge may be closed-minded when it comes to processing contrary information and unable to process or analyze relevant information.[1] Audiences that are well informed and have strong feelings are prepared to defend their attitudes from attack; they process information in a biased manner by favoring supportive material and rejecting opposing information.[2] Informed negative audiences will probably be selective about what information they listen to, listening for weaknesses in the opposition. Uninformed audiences are likely to attend to all information because they lack the advance knowledge to discriminate between supportive and contrary information.[3] As a speaker, it will be easier for you to evoke change in an uninformed negative audience than an informed one.

- **Attitude toward the Topic** Audiences obviously are negative when a position is advocated that they see as detrimental to them. For example, talking to a group of managers about having to make budget cuts and possible layoffs of managers would evoke a negative response; so would trying to convince a small community that a new mall will not destroy its ecology or quality of life. You need to carefully consider not only the impact of your topic and position on audience members but also their perception of the impact. (Sometimes audiences perceive a speaker's position as detrimental when it really isn't.) You can also anticipate a negative reaction because of

passive negative audience A knowledgeable audience that opposes what the speakers are advocating and has little or no interest in the topic.

active negative audience An audience that is knowledgeable, interested, and opposed to what the speaker advocates.

the nature of the audience and their reason for assembling, as with the representative of the mall developer. Certain topics can also be identified as likely to evoke negative reactions, such as raising taxes, closing a local school, cutting athletic programs from a high school, increasing college tuition, or censoring the coverage of news events.

Think about a strong attitude you have toward an issue. Why do you have that attitude and why do you hold on to it? How people come to hold the views they do and why they hold on to them has been the subject of intense research for decades. These factors provide a foundation on which to generate strategies for changing those views. A number of factors have been found that affect the adoption, mainte-nance, and changing of people's attitudes—including a drive to be accurate and a desire to hold attitudes that reflect positively on a person's self-image—that are con-sistent with a person's values and behaviors, that a person can defend, and that allow an individual to affiliate with desired groups.

One goal people have is to be right. We like being accurate; we like to have correct facts, and to be able to share those facts with other people. The more important the issue, the more we want to be correct.[4] People don't like to hold attitudes or even express opinions that are wrong; therefore, one way to change someone's opinion is to prove he or she is wrong. For listeners who don't scrutinize information very much, highly credible sources are more likely to change listeners' attitudes than less credible sources.[5] One problem with being wrong is that it makes us look silly—we lose face, which has to do with another goal we have in holding attitudes: we want to maintain a positive image. We are often embarrassed when we discover that something we've been claiming is true turns out to be wrong. For example, you've probably argued with your friends that a particular actor was in a movie or TV show, only to have someone get a list of the cast and show you that you were wrong. Along with protecting their self-image,

● **TABLE 16.1**   Qualities of Passive and Active Negative Audiences.

Passive Negative Audience	Is knowledgeable about the issue
	Opposes the speaker's position on the issue
	Has lost interest in the issue
	Thinks, "I don't care about this issue any more, though I have learned a lot about it, and I disagree with what the speaker is saying."
Active Negative Audience	Is knowledgeable about the issue
	Opposes the speaker's position on the issue
	Has interest in the issue
	Thinks, "This issue is important to me, I have learned a lot about it, and what I've learned contradicts the posi-tion advocated by the speaker."

Italics highlight the differences between these two audiences.

people also like to hold attitudes that are consistent with how they see themselves, both in terms of their other attitudes and also in terms of their values and behaviors.

Back to the strong attitude you were thinking about a moment ago. Can you explain to others why you hold that attitude and why you believe it is correct? If you can, you are more likely to retain that attitude; if not, it is more susceptible to change. Generally, we are more likely to hold onto attitudes that we can defend. While we hold attitudes without strong reasons because of impressions, gut feelings, or biases, those attitudes are more susceptible to change than well-grounded ones. Remember that having knowledge and well-developed reasons for your attitudes increases your ability to counter any attack on those attitudes. Suppose you have a gut feeling to support Mitch Baker for student president, but don't have any good reasons. In talking to your group of friends, you find they are all supporting the other candidate, Jasmine Duncan, and have several good reasons why. Are you likely to continue supporting Mitch? Probably not.

• **Interest in the Topic**   Finally, you need to determine, as best as you can, the level of audience interest. Active negative audiences are more likely to engage in counter-arguing, seeking information to support their position, and participating in discussions of the issue. On the other hand, passive negative audiences have a negative attitude toward an issue but have lost interest in it; in this way they represent a negative audience that is also apathetic. These audience members don't want to think about the issue anymore, don't want to discuss it, and probably withdraw from situations where it is considered. You've probably faced this many times in your life when a parent has denied your request for something, and your continued efforts to present new arguments were met with your parent declaring, "I don't want to hear any more about it!" Obviously the first challenge here is to get the listeners to listen—to arouse their interest so you can present your case. Many of the strategies we discussed in Chapter 15 for dealing with apathetic audiences can be applied to this audience; however, once you have gained their attention or interest, you will then need to apply the strategies discussed in greater detail in this chapter for overcoming their negative attitude toward the topic.

You may wonder why a person would even bother to attend a presentation toward which they have a negative predisposition. Wouldn't a person with a negative attitude toward the speaker's position just stay away? Part of understanding a negative audience is to fully appreciate the factors that have lead them to attend your presentation.

Reasons Negative Audiences Attend Presentations

There are any number of motivations that cause people to attend a presentation toward which they have a negative reaction, we will discuss three, as follows.

Mandatory Attendance   In Chapter 6 you read about mandatory and voluntary audience motivation to attend a presentation. Sometimes audience members attend presentations as part of their responsibilities and are subject to presentations for which

In responding to this audience, a speaker needs a keen understanding of their attitudes, interest, and knowledge of the issues. ●

they have a negative predisposition. This might include a business meeting where a person opposes the issue or proposal being advocated, a club or organizational meeting where decisions are being made that a person opposes, or a required class on a subject a person dislikes (see Act and Reflect 16.1). In each of these instances, the audience might hold negative attitudes toward the topic or the speaker that will have a dramatic impact on the way those members listen and respond to the speaker's message.

ACT&REFLECT

16.1: Resistance

ACT • Rank the following issues from 1 to 6, giving 1 to the topic you believe your classmates would most oppose and 6 to the least.

_____ Increasing tuition

_____ Increasing student fees

_____ Adding an additional course requirement in creative writing for all students

_____ Raising the drinking age to twenty-four

_____ Requiring drug testing of all students for continued enrollment

_____ Requiring two years of civil or military service from all students after graduation

REFLECT • In what ways would your strategies to gain support differ in relation to the level of resistance that your rank order reflects?

To Present Their Own Views and Influence Others The school board in our community had created a plan to cut the budget that included reducing support for the music and art programs throughout the district. Parents and students attended an open hearing in the hope of convincing the school board members to reconsider their plan and continue support for the arts.

The most effective school board members and parents anticipated the arguments and sentiments of their listeners. Acknowledging the divergent views of listeners and responding to those views can increase the possibility of quelling negative attitudes that may be motivated by people's fear of not being able to achieve their goals. One strategy for dealing with a negative audience is to propose solutions that allow everyone to achieve at least some of their goals such an approach may reduce the prevailing negative attitudes.

To Learn about the Opponent A third reason negative audiences might attend is to learn the "opponents'" arguments. In essence, negative audience members might actually be on a subversive intelligence-gathering mission (okay, so maybe we're being a little melodramatic here). Nonetheless, we often listen to presenters of opposing views so we can be prepared to counter their arguments. Listening to the evidence and claims in support of an opposing position better equips you to develop your own arguments and find counteracting evidence (see Act and Reflect 16.2).

Moving the Audience along the Continuum of Resistance: Persuading

The negative audience's level of opposition can be placed on a continuum from strongly opposed to mildly opposed. While any given audience may be made up of

ACT&REFLECT

16.2: Observing Negative Audiences in Action

ACT • Think about a meeting you have attended in which a person advocated a position contrary to that of the majority of the other members. Think about the behaviors and reactions of other members that reflected their negativity toward the issue.

REFLECT • On the basis of the comments and behaviors of the negative participants, what would you conclude was the motivation for their negative attitudes? How did the presenter respond to these individuals? What factors contributed to the presenter's success or failure? What could have been done to improve the presenter's success?

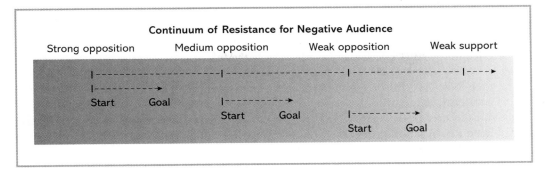

● **FIGURE 16.1** Continuum of Resistance for Negative Audiences.

individuals who vary in their levels of opposition, you can still generally identify the position of the majority and, most important, of the decision-makers on whom you might be focusing. For any single presentation, you can expect the audience members to move a limited distance along the continuum. For a strongly opposing audience, this might mean reducing their level of activity in support of their position but probably not changing their view. For example, in making a presentation to a group of students who are on probation after being caught driving while under the influence (DUI) of alcohol, you would be unlikely to convince them to totally abstain from alcohol. However, you might be able to convince them to be smarter about their drinking, perhaps to have a designated driver, to give someone else their car keys if they are at a bar, or to limit their drinking to Friday or Saturday night. Accomplishing any of the suggested changes would be a reasonable goal with such an audience. Figure 16.1 illustrates the movement of an audience from their preexisting level of opposition to one that is less opposing.

Goal Setting for Negative Audiences

The goals you set in presentations to negative audiences are directly related to where the audiences fall on the continuum of resistance. You should (1) decide what attitude or behavior you would like your audience to adopt, (2) decide how far your audience is from that goal, and (3) develop a strategy for moving the audience toward your goal. Speakers generally recognize the futility of trying to convert opponents to partisans by means of a single speech. Instead, speakers seek to neutralize the opposition or weaken commitment. If the opposing attitude is well entrenched, speakers may feel that they can do no more than raise doubts about the arguments or evidence supporting the opposing attitude. If the opposition is extreme, speakers may sense that the best that they can accomplish is a reduction in the intensity of the opposing attitude.[6]

In establishing your goal for a negative audience, consider the specific behaviors and attitudes you are seeking to change through your persuasive strategies. As we've asked before, "When you are done with your presentation, what do you want from your audience?" In some instances, you might seek only to alter their attitude, perhaps reducing their feelings of opposition toward your position. At other times, you might seek to change a specific behavior. Changing behavior usually involves changing some underlying attitude as well. Trying to convince the group of students serving probation for DUI to use a designated driver in the future seeks a change in their behavior, but it requires changing their attitude about their invulnerability to accidents, harm, or incarceration. It requires changing their attitude about relying on another person to keep them safe. In setting a behavioral change as your goal, you need to carefully consider the underlying attitudes and craft your presentation to alter those attitudes.

You might have the impression that it is you as the speaker or your message that changes an audience's attitude. Your role and your message may actually be only the indirect cause of such changes. The **cognitive response model** maintains that the listeners are active participants in the persuasive process because they think about what they hear.[7] In essence, the speaker doesn't really change the listeners but activates their thoughts, hopefully in the direction the speaker desires. This is similar to that part of the elaboration likelihood model that includes both the arousal of cognitive processing in those who are involved in the issue and the use of peripheral factors in those who are uninvolved. There are good things and bad things about activating a person's thoughts on an issue. The bad aspect is that speakers' presentations to negative audiences may stimulate counterarguments in their minds, counterarguments that result in further rejection of the idea.[8] The good news is that the thinking might evoke the audience's consideration of new information, new perspectives, new arguments, and new issues that might result in change toward the speaker's position.[9] The amount of thought listeners engage in varies, as does their ability to pay attention and consider the information the speaker provides.[10] As a speaker, you should consider how to strategically evoke thoughts in the audience that will result in more support for your position.

Strategies for Presenting to Negative Audiences

Moving a negative audience from their original position to the one you would like them to adopt is an extremely challenging and complex task. How do you get your friends to go along with something you want? What do you say to get your parents' permission for some activity they oppose? What do you tell your boss to achieve a change in your work schedule? You've probably developed your own personal repertoire of strategies, some more successful than others. A multitude of theories and strategies have been developed to overcome audience resistance to change. The following sections place some of the more significant strategies into four categories: foothold strategies, support strategies, psychological strategies, and organizational strategies. Exposure to this wide range of strategies should prepare you for selecting and applying the best strategies to fit the negative audiences you encounter.

cognitive response model An approach to persuasion that maintains that listeners are active participants in the persuasive process because they think about what they hear.

Foothold Strategies

While the positive audience is willing to listen and the neutral audience has to be convinced to listen, the negative audience may not hear anything you have to say, thus undermining any attempt to convince them of the merits of your position. There are some negative audience situations that are probably hopeless, making a presentation to them usually done for some other reason than trying to persuade them to change their views. Those listeners who are on the extreme side of the continuum of resistance may be such an audience. Those with strong negative views are less inclined to seek additional information; they have already made up their minds and don't want to confuse the issue further.[11] You need to start with **foothold strategies** that allow you to gain initial openness and interest in listening to you and to your message. The following strategies can be used.

Establish Common Ground   One of the primary principles of negotiation involves identifying the common goals of the two adversarial parties. In some ways, presentations to negative audiences are like negotiations, except that only the presenter talks, and he or she must anticipate the listeners' responses, criticisms, and concerns. Regardless of a person' support or opposition to the Iraq war, there was a shared common interest in protecting U.S. military personnel. That common interest often served as the starting point for many speakers when facing negative audiences. Discussing the common ground increases the audience's attention and willingness to listen, at which point the speaker can begin to introduce issues and arguments that challenge the audience's existing views. The stronger connection you can make between the points you raise and the common ground, the better chance you have of influencing the audience. Each time you introduce a controversial point, you might need to retreat to discussing the common ground again to regain audience acceptance. The following is a hypothetical example of the use of this strategy in a presentation to a group of undergraduates about attending graduate school:

> I remember that when I was finishing up my undergraduate degree I was so ready to be done with school. I couldn't believe that after all those years of schooling, it would finally be over. I couldn't imagine going on any further—I felt burned out about school. I suspect many of you are probably having similar feelings and are looking forward to your last day of classes. But a funny thing happened to me during my last year. I started getting excited and doing well in my senior classes. I also realized there was a lot that I didn't know about my discipline. After reading one of my papers for class, a professor told me I should think about going to graduate school. I also found out it took about two years to get a master's degree, taking just three classes a semester. The department offered a number of assistantships that would cover my tuition and expenses, as long as I didn't party too much.

foothold strategies Specific strategies used to gain initial audience openness and interest in listening to speakers and their messages.

Demonstrate Understanding and Respect for the Audience's Position This strategy was illustrated implicitly in the foregoing example. You need to connect with the audience as well as you can, despite their negative attitudes, by showing your understanding and respect. People need to feel they are understood, especially in situations of conflict or disagreement. They are more inclined to listen to someone who understands, acknowledges, and appreciates their views, even if they disagree with that person. You've probably been frustrated by someone who proclaims you are wrong about something without even knowing your reasons. On the other hand, you are more open to listening to someone who is able to display empathy or understanding while also expressing disagreement. To accomplish this in presentations, you need to make statements about the audience's perspective, the reasons for their position, their concerns, and their objections to your position. Obviously, you need to be accurate in making such claims about the audience, and you need to present them in a respectful manner. There are times when we react negatively when others say they know what we're thinking (even if they do). The earlier example from a presentation on graduate school included an attempt to show this understanding but in a qualified, nonthreatening manner. Look back at the example and see if you can spot it. As you prepare your presentation, seek feedback from one of the typical audience members about your understanding of their potential reactions to your intended comments. In the graduate school example, the line that begins "I suspect many of you are probably having similar feelings" demonstrates the speaker's understanding of the audience.

Keep the Brain in Mind Our earlier discussion of the mind focused on increasing retention of information; however, a negative audience may actually resist your efforts to help them retain your arguments, stories, and information. The challenge, then, is to get their attention early and clear a path for the journey of your message through their minds. Your message must attract listeners' attention in order to pass through the first filter, the reticular activating system (RAS).[12] To overcome this daunting barrier, concentrate on attracting the audience's attention in such a way that the negativity you are facing is at least temporarily set aside. There are two ways you might achieve this goal:

1. You might present an issue that you know you and your audience agree on, despite their negativity toward you and the balance of your viewpoint. When FBI director Robert S. Mueller spoke to the American Civil Liberties Union to defend the FBI's record on civil liberties, he began his presentation by remarking that the ACLU should thank the FBI for helping to boost ACLU membership.[13] The remark brought laughter and a standing ovation from the initially hostile audience.

2. Although research on the effect of laughter as a means for achieving speaker goals is unclear, getting the audience to initially laugh attracts their attention.

Once the listeners' initial RASs allow your comments to be recognized above all of the other stimuli, your message passes into the short-term memory.[14] Then, for approximately five to thirty seconds, you have another opportunity to convince them to invest the time and effort to listen to what you have to say. How can you take advantage of this time? At this point, acknowledge that you are aware of the position of your negative audience, as well as indicating that you understand why they feel as they do. In other words, establish empathy with them.

Now, as the message moves into the short-term memory, you have the opportunity to present your view to your audience. Identify the key reasons you want to convey to them. Use techniques that will draw them into your presentation. Do you have examples they have experienced that will draw them in? Can you discuss events of concern to them in their terms? Continue to establish empathy as you present your views.

Because you are presenting to an audience that has its own agenda, an audience that feels commitment to an issue differently from how you would wish, it is particularly important that you continue to frame your message in terms of what is important to them. They need to feel that your message relates to them. Such efforts help to move information into their long-term memory.

Think about the last time someone was able to talk you into changing your mind about something. What did he or she say that made you change your mind? You probably thought about a situation that involved someone with whom you have a positive relationship and to whom you listened as he or she explained the opposing position. You were probably in a conversation and explained your point of view, to which the other person provided reasonable counter-arguments. Perhaps the other person had evidence that refuted your position or had enough credibility that you accepted his or her word. A significant advantage of trying to sway someone's mind in an interpersonal interaction is that the speaker can discover the underlying reasons for the listener's position and thus directly challenge those reasons. In a speech you need to anticipate and adapt to the thoughts and feelings of your audience.

Consider Multiple Presentations Sometimes gaining a foothold is part of a larger strategy that involves giving multiple presentations, each building upon the others. A single presentation is limited in how much change you can accomplish, and you might accomplish a greater change if you have the opportunity to make several presentations to the same audience.[15] For each presentation, you can set a goal of moving the audience a little bit more toward supporting your ultimate goal. Gaining support from colleagues in a series of business meetings may involve establishing a series of narrower goals for each individual presentation in order to accomplish the larger, overall goal. You've probably evoked this strategy when trying to talk your parents into giving you permission for some activity they oppose you doing. You whittle away at their objections over time, slowly moving them from their strong opposition to eventually supporting your request. This strategy involves establishing a series of narrower goals within the context of your overall goal, though it is limited to situations when you have more than one opportunity to talk to your audience. You might actually make arrangements that help in implementing this strategy. Rather than requesting one opportunity to talk to a group, you might propose a series of meetings, setting a goal for each meeting of what you would like to accomplish en route to your ultimate goal. Two strategies commonly used to accomplish this are "foot-in-the door" and "door-in-the face."

The **foot-in-the-door strategy** involves asking for a lot less than you really want in order to gain initial acceptance by the audience and then later make the more substantive request. You can make a series of small requests that creates an "agreeing" mindset. The logic is that once I've gotten you to agree to several smaller requests, you are more apt to agree to a larger request. Even negative audiences may be open to agreeing to some small, relatively insignificant request. The manager who is advocating personnel cuts might start with a proposal to simply not rehire a few employees who have left and monitor the impact on production and profits. Once that proposal is agreed to, the manager might make another presentation later with requests for larger cuts.

The **door-in-the-face strategy** involves asking for a lot more than you really desire and settling for less, which was what you really desired anyway. Again, the manager might argue for a 35 percent layoff in order to improve profitability. At a subsequent meeting, the manager might revise the proposal and suggest that a 20 percent reduction could provide the margin necessary to accomplish the goal. The initial large request provides a framework that makes the smaller request more acceptable. You might have faced the use of this technique with solicitations from organizations that initially ask you to donate one hundred dollars, which you refuse; when they suggest ten dollars, you decide that would be okay.

Psychological Strategies

Humans have unique ways of processing and responding to information—they are far from objective, rational, and perfect in either their actions or decisions. The following list of strategies is based on our understanding of how people process information and make decisions. The better understanding you have about how people behave and respond to messages, the more effective you can be in developing effective presentations to negative audiences.

Appeal to Values and Needs Your understanding of the psychology of humans will help you develop arguments, make appeals, and implement strategies that directly relate to

foot-in-the-door strategy A foothold strategy that involves asking for a lot less than you really want, in order to gain initial acceptance by the audience, and then later making the more substantive request.

door-in-the-face strategy A foothold strategy that involves asking for a lot more than is really desired but settling for less, which was what was really desired anyway.

their interests. Suppose you were making a presentation to your classmates, asking them to volunteer to donate their blood at an upcoming school blood drive. Most people think donating blood is a great idea—for someone else to do. In analyzing their negative reaction to the proposal, as discussed in the last section, you might identify reasons they are reluctant and address those. However, by knowing what is important to them, you also can develop arguments and appeals to offset their objections—arguments and appeals based on your knowledge of them. So what do you know about your classmates that could be used to move them to volunteer? Are they committed to the community and humanitarian causes? Do they take pride in helping others or feel a moral obligation to do so? Do they like to be part of the crowd? Or do they like free cookies?

Negative audiences are likely to be skeptical of appeals, so your appeals need to be clear, strong, and well supported. Appealing to a sense of moral obligation to convince students to donate blood would require some evidence that donating blood fulfills this obligation. This might include the use of testimony from student donors about their sense of moral fulfillment or from clergy indicating that such acts are a moral obligation. In considering appeals to negative audiences, you should review the material in Chapter 9 on needs and motives. In addition, audiences often hold certain attitudes because they serve an instrumental purpose that allows them to fulfill their needs.[16] The resistance to donating blood serves the need to protect oneself from harm. As a presentational strategy, you want to demonstrate either that the attitude is not meeting the intended need, or that more important needs are being sacrificed.

Identify and Respond to Inherent Concerns and Objections What are the concerns people have when considering donating blood? People worry about it hurting, about feeling faint, about infections, about not having enough blood to share, about not having enough time, and more. All of these concerns contribute to the negative response to the request. Once you identify and appreciate the concerns, you can address them and hopefully reduce their impact. For example, some people really don't know how much blood they have in their body, how much blood is drawn, and what the impact the removal of a pint of blood will have on a person. Knowing this concern allows you to provide information to educate and allay their fears. However, you will need to have highly credible sources and to demonstrate your own knowledge if you are to overcome these concerns. Even then, irrational concerns are not easily overturned by rational means; you might provide strong evidence, yet certain audience members will still believe they don't have enough blood to donate.

Appeal to Desires for Group Membership We tend to acquire and sustain attitudes, beliefs, and values that allow us to affiliate with desired groups. Changing your support to a candidate your friends had reasons to support also helps you retain your affiliation with those friends. What might happen if you continued supporting Mitch while your friends actively campaigned for Jasmine? Your relationships could be damaged. We seek out groups who share our attitudes, but we are also more inclined to adopt the attitudes that are held by groups with which we identify. What strategy might be developed on the basis of this principle that would help us change a person's attitude? You show how the listener can gain membership in a desirable group by adopting the attitudes of that group. Another strategy would be to point out to the audience how their affiliated groups already possess the attitude or are engaging in the action. For example, audience members are more likely to donate blood if they believe that most of the members of one of their peer groups, such as their Greek housemates, teammates, club members, or church group, are donating blood.

Create a Favorable Frame for the Message "Is the glass half full or half empty?" That question is often used to demonstrate whether a person is an optimist or pessimist; however, it also reflects a matter of perspective. To get the pessimist to change his or her mind, a speaker might say, "You need to look at it from another perspective; you've got a lot more than you'd have if the glass were totally empty!" The underlying strategy is to frame the issue in the context of attitudes, beliefs, and values that you know the listeners already hold.[17] **Message framing** involves creating a context for the message that works in the speaker's favor—creating a particular perspective or mind-set from which to consider a message. As with changing the pessimist's view to the glass being half-full, you can attempt to change the known focus of your listeners. For example, rather than discussing an audience's view that increased tuition will make going to college too expensive, you could focus on how a tuition increase will improve the quality of their education, increase the course offerings they need, and increase scholarships available to the students.

Negative framing involves painting a picture of harmful consequences related to some issue, while **positive framing** focuses on benefits. In making a presentation promoting the use of bicycle helmets, a negative frame could be created by citing the annual number of deaths and injuries due to head injuries and discussing the sadness felt by families who have lost a member because of a failure to wear a helmet. A positive frame might involve discussing the low costs of today's helmets, the attractive designs they come in, or the ease of use. The effectiveness of the negative versus positive framing depends on the situation and listener predisposition.[18] A lot of the research on message framing has been done on public service announcements (PSAs) that are aimed at changing people's health behaviors. Negative framing (loss-framed) has been effective in promoting early detection behaviors (breast self-exams, mammograms, and HIV testing) while positive framing (gain-framed) has improved preventative actions (using infant car restraints, exercising, and using sunscreen).[19]

Apparently people are more inclined to make a risky choice when the issue is framed in terms of loss (negative frame) and are averse to making risky choices when the issue is framed in terms of gains (positive frame).[20] How can you use this information when speaking to an audience that opposes your position? The answer depends on your goals and what information you have available. The manager who is attempting to get other managers to support a downsizing of personnel, including managers, could explain the choices as follows:

message framing Creating a particular perspective or mind-set from which to consider a message.

negative framing Message framing in which the speaker paints a picture of harmful consequences related to some issue.

positive framing Message framing in which the speaker paints a picture of the benefits associated with an issue.

A speaker can frame the audience's perspective. Picture 1 is of an old woman with her chin on her chest. Pictures 2 through 7 help the audience reframe until they see the picture of a young woman looking to her left. ●

A Question of **Ethics**

The strategies discussed in this section can be used in ways that are considered unethical. Examine these two examples and decide if you believe the speakers are ethical.

1. "Patriotic Americans support the president's decision to go to war. Opposing the president makes you un-American."

   This speaker is using identification, being a "patriotic American," as a way to sway attitudes. To what degree do you feel employing such a claim is ethical?

2. "A lot of you think that the impending budget cuts mean the quality of our product and services will suffer. However, look at this as an opportunity, as a chance for us to show how creative and industrious we can be in the face of challenge. These cuts will help us decide on priorities and become more efficient. We will become stronger, not weaker."

   In this attempt at positive framing, the speaker is painting the glass as half full. To what degree is the speaker being ethical if he or she knows that there will also be layoffs, cuts in wages, and cuts in benefits?

Positive framing: For the last two quarters, expenses have exceeded sales income by 15 percent. We can downsize personnel by 20 percent without harming production or quality and continue providing long-term job security for 160 employees. This cut would equalize expenses and income, allowing us time to develop strategies for increasing sales. The other choice is do nothing and gamble the economy will improve, but if the gamble is wrong, we could be bankrupt within a year, with all two hundred employees losing their jobs.

Negative framing: Everyone's job is in jeopardy right now because our sales continue to lag behind our costs by 15 percent each quarter. We could all be on unemployment in a year or less if we don't do something soon. Our choice is to do nothing and hope that the economy improves, which seems like about a fifty/fifty proposition, or we can cut our expenses by laying off forty employees and return to solvency right now.

Which of those two messages would be more likely to influence you to accept the plan to lay off employees? Message framing theory predicts that positive framing encourages listeners to make the less risky decision, which would be to lay people off and preserve the company. Those who listened to the negatively framed message should be more inclined to take the risky decision, which would be to not lay anyone off and gamble on the economy improving. So, in this instance, using a positive framed message would be the better strategy. The success of framing depends on such factors as how much listeners actually process and accept the frame you provide;[21] how much effort the listeners are willing to exert in thinking about the frame;[22] and people's involvement with the issue (see Act and Reflect 16.3).[23]

Use Fear Appeals "If you don't study harder and get good grades, you won't get a good job." "Searching everyone's luggage before boarding the plane is necessary to prevent death and destruction from a smuggled bomb." "Unless you exercise regularly, you are likely to develop heart problems." These three statements represent a form of negative framing but, more specifically, the use of fear appeals. **Fear appeals** are persuasive strategies that use the emotion of fear to change behavior or attitudes by linking undesirable consequences to specific actions or inactions. Fear appeals usually take the form of some threat—that is, a statement that some action or inaction will result in an undesirable outcome. Persuasion occurs when listeners adopt the requested change to avoid the outcome. Part of the strategy involves trying to create a fear appeal message that evokes an emotional state of fear for which the speaker provides the relief.[24] However, creating an aroused state of fear in an audience is not easy, though an uninformed audience might be expected to be more vulnerable than an informed one. Fear appeals involve both emotions and cognitions—the arousal of fear and then a logical argument in support of action to alleviate that fear.

The extensive research on fear appeals has produced conflicting results attesting to the fact that threats don't automatically change behavior. If that were the case, there

fear appeals Using the emotion of fear to change behavior or attitudes by linking undesirable consequences to specific actions or inactions.

ACT&REFLECT

16.3: Creating Message Frames

ACT • For each of the following situations, create an appropriate negative and a positive message frame.

Topic	Positive Frame	Negative Frame
1. Asking a local business association to donate money to support a student organization's project		
2. Convincing PTA members at your child's school to volunteer for the school carnival fund-raiser		
3. Convincing your classmates to attend local performing arts events such as plays, a classical concert, or dance recital		

REFLECT • For which of these was it easiest to create a positive frame? A negative frame? Which was the hardest to create a positive frame for? A negative frame? Why?

---

would be no drunk drivers, no one smoking cigarettes, a decrease in obesity, and so on. People have a lot of defense mechanisms to fight fears and thus reject fear appeals. Human reactions to fear and threats are complex and thus challenging to utilize in presentations, but there are some general principles for you to consider when addressing negative audiences.

- First, not everyone is threatened by the same thing. Have you ever gone to a "scary" movie during which some people anxiously sat on the edge of their seats while other people laughed? We're not all frightened by the same thing—this is strongly related to our needs. Knowledge of the audience's beliefs, values, and attitudes is critical to developing effective fear appeals.

- Second, threats vary in severity.[25] You might be able to create fear in your audience, but is it a large enough fear to overcome their resistance? Again, scary movies provide a nice example; some are more frightening than others. Those that are scariest have the greatest impact on us. Similarly, the greater the threat you can create, the greater the likelihood the audience will act. Part of the severity is also linked to the timing of the threat. Teenagers are unlikely to feel threatened by the collapse of the Social Security System, while those approaching retirement are. The closer a threat is to actually occurring to us, the more frightening it is.

- Third, there is an exception to the second principle, in that too much fear can work against the speaker, creating a **boomerang effect**: the audience gives up rather than rallying.[26] If the speaker portrays too pessimistic a picture, the listeners may simply adopt a defeatist attitude and give up rather than act. After hearing the report about how bad the company's financial situation is, the managers might simply give up and refuse to act because they believe any action would be fruitless. The boomerang effect occurs when the threat is seen as overwhelming, when there is a lack of faith that the proposed solution will work, or when the audience members feel incapable of making the change. In making a presentation, the speaker must be sensitive to controlling for this effect by building a case that shows the threat can be managed and that the audience members can manage it. Such presentations have probably been made innumerable times during half times when teams are losing by an extraordinary margin and the players want to give up.

- Fourth, we have to believe that the threat is real and that it is a threat to us. The layoffs mentioned in the earlier scenario will be very threatening to those who think they are most vulnerable to being fired and not threatening to those who feel secure. Research on the persuasive impact of health messages on stress found that when people felt vulnerable, they expressed a higher likelihood of participating in the suggested action, sought more information on an optional stress management training program, and subscribed for the training more.[27] To combat these feelings of vulnerability, however, people take on an air of invulnerability as a defense against some threats, proclaiming, "That won't happen to me." Can you think about any threatening messages you have fended off with such a proclamation? As a speaker, you need to show that the listeners are very much in danger, but in doing so, you also need to be prepared to address the defensive or coping strategies they invoke. You have to convince the audience that they really will be affected so you can combat such responses as "I won't get AIDS when I have sex," "I can drive all right even when I've had a few drinks," or "I don't really need sunscreen to avoid skin cancer." Another defense mechanism that might be used against you is denial—the audience members may simply tune you out because they don't want to hear about the threat.

- Fifth, for a threat to result in some desired change, two things have to happen: the listeners must believe the action you are suggesting to eliminate the threat will actually be effective (this is called response efficacy), and they must believe they are capable of it (this is called self-efficacy).[28] Again, in the layoff scenario, to what degree do the fellow managers feel that cutting 20 percent of the employees will produce financial stability and to what degree do they feel they can actually make the cuts (perhaps there are union contracts that prevent this action)?

boomerang effect When a speaker instills so much fear that the audience gives up rather than rallying.

In summary, fear appeals and threats can be a powerful strategy for changing audience attitudes and behaviors. To be effective, the threat needs to be perceived as real to the audience, a solution must be provided that they are convinced will reduce the threat, and they need to believe they are capable of implementing the solution. Accomplishing each of these steps depends on how well you know the audience and adapt your appeals to that knowledge, the quantity and quality of your evidence, and the soundness of your arguments connecting actions to threat avoidance.

Before you start trying to scare all your audiences into adopting your position, remember that sometimes positive framing can be more effective than the negative framing reflected in fear appeals (see Act and Reflect 16.4). One study found students more likely to increase their exercising after hearing a positively framed message from an expert than after hearing a negative one.[29]

The child in the photo behind the speaker died in a car driven by her drunk mother. Does it work as an effective fear appeal? ●

Support Strategies

Maybe you're now thinking, "I know the needs this audience has that I can connect to. I can frame the issue in my favor, and I can show the audience members that their friends are all taking the position I'm advocating. I'm ready to make my presentation." Not so fast, grasshopper! You still need to think about the best way to support a presentation to a negative audience. They are likely to be cautious and skeptical of the information and support you provide. Here are some strategies on how to best incorporate support into a presentation to a negative audience.

ACT&REFLECT

16.4: Fear Appeals

ACT • For each of these audiences and topics, create a fear appeal that you could use.

1. Convincing a high school group to practice safe sex (or abstain)
2. Convincing your classmates to enlist in the military service after graduation
3. Convincing your work colleagues to volunteer to help at the local food pantry

REFLECT • Which of these appeals do you think would be most effective? Least effective? Why?

Select the Most Effective Form of Support You can use stories, narratives, and other qualitative forms of support effectively to influence negative audiences. Stories can evoke certain emotional responses in support of a speaker's goals, but negative audiences may perceive such appeals as manipulative. Imagine a low-credibility speaker telling you a story about how his poor widowed grandmother struggled to make ends meet because her husband hadn't bought enough life insurance; therefore, you should purchase a policy. Would you be moved by the story? Negative audiences are likely to be guarded as they listen to such stories and somewhat immune to emotional appeals. However, good stories have staying power and are more likely to be retained than statistical evidence.[30] Remember that a good story is one that has coherence (makes sense) and fidelity (is believable). Negative audiences will be more critical, so the speaker must work harder to establish the credibility of the story. You can increase retention of your message with the use of a meaningful metaphor (see Act and

Everyday Example

State Senators Address a Negative Audience

The following article describes a news conference in which two state senators in New Mexico faced a negative crowd opposing the proposals they advocated. See if you can identify what led to this being a more positive situation than anticipated. What additional strategies from this chapter might the senators have used?

We live in an era of sound-bite politics. Policy debate too often is reduced to a noisy, *Crossfire*-like exchange of talking points and sloganeering. Public interaction with public officials frequently consists of hand-picked supporters asking pre-screened, softball questions.

Considering that, something refreshing happened at the Roundhouse this week.

Two state senators from the social-conservative wing of the Republican Party—Bill Sharer of Farmington and Mark Boitano of Albuquerque—did something that too few politicians do these days. They went out among the public and had civil, but serious, conversations with people who they knew passionately opposed their political philosophy.

The occasion was a Valentine's Day news conference featuring GOP lawmakers talking about a package of bills they contended would encourage the institution of marriage and discourage divorce.

Among the proposals: Reduce the $25 marriage license fee for couples who take marriage-education programs; require 10 percent of federal welfare funds received by the state to be used to encourage two-parent families; require that divorcing couples with children—or those in which one spouse doesn't want a divorce—go to pre-divorce counseling classes; and provide $200,000 to community groups and religious organizations for a range of educational programs and advertising campaigns to promote marriage.

The issue of gay marriage wasn't even mentioned by the senators and other speakers at the news conference.

But it was very much on the minds of a majority of audience members. Monday also was Lesbian, Gay, Bisexual and Transgendered Lobbying Day at the Capitol.

Dozens of those who came to lobby against bills that would prohibit same-sex marriage—including Senate Bill 587, sponsored by Sharer—showed up at the Republican event on the west side of the Roundhouse. The speakers looked out to a crowd with large signs reading "Love = Love" and "All Love is Equal" and a poster with photos captioned "The Faces of Gay and Lesbian Families."

To fully appreciate this, you've got to realize how radically different this scene was from the typical Roundhouse "news conference." Usually, these exercises are preaching-to-the-choir pep rallies where the audience consists primarily of true believers who applaud at all the right places.

Monday's event had the potential to become just another screaming battle in the culture war. It didn't. There were a couple of instances of mild heckling from a few in the crowd. And a few times when a speaker said something about strengthening marriage, and some audience members responded, "For us too."

"I didn't feel much hostility at all," Boitano said immediately after the event. But heck, he had just received loud applause from both straights and gays in the crowd when he concluded his talk by saying love is the most powerful force in the universe.

Sharer later told me he was prepared for much worse. "I thought they might throw tomatoes at us," he said. I think he was only half-joking.

Nobody threw anything, but several people wanted to let the senators know how they felt about same-sex marriage and how legislation would affect their lives and their families.

They approached both Sharer and Boitano, and some interesting conversations ensued.

Despite the friendly tone of Monday's encounters, it's not likely anyone changed his or her mind on the issue.

The activists will continue to fight Sharer's bill. And Sharer and Boitano still are going to vote to define marriage as being only between a man and a woman—though Sharer held out the possibility he could back Sen. Cisco McSorley's SB 576, which would establish "domestic partnership" licenses that would give unmarried couples the same rights and benefits of married couples.

At one point Monday, Mary Ellen Capek, a lesbian who was married to her partner in Canada, asked Sharer: "How do we get past stereotypes?"

I can't help but think both sides made some steps in that direction that day.

Source: Steve Terrell, "Senators' Marriage Proposals Spark Rare Talks," *New Mexican,* February 17, 2005.

Reflect 16.5). The very act of using metaphors can have the added benefit of actually increasing a speaker's credibility.[31]

Researchers are at odds about whether stories are more effective in persuading audiences than statistics.[32] There are a number of factors that have lead to different research results, but ultimately, the best advice would be to use both. Providing statistical evidence and specific examples appears to have more persuasive impact than the use of either form of support by itself.[33] Such a strategy makes sense, given the diversity found in most audiences; some listeners may be more responsive to the statistics and others to the stories. Stories and statistics can complement each other. Statistics can become more meaningful when connected to an effective illustrative story, and the generalizability of a story can be enhanced when it is connected with

ACT&REFLECT

16.5: Elaborating Metaphors for Negative Audiences

ACT • Assume you are facing a negative audience for each of the topics listed. For each topic and metaphor, identify three ways the metaphor can be extended to further illustrate important points about the topic.

Example: Graduate school is a safe harbor during a storm. **Extensions:** (1) protection from the storm—avoid being unemployed during bad economic times; (2) opportunity to improve the boat and make it more seaworthy—improve your skills and marketability; (3) chance to visit with other captains about good fishing spots—opportunity to network with other graduate students.

Topic and Metaphor   **Extensions**

1. Drinking is a plague on college campuses.

2. Studying is an investment in your future.

3. Donating blood is a gift you give that costs you only time.

REFLECT • Think about what type of evidence you would need to make each of the extensions more powerful. What metaphors might work for the topics you are considering for your next presentation?

relevant statistics. Here's an example from a 2003 speech given by Tony Blair, as prime minister of England, to the annual meeting of his Labour Party:

> Yes the cynics say, "New Labour's been a great electoral machine but you've done little with it."
>
> I could recite you the statistics: The lowest inflation, mortgage rates, and unemployment for decades. The best ever school results, with over 60,000 more 11 year olds every year now reaching required standards in English and Maths. Cardiac deaths down 19 per cent since 1997, cancer deaths 9 per cent. Burglaries down 39 per cent.
>
> But it's not statistics that tell us what has changed, it's people.
>
> The lone parent I met, for years unemployed and unemployable. Now not just in work through the New Deal but winning promotion.
>
> What mattered to her most? Not the money alone but the respect her child gained for her, seeing her work, grow in confidence, becoming a role model. One of two million people the New Deal has helped since 1997. That's what this Labour government has done for Britain.
>
> Or the children I met this month at a brand new academy in Thamesmead in one of the most deprived estates in the country.[34]

Be Psycho-Logical. Blending logic with an understanding of how people think and make decisions has been labeled the **psycho-logical approach**—that is, realizing that pure logic in and of itself will not necessarily lead to change if you have not taken into account the way your listeners think.[35] Decisions are the product of logical consideration, emotional investments, and biased reasoning. The most effective presentations are responsive to all of these: presenting solid arguments, incorporating relevant narratives, and adapting to biases. This psycho-logical approach is one reason you can use enthymemes to persuade an audience—they already know elements of the argument and don't need you to spell them out. However, with negative audiences, the speaker might want to clearly identify all of the elements of the argument rather than depend on the audience to fill in the missing element.

Utilize Reluctant Testimony Negative audiences are going to be skeptical of what the speaker says; therefore, you should draw from sources that are highly regarded and trusted by the audience. Failing that, sources speaking in your favor who are seen as unbiased can also influence the audience. **Reluctant testimony,** occurring when a person speaks against his or her own previous interests, can also prove to be a powerful form of support. You've probably seen lots of commercials in which a smoker speaks against smoking, a drug user warns about the dangers of drugs, or an alcoholic discourages excess drinking. These individuals are usually seen as more trustworthy than biased sources. Researchers who applied the cognitive response model (stimulating thinking about the message) to studying reluctant testimony discovered that audiences responded with more positive thoughts and fewer unfavorable thoughts, leading to more persuasive impact.[36] They found a similar impact from both reluctant and unbiased testimony.

Build on Known Arguments You can use logical appeals and argument when addressing audiences who base their opposition on their knowledge of the issues. However, such appeals are less successful with audiences who lack knowledge and base their opposition on emotional responses or biases.[37] Knowledgeable negative audience members listen critically and generally are tuned to information that supports rather than opposes their position, making the task of changing their position even more difficult. One approach is to begin with the arguments supporting their position that are known to the listeners. As you discuss those arguments, you can present specific counterarguments that are bolstered by evidence that is clear, strong, and perceived as fair and credible. In this example, the speaker's goal is to convince a classroom full of college seniors to delay entering the workforce and continue their education in graduate school.

> In your last year of college, most of you are excited by the prospect of completing your degree and getting a job. Gaining the bachelor's degree means you can expect a much higher average income than if you didn't get your degree, and that fact has motivated many of you through college. According to the 2000 U.S. census, the average income for all those with bachelor's degrees was $52,200.[38] However,

psycho-logical approach Persuading listeners with a blend of logic and an understanding of how people think and make decisions.

reluctant testimony Testimony of a person speaking against his or her own previous interests.

the average income for those with master's degrees was $62,300. That means that going to school for just two more years means you can expect an extra $10,100 a year. An extra $10,000 a year—do you think you could use an extra $10,000 a year?

In this example, rather than attempting to refute the students' expectation of making a good salary after they finish their bachelor's degrees, the speaker uses their underlying desire for a decent income as an argument for continuing toward a master's degree. Do you think this would be enough to convince students to continue their education? Does it convince you? Such an argument could lead to the audience doing further investigation of the pros and cons of continuing their education. On the other hand, as we've discussed before, people's decision making and attitudes often have an emotional component that is not addressed simply by logic. The prospect of "enduring" two more years of course work might generate a strong emotional reaction that the speaker would also need to address. Logic alone is often insufficient to persuade.

One effective argumentative strategy is to get your audience involved in your message. ●

Create and Use Arguments The conditions needed to make an effective argument are similar to those for effective evidence: the audience needs to recognize you are presenting an argument, needs to think about your argument, needs to accept each of the elements of the argument as valid, and needs to accept the logic connecting the elements. If these four conditions are met, an audience should feel compelled to accept your argument; however, the psycho-logical approach reminds us that the mere fact that we've made a great argument doesn't mean the audience will agree. Many a teenager has suffered through the struggle of giving a solid argument to justify a request only to have a parent still deny it. When pressed as to why, the parent usually replies, "Because I said so, that's why!"

You can help your audience recognize that you are presenting an argument by being explicit and by identifying the elements. For example, "I know you don't believe your drinking is harmful, but let me explain how you are harmed and provide evidence in support of this claim . . ." Getting a negative audience to think about your arguments is more challenging and, at times, impossible. Prejudiced listeners will simply turn off their attention. You may have to give an argument supporting why they should listen to your argument. In essence, you need to establish a need for them to listen, as we discussed in relation to Monroe's motivated sequence. Here's an example of creating a need to listen to your arguments that we wrote; it is based on actual occurrences we researched:

So why should you listen to me today as I discuss drinking problems in college? One reason to listen is because your life might depend on it and other people's lives might depend on it as well. University of Wisconsin sophomore Mark Mueller's body was found on New Year's Day, 2003; he had fallen and hit his head after drinking the night before. Jared Dion of the University of Wisconsin LaCrosse drowned in the Mississippi after a night of heavy drinking. Marlon Blue of Northern Illinois University was found dead in a retention pond on his campus after a night at the bars. None of these individuals probably considered how drinking might affect him, but it did. Let me explain some of the issues related to college drinking that relate to your own safety.

To encourage listeners to process your arguments, you may need to lead negative audiences clearly through them. You should present each of the three elements of your inductive or deductive reasoning. The negative audience will be most critical of your arguments and of how well you connect the evidence to your conclusion. Again, you should articulate each of these three elements clearly to the negative audience. The audience's evaluation of the validity of the elements and the degree to which the elements connect depends on how strong your thinking and construction of arguments has been.

Table 16.2 shows a set of specific argumentative strategies that were identified several years ago by communication scholars Rod Hart, Gus Friedrich, and William Brooks.[39] Each strategy represents a type of appeal that can be used as an argument for action. These strategies are often found in our daily interactions with other people. Each type of appeal is followed with a definition and example of the way a

● **TABLE 16.2   Argumentative Strategies.**

Inclusion	The process of connecting the immediate audience's attitudes, values, and goals to those of a prized reference group	"Our candidate has been endorsed by the United Auto Workers, the American Federation of State, County and Municipal Workers, and AMA, and the American Bar Association. Won't you join these groups in support of . . . "
Maximization	The attempt to demonstrate graphically the superiority of the speaker's proposal over that of competing propositions	"This proposal will produce greater profits, increased market share, stronger innovations, and more company growth than any other proposal before you today."
Minimization	The process of deprecating the views of those opposing the speaker and/or of slighting apparently detrimental aspects of the speaker's proposal	"The 20 percent higher cost of my proposal than the others isn't that big of a deal when you look at the relative long-term benefits. Those who oppose this proposal are failing to plan for the years to come."
Association	The method whereby the speakers show relationships between themselves or their proposals and beliefs that are positively valued by the listener	"My proposal to support a new high school is based on my belief in providing the best education we can for our children, a value I know you share. Building a new high school is building for the future."

● **TABLE 16.2** (Continued)

Disassociation	The process by which speakers depict the lack of relationship between themselves (or their proposal) and beliefs that are negatively valued by the listener	"Do you want layoffs? Do you want wages lowered and fewer benefits? Do you want longer hours and no overtime pay? My plan to modernize the plant will ensure the company's health and your health."
Simplification	The method whereby speakers reduce the positive aspects of their proposals (or the negative aspects of their opponents' proposals) to its lowest common denominator	"Ultimately the decision about whether you make a pledge to reduce or abandon drinking alcohol comes down to one question: how much do you value your long-term health and safety?"
Unification	An attempt to demonstrate graphically the underlying similarity among a series of otherwise disparate elements	"Living longer, enjoying your life, having a positive attitude about yourself, and looking good are all products of adopting a sustained exercise program for yourself."
Involvement	The actual or simulated attempt to engage the audience directly in communicative interaction	"Raise your hand if you would like to live to be one hundred? Now raise your hand if you engage in at least thirty minutes of exercise three times a week."
Gradualism	A technique whereby speakers argue that the acceptance of their proposals does not necessitate radical restructuring of an audience's belief system	"I'm not asking you to start running ten miles a day. Try running just one mile at your own pace; two days later, just walk a mile. Every other day, extend your run and walk a little more."
Overkill	The often subtle procedure by which speakers ask for far more attitude change than they can hope to get in order to at least obtain some concession from their audiences	(Door-in-the-face) "We would like you to volunteer to work at least two hours each day after school or work. However, if you can't manage that, many of our volunteers come one day a week for three hours, and maybe that would work for you too."
Projection	A common device whereby speakers hypothesize the outcomes of audiences' wrongly following the course of action they oppose and/or rightly embracing the proposal the speakers endorse	(Visualization) "You've finished donating blood and have a small Band-Aid on your arm. As you leave, you look around at the other people donating and feel proud that you are helping someone in need. You feel a sense of satisfaction knowing you have made a difference."
Elimination	The process by which speakers successively set aside alternative approaches to the solutions they support (often accompanied by minimizing strategies)	"So what are your exercise options? Treadmills are cumbersome and expensive. Health clubs make people feel self-conscious. Swimming requires access to a pool. Jogging is ideal because the only cost is a good pair of shoes."

Type	Definition	Example
Idealization	An abstracting technique by which speakers suggest that certain super-ordinate goals are more important than any disagreements the speakers and their listeners might harbor.	"We have frequently been divided about issues of policy or procedures, but today we are faced with a more grave issue—ensuring the continuation of our program. Agreement with this proposal will show our commitment to a shared vision."
Legitimization	The tangible counterpart to the ideal-ization strategy whereby speakers argue that some person, document, or institution demands the ac-ceptance of the speaker's proposal	"Your own morals and values may lead you to condemn pornography, but our Constitution guar-antees freedom of expression. Once you start putting restrictions on such expression, you risk losing your rights to all expression.
Self-Deprecation	A frequently used persuasive strategy in which speakers admit to certain inadequacies in order to build reci-procity between themselves and their listeners	"Did I make a bad decision in endorsing the Johnson contract? Yes, but I learned from that—get all the facts and input of other departments; that's what I have done. The proposed Smith contract is a good choice."
Apprehension	Better known as the fear-appeal approach; a device whereby speakers graphically illustrate a threatening set of events or depict the deleterious consequences of an audience's not following the speaker's advice.	(Fear appeals) "One night of fun at the bars can lead to a lifetime of horror—perhaps haunting nightmares of those killed when you lost control of your car, perhaps facing a lifelong disability because you wrapped your car around a telephone pole. Don't drink and drive. Use a designated driver."

Source: Reprinted by Permission of University Press of America.

speaker might apply the strategy. Your topic and the nature of the issues you are cov-ering are likely to determine which strategies to apply. As you study the list, consider the appropriateness of each strategy to your next presentation and what to say to establish the argument. See also Act and Reflect 16.6.

Organizational Strategies

All right, now you're thinking, "Surely, now that I've learned about support stra-tegies for use with negative audiences, I'm ready to give my speech." Sorry, you're not quite there yet, eager speaker. You still need to consider the best way to organize the presentation to maximize your effectiveness. Your decision about what structure to use can significantly impact the success of your presentation to a negative audience, as we discussed in Chapter 11. How will the audience respond to the organization of the material you have to present? What are your alternatives? Each part of your pre-sentational structure should be designed to help you achieve your goal. This section provides both overall organizational strategies, as well as those specific to the intro-duction and conclusion.

ACT&REFLECT

16.6: Applying Argumentation Strategies

ACT • For each topic, briefly describe how you would apply one of argumentation strategies from Table 16.2 to win support from your classmates. Use a different strategy for each topic.

Topic	Strategy	Application
1. Increasing study time		
2. Support a tuition increase		
3. Donate blood		
4. Go to graduate school		
5. Your own topic (specify)		

REFLECT • Which of the strategies you chose do you think would be most effective? Why? Which would be least effective? Why? For your own topic, what other strategies might be effective?

Strategic Selection of the Organizational Framework While we've introduced you to a large number of organizational choices, some of them work better than others when speaking to negative audiences. We discussed organization frameworks that work particularly well with such audiences and as frameworks for persuasive presentations in detail in Chapter 11, most notably:

- Agree-disagree pattern
- Two-sided refutational framework
- Reflective thought sequence
- Elimination of alternatives (method of residues)
- Scientific problem solving
- Monroe's motivated sequence[40]

Each of these organizational frameworks may need further adaptation to fit your goals. For example, in using Monroe's motivated sequence, you might develop one point in a presentation to a negative audience using the entire sequence but devote only one sentence to each of the steps that make up the sequence. On the other hand, because the motivated sequence is a rather complex structure, you might select only parts of it to fit your needs. Perhaps selecting only the "need" and "solution" steps would create an entire presentation that would suit your particular needs with the negative audience.

In deciding which framework to use, consider the specific qualities of your audience and their responses to your topic. Once you have chosen that framework, you will need to think about each part of it. For example, in some frameworks there is a point when you inform your audience of the nature of the problem. How will you organize that part of your presentation? For assistance in making this decision, look to the other organizational frameworks we have discussed. You might find, for example, that chronological order, an organizational framework we discussed for helping audiences learn, would be the most effective means to help your negative audience learn more about the situation. In order to convey your viewpoint to them, repetition of a key theme or point could be an effective choice.

When you find yourself planning a presentation to a negative audience, you are faced with an array of organizational options. Don't be afraid to "pick and choose" from as many of the frameworks as you need to create the most effective presentation you can for this special circumstance.

Narrow Your Focus Research demonstrates the people with strong views on an issue will listen and even remember opposing views, but in doing so, they are constantly developing counterarguments to what they hear.[41] This phenomenon means that you can actually defeat your own goal by causing the audience to become even more entrenched in their attitudes than they were before you spoke. In essence, the harder I try to pull you in a given direction, the more resistance you muster to oppose my pull. Thus, when I'm done pulling, you have developed additional strength. So how do you present arguments without causing greater audience resistance? One option would be to present only a few select arguments—those that are the strongest and most difficult to refute. A long list of arguments both weak and strong allows the opposer to focus attention on developing counterarguments to the weak arguments while ignoring the strong. With the most extreme audience, your goal is to gain incremental changes rather than wholesale ones, which you might best achieve by using narrowly focused arguments.

Adapt the Introduction When planning the introduction to the negative audience, it is important to make every word count, because you not only are trying to achieve your own communication goal with the audience but also must scale the barriers that surround their opposition. However, if you spend too much time on the introduction, you lose the advantage of grabbing the audience's attention, and you allow time for them to regenerate their negative attitude.

Here's how the five components of the stock introduction can apply to negative audiences:

> *Attention-grabber.* You will need a thoughtful attention-grabber that does its job well. As we have indicated, it is helpful if the presenter can establish common ground with the negative audience.

Audience relevance. You can do this as you are establishing audience relevance, because this will demonstrate to the audience that you are sensitive to their viewpoints.

Credentials. Whether you should present your credentials is another judgment call. If the audience knows who you are, the fact that they already know your credentials may only exacerbate their negative attitude. However, if there is a relevant fact they are unaware of, consider divulging this point. For example, if you are speaking to the local Harley-Davidson club in favor of legislation that requires motorcycle helmet laws, it could be advantageous to their reception of you to disclose that you are certain your life was spared because you were wearing a helmet when your motorcycle was hit by a car.

Thesis. What about divulging your thesis? Your audience may be negative because they know, or believe they know, your viewpoint. If they already know your thesis, as with your credentials, you might be stating the obvious, exacerbating their negativity. If you have developed a reputation as an advocate for a cause or a particular position that is inconsistent with your audience's view, it is probably unnecessary for you to state what your audience already knows. You should state your thesis when it differs from what your audience expects. A company CEO who is expected to announce a plant shutdown but instead announces a major salary increase for employees would be wise to disclose this thesis early.

Preview. Preview your major points for the audience, but do so in a more general rather than specific way. Some of the organizational frameworks, such as the method of residues or the two-sided framework, could have a number of major points. When this is the case, rather than previewing each of these points, it makes most sense for you to preview in a more general way: "Let's take a look at some of the possible solutions we've discussed and see which are best suited to our problem." Or "On the basis of the discussions we've all participated in, it appears that three possible solutions have presented themselves." A general preview of this type allows your audience to be informed enough to listen to and follow your presentation.

Adapt the Conclusion Don't underestimate the potential of the conclusion to restate or reinforce any points you made during the presentation, as well as concluding in a memorable way. If applicable, restate what it is that you want your audience to recall, and develop an effective means to say "The End." However, in addition to either or both of these components of the conclusion, a recognition of the goodwill of the audience may be in order.

Address the audience's final state of mind and their goodwill. Consider the amazing event that has just occurred: you have made a presentation to an audience who "merely" disagreed with your viewpoint, or was antagonistic toward you personally, or, in the worst-case scenario, was downright hostile. What does this mean? It could mean you have effected a change in the audience's attitude and established a relationship with them, or that you had no impact and they have simply been acting courteously. Nonetheless, the bottom line is that they are still with you in some way, and you should confirm this goodwill. Let them know you appreciate their consideration of you and/or your message: "I am pleased to have had the opportunity to discuss my views with you." Or "I hope we can find common ground to work together in the future." A statement that confirms your willingness to interact or collaborate further with the audience is a fitting addition to the conclusion.

Be willing to engage the audience. A telling point about your character as a speaker is your willingness to respond to their questions and comments. Don't leave the area too quickly. After you have concluded your presentation, pause, take a breath, make eye contact with your listeners, and state deliberately, "I'd be happy to hear your comments and your questions." Think about the implications of this tactic. You have already demonstrated your courage and your conviction regarding the views you have expressed. To be willing to remain and interact with your audience after you have completed this act of courage simply emphasizes the worth of your opinion and the strength of your character. Don't take the chance of destroying this powerful image and important relationship you have created with your negative audience. Immediate follow-through is imperative to your entire message.

● GETTING TO WORK

What follows is the information conveyed in this chapter in encapsulated form.

Preliminaries: To Be Determined

How much interest in and knowledge of your topic does the audience have?

What is your audience's attitude toward what you are advocating? How resistant are they?

Your overall goal is to move the negative audience along the continuum of resistance. What is a reasonable goal, given the audience's attitude?

Why is the audience there?

Strategies for Addressing Negative Audiences

Foothold Strategies

Identify what you have in common with the audience that you can present and build on.

Describe your understanding of their viewpoint and your respect for their position.

Work toward gaining the audience's attention, interest, and receptivity to what you have to say.

If your presentation is part of a long-term strategy, what might you ask for to get in the door, or to get the door in the face?

Psychological Strategies

Identify and discuss how the audience's values and needs can be met by supporting your position.

Directly address any concerns or objections the audience has about your position, when appropriate.

Identify groups that your audience belongs to or wants to belong to that support your position.

Describe a scenario involving your position that the audience will see as a positive frame.

Identify and present any real dangers or harms to the audience that might occur if they do not adopt your position. What evidence do you have to support this?

Support Strategies

Present stories and metaphors that reflect positively on your position and that the audience can identify with.

Incorporate credible and/or reluctant testimony that supports your position.

What arguments does the audience use in support of their position? Build on those arguments to support your position.

Examine the list of typical argumentation strategies and select two or three that can be incorporated in support of your position.

Organizational Strategies

Organize your presentation according to the framework that best fits the issue, the situation, and the audience.

Narrow your focus—present the fewest possible key points that have the greatest possible impact.

Incorporate the five components of a stock introduction (attention-grabber, audience relevance, credentials, thesis, and preview) that best fit the situation.

Conclude your presentation with a review, and a memorable finale; make a statement of goodwill; and invite questions and comments.

SUMMARY

Passively negative audiences have knowledge of the issue and oppose the speaker's position, but have lost interest; actively negative audiences have knowledge, oppose the speaker, and continue to have an active interest in the issue. Understanding the reasons people hold attitudes can help in developing effective strategies. People hold on to attitudes that they believe are correct, that make them look good, that are consistent with their values and behaviors, that are defensible, and that allow affiliation with a desired group. Some of the reasons audiences are likely to attend a presentation when they oppose the speaker's position are that their attendance is mandatory, that they seek an opportunity to express their views and influence others, or that they want to gain information about the opposition. Persuading a negative audience involves recognizing their level of resistance and setting a realistic goal of how far you can expect to reduce their opposition. Recognizing the level of resistance allows you to determine the degree to which your goal involves influencing attitudes and/or behaviors.

There are a number of strategies that can be employed when addressing negative audiences that can be placed into four categories: foothold strategies, psychological strategies, support strategies, and organizational strategies. Unless an audience is interested in what you are speaking about, they will not listen; therefore, you must gain a foothold by stimulating interest. Establishing a common ground with the audience, and showing respect and understanding of their position can help you connect with the audience and influence them to listen to you. Adapting to the functioning of the mind also involves gaining attention and opening pathways to long-term memory. Accomplishing goals might involve a series of presentations rather than a one-shot attempt in which such strategies as "foot-in-the-door" or "door-in-the-face" are employed.

Some psychological strategies you can use in presentations to negative audiences are appealing to their values and needs identifying and responding to concerns and objections, showing a connection with desired groups, creating a favorable frame of mind in which the message is considered, and using fear appeals.

Narratives and metaphors appear to aid in persuading, particularly when arousing emotional responses. The use of statistics appears to work with some audiences more than others and might best be coupled with the appropriate use of narratives. Logical appeals and arguments are appropriate with knowledgeable audiences, who tend to listen more critically. Start with arguments the audience already knows before introducing new ones. Sound arguments have staying power, in that when an audience is considering the content of a presentation, the strength of a logical conclusion will endure. However, people don't operate on logic alone, and being psychological involves considering how people are influenced by their biases and emotions. A number of argumentative strategies can be employed to effect change, such as involving the audience, using gradualism, systematically eliminating alternatives, admitting your own inadequacies, and projecting future outcomes.

In addition to all the organizational frameworks recommended for presentations to negative audiences, you need to consider the internal workings of the framework you select. Is there an organizational framework that is recommended for either the positive or neutral audience that might help you to organize one point of your speech to the negative audience? Besides the overall structure of your presentation, don't forget to organize the major points of your organizational framework. The presentation might also be strengthened by focusing on a few central points. The stock components of the introduction and conclusion work to orient the audience to the presentation and to end it in a memorable manner. In the case of the negative audience, carefully consider which of the components will assist you in previewing and reviewing your message in the most effective manner for them.

VIDEO EXPERIENCE

1. Citizen appeals to city government or other agencies often involve making appeals and trying to persuade listeners (often a board or council). In the first video example, a citizen of Wichita, Kansas, is asking the city council for better animal control because of stray dogs. See if you can identify the strategies, appeals, and arguments he uses in trying to gain the support of the city council.

2. In the second video, a student makes a class presentation addressing the issue of home-schooling. The student surveyed audience members prior to the presentation, confirming that a majority of the other students were not supportive of home-schooling, along with identifying some of their concerns. Listen to the strategies she uses to address those concerns. How well do you think she addresses them? A transcript of this presentation is included at the end of this chapter.

THINKING BACK, THINKING AHEAD

1. Create a list by brainstorming as many situations as you can think of in which the audience was negative at the beginning of the presentation. Next to each, identify where the audience stood in terms of the two dimensions of support/oppose the speaker's position and interest/no interest. Label each audience as an active or passive negative audience. Create a line for each situation to indicate the level of the audience's resistance and indicate where the audience started and where they were when the speech was done. For those who changed, indicate what the speaker did to accomplish this.

2. For each of the following situations, identify at least two specific strategies from this chapter that you could apply to reduce the audience's negativity.

   a. As part of a course, you are required to make a presentation advocating that all college graduates serve two years of government service (in the military, Peace Corps, or other program).

   b. A group of employees are being required against their will to attend your training session on some topic relevant to your specialty.

   c. You are speaking to a group of high school seniors whose parents have forced them to visit your campus. They have visited the campus of another school similar to yours (could be an in-state rival if you have one), and that other school is the one they really want to attend.

   d. You are making a request to your church's administrative committee, which is made up of older church members, for funds to support a one-week mission trip by college students to Mexico. This committee has not been supportive of college student activities and believes church repair and maintenance are a greater priority.

3. You are giving a presentation to this class arguing for the adoption of some action or attitude (you decide on one that is appropriate) that the majority of the class opposes. You are limited to five minutes to talk about this topic. What would be the first thing you would tell your audience? What strategies would be best to use? Why?

4. Keep a log of the presentations you have attended or seen on TV at which a negative audience has been in attendance. How do presenters respond to the negativity? Have you witnessed a presentation in which the speaker responded to the negative audience negatively? What was the result? What do you learn about ways presenters can and should respond to negative audiences?

5. Identify two potential topics for a speech to your classmates that you are reasonably sure they would oppose. For each topic, identify how you could apply each of the following strategies:

   a. Common ground

   b. Values or needs

   c. Concerns and objections

   d. Negative frame

   e. Fear appeals

   f. Building on known arguments

Sample Speech

Presentation to a Negative Audience   MSL

The speaker surveyed the students prior to the presentation, revealing opposition to her position in support of home-schooling. She was able to determine some of the reasons for the listeners' opposition and address those concerns directly in her presentation. The audience was a somewhat active negative audience—they had some knowledge of the issue, and they opposed the speaker's position, but they had some interest.

Benefits of Home Schooling
Katelyn Verhoef, student, Iowa State University, fall 2004

To get to grade school or high school, you may have driven or you may have walked. Well, all I had to do was walk down a flight of stairs and I was there. That's because I was home-schooled. My parents started home-schooling me in 1996 when I was going into fourth grade. At the time home-schooling wasn't a very popular thing. Not many people knew about it, and there were concerns that my parents were ruining our lives. Statistics have shown though from the U.S. Department of Education, National Center for Education, that there were 850,000 home-schoolers in 1999. That number is up to, from 2003, 1,092,000. This makes up about 2.2 percent of the school-aged children from ages five to seventeen. So home-schooling has been growing in popularity since I started home-schooling; however, it's still not as popular, obviously, as public school or private school. I know a lot of you have concerns about home-schooling from the surveys I received, especially in the area of education, socialization, and just generally how they end up as adults. So let me talk about those and hopefully leave you with a positive outlook for home-schooling. Some day you guys might have kids and you'll have to decide how you will educate them.

How well does this get the audience's attention?

Let's start out with education. People tend to be concerned about parents educating kids because they said they're not certified and not qualified. Well, there's a study called *Home Schooling Works,* by Dr. Lawrence M. Rudner, who's with the College Library and Information Services, University of Maryland, College Park. He's been involved with quantitative analysis for over thirty years and has served as professor and a branch chief for the U.S. Department of Education, and this is what he found. [Displays an overhead of research graphs] He used the PDS test, which tests knowledge basically of home-schools in both fourth grade and eighth grade. The blue [points to bar on graph] is at least one certified teacher and the red is no certified teacher. He found no significant difference.

To what degree does this demonstrate understanding and respect for the audience's positions?

There was also another study done by Dr. Brian D. Ray, Ph.D., president of the National Home Educational Research Institute. [Displays another bar graph] He found the same results; this is for a basic battery test, except he also compared them to public schoolers. Home-schoolers with the parents certified got an 88 percentile rank, home-schoolers without certified parents got an 85, and public schoolers had a 50. That's significant difference.

What's your evaluation of this source? Has the speaker adequately established his credibility?

There's also statistics showing that home-schoolers can have higher ACT scores than normal schoolers. In 2000, according to the National Center for Policy Analysis, the national average on the ACT for 2000 was 21 nationally out of a possible 36,

What is the underlying argument and logic the speaker uses here? How effective is it? What would make it more effective?

(continued)

Sample Speech to a Negative Audience continued

Here the speaker cites specific examples from her own experience. What impact would this have the other student listeners?

while children taught at home averaged 22.8. My friends who are home-schooled tended to have higher ACT scores, too. Micah Van Mersbergen, he's a junior here majoring in mechanical engineering and agricultural engineering, had a 34. I had a 33. My friend, Richard, he's a senior in high school, home-schooled in Oskaloosa, Iowa. He had a 35. So, education tends to be a little bit above average.

The speaker shows an understanding of the audience's view and also uses the argumentation strategy of self-deprecation. How well does this lower resistance?

Also there was huge concern among you in the surveys concerning socialization. I understand that concern because since they're home-schooled at home they don't get the interaction that you guys got with all the kids your age. But home-schoolers get more of an education with people that aren't their age, like their parents and their younger siblings. Home-schoolers tend to be involved in a lot of activities that they do the socialization with children their age. So it's not so much of a concern.

How well does this counterargument that home-schoolers are involved in activities and the accompanying evidence work to overcome the audience's concern about home-schoolers' socialization?

[Displays an overhead bar graph of study results] This study is also done by Brian D. Ray for an article entitled, it's the same article. He found that 98 percent; of home-schoolers participated in more than two activities, and this data was collected for more than 5,400 home schoolers. So as you can see [pointing to overhead] they were involved in normal things like Scouts, ballet and dance classes, 4-H, volunteer work, Bible clubs, music groups. They played with people outside the family. As you can see, they have a lot of social activities. Home-schoolers are involved in a lot of social activities.

There was a study done by Dr. Larry Shyers, who is a psychotherapist and the chairman of the Florida Board of Clinical Social Work, Marriage and Family Therapy and Mental Health Counseling. He compared the behaviors and social development test scores of two groups of seventy children, ages eight to ten. One group was being educated at home and the other group wasn't. He found that home schoolers didn't seem any different from the other group—from the group who were going to public or private school. He also found that they tended to have less behavioral problems than the regular schoolers. From this he concluded that the results seemed to show that a child's social development depends more on adult contact and less on contact with other children as previously thought.

How does the speaker apply association and idealization strategies in support of home schooling in this section of her presentation?

Children seem to have pretty good education from home schooling and socialization, but the real test is how are they going to turn out as adults. Are they going to be productive? Are they going to be good citizens? My following graphs are all from Dr. Brian D. Ray's research, and this is fairly recent research, it came out in 2003. It's called "Home Schooing Grows Up." Over five-thousand people who had been home-schooled for more than seven years were studied, or surveyed, sorry. This is what they found. Of the people in the eighteen-to-twenty-four group [displays overhead chart and points to each bar as she talks], this is beyond graduation, the first one, the blue is home-schoolers, and the red is not-home-schoolers. This one is some college but no degree, and as you see it goes up to about 50 percent. Home-schooling is way higher. This one is associate's degree. This one is bachelor's degree. This one is graduate or professional but no degree. This one is master's. There wasn't a doctorate degree— keep in mind these are eighteen-to twenty-four-year-olds. Professional degree as an MD or JD and then there's also other. The other is like vocational tech school or did not graduate from high school. So that's the only one that home schoolers scored way lower than the general population.

Since there was a election recently I wanted to also show that home schoolers tend to be more civically involved as adults than regular schoolers. This chart [displays bar chart] is from the same study. General U.S. is about fifteen million that they studied; then home educated were about five thousand that they studied. And it says voted in national, state election in U.S. in past five years. As you can see in the eighteen-to-twenty-four group, twenty-five-to-forty-nine, and forty-to-fifty-four group, home-schoolers generally vote more often than non-home-schoolers.

◄ *What type of argumentative strategy does the speaker use here?*

Home-schoolers tend to be more happy than the regular population. This is happiness quotient [displays overhead pie chart]. Blue is very happy, brown is pretty happy, and red is not too happy. As you can see, home-schoolers have a lot more blue, which is very happy, and the general population has a lot of brown, which is fairly happy.

So as you can see, home-schooling tends to be a fairly good education. It gives them a good education. It gives good socialization skills. It makes them into pretty good adults. I know you all have never been home-schooled, so you don't have experience or anything, but I found it to be very beneficial to me—I made lots of different fiends I would have never made. I've enjoyed the independence. I've enjoyed all the opportunities I've had. I started working in a nursing home when I was sixteen. I would have never had that opportunity because it takes a lot of time and energy. Someday you all are going to have to decide how to educate your kids, and home-schooling is a good option. It's very easy; all you have to do is stay home and educate your kids. Do you have any questions? I would be happy to answer your questions.

◄ *The speaker shares personal stories about her experience as a home schooler and uses the association strategy. To what degree are these strategies effective here?*

Additional Questions to Consider

1. To what degree did the speaker move you along the continuum of resistance toward her position?
2. What aspects of the speech had the greatest influence on you?
3. What additional strategies might the speaker have used to support for home schooling from an audience who were primarily educated in public schools?
4. The speaker didn't make any direct fear appeals (such as the negative aspect that might be associated with attending public school). To what degree to you believe this was or wasn't a good decision by the speaker?

NOTES

1. W. Wood, N. Rhodes, and M. Biek, "Working Know-ledge and Attitude Strength: An Information-Processing Analysis," in *Attitude Strength: Antecedents and Consequences,* edited by R. E. Petty and J. A. Krosnick (Mahwah, NJ: Erlbaum, 1995), 283–313.

2. Wood, Rhodes, and Biek, "Working Knowledge and Attitude Strength."

3. Wood, Rhodes, and Biek, "Working Knowledge and Attitude Strength."

4. M. Heesacker, R. E. Petty, and J. T. Cacioppo, "Field Dependence and Attitude Change: Source Credibility Can Alter Persuasion by Affecting Message-Relevant Thinking," *Journal of Personality, 51* (1983): 653–665.

5. Heesacker, Petty, and Cacioppo, "Field Dependence and Attitude Change."

6. T. Clevenger, *Audience Analysis* (Indianapolis: Bobbs-Merrill, 1966).

7. R. E. Petty and J. T. Cacioppo, *Attitudes and Persuasion: Classic and Contemporary Approaches* (Dubuque, IA: Brown, 1981). W. Benoit and M. J. Smythe, "Rhetorical Theory as Message Reception: A Cognitive Response Approach to Rhetorical Theory and Criticism, *Communication Studies, 54* (2003): 96–114.

8. A. H. Eagly, P. Kulsea, L. A. Brannon, K. Shaw, and S. Hustson-Comeaux, "Why Counterattitudinal Messages Are as Memorable as Proattitudinal Messages: The Importance of Active Defense against Attack," *Personality and Social Psychology Bulletin, 26* (2000): 1392–1408. A. Lieberman and S. Chaiken, "Defensive Processing of Personally Relevant Health Messages," *Personality and Social Psychology Bulletin, 18* (1992): 669–679.

9. Benoit and Smythe, "Rhetorical Theory as Message Reception."

10. Benoit and Smythe, "Rhetorical Theory as Message Reception."

11. R. E. Petty and J. T. Cacioppo, *Communication and Persuasion: Central and Peripheral Routes to Attitude Change* (New York: Springer-Verlag, 1986).

12. A. R. Damasio, *The Feeling of What Happens: Body and Emotion in the Making of Consciousness* (New York: Harcourt Brace, 1999).

13. "FBI Chief Defends Agenda," *Boston Globe,* June 14, 2003, retrieved from Lexis-Nexis, at Iowa State University.

14. D. A. Sousa, *How the Brain Learns* (Reston, VA: National Association of Secondary School Principals, 1995).

15. Eagly et al., "Why Counterattitudinal Messages Are as Memorable as Proattitudinal Messages."

16. S. R. Lundgren and R. Prislin, "Motivated Cognitive Processing and Attitude Change," *Personality and Social Psychology Bulletin, 24* (1998): 715–727.

17. W. Wood, "Attitude Change: Persuasion and Social Influence." *Annual Review of Psychology, 51* (2000): 539–570.

18. R. E. Petty, D. T. Wegener, and L. R. Fabrigar, "Attitudes and Attitude Change," *Annual Review of Psychology, 48,* (1997): 609–648.

19. R. M. Perloff, *The Dynamics of Persuasion: Communication and Attitudes in the Twenty-First Century.* (Mahwah, NJ: Erlbaum, 2003).

20. P. Salovey, T. Schneider, and A. M. Apanovitch, "Message Framing in the Prevention and Early Detection of Illness," in *The Persuasion Handbook: Developments in Theory and Practice,* edited by J. P. Dillard and M. Pfau (Thousand Oaks, CA: Sage, 2002), 391–406.

21. A. J. Rothman and P. Salovey, "Shaping Perceptions to Motivate Healthy Behavior: The Role of Message Framing," *Psychological Bulletin, 121* (1997): 3–19.

22. S. M. Smith and R. E. Petty, "Message Framing and Persuasion: A Message Processing Analysis," *Personality and Social Psychology Bulletin, 22* (1996): 257–268.

23. A. J. Rothman, P. Salovey, C. Antone, K. Keough, and C. D. Martin, "The Influence of Message Framing on Intentions to Perform Health Behaviors," *Journal of Experimental Social Psychology, 29* (1993): 408–433.

24. Daniel J. O'Keefe, *Persuasion: Theory and Research,* 2nd ed. (Thousand Oaks, CA: Sage, 2002).

25. K. Witte, "Putting the Fear Back into Fear Appeals: The Extended Parallel Process Model," *Communication Monographs, 39* (1992): 329–349.

26. Wood, "Attitude Change." Witte, "Putting the Fear Back."

27. E. H. H. J. Das, J. F. F. de Wit, and W. Stroebe, "Fear Appeals Motivate Acceptance of Action Recommendations: Evidence for a Positive Bias in the Processing of Persuasive Messages," *Personality and Social Psychology Bulletin, 29* (2003): 650–664.

28. Witte, "Putting the Fear Back."

29. L. W. Jones, R. C. Sinclair, and K. S. Courneya, "The Effects of Source Credibility and Message Framing on Exercise Intentions, Behaviors, and Attitudes: An Integration of the Elaboration Likelihood Model and Prospect Theory," *Journal of Applied Social Psychology* (2003): 179–197.

30. Kazoleas, "A Comparison of the Persuasive Effectiveness of Qualitative Versus Quantitative Evidence: A Test of Explanatory Hypotheses," *Communication Quarterly, 41* (1993): 40–50.

31. J. W. Bowers, and M. M. Osborn, "Attitudinal Effects of Selected Types of Concluding Metaphors in Persuasive Speeches," *Speech Monographs, 33* (1966): 147–155.

32. E. J. Baesler, "Persuasive Effects of Story and Statistical Evidence," *Argumentation and Advocacy, 33* (1997):

170–175. F. J. Boster, K. A. Cameron, S. Campo, W. Liu, Wen-Ying, J. K. Lillie, E. M. Baker, and K. A. Yun, "The Persuasive Effects of Statistical Evidence in the Presence of Exemplars," *Communication Studies, 51* (2000): 296–306. L. L. Lindsey and K. A. Yun, "Examining the Persuasive Effect of Statistical Messages: A Test of Mediating Relationships," *Communication Studies, 54* (2003): 306–321.

33. Boster, et al., "Persuasive Effects of Statistical Evidence."

34. Tony Blair, presentation to the annual conference of the Labour Party, Bournemouth, September, 30, 2003, retrieved from the Labour Party Web site, at www.labour.org.uk/tbbournemouth.

35. R. P. Hart, G. W. Friedrich, and W. D. Brooks, *Public Communication* (New York: Harper & Row, 1975).

36. W. L. Benoit and I. A. Kennedy, "On Reluctant Testimony," *Communication Quarterly, 47* (1999): 376–387.

37. Wood, Rhodes, and Biek, "Working Knowledge and Attitude Strength."

38. Statistics from U.S. Census Bureau, "The Big Payoff: Educational Attainment and Synthetic Estimates of Work-Life Earnings," July 2002, retrieved from the U.S. Census Bureau Web site, at www.census.gov/prod/2002pubs/p23%2D210.pdf.

39. Hart, Friedrich, and Brooks, *Public Communication.*

40. A. H. Monroe, *Principles and Types of Speech* (New York: Scott Foresman, 1935).

41. Eagly et al., "Why Counterattitudinal Messages Are as Memorable as Proattitudinal Messages." A. Lieberman and S. Chaiken, "Defensive Processing of Personally Relevant Health Messages," *Personality and Social Psychology Bulletin, 18* (1992): 669–679.

Chapter 17

Making Presentations on Special Occasions

To Recognize and Remember

Your Majesties, Members of the Norwegian Nobel Committee, Excellencies, Ladies and Gentlemen,

It is with a deep sense of gratitude that I accept this prize. I am grateful to my wife Rosalynn, to my colleagues at The Carter Center, and to many others who continue to seek an end to violence and suffering throughout the world. The scope and character of our Center's activities are perhaps unique, but in many other ways they are typical of the work being done by many hundreds of nongovernmental organizations that strive for human rights and peace.[1]

—*Jimmy Carter, Nobel Lecture, Oslo, December 10, 2002*

Without reading the source or event for this quotation, you probably guessed this was a speech given on a special occasion. Maybe you arrived at this conclusion by noticing the speaker's praise of various individuals; perhaps you caught the emphasis on the antithetical qualities of "the unique" and "the typical"; or maybe you were inspired by the possibilities of a better world, free of violence and suffering. These qualities found in Jimmy Carter's Nobel Prize lecture are typical of a special kind of presentation known as the special occasion speech. This type of speech differs from other speeches we have discussed. Previously our focus has been on the nature of the audience and various approaches to consider when presenting to different audiences. With a special occasion speech, we look at ways to organize and phrase messages that celebrate special events—occasions.

It's difficult to imagine many occasions more special than receiving the Nobel Prize for Peace, unless it would be receiving the Nobel Prize in any of the other categories or an Academy Award or a Pulitzer Prize, or being inaugurated as president of the United States. Those are certainly major special occasions. In our private lives we observe smaller but equally important special occasions: a wedding anniversary, a memorial service, a retirement party, or the introduction of a guest speaker are only a few of these. Although they occur on a smaller scale, family, professional, and other events are of equal importance in their observation of the accomplishments of individuals we wish to recognize and celebrate. ●

If you believe you will never find yourself in the position to give a special occasion speech, that will only be the case if you have no need to pursue a career, if you have no family, or if you live on a desert island where there is no one to socialize with. "Everyday people" might not be inaugurated president of the United States, nor do they receive Academy Awards or Nobel Prizes, but they do attend funerals or memorial services, and they celebrate anniversaries, weddings, retirements, and other important events by which people mark their lives. Everyday people (like all of us) introduce guest speakers, and they present and accept awards. And there are many occasions when "everyday people" find themselves expected to say some special words for an occasion. The father of one of us was once called on to present a gold watch to a retiring colleague. Dad fretted for at least six months about his capability to handle this task. Whether the uncertainty is due to being singled out to present or to the lack of organizational frameworks for special occasion speeches, such events do present their own special challenges. Aristotle guides us in preparation of those special, often emotional, sometimes nerve-wracking, celebratory moments in our lives.

The Ceremonial Oratory of Display: Epideictic Rhetoric

Ceremonial speaking, or **epideictic discourse,** originated in Greek antiquity.[2] The word "epideictic" comes to us from the Greek word *epideiktikon,* meaning "demonstrative." Aristotle differentiated the epideictic speech from political and legal discourse by describing it as "speeches that do not call for any immediate action by the audience but that characteristically praise or blame some person or thing, often on a ceremonial occasion such as a public funeral or holiday."[3] There are a number of characteristics that, when merged, make up presentations that are considered special occasion or **epideictic speeches:** first, such speeches offer praise or blame; second, the speaker enhances or amplifies the accomplishments of the person or the qualities of the event that is the focus of the speech; third, the time frame of the speech is the present but encompasses past and future; fourth, the audience's role differs from other types of presentations; finally, the importance of the event or ceremony motivates the speech.[4]

How do each of the principles Aristotle identifies assist us in creating special occasion speeches? The first consideration is the cause for which an individual or occasion is singled out as special.

Principle 1: Demonstrating Praise or Blame

Although Aristotle defined the epideictic speech as one praising or blaming an individual or event, this special type of presentation characteristically focuses on praiseworthy rather

epideictic discourse Ceremonial speaking.

epideiktikon Greek word meaning "demonstrative."

epideictic speeches Presentations given on special occasions.

than negative occasions.[5] Even in instances when a seemingly negative quality is divulged, it is typically given a positive spin. For example, a speech recognizing "the teacher of the year" might mention the recipient as being "stubborn," from the standpoint that she "was totally stubborn about protecting the welfare of her students, who, she was convinced, were worth their weight in gold."

When you find yourself in the role of giving a special occasion speech, a first step is to identify qualities of the person or characteristics of the event that are relevant to the occasion and connect these qualities to examples that praise the person or event. In addition, the focus of the celebration should be elevated or amplified.

Principle 2: Amplification

Amplification is the process of individualizing and enhancing the accomplishments and/or qualities of the person or event celebrated. To introduce an Olympic athlete as the gold medal–winner of his or her sport is an example of amplification. To state that the gold medal–winner set an Olympic record further amplifies his or her accomplishments. When a person is described as "the first one . . . ," "the only one . . . ," "the most accomplished . . . ," "the greatest . . . . ," "the hardest fighter . . . ," "the one nominated more than anyone else . . . ," "the one who received the most awards . . . ," each of these phrases amplifies. Aristotle believed special occasion speeches should slant heavily toward amplification.[6] If a person's actions could not be amplified on his own merits, Aristotle advocated creating a comparison to others. In another Nobel Prize example, when Nobel Prize–winners of the Western Hemisphere were greeted at the White House, President John F. Kennedy said:

> I think this is the most extraordinary collection of talent, of human knowledge, that has ever been gathered together at the White House, with the possible exception of when Thomas Jefferson dined alone.[7]

Although President Kennedy apparently chose not to amplify individual Nobel laureates, the comparison to Thomas Jefferson was a strategy to highlight their accomplishments. The time frame of special occasion speeches also adds an unusual and interesting dimension to this type of presentation.

Principle 3: Celebrating the Present

When Jimmy Carter accepted the Nobel Peace Prize, he praised those who had worked in the past to end violence and human suffering, as well as challenging listeners to continue to work in the future on behalf of human rights. Although special occasion speeches focus on current activities or existing qualities, they recognize past accomplishments and suggest future possibilities through a framework of shared human values.

The recognition of human accomplishments that occurs in the present evokes past accomplishments that become the basis for promoting a vision of a better life, "of a world that could

amplification The process of individualizing and enhancing the accomplishments and/or qualities of a person or event being celebrated.

A Question of **Ethics**

Principles 1 and 2 of Aristotle's epideictic discourse speak to the need to demonstrate praise or blame and to include amplification in ceremonial speeches. Principle 1 states that the positive qualities of a person should be the focus of a ceremonial speech and that if negative qualities are known about the person being celebrated, they should be presented with a "positive spin." Principle 2 states that methods should be identified to enhance the qualities or accomplishments of the person celebrated. This means that characteristics about the person could be embellished for the sake of the ceremonial occasion. Is it possible that by following the principles you could amplify or demonstrate praise to the point that you were discussing characteristics the person simply did not possess? At what point does adhering to these principles become unethical? That is, when you give a ceremonial speech, how would you differentiate between adhering to the principles and committing the unethical action of being deceitful to your audience by describing qualities the person in your speech did not possess?

be."[8] Dr. Martin Luther King's "I Have a Dream" speech was a protest of "Jim Crow" statutes that mandated segregation of public facilities. However, Dr. King's "dream" of freedom, equality, brotherhood, and justice served to remind Americans of the struggle for civil rights and also outlined an American future to aspire to.[9] The speech was given at a huge civil rights rally in Washington, D.C. (in the present); to illustrate unjust laws (in the past); and to present a vision of Dr. King's dream (in the future). Here we also have an example in which, rather than offering praise, censure of the statutes was a central focus of the speech.

Though the immediate goal of a special occasion speech is to recognize a person or event, in doing so, there are equally important long-term goals of confirming and promoting "adherence to the commonly held values of a community with the goal of sustaining that community."[10] In this case, "community" refers to a group of people: a family, a business organization, attendees at a Labor Day rally, or other members of a recognized group of people. As you prepare your next special occasion speech, consider the virtues and values displayed by the individual(s) recognized. How can these qualities serve as examples to your audience of values they adhere to?

Principle 4: Role of the Audience

Because you have read this book, you know it is the nature of the audience that informs and influences many of the decisions a speaker makes in planning and giving a presentation. It is also the audience on whom the speaker intends to have an influence to reach his or her communication goal. However, when preparing a special occasion speech, the audience does not hold this central position that informs the speaker's decisions.

Although a special occasion speech can certainly inspire an audience or cause them to reflect on past events with the intention of working toward a better life, the roles of speaker and audience are not so clear-cut with the special occasion speech. In fact, Aristotle saw the principle characters in the special occasion as the speaker and the person receiving the recognition, with the audience assuming a spectator-like role. Others who have written about special occasion speeches indicate that the audience is likely to know the qualities of the person being recognized; the speaker is not likely to be informing the audience of something they did not know, or telling them something "newsworthy."[11]

For you, this slightly different role for the audience means it is not so crucial for you to consider your audience in the ways we have suggested earlier. There will certainly be times when your audience may not be knowledgeable, or may be inconsistently knowledgeable; however, you do not present the speech as though you are informing the audience but rather as though you are stating common agreement and recognition with the audience that the individual being honored possesses certain admirable qualities, as highlighted in the speech.

On the other hand, if you know your audience will not be knowledgeable about the person, what can you do? In one instance, the recipient of a university honorary degree was considered a giant in genetics, his area of expertise. Although his name was not well known outside his field, the results of his work affected the daily lives of many of the listeners. The challenge was to state his accomplishments in such a way that they were amplified, and also in a way that informed the audience of the individual's accomplishments without embarrassing him. Because the person was a geneticist, his work had influenced agricultural practices that many in the audience knew about. Therefore, examples of the way his work had benefited agriculture were included in the speech.

On many occasions, audience members are in attendance because they know the person or cause that is being celebrated. In those instances, identifying outstanding accomplishments serves to confirm and strengthen the fabric of a group of individuals who make up a community, whether it is the community of a business or campus organization or the world community.

Principle 5: The Occasion

Most often, a special occasion results in a special presentation; at other times, an event requiring a special presentation results in an occasion. Either way, the event and the speech are connected. Ceremonial occasions include "traditional" events, such as holidays, as well as more "special" circumstances, such as funerals.[12] This means that the occasion itself might be the motivation for a ceremonial speech, such as the dedication of the monument in memory of World War II Veterans in Washington, D.C., or a Fourth of July celebration. An individual's accomplishments might also be the motivation for a ceremonial speech; or an event involving your family, your professional colleagues, a church or community organization, may also be the occasion for a ceremonial speech (see Act and Reflect 17.1).

A special occasion speech should make note of the occasion for which it is given. Whether it is the two-hundredth anniversary of the signing of the Declaration of

ACT&REFLECT

17.1: Paying Attention to Special Occasions

ACT • Attend as many different kinds of special occasions as you can schedule: the dedication of a building, a guest speaker, a retirement reception, an awards ceremony, a baby shower. Can you identify the five principles of epideictic discourse in each of the special occasion speeches you hear at these events?

REFLECT • How does each of the five principles contribute to the celebration? As an audience member, did you find the special occasion speech to be an inspiration to yourself personally? How so? As a presenter, what ideas did you hear that you might incorporate into a special occasion speech?

Independence or a fifth high-school class reunion or a Mother's Day brunch, these are the motivations for special occasion speeches, and they are worthy of mention in the speakers' comments.

Generally a special occasion speech results in a merger of all of these five characteristics. However, special speeches for special occasions require their own considerations.

Special Occasions

Speeches of Welcome and Introduction

Speeches of welcome and introduction are similar in their goals, with the exception that a speech of welcome is made to any special guest, whereas a speech of introduction introduces a guest speaker to an audience.

Speeches of Welcome A **speech of welcome** could be made at the beginning of a special meeting or conference or to welcome a special guest to a meeting or other event. A speech of welcome might also be used to demonstrate appreciation to attendees at an event that observes a special occasion. When you are the person welcoming the guest or guests, your comments should take into account the following considerations:

Clearly identify the person or group being welcomed and the occasion. "As we dedicate our new communication building, we are pleased to welcome the alumni whose generous support made this building possible." Identify the guests by name and ask them to rise.

Affirm shared values. Identify the values of your organization as well as the values of the person or persons being welcomed and demonstrate the manner in which those values

speech of welcome Speech made to an individual who attends an event as a special guest.

are consistent or in which they complement each other. "Your continued support of this state-of-the-art communication facility demonstrates your commitment to the education of young people in this state, a pursuit we all agree is imperative to our future."

Express appreciation for the guests' attendance. "We welcome you and we express our deepest gratitude for your ongoing interest and your generous support."

In Ashley's classroom special occasion speech, she welcomed new and returning members, parents, and leaders to the first meeting of a 4-H Club. She discussed her own remembered experiences as a new member and the worries she had about making friends, before reassuring the new members that they would find smiling faces and helping words. The shared values she affirmed are the components of the 4-H motto: "Head, Heart, Hand, Health." She listed examples of ways the club has followed the motto through special service projects to the community, senior citizens, and the local library, and then she listed some of the projects scheduled for the coming year. She closed by repeating her welcome and inviting everyone to gather for refreshments.[13] See Act and Reflect 17.2.

A speech of welcome or introduction should be tailored to fit the honored individual. ●

ACT & REFLECT

17.2: A Speech of Welcome

ACT • Watch Ashley's welcoming speech to the first 4-H Club meeting of the year. She describes her own feelings of hesitance as a new member herself when she was younger. When she discusses the club values, she also informs new members of the service projects of the club.

REFLECT • Why is Ashley discussing her own hesitance? In this speech of welcome, what do you think is her reason for focusing on herself rather than on her listeners? What is the benefit of integrating the club's values with the service projects? Besides being a special occasion speech of welcome, which type of audience that we have discussed in this book is Ashley speaking to? To what extent do you feel her decisions about the content of this speech meet the needs of that audience?

Speeches of Introduction A **speech of introduction** introduces a guest speaker. You may be introducing a guest speaker for one of your classes, or you might have the responsibility of introducing a speaker for a special campus event or a conference.

Cordially greet the speaker and identify him or her by name, including the formal title of your guest. State the individual's name as soon as possible in your introduction: "It is a pleasure to welcome Dr. Marion Jones, our special speaker for tonight."

State your speaker's credentials and mention her or his name several times. "Dr. Jones is the national president of our organization, the Student Humane Society (SHS). Dr. Jones has devoted her life to improving conditions in animal shelters and pounds. She is known internationally for her work. Dr. Jones also . . ."

Connect the values of your organization to those of your speaker. "As members of the local chapter of SHS, our mission is consistent with the goals Dr. Jones espouses."

Welcome the speaker and confirm the value of her or his presence. "I know I speak for everyone here when I say, 'We welcome you and we eagerly anticipate your message.'"

Lead the audience in applause. How do you encourage an audience to applaud? Sometimes the sound of your voice is a clue to the audience that applause is expected, as are the words you speak. To ensure that the audience applauds at the right time, give them a cue: Raise your hands slightly so they are visible to the audience. Slowly begin to applaud, and the audience will follow your lead.

MSL

Dr. Anthony Pometto introduced a keynote speaker who was well known by his audience at a professional meeting, by stating that it was his pleasure to introduce Dr. Charles Bourland. Because the audience was well acquainted with the speaker, Dr. Pometto affirmed the speaker's credentials by nicknaming him "Dr. Space Food" and expressed his appreciation for the contributions Dr. Bourland had made to the organization. He described the special experience the audience was about to enjoy and closed by naming Dr. Bourland and reminding the audience of his thirty years of experience with NASA.[14]

Speaking to Honor and to Remember

Speeches to honor and to remember amplify both the lives and accomplishments of individuals. The major difference is that a speech to honor recognizes a living person, whereas a speech to remember recognizes a deceased person. Speeches to remember are also called eulogies.

Speaking to Honor The **speech to honor** recognizes the accomplishments and key events in the life of a living person. Organizations make such speeches to members who have made contributions to them or whose accomplishments reflect well on the organization. The speech may be accompanied by the presentation of a plaque, small gift, or other memento marking the occasion, but it is the person's accomplishments that are the focus of the presentation. When you are called on to present a speech honoring an individual, there are a number of considerations to guide you as you prepare your presentation:

Identify the values of the organization or group honoring the individual. "Our organization of volunteers has

speech of introduction Introduces a guest speaker to an audience.

speech to honor Recognizes the accomplishments and key events in the life of a living person.

ACT&REFLECT

17.3: Introducing and Concluding a Special Occasion Speech

ACT • The body of Kasey's special occasion speech focuses on the components we have indicated should be included in a speech to honor. Watch Kasey's speech and pay attention to the introduction and the conclusion. How does Kasey construct his introduction? His conclusion? Do these follow the guidelines we have given in another chapter? What components do you hear in Kasey's speech? What do you not hear?

REFLECT • How effective did you find the introduction and conclusion of Kasey's speech? Did the introduction attract your attention and interest? Did the conclusion say "The End" in a memorable manner? What have you learned from this example about constructing introductions and conclusions for special occasion speeches?

worked tirelessly since its inception to make the lives of hospitalized children more comfortable."

Identify the accomplishments and/or contributions of the individual. "Among our most devoted and active volunteers we count Tyrell Carr, who has worked tirelessly to raise funds for our organization, to train other volunteers, as well as giving his time to the children."

Connect the values of the organization to the accomplishments of the individual being honored. "Tyrell is not just a volunteer for our organization; some might say Tyrell is our organization. In him we see all of the fine traits for which this organization stands."

Express appreciation. "For his good works, we honor Mr. Tyrell Carr."

Lead the audience in applause.

For Kasey's classroom special occasion speech, he presented an award to a convenience store manager at the convenience store national meeting. He identified the values of the convenience store as excellence, professionalism, and convenience. He gave examples of the manager's work that illustrated those values: the manager's accomplishment of building the local convenience store into the leading convenience store in the area; the new products she began to carry in the store, and the implementation of a "pay-at-the-pump" plan.[15] See Act and Reflect 17.3.

Speaking to Remember (Eulogy) A **speech to remember,** also known as a **eulogy,** is given in memory of a person who has died; the speech may be presented at a funeral or memorial service. A eulogy recalls a person's admirable qualities by describing events in the person's life or actions or qualities of the person. Listeners should feel inspired to strive to acquire the qualities of the person.

speech to remember A speech presented at a funeral or at a memorial service for a person who has died.

eulogy Same as a speech to remember.

A eulogy will be meaningful to listeners if the remarks are personal and offered from the heart. ●

Limit the number of qualities remembered or events described. Unless you know that you will be the only person to speak, the time will be shared with others. If there is one outstanding quality you wish to highlight, that is sufficient: "He was the most generous person I ever met."

Personalize the events or experiences you are relating by giving examples. "I remember a time he literally gave the shirt off his back to a person who needed it."

Conclude your remarks with a brief summary of the qualities the person possessed and add a dignified personal sentiment. "He taught me the value of giving. I am a better person for it, and I will never forget him."

Mandy gave her classroom special occasion speech to remember her friend who was killed at the age of nineteen in military action. She fashioned the eulogy around the Marine motto, *Semper fidelis,* meaning "always faithful," telling how her friend exemplified the quality of being always faithful to his family, friends, community, brothers in the Marines, and himself. She illustrated his sense of humor with an account of him dressing up as Santa Claus and passing out his broken old toys to his classmates. The third quality Mandy discussed was his selflessness, which she said had taught her to be selfless (see Act and Reflect 17.4).[16]

ACT&REFLECT

MSL **17.4: The Role of Delivery in a Speech to Remember**

A C T • Watch Mandy's speech in memory of her friend. Listen to her voice. On the basis of the dimensions of vocalics that we discussed in Chapter 4, how would you describe her voice as she gives this speech? What do you notice about her pitch range, her volume, her fluency?

R E F L E C T • How do the qualities you notice in Mandy's voice contribute to the effectiveness of this special occasion speech?

Speeches of Farewell

In our transient society, you might often find yourself searching for the words to bid farewell to a friend, a neighbor, a colleague, or some other person. In addition to saying goodbye, a **farewell speech** serves a number of other functions, particularly praising and amplifying the person's qualities. See Act and Reflect 17.5.

Reflect on the positive contributions the person has made. "Whether we needed a cheerleader for our team or a tireless volunteer to plan the company golf tournament or a fun person to eat lunch with, Toshiba was always the person everyone turned to."

Express regret at the person's leaving. "Toshiba has made the decision to move on, and we will be hard pressed to find another person who can do all that she did, always with a smile."

Wish the person good luck in his or her new life. "We will miss our colleague and friend, but we have to admit, Toshiba has landed a great new job, and we wish her the best."

Make a prediction about the positive contributions he or she will make in the new setting. "We know the people she will work with at her new job will come to think of her as highly as we do."

Express final regret at the person's departure. "Toshiba, we wish you luck, but we will miss you. The door is always open if you want to come back here."

Toasts

A **toast** is a very brief speech expressing optimism or good luck. Toasts are given at weddings and other celebrations, and often a glass is raised as the toast is presented. When proposing a toast, it is best to be brief. Toasts may or may not be scheduled in advance, but it seems when one is given, spontaneous toasts follow.

State the name(s) of the individual(s) or the occasion of the toast. This is as simple as saying: "Ben and Mary, now you are husband and wife." As you state the name(s), look directly at the person(s).

Describe a positive quality of the event or person(s) being toasted. "There were never two people better suited to each other: you are the yin and the yang." As you proceed with the toast, direct your eye contact to the entire audience.

Briefly describe your optimism and good wishes for the future. "I wish for you both a long married life of happiness and laughter."

Raise your glass and repeat the recipients' names. "To Ben and Mary."

Karen was assigned to prepare a toast for her classroom special occasion speech. The toast she prepared was on the occasion of a young friend's twelfth birthday. The positive

ACT & REFLECT

17.5: Bidding Farewell

ACT • Although we give the guidelines for a speech of farewell for instances when you bid someone else farewell, it is also possible that you might give a speech of farewell to say good bye on behalf of yourself. Select a group of colleagues, friends, classmates, or another group as your audience. Using the guidelines given here for developing a speech of farewell to someone else, develop a speech that you would give to say farewell yourself to your selected audience.

REFLECT • What do you see in the differences of a speech of farewell to someone else in comparison to a speech of farewell from the speaker to the audience?

farewell speech A speech given on the occasion when an individual leaves a place of business, neighborhood, etc. to begin in another location.

toast A very brief speech expressing optimism or good luck.

ACT & REFLECT

17.6: Planning a Toast

ACT • Listen to Karen's toast. Remember that one of the principles of ceremonial speaking is celebrating the present while recognizing the past and focusing on the future.

REFLECT • How does Karen implement the principle of "celebrating the present" in this toast? What details does she include in her toast that build on the past and focus on the future while toasting the birthday party?

qualities of the friend that she noted were her sense of adventure and humor and her determination, which had helped her to become a better reader and to overcome her shyness. Karen expresses her optimism and good wishes by affirming her satisfaction in watching her friend "along the way" and gives her her best wishes for a great future and "another year filled with sunshine (see Act and Reflect 17.6)."[17]

Award Ceremonies

Presenting an Award Organizations often present awards to individuals whose accomplishments exemplify the organization's values or further its goals. An **award presentation** is often a major speech in itself. The amount of time you will have for the presentation will depend on the type of event, as well as other proceedings scheduled. Generally, you can expect to speak for several minutes, and you should amplify those of the individual's accomplishments that have motivated the presentation of the award. When you present an award, do the following:

Identify the values or goals represented in the award. "The honorary doctor of letters is the highest award given by our university to exemplify an individual whose work has improved the quality of life for humankind."

Describe the qualities of the individual who has been selected to receive the award; demonstrate that the individual is worthy of it. "Natalie Weinsetel is honored today for her talents as a poet, for her ability to speak to all cultures through her verse."

After you have described the accomplishments of the award recipient, introduce the individual who will receive the award. "Ladies and gentlemen, it is a pleasure to present the honorary degree of doctor of letters to the poet laureate of the United States, Ms. Natalie Weinsetel."

Lead the audience in applause as the recipient rises to accept the award. "Please join me in honoring Ms. Weinsetel."

If the recipient is to be given an award, that is, a trophy or plaque, when the individual comes forward to receive it, shake hands with him or her.

Ross presented the International Unity Award for his classroom special occasion speech. He briefly described the purpose of the award—to end human suffering—and listed previous recipients of the award. Most of his presentation centered on the individual to whom the award was to be presented. He noted that the recipient would be the first woman to receive the award, which was given in recognition of her work to enhance the quality of life in countries such as Kuwait or Iraq by providing educational opportunities for children in those countries.[18] See Act and Reflect 17.7.

award presentation A speech that precedes the presentation of an award.

Award Acceptance is every bit as important as presenting an award. An award recipient minimizes his or her actual accomplishments and maximizes the importance of carrying on the values inherent in the award and continuing the work that has resulted in receiving it (see Act and Reflect 17.8).

Express appreciation to the organization for their assessment of your worthiness. "I am humbled by the recognition you have given me at the close of our most successful football season."

Discuss the values inherent in the award. "This award recognizes the importance and the value of collegiate athletes to serve as role models for young athletes."

Compliment the value of the organization that sponsors the award. "Your organization has done so much for the welfare of young people in this community, including its work with young athletes."

Proclaim that it is an honor to receive the award. "It is an honor to be recognized by you. I also receive this award on behalf of my teammates, for they are also fine role models."

ACT & REFLECT

17.7: Role of the Audience on a Special Occasion

ACT • Watch Ross's award presentation speech. Some experts assume that the audience already knows the accomplishments of the recipient of an award, implying that it is unnecessary to tell them something they already know in the presentation speech. However, it is always possible there are people in the audience who are unfamiliar with the nature of the award or with the accomplishments of the recipient, or both.

REFLECT • How does Ross accomplish the dual task of informing audience members who might be unaware of the nature of the award while describing the accomplishments of the award recipient? In what other ways does Ross acknowledge the audience?

In her classroom special occasion speech, Amy accepted the unity award that Ross presented. In her acceptance speech, after expressing appreciation for being chosen to receive the award, she recognized the values symbolized by the award, to end human suffering and to bring world peace. She described projects of the sponsoring organization, such as providing job opportunities around the world, as reflective of the values of the award. When she proclaimed the honor she felt in receiving the award, Amy also recognized teams around the world who were working on her behalf.[19]

Nominations

A range of customs determine the nominating procedures for organizations for electing officers. Sometimes nominating occurs on an impromptu basis, and individuals nominate colleagues spontaneously. A nomination can also be planned in advance, similarly to other presentations. The same is true for accepting a nomination: the nominee may respond in an impromptu or more formal fashion. Whatever the circumstances of the nomination process, there are a number of components that should be included.

Speech to Nominate Whenever possible, ask the permission of the nominee in advance of your nomination: "You would make a great parliamentarian. May I nominate you at the

award acceptance A speech given in appreciation by an individual who receives an award.

Everyday Example

Sad-Eyed Legend in the Lowlands

This article describes the presentation of an honorary doctor of music degree to the musician Bob Dylan. According to the article, Mr. Dylan did not speak after receiving the award; however, we believe the recipient of an award assumes as much responsibility for the occasion as does the presenter of the award. What would you have suggested Mr. Dylan say in his acceptance speech?

Bob Dylan accepted an honorary doctor of music degree Wednesday from Scotland's oldest university. "Many members of my generation can't separate a sense of our own identify from his music and lyrics," professor of English Neil Corcoran said in an awe-struck address. Founded in 1413, Saint Andrews counts among its students Prince William, second in line to the throne. Dylan has accepted only one previous honorary degree, from Princeton in 1970—a ceremony memorable in part because of a noisy invasion of cicadas. Dylan didn't seem to have anything to say Wednesday, but maybe "Day of the Locusts," a song inspired by the Princeton commencement, sums it up:

I put down my robe, picked up my diploma,

Took hold of my sweetheart and away we did drive,

The recipient of an honor or award has a responsibility to be gracious about receiving the honor or award. ●

Straight for the hills, the black hills of Dakota,

Sure was glad to get out of there alive.

Source: "People in the News," compiled by Michael Corey, *Des Moines Register,* June 24, 2004, p. A2. © 2004, reprinted with permission of the *Des Moines Register.*

ACT & REFLECT

17.8: Accepting an Award

ACT • For a speech to accept an award, we have suggested that the recipient should minimize attention to himself or herself. Watch Amy's acceptance speech. Identify the parts of the speech: what parts express appreciation, discuss values, compliment the sponsoring organization, and proclaim the award is an honor to receive.

REFLECT • At what points does Amy minimize attention to herself by discussing the accomplishments of others? How important do you think it is when accepting an award to discuss your own accomplishments versus giving others credit?

meeting tonight?" If the person prefers not to be nominated, honor his or her wishes. If the person agrees to be nominated, there are several components you should include in your nomination speech:

Cordially state the name of the person being nom- inated and the position for which the nomination is submitted. "It is my pleasure to nominate Wanda Johnson for the office of parliamentarian of this organization."

Briefly summarize the duties of the position for which the nomination is being made. "As we all know, the role of parliamentarian in this group of outspoken members is key to our ability to conduct our business."

Present the nominee's accomplishments, previous experiences, or other qualities that make the person worthy of the position. "Wanda is an excellent choice to fill the role of parliamentarian. She has currently served in that role for other campus and community organizations,

I would like to thank my-
Psychiatrist
Therapist
Orthodontist
Astrologist
Publicist
Manucurist
Stylist
Pedicurist
-I LOVE
YOU ALL

© www.CartoonStock.com

and even now is parliamentarian for the campus student government; she is a certified parliamentarian; she is known for her objectivity and her analytical skills."

Restate the nominee's name and the office for which he or she is being nominated. "I am pleased to nominate Wanda Johnson for the office of parliamentarian of our organization."

For her classroom special occasion speech Shannon nominated a friend to receive an award given by the "Friends Forever" organization. She first named the award for which she was nominating her friend. She listed her friend's qualifications for the award: the ability to listen, involvement in the friend's life, the capacity to forgive and forget, endurance, remembering. She gave examples of the ways in which her friend exemplified these qualities and stated that she hoped the organization would select her friend for the award.[20] See Act and Reflect 17.9.

Speech of Acceptance or Regret If you know in advance that you will be nomi- nated, your speech is likely to be one of **acceptance.** In some instances, you might not be aware that someone plans to nominate you and you do not wish to be a can- didate for the office. In this instance, you graciously extend your **regrets.**

Whether you offer acceptance or regrets, thank your nominator and express your honor at receiving the nomination. "It is a surprise and an honor to be nominated for this important office. I thank Ruth Jones for nominating me."

If you accept the nomination, indicate your intentions to carry out the duties of the office to the best of your ability, if elected, and indicate what your priorities will be. "If elected I will strive to meet the expectations of this organization as I carry out my duties in these ways: . . . "

If you are unable or unwilling to accept the nomination, briefly indicate why. "Unfortunately, due to other obliga- tions, I will not be able to serve at this time. I respectfully request my name be removed from the nominees."

acceptance A speech given to accept a nomination.

regrets A speech given to decline a nomination.

ACT&REFLECT

MSL 17.9: A Speech to Nominate

ACT • We discussed the speech to nominate in terms of nominating an individual for an elected office in an organization. Shannon has used the format of the nomination speech in a slightly different way, to nominate a friend for an award. Watch Shannon's speech.

REFLECT • Identify the major points of Shannon's speech and listen to the way she develops each of these points. Using her speech as a pattern, develop your own speech in which you nominate someone for an elected office in an organization to which you belong. What qualities do you hear in Shannon's speech that are not suggested in the discussion of the speech to nominate? How could you use these ideas in your speech to nominate?

Whether or not you accept, thank your nominator for nominating you. "I thank Ruth Jones for her nomination. I am humbled by her confidence in my ability to carry out this important duty."

For his classroom special occasion speech Collin gave a speech accepting his nomination for vice president of his fraternity. He thanked his nominator for the flattering nomination and then briefly described his own history as a member of the fraternity. He outlined three priorities he would follow if elected: to strengthen and regulate committees, to attend interfraternity council meetings, to work well with others. Before thanking his nominator a second time, he wished his opponents the best of luck in the election.[21] See Act and Reflect 17.10.

Dinner Speeches

Of all the special occasions a person might encounter in a lifetime, the special occasion speech that most closely resembles other types of speeches we have discussed is the **dinner speech.** As its name implies, a dinner speech is a speech given after a meal. The speech could be given at the annual meeting of a professional organization, at a convention, at the holiday dinner of a business organization, or as part of a service organization's regularly scheduled meeting. As the dinner speaker, you have the aftermath of the meal as your formidable competition. After enjoying a meal, your audience could be sleepy. If alcohol has been served, the possibilities of having a drowsy audience increase further. Some audience members may continue to eat their meal while you are speaking, finishing their dessert or drinking coffee. On top of all of these distractions, servers might be clearing tables. What to do? The qualities of the epideictic speech Aristotle has given can be particularly helpful in preparing a dinner speech.

Recognize the occasion. If there is not an occasion, create one. What is the occasion of the meeting? Is it the annual conference of your professional organization? If so, what are its values and goals? Is it the monthly meeting of a community service organization? If so, what contributions does it make to the community? Is it the holiday banquet of a large company? Has the year been successful for the company, in terms of economic gains or organizational changes? Is it an end-of-year athletic banquet? What are the athletic teams' records? Have athletes been recognized at state or national levels? Often dinner speakers present at an event that is already a celebration or occasion.

If the presentation does not coincide with an occasion, look to the organization's charge or goals to help you create

dinner speech A speech given after a meal.

Everyday Example

Richardson to Kerry: Don't Consider Me for a Running Mate

How closely does New Mexico governor Bill Richardson follow the format suggested here for a speech of regrets? Is anything omitted? How would you suggest Governor Richardson modify his regrets?

New Mexico Gov. Bill Richardson, one of the country's top Hispanic Democrats, on Thursday told John Kerry he no longer wants to be considered as a possible running mate.

Richardson said he wants to keep a promise to the people of New Mexico to serve a full, four-year term and noted that Kerry has "numerous experienced and talented leaders" from which to choose a vice presidential candidate.

"It is with that knowledge and comfort that I must tell you that I respectfully remove myself from the selection process and withdraw my name from consideration for the vice presidential nomination," Richardson said.

Source: "Richardson to Kerry: Don't Consider Me for a Running Mate," *Ames Tribune* (Iowa), July 2, 2004, p. A6.

an occasion. The purpose for doing this is that the after-dinner speech needs a theme. The dinner speaker for a professional organization might discuss the way the values of the organization are reflected in its accomplishments or specific members' accomplishments. A dinner speaker for a community service group might talk about the group's accomplishments in the community; attendees at the holiday banquet for the large company might expect to hear a dinner speech on the impact of change on their business; the dinner speaker at the athletic banquet might discuss the connection of athletics with the development of personal character. Unless you have been asked to speak about a particular topic, or on behalf of a specific occasion, look for themes or values embraced by the individuals in attendance at the event to create the occasion.

Present the dinner speech in a positive light. Seek opportunities to offer praise. Remember that a dinner speech happens after a dinner or some other meal. At the least, you might be battling drowsy listeners distracted by the aftereffects of too much food. At the worst, you might find yourself competing with the noise of rattling dishes. Is there a lighthearted or humorous way you can present your topic? If you are one of those people who can't tell a joke, then don't. But there must be stories related to your theme that your listeners would enjoy hearing.

Don't assume that your dinner speech cannot or should not have a serious point. You might be speaking to a service organi-

17.10: Responding to a Nomination

ACT • Watch Collin's speech and identify the areas in which he indicates he will accept the nomination and his plans if he is elected.

REFLECT • What if Collin had extended regrets to the nomination? How would you convert his speech to a speech of regrets? Could you use the three priorities he lists in some way in a speech of regrets? How would you do so?

zation about meeting greater community needs in the future. Tell stories of good works by the organization in the community to inspire your listeners to take on the challenge they will face. Maybe the business organization suffered a severe economic setback during the year. Find some way to put a positive spin on the events. Look toward the future as a time for growth and renewal. Perhaps the professional organization is losing membership. Talk about the need to rebuild membership and suggest ways that can be done. Maybe the athletic teams suffered their very worst year. What good came from the year? What lessons could be learned and what awesome games were played by the athletes despite the losing year? You needn't kick discouraging experiences under the rug, but instead present your message as positively as you are able, praising individuals' accomplishments in the face of adversity.

Amplify group and individual accomplishments. A dinner speaker presenting at the annual conference of a professional organization traced the history of the organization through the contributions of many of the individuals who were in attendance. She described how the organization had first started because a few individuals felt there was a need for members of the profession to meet and talk regularly; she listed organizational milestones initiated by other members; she praised the accomplishments of leaders of the organization. In giving a timeline of the history of the organization, she managed to name many of the people in the room, recognizing them by telling stories of their work and amplifying their personal efforts and the contributions they made to the organization.

Because a dinner speech is often a very public event, possibly attended by a large number of people, the size of the event and the amplification of accomplishments should be consistent. In other words, a "big event" should be reflected in accounts of "big deeds" of both individuals and the group or organization. Don't fabricate individual or group accomplishments, but at the same time, do not minimize. If an athletic team has won its first meet in fifty years against a rival team, be sure to amplify that awesome accomplishment. Be sure to name individual players whose moves contributed to the win. If the business organization has experienced the greatest increase in profit in its history, talk about that. What led to the increase? Who were the indi-

Dinner speakers may need to overcome interference generated by listeners finishing their food and tables being cleared. ●

viduals whose sacrifices for the company resulted in the profits? Put them in the spot-light. Did the community organization receive national recognition that had never before been given to an organization in your state or town or country? Amplify that accomplishment along with the individuals in the organization who made it possible.

Recognize the audience. As you are praising positive events and applauding indi-viduals who have made noteworthy contributions, name names as often as you can. In telling the stories that bring alive the events you are amplifying, name persons who participated in those events or were key figures in those stories. Don't be hesitant to describe the football team's strategy by calling players by name as you describe their actions. At the same time, don't limit the individuals you recognize by name to a few, unless the dinner is held in their honor. If you plan to offer recognition for several categories of accomplishments, try to recognize as many individuals as possible. For example, if you are honoring the volunteer who worked the most hours during the year and the volunteer who was voted the most positive person to work with and the volunteer who raised the most money over the year, it is better if the same person is not recognized for all of those honors. If the same individual is the recipient of all of the honors, it might be better to honor the individual and talk about his or her con-tributions to the organization. You might be speaking to a roomful of volunteers who all feel they made a contribution, and they deserve to be recognized as well.

An additional way to recognize the audience is to use inclusive pronouns: "you," "we," "our," "us." Even if you are not recognizing everyone by name, you are includ-ing everyone through your pronoun usage.

Celebrate the present. As you have seen in the examples we have used in this dis-cussion of dinner speeches, although the celebration occurs during the present, that celebration is often justified by looking back to the past and by looking forward to the future. In effect, the event at which the dinner speech is given is a "hinge" event, that is, it is a transitional event between the past and the future.

When you look to the past, identify the key events that have contributed to the current status of the audience or the organization. Discuss the future as a time to move ahead or beyond the events of the past. Discuss the past as a time when adver-sity was overcome or important lessons were learned. Discuss the future as a time to set and achieve goals and to grow.

Organize your dinner speech with an introduction, a body, and a conclusion. A din-ner speech should be built around a speaker's goal and a thesis. Review the guidelines for constructing speeches to help yourself select an organizational framework and to incorporate your points in an organized format. Introduce your topic so the audience knows what you are discussing and why. In the body of your presentation, make several clear points that support your theme. Conclude your presentation by restating the con-nection of the group with your theme.

Use notes, but be audience oriented in your delivery. The best dinner speech is one the presenter is able to give in "prepared conversational" delivery. However, in some instances, the dinner speech is published and disseminated to other audiences, and a manuscript is requested. If you are speaking at an event where a copy of your speech has been requested, develop your notes with the priority of making a connection with your audience. If necessary, you can construct your speech in manuscript form after you have presented, or you can request that your speech be taped and transcribed.

ACT & REFLECT

17.11: Analyzing a Dessert Speech

ACT • Watch the speech given by Dr. Charles Bourland, NASA food scientist.[22] The speech is accompanied by a slide show, with Dr. Bourland narrating the slides with accounts of his experiences on the recovery crews of *Apollo 12, Apollo 13*, and the first Sky Lab. Notice Dr. Bourland's delivery style and the audience's response to him.

REFLECT • Using the guidelines we have given here for a dinner speech, analyze Dr. Bourland's speech. Which of the guidelines do you see used in Dr. Bourland's speech that help him create a speech that both he and his audience enjoy?

When you are contacted to give the dinner speech, you will likely be informed of the expected length of the speech. As you prepare your speech, don't abuse the time limit you are given; in fact, if you can compose a speech that is slightly shorter than the time limit, your audience will appreciate your consideration. Be prepared to make cuts in your speech at the last minute. If your presentation is part of a monthly meeting, the group could have organizational business to conduct that takes longer than anticipated, and you might be asked to cut your presentation accordingly. Even if you are not given a specific length of time for your presentation, be brief. A ten- or fifteen-minute dinner speech is long enough to expect listeners to stay alert. Time is of the essence for dinner speeches, and dinner speakers must be prepared to be flexible. See Act and Reflect 17.11.

● GETTING TO WORK

Due to the special nature of ceremonial speeches, you have a certain "creative license" for preparing the speech; however, there are also some constraints you should adhere to, and we have outlined these for each type.

Guidelines for Preparing Ceremonial Speeches

1 When you are preparing a ceremonial presentation, you may include the following procedures or conventions any way you wish, but include all of them. When you have several qualities or values or experiences to discuss, be sure to organize these components according to some basic conventional structure.[23] For example, if you wish to showcase a number of accomplishments of the award recipient, arrange these accomplishments in chronological order. If you have a series of stories to tell about a person who is being roasted or toasted, arrange the stories in order of least to most important so that you can end on a strong point. Your audience should be able to identify a basic organizational framework in your presentation, in addition to appreciating its creative qualities.

2 Aristotle made two other suggestions regarding special occasion speeches that might be helpful.[24] First, remember the importance of the voice when giving ceremonial speeches. As you may have noticed, a ceremonial speech is really a performance, and if you are reading your speech, if you are too careful with your words, or if your voice is not consistent with your words, the effect of your message will be diminished. Also, despite the advice to organize your ceremonial speech in some recognizable format, Aristotle felt that part of the charm of a ceremonial speech lay in the unexpected. A eulogy, for example, might begin with a humorous story illustrating an endearing quality of the person being remembered. An award presentation might include an unrelated but complimentary story about the recipient.

3 The freedom inherent in a ceremonial presentation does not imply that you should not give the presentation thought and planning. Because you are left to your own devices, planning and creating a ceremonial presentation becomes all the more challenging and important. In many instances, you are giving the presentation because you are the individual who is best acquainted with the person who is being recognized. Despite your relationship with the person, to create the "right" message, you must spend a certain amount of time and thought to identify the best stories and qualities that represent the person who is the focus of the speech. You might find it helpful to interview others who know the person. All of this takes some time.

4 Don't hesitate to be personal as you create a special occasion speech. On the occasion of the *Challenger* explosion, President Ronald Reagan spoke at a memorial service in Houston to remember the seven astronauts whose lives were lost. Mr. Reagan named each astronaut and made a personal comment about each, saying for example: "We remember Judith Resnik, known as J.R. to her friends, always smiling, always eager to make a contribution, finding beauty in the music she played on her piano in her off-hours."[25]

5 A ceremonial speech is also an excellent opportunity to use figurative language. Your knowledge of metaphors, analogies, and other figurative language adds to the meaningfulness of these special messages as they are spoken to the audience. In the same eulogy, President Reagan used an analogy comparing the astronauts to early pioneers:

> We think back to the pioneers of an earlier century, and the sturdy souls who took their families and their belongings and set out into the frontier of the American West. Often, they met with terrible hardship. Along the Oregon Trail you can still see the grave markers of those who fell on the way. But grief only steeled them to the journey ahead.
>
> Today, the frontier is space.[26]

6 With all ceremonial speeches, because they are part of a ceremony, you will not lose your effectiveness, nor will you be less appreciated, if you are brief. Say what is important to be said, say it graciously and sincerely, but say it briefly. The bottom line with a ceremonial speech is that you are showcasing a person, and the audience should see that person through your message.

SUMMARY

When preparing and presenting a speech for a special occasion, presenters have a certain amount of creative license. The organization of a type of speech depends on the occasion and the person being recognized. However, despite the freedom to create that this type of speech affords, there are five principles that guide the presenter.

Special occasion speeches are events when an individual or event is praised. When an individual is recognized, the speech should identify commendable qualities or values that are shared by the audience. You should present stories and personal experiences that illustrate these qualities. Similarly, when an event is celebrated, you should present the values the event represents. The accomplishments of a person recognized should be amplified or enhanced, so the person is "set apart" from others who are not recognized. Although special occasions are happening in the present, the special occasion speech draws on past events to illustrate and define the occasion and provides inspiration to the audience toward a better way of life or a better future. The role of the audience differs from what it is at other types of

presentations. The audience assumes an observer-like role as the presenter speaks to and about the person who is recognized.

As the name of this type of presentation implies, the special occasion speech is motivated by an existing occasion such as a traditional event, or it creates an occasion through its delivery, such as the presentation of an award or honor. Common types of special occasion speeches are speeches of welcome and introduction; speeches that honor and remember; speeches of farewell; toasts; presenting and receiving of awards; speeches to nominate and speeches to accept nominations—or extend regrets; and the dinner speech.

VIDEO EXPERIENCE

Watch the four special occasion speeches: Laura speaks at a meeting of the Dave Barry Fan Club; Katie speaks at her father's fiftieth birthday party; Crystal is the speaker at a volunteers banquet; Jessica presents to the committee on teaching excellence.[27] The "occasion" for which all of these special occasion speeches is given was created by the students as part of their class assignment. First, identify the occasion for which the speech

was given; second, identify the parts of the speech to determine whether the speakers included all of the areas suggested in this chapter; third, listen for the principles of epideictic rhetoric. What feedback would you give to each speaker? That is, what do you feel are strengths of each speech and what, if any, suggestions would you give the speakers for modifying their speeches?

THINKING BACK, THINKING AHEAD

1. You might be thinking that much about special occasion speeches has to do with saying nice things about people, and that is certainly true. How can you use what you have learned about special occasion speeches to enhance your personal or professional relationships? Although special occasions occur more often than we might typically think, the opportunities to use the principles of special occasion speeches in our relationships arise daily. Identify qualities of special occasion speeches that could become a part of your communication repertoire and see what positive results you create in your relationships!

2. We've pointed out that special occasion speeches are times when some personal qualities must be presented in a positive manner. Television and radio often give us examples of less-than-positive qualities being given a more positive spin. Listen closely to the ways talk show hosts and television interviewers speak to and about guests so that their questions and comments are presented positively.

3. Begin a file of jokes, sayings, poetry, quotations, and even speeches that you could use for inspiration the next time you are called on to give a special occasion speech.

4. Observe the ways that speakers perform certain actions that accompany special occasion speeches: the presentation of an award, shaking hands with an award recipient, the focus of eye contact, the sound of the voice, the raising of a glass at a toast. All of these are important nonverbal aspects of special occasion speeches. What do you notice about the presenter's nonverbal actions that enhance the occasion? That detract from the occasion?

5. Focus also on the recipients' actions when receiving an award or other recognition. How do recipients' respond to words of praise, regarding their facial expressions and posture? How does a recipient demonstrate gracious acceptance without appearing immodest?

NOTES

1. J. Carter, Nobel Lecture, December 10, 2002, retrieved from Nobel Prize Web site, at www.nobel.se/peace/laureates/2002/carter-lecture.html.
2. Aristotle, "Rhetoric," translated by W. Rhys Roberts, in *The Rhetoric and the Poetics of Aristotle* (New York: Random House, 1954).
3. Aristotle, "Rhetoric," translated by George A. Kennedy, in *Aristotle on Rhetoric* (New York: Oxford University Press, 1991), 7.
4. W. H. Beale, "Rhetorical Performative Discourse: A New Theory of Epideictic," *Philosophy and Rhetoric 11* (1978): 221–246.
5. Beale, "Rhetorical Performative Discourse." 221.
6. Aristotle, "Rhetoric," trans. Kennedy, 243.
7. John F. Kennedy, remarks greeting Nobel Prize–winners of the Western Hemisphere, White House, Washington, D.C., April 29, 1962, retrieved from Kennedy Library Web site, at www.cs.umb.edu/jfklibrary/jfkquote.htm.
8. C. M. Sheard, "The Public Value of Epideictic Rhetoric," *College English, 58* (1996): 765–794.
9. L. E. Rohler, "Martin Luther King's 'I Have a Dream,'" in *Great Speeches for Criticism and Analysis,* edited by Lloyd Rohler and Roger Cook (Greenwood, IN: Alistair Press, 1988), 329–336.
10. Sheard, "Public Value," 766.
11. Beale, "Rhetorical Performative Discourse," 237.
12. Beale, "Rhetorical Performative Discourse," 239.
13. Ashley Osgood, speech given on a special occasion, December 6, 2004.
14. Anthony Pometto, introductory speech, to introduce keynote speaker Dr. Charles Bourland, NASA Food Technology Commercial Space Center meeting, Ames, Iowa, April 21, 2004.
15. Kasey Pfabb, speech on a special occasion, December 3, 2004.
16. Mandy Sadowski, speech on a special occasion, December 8, 2004.
17. Karen Tarara, speech on a special occasion, December 6, 2004.
18. Ross Kelderman, speech on a special occasion, December 3, 2004.
19. Amy Diekevers, speech on a special occasion, December 3, 2004.
20. Shannon Kirton, speech on a special occasion, December 8, 2005.
21. Collin Schmidt, speech on a special occasion, December 6, 2004.
22. Charles Bourland, retired food scientist with NASA, keynote speech, NASA Food Technology Commercial Space Center, meeting, Ames, Iowa, April 21, 2004.
23. R. P. Hart, *Modern Rhetorical Criticism* (Glenview, IL: Scott Foresman, 1990), 164.
24. Aristotle, "Rhetoric," trans. Kennedy, 260.
25. R. Reagan, "A President's Eulogy: Remarks at a Memorial Service Held in Houston," January 31, 1986, retrieved from Web site, at http://ohiopowmia.com/space/eulogy.html.
26. Reagan, "President's Eulogy."
27. Laura Johnson, speech on a special occasion, December 8, 2004. Katie Dencklau, speech on a special occasion, December 8, 2004. Crystal Nord, speech on a special occasion, December 3, 2004. Jessica Culhane, speech on a special occasion, December 6, 2004.

Sample Everyday Presentations

The following transcripts aren't from particularly famous orators or noted speeches but rather are a sample of everyday presentations—the types of presentations you might make. While they are more formal than many everyday presentations, these speeches reflect speakers' efforts to impact different types of audiences in different situations. These speeches are intended as samples of everyday speeches for your analysis and discussion. Consider what you have been learning from this text and from your class as you consider each transcript. Try to imagine the audience and their reaction to the speaker's message. Think about what worked and what else could have been done to help the speaker achieve his or her goals.

Presentation to a Positive Audience

Policy and Development in the Telecommunications Industry
by Linda P. B. Katehi, Dean of Engineering at Purdue University

Dr. Linda P. B. Katehi presented the following comments at the opening of the third day of a conference on issues related to telecommunications sponsored by the Telecommunications Industry Association. Her audience consisted of those people interested in issues related to telecommunication policy and development. They were a positive audience; she delivered a presentation geared primarily to inspire. (Presented at SuperComm 2005, June 8, 2005.)

Good Morning!
    My name is Linda P. B. Katehi, and I'm the John A. Edwardson Dean of Engineering at Purdue University. It's an honor to be here with you at the beginning of today's schedule.
    In 1876, the president of Western Union was offered exclusive rights to the telephone. The offer came from Alexander Graham Bell for $100,000. The president responded, "What use could this company make of an electrical toy?" He then distributed an internal memo to company employees which read, "This telephone has too many shortcomings to be seriously considered as a means of communication. The device is inherently of no value to us." I'm glad to see that society did not adopt this view of the telephone.
    Innovation and discovery in the last century brought great change to our world—from Purdue alum Neil Armstrong's first step on the moon that launched the space age—to an invention as simple as the safety belt for automobiles. As we gather at the beginning of a new century—that has the potential to be the greatest one hundred years of humankind—there's

no doubt that engineers of tomorrow will lead the way. When considering the engineering profession of the future and the education needed to prepare the engineer of 2020 and beyond, there are important statistical projections to keep in mind: By 2050, 8 out of 9 billion people will be in developing countries, while the economic growth of these developing countries will be only 2 percent below the expected economic growth in the developed world. In 20 to 30 years, the most popular language will not be English and what are now considered U.S. industries will not exist in their present form. By 2050, the greatest social problem occupying the world will be poverty, and its primary impact will be on the female population. It's very easy to conclude that the U.S. engineer beyond 2020 will have to address a totally different set of problems from the ones we solve today.

It's expected that the U.S. engineer beyond 2020 will be based abroad, will have to travel, physically or virtually, around the world to meet customers and interact with them using advanced means of communications. The U.S. engineer beyond 2020 will have to know how to address or solve a variety of problems: from creating new means of communication to solving poverty and healthcare; to providing transportation; to addressing the environment; to accommodating new technology breakthroughs, breakthroughs that result in the United States' ability to innovate.

In an increasingly global and knowledge-driven economy, technological innovation (the transformation of knowledge into products, processes, and services) is critical to competitiveness, long-term productivity growth, and the generation of wealth. A newly published report by the National Academy of Engineering (NAE) on *Assessing the Capacity of the U.S. Engineering Research Enterprise,* states that leadership in innovation is essential to U.S. prosperity and security. But there are some alarming trends that threaten the sustainability of the U.S. research enterprise. Among the trends listed in the NAE report is an erosion of the engineering research infrastructure due to inadequate funding over the last two decades. The United States is at a tipping point—either we will remain an innovator of new products, new ideas, and high technology, or we will become consumers of innovation produced elsewhere.

In his book *The World Is Flat,* Thomas Friedman notes that "advanced telecommunications, logistics, and trade liberalization have taken down all boundaries to the flow and exchange of ideas," and all international markets are now competitors and collaborators. I agree with Friedman's assertion that "American individuals have nothing to fear from a flat world, provided we roll-up our sleeves, be ready to compete, get every individual to think about how he or she upgrades his or her educational skills, and keep investing in the secrets of the American 'sauce.'" The American Dream, as some of us refer to it.

The secret to America's "sauce" is our research and development capabilities maintained through engineering and science. The NAE report also mentions that "Without engineering research—innovation, especially groundbreaking innovation that creates new industries and transforms old ones—simply does not happen." Innovation happens in industry, government research labs, and universities. Today, industry accounts for two-thirds of the nation's research and development expenditures, and more than 90 percent of patents issued in the U.S. However, the focus, today, is on short-term applied research (NAE, p. 21). Without restoring long-term engineering research in industry to a substantial level and sustainable level, the economic health of our country is threatened.

In Indiana, we recognize the importance of creating partnerships between business and higher education in remaining competitive on the global stage. An analysis of the Indiana Manufacturing Sector was recently published, and in this report it was noted that "leading economy states are those that promote strong investment in science and technology and the commercialization of innovations." Through innovative manufacturing and Purdue's research capabilities, Indiana is optimizing its ability to develop new products and processes. We are doing this by investing wisely in our state's educational system, and in science and technology research. However, the ability to innovate requires much more than research; investment and research-infrastructure requires an organizational structure that values and accepts a multiplicity of ideas, respects differences, believes in equity, emphasizes collaboration and teamwork, and does all this with a sense of professional responsibility. Organizations that enlist diversity in team building will succeed in developing tomorrow's breakthrough ideas.

There is little doubt that diverse teams have a greater chance of coming up with unique ideas because members have different cultural backgrounds. Diversity in teams encourages creativity and a better ability to solve the great challenges our society faces today. Those who will lead us in building the U.S. engineering research enterprise tomorrow are the students in our classrooms today. We share the responsibility to prepare these future innovators to work in a world that is highly competitive, where borders no longer separate us from one another, and where diversity is paramount. As one of just 16 female deans of engineering out of 350 engineering deans in this country, I cannot emphasize enough the importance of encouraging women and underrepresented minorities to enter the engineering profession. Not doing so would compromise diversity within this profession and we would pay an opportunity cost in new products not built, in new designs not considered, in constraints not understood, new processes not invented and in ideas not generated.

Our response to the challenge of maintaining the United States' leading edge in technology and innovation must be bold. I'm reminded of America's response to challenges posed during the Industrial Revolution. As our economy was transformed, our leading edge was maintained through policies such as the Morrill Act of 1862. With the establishment of land-grant universities like Purdue, American agriculture was modernized and our nation's ability to produce knowledge and human capital was sustained. Once again, we find ourselves at a crossroads in history—operating within a new economy—and we'd better roll up our sleeves and get busy.

Thank you for your attention and enjoy the rest of this session.

Presentation to a Neutral Audience   MSL

A Student's Report to the Board of Trustees
by Charles Maddox, President, Student Government Association
of Austin Community College

This presentation was given by Charles Maddox while he was the president of the Student Government Association of Austin Community College. This speech was delivered on October 3, 2005, after the Gulf Coast was devastated by hurricanes. Maddox is addressing the board of trustees as part of the monthly board meetings at which different associations on campus provide activity updates. The response to these reports is generally neutral, and the speakers' primary goal is to provide information. Evaluate the speech in terms of how well the speaker recognizes and addresses the neutral audience. What other strategies might the speaker have adopted?

Good evening Dr. Kinslow, Madam Chairperson, and distinguished members of the board and those in attendance. I'd like to express this opportunity right now to inform you on the state of the student government. You may not know it stepping outside with the temperature that fall is upon us and change is in the air. Change is the only constant in life and as day turns to [night] and year to year, change both that we plan and change that is unexpected.

Sometimes unexpected change is unwelcome and destructive, but like all change it has its place both in our plans and in fates. Other times change is the only remedy, as our needs expand and our responsibilities increase. Change unites and it strengthens. The devastation and suffering brought on by hurricanes Katrina and Rita have been unparalleled in American history. We did not seek, we did not ask for, nor expect the magnitude of change that was wrought by the forces of nature. Many of our brothers and sisters have been misplaced; all their plans for their lives, their goals for their lives, were temporarily set back. We applaud the administration and faculty for their generosity and their kindness and their support of our brothers and sisters from the coastal region to ensure that their educational goals shall not end and that this unwarranted negative will be traded for a rewarding positive change in all of our lives.

The current participation in student government for awhile now has been expanding exponentially. In my first student government meeting in September of 2004 there were only six active students on the roster. Today that number is nearly tenfold and more applications are coming in daily from eager students. At this time last year the student senate was in existence on paper only. Today, the student senate is an active recipient of the voice of the students and a vital participant in serving the student body. As our numbers grow, so do our responsibilities. At this time we are amending our constitution to help [show and] strengthen our organization and show the changes that have been made. Change also helps bring us together. In the spirit of campus unity and student cooperation, Phi Theta Kappa has joined the student government to entertain the students of ACC safely and jovially during Halloween. The party is set for Friday, October 28, on the Rio Grande campus from 7 p.m. to 9 p.m. All members of the board, those in attendance, are invited; however, there is a strict dress code, you must show up in costume.

Mayor Will Wynn's office has brought representatives together from the student bodies of local institutions of higher learning for the benefit of the students as well as the citizens of the city of Austin. Representatives from Texas State, Houston-Tillotson, Concordia, Saint Ed's, U of Texas, and of course Austin Community College have united to convey the concerns and construct the solutions that face our campuses and students in one unified voice so that the next generation will be ready to assume the responsibilities of leadership and the duties of citizenship. Senators Joshua Moore [and] Scot Agere of the Pinnacle campus, Senate chair AJ Dennis, President Michael Sanchez and myself have represented and served the faculty, staff and administration and student body of ACC with distinction, dedication and honor.

The only thing in life we can expect to happen always is change. Change of the seasons though it may not happen right now, change of lives, change of organization. Change allows us to evolve, to mature, and see the opportunities that were not there before. While change is not always welcome nor do we easily find the wisdom in such change, we can always take comfort in the wise words of the book of Ecclesiastes or of the Turtles, if you're a child of the sixties: "There is a season and a time to every purpose under Heaven." Thank you very much for this time. [After the presentation the board discussed and joked about the final reference and concluded it was a group called the Byrds and not the Turtles that sang the words.]

Presentation to a Negative Audience I

Concerns about the Army's Plans for the Honouliuli Preserve
by Nat Pak, Volunteer Coordinator of the Nature Conservancy

The following presentation was made by Nat Pak, a member of the Nature Conservancy, at a "scoping meeting," at which the United States Army sought public input about a plan to modify and expand part of an army base in Hawaii. The meeting was done to fulfill the Environmental Protection Agency process for land use. The speaker raises questions about the proposal and questions the army's use of the land. The speaker actually presents two speeches; the first is as a spokesperson for his organization, and the second as a public citizen. While a panel of Army personnel hosted the event, the audience was made up of a number of individuals who were opposing the plan. To whom does the speaker address his comments, and to what degree is he effective in doing so?

My name is Nat Pak. I'm the volunteer coordinator of the Nature Conservancy, which is a private nonprofit organization. The good folks from the Army have already heard our concerns and apparently have already acted on some of them. So I will present this testimony from the Nature Conservancy for the benefit of the members of public attending this meeting who may not be familiar with the Nature Conservancy, Honouliuli Preserve and the ways that the Army's plans may affect the native plants, animals and natural communities of the preserve.

The Nature Conservancy of Hawaii has serious concerns regarding the Army's proposed acquisition of the northern portion of our Honouliuli Preserve for use as a small arms qualification range.

Honouliuli Preserve extends for about 3,700 acres along the southern Waianae Mountains and down the east slope above Makakilo and Kunia. At its northern end it is adjacent to Schofield Barracks.

Because Honouliuli contains more than 70 rare and endangered species and some of Oahu's last remnants of diverse native ecosystems, the Estate of James Campbell granted the Conservancy a long-term conservation lease of the preserve.

Protection of rare species and the native forest which they live is our number one concern. In 2001 Honouliuli Preserve in its entirety was designated as critical habitat for the Oahu 'elepaio, a native endangered forest bird.

Soon the preserve will be proposed for critical habitat for endangered plants. In addition, the area of the preserve identified for acquisition overlaps with areas in the Makua implementation plan. There are also significant Hawaiian cultural sites in the preserve.

Since 1990, the conservancy has expended about $2.5 million to conduct resource management and community outreach activities at Honouliuli. For the past three years this work has been concentrated in the northern part of the preserve due to the higher chance of species survival and the ease of access.

This is the same part of the preserve now proposed for acquisition. Earlier this year we completed a 110-acre fence in this area of the preserve to exclude pigs funded by a grant from the U.S. Fish and Wildlife Service. Maintenance followup management is required by the grant agreement for at least 10 years. In the near future we hope to fence an area near Pu'u Hapapa to protect one of the most robust populations of endangered tree snails remaining on the island.

Threats to Honouliuli Preserve include wildfire, animals such as feral pigs, invasive weeds and human disturbance. Consistent and intensive management in the form of fencing, weed control, effective predator control, planting native trees and seed collection is required to protect the area's many rare and endangered plants and animals and to restore native Hawaiian forest.

For these reasons the conservancy has specific concerns about the size of the acquisition, the types of training that may occur and the resulting impact on access, erosion and wildfires. We also have concerns about the spread of weeds and damage to restoration sites.

The Nature Conservancy recognizes the U.S. Army as an important and valued conservation partner in Hawaii. We are working together to find a way to accommodate the Army's training needs without damaging the important and natural cultural resources in Honouliuli.

For those interested in learning more about Honouliuli Preserve, please see me for a recently produced booklet that describes its natural and cultural history.

I'm now going to add my personal concerns which, for the record, are mine alone and not those of the Nature Conservancy. I'm not here to question the Army's need to transform itself or our country's need for a transformed Army. Nor am I here necessarily to question whether those needs must be met by acquiring more land. I am concerned, however, that the needs of our country and the Army are very much the product of specific times and circumstances and can be expected to change with events, leadership and public opinion.

We've heard from Mr. Borne that who may predict what the needs of this country and its Army will be in the future. We've heard from Ms. Ockerman that it's—we can only speculate on whether the Army will be subject to environmental laws in the future.

The needs of the native plants and animals of Honouliuli Preserve and elsewhere, however, are timeless and unchanging. They will always need that particular piece of land and the care of those entrusted with its management to survive.

Despite the fact that the Army currently does an excellent job of managing the natural resources on its lands in Hawaii, it has not always been the case. Nor may it always be the case. It is not the Army's mission to protect these native plants and animals, nor should it be. But neither should it be entrusted with their protection in perpetuity.

I do not believe that the Army is capable, nor would it wish to take on this responsibility forever. The decade or so since the end of the Cold War or the half century or whatever that the Cold War lasted, that's a mere heartbeat in the life of the land. It's better to let the organizations and individuals committed to protecting our natural heritage for generations and generations to come to continue their work in the only places left where they can make a difference.

As for specific concerns I'd like to see addressed in the EIS, I was not aware that this meeting was that forum, but I will submit them in writing.

Thank you for this opportunity to comment.

Presentation to a Negative Audience II

Budget Priorities for Clemson University,
by Jim Barker, President of Clemson University

In this presentation, Jim Barker, the president of Clemson University, addresses the Higher Education Subcommittee of the House Ways and Means Committee of the South Carolina legislature. The address was intended to identify the budget priorities of Clemson University and was given at a time when the state budget was very tight and there had been cuts in university funding. While the listeners might be neutral or even positive, the speaker develops the presentation as though they were negative and seeks their support for several specific initiatives. How effective do you think the speaker is in making his case for support? What did he do well?

Thank you for giving me the opportunity to speak with you today and offer information about Clemson University's budget priorities.

First, let me say that as we present these priorities, we understand that the state continues to face serious financial difficulties. In such times, your task is to ensure that every dollar the state spends is a good investment. I know that you believe higher education is a good investment for the people of South Carolina; that's why you serve on this committee and have been so supportive of Clemson and other institutions in the past. We ask first and foremost for your continued advocacy of higher education or a priority for South Carolina.

I'd also like to thank you for your support of the research university regulatory reform bill last year. This is an important initiative for economic development, and we ask for your continued support as the proposals move through the Senate.

The regulatory reform bill is an important next step in our progress toward building a knowledge-based economy for South Carolina. We have seen this year that state investments in research universities pay off. Since the academic year began, we have broken ground for a 400-acre automotive research campus that promises to make South Carolina the center of the automotive and motorsports industry, and announced plans to invest $70 million over the next five years at the Clemson Research Park in Anderson County to help build an advanced materials economic cluster in the emerging photonics industry. Both of these initiatives will create new jobs for South Carolinians. But while support for research is increasing, funding for basic academic programs continues to decline. Our top budgetary priority is simply to maintain current base funding for educational and general programs. Since 2001, we have lost a fourth of our state E&G funding, and the result has been increased tuition, internal budget cuts, and the loss of faculty and staff positions.

As you know, Clemson University's goal is to be one of the nation's top 20 public universities. Why? What does that mean to students? Our research shows that it means smaller classes, more one-on-one interaction with faculty, a better chance of graduating on time, higher starting salaries and a better chance of getting into the nation's top graduate programs. For the state, it means a higher level of research productivity that translates into a knowledge-based economy and more jobs for South Carolinians.

Even as we have lost state funding, we have seen quality improvements at Clemson. Part of the reason is that we have raised tuition substantially to protect academic quality. Another reason is that the internal budget cuts we've made have been strategic and thoughtful. We have not done across-the-board reductions. We have protected priority areas as much as possible and have continued to invest in quality initiatives.

However, we are concerned about increasing costs to our students, and we believe we have reached the limits of what we can cut internally without significant personnel reductions and program cuts that will directly impact the classroom. Stable base funding will minimize tuition increases and protect program quality.

While we are on the subject of base funding for core programs, I must express my deep concern with the Governor's proposed budget, which includes an unprecedented 41 percent cut for Clemson's Public Service Activities. I know that this committee's charge is to address academic priorities, but at Clemson, our PSA programs are integrally connected to academics. We will have an opportunity next week to present the PSA budget, so I will not go into detail at this time. But I can tell you that the budget cuts proposed for PSA will have a devastating impact on our academic programs, especially in the College of Agriculture, Forestry and Life Sciences. Many faculty members have joint PSA and teaching assignments, and the loss of those positions would have a direct impact on degree programs currently serving more than 2,000 students.

Our second priority is a cost-of-living increase for state employees. We share the General Assembly's concern about the fact that state employees are financially losing ground. Clemson's greatest resource is its faculty and staff. We encourage you to give every consideration to a cost-of-living increase or, at a minimum, funding to offset the recent increase in the state health insurance premium.

We also have a list of programmatic priorities that are outlined in the materials you have in front of you. For the most part, they are the same priorities that you have seen for the past two years, so I will not take your time to go through them one by one. However, I would like to touch briefly on two. Last year, we requested $1 million to build a center of excellence in wireless communication. We received $500,000 in nonrecurring funds, and we value that support. We ask for your continued support for this program, and would point out that it was included as a priority in Governor Sanford's executive budget proposal.

The second program that I would like to mention is one that was not on our list last year but is a high university priority. We seek $250,000 for our Emerging Scholars Program. This outreach program aims to make higher education accessible to students in schools with the lowest college-going rates in the state. By starting early and bringing these students to campus for summer experiences over two years, we demystify the college experience and completely change their self-concept. They come to us assuming they could never even think about college. When they leave, they fully expect to come back as a full-time, degree-seeking student. We hope that many of these students will attend Clemson, but the goal of the program is to get them into college—any college. That's how you break the cycle of poverty and underachievement.

The Emerging Scholars Program is important to South Carolina and it is important to me, personally. You see, I am the first person in my extended family to go to college. I remember how mysterious and inaccessible college seemed to be. I had never been on campus, eaten in the dining halls or gone to college classes. I was very fortunate that I found mentors to help me understand college and apply and visit campuses; so that I came to believe I could attend and be successful on a college campus like Clemson. The Emerging Scholars Program would have been a tremendous help to me, and Clemson is determined to make a difference in the lives of first-generation college students. I encourage you to read through this material and let me know if we can provide anything else that will help you with the very difficult task that you face.

We appreciate your attention today, and the service you provide to the state every day.

Index

Audience (*cont.*)
conveying presentational structure to, 190–191
cultural composition of, 34, 157–158
demographic characteristics of, 34, 149–150, 151, 152–153
demonstrating understanding and respect for position of, 428
detached (*See* Detached audiences)
in determining type of support material, 196–198
disposition of, 150, 152
diverse, 74–75, 89
establishing relevance of, 318–319
ethical considerations for members of, 75–78
ethics in interacting with, 72–74
for everyday presentations, 4–5
extending personal greeting of, 311–312
gaining attention of, 311
hooking attention of, 403–404
influencing in conclusion, 324–325
influencing without controlling, 72–73
informing, 362–363
inspiration of, 363–364
involving and connecting topic to, 401–402
knowledge of, 33–35, 152
maintaining or establishing positive relationship with, 16–18
mixed, 22–23
motivating, in introduction, 42–43
motivational characteristics of, 150, 152–153
moving, along continuum of resistance, 424–425
negative (*See* Negative audience)
neutral (*See* Neutral audience)
open (*See* Open audience)
organizing presentations for, 278–286, 286–292, 292–299
passive (*See* Passive audience)
personally involving, 146
positive (*See* Positive audience)

providing opportunities for, to process information, 147
relating differences in, 158–159
responding to
after presentation, 345–350
during presentation, 342–345
responding to questions from, 340–342
role of, 462–463
showing relevance of information to, 147–148
supportive (*See* Supportive audiences)
understand and adapting to context of, 11–12
visualization and, 235
voluntary, 150, 152, 153
Audience analysis
achieving immediacy through, 140
planning sheet for, 162
Audio aids, guidelines for presenting with, 261
Audiotapes, 260–261
Award ceremonies, 470–471

B

Bandwagon effect, 379
Behavioral flexibility, demonstrating, 158
Beliefs of listeners, 155–157
Belonging, need for, 232
Blair, Tony, 440
Blame, demonstrating, 460–461
Books, 174
Boolean logic, 171–173
Boomerang effect, 436
Breathing, 50–52
Brokaw, Tom, 139
Burned out, 396–397
Bush, George, 133
Bush, Laura, 348–349

C

Cacioppo, John, 207
Captive audience, 150, 152
Carter, Jimmy, 459, 461

Photo Credits